Magix Movie Edit Pro 2014 Revealed

Revealed

Jeff Naylor

Magix Movie Edit Pro 2014 Revealed

ISBN number 978-0-9564866-6-0

Published by
Dtvpro Publishing
32 Dinmore
Bovingdon, Hemel Hempstead
Herts, HP3 0QW

First edition published June 2014

POD file 1.0

Software used: Movie Edit Pro Ultimate 13.3.0.8

For downloads, updates and support please visit

www.dtvpro.co.uk

Introduction

Movie Edit Pro is a powerful program. In fact, it's far more powerful than it first seems to be, with features that aren't available in many programs of a higher price. My initial impression was that the editing functions were complex, but they turned out to be very flexible and worth the learning curve. To that end this book concentrates on using the Timeline and Storyboard. I also think that a few the translations from German leave something to be desired, so hopefully I've cleared those up! I find the program very stable in comparison to others I have used, with a high level of support from the in-house programming team.

Another advantage is that if your hobby turns professional at some point, the sister program Video Edit X6 can handle broadcast quality operations and is so similar in function that nothing you learn while using MEP will be wasted.

I want you to use this book as an alternative to wading through the manual, and the instructions are often illustrated by examples so that you can practice *Learning by Doing* wherever possible. If you are completely new to video editing, or at least Movie Edit Pro, then I'd encourage you to start at the very beginning.

I hear of people who work for months on their first editing project. They learn as they go, perhaps doing things the long way round at times, but getting great pleasure from it as they do so. Unfortunately, a few of those find themselves up a cul-de-sac. By making some short projects with me before embarking on your masterpiece, I hope you will avoid the dead ends.

I want this book to show you how to edit video, for which MEP is a means to an end. The pleasure should come from creating movies.

You can still use this book as a reference. I've included a comprehensive index and the chapter descriptions will also help you navigate your way around.

What you need to use this book

The first six chapters require nothing more than a suitable computer and a physical copy of Movie Edit Pro. If you have a downloaded version, you will need a few small sample files that you can download from the Internet.

Further into the book some of the projects will use features not available on the standard version, but I will make this clear. You will also need more sample material which can be freely downloaded or sent to you on a Demo DVD (at cost price) if you have a slow Internet connection. If you have used earlier books in this series you will already have the largest file required.

About the Author

Jeff Naylor has worked in broadcast television since leaving school. In the 1980s he also developed an interest in personal computing which led to the publishing of several programs and books.

He began using video hardware and software in the late 1990s as a means of making showreels for his directing work.

He has been determined to find constructive solutions to his editing problems since recovering from a Spinal Tap moment in 1999 when the computer very nearly went out of the window.

Author's acknowledgments

I've been helped greatly by John Bagnall in the writing of this book, who has checked all the projects and pointed out many areas that needed correction or further clarification.

Huge thanks also to Fiona for her diligent checking of the text, and pointing out where I'd resorted to techno babble!

The online Magix community have helped me with some of the more quirky aspects of the program, and the Magix employees responded quickly to bug reports.

My final thanks go to my Mother for constantly asking how I was getting on with the book.

Thanks Mum.

By the same author: **Pinnacle Studio 15 Revealed**

Pinnacle Studio 16 Plus and Ultimate Revealed

Videomaking - The Grammar Revealed

Pinnacle Studio 17 Plus and Ultimate Revealed

Contents

The Flight Movie Rough Cut...187

Audio Editing...235

Advanced Transitions

Fine Tuning with the Trimmers.................................359

Advanced Techniques...381

Media Management...417

Importing Media..431

Some Basic Principles

Video editing programs work somewhat differently to other programs that you might use on a computer, and understanding how they operate can save a lot of confusion. In addition, having a clear concept of how video is stored as a digital file will help you to troubleshoot issues you may have when working with the many different types of files that abound today. If your knowledge in this area is a bit sketchy, I'd urge you to read this chapter before diving into the rest of the book. Even if you think you have a good grasp of the principles there may be some valuable nuggets of information, so please come back to this chapter when your impatience to start editing has subsided!

How a Video Editing program differs from other types of data manipulation

When you work with a word processing program, you will often create a document from scratch. OK, you might start with a template of some sort; the layout of the page could be pre-defined, there may even be some text already present – your name and address and the date might be part of a letterhead template. However, the original content of the letter is typed into that document by the user and the file that is used to store the document contains the actual letters of text stored in a digital format. Even if you have copied the text from somewhere else and pasted it into your document, the text is added to the document file.

If you open a partially written document file in a word processor, add or delete a few words and then save the document again, you have made a permanent change to the document. If you don't want to change the original document you can perform a "Save As" operation on the edited document file and give it a new name, but if you just allow the program to overwrite the original document, any bits of text that have been removed are lost forever. (In reality, modern sophisticated programs may offer ways to recover the data, but that can't be relied on.)

Other programs operate on "data" that isn't created by the user within the confines of the program. Consider a photo editing program. You have taken a photo with your camera which has stored the picture as a digitally encoded file. You transfer that picture file to the hard drive of your computer. It's most likely in a format called "JPEG" but could be in one of dozens of other formats. As long as your computer's operating system knows how to decode the file it can display the picture for you. When you open the picture file in a photo editing program that also understands the JPEG format, that program can not only display the picture, but allows you to edit it. You can crop it, alter the exposure or modify the picture in many other ways, depending on the sophistication of the program. However, when you have made the changes, you need to re-save the file. Although the program will probably warn you of what you are about to do, if you save the modified picture with the same name, in the same format, you will destroy the original file. You may be able to recover the original picture (it might still be in the camera memory), but then again, you might not.

Photo editing process

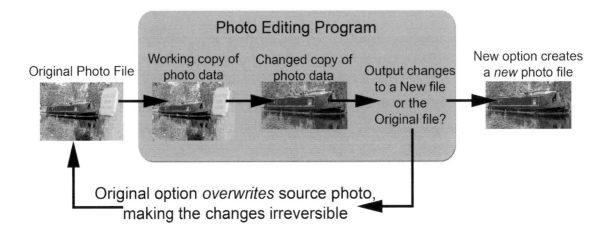

The above process is called "destructive" editing. It's quite easy to avoid destroying the original picture file by careful use of "Save As" and alternative file names, but when you are manipulating a picture file, you are manipulating the data from that original picture.

Let's consider a more sophisticated use of an editing program, where you are using it to create a new object – for the sake of this example let's assume you have taken a picture of a child's birthday party and you want to produce a Thank You card with some text superimposed. You start a new, untitled picture and set the size to something suitable for printing. Now you **import** the picture from the file already saved on your computer. You find the picture is the wrong size and shape, so you shrink and crop it to fit the card, and then add some text using a tool in the editing program. You have made a new object, and you save the whole thing to a new file with a name that bears no relation to that of the photo that is part of the card. Even the file format will be different – if you use Photoshop, for example, the default file type will be .PSD, and not a JPEG.

When you are working on the Thank You card, the editing program contains data relating to the picture, but once you save and reload the card from the publishing file, only the shrunken and cropped picture data is available to the program. If you delete the original, full size, picture file from your computer you can still load the publishing file containing the card and that will hold some, but not all, of the picture data.

Publishing program process

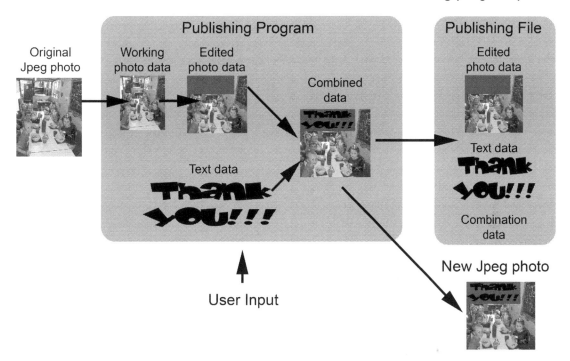

This more sophisticated way of working is still potentially "destructive" editing if you overwrite the original JPEG. More importantly, it is potentially destructive in another way.

Let's assume someone else wants to print out the card. You can just give them the Publishing file and if they have the same program as you, they can do so - they don't need the original JPEG. But what if that person wants to change your cropping because you have cut their child out of the frame? With only the Publishing file there is nothing that can do about your editing because the part of the photo with their child in is not stored in the file you gave them.

This model is one which, in my experience, some people believe applies to non-linear video editing programs. It's an understandable assumption, but not normally how a video editing program works.

Video data takes up far more storage space than text or even pictures, so it makes sense to leave the video data on the hard drive and not try to embed it in the file that defines the edited version of the movie. The Movie project file that you save during, and at the end, of an editing session won't contain any video; neither is it likely to contain any pictures or music. There may be some raw data such as titles, but this will depend on the program.

So what does this Movie project file actually contain? Apart from information about how the movie is set up, it is mostly data that points to other files.

Let's return to the example of writing a letter. If a word processor operated in the manner of a video editing program, the text would be stored as separate files and the document file for a letter would be a set of instructions defining which parts of those files make up the letter, and in what order they are arranged. Translated into "English" the document file would be a set of data something like the following:

- The document uses a page size of A4 and the default text colour is black.

- It starts with the first word of the file *Home address* which is stored in the *My Documents* folder of the *C: drive* and uses the next 21 words. This text is right justified.

- Insert two blank lines

- The next word is the fifth word from the file *Letter to John* which is stored in the *My Documents/Letters* folder of the *C: drive* and uses the next 300 words. This text is left justified.

Now, while this is an unnecessary complication for a word processing program, there are a few advantages. The files *My address* and *Letter to John* can be huge, but the document file can be small. The files *My address* and *Letter to John* are also in no danger of being overwritten and can be kept in any accessible location as long as they can be read by the program.

What if you want someone else to read your letter though? If they don't have the same editing program as you, then it's no good sending them the document file. Even if they do have the same program, they will still need access to the text files referenced in the document file. So what you need to do is **Export** the letter. You might print it out, or you might make a new file that any computer can read – a simple text file (with the suffix *.txt*) or perhaps a Printer Definition File (PDF file with the suffix *.pdf*). In the case of the text file, it would only contain the bits of the text specified by the document file – for example, it won't contain the first four words of the *Letter to John* file because they are only contained in the original text file. The export started at the fifth word.

Now let us take the above model and apply it to a video editing program so you can begin to see the advantages. None of the large assets – video, audio and picture files – that you use in the creation of a movie project need to be embedded in the file defining the movie. What is more, the computer only needs to bring the portions of the assets that it needs to display at any one time into the computer's fast RAM memory, leaving them stored on the hard disc. As long as it can access the assets quickly enough to show the movie in real time they can stay in their original locations.

Non-linear editing process

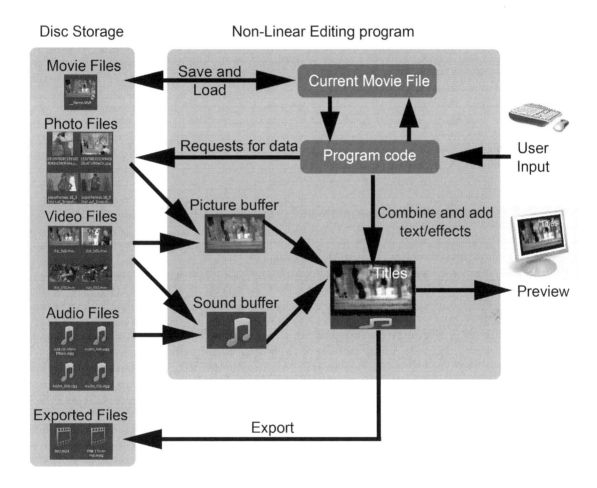

Our Movie project file might translate into something like this:

- This movie has a resolution of 1920 by 1080 pixels and a frame rate of 25 frames a second.

- It begins at 00:00:00:00 (0 hours, 0 minutes, 0 seconds and 0 frames)

- At this point display the text "My Spanish Holiday" in Arial font, yellow 48 point centre justified over a black background.

- At 00:00:05:00 (5 seconds) fade out the text over a duration of 00:00:00:12 (12 frames – nearly half a second)

- At 00:00:6:00 (6 seconds) play the video from the file *28_6_13_01.AVI* stored in the folder *Holiday Videos/Spain 2013* on the D: drive, starting at 00:00:28:05 (28 seconds 5 frames in) for a duration of 00:01:15:00 (1 minute 15 seconds). During this shot, apply the video effect "Auto Colour Correction".

If you use a media playing program such as iTunes or Windows Media Player, where a playlist points to music files rather than contains them, the above concept will be familiar to you. An editing program is just more selective and can choose sections of a video or audio files rather than the whole file.

Exporting and previewing

Just as in the earlier word processing example, when you want someone else to view your edited movie, if they don't have the same editing program as you have used, you will need to export the movie. Even if they did have the same software, they would need access to all the files referenced in the movie project, even if the files are very large and you have just used short fragments. However, in much the same way as a letter might be printed out or saved in one of a number of computer readable forms, movies can be exported in a number of ways. In the earlier days of software video editing, exporting was normally achieved by re-recording the movie onto a videotape. Nowadays if you wanted to send someone a copy of your edited video to be played through their TV you would burn it to a DVD or increasingly likely, you would create a new video file that can also be played by a computer or uploaded to a video sharing site such as YouTube.

Playing an edited movie within an editing program or exporting it to a file both use the source files in the same manner. In the case of playback to a screen, it needs to happen at the same pace (or frame rate) as the video was shot at. For export to a file it has to re-encode the video data into a new file and this may take more computer power than simply displaying the pictures. However, it doesn't really matter if it takes 30 seconds or 2 minutes to export a movie with a duration of one minute.

Real time preview may be affected by other factors though. Let's assume we are happy with our "My Spanish Holiday" movie and want to preview it from the beginning. With the cursor at the start of the movie, when we press the play control, the program generates the title specified, then after 5 seconds it fades it out over half a second.

Another half a second of a blank screen is sent out before the program begins playing the first video file from the hard disc, starting at the point specified.

One factor that may stop you being able to watch the edited movie in real time is the manner in which the source video is stored on the hard disc. If the data is in a very raw state it will be stored as a large file and even the latest computers will struggle to read that amount of data from the hard disc in the time it needs to achieve real-time playback. To avoid that problem almost all video files have their data compressed in some way so that they can be read faster than required. However, some types of compression are so complex that the video information cannot be decoded by the computer's processor quickly enough – depending on the power of the computer and the sophistication of the editing software.

Compression and playback

Hard Disc Storage	Typical transfer speed 4Gb per minute	System Memory	Decompresssion time for 1 minute of video	Real Time Playback
Uncompressed 1 minute=8Gb	✖	Uncompressed	5 seconds	✔
Lightly compressed 1 minute=50Mb	✔	Lightly compressed	20 seconds	✔
Heavily compressed 1 min=15Mb	✔	Heavily compressed	80 seconds	✖

Therefore, if a video file is too lightly or heavily compressed it can overwhelm the capabilities of a computer to play it back smoothly. It is more likely that you will be trying to work with files that are heavily compressed than files that are simply too big, so CPU power may prevail, but not everyone can afford a very fast machine.

However, in addition to being able to fetch and decode the video data quickly enough, there may be other things that will hinder real-time preview. In the Movie project file I described earlier, you will notice that I specified an effect, "Auto Colour Correction" to be added to the shot starting at 6 seconds. The video editing program needs to calculate and apply this effect to the video data after fetching it from the hard disc but before outputting it to the screen. We will have a problem here if the effect takes a long time to calculate and apply to the video data. If it takes more than one second to add the effect to one second's worth of video, we can't play it back in real time – it is going to slow down and appear jerky.

Proxy and Preview files

What's the solution to the playback problem then? We have to be able to preview our video projects in real time in order to make any creative decisions or if we want to "print" them back to a tape. Two strategies are used to achieve this.

The old-school approach is called **Proxy Editing**. Magix Movie Edit Pro 2014 has now implemented this method so that you can work with 4K resolution files, and its broadcast-capable big brother, Video Edit Pro also has the facility. With proxy editing activated, any file you import has a shadow file (a proxy) generated. This file uses a medium compression format that will play back smoothly for preview purposes, and is used in place of the original file when you want to preview the project. In order to avoid encoding losses, when you export your movie, the original files, and not the proxy files, are used to produce the final movie.

Proxy editing isn't a complete solution, because it is still possible to overload a video clip with effects that can't be calculated quickly enough for real time playback. The more selective approach is called **Preview Rendering**. With this feature, any areas of the movie that aren't going to preview smoothly can be exported to a new temporary video file which is used for preview. In some circumstances, these temporary files can be used for export to save you time at that stage. We will see how preview rendering can be used selectively later in the book.

So, if you have added some pretty complex effects and transitions to some parts of your movie, these may need to be preview rendered. If there are some clips using a highly complex compression scheme that your computer struggles to play back in real time, these can be preview-rendered as well. Perhaps whole sections of the movie don't need this treatment, though, saving you the time it takes to re-encode everything.

Why "non-linear"?

You may have noticed me using the term "non-linear" without actually explaining what it means.

Before the advent of video, movie editing was non-linear. Film is little more than a series of individual photos on a strip of celluloid. Making a movie from a bunch of film clips allows you to build it up in sections and rearrange it with ease. Changing the finished product was easy too – you could cut bits of film out of the movie and repair the gap, or split the reel at a certain point and splice in a new section. So, the process isn't *linear*, in a straight direction – you need not start at the beginning and work methodically to the end.

A series of frames

Video used to be only recorded on tape, with the movie starting at the beginning of the tape and ending at the end. To edit your movie you copied across the bits you needed from a playback machine to a record machine in the order that you wanted them to appear. If you then decided to change your mind and swap two parts of the movie around, you had to go back to the point where your changes began and remake the whole movie from that point on. (OK, if you are familiar with audio tape recorders you might ask why video tape couldn't be spliced in the same way. It could, but it was an extremely delicate operation that didn't always work, and risked destroying the recording.)

However, once it became possible to store video data on a hard disc rather than a tape, non-linear Video editing became a practical proposition. What's more, because a Movie project file is nothing more than a complex playlist, you don't even need to move the video data around in the computer memory or on the hard disc – you just change the playlist. So in many respects it's faster and more flexible than film editing.

Storing and replaying moving pictures

Those digital files on your hard disc are nothing like a strip of celluloid with a series of still pictures on them, but the underlying principle of recording and playing back moving pictures is the same. We won't concern ourselves with how a strip of film is created, but through the wonders of lenses, light-proof housings, opening and closing shutters and chemical reactions, it consists of a series of semi-transparent images, each one taken

a very short time after the other. If these images are projected onto a screen by shining a light through them in rapid succession, the human eye and brain isn't aware that they are individual pictures and any movement that occurs in the subject matter appears as natural movement. Each one of the images is called a frame.

The frame is the fundamental unit in film, television and video. The number of frames shown each second varies, unfortunately. Conventional feature films record and display 24 frames a second. The television system created in the USA (NTSC) uses 30 frames a second (actually, slightly less – 29.97 frames a second for technical reasons) and the European (PAL) system uses 25 frames a second. There are historical reasons for these incompatibilities, (and some other video standards as well). The basic principle, though, is that if you can show still pictures quickly enough, one after the other, the brain is tricked into thinking they are watching continuous action.

Scanning

There is a further complication with video. I really need to mention it now rather than glossing over the issue, but if this section confuses you, come back to it when you need to understand the difference between progressive and interlaced video.

Historically, a video picture was recorded by scanning a thin line across an image projected by the camera lens onto the face of a "Camera Tube". The scanning started top left and "read" the values across to the right of the picture, then moved down the image and scanned another line. Because of technical limitations, a better picture resulted if the first pass scanned alternative lines making up half the image, then a second pass went back and scanned the gaps between the first set of lines.

So, in a Top Field First (TFF) scanning system the first pass, called a **field**, scanned lines 1,3,5 and so on, and the second pass scanned a field consisting of lines 2,4,6 and so on.. The two fields were also played back like this, so instead of there being 30 (or 25) frames per second, there were 60 (or 50) fields per second. Just to make matters more complex, some types of cameras scan lines 2, 4, 6…. and then return to 1, 3, 5… thereby using a Bottom Field First scanning system.

These scanning schemes are called **Interlacing** and many TV broadcasts are still stuck with them today. They hark back to the days of not just camera tubes but also vacuum tube displays (CRTs – Cathode Ray Tubes). The alternative scanning scheme is called **Progressive** because the scanning progresses through the lines sequentially – 1, 2, 3, 4, 5, 6… and so on.

Interlacing example with a low resolution format

Full Resolution

40x30 resolution

Lines   Top Field   Bottom Field   Lines

1 →
3 →   ← 2
5 →   ← 4
                                             ← 6

Bottom field extrapolated to a full frame has only 15 lines of vertical resolution

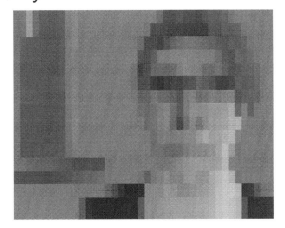

Most readers of this book will be watching video on solid state displays – the flat panel display of a Plasma, LCD or LED TV, or a computer, tablet or phone screen. These are natively progressive devices that don't need interlaced signals, but it is often best to let them convert the signals themselves rather than doing it beforehand. Converting interlaced video to progressive doesn't automatically make it "better" and if not done carefully can make it look considerably worse. Problems start to occur when you try to show two fields at the same time, but a part of the scanned image has moved between scanning the first and second field. In the worst case, you might have to drop a whole field of information, resulting in half the vertical resolution of the scanned image. The screenshot illustrates this with a low resolution picture - 40x30 pixels - to make the example clearer. (It's not far off the resolution of very early mechanical scanning systems, though!)

To keep things simple, let's forget about interlaced video for the rest of this chapter!

Still pictures as digital files

When you print out a photograph taken with a digital camera, it is nothing more than series of coloured dots that blend into each other. The quality of the picture is a function of how accurate the colour of the dots is, and how many there are to the square centimetre or inch. The same is true when you display the digital photo on a TV or computer screen, except that the screen has a fixed number of dots – or **Pixels** (picture elements) – to the square centimetre or inch. If we enlarge our view of the photo, we can see the individual pixels that make up the photo.

I have a digital stills camera that can take a photograph with a resolution 1920 pixels wide and 1080 pixels high – that's just over 2 million pixels or 2 **Megapixels**. In order to represent all the colours and degrees of brightness the screen can display we need to use three bytes of digital data for each pixel (red, green and blue in the range 0-255 each). So, to store a bitmap of that photo the camera needs to use 6 million bytes – about 6Mb.

A bitmap is a very inefficient means of storing picture data, although it is the most accurate. Most photographs are going to have areas that are exactly the same colour and brightness so you can start compressing the information by defining areas of the image that have the same value. If you aren't too fussy about the meaning of "same value" or very fine detail you can compress most photos by quite a lot. Far better compression schemes are possible using more advanced mathematics, of course. The highly popular **JPEG** scheme (Joint Picture Experts Group, file types *.jpg* or *.jpeg*), for example, uses Discrete Cosine Transformation, which I'm not going to attempt to explain as I'm not sure I understand it sufficiently myself!

Video as digital files

A very inefficient way to store a video picture is as a series of bitmaps, each one defining one frame. For good quality video you need at least 24 bitmaps for each second of video playback. There is a format that stores video in this manner; it's called Uncompressed AVI (Audio Video Interleave, file type .*avi*). As the acronym implies, AVI files contain audio as well as video data, and as you might guess, they are pretty big. A program I use to create animations, iClone, produces high definition uncompressed AVI files and 1 second of video needs 178Mbytes of memory to store. These types of files are so large that they cannot be fetched from the hard disc of a computer quickly enough to be displayed in real time.

I've already pointed out that there are perfectly good ways to compress individual pictures, so it seems obvious that compressing each frame using a method such as JPEG encoding is going to make video files smaller. This is called Intraframe encoding because all the compression is applied within the individual frames. The most common example of an intraframe video compression scheme is DV-AVI – the first digital video cameras available to consumers. Here each frame is compressed, but a DV-AVI file contains each individual frame as a separate image.

Intraframe video compression

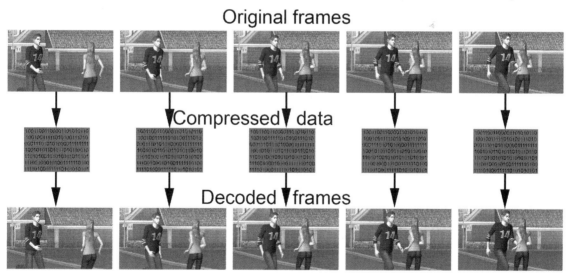

Original frames

Compressed data

Decoded frames

DV-AVI files are only "standard" definition, with the same number of pixels in each frame as regular TV broadcasts, and the compression applied to the individual frames is such that the pictures don't quite meet the high standards required by most broadcasters – although DV cameras are used for news gathering. The files are still big, but not so big that they can't be read from a computer hard disk in less than real-time – so they can be played back smoothly.

The compression applied to the individual frames of video is relatively light as well, comfortably within the power of a computer to decode and re-encode without significantly slowing down playback.

Interframe compression

DV-AVI files and similar intraframe compression methods still produce files that are too big to be sent over the Internet or via transmitters – there is just too much data. The next step in compression techniques for video looks at the similarity between adjacent frames in much the same way as still picture compression looks at the similarities between adjacent areas. Imagine a video of a newsreader sitting at a desk with a picture behind them. The only differences between the subsequent frames are small movements of the newsreader's head. So, by only recording the *differences* between frames, the amount of data needed is reduced enormously. This is a very extreme example; video with lots of movement, either by the subject or the camera, can't be compressed so much, but there are still savings to be made.

The most common form of interframe compression is currently **MPEG-2** (Motion Picture Experts Group type 2, file type *.mpg* or *.mpeg*). The video consists of "Groups of Pictures" (GOPs). These are generally around 12 to 15 frames in length. The first frame is called an I-frame, and, although compressed, holds all the data needed to reconstruct that frame. I-frame stands for intra-coded frame – all the compression is within the frame just as in DV-AVI. The rest of the GOP is made up of P-frames and B-frames. P-frames - predictive-coded frames - refer to data from the previous I or P frame when compressing data. There are normally 3 or 4 P-frames in GOP. B-frames (Bidirectionally-predictive frames) refer to data from frames both before and after it.

If, like me, you struggle with the concept of how that all works, the important point to grasp is that for MPEG-2, there is only one high quality, accurately compressed frame every half second or so. Every eighth of a second, there is reasonable quality data in the shape of a P-frame. The rest is the result of a very sophisticated compression scheme. Or, if you prefer, Smoke and Mirrors.

Another useful fact to know is that MPEG-2 compression works by dividing frames up into blocks of pixels. Sometimes it can look at two successive frames and say "the block of 16x16 pixels that were in the top left corner of the frame have now moved five pixels right and two pixels down". The difference between them is all that needs to be recorded. Even if the blocks aren't exactly the same, the principle can be applied. Clever, eh?

Simplified interframe compression scheme with a GOP of 4 frames

Original frames

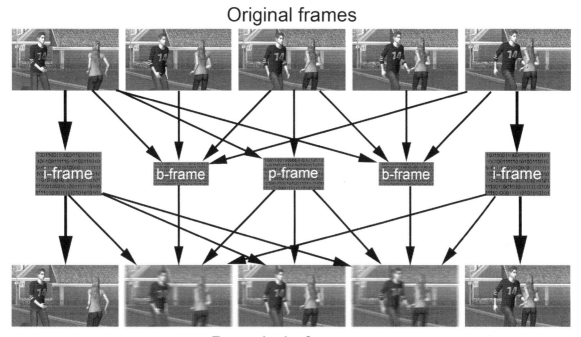

Decoded   frames

This fact explains why, when MPEG-2 compression is very high or has gone wrong, the video picture tends to turn into square, blurred blocks.

Bitrates

When compressing a video file, the resolution and frame rate may be fixed but you can vary the amount of compression by altering the **Bitrate** – the number of digital data bits used to represent a second's worth of video.

MPEG-2 can use variable compression. If the video gets a lot of movement, it can reduce the compression to try to keep up with the large changes. You can also specify the Bitrate of the compression to suit your own purposes.

DVD quality MPEG-2 video uses about 6000 Kilobits to represent a second's worth of video, although this may vary depending on the content if the encoding uses variable Bitrate – compressing video with less movement more than sections with lots of movement.

Sometimes the words **"Data Rate"** are used instead of Bitrate just to confuse us. That might not be measured in bits, but bytes or something else. So when we look at data rates, let's make sure we are comparing like with like. A Kb is a kilobit. A KB is a Kilobyte - eight times more, so be sure to check if the b is upper or lower case. Some people just love trying to confuse the general public, and whoever came up with those abbreviations wasn't trying to make it easy!

MP4, H.264 and beyond

MPEG-2 is still too big to use over the Internet and get decent quality. Other formats, including MP4 (Motion Picture expert group, type 4, file type .mp4) video, use more advanced compression schemes with a correspondingly larger need for computer power to encode and decode the images. The current favourite for compression is a scheme called H.264, used by AVCHD cameras, Blu-ray discs and much more. Although specialist hardware can handle this format relatively easily it can put a great deal of strain on a normal computer's CPU, making smooth playback difficult. It's particularly tough for editing programs to extract single frames, which media playing software doesn't need to do. If you are puzzled that Windows Media Player can play back your new camera footage smoothly, but your editing software can't, that's why.

Recent computer hardware and software have caught up with the requirements of H.264, but technical advances and the desire for higher resolution video mean that a new standard – H.265 – is on its way. This aims to halve the Bitrate of video for a given resolution and quality. At the time of writing dedicated hardware encoders and decoders are being made available, but the current generation of CPU based hardware may have to rely on proxy editing to handle the video smoothly.

Containing file types

I have often read – and answered questions about – video file types that don't behave properly within a video editing package. Media playing software has a great advantage because it only needs to partially decode the files – and often you don't realise that you have to wait quite a while for the playback to get going. Another reason, though, is that two files may appear to be of the same type, but contain radically different content. Even an old format such as AVI is just a **Container** – the streams of data within it can use different compression methods. These schemes – known as **CODECS** (compression/decompression) may not be compatible with the editing software of your choice. Even DV-AVI has two types.

MP4 and M2TS are two types of container that can use, amongst other schemes, MPEG-2, MP4 (simple) and H.264 compression. MOV, the Apple format, is even more indiscriminate, and may be a **Wrapper** for many combinations of video and audio compressions schemes.

Time to start editing…

I've singled out the above topics from experience of answering questions about consumer video editing over the years; they are the areas that cause the most confusion. There are many other bits of technical knowledge that you may find interesting (or at least useful) when you use an editing program, but I will introduce those as and when they are relevant to the functions under discussion. Let's Launch Movie Edit Pro!

Introducing Movie Edit Pro

The next few chapters aim to familiarise you with the basic functionality of Magix Movie Edit Pro. I'd recommend you explore the program with me by having it open in front of you as you read through. At various points there will be a bullet point list with instructions to follow so that I can demonstrate various aspects of the program – we will import, explore, rearrange and edit a few clips as we go along. Even if you skip some parts of these chapters I'd encourage you to try the practical sections.

Program versions

There are three versions of Magix Movie Edit Pro. The basic version is still a pretty capable piece of software, so it won't be until later in the book that owners of that version will be unable to complete a few of the examples – when I describe features which are restricted to the higher versions I will mention it in the text.

The Plus and Premium versions only differ from each other because of the addition of some high-end plug-in effects to the Premium version. There is also a truly professional version of the software, named Video Edit Pro X5, which resembles the consumer versions in many ways (it can even load projects made in MEP), so this book could be used as an introduction to that version, but I'm not going to include any of the VEP X5 features and differences here.

I'm also going to assume you have installed the program successfully using the standard settings and locations and applied any service patches that are available. If you are having issues I'd encourage you to use the Magix support system, which in my experience is very helpful.

Resetting the program

When you first run Movie Edit Pro it will normally present you with a dialogue box similar to that shown in the *default opening dialogue* screenshot overleaf. However, if you have already used the software before you started this book, it's quite possible that you have modified the setting from the default. If you are having trouble following what I'm describing in this chapter, you might want to set the program to its default settings.

This is nice and easy to achieve in MEP, because there is a specific command to do just that. Close the dialogue box if it is there, then look in the drop-down *File* menu. Here, select *Settings* and the bottom option, *Reset program settings to default…*; the program will then restart and you will see the dialogue box.

Resetting the program defaults

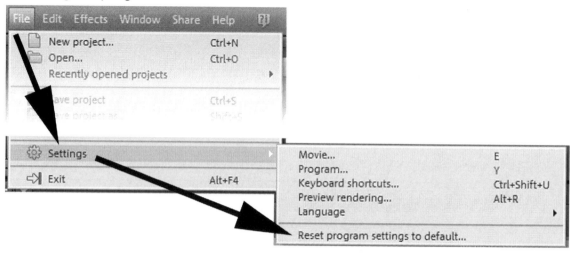

Default opening dialogue

The opening dialogue asks "What do you want to do?" and offers you three choices. It also has a button that lets you view the Intro video.

The default opening dialogue (Plus and Ultimate versions)

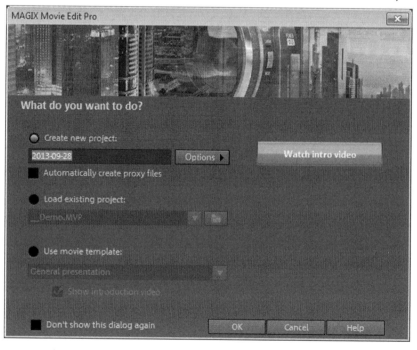

The first, pre-selected, option is to *Create a new project*, and by default this gives your project a name corresponding to the current date. If there is already a project with that name an incremental suffix (for example, -*02*) is added. My advice is for you to change the date to something more descriptive before starting a new project, although you can always do this later on by choosing *Save as* or simply renaming the project when you close the program. Beneath this option is a checkbox that will force the new project to use proxy files. This feature isn't available in the basic version and we won't using this option until much later in the book.

The second option is for you to *Load an existing project*. Select the radio button for this option and you can open the drop-down box to see a list of recent projects, or you can use the folder icon to locate projects anywhere on your computer, using a standard Windows "open" dialogue.

The third option is to *Use movie template*. Again, this isn't a feature available in the basic version. If you want to have a bit of fun and knock together something quickly you might find templates interesting. They can be chosen from the drop-down box and the option choices include viewing a short introduction video, so it is fairly self-explanatory. I'll be honest and say this isn't my idea of creative movie-making and I suspect you may find the limitations somewhat restrictive after a while.

If you want to skip the whole opening dialogue box, you can disable it by using the checkbox at the bottom. When you open the program or select *New project* from the file menu you will get an empty project with the default options. This isn't such a bad idea because there are many other ways of choosing movie settings or loading existing programs. Also, it's easy to restore any disabled dialogue boxes in *File/Settings/Program/System* by using the *Reactivate Dialogs* button.

Incidentally, in the same *System* panel you will find a checkbox with the function to *Shade program screen when opening dialogs*. I like to work with this feature turned on as it helps the dialogue boxes stand out. Your preference might not coincide with mine!

Project options

When you create a new project from the *What do you want to do?* dialogue, you also have an *Options* button. Click on this and you get two new sub-options.

The first sub-option relates to setting up a project folder. I will

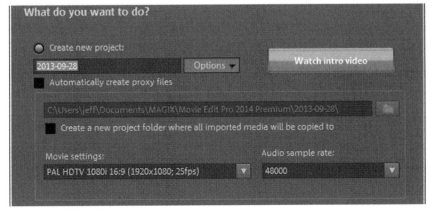

discuss this feature later (page 422) , and we won't use it before that, so leave the *Create a new project folder....* checkbox deselected for now.

The second sub option allows you to change the project settings – resolution, frame rate, aspect ratio, and the audio sample rate. For now, the default values are OK. We can always change these mid-project using the *File/Settings/Movie/Movie Settings* box, where there is also a checkbox to set the defaults - *Use settings as presets for new movies*.

It's highly likely that you will normally want to use the same settings. When you installed MEP you were asked which video standard you wanted to use – PAL/50hz for Europe or NTSC/60hz for North America. You will want to work in High Definition if you have suitable video sources or are using still photos and your computer is powerful enough. So when you get used to the program you may want to modify the default project settings. For now, though, leave them as they are so I can demonstrate another feature shortly.

So, in summary:

- Run Magix Movie Edit Pro.
- If you don't see the opening dialogue "What do you want to do?" box, use the *File/Settings/Reset program to default settings* option and the program will restart, displaying the dialogue box.
- Change the name in the *Create new project* box to "*My Test Project*".
- Click *OK*.

Program Layout

You should now see something very similar to the screenshot on the next page.

This is the Edit screen. The whole program is contained in a standard window with the top border – the title bar - showing the name of the program on the left and standard resizing icons on the right. You can use these windows icons to minimize, shrink, maximise or close the program. While shrunk down, the program window can be resized and dragged around like any other normal Windows program. If you use the X to close the program with a newly created, empty and unsaved project on display you will lose it, but this isn't a great hardship because once you have done any work at all, you are prompted to save your work before the program closes.

The Edit screen has five areas:

1. The top of the window displays a Magix logo, a small group of tool icons, a set of drop down menus and three tab buttons for switching modes.

2. Top left is the **Program monitor**. Here you can display and play source material and the movies you are making

3. Top right is the **Media pool**. This is where you can find all the video, photo and audio content to use in the movies and projects you make, along with titles, transitions and effects that you might also want to add.

4. Below these two areas, spanning the width of the screen is the **Project area** where you compile and edit the source material into movies and projects.

5. At the very bottom is an information bar. Much of the time you will only see the legend *CPU* there, but at other times it displays data about the progress of operations or expanded information relating to the currently displayed tooltip.

Areas 1 and 5 are fixed in size and anchored to the top and bottom of the Edit screen. The other three areas can be resized and even undocked from the edit screen.

The Edit Screen layout

The Active Window

If a window is active it is said to have the focus. When you use the mouse on a particular area it becomes active, so whichever window you click on automatically gets the focus.

If you are a fan of keyboard shortcuts – and I am – then it's not always immediately obvious which area you are operating on, and some keys work differently in different modes. To help you know which window is going to respond to your key presses, a thin blue line shows at the top when it has the focus.

This only applies to the three central areas, The Menu and Information areas don't show the blue line when active, but the last used window will remain active for the purposes of keyboard shortcuts.

To show the blue line in action, click on the centre of the Program monitor, the Media pool and the Project area in succession and watch the blue line appear over each one in turn.

Rearranging the layout

The four-way mouse cursor

You can change the relative size of the three central areas without undocking them. For the majority of users this is the easiest way to arrange the screen to suit the task in hand. For example, when you want to look at the quality of a video source you need the Preview screen to be as large as practicable, but when searching for new content you can display more material with an expanded Media pool; if you are working with a complex movie you may need the project area to be enlarged.

Hover your mouse over any boundary of the three areas and the cursor changes to a double-headed arrow. Left click, hold and drag and you can move the boundary. Try this on the junction of the Preview and Media areas and by dragging left you can increase the area available to the Media pool at the expense of the Preview monitor. Also try dragging the top edge of the Project area with a vertical double arrow – notice that both the preview and media areas shrink or expand in sympathy.

Even more control is available if you hover over the junction of all three areas – where you can generate a four-way arrow cursor and drag all three areas simultaneously. This is the most common way of altering the arrangement and I'd encourage you to use it rather than struggle to see the area you are concentrating on at any particular time.

Resetting the layout

If you have adjusted the layout and want to return to the standard arrangement you can of course readjust the areas manually. There is also an option in the drop-down menu –

Window/Window arrangement menu

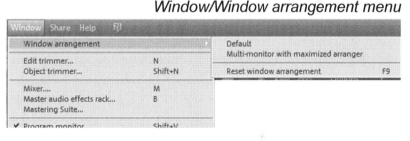

Window/Window arrangement/Reset window arrangement – but this isn't anywhere near as convenient as using the keyboard shortcut F9 (function key 9). Although I like using keyboard shortcuts I never can remember all of them. However, the F9 key is one I'd recommend you get used to using because once it becomes second nature it not only saves you time, but encourages you to resize the Edit screen areas in the first place.

F9 works in all circumstances, restoring the program to full screen with the default arrangement. It even maximises the program after you have used the Minimise command, as long as you haven't selected another program window.

Undocking the areas

Further customisation of the layout can be achieved by dragging the individual areas to undock them from the Edit screen. At the top of each area is a movement bar – a title bar without any text. At the far left of each area is a maximise icon which you can click on to make the individual area fill the computer screen. Try this on the Media pool to see the effect, then click on the minimise icon occupying the same position to shrink it back into the Edit screen. If you just drag the grey bar a short distance though, you will see the area undock itself. Now you can drag and resize it without it affecting the other two areas – you can even drag it outside the Edit screen if that isn't displayed full screen or you have two monitors attached to your computer.

If you right click on the grey bar for each area a small but useful context menu appears. *Bring to front on mouse click* can be checked or unchecked and alters the behaviour if you have arranged the areas to overlap each other – they stay partially hidden when you select them if you uncheck this option.

Even if you don't have a particularly large monitor this feature has its uses. Many editing programs have the Preview screen on the right and not the left, so if you are used to this layout you can swap the Media pool and the Preview monitor, and if you let them snap back into position you can even use the four-way icon to resize the windows as usual.

With a large monitor, or even better, dual monitors, you can customise the layout to your heart's content. The only issue is that you can't save a customised layout so if you get used to working in a particular way you will have to set it up each time you launch MEP – and you can't use the F9 key because it destroys your carefully set up layout. (The professional version, Video Edit Pro X5 does allow you to save new layouts, by the way.)

Dual Monitors

If you are lucky enough to have two monitors attached to your computer (or like me have a second display plugged into a laptop) then you can select *Windows/Window arrangement/Multi-monitor with maximised arranger*. I highly recommend you use this mode if you have the hardware, although I'm afraid the screenshots in this book won't always match.

Dual screen default layout

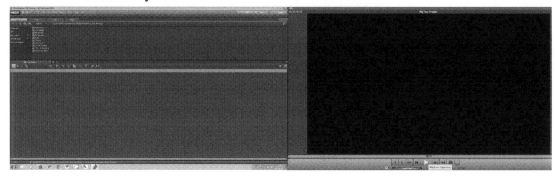

The screenshot shows how the windows are arranged with two monitors – Media pool and the top of the main display, Edit area below, with the Preview monitor full screen on the second monitor.

The great thing about using this mode is that it is a preset – which is to say that you **can** use the F9 key to reset the layout.

Exploring the interface

Area 1 in our list, along the top of your screen, is laid out in a way which should be familiar to any Windows user.

The Magix logo appears on the far left, followed by five shortcut items that are also duplicated in the drop down menus – New project, Open project, Save project, Program settings and Context help. This area is called the **Upper toolbar**. Hover your mouse over any of these tools and a tooltip will also inform you of the keyboard shortcut you can use to activate the tools.

The upper toolbar and a typical tooltip

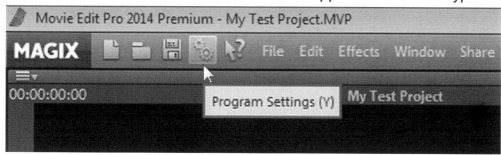

Tooltips are a very useful reminder for many functions in MEP; they operate in many areas of the program, not just the toolbars. Sometimes they just tell you the keyboard shortcut but at other times they describe the function of the tool you are hovering over. This makes them a useful way of exploring the program and if you have any doubts that you are about to use the right command you can check by waiting for the tooltip to confirm what will happen.

The information bar at the bottom of the Edit screen (area 5 in our list) often shows an expanded version of the currently displayed tooltip, so if you don't quite get the meaning, take a look at the bottom of the screen.

The **Context help** feature takes the help a step further by changing the mouse pointer to a question mark – so when you click on a program area the relevant section of the Help file is displayed in a new window.

Keyboard shortcuts are important when you start to become more proficient with any software, and are particularly useful when editing video. I'm not advocating you try to use them all the time - the use of CTRL-O instead of using the menus to open a new project is a step too far perhaps, but at the other end of the scale using the space bar to stop and start video playback is a real time saver. In between there are many shortcuts that you may find useful, particularly if you are performing repetitive tasks. Movie Edit Pro allows you to customise the shortcuts, and you can even save, load and reset the settings as well as use schemes from other editing programs. All this can be done from the *File/Settings/Keyboard shortcuts* option.

Before looking at the Menu option, let's take a look to the right of area 1.

The Edit workspace tab

The three workspace tabs

Three tab buttons are there that allow you to switch to workspaces other than the Edit screen. The first tab is Edit, and should currently be highlighted. It's the workspace you will spend most of your time using.

Burn

Clicking on this tab opens up a whole new interface.

The Burn screen

You will need to use the Burn screen when you want to export the current project onto media that uses menus – DVD, AVCHD and Blu-ray discs. There are other options available here as well. If you are only interested in making movies to put on the Internet or send as files you may never need to use this screen. It is a very powerful feature and I'll be covering it in detail later in the book. When you are in the Burn screen the workspace tabs in the same place as they are in *Edit* , so to return to there, click on the Edit tab.

Export

The third tab brings up a child window over the top of *Edit* or *Burn*, rather that a complete workspace. *Export* offers you all sorts of options to output your current movie, apart from making discs with menus.

The Export screen

There are six options, including the ability to upload directly to YouTube, Vimeo and Facebook. Despite all these options, the Export screen is a simplified wizard that will give you easy access to the popular export types and isn't obligatory. Output can be achieved

without opening the Export screen - for example exporting to file is possible from the file menus and gives you more choices. Again, exporting is a complex subject that has its own chapter devoted to it later in the book.

To escape the Export screen you need to use the Close button or the X at the top of the window.

If you have followed any of the above, your screen may not look like the screenshots I'm about to use, so let's restore the display:

- If a box with the title *Finish movie* is open in front of the main edit or burn screen, click the close button.

- If the *Burn* tab is highlighted, click on the *Edit* tab.

- If you have more than one monitor, drag the Edit window to the main monitor (or the largest one if they are odd sizes).

• In the menu *Window/Window arrangement* select *Default*

If at any point you resized the window or rearranged the areas, use the F9 key to reset the layout to the default display.

The Menu Bar

To the right of the upper toolbar are the Windows style **Drop-down menus**. Here most of the program functions are arranged into groups according to their function. If the function you want can't be found in a drop-down, then you will either find it in a **Context menu** or it doesn't exist. If you aren't sure what a context menu is, you probably know it as a Right-Click menu – the list of commands that come up when you right click on a specific area of a program. We will look at these as and when we need the functions. What follows are the highlights of the drop-down menus and concepts you need to understand in order to use them.

File Menu

File doesn't just deal with saving and loading projects, as you can see when you open it up, but the first few options are related to file operations.

The File menu

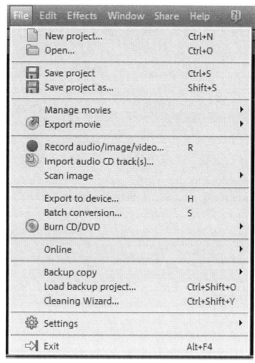

New project, Open, Save project and *Save project as...* are fairly self-explanatory, although note that they do refer to Projects and not Movies – more of which in a moment. *New project* will open the "*What do you want to do?*" dialogue box unless you have disabled it.

Assuming you have saved at least one project, there will also be a *Recently opened projects* command, which lists projects you have been working on recently and allows you to open them without having to browse. If you have just reset the program as I suggested, the list will have been reset so there won't be anything to load.

Let's just use the file menu to test these features, because although we have started a new project, it isn't saved yet.

- Click on the File menu and select *Save project*.

- If you haven't already saved the project, you will get a Windows *Save as* dialogue box with the project name you chose already filled in in the file name box.

- If you used another name when you started the project, change the file name to *My Test Project*.

- Click on *OK*.

- If you have already made a project with this name, you will be warned and offered the chance to overwrite it. If you don't want to, use a different name and make a note of the name.

Now when you look in the File menu you will see a *Last opened disc projects* entry for My Test Project

From now on, you can use the CTRL-S option to quickly save the project in its current form.

Movies and Projects – the difference

The third section of the file menu has two commands specifically for Movies. It is important to realise that Projects and Movies are two distinctly different things in Movie Edit Pro.

A **Movie** is a description of a sequence of objects such as videos, photos and audio. It can also include text, effects, transitions. The file type for a movie has the extension .MVD. As I hope I made clear in the first chapter, a movie file doesn't contain any videos, photos or audio, just references to the source files it uses.

A **Project** consists of one **or more** movies. The file type for a project has the extension .MVP. Again, the project file doesn't contain any of the source files, but what is effectively a playlist for each of the movies it contains.

If you are just making a single movie in MEP, you still start a project. So why is there a distinction? The first advantage is that when you make a DVD, AVCHD or Blu-ray disc, it can contain a number of different movies reached through various menus. A project can contain all those movies. Secondly, you can build up a complex movie from a collection of simpler movies, copying and pasting from one movie to another, or do the reverse and make a highlights movie from a selection of longer movies but still have the whole construction open as a single project.

In most of this book I'll be mainly demonstrating techniques with just one movie contained in the project at any one time, when the terms can be considered to be interchangeable, but please bear in mind the difference.

If you are confused by this, things will become clearer when we examine the Edit area of the program, where movies are displayed in the Arranger, but you can also switch between these movies using tabs. So I'll discuss the sub-commands of **File/Manage movies** later.

Schematic view of Projects

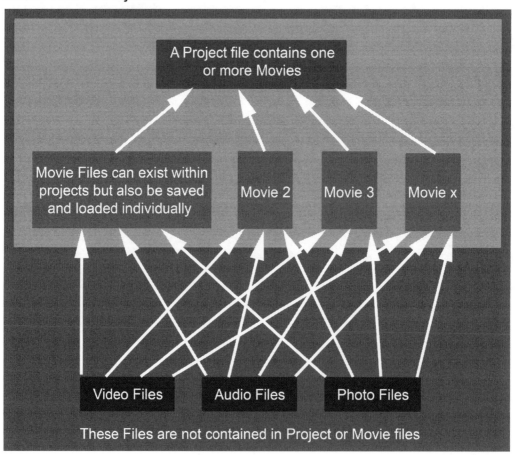

A Project file contains one or more Movies

Movie Files can exist within projects but also be saved and loaded individually

Movie 2

Movie 3

Movie x

Video Files

Audio Files

Photo Files

These Files are not contained in Project or Movie files

Other File Menus commands

File/Export movie allows you to make a file from the currently selected movie, either as a video, audio or photo file. There is a huge range of options here so you can use a suitable format for the target playback device and how you are going to store and send the file. This command overlaps in function with some of the Export screen options.

The fourth section of the File menu concerns itself with bringing source material into Magix so you can use it in your projects by recording, importing or scanning. I'll cover this in detail in the Import chapter.

Section five contains three utilities. *File/Export to device* combines a number of suitable export presets with a wizard that will copy the resulting file to a hardware device such as a camera or smartphone. *File/Batch conversion* is a useful tool for remaking a group of files already on your computer in a different format – perhaps something that will be easier to edit, playback or store. *File/Burn CD/DVD* has a number of options for creating and copying optical media.

If you want to make use of the Internet based features offered by Magix you can use *File/Online*.

The seventh section concerns backups and media management and can help you keep your hard discs organised and free of clutter.

Backup copy is the option you should use for making safety copies of your projects or movies that include all the source material you have used. I hope I have made it clear that just saving a project or movie file isn't enough for a full backup that can be moved to another computer, as these file types don't include any video, photos or audio. Using this option you can put everything you need to recreate the project or movie into one folder on a hard disc, or burn the component parts to an optical disc. You also have the option to retrieve the project from the disc. The optical disc functions use the sub program Speed 3 for CD/DVD operations; this sub-program is also opened when you use the Burn CD/DVD option.

Load Backup project takes you to the location that MEP saves backup files of your projects. If you haven't changed the settings, MEP automatically saves a backup of your project file every 10 minutes – assuming you have made any changes in that time. Personally, I prefer to set this to a shorter duration if I'm working on a complex project that might have a tendency to crash – but you may find the interruption distracting. To alter the setting, go to *File/Settings/Program/System*. You can even turn off automatic backup, but I wouldn't recommend it!

Backup files use the project name and have the extension *_BAKx_MV_* where x is an incremental number. Magix only makes 10 backups before reusing the numbers so you also need to look at the date the file was modified to work out which is the latest file. Backup files are stored in the Projects location specified in the

File/Settings/Program/Folders dialogue box. If in doubt, you can always use a Windows OS search to find any backup files.

Cleaning Wizard

Lots of files are generated by MEP that only have a temporary purpose, and however tidy minded you are, once you have made a few projects you will find your hard disc becoming cluttered. The Cleaning wizard helps you spring clean your hard discs. It's a powerful but complex tool that is easier to use when you understand the functions of the various file types – a subject covered later in the book. See page 428.

We have already taken a brief look at some of the all-important *File/Settings* menu entries and will examine others in greater detail as and when we look at the program functions they control. You can even change the language setting here should you want to practise your bi-lingual skills!

The Edit Menu (Plus and Ultimate versions)

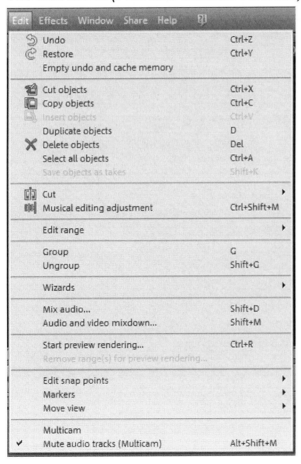

The last option in the File menu lets you quit the program.

Edit Menu

The items here mostly affect the movie you are making.

The first item is probably one of the most useful functions in any program, particularly while you are experimenting – *Undo*. I use it so often that the keyboard shortcut is second nature to me, and fortunately it is one of the Windows standards – CTRL-Z.

When I first used Movie Edit Pro I was surprised to find that you could only use undo 9 times.

Fortunately, if you go to *File/Settings/ Program/System*, you can set the number of allowed Undos to a much higher number – I work with 30. There is probably a memory/performance penalty in storing more undo data but I can't detect it on my computer (a 64-bit OS i7 with 8Gb of RAM). If you find your computer slowing down you might want to stick with the default setting – and it's also possible to use the option in the Edit menu *Empty undo and cache memory* option to free up the RAM used to store the Undo steps and anything currently stored on the clipboard – the "place" things are put when you use *Copy*.

Restore (sometime called Redo) reverses the effect of Undo. I mostly find I use it when I've accidentally used CTRL-Z too many times. The keyboard shortcut is CTRL-Y.

The next set of commands includes mostly Windows standards – *Cut*, *Copy*, *Insert* (normally called *Paste*), *Delete* and *Select All*; these use the normal keyboard shortcuts for Windows. *Duplicate Objects* (D) is a slightly odd one with different behaviour in different editing modes. We will look at that later – there are alternatives as well.

Edit/Save objects as takes requires a full explanation later on, but briefly, **Takes** are objects that point to a real file, but often with modified start and end points and possibly with effects added. They are effectively shortcuts – a one object playlist, if you like.

Of the remaining items in the Edit menus, most are best described in context, when we have actually got something to edit. They are introduced in the later chapters, but please also use the index to see where they are discussed in detail.

Wizards are effectively sub programs that perform specialised creation functions.

Slideshow maker will automate the creation of a movie consisting of still photos and music.

Music generator allows you to create music automatically.

Travel route generator is a fairly niche tool, only available in Plus and Ultimate, that can take a map and draw a route around it for you.

The last two items in the edit menu concern Multicam mode. Again, this isn't available in the basic program. It's a very specific editing layout that lets you cut between two cameras, normally used when you have shot the same action from two different angles and want to cut them together "as live". This very useful tool was what first attracted me to the Magix range of NLE software and I will cover it more extensively later in the book.

Effects Menu

Altering the source material in any way other than choosing the start and end points you use in a movie normally involves adding an Effect. These can be something really simple such as making a video clip a little brighter or cropping a photo to improve the framing, right through to multi-layer overlay, distortions, movements, speed changes and more.

There is very little in the drop-down Effects menu that doesn't appear in the Effects tab of the Media pool or as context menu command, but one feature deserves special mention here.

Master Effects

Effects settings movies is a useful tool if you want to add a global effect to a whole movie. You are most likely to use this command for small corrections rather than anything radical. Perhaps when you make a DVD from your video camera footage it appears too dark or the wrong colour when played back on the TV, or photos are cropped so you don't see the whole image.

The Master Effects panel

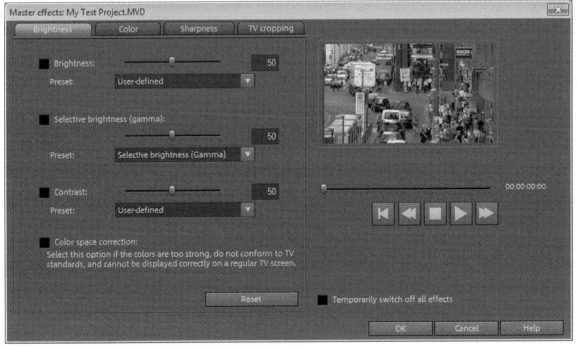

When you use this command, a box opens entitled *Master effects*. The right side of the box has a preview screen, scrubber and simple transport controls so that you can preview the global effect on the whole movie. A small checkbox allows you to enable or disable any corrections you have made so that you can compare "before" and "after" in the preview window. *Temporarily switch off all effects* is just that – temporary. You can't use it to disable Master effects; you have to reset them.

The left side of the box has four tabs, each of which has a reset button so you can ensure you can disable any changes.

Master effects color tab

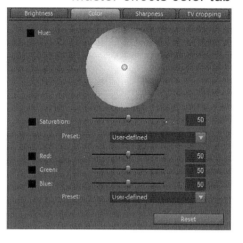

Brightness contains sliders and drop down pre-sets for brightness, gamma (which affects certain areas of the brightness) and contrast. *Color space correction* is a checkbox that allows you to reduce the range of colour so that it can display properly – if somewhat washed out – on any TV screen. At the extremes of colour reproduction, conventional printing is capable of using a wide range of colours but they are don't match those that computers and TVs are capable of. Additionally broadcast standards limit the range of colours so that all TV sets can reproduce them.

Color allows you to adjust the overall Hue, Saturation (the amount of colour – no saturation is equal to black and white) and the relative red/green/blue levels. If you have shot a whole movie with a camera set to the wrong colour temperature setting, for example, it can be fixed here.

Sharpness allows you to enhance pictures, and sometimes that can also mean making them *less* sharp to disguise patterning or "noise" in the video – detail that shouldn't be there. Taking a look through the pre-sets here is a good way of understanding how the various controls interact to achieve improvements.

The Sharpness tab

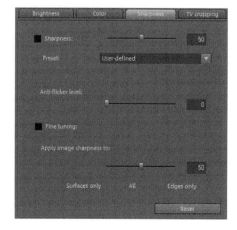

For example, reducing high frequency variations in a otherwise "flat" (surface) area will hide video noise.

The *Anti-flicker level* option only works on still images where the very sharp edges of downsized pictures can flicker, particularly if you add a movement effect.

The *TV Cropping* tab addresses an issue that affected many TV sets in the past, but with the decline of CRT TV displays is less of a problem. However, even modern flat panel displays can suffer from a problem of excessive overscan, resulting in you not being able to see the full picture.

Early TV sets never showed the whole picture that was broadcast in order to avoid showing the flickering lines around the analogue signal. A poorly set up TV would show even less than it was supposed to. In order to accommodate this all broadcasters, even today, obey rules about "cut-off". Any important text that has to be read must fall within a central zone, although other important visual elements are allowed a little more room. So, a properly shot TV programme should never have missing information even on an overscanning TV display.

As a hobbyist, you may not have obeyed these rules, so you might want to shrink your video at the last stage. An additional problem is caused by computer screens showing the entire video picture, so you become more aware of what is missing. Finally, DVD players, in conjunction with TVs, often have arbitrary "auto" settings to avoid the viewer ever seeing black borders, and these can make the cut-off even worse.

This last problem can also distort the shapes of objects, making circular items look oval. If you can find the correct settings between your DVD player and your TV, and you take care when shooting and placing titles on your movies you shouldn't really need to shrink the final output, but if you do, the TV cropping feature will help you do so.

There is a short project that you can burn to a disc to check what settings will be best for your DVD/TV combination. In my copy of MEP the name of the movie has been mistranslated - it's actually called _TV anti cropping. You can then input the figures into the parameter boxes. Three check boxes at the bottom allow you to choose if you want to crop photos, videos and all tracks.

Note that this feature does not shrink titles. When you create a title it is possible to force the text to fit within the safe area (it's an advanced setting), so there should be no need. Also, TV Cropping allows you to display a white safe area line in the preview monitor at all times – just check the *Show TV screen area in preview monitor* box – so, when using graphics or reframing photos, you can be sure your composition complies with broadcast standards.

The Master Effects Cropping tab

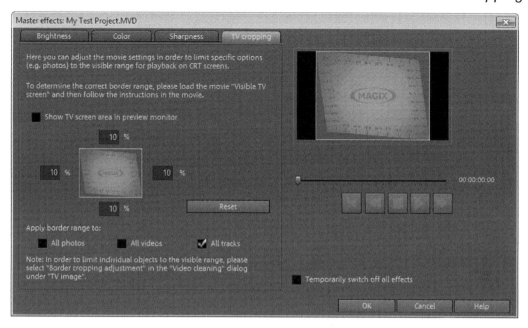

More Effects

Returning to the effects menu, the first two functions in the *Effect/Video Object effects* menu don't appear in the Media pool – *Scene detection* and *Stabilisation*. We will cover how these work when we make the *Flight* movie.

The next section actually applies to Photos. If you have Plus or Ultimate, you can open a selected photo using the supplied photo editing program **Xtreme Photo Designer**, or if you dive into the setting menu you can make this option work with a photo editing program of your choice that you may be more comfortable with. *Save*

The Effects/Video objects effects menu (Plus and Ultimate)

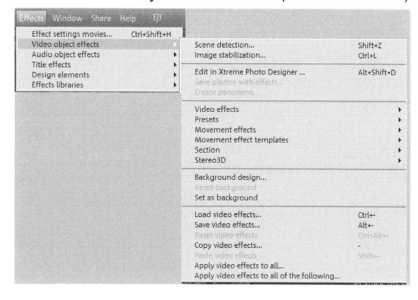

Photos with effects saves a new copy of the selected photo with the effects you have added permanently applied. *Create Panorama* opens a Wizard that lets you stitch two or more suitable photos together to make a continuous photo – normally used when you can't get the whole view in one shot, but also useful for blending normal pictures together.

The final three sections of the *Effects/Video object effects*, and all of *Effects/Audio object effects*, *Title effects*, *Design elements* and *Effects libraries* menus are duplicated in the Media pool, when using the context menus on objects or by having their own toolbar button; they will be covered in detail elsewhere.

Window Menu

The Window menu (Plus and Ultimate versions)

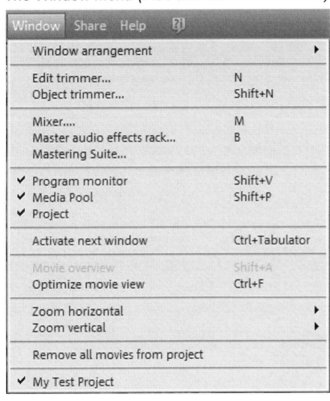

We have already looked at the first few entries in this menu - the *Window arrangement* sub menu options, used to set and reset the basic Edit screen layout.

Edit trimmer and *Object trimmer* open a tool for frame accurate editing, while the next section brings up powerful audio mixing tools.

Program monitor, *Media pool* and *Project* can be clicked on to check or uncheck the entries – hiding and revealing the relevant dockable components of the edit screen. If you are working with a large or with dual monitors and have undocked the Edit screen areas this can be a useful tool.

Activate next window moves the focus to the next area, the same effect as clicking on it, so you are unlikely to use this option, but you might want to use the keyboard shortcut – CTRL-TAB.

Movie Overview is a feature you are unlikely to use until your project gets quite complex and you are using Timeline mode. It switches the Program monitor away from its normal function of displaying source material or the current position of the movie you are editing and instead displays a graphical representation of the entire movie. You can then draw boxes around parts you want to display or click on individual clips to show them maximised in the Project area. When we get a decent sized project in place I will describe how to use this method of navigation, but for now, if you find yourself looking at something confusing in the Program monitor, you may have accidentally activated this mode.

Apart from using the menu, this mode can also be activated – and deactivated – by the furthest right icon under the program monitor, or toggled on and off with the keyboard shortcut SHIFT-A - most likely that's how you got there by accident!

Optimise movie view resizes the display in the Program window to show the whole project. The two Zoom commands contain options for resizing the view. Again, you are more likely to use the keyboard shortcuts, mouse or the tools in the program window instead of the menu options.

Movie Overview and the Program monitor button

Window/Remove all movies from project is in an odd place, in my opinion. There is actually a context menu option to manage the various movies in the Project window so it seems odd that this one is here. If you want to reduce the number of movie tabs in the project window to zero, you can use this command.

If you only have one movie open in the project window, the last entry in the Window menu will be the title of that movie. If you were to have more than one, you could select the active movie by selecting it here – not something that is particularly useful because the same task can be achieved by clicking on the desired movie tab.

Share Menu

This offers a number of options for exporting your movies to the Internet, interfacing with Magix own Internet services and burning files to optical disc (again!).

When it comes to using YouTube or Vimeo, although you can use these methods, it's often better to make your files and then use the sharing site's own upload routines when posting your files. The reasons for doing this are two-fold. Using MEP to do the upload ties up the program when you could be getting on with more editing.

The Share menu upload options

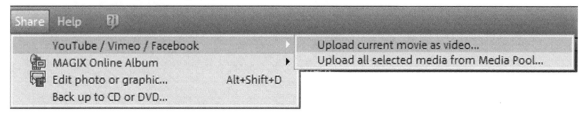

Additionally, the video sharing sites sometimes change their APIs – the interface another program uses to perform the upload. So there may be times that the upload doesn't work, while Magix prepare a patch. Some guidelines are discussed as to the best file formats to use when manually uploading when we look at Exporting.

Help Menu

The Help menu

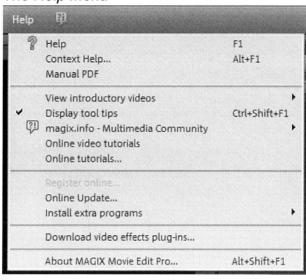

This is where you can find many resources for training and using the program, including help files and links to Internet based help. Switching on the *Context Help...* tooltip is possible here – but the keyboard shortcut ALT-F1 or the upper toolbar tool are quicker ways to access this. You can switch off Tooltips from here as well.

Some items aren't strictly "Help". You can register the program and check online to see if your program is completely up to date, although the very latest patches, perhaps not fully tested "beta" patches, may not be available unless you visit the Magix website manually. There are options for installing extra effects such as the additional plug-ins that come with the Ultimate version, and free extras available from the Magix website. Finally, the *About* option allows you to check the version you are running and your serial number, as well as displaying a considerable amount of copyright information.

The last menu item is a question mark that can connect you straight to the Magix website to ask a question. If the answer is already in the database, this can be a useful feature, but if it isn't it might take some time!

The Media Pool

The Media pool is where Movie Edit Pro displays the stuff – media, transitions, titles and effects – that you want to use in your movies. The most complex part is the **Import** section, which you select with the left-most tab. It's a very flexible browsing and searching tool that works in a similar way to Windows.

Import

Click on the Import tab. Here you can locate any media – videos, photos or audio that is already on your computer. You can also select and preview it in the Program monitor and pre-

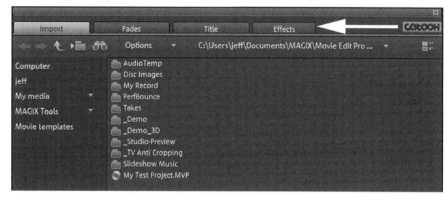

Media pool with the content tabs indicated with an arrow

trim it – by which I mean choose the start and end point – before you include it in your movie.

It is possible to open a standard Windows Explorer window outside of MEP and drag your source material to the Timeline, but you won't be able to pre-edit the clips, so it is worth learning to use the Media pool/Import screen.

The toolbar across the top starts on the left with three navigation icons – Back, Forward and Up. Click on the next icon that looks like a folder – the tooltip says Folder tree view. Click on it a couple of times to see the display beneath the icon switch between a simple list of locations and a tree view.

For now, choose the simple List view. The locations showing are all Links, and by default there should be five main links. The list can be customised so that other links can be added, re-arranged or deleted but the five defaults are fixed and stay at the top of the list.

You should see Computer at the top of the list. Under this will be the name you used to log into Windows. The next item should be My media, and alongside will be a small triangular expand/contract button. These buttons are important. Wherever you see them, it means that there are sub-options that can be revealed by clicking on the button. If you want to collapse the list to tidy up the display, click on the button again.

These first three links all point to locations on the computer of your hard disc – Computer being the most obvious. Your user name ("jeff" in the example screenshots) points to the My Documents location for the current user. If you haven't set up a specific user account then that may be the "name" of the computer.

Using the expansion arrow to display the contents of My media

My media doesn't show anything until you open up the sub-options. Here you will find some useful predefined locations. In particular, if you have customised some of the locations in File/Settings/ Program/Folder the links here will reflect your custom locations – for example, change the default recordings location to D:\Magix recordings (to save your captures to a second hard drive) and the My media/Recordings link will change to point to the new location.

Magix tools lists places on the Internet where you can find source material or locations where you have already put downloaded objects. Movie templates is another way of loading the templates you had the chance to do in the "What do you want to do?" Opening dialogue box (if you own Plus or Ultimate).

Creating a new link in the Media pool list

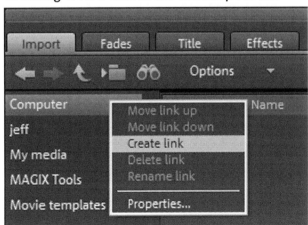

If that's all you see, you haven't created a Custom link yet. Right click on any of the other links and the context menu will only offer you one option – *Create link*. Let's do that now – it will come in handy shortly:

• Right click on *Computer* and select *Create link* from the context menu.

•In the Windows Browse for folder box, select Computer/C: (your main drive may also have a name, but it will be called C:).

- Click on *Make New Folder*.

- In the text box, name the new folder *Revealed Video* and press *OK*.

- A white rename box will appear in the Media Pool Links area pre-populated with the title *New link*. Change this to *Revealed Video* and then press Enter.

The Link context Menu

Right click on the link and you will see that you have the chance to rename, delete or manage it – if there were more than one you could re-order the list. Properties opens a Windows information box relating to the location the link points to.

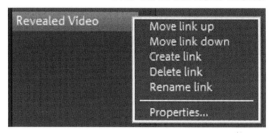

As you click through the links – Computer, User, My Media – you will notice that the contents of the pane to the right change, reflecting the contents of the location the link refers to. I'll call this the browser pane from now on. The important difference between using the browser pane and a normal Windows Explorer window is that only the relevant objects on your hard discs and removable storage media, such as memory cards and optical discs, are displayed. You will also see any files that could be used as objects in your movies such as video, photo and audio files that are compatible with the program. What you won't see are irrelevant files – text files for example.

The browser display tool

You can how this content is displayed, using the tool at the far right of the toolbar – Display options. Select Computer in the list and select each option in turn to see the difference.

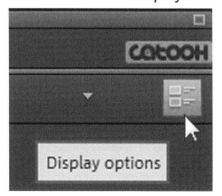

List is a simple, compact display. Details shows more information about the locations, organised in columns. In both these modes there is a small icon indicating what type the object is. Videos show as film frame, Photos are a coloured picture frame, Audio files are shown as musical notes and Takes displayed as a star.

Large icons gives a clearer graphical display – and in the case of videos and photos you get to see proper thumbnails. When Large icons is selected, a new tool appears on the toolbar to the left of Display options; the + and – sign opens a slider that allows you to alter the size of the icons, which is particularly useful when displaying the thumbnails.

Large icons view with the size control arrowed

Now I have described the basics, we can experiment with the navigation controls. Select Computer in the list and if you see something other than a simple list of hard drives and optical drives, click on the upward pointing arrow tool third from the left. This should take you up one level at a time until you see the text Workspace on the toolbar – now you are at the top level!

Double-click on the C drive and try to find a video clip by drilling down through the folders. Try clicking on Users to open that folder, then Public, then Public Videos. If there aren't any clips there, try your own user profile. If you fail to find any video clips I'll show you how to get some in a moment.

Switch the view to Large icons and alter the size slider to see how much clearer the icons and thumbnails can be made.

Clicking on the Up arrow tool should return you to the workspace level (Notice that the tooltip is a little misleading here – the keyboard shortcut is the backspace key). However, now we have a bit of a browsing history and so the back and forward arrows, the two tools on the far left of the toolbar, will allow you to explore the locations you have already visited.

Yet another way to navigate around the locations is provided by the drop down arrow to the right of the text displaying the current location in the toolbar – click on that to see a list of recently used locations and click on one to open it in the browsing pane.

Searching for a file is achieved with the "binoculars" icon in the toolbar. This opens a new pane in the List/Tree view area. There are plenty of selections here to help you track down what you are looking for – the pattern pretty much follows that of a Windows search, and as the search depth drop-down box shows, locations that have been indexed by Windows are included in the searches.

The time has come where we want to look at some video. Shortly we are all going to need to be using the same sample clips, so let's look at how to use the media pool to move some video around.

The search tool in action

If you bought the boxed version of the program, you will have the demo project available to you – the footage of the cycle courier in the city streets-but we will need to convert it. If you bought the download version you may not have this footage, but you can download if from my website www.dtvpro.co.uk. Even if you have a poor Internet connection these particular clips should be small enough to download comfortably. If all else fails I can provide a Demo DVD that contains all the files you need to use this book. These can be bought via the same website. The charge for the DVD is to cover costs rather than make a profit (I'd like to include the DVD with the book, but the way small scale publishing works.

To download the clips from the website:

- Open your Internet browser to find the website www.dtvpro.co.uk and navigate to the page for this book's downloads.

- Follow the instructions for the browser you are using to download the three files clip_020.wmv, clip 021.wmv and clip_058.wmv into the default download location.

- Open the default download location in Windows.

- Hold down CTRL and click on each of the three files in turn so they are all highlighted.

- Right click on one of the files and select *Copy* from the context menu.

- Now return to the Magix program.

- Click on the link *Revealed Video* we created.

- Right click anywhere empty in the browser pane on the right and select *Paste* from the context menu.

- Wait for Windows to copy the files into the hard disc location we set up earlier.

If you have the DVD:

- Insert it into your DVD drive.

- Click on the DVD icon in the browsing pane to open the DVD.

- Click on the folder *My Test Project Clips* to open it.

- There will be three clips there. Select all three.

- Right click on any of the selected clips to bring up the context menu.

- Select *Copy*.

- Click on the link *Revealed Video* we created.

- Right click anywhere empty in the browser pane on the right and select *Paste* from the context menu.

- Wait for Windows to copy the files into the hard disc location we set up earlier.

From the above two workflows, you can see that Copy and Paste works between Windows Explorer and the Media pool. Note, though, that you need to use the right-click context menu in the Media pool – keyboard shortcuts don't work in the same way as they do in Windows.

If you don't have an Internet connection and don't have the Demo DVD, see if you have the demo project available in MEP. Click on the link *My media/projects* and look for a folder called _Demo. If it is there then you can proceed as follows:

- Double click on the _Demo folder to open it. Find the following files and CTRL-click on each one to highlight them all :- clip_020.mxv, clip 021.mxv, and clip_58.mxv.

- Right click on any of the clips to bring up the context menu

- Select *Copy*.

- Click on the link *Revealed Video* we created.

- Right click on a blank area in the browser pane on the right and select *Paste* from the context menu.

- Wait for Windows to copy the files into the hard disc location we set up earlier.

This workflow shows that you can also copy and paste between Windows locations using the Media pool alone.

Important Note:

At the time of writing, there is a thumbnail bug in Movie Edit Pro build 13.0.2.8. Although it is limited to .mxv files, it makes the following demonstrations somewhat confusing as you may see the wrong thumbnails in the Storyboard. There also appears to be issues with clip durations. Therefore, for consistency I recommend that you now convert the mxv clips to wmv files using the Batch Conversion wizard. Refer forward to page 476 where I describe in detail how to do this.

OK, now we definitely have some video to play with!

Click on the Revealed Video link to open the location if it isn't already and then right click on some blank space in the browser pane to bring up the context menu. This has 8 options and possibly some navigation links at the bottom.

At the top of the menu are three options that duplicate the role of the Display options tool we used earlier. Select Large icons and adjust the size slider to about the half way position so your display is similar to the screenshot.

Notice in particular that when you hover your mouse over a video file (or indeed a photo or audio file) a small blue toolbar appears. This happens regardless of the display mode but it is clearer when larger

The Browser context menu

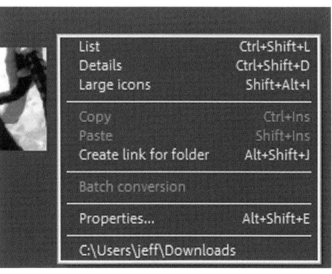

thumbnails are used. These are important tools and we will look at them in detail when I introduce the program monitor.

Copy and paste should be obvious in function – we have just used them. Create link for folder is a handy option – use it to give whatever folder location you have open in the browser pane a custom link in the List view on the left. You don't have to give the link a name either – although you can rename it if you wish. Batch conversion only works if a file or files are highlighted – as I mentioned earlier it can be used for converting files to different formats. Properties opens a Windows Properties box for the current location.

I have yet to describe one function on the Media pool Import toolbar – Options. This brings up a 13 option context menu – which is the same menu you get if you highlight a thumbnail, folder or other icon and right-click, although this may have some additional navigation options tagged onto the bottom. Many options are the same as the context menu for the location, but you can Delete and Rename objects, see the properties for the object rather than the location, Create a new folder, open the CD/DVD burning wizard and export to the Magix online services.

The Options menu

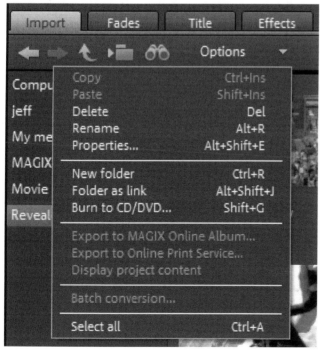

Display project content is a handy little tool that shows you what objects are included in a project – but you need to use it on a project file. There isn't anything to see in our test project right now, but if you have the demo project available you could try it out on the _Demo.MPV file. It's a good way of finding a specific file you know you have used in an old project and including it in a new one by dragging it from the media pool to the Project area.

One option available in the longer context menu is Select all – along with the hint that the keyboard shortcut for this is CTRL-A. This will select all the objects in the current pane for you to carry out further operations – copy, drag, delete and so on. This is a very handy tool.

Selection – Windows and all

I'm going to discuss Windows selection techniques for a moment. These apply to most Windows programs including MEP as well as the Operating system, and you may well use them already, but I'm surprised at how many people don't know all of them. In other sections of the book I'll use the phrase "Windows multi-selection" or just "multi-select" when you can use them. If you would like to try them out use the three files in the Revealed Video view.

Single-clicking on a single object in the current window selects it.

Holding down the CTRL key and single clicking adds that item to the group selected.

Single clicking again without CTRL starts the selection process over so you only have one object selected.

With a group of objects selected, holding down CTRL and clicking on an object de-selects just that object from the group.

Clicking on one object, then holding down the SHIFT key while clicking on another object selects all the objects in the range between the two objects.

Using the mouse to draw a selection

CTRL-A selects all the objects.

You can also use the mouse. Click and hold on a blank area of the window and then drag to create a "Lasso" or "Marquee" – sometimes called a bounding or selection box – and all the objects that are touched by the area you draw are selected. (Sadly, the Windows option of using the CTRL key to add further areas selected by the mouse doesn't work in MEP)

As we will see later on, these techniques don't just work in the Media pool – you can use them in the project area as well.

Tree View

Tree View

Switching to Tree view – the fourth toolbar icon from the left – shows the current location within the context of the structure of your hard disc.

This takes up more space but is a clearer way to navigate around. The triangle icons again indicate if there is further content but in this case if they are pointing to the right the branch of the tree isn't open, if they are point down and right, the branch is open. Clicking on the triangle opens and closes the branch.

I tend to only use tree view for the initial location of objects. If I'm going to use that particular branch of the tree often I turn the folder location into a link so I can use the basic view. A lot depends on how organised you are. However you want to work, the tree view takes up valuable space, so it's often worth switching it off so you can make your object thumbnails bigger or fit more of them into the browser pane.

The other Media pool tabs

Fades, Title and Effects tabs allow you access to the fades (transitions), titles and effects as well as letting you change the parameters, and in the case of titles create one from scratch. Each has a list view on the left, but the contents of the right hand pane vary – sometimes there are objects you can add to your movies, but often there are controls. The Media pool becomes an editor in many circumstances. We will explore these functions in detail later.

The Catooh button is a shortcut to the online facility that can also be reached via the File/Online menu. You can use it to download free and paid for content to add to your movies, which gets placed in the Media pool links under MAGIX Tools/Downloads/Photo and video folder location.

Let's look again at the blue toolbar that appears when you hover over a media files. There are three tools that act on the current media object; left to right they are **Preview**, **Send to the Program monitor** and **Send to the Edit area**.

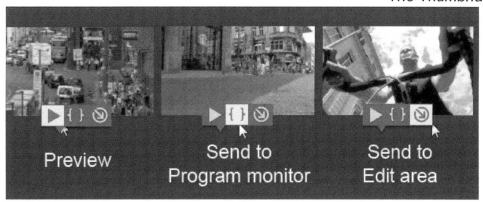

Preview   Send to   Send to
               Program monitor   Edit area

Introducing the Program monitor

We have finally got to the point where we can see the Program monitor in action! Let's first look at what the Preview tool does:

- Select the Revealed Video link in the Media pool.

- Click on the icon at the far right of the Media pool toolbar and select Large icons.

- Click on the size tool to the left and adjust the slider to about half way.

- Hover your mouse over the thumbnail with the title *clip_20.mxv*. A blue toolbar appears at the bottom of the thumbnail.

- Click on the Preview tool.

What do you see? I see the wide shot of the cyclist playing in the Program monitor display window on the left. It's only seven and a half seconds long, so don't blink! I'll describe the Program monitor in detail shortly but one point I'd like you to note is that the title of the clip has appeared above the display of the clip. This tells you what you are looking at, and while that may seem obvious at the moment, it is a significant piece of information.

Double-clicking on an object in the Media pool/Import area normally has the same effect as pressing the play tool. However, you can change the behaviour in the Settings/Program/System panel so the double-click behaviour is to Send to Arranger – or as it is called in some areas of the program, Send to Edit Area. My preference is to stick with the default and through the book I'll assume you have as well. Like other defaults that can be altered, if you've come from a different program and have its behaviour engrained in you then you might want to change Magix's settings.

If you want to browse an audio clip by using either the Preview tool or by double clicking on the item, then you will hear the sound play, along with a graphic representation in the Program monitor. However if you select a Photograph then just the Photo will appear in the monitor.

Now for Send to Program monitor:

- Repeat the first three steps above if required so you can see all three clips.
- Hover your mouse over the thumbnail with the title clip_21. A blue toolbar appears at the bottom of the thumbnail.
- Click on the middle tool that looks like a pair of curly brackets, or braces.

In this case, the video won't play but it will replace the previous clip in the Program monitor window. Note that the title has changed, but another significant difference is the blue bar that appears under the display – this is the range indicator, which we will explore in a moment.

Again, you can move an object from the Media pool to the Program monitor without using the tool – but in this case, there is a slightly different outcome. Click on a file, hold down the mouse button and drag the file to the Program monitor viewing area and the file is loaded into the monitor, but when you do it this way, the range indicator isn't set. This is a subtle difference which may be useful for some people's workflow.

Introducing the Edit area

The final tool involves the use of the lower window – something else that you might be wondering if I'd ever get round to describing.

Before we start using it I'm going to have to check something in case you didn't reset the program before starting work – the display mode of the Edit area at the bottom of the edit screen. Look at the screenshot. The first icon of the edit area toolbar needs to be highlighted – its tooltip will say Storyboard mode if you hover over it. In Storyboard mode objects placed in the movie are represented by blocks of equal size, surrounded by various icons. That's the mode I want you to use at the moment, so click on it now.

I'd also like you to do one other check. The 13th tool – that's the final one of the central group - should look a bit like this: { _+}

The relevant Edit area tools

You can compare your screen with the screenshot or hover your mouse over the icon to get the tooltip, which should say Automatic application. If it doesn't, click on the small drop-down arrow to the right and select the top item in the list.

OK, now I can show the Edit area in action!

The Send to Edit area tool:

- Repeat the first three steps again if required so you can see all three clips.
- Hover your mouse over the thumbnail with the title *clip_58.mxv*. A blue toolbar appears at the bottom of the thumbnail.
- Click on the right-hand tool that consists of a circle containing a diagonal arrow.
- What will probably happen at this point is an annoying dialogue box will appear telling you something about the project and clip settings not matching. For now, select the *Adjust* button.

The video clip will appear in the Program monitor – but some other significant things will have happened:

A thumbnail of the clip will have been placed in the Edit area.

The blue range indicator will have disappeared from below the Program monitor display.

The name of the project will have replaced the name of the clip above the display.

The project name will have acquired the addition of an asterisk indicating the project has changed but hasn't been saved.

So now the Program monitor is no longer displaying an object in the Media pool, it is displaying the Movie being made in the Edit area.

Currently the movie only consists of one clip, but nevertheless it is a movie. The clip that is included in the movie is flagged with a red dot in the Media pool.

I want to make the movie just a little more complex, and show you another feature of the Import tool:

- Use Windows selection to multi-select the first two clips in the media pool – *clip_020* and *clip_021* – so that they are highlighted.

- Now hover your mouse over either of the clips so the blue toolbar appears.

- Click on the **Send to Edit** tool again.

- Two more objects should be displayed at the end of the Storyboard.

We now have a proper movie, consisting of three whole clips! It is being displayed in the Program monitor, and we know that because the project title – My Test Project – is displayed above the video.

So, you can send a whole bunch of clips to the movie in this way, just with one mouse click.

Notice that the three clips in the movie are in the order we sent them – the third clip is the first in the movie, then the other two clips were added to the end of the movie in the order they appeared in the Media pool. This is a function of using the Send to Edit area tool with Automatic application selected as the Insert mode – the clips get appended to the end of the movie.

The three clips in the edit area

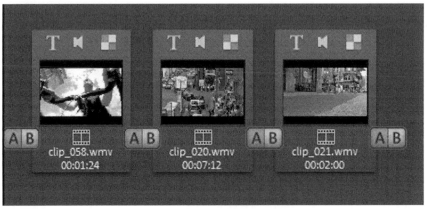

If you don't want to put the clips at the end of the movie, you can use another Insert mode or just drag and drop them – even if they are a multiple selection. This allows you to choose where you place them. We need to understand the Edit area clearly before we use this approach. Before that, there are a lot of powerful tools associated with the Program monitor that are worth exploring.

Best practice for saving projects

Now we have a movie, we ought to consider saving it. If something goes awry it's then just a case of reloading it rather that starting from scratch.

As I said earlier, our movie is contained within the project as a form of playlist. If you have made changes to the playlist in any way since the last time you saved it, you will see an asterisk after the project name as displayed on the title bar for the entire program, and the movie name displayed above the Program monitor when it is displaying the contents of the edit area.

Let's just save the project:

- Hold down the CTRL key
- Press the S key

That's it – the asterisks should have disappeared until you make another change. If you struggle to remember too many keyboard shortcuts, you can use the File/Save project command instead of CTRL-S.

There are very few downsides to saving as you go along, particularly if you have set the Undo level to something a bit higher than the default. Some programs forget the Undo history when you save, but MEP doesn't. When you reload a project, sure, the undos aren't available, but then you are unlikely to close the project in the middle of your creative flow.

Movie Edit Pro's automatic backup can't be relied upon to save the program at significant moments, so unless you have it set to a very frequent level you are always in danger of losing a little work if the program crashes.

Better still, make incremental saves. Every so often do a "Save as" instead of a "Save" and add a number to the end of the file name, or even a description. For example, say you have made the body of the movie and you are thinking of adding some titles – save the program and My Test Movie 1 or My Test Movie before titles. That way, if something in the project gets corrupted or you have a radical change of heart about the content, there are points that you can step back to without having to rely on Undo or starting from scratch.

The Program Monitor

Having looked briefly at the program monitor in the context of the Media pool, let's now look at all the features, one at a time.

3D modes (Plus and Premium only)

At the very top of the Program monitor the grey movement bar we used to undock the pane has an icon on the left that controls the viewing mode. Click on it for a drop down menu and ensure that Standard (2D) is selected.

If at any time you see an odd display, you may have been switched to one of the 3D viewing modes. There is a section about 3D later in the book, but in brief, wherever you see the glasses icon, it indicates 3D settings. Cycle through the other types of display if you wish, to familiarize yourself with the other display modes, and

The 3D display mode menu

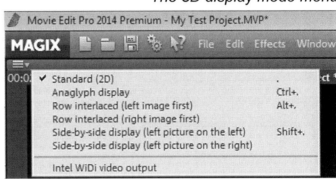

then return to 2D. If you have an Intel WiDi adaptor, you can enable it here.

Changing the view

Switching the content of the monitor is achieved with the mouse:

- Double click on clip_020 in the Media pool to play it (or use the Preview tool if you have changed the default behaviour).

- When it ends the monitor will display black briefly. It will then return to the first frame, with the clip name still showing at the top.

- To switch to monitoring the current movie, click on anywhere in the edit area and the clip name will change to the movie name.

- Depending on where you click, you may still be monitoring the previous clip. If you do, just press the space bar twice to bring up the display from the Movie.

Timecodes

The bar that currently displays the movie name also has two timecodes displayed on either side. To the left is the time of the current frame, to the right is the overall duration of whatever is being displayed or a range if that is active. Timecodes take the format hours, minutes, seconds and frames, where the number of frames in a second will depend on the video standard of the movie or video clip.

Further information is also placed just below the video display. The clip, project or range duration is shown as a number without superfluous leading units – if there are zero hours or minutes, for example, they aren't displayed.

The Playback marker

Timecodes and the Playback marker

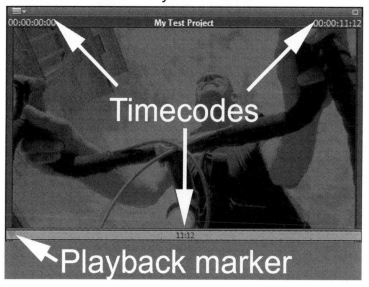

As we are now looking at the movie, the right-hand timecode should read 00:00:11:12 – the movie's current duration. The left-hand timecode will show the position of the orange downward pointing marker below the display. Magix calls this triangle the Playback marker when displayed in the program monitor. If you have used other software you might know it as the scrubber or playhead:

- Press the END key on your keyboard and the Playback marker will move to the end of the movie.

- Now the left-hand timecode will read the same as the duration on the left.

- Press the HOME key on your keyboard and the Playback marker will move to the start of the movie.

- Now the left hand timecode will read zero.

- Press the spacebar; watch the Playback marker move and the timecode increment as the movie plays.

Moving the Playback marker

Dragging the Playback marker with the mouse is one fundamental way of locating a part of a video clip. The action is often called scrubbing, so the *Playback marker* is often called the *Scrubber* in other software. This also applies to the marker and cursor when we work in the edit area. At times I may use Scrubber interchangeably with Playback marker or Cursor.

In many circumstances dragging the marker is sufficient but there are numerous other ways to move it, including more keyboard controls. I'm going to demonstrate some of them in conjunction with using another tool. One method that I hardly use is to type numbers directly into the boxes, but this is possible if you take a little care.

Setting Ranges – In and Out points

I've already shown you the blue range indicator when we put a clip into the Program monitor, but we can also bring the range indicator into being when working on a movie. The left hand edge of a Range is called the In point, the right hand edge is an Out point.

Please note that these terms don't just apply to ranges. Untrimmed clips don't display ranges, but the first frame is still called the In point, the last frame is the Out point. Trimmed clips within the movie also have In and Out points.

Setting a range is a very important tool in MEP, particularly when working on source material. There are a number of ways to do it; some are accurate, some are convenient, and an accomplished editor will use more than one method.

First of all let's use the mouse:

- Click on the bar that contains the Playback marker about a quarter of the way from the left.

- The marker moves there and you will either see the close shot of the cyclist or the wide shot.

- Click, hold and drag the marker until you find the exact first frame of the wide shot.

- Release the mouse button.

- Click on the opening curly bracket tool on the transport console below – it's the first button on the left.

Setting the In point

- We have set the In point of the range – an opening curly bracket appears beneath the Playback marker.

- Click on the bar to move the Playback marker to about three-quarters along the movie.

- Drag the marker to locate the very last frame of the high wide shot before the low long shot.

- Click on the closing curly bracket tool on the transport console below – it's the second button on the left.

Setting the Out point

- We have set an Out point for the range. A closing curly bracket appears under the marker and the area between the two markers is coloured blue.

If you got this spot on, the timecode in the middle of the blue area will say 07.11

You can also adjust the In and Out points of a range by dragging the curly brackets once they are in place.

- Click somewhere in the middle of the range to move the Playback marker out of the way.

- Hover over the In point marker at the start of the range to get a double headed cursor.

- Click and drag the In point left so the range duration extends to 9 seconds.

- Release the mouse button.

Notice that as we did this, the Program monitor showed the exact frame as we dragged the markers.

Accurately selecting the exact frame by dragging the markers with the mouse can be a bit tricky. There is a tool in the Program monitor that can help you. Immediately below the Playback marker and range area is a thin dark grey line. Look more closely and you will see small "handles" at the left and right edges:

- Hover over the left-hand handle to generate a double headed mouse cursor.

- Click, hold and drag the handles to the right. The dark grey bar shrinks equally on either side.

- Keep dragging until the slider is about a third of the size of the entire width of the Program window.

Zooming the timescale in the Program monitor

- The blue range bar completely fills its own area and the In and Out points disappear off the edges.

- Release the mouse button and click and hold on the centre of the slider.

- Slide it left until the In point appears and then release the mouse button.

- Now drag the Playback marker and find the start of the wide shot again. You will have less range but more accuracy. Reset the In point.

- Drag one of the slider handles to restore it to its full width.

If you are a "mouse" person, there is a more convenient and accurate way to adjust the Playback marker without having to constantly be adjusting the scale view. Before I show you that, let's get rid of the range.

Removing the range

It's rarely a problem that a range is set, but it can clutter the view a little. If you want to remove the blue bar from the Program monitor, double click on it. The bar disappears and the In and Out point markers disappear. Easy, eh?

The Jog wheel

At the very bottom of the Program monitor beneath the Transport console are four controls. The one on the left is a Jog wheel. At the same time as demonstrating this feature, let me also introduce the keyboard short cuts to set the In and Out points:

Hover your mouse over the Jog wheel click and hold.

- Drag the mouse slightly to the right and stop

- As you do so, the Playback marker moves a few frames to the right and then stops.

- Drag it back to the left a short distance and the marker and display follow suit.

- Locate the first frame of the wide shot again.

- Don't bother to release the mouse button, just press the I key with your other hand to mark the In point

The playback marker doesn't move the same distance as you move your mouse, which makes this jog wheel operation very accurate. For short distances it doesn't matter that the mouse cursor strays away from the wheel tool. However, if you want to jog a long way, you might run out of space. This is when you can use the SHIFT key:

- With the mouse button still held down, try to jog to the end of the wide shot.

- You will find the mouse getting near the right edge of the program window. For longer distances you would run out of room.

- Jog back to the left.

- Press and hold down the SHIFT key.

- Now jog to the right. You need to move the mouse far less.

- When in the vicinity of the Out point, release the SHIFT key.

- Continue to jog to locate the Out point – the control has returned to its original sensitivity.

- When you have found the last frame of the wide shot, press the O key on your keyboard to set the Out point.

Let's take a break from setting In and Out points while I show you the other ways of playing clips and moving the Playback marker. As you explore them, consider what tasks they might be more suitable for.

The jog and shuttle controls

Jog

Shuttle

Shuttle

To the right of the Jog control is a Shuttle slider. For longer movies and clips, this is a better control to use:

- Click and hold on the knob in the middle of the Shuttle slider.

- Drag it just a little way to the right. Playback commences in a forward direction, but at a very slow speed.

- The further you move the knob to the right, the faster the playback.

- Soon you will reach a very fast playback speed – it's indicated by the tooltip as 99 times real playback speed. You will also reach the end of the movie!

- Return the knob to the left. The Playback speed slows down.

- Once past the centre position, the playback goes into reverse.

A certain amount of accuracy may be needed for frame accuracy, so you might want to switch to using the Jog wheel for the final location of a frame, but over longer distances the shuttle control is a good tool. If you are searching a particularly long clip or movie, you might even want to use the SHIFT key, which speeds up the shuttle by another factor of ten – warp speed 990x real time!

The Transport console

The row of buttons above the Jog and Shuttle controls are called the Transport Console. We have looked at setting In and Out points with the first two controls on the left.

Transport controls

The third button moves the Playback marker to the range. If no range is set it goes to the start of the movie.

The fourth button moves the marker to the start of the clip or movie, regardless of the range setting.

The fifth button is the Play control. A very significant keyboard shortcut for this control is the Space bar. Click the button or press the Space bar and the movie or clip starts playing at the current Playback marker position and will continue to the end unless you stop it.

While the video is playing, you will notice the Play icon changes to a square Stop icon. Clicking it, or pressing space, stops the playback.

Should I Stay or Should I Go - back?

With MEP set to its default setting, when you stop playback, the Playback marker returns to the original position. If you have used other video editing software in the past this behaviour will either be what you expect, or it will be annoying because you will be used to the marker stopping at the point you pressed stop.

If you have no preconceptions about how this control should work, I suggest you leave it in the default mode. There are other ways of halting playback that leaves the marker in the stop position. I will describe them a moment.

If it really annoys you that the marker returns to the starting position, disable the behaviour. Select *File/Settings/Program/Playback/Arranger/Spacebar behaviour* and check the *Spacebar stops at current playback position* checkbox. This also modifies the play control behaviour as well.

The sixth button is for range playback – press it and the playback starts at the range In point and ends at the Out point, then the marker returns to where it was. This has a number of uses – I use it to remind me exactly what I have marked, for example.

The seventh button moves the Playback marker to the Out point of the current range.

The last two buttons to the right aren't really relevant at the moment - the red button opens the recording dialogue for bringing video and audio sources into the program. Ignore it for now.

The final control switches the monitor to viewing the project as mentioned earlier. It only works in certain Edit modes.

Using the Keyboard

The Up and Down arrow keys can be used as a supplement to the space bar. The Up arrow plays the video from the current playback position. If the video is playing (however you started it) and you press the Up key, playback stops and the playback marker returns to the position it was before you began playback. However, if you start playback (by any means) then press the Down arrow, playback stops but the marker remains where it is. So, if the dilemma of how to configure the Space bar is too much for you, you can sidestep the problem and use the Up and Down arrows instead!

The J, K and L playback key function is implemented in almost all good video editing programs, but from reading forums I get the impression that few hobbyist editors use them. They really can move your editing up to a more efficient level if you make the effort to learn their function:

- Press the Home key to move the playback cursor to the start of the movie.
- Place your index finger over the J key so that your middle and fourth fingers rest on K and L.
- Press L once. The movie starts to play at normal speed.
- Press J once. The movie starts to play backwards.
- Press K. The movie stops playing and the marker stays where it is.

Ok, now let's try some multiple key presses:

- Press J and let the movie play to the beginning.
- Press L twice in succession. The move starts to play forwards but a double speed.
- Press J once. The forward playback carries on, but back to normal speed.
- Press J again. The playback goes into reverse.
- Press J a few more times. Playback increases in speed until you very quickly reach the start of the movie.

With these features, it's possible to explore long clips easily, slowing down as you approach or overshoot your target. For greater accuracy, you can slow the playback down by using the SHIFT key:

- Hold down the SHIFT key and press L. Playback starts in slow motion.
- Press the L key a further 3 times to ramp up the speed to normal.
- With SHIFT still held down, press J. Each time you do the playback slows down.
- After 4 key presses, the playback reverses.
- For the K key to work, you need to release the SHIFT key.

So with a bit of practice, you should be able to navigate your way very efficiently through video clips, both short and long. The final frame selection is still a bit hit and miss, though. For this, the arrow keys can be used.

Jogging with the keyboard

To step the Playback marker one frame forward, press the right arrow key on the keyboard. One frame back? The left arrow. If you press and hold, playback happens in real time.

Holding down the CTRL key as you jog makes the steps five frames at a time – and holding down the arrow keys with CTRL results in fast forward or reverse playback.

Also, if you want to stop and start playback your fingers are very near two additional shortcuts. The Up arrow starts normal playback, the down arrow stops it.

Jogging with the mouse

If you click on the jog wheel under the program monitor, the scroll wheel on the mouse becomes active for jogging along the video displayed. You can hold down the SHIFT key to change the rate of jogging as well. If you click back on the Timeline the wheel reverts to it's normal behaviour of scrolling the Timeline view. Incidentally, if you hold down CTRL, audio scrubbing is activated.

So with all those methods of moving through clips and movies, you should find one to suit you. What's more, there are other keyboard shorts I haven't mentioned because I don't want to overwhelm you (the = key starts playback as well, for example). If you are very fixed in your ways, the keyboard is fully customisable or you can load presets for other editing programs.

Efficient editing – setting In and Out on the fly

Now I've fully explained all the methods of playback it's worth pointing out that you can set In and Out points even when the video is playing. You don't have to stop the playback - pressing I or O or using the Transport console tools sets the appropriate In or Out point and the playback isn't even interrupted.

So if you are playing a video and making a rough judgement as to what part of the clip you want to use, you can keep pressing the I key until the action begins. The same applies to setting the Out. Has the action finished? Probably – press the O key. Whoops no, there is a little bit more, press O again.

If you have a lot of clips to process and are going to polish the movie later on, this can be a real time saver, rather than carefully jogging to find the precise frame.

Adjusting the display

The Program monitor is normally set to a convenient size in relation to the Edit screen layout. We have seen how you can adjust the arrangement to suit your current task.

At times, you may want the video to fill your PC monitor screen – you just want to assess the clip or movie and sit back without peering at a small area of your desktop. The maximise icon at the top left of the monitor can do this, but you don't need to be that precise:

- Double-click on the video in the monitor. The Program monitor expands to fill your PC display.

- Double-click again. The display returns to its previous size.

- Hold down the ALT key and press Enter. The monitor expands again.

- Press the ESC keys and it returns.

So, you can use both mouse and keyboard routes in and out of full screen display.

Most of the time, we want to see video or photos full frame within the frame size of the Program monitor, but it is possible to zoom in and out as well as move the display manually, you can do this with the mouse and CTRL key:

- Hold down the CTRL key and hover your mouse over the video area of the Program monitor.

- The mouse cursor turns into a hand. If it doesn't, move the mouse slightly.

- Use your mouse wheel to zoom into the video.

- Now click, hold and drag to reposition the view.

- With the hand cursor showing, double-click to restore the view.

This feature is particularly useful if you want to examine some detail of a video or photo without disturbing your window layout and you can't switch to full screen because you are adding effects, for example.

Program monitor viewing size

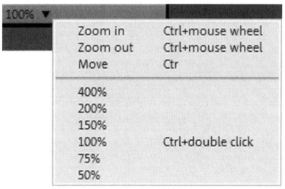

The current zoom level is displayed at the bottom of the monitor and will normally say 100%. Alongside the zoom percentage is a small drop-down arrow that you can use to open a submenu that covers the above operation and has some fixed size presets you can select.

This control should not be confused with setting the resolution of the display. If you have a full HD PC monitor then it will have a resolution 1920*1080, so displaying full HD video in just the top left-hand quarter won't do the video resolution justice. You cannot judge the finer details unless you switch to full screen. With two monitors one can be dedicated to the Program monitor but many people will only have one screen.

This isn't normally an issue during the editing of an HD movie – if you have any concerns about a particular shot being usable you can quickly check it by switching briefly to full screen – perhaps finding the point where it becomes unusably out of focus.

If your movies are of a lower resolution – 1280*720 or Standard Definition then MEP allows you to adjust the size of the Program monitor to a fixed resolution so that you can match it to the native resolution. So if you have a large monitor and are editing SD video, you can be sure that the preview is showing you as much detail as possible and there is no point in making it larger.

This feature is available from the context menu if we right-click on the Program monitor. The first entry is another way to switch to full-screen preview. Next we have a choice of preset resolutions to match your source footage or movie settings, including an option for custom settings, but the next section down is more likely to be of use to you.

Program monitor Context menu

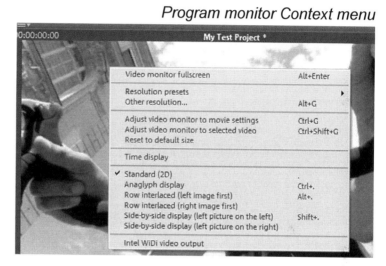

Adjust video monitor to Movie settings will resize the resolution of the program monitor to match the movie, so you can judge the quality of the final output. If you try to use this with full HD video you will be warned that you are about to do something somewhat impractical – because you won't be able to see anything of the rest of the Edit screen!

Adjust video monitor to selected video uses the currently highlighted video object on the Edit area as a template for the size of the Program monitor, so if you have mixed resolution sources in your movie you can size the preview to suit the clip you are currently working on.

Adjust to default size has the same effect on the monitor as pressing F9, but doesn't affect the other areas of the Edit screen.

Show Time - displaying timecode

If you find the small timecode display top left of the program monitor too small, you can add timecode to the movie by using one of the special titler presets. Using the context menu option Time display switches the Media pool to the location where the presets are stored. (Earlier versions actually had a secondary timecode generator, but this was dropped in the 2014 version.)

The final set of context menu commands duplicate the 3D display mode options available from the 3D display mode icon at the top of the monitor.

Full screen preview context menu

There are a few differences in the menu options you get when you right click on a maximised Program monitor. The preset size choices aren't there, but a useful command is in their place.

Stretch video picture to full size makes sure that whatever the resolution of your movie or source material it will fill the screen. The other addition is Show transport controls. If you have a 1920*1080 PC monitor and you are working with full HD video, including the transport controls causes the video to shrink to a size a little less than full HD. If you are comfortable with using the keyboard (even if it's just the space bar) then you can turn off the transport console so you see the video in its native resolution.

Preview quality

Program monitor quality settings

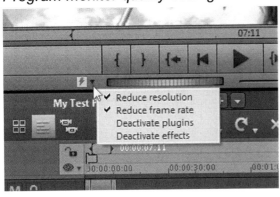

There is a further control over preview resolution available as a tool at the bottom left of the Program monitor – it is shaped like a lighting flash. When it is highlighted, the quality may be reduced.

There are more ways of controlling preview quality here than in previous version of the program, but unless you are using the WiDi connection, the only one you might need to use is the Reduce resolution setting.

It's easy to get this muddled up with all the other resolution controls, but this tool has no effect on the number of pixels that make up the preview area.

The purpose of this control is to reduce the load on your computer by displaying any video at half resolution, thus allowing smoother playback on less powerful machines. If you are using a complex video format you may struggle to preview your movies, particularly when they have effects added. There are a number of things you can do to help achieve smooth playback without upgrading your hardware, and switching to half resolution is one of them. Also see Preview rendering, Preview settings and Display options for further tools.

If you don't struggle with playback smoothness under normal circumstances, then you should use Full resolution. Once you add a lot of effects or plug-ins, then this setting probably won't make much difference anyway, so you will end up using Preview rendering.

If you want to see the true effect, try zooming the display into 400% and then switching settings – its effect will then be very noticeable.

The other options may help you with a WiDi display, but don't lead to a good editing experience.

Let's do some editing - Pre-trimming

We have already sent three clips to the movie, but because they came from the Import window of the Media pool, we ended up with the whole of each clip. It will probably seem obvious to you when I say we can adjust the clips once they are in the movie – after all, this is an editing program! However, putting a vast amount of material into the movie and then sorting it out isn't a particularly efficient way of working. In particular, if you have a plan for your movie you might already know which parts of the clips you are going to use. Additionally, some clips might have a lot of unusable material that you have no intention of using, so it would make sense to cut it out before you even put it into your movie.

We have seen how we can move a clip from the Media pool to the Program monitor. I've also shown you how we can set a range between an In and an Out point on that clip in the Program monitor. The final step is to move the trimmed clip from the program monitor to the movie – and that can be simply a case of dragging it with the mouse from the monitor to the movie. When you do this, only the section of video between the In and Out point gets added to the movie.

In this following example, let's assume I want to pre-trim clip_020 because I only want to use the first 6 seconds.

Here is how to carry out pre-trimming:

- Click on Clip_020 in the Media pool/Import window to highlight it.

- Either drag the clip across to the Program monitor window or use the toolbar brackets tool to send it there.

- What I'm aiming to do is to end the clip once the cyclist has finished turning and is moving in a straight line.

- Use any of the methods I've outline to move the Playback marker into the right area.

- However, once in the vicinity, use the arrow keys to get the top left timecode to read 6 seconds exactly. This is akin to selecting a very accurate Out point, and it means our projects will match. For reasons I'll explain later, don't use the jog control yet.

- Once you have found the point, press the O key or use the transport console to set an Out point.

- A blue Range indicator may now already extend from the beginning of the clip to over three quarters of the width of the Program monitor.

- If it doesn't, set an In point at the start of the clip. The timecode on the range should now read 06:00.

- Click, hold and drag the video in the Program monitor down to the blank area to the right of the three clips already in the edit area, then release the mouse button.

We should now have four clips in the movie.

Before we turn our attention to the Edit area, please save the project as *My Test Project 2*.

The movie so far

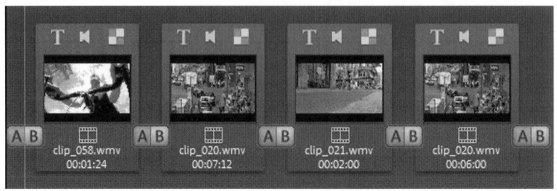

The Edit Area

In case you have jumped here, skipping some of the earlier steps, it's worth reiterating that we are currently working in Storyboard mode. If your screen doesn't look like the screenshots, click on the Storyboard mode icon furthest left on the Edit area toolbar.

The Movie tabs

Our project only has one movie in it at the moment, and at the top left of the edit area is a tab that proclaims what looks like the title of the project – or is it? The first movie in a new project takes the same name as the project, but that can be changed:

- Right click on the title My Test Project in the edit area in the lower part of the screen.

- Select Rename movie in the context menu that appears.

- Change the title to My Test Movie in the text box and press Enter.

- The new name appears on the tab.

Movie tabs context menu

To the right of the movie tab are two smaller tabs, The first one has a + sign on it and opens a new movie tab:

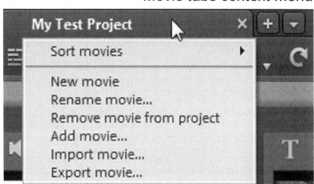

- Click on the + sign. A new full size tab appears with the title My Test Project 2.

- The plus tab is still there, just further along. Click on it again.

- The third movie takes the title My Test Project 2 – 01.

- Click on each of the new tabs to see an empty movie in the area below.

As you can see, the automatic naming scheme uses the project name as a base, and then adds incremental numbers to avoid duplication.

The small tab on the furthest right has a drop down arrow that opens up a slightly longer context menu than the one we have just seen. The top set of entries are the names of the movies in the project, with the currently selected having a check mark. We can click here to select a different tab if we wish.

Sort movies offers a set of options to re-arrange the order of the movie tabs. This isn't just for cosmetic reasons. When we look at making optical discs with menus, we will see that the order of movies here is reflected in the order that they will appear on the menus and the disc itself:

- Click on the drop-down menu tab and check My Test Movie.

- Click on the tab again and select Sort Movies/Move forward.

- The tab for My Test Movie moves to the right.

New movie has the same effect as clicking on the + tab, and we have already seen what Rename movie does. Remove movie from project does what it says it does:

- Click on the My Test Project 2 – 01 tab to select it then open the drop-down menu or right click for the context menu.

- Click Remove movie from project.

- Unless you have already disabled it, a dialogue box comes up warning you of the consequences of deletion. As this movie is empty, you can ignore the box and just click Delete movie.

- Click on the first tab My Test Project 2.

- Click on the X in the right corner.

- The same dialogue appears. Click Delete movie.

- Both of the new movies we created will now have been removed.

The final three options are Add movie, Import movie and Export movie. To demonstrate these clearly we need to start with the last option.

- Open the movie tabs drop-down menu again and select Export movie.

- In the Windows dialogue that opens, note that the file type is MVD (for movies), not MVP (for projects).

- Change the save name to Copy of My Test Movie and Save.

- Open the drop-down menu again and select Import movie. Find Copy of My Test Movie.MVD in the windows dialogue and open it.

- Read the dialogue box and then click Ok.

We have now loaded an additional movie into the project. It happens to be a copy of the original movie at the moment, but we can change either one of the movies and those changes will be stored in the project file. However, nothing we do to the Copy of My Test Movie will be saved in the Movie file – the MVD file – unless we specifically use the Export movie command.

From this, I hope you can see how important it is to understand the difference between a Project and a Movie. To reiterate from earlier, a project consists of all the movies held within the tabs as well as other information such as what order the tabs appear in across the screen. If we happen to have exported one of the movies (perhaps to use in another project) then any changes we make in that movie tab within the project will be saved when we save the project, but the changes will be only saved to the project file, not the movie file.

The Export movie file dialogue

The final option in this menu is Add Movie.

- Ensure that Copy of My Test Movie is selected as the current movie.

- Open the drop-down menu and select Add Movie. You will see that the dialogue that opens has the title Append Movie.

The Append Movie dialogue

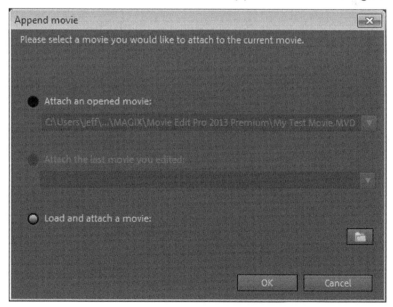

- Three radio buttons offer you a choice of movies to add.

- Select the final button, Load and attach a movie, then click on the browse folder on the right.

- Find Copy of My Test Movie.MDV and open it. Read the first warning box and then click on New Name.

- Read and then dismiss the next warning dialogue box.

- Drag the Append movie dialogue box that is still present away from the edit area so you can see the movie tabs.

What has happened so far is that a renamed copy of the copy has been added as a third project, but the process isn't over yet. The name of the movie is below the active radio button in the dialogue box and we still have to click on OK to close it:

- Click on the OK button.

If asked if you want to do a save at this point, do so.

Now what has happened? The new tab we have created has disappeared again, but if you look at the content of the Copy of My Test Movie, you will see there are eight clips, not four – the selected movie has been added to the end of the movie that was current when we began this process.

The result of Append Movie

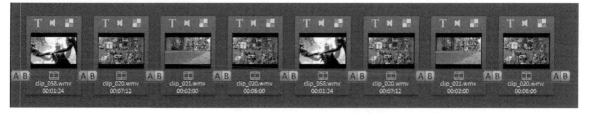

So, Add movie allows you to select a movie that has been saved before and add the content of that movie at the end of the current one. During the process it happens to open a temporary copy of the saved movie, and then closes it again. This confused me at first as I thought the command wasn't doing what I expected. It was, but in two distinct stages!

What if we were to use the first radio button option to use another movie that is already open in a project tab? This is quite a destructive process because we can't use Undo, so to begin with I'm going to suggest you save the current project:

- Use the File menu or CTRL-S to save the project.

- Highlight the first movie (My Test Movie) and open the drop-down menu.

- Select Add Movie, Check the first radio button of the dialogue, Attach an opened movie.

- The only entry in the drop-down list associated with the first button should be Copy of My Test Movie. There will be a Windows path for the default location for projects and movies prefacing the filename.

- Click on OK. Notice that the dialogue box warns you that the open movie you are about to append will be closed. You have the chance to save it, but there is no need to bother in this example.

We will now only have one movie open – My Test Movie. When you examine it – and you may have to use the scrollbar at the bottom of the Edit area to do this – you will see it contains 12 clips; four from the original movie and eight from the copy.

So this is how you add movies together. However, it's also possible to copy and paste from one tab to another, which you may prefer, because the Add movie option always puts the new content at the end of the current movie, whereas using copy and paste you can be selective about which parts of the source movie you use and chose the destination for the paste operation.

Now, in the process of restoring the project we just saved, you will see some dialogue boxes that show you can also add projects together.

- Open the main File menu and hover over the Last opened disc projects option.

- My Test Project 2 should be at the top of the list that appears.

- Select it by clicking. The box that appears offers you the chance to leave the current project open and add the new project.

Close/Add Dialogue box

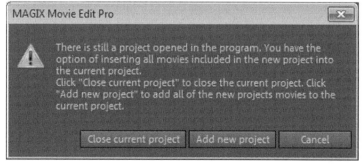

- If we did so, the movies in the project we were about to load would be added to the ones that are already open. Instead click Close current project.

- The next warning tells us we are about to close a project that hasn't been saved. Normally you would go along with this, but in this particular case we are loading an earlier version of the same project.

Choice of saving the current movie

- Click on Don't save, otherwise we would save the changes we don't want and then reload them!

- Finally, use one of the methods I showed you earlier to delete the second movie – Copy of My Test Movie – and save the program again.

The movie should be back the the state in which we saved it near the start of this chapter.

Storyboard view

We should now be seeing something very similar to the screenshot. This is Storyboard view, and previously I showed you how to use the tools on the left of the Edit area toolbar to switch to it. Below the toolbar is the arranger area which currently has four objects representing the four clips we have added from the Media pool.

The current project in Storyboard view

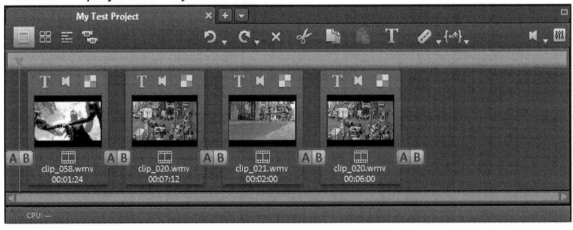

The Storyboard is only really suitable for simple editing, but even if you are about to embark on a complex project, don't dismiss it as worthless. Some very important principles are common to both the Storyboard and the Timeline, and they can be demonstrated more clearly in the Storyboard view, so don't think you are wasting your time learning to use it. Also, it's far easier to work on the structure of a movie, and in particular a slideshow, in Storyboard mode.

The fine adjustment of clips is easier using the Timeline, but we haven't got to that stage yet, and the most powerful tools of all – the Object and Edit trimmers work in either mode anyway. As the Storyboard only displays objects on the first track of a movie, you can't control elements placed on other tracks – titles, overlays, split audio and music. However, the current movie has none of those elements, so I'm going to use it to give an overview of using Storyboard mode. Some of the tools I introduce are also very relevant when you work in other modes, so even if you think you might not use the Storyboard much, don't be tempted to skip too quickly through the rest of the chapter! I'll be using later when we make a more complex project too.

Objects on the Storyboard

The first thing to note about the four clip objects that are displayed is that they are all the same width – each one occupies the same amount of space regardless of its duration.

- Click on the second of the objects to make the Storyboard active.
- Press the Home key. The Playback marker moves to the start of the movie in the Program monitor.
- Another Playback marker appears on the bar between the toolbar and the Storyboard. Beneath it an orange line extends through the Storyboard. This is the Playback cursor.
- Use the Play button or press Space and watch the playback marker and cursor in the edit area.

Notice how the playback cursor splits - a second copy showing the current playback position. When you stop playback using the Down Arrow or K keys the main cursor will catch up. If you use the Space bar the second cursor will return to it's start position, unless we have changed the program setting as discussed in the Program monitor chapter.

As each object is the same width but represents a video clip of a different duration, during real-time playback the cursor has to travel at different speeds to cross each object. So it moves quickly across the first object, taking 1 second 24 frames to do so. The next object represents over seven seconds of video, so the cursor has to travel nearly four times slower.

The only way to tell the duration of each clip is to look at the duration information on the object, or actually play it.

Navigating the Storyboard

Clicking on any object in the Storyboard selects it, with the selection being indicated by a blue border.

- Click on the last clip in the movie.

- A blue border appears around the object.

- The Storyboard Playback cursor jumps to the gap between clips 3 and four.

The highlight around a selected object

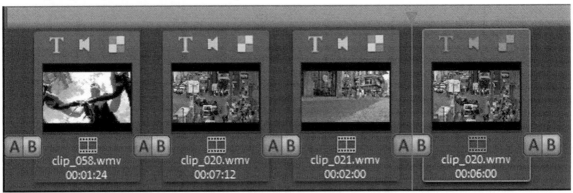

It's worth noting that there is sometimes disconnected behaviour between the Playback cursor and the selected object. Selecting an object moves the cursor, but moving the cursor doesn't change the object selection.

With the Storyboard active, the Left and Right keyboard arrows behave in a different way to how they operate in the Program monitor. Using them selects the Storyboard object to the left or right respectively. The Playback cursor jumps to the gap in front of the selected object. If you want to revert to single frame jogging you have to make the Playback monitor the active window by clicking on it or using one of the transport controls. As I've already mentioned, you can check which window is active at any time by looking for the thin blue line at the top of the window.

Currently, with only four objects in the movie, all of them can be seen. If there are more than can be displayed, a scroll bar would appear beneath the objects. You can then drag this to move along the Storyboard. Also, the Home and End key help speedy navigation. Finally, if your mouse has a scroll wheel, you can use that to move left and right along the Storyboard.

Storyboard object icons and tools

Every object has seven items displayed on it.

The "T" icon opens the Title editor so that you can add titles. In Storyboard mode it is easy to edit the text, look and position on screen of a title, but positioning it in time is much easier to do in the Timeline mode.

The speaker tool would allow you to adjust the level of any audio associated with the object. In the current project there isn't any audio, so the tool just gives an error message. Making sophisticated adjustments to audio is also best carried out using other tools.

A video object thumbnail

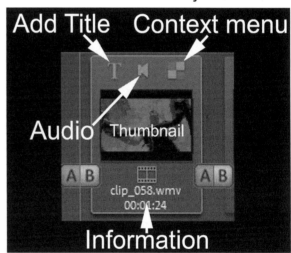

If the object were a photo rather than a video clip, the speaker tool would be replaced with one that rotated the photo 90 degrees clockwise – so you can switch from landscape to portrait or even flip the photo upside down.

The checkerboard icon has the same effect as right-clicking and opening the context menu. This is the same context menu as you get in Timeline mode.

Two items that may be of particular use with video in Storyboard mode are the Edit trimmer and Object trimmer because they are the only good way to adjust the duration and the In and Out points, while in Timeline mode they are used for fine adjustments. I'll give a detailed account of using the trimmers later. In fact every entry here is covered in detail elsewhere – most of them will work much better in Timeline mode anyway so it's in that context that I will explain them.

If the object is a photo, there is a context menu tool to Change photo length. This is genuinely useful, and can be applied to one, all or a selection of photos.

In the middle of each object is a thumbnail that helps you identify it. A video object shows the first frame and a photo shows the orientation. They are shown full frame even if video effects have been used to manipulate the size and position, but other effects such as colour correction do show up.

Titles will be black, and audio will show a waveform, but it's important to note that you cannot actually add these items directly to the Storyboard. If you can see them, they must have been placed on track one in Timeline mode before switching to the Storyboard view.

Beneath the thumbnail an icon shows if an object is a photo (camera icon) or a video clip (filmstrip icon). Underneath that is the filename of the object and at the very bottom is the duration.

Transitions on the Storyboard

Between each object is a small orange/blue icon with the letters A and B. This is used to represent a transition. By default, transitions are set to be a simple cut – an instantaneous switch from the outgoing video – the A source – to the incoming video – the B source. So, the currently displayed icons all represent cuts.

The Transition menu

Let's change one of those cuts to another type of transition:

• Press the End key to move the Playback cursor to the end of the movie and note the duration. We have four clips and the total should be 17 seconds 12 frames.

• Click on the middle cut icon between clips 020 and 021. This will reveal a new menu.

• Note that the first entry, Cut, is checked. Click on the second item, Crossfade.

- The area around the transition plays, and you can see the outgoing wide shot (A) transition into the low angle shot (B) using a dissolve from one source to the other.

- The transition icon has changed to the crossfade icon.

- Press End again to see that the duration of the movie has reduced to 16 seconds 12 frames.

The Crossfade icon

There is an extremely important principle at play here. I'll mention it a number of times through the book, because often editing programs deal with transitions in such a seamless way that people don't realise what happens when you add one.

Because the outgoing video needs to overlap the incoming video to create the transition – they need to play at the same time – the duration of the movie needs to shorten by the length of the transition. MEP has chosen to automatically overlap the video sources by one second because that is the default duration of transitions.

Before the next step, I want you to save the project with a new name:

- Use the File menu to Save as… My Test Project 3.

Now we can do something destructive! Let's alter the duration of the transition:

- Click on the new crossfade icon and select Set transition length.

- In the dialogue box that appears, drag the slider all the way to the right – 20 seconds duration.

- Click on OK and Play the movie.

The Set duration tool

That wasn't a twenty second crossfade, was it? Check out the duration of the movie again – it should now read 15 seconds 13 frames. So what happened? The clue is in the duration information of clip_021. Looking at the Storyboard object information you can see that it has duration of 2 seconds. If you step through the transition a frame at a time, you can see that only the very last frame of clip_021 is clean of the crossfade.

So the overlap can't be more than one frame less than the material available otherwise the transition won't have completed before the video runs out. The program has automatically truncated the duration to what is possible!

I want to describe using transitions in more detail, particularly in adding them in batches and globally adjusting the durations, but it's best done when we make a slideshow. As with most editing functions though, Timeline mode offers more power.

Gaps in the Storyboard movie

We don't have any gaps in our movie at the moment. In fact, if we start in Storyboard mode and never switch out of it, it seems to be impossible to create a gap. MEP deliberately closes up any gaps we create when we delete objects from the Storyboard.

If you want to create a gap you will have to do so in Timeline mode. Having done so, either deliberately or by accident, switching back to Storyboard presents us with a problem. Let's jump ahead briefly to show you what I mean. Please don't be distracted by the wonders of the Timeline at this point!

- Click in the Timeline mode icon third from the left of the Edit window toolbar.

- Notice that the transition we created shows at the end of the second clip.

- Click on the second clip on track 1 so that it turns yellow.

Clip 2 highlighted in Timeline mode

- Press the Delete key.

Clip 2 removed

- Study the Timeline. There is a gap between the first two clips now left on track 1.

- Switch back to the Storyboard view by clicking the first icon on the toolbar

The gap icon in Storyboard mode

You should see something very similar to the screenshot. There are only three clips, because we have deleted one. Play the movie from the start, though and you will see that there is a gap which just shows as black video, during which the Playback cursor pauses for the duration of the clip we have removed.

So, how do we know there is a gap? Look at the transition icon between the first two clips on the Storyboard and you will see it has changed. Click on it to open the menu and you will see that it is now a Thru black transition. This gives us the clue we need.

- Click on the transition icon between clips 2 and 3

- Change the transition to Thru black.

- Play the movie.

Normally, if you add Thru black as a transition in the Storyboard it will fade up the outgoing video and then immediately fade in the incoming video, reaching black level for just a single frame. However, if the gap has been created in Timeline mode, you can't be sure exactly what is going on.

In reality, gaps and the Storyboard don't mix well, but in a single track project you are unlikely to want to have significant areas of black video. If you do want to use black level it is probably best if you create a black photo to use.

If for some reason you find yourself with an unwanted gap in Storyboard mode, it is quite easy to get rid of:

- Click on the transition icon between clips 1 and 2
- Select Cut (no fade)
- The icon reverts to a cut icon and the movie duration reduces.
- Play the movie and the gap has gone.

Rearranging objects in Storyboard mode

Let's get back to where we were before I showed you a brief glimpse of the Timeline:

- Revert to the project by opening My Test Project 3, closing the current project and declining the offer to save it.

Rearranging is what the Storyboard is really good at, and Drag and Drop is my tool of choice for rearranging objects:

- Click and hold on the second object from the left – the full duration wide shot.
- Drag the clip to the right. Notice in particular the red line that skips between the gaps indicating where it can be dropped.

Dragging clip two to position one

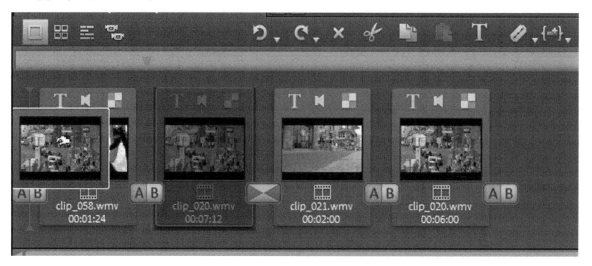

- Drag left and right to see the four places that you can drop the clip. Settle on the first position furthest left and release the mouse button.

We have moved the second clip to the first position. Notice that the crossfade transition remains attached to the end of the clip we have repositioned.

You can also move multiple selections of clips:

- Click on the second clip, hold down CTRL and click on the third clip. Both should now be highlighted.

- Click, hold and drag either of the highlighted clips to the end position on the movie.

So, you can see how convenient it is to rearrange objects on the Storyboard. You can't drop the objects anywhere that would involve them splitting other objects and you can work on groups of objects, not just individual ones.

The current state of the movie

Storyboard toolbar

Nearer the centre of the Edit toolbar are a group of nine tools. The number of tools will vary between display modes, although the tools that they invoked may still exist even if the tool icons don't.

The first three tools exist in all four modes. Let's skip

The Storyboard Toolbar

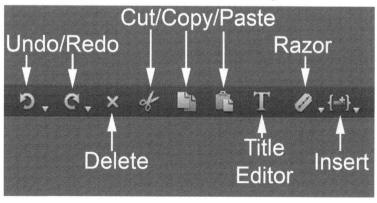

the first two tools for a moment. The third tool is Delete – the x icon. Hover over it and you will see that the keyboard shortcut is the obvious choice of the Delete key.

- Click on the first object in the Storyboard – the untrimmed wide shot with the duration of 7:12.

- It will show a blue border and the icons within the object will also turn blue.

- Click on the X (delete) tool. The object disappears from the project, along with the crossfade icon.

- Now highlight the first object – the 6 second trimmed wide shot - if it isn't already. Press the Delete key.

- Multi-select the last two clips so that they are both highlighted. Delete again.

We are left with an empty movie. So the Delete function is pretty obvious in the Storyboard, and you can use multi-selection as well.

Now I've made you destroy the project, I can demonstrate a feature of the first two tools on the left. These are Undo and Redo, but they have a bonus feature over using the Edit menu options or the keyboard.

Click in the small downward pointing arrow to the right of the Undo tool.

A list appears with at least three items – all of the first three Delete.

If we were to click on the top item in the list we would just undo the last action – in this case the last delete operation.

The Undo tool History list

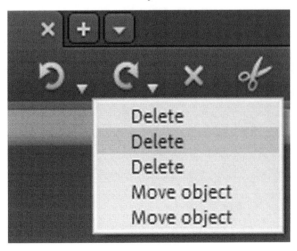

Instead, click on the second Delete. Three objects return to the Storyboard.

Investigate the drop-down list again, as well as the one to the right of the Redo tool. You can see that the Undo history is available in these lists, so you can jump straight to a particular operation. A string of Deletes might not be much help, but if there were other items it would be easy to jump to a particular point in the editing history – both forward and back.

The next three tools are Cut, Copy and Paste. These tools don't appear on other toolbars, because you can always use the Windows standard shortcut keys. Cut removes the selected object or objects from the Storyboard and places them on the clipboard. Copy puts a copy on the clipboard. Paste places whatever is in the clipboard onto the Storyboard.

The destination of the objects on the clipboard is determined by what is selected on the Storyboard.

- Click on the last clip to highlight it.

- Click on the Copy icon or press CTRL-C.

- Click on the first clip to highlight it. The Playback cursor moves to the position in front of the clip.

- Click on Paste or press CTRL-V.

- An additional copy of the last clip is placed at the beginning of the movie.

- Drag the Playback cursor to the end of the movie and Paste again.

- Notice that the destination of the paste still remains as the point before the highlighted clip and not the playback cursor.

There isn't a significant difference between using Drag and Drop or Copy and Paste when working in Storyboard mode. You can choose whichever suits you. Personally, I like the visualisation of Drag and Drop.

Duplicate

I know this doesn't appear on the toolbar, but having just mentioned Cut, Copy and Paste this is a good point to show you what the Duplicate tool in the Edit menu does.

Duplicate is in the File menu

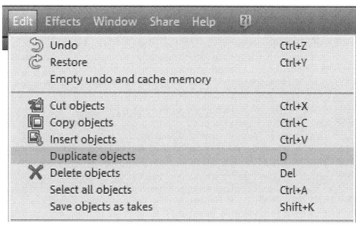

- Click on the last clip again.

- Open the Edit menu and select Duplicate objects.

- An identical copy of the selected clip is added in front of the selected clip.

- Press the D key. Another copy appears.

- Multi-select the last two clips and delete them.

So, it's effectively a Copy and Paste in one key press or mouse click, but the destination is fixed. You can also multi-select objects for duplication.

As I said before, there are other ways of duplicating clips, but only when we are in Timeline view.

The Razor tools

The razor is one of the most important tools for editing, and Movie Edit Pro has a number of variations of the razor tool that makes it more powerful than some other editing software. Let's start, however with the basic operation which you may be able to predict from the tool's name and icon.

The basic function of the razor is to split or slice a single video clip into two separate clips – just as you would use a razor blade to cut an audio tape or a splicer to cut a film clip in two (and I realise that there are whole generations of people who won't know what I'm on about!).

- Beside the Razor tool is a small drop down menu arrow. Open it and check the top option, Split, is selected.

- Notice the tooltip says the keyboard shortcut is T.

- Use your video previewing skills to park the Playback cursor 10 frames into the first clip in the movie.

- Click on the Razor tool.

We now have six clips on our Timeline.

After the first Split

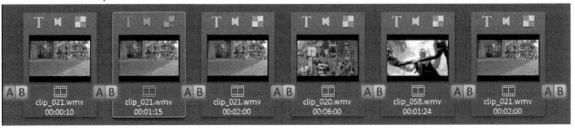

The first clip consists of the first 10 frames of clip 021. The second clip contains the remaining one second and 15 frames. Check out the durations at the bottom of the objects to confirm.

- Play the start of the movie; you won't even be aware that there is a cut between clips one and two – the video plays seamlessly.

- To see where the split occurred, drag clip two to the start of the movie and play the movie again; you will see three bits of action, all from three different parts of the same video footage.

- Select the first two clips and delete them – we should still have a full copy of clip 021 at the start of the movie.

A commonly used technique is to use the split tool to slice a section off the start or end of a clip, then throw away the unwanted bit. It's the same as setting a new In or Out point, but it takes two actions to achieve. If you can get used to using the keyboard shortcuts, or you are going to be setting a whole series of new In or Out points, then two additional razor modes will save you time.

- Set the Playback cursor to 10 frames into the first clip on the Storyboard.

- Open the dropdown menu beside the Razor tool

- Hover over the second entry and note that the keyboard shortcut is Z.

Switching to Remove Start mode

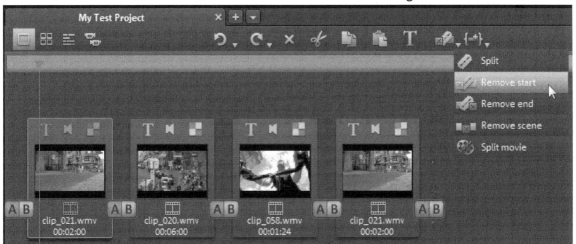

- Click on the tool. Remove Start becomes the default razor tool icon.

- The first clip reduces in length by 10 frames and if you compare it with the last clip you will see the frames are missing from the start of the clip.

The Razor tool Remove scene end is identical in function, except it removes the portion after the Playback cursor, rather than before it. The keyboard shortcut is U.

Remove scene

Two other tools appear in the drop-down list associated with the razor. Neither of these use a razor blade in their icon.

Remove scene isn't really important in Storyboard mode, because deleting a clip causes the gap left behind to be automatically closed up. When in Timeline mode we can use it to force this behaviour, as we will see later. For now, let's just test it to remove the first clip of the movie:

- Click on clip 1 – the trimmed version of clip_021 – to highlight it.
- Open the drop-down next to the razor tool and hover over the Remove Scene icon.
- Notice the tooltip informs you that the shortcut is CTRL-Delete.
- Click on the tool. The first clip disappears just as if you have pressed Delete or used the X tool.
- Notice that the Remove scene tool icon is now where the razor icon was before.

If you play the Timeline now, you should see that the edited sequence now makes some sort of sense.

We've made a movie!

While we have been looking at the functions of the program, I've been slowly manoeuvring the movie into a believable cut sequence. If you play the three clips from the start, they should consist of:

The first six seconds of Clip_20. The cyclist appears in the background and turns a corner.

All of Clip_058. This close shot of the cyclist is taken from such an angle that we cannot see any important geography.

All of Clip_21. A low angle wide shot of the cycling.

The buffer shot of the cyclist disguises the fact that the two wide shots are of completely different streets. Cutting away from the first wide shot before we fully establish the buildings on the left of frame also helps the illusion that these shots depict real time.

So, please save the project at this point! Let's also make this an incremental save by giving it a new name instead of using the same one:

- Use File/Save as… to open the Windows Save as dialogue box.

- Change the file name to My Test Project rough cut 1.

- Click on Save.

Rough cut 1

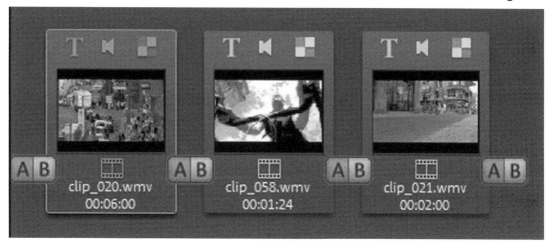

By the way, if you want to cheat, these project files are all available on the website and Demo DVD.

Split movie

This is an interesting tool, more likely to be of use when creating optical discs, but with other potential uses.

- Position the playback cursor about halfway through the second clip, the close shot of the cyclist.

- From the drop-down menu, select the Split movie tool.

Whoa, what happened there? The project area now has two movies. The first one has the same name as the original and consists of two clips. If you look at the duration of the second clip, though, it's about half the duration that it was before.

Switch to the other movie tab – it should have been named My Test Movie_01. By default, this is likely to be displayed in Timeline mode, so use the toolbar to switch to Storyboard.

The second movie in Storyboard mode

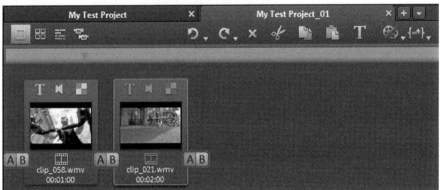

There you will see the second half of what was originally the middle shot, and all of the last shot. The original movie has been split at the point of the Playback cursor and the section after the split placed in a new movie.

- Before we carry on, reload the rough cut we saved on the previous page.

The Insert tool and the V key

We have already looked at one form of the Insert tool – when we used the Insert into movie to put the clips from the Media pool into the edit area. Because we are in Storyboard mode and we have set the Insert mode to Automatic the clips always go at the end of the movie – where they cause the least disruption!

Instead of using the Media pool thumbnail toolbar – the blue bar that appears over the objects when we hover over them – we can also use the V key or click on the Insert tool – the last item of the central group of tools.

As long as the Media pool window has the focus – you can see it is active because of the thin blue line across the top – then whatever item is highlighted will go to the Movie when we use the Insert tool.

The Program monitor itself doesn't have a tool to send its contents to the movie. You will remember that when we wanted to send a trimmed clip to the movie earlier, I got you to use drag and drop. Without muddying the waters too much at this point, I want to point out that different rules apply to Dragging and Dropping from the Media pool or Program monitor or within the Storyboard itself. For now, though, let's stick with describing Insert – but bear in mind I'm only describing the use of the Insert tool or the V key.

Let's repeat the process of trimming and adding clip_020 to the movie using the Insert tool on the Storyboard to bring in a trimmed clip from the the program monitor. In the following set of instructions I'm going to include a couple of deliberate mistakes as well:

- With My Test Project rough cut 1 open, delete the first clip on the Storyboard – the high wide shot we trimmed to 6 seconds.

- Send, or Drag and Drop, clip_020 from the Media pool to the Program monitor.

- Trim the clip so the In point is at the start and the Out point at 6 seconds exactly.

- Let's deliberately switch to the Storyboard as if we forgot to set the destination beforehand. Click on the second clip, and then use the left arrow to highlight the first clip.

- The Playback cursor is at the start of the movie, which is where we want the clip to go.

- Unfortunately, clip_020 is no longer in the Program monitor as that has switched to the Storyboard.

- Drag and drop clip_020 from the Media pool to the Program monitor again

- The clip returns to the Program monitor. More importantly, the trimmed range is still in place!

- Click on the program monitor to make it active – the blue bar appears at the top.

- Press V or click the Insert tool.

Well that nearly worked, didn't it? Unfortunately, the clip went to the end of the movie because we are still in Automatic mode. We will investigate what mode we should have used in a moment.

By making you reselect the Storyboard to change the target (something that you are likely to do unless you are a very methodical person) you lost the focus, but I showed you how to get it back without losing the trim points. That's something I do all the time!

A word of warning though. If you switch to another clip in the Media pool, or start setting ranges within the movie, the program will forget the trim setting for the first clip, so you still need to be a little methodical. Best practice is to always set up the Storyboard (or Timeline) destination before selecting and setting up the new clip you intend to Insert.

Selecting Single Track Ripple

Let's now see what happens if we change the Insert mode:

• Open the drop down arrow to the right of the Inset tool and click on the second item down, Single-track ripple. It becomes the active tool.

• Delete the last clip on the Storyboard that is in the wrong place.

• Select the first clip so it is highlighted.

• Send, or Drag and drop, clip_020 to the Program monitor.

• If you have lost the trim points, trim the clip again so the In point is at the start and the Out point at 6 seconds exactly.

• Check that the Program monitor has the focus (the blue bar at the top).

• Click on the Insert key or press V.

Good – that's what I intended to do. The Single-track ripple Insert mode sends the source object to the current Storyboard position, and moves the other clips along. By the way, it doesn't matter if the clip is playing when you use Insert; as long as the trim range is there and the monitor has the focus, Insert will send the range to the movie.

Ripple in this context means "move everything later in the movie along to make room". This happens in Storyboard automatically when you drag and drop, so it doesn't seem unusual, but remember we can only see one track of the movie at the moment.

If you have added some titles to your Storyboard movie, they are occupying other tracks – ones we can't see. In this case, Single-track ripple is normally a BAD IDEA! If you insert a clip, the objects on the main track will move to make room, but the titles – or anything else on other tracks – will stay put and the relationships between the objects will be destroyed. For example, if you had put a title with someone's name over a shot of them, then inserted a shot of someone else in Single track ripple, you could end up with the name title over the wrong person!

Multi-track ripple moves the object on ALL the tracks down so you won't lose sync with other tracks. It's a bit long winded to demonstrate this right now, and will be covered in detail when we are in Timeline mode, so let's just say it's by far the best mode to use in Storyboard mode even if you don't think you are using more than one track.

Insert keyboard shortcuts

Before we look at the other two modes in the drop-down menu, there is a difference about the keyboard shortcuts that you should know about. While the V key has the same effect as clicking on the currently selected tool, you can change the mode and perform the functions at the same time with other keyboard shortcuts. So, with Single-track ripple selected, if we press the key "1", the mode switches to Automatic and then the selected clip is inserted in automatic mode. The key for Single track ripple is 2, for Multi-track ripple 3.

Let's try Multi-track ripple using the keyboard shortcut:

- Click on the first clip in the Storyboard and delete it.

- Hover over the Insert tool. The tooltip should say Insert track (2).

- In the Media pool drag clip_020 to the program monitor. The In and Out points should still be set.

- Click on the Program monitor to highlight it.

- Press the 3 key (in the main area, not on the number pad).

Because of the current view and state of the movie, this should have the same result as before, but notice that the Insert tool icon has changed to the Multi-track ripple symbol. Just to prove the mode change occurred before the Insert:

- Press the 1 key.

- Notice that the clip has also been inserted to the end of the movie and the mode icon has changed back to the Automatic insertion icon.

- Leave the new clip at the end of the movie – we will use it to experiment with.

Exchange

The fourth mode of the Insert function swaps the currently selected Storyboard object with the object selected in the Media Pool or Program monitor. If the objects are of different durations, then the duration of the movie is altered:

- Highlight the last clip in the movie – the extra copy of the trimmed wideshot.

- Press the End key to send the Program cursor to the end of the movie. Check the Movie duration top left of the Program monitor – it should be 15 seconds 24 frames.

- Click to highlight clip_058 in the Media pool, then press the 4 key on the main part of the keyboard.

- The last clip of the movie is replaced with the close-up of the cyclist. This clip is much shorter and if you check the movie duration, you will see it is now 11 seconds 23 frames.

- The Insert mode icon has changed to represent Exchange.

Exchanging the last clip

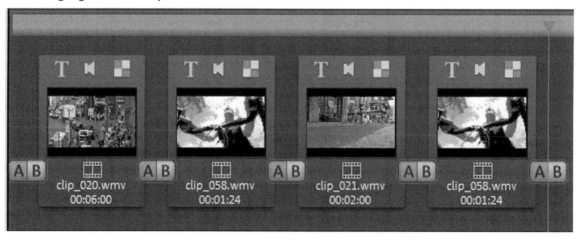

Let's try something else to demonstrate Exchange and its effect on the movie:

- Select the first clip in the movie – the 6 second wide shot.

- Highlight clip_020 in the Media pool and use the Send to movie tool.

- Because the Insert mode is now Exchange, and we have selected the untrimmed clip, the first shot of the movie changes to a duration of 7 seconds 12 frames.

- If you want to check the duration of the movie, you will see it is 1 second 12 frames longer than before – the difference between the trimmed and untrimmed clips.

- Select the first clip of the movie again, if it isn't already selected.

- Drag clip_020 from the Media pool to the Program monitor.

- Click on the Program monitor to make it active.

- The In and Out points should still be set to 6 seconds. If for some reason you have lost the range setting, reset it to 6 seconds durations as before.

- Click on the Insert tool or press the V key.

The first clip in the movie should revert to a 6 second duration. This is also good demonstration of the difference between using the Program monitor and the Media pool as the source.

If there is content on other tracks, using Exchange will ripple all the tracks in Storyboard mode, so it doesn't destroy the sync. This includes moving the content back to the left if you exchange a long clip with a short clip.

Overwrite

The final Insert mode makes space in the movie by cutting a gap that is of the duration required then putting the new clip in that gap. Unless you send the new clip to the last shot in the movie and it is longer than the original, your movie duration will stay the same.

- Highlight the last clip of the movie – the additional close shot of the cyclist.

- Restored the trimmed wide shot to the Program monitor and click to make it active

- Press the 5 key. The Insert mode icon changes to Overwrite and the last clip changes to the trimmed wide shot.

This isn't a good example of what Overwrite does because the duration of the movie has extended to 15 seconds 24 frames, but now try the next demonstration:

- Select the last clip of the movie again. The Playback cursor should be between the third and fourth clips.

- Hover over clip_021 in the Media pool so the toolbar appears.

- Click on the Send to movie tool.

Overwriting part of the last clip

When you examine the end of the movie now, there are two thumbnails where there was just one. Look at the durations, however. The clip that has been inserted has the same duration as it does in the Media pool – 2 seconds. The last clip is only 4 seconds long now. If you compare the first and last clips of the movie, you will see that the first two seconds have been overwritten – the cyclist is already entering the crossroads at the In point of the clip.

So there is no sign of the beginning of clip_020 now because it has been obliterated by the replacement – it's been overwritten! If you want to check the movie duration again, you will find it is unaltered.

I'd like you to perform an Overwrite once more:

- Using the methods I've demonstrated above, Overwrite the penultimate clip of the move (a copy of clip_021) with clip_058.

Now the movie has six clips in total, but look at the durations of the last three. It just so happens that clip_058 is only one frame shorter than clip_021, so now the penultimate clip is only one frame in duration! Play the end of the movie to see what a single flash frame looks like – blink and you will certainly miss it.

However, the Storyboard gives this single frame object just as much prominence as any other clip. In Timeline mode, a flash frame may be very hard to spot. In Storyboard mode, it's very easy. Bear this in mind if you are trying to debug your movie.

One frame clip occupying the same space on the Storyboard as a 4 second clip

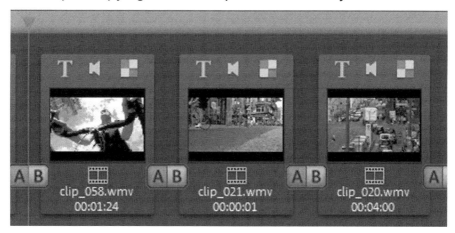

Drag and Drop, Storyboard, and the Insert mode

One of the important things to realise about Drag and Drop is it behaves differently depending on which view you are using.

In Storyboard view, Drag and Drop always works in Multi-track ripple mode, whatever Insert mode you have selected. You can't destroy the sync between the track on view and any "hidden" tracks that there might be. That applies regardless of where you are dragging the source material from – the Storyboard, the Media pool or the Program monitor.

This also means that in Storyboard view, you can't use Exchange or Overwrite when Dragging and Dropping. These functions are restricted to using the V key or the Insert tool. It's important to realise that this isn't the case in Timeline view, as we will see later.

Drag and Drop and Windows

While we are on the subject of Drag and Drop, I should mention another feature. I demonstrated earlier that you could use a Windows Explorer window as a source when copy and pasting to the Media pool. You can't copy and paste from an Explorer window to the Program monitor or your movie, but you can Drag and Drop. So, if you want to bypass the Media pool for whatever reason, it is possible.

I'm not encouraging you to use this workflow at this point – it's only really practical if you have dual PC monitors, in my opinion, but it's an interesting feature that you might consider.

Audio tools

The Audio Tool Icons

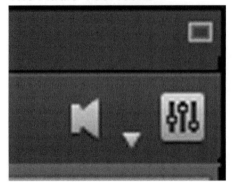

There are a couple of tools at the far right of the edit area toolbar that I haven't mentioned yet, and in the interest of completeness, I should point out that they are audio functions.

The furthest right opens a new window containing a very comprehensive audio mixing panel. The other icon controls the scrubbing mode – what you hear when previewing the movie at anything other than normal playback speed.

We haven't used any audio yet, so I'll describe how these tools work when we look at editing sound in more detail.

Storyboard recommendations

To recap,the Storyboard has its uses, but it also has some serious limitations. I think the best time to use it is when you are compiling a series of photos or shots, but before you start working with the audio or adding titles. Slideshows in particular benefit from the layout and the tools to add transitions.

Once you have added any extra audio or titles, I'd suggest you steer clear of the Insert modes other than Exchange. Stick with Drag and Drop and you shouldn't do any inadvertent damage to the sync of the movie.

Switching back to Storyboard mode is sometimes a good idea if you want to make structural changes to the story your movie is telling. However, there is another viewing mode that is even better for that, and we will look at that next.

Scene overview

Before we move to the next viewing mode, let's restore our test movie to it's correct state. If you have followed the previous section to the letter, there will be six clips on the Storyboard:

- Multi-select clips 4, 5 and 6 and use the Delete tool, or

- Load the saved project My Test Project rough cut 1, closing the current project and not saving it.

You can carry out the following tests with random clips instead if you wish.

- Click on the second tool icon from the left – Scene overview.

Scene Overview

The only changes to the display happen in the lower half of the screen. The central block of tools on the toolbar have reduced in number from nine to six, the clip thumbnails will have shrunk in size and all the icons will have disappeared apart from the file names under the thumbnails.

Calling this viewing mode Scene overview can be a bit confusing if you are used to using the term Scene in terms of movie storytelling. A scene in a movie or TV program can consist of a number of shots that portray a single event that purports to be in real time – the "Shower scene" in the Hitchcock thriller Psycho has over 50 cut shots, for example, but it is still considered to be one scene. However, overview is certainly the right term.

The important control when working in this mode is a slider situated bottom right of the window.

- Click, hold and drag the slider to the far right. The thumbnails get quite large – larger than the Storyboard thumbnails.

- Now alter the relative sizes of the edit screen windows by using the four-way arrow that appears when you hover over the junction of the windows.

- You will see the thumbnail sizes adjust a little to try and make the best use of the space available to them.

- Reset the Window arrangement with the F9 key. The thumbnails don't change size.

Being able to make the thumbnails larger and reduce the clutter of all the icons makes it easier to see what the shots are, but isn't really what Scene overview is all about.

- Drag the slider to the far left. The thumbnails are just about discernible.

- Click on the first clip and then use the multi-selection command CTRL-A to select all three clips.

- Press CTRL-C (copy) and then press CTRL-V nine times in succession. The overview window now has 30 clips, or shots, in view. Unless you have a particularly small PC monitor, you should be able to see them all.

- Adjust the thumbnails size again – this time try the + and – tools either side of the slider.

- Making the size too large will eventually mean you can't see the whole movie.

You can use the vertical scroll bar to navigate to the hidden part of the movie or you can adjust the window arrangement to make more space. For most movie and monitor sizes there will be a setup which allows you to see a significant chunk of the movie, if not the whole thing.

Overview of a large movie

Navigating the Overview

We can click on the thumbnail to select and then use the keyboard arrow keys to move the selection. Notice that the Up and Down arrows move you to the next row of clips, while the Left and Right arrows have the same function as they do in Storyboard view. As with the Storyboard, its the Overview area, and not the Program monitor, that needs to have the focus (indicated by the blue line at the top of the screen) for these keys to work.

The currently selected clip has a blue border. There is also an outer border of an orange line, and this is the equivalent of the Playback cursor – it tells you what is currently being displayed in the Program monitor.

- Click on the first clip in the Overview, then press the space bar to start playing the movie.

- Watch the orange border progress down the series of clips as the movie plays.

- Press the K key to freeze playback without returning the Playback marker.

So, you can see that the currently previewing clip is marked with the orange border, but the currently selected clip is marked with a blue inner border, and the two things can be different. The selected clip is the source for a Delete, Cut, Copy or Drag and Drop operation.

Transitions and gaps

The very simplistic nature of the Overview means there is absolutely no indication whether transitions, or even gaps, are present in the movie. The only way to tell is to play the movie.

This makes the Scene overview mode a bit dangerous to use for re-arranging a movie when transitions are involved, but like Storyboard, the transition or gap remains attached to the outgoing point of any clip you decided to move.

Rearranging objects in Scene overview mode

Let's take a look at how convenient the overview mode can be for re-ordering your movie:

- Click and hold on the fourth shot in the movie – the second copy of the high wide shot.

- Drag left and down. Watch the red bar show you the destination. Place the bar after one of the later close shots of the cyclist and release the mouse button.

More complex operations are possible:

- Click on the second close shot of the cyclist – the fifth shot in the movie.

- Now hold down the CTRL key and click on all the other close shots – other than the very first one.

- You should have multi-selected nine clips, all the same shot and all highlighted in blue.

- Click and hold on any of the highlighted clips and drag it around the screen – you will see a red bar indicating the destination appears in the spaces between clips.

- Drop the clips at the very end of the movie.

That shows how effective using multi-selection and Drag and Drop within the movie can be. Here's another example using delete:

- Click on the fourth clip in the movie.

- Hold down SHIFT and click on very last clip.

- Click in the X tool in the toolbar, or just press Delete.

- Our movie should be back to the original three clips.

Obviously, these techniques aren't just restricted to multi-selection – we manipulated just one clip to start with - but it does show off the power more clearly. One of the main benefits of using the overview is that you can drag and drop over a much greater range than is possible to view clearly in Storyboard view.

The Scene overview Toolbar

I mentioned that the toolbar is missing three tools. These are Cut, Copy and Paste, but as I've just shown, these features still actually work if you use the Edit menu or the Windows shortcut keys. I can only speculate why these tools are missing - perhaps Magix want this mode to have a less cluttered look?

All the other tools behave in an identical manner to the way they work in Storyboard mode, and the same notes about using Insert as opposed to Drag and Drop are all relevant.

Timeline Editing

We have now arrived at the most useful viewing mode. Other modes have some limitations but offer simplicity, but once you get used to Timeline mode, you will probably use it for almost all your video editing. It's important to realise that some of the tools we have looked at – Insert and Drag and Drop, for example – behave differently in Timeline mode. Let's switch to it now:

- With our *My Test Project rough cut 1* movie of three clips in the Scene overview or on the Storyboard, click on the third icon on the Edit area toolbar – it has the tooltip Timeline mode.

- Press CTRL-F to optimise the Timeline view.

If you have skipped here, you may want to load the movie from the website or the Demo DVD (it's in the *My Test Project files* folder along with the other stages of the project).

Timeline view of our rough cut with the view icon indicated with an arrow

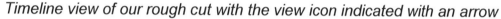

Navigation and viewing

In Storyboard and Scene overview modes, once the edit area has the focus and an object is selected you can use the keyboard arrow keys to change the selected object. This isn't possible in Timeline mode – you have to use the mouse to change the selected clip because the arrow keys retain their jog and playback functions.

The disconnection between clip selection and the Playback cursor is normally even greater in Timeline mode than the other modes, because selecting a clip does not move the Playback cursor. When I first moved to Movie Edit Pro I found this behaviour rather inconvenient as I was used to the cursor moving with the selection. I then discovered that it is possible to change the behaviour. However, if you decide to do so, let me just say that having worked in both modes, I now find the default behaviour more powerful in some circumstances – Copy and Paste being one of them. Please bear this in mind, but if you want to change the default, you can do so in File/Setting/Program/System/Other, where there is a checkbox for Move play cursor when object is selected.

In Storyboard each object is a fixed size. In Scene overview you can alter the size of the objects but in both modes you have to use scroll bars to view large movies. In Timeline view the width of the objects vary with their duration, but you have the ability to change the scale of the Timeline, so scroll bars aren't always required.

Immediately above the three clips is a timescale. It runs from zero seconds to ten seconds, although you can't currently read 10 seconds as the labels are right justified and run off the edge. You can see that the first clip is six seconds in duration by looking at where its right hand edge aligns with the timescale. The number above the timescale is the range duration, but currently there is no range set so it is the movie duration.

Timescale and range duration

View controls and menu entries

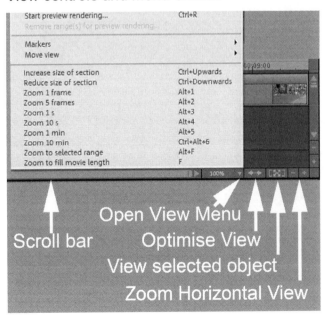

Take a look at the scroll bar at the bottom of the window as well. Currently it should fill the width of the space available. An important principle here is that the size of the scroll bar isn't linked to the scale of the Timeline. To the right of the bar are controls to alter the view.

There are a number of ways to change the horizontal scale:

• Click on the + and − icons at the far right of the scroll bar. Watch the percentage figure change in the small box just to the right of the bar, and the numbers change on the timescale.

• Click on the small drop-down arrow beside the box. This menu can also be opened as a context menu by right clicking on the timescale or the scrollbar.

- Select Zoom 10 seconds, or use the shortcut ALT-4.

- The timescale changes to 10 second units, and the clips in the movie shrink to match the scale.

- Press the F key – without CTRL. The timescale is altered again so that the movie fills the view, but note that the scroll bar isn't now occupying all the space allocated to it.

- Drag the scroll bar or use the arrows either end to see the empty space to the right of our movie when viewing at this scale and scroll bar size

- Click the double-headed arrow tool on the bottom line – the scroll bar returns to full size. This tool has the same effect as using CTRL-F.

So there are plenty of ways to scale the view. If you look at that context menu again you will see even more – CTRL Up and Down arrows for example. Perhaps even better is to consider using the mouse wheel. Using the wheel moves the scroll bar, using the wheel in conjunction with CTRL alters the timescale.

Moving the Playback cursor

The most obvious way of moving the playback cursor is either to drag the marker or just to click on the timescale above the top track where the marker resides - the cursor jumps to that point.

If you find that a bit fiddly, consider if you want to set the Move play cursor when object is selected box as mentioned earlier – then all you need to do is click on an object and the cursor will move to the start of that object.

However, there are many other ways to move the cursor as well. The timescale context menu has a submenu to Move view.

The Playback cursor movement menu

To next object border	Alt+W
To previous object border	Alt+Q
To movie start	Home
To movie end	End
To beginning of range	Ctrl+Home
To end of range	Ctrl+End
Page to the right	Page down
Page to the left	Page up
Snap unit to the right	Ctrl+Page down
Snap unit to the left	Ctrl+Page up
To next project marker	Ctrl+Shift+Page down
To previous project marker	Ctrl+Shift+Page up
To next scene marker	Shift+Page down
To previous scene marker	Shift+Page up
To next chapter marker	Alt+Page down
To previous chapter marker	Alt+Page up
To next marker	W
To previous marker	Q
To next empty range	Unknown
To previous empty range	Shift+Unknown
To next selected object	Shift+W
To previously selected object	Shift+Q

Reset selec
Edit range
Start previe
Remove ra
Markers
Move view

This has an almost overwhelming list of commands, all of them with keyboard shortcuts. They all move the Playback cursor. Personally I find the mouse is often sufficient for this task, but I also use some of the keyboard shortcuts.

We have already seen how Home and End can be useful for moving to the beginning and end of a movie. Two other keys that perform the same function if no markers are set are Q (Home) and W (End). Using these in conjunction with other keys makes for a very convenient way of moving the cursor, and of particular interest is that the cursor snaps to a distinct position.

ALT and Q/W moves to the beginning or end of the next object.

SHIFT and Q/W moves to the next selected object – multi-selections included.

CTRL and Q/W moves to the next object and selects it. This last option is therefore the same as using the arrow keys in Storyboard or Scene overview mode.

You can use Q and W for moving between all the types of markers but we need to know what markers are.

Timeline Ranges and Markers

Above the timescale are two more strips that only appear in Timeline view. I've already mentioned that the top one holds a range indicator; the second one is where markers are placed. Alongside the top strip is a padlock tool which has an effect on both the ranges and markers.

Markers are placed in the strip below the range area. To be pedantic, the range In and Out points count as markers as well, as we will see in a moment.

There are three types of Markers. **Project markers** are general purpose tools that users set for their own purposes. Project markers can be given titles to remind you where you might need to come back and do some work, or can be used as navigation or alignment guides. **Chapter markers** are used for setting navigation points for menus in DVD, AVCHD and Blu-ray discs. You won't meet **Scene markers** until we do some scene detection with the next movie we make - they look like chapter markers but are orange, not blue, and are associated with a video object, not the Timeline.

Setting project and chapter markers can be done from the Edit/Markers menu or with keyboard shortcuts:

- Use the Program monitor to find the point in the first clip where the cyclist is in front of the white van. He begins to be obscured by the lamppost at exactly 3 seconds.

- Let's assume we want to come back to this point and add a sound effect later on.

- With the Playback cursor at that point, press CTRL-Enter.

- A Rename box appears. Enter *Car horn?* And press OK.

Naming the marker

- A blue symbol with the number 1 appears in the marker strip, with a text label alongside.

We can drag this new marker to a new position, or right click on it to bring up a context menu to rename or delete it.

The marker in place

Let's also set a chapter marker:

- Set the Playback cursor to the start of clip two.

- Press SHIFT-Enter. A blue flag icon appears immediately in the marker strip.

Chapter marker

There is no text label associated with this chapter marker, but if we right click on it and use the context menu to Rename it, one can be added.

Timeline ranges are similar to the ranges we can set in the Program monitor, but while those ranges had a very specific use – pre-trimming clips – Timeline ranges can be used in various ways. For example we can export the whole movie or just a section marked by the range. Ranges can be used to define a section of the Timeline that you want to pre-render to help preview playback. Perhaps most useful, we can select a section of the Timeline and carry out editing operations on that range – often with behaviour that is very helpful. In fact, range editing can achieve some tasks when re-arranging movies that are more long-winded using other methods, so I'd encourage you to start using ranges now.

We can set a range in a number of ways:

- Check that the padlock tool is unlocked – it is coloured red if it is locked.

- Click on the range area, roughly in line with halfway along the first clip.

- An In point curly bracket appears where you clicked and an Out point curly bracket is placed automatically at the end of the movie.

- The area between the In and Out points is coloured blue and the duration of the range is displayed in white in the middle of the range.

- Click, hold and drag the In point until the range has a duration of 5 seconds.

- Set the Playback cursor to the end of clip two (ALT-Q/W is a good way to do this).

- Press the O key to set an Out point. The range reduces to 3 seconds

Setting a range

So, you can click or use the I and O keys to create a range, and use the I and O keys or dragging to modify the range. Like the range in the Program monitor, double clicking clears the range. Additionally, if you have set a range and click to the right of it, a new range occupies the width of the Timeline view.

There are numerous things we can now do with that range, and if you want to get a preview of some of them, take a look in the Edit/Edit range submenu. I'll cover range operations in context when we look at Timeline editing, pre-rendering and exporting.

One important point about that padlock tool – it stops you moving the range In and Out markers by dragging or clicking. **IT DOES NOT** stop you using the keyboard or menu to reset them though!

So with three of the four types of markers in place – range, project and chapter – try using the Q and W keyboard shortcuts for navigation. You can skip forwards and backwards along the movie with ease, stopping only at points that you have marked yourself. Very handy, don't you think?

There are even more sophisticated navigation shortcuts available, where you can choose to skip between just one type of marker, but I tend to have trouble remembering them. If your marking schemes get so complex that Q and W aren't sufficient, you can look them up in Edit/Move view!

Preview rendering

In the first chapter of this book I talked about pre-rendering as a strategy to achieve smooth preview. While the project we have on the Timeline should not stress your computer, I just want to briefly show you the controls, although I'll explain how to use them properly when we start adding effects to our movies.

Preview rendering dialogue, with the eye icon arrowed

Below the padlock is an Eye tool icon and a drop-down arrow:

- Set the Playback cursor to the start of the movie.

- Click on the Eye tool. The program scans the Timeline. In this case it is so short you probably won't see anything happen.

- After a moment a message appears telling you that in the program's opinion you don't need to do any preview rendering.

- Set a range on the Timeline for the whole movie and click on the Eye icon again.

- This is how you force rending to happen. The Auto option will look for critical areas again, but if you click on Range the blue area is rendered. Do that now.

- A thin red bar appears immediately above the top Timeline track, spanning the range.

- A rendering information message flashes up at the bottom of the screen.

- After a few moments, the thin red bar turns green.

Render indication

Green render bar

So, the section of movie covered by the range has now been converted to a new, separate, relatively low compression video file which will be used for preview instead of the original source material.

Opening the drop down arrow reveals how we can remove this rendered range:

Render menu options

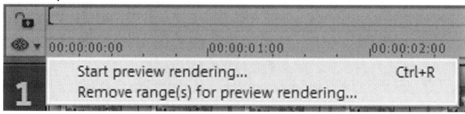

- Open the drop-down arrow and select Remove range(s) for preview rendering.

- A dialogue box warns you of what is about to happen. Select Yes.

- The green bar will disappear

Track management

When we started this project many pages ago, I asked you to just the accept the default project settings. This probably means we have 32 tracks, which is far too many for most projects. Having more tracks than you need just makes navigation awkward, so before I set about describing how we manage the tracks, let us get them down to a manageable number!

- Open *File/Settings /Movie* and ensure the the Movie setting tab is selected.

- Under Number of tracks there is an entry box and a selection of radio buttons with fixed numbers of tracks.

- Select 4 tracks as this is the minimum and click on OK.

Setting four tracks

Obviously, if we wanted a number of tracks that wasn't catered for by the pre-sets, we could use the entry box. It's probably best to start with the minimum number of tracks you think your project will need and if you decide you need another one, use the small tool at the very bottom left of the program window alongside the scroll bar to Add Track.

The Add track tool

Track height

With four tracks in the project, most default screen layouts should be able to display all the tracks without them falling off the bottom of the Arranger. If they do, then you can use the vertical scroll bar on the right to move the window up and down. However, it's probably better to customise the track heights. On the left are the track headers, numbered 1 to 4. At the moment, only track 1 has any content, so the other numbers are dimmed. If you look very closely between the tracks there is a small handle which indicates that the tracks can be resized:

Using the track header tab to resize the track height

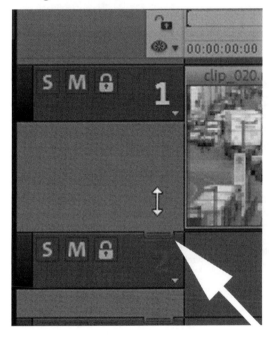

• Hover over the boundary between tracks 1 and 2. A double headed vertical cursor should appear.

• Click and drag to resize the track. Notice when you shrink it as much as possible the thumbnails on the clips disappear.

• Enlarge it again so you can see the thumbnails.

The track headers also have a small drop down arrow that opens a two entry menu. Opening this menu is also possible with a right click on any other blank part of the header. There are two entries, and the first, dealing with multicam, will be dealt with later. Track height is the one we are interested in at the moment:

Track height menus

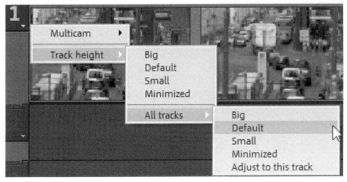

• Hover over the track 1 header and open the track header menu.

• Select Track height/Big.

• Use the same technique to set track 2 to Small and tracks 3 and 4 to Minimised.

- Resize the window arrangement so that you can see all four tracks. Use this opportunity to arrange the Program monitor so it doesn't have wasted space around the display.

- Set the Media pool to Large icons and zoom the size so that the video thumbnails are about half the height of the window.

Now you have a window that is optimised, but it's quite easy to destroy the layout. However, the track layout and window arrangement are saved with the project. Let's demonstrate this along with using the mouse wheel to resize tracks:

- Save the project as *My Test Project rough cut 1 display optimised.*

- Now use the mouse wheel to resize the tracks.

- Hold down the SHIFT key and roll the wheel towards you. The tracks all minimise.

- Roll the wheel away from you. The all get bigger. Set them so they fit in the window.

- Unfortunately, the tracks are all the same height now!

- Reload the project we just saved, closing the current project and declining the offer to save it.

We should have restored the layout to that saved. The Media pool settings aren't restored if you change them and in later screenshots I will revert to the smaller version for clarity, but the track layout will be preserved.

The mouse wheel vertical zooming function (SHIFT-wheel) always centres on the track at the top of the window. In conjunction with using ALT-wheel for vertical scroll and CTRL-wheel for horizontal scroll you have a very useful set of tools for navigating projects with many tracks.

The track header menu option Track height/All tracks allows you to set the tracks to a uniform size of your own choice. If you want to match the height of all the tracks to the current track, then use Adjust to this track.

One temporary control which can be used to alter the track height is contained on the lower toolbar alongside the horizontal scroll bar. To the left of the + and − tools is the Zooms current object button.

- Highlight the first clip in the movie.

- Click on the Zooms current object tool.

- The Arranger view adjusts to fill the window with the object selected.

Without thumbnails, this isn't a particularly useful tool for video clips. For audio, however, it is a great way to see the waveforms clearly for editing.

With the clip still yellow, press SHIFT-F. The Arranger will return to its original layout.

Track header tools

The track headers contain a number of tools apart from the identifying numbers.

On the far left of each header is a dark bar that is empty at the moment. When we start looking at audio, you will see a small level meter here unless the track is completely minimised.

The track header tools

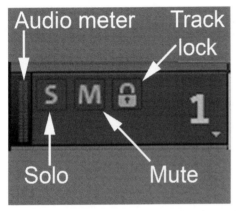

The next two buttons are Solo and Mute. Although this is audio terminology, in this case it applies to video as well.

If you click on the S button and light it, then only tracks that are activated will be seen and heard.

If you set the M button, you won't see or hear the "muted" track at all. I'll demonstrate these features shortly.

The next tool is a padlock. Clicking this locks the track so you can't edit or move it in any way. When the padlock is on, the icon is black in a white box.

You can name the tracks:

- Double-click your mouse in the blank area under the three tool icons on Track 1.
- A white text entry box appears.
- Enter the text Main Track and press Enter.

Renaming track 1

- It's possible to do this to all the tracks, replacing the label Track: with a more descriptive title.

Clip representation

We should still have three video objects spread across the top track of the arranger window. The clips will be represented by a series of thumbnails on a blue background and the clip name in the top left corner. As mentioned earlier, each clip occupies a horizontal space that is proportional to its duration. We know that the first clip is six seconds and the others are about 2 second each. The total movie time is just under 10 seconds and therefore the first clip occupies about 60% of the width of the movie as displayed.

Press the space bar and watch the movie play in the Program monitor. The Playback marker and cursor travels across the clips at a linear speed (unlike the way it does in Storyboard or Scene overview modes).

The long clip will be made up of a series of thumbnails, each showing a video frame that approximates to its position. The narrower the track height the more thumbnails you will see. This is the default display mode. The two shorter clips will just have a thumbnail at the beginning and end, representing the first and last frame of the video. If you are working with a small PC monitor or the clip is too small, you may only see the opening frame, perhaps even only partially displayed.

Simple Video object display

Some video editing programs don't represent a video clip as a series of thumbnails, restricting the display to either the first and last frame, or even just the first frame. Some editors allow you to switch off thumbnails completely.

There are two reasons for this. Historically, less powerful computers may have struggled to create and refresh the thumbnails without slowing down program operation. The other reason is that it can lead to a cluttered display. When we come to use track curves and keyframes later on, you may find the thumbnails quite distracting.

If you are used to working with an editor that doesn't display continuous thumbnails, Movie Edit Pro allows you to switch to a simple display mode that restricts the thumbnails to the first and last frame. The one disadvantage of this mode occurs if you are working with clips that contain internal cuts – they are much harder to spot. However, in this book I'm going to treat material like that to scene detection before working with it. Additionally, not only am I personally used to editing without continuous thumbnails but it would make the screenshots in this book more cluttered, so I'm going to switch to simple mode, and I'd encourage you to do the same.

- Use the File menu to open Settings/Program or press the Y key.

- The Program setting dialogue box opens

- Select the third tab, Video/Audio

- Bottom left is a box entitled Timeline. Check the box for Simple video object display (first and last).

- Close the dialogue box with the OK button.

- If you decide you don't like working this way, by all means switch back, but bear in mind that your screen may not always match mine.

Object colours

By default, video and photo objects on the Timeline have a blue background. Other types of object use different colours to help you differentiate them. When we use titles and audio you will see that they are coloured purple and green respectively.

When we select a clip, it changes colour:

The first clip selected (it's yellow!)

- Click on the first clip on the Timeline.

- The background colour turns yellow.

The selection colour is always yellow, but clips on the Timeline can have their normal background colour changed to a custom colour. This is a feature that is useful for more complex projects, helping you to identify particular clips or groups of clips. Here is how you would change the clip colour:

- Right-click on the first clip. The object context menu appears.

- Select the last option, Object properties.

- Make sure the first tab General Information is selected.

- Click on the Background colour box. A standard Windows colour selection box now allows you to choose a new colour.

Importantly, if you have more than one clip selected, you can change the colour for a whole group at the same time.

You may notice two other items that you can change in the Object properties box. Entering a new name for the clip doesn't change the filename displayed in Timeline view, but it does in Storyboard and Scene overview modes. You can also change the aspect ratio of a clip or selection of clips. This is most likely to be of use when the original video has had its aspect ratio detected incorrectly in the first place.

How to change a clip colour

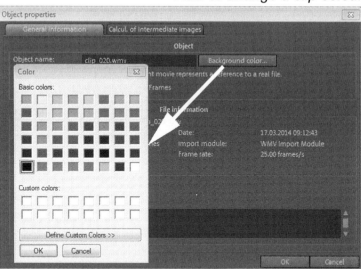

Object selection

Before we start working with clips, I just want to check that you haven't accidentally changed the mouse mode. It should, by default, be in Mouse mode for single objects, This is a tool that only exists when you are in Timeline mode - it's the ninth from the left of the central group of tools on the toolbar as shown in the screen shot. If that isn't the case, press the number 6 key on your main keyboard to switch it to that mode. There will be an explanation of the other modes shortly. We will take a closer look at the new Timeline toolbar later.

If you want to select more than one of the objects on the Timeline, you can use one of the various Windows multi-selection methods. This introduces another colour to the Timeline. The last selected clip will use the normal primary yellow

Mouse mode for single objects

colour, while any additional clips in the selection will be a paler yellow. In some circumstances you need to know which one is the primary clip – when clips are snapping to boundaries, for example. So it's the brighter yellow object that you need to keep an eye on.

One method of multi-selection doesn't work in either Storyboard or Scene overview. In Timeline mode, however, you can draw boxes to select objects in the same manner as you can when working in the Media pool Import window:

- Scale the Timeline to fit the content (CTRL-F is the quickest way).
- Hover you mouse below the middle of the first clip.
- Click, hold and drag left and up. You will begin to draw a Windows selection box (sometimes called a lasso or marquee tool) – a dotted rectangle.
- Use the mouse to include a part of all three clips and release the mouse button.

You can now subtract or add further clips by using CTRL-click. You will notice that in the default mouse mode you can't start to draw a rectangle on a clip, only on a blank part of the Timeline. There is a mouse mode which allows you to work round this issue which we will see shortly.

The Timeline transition tool icon

The Timeline has the same basic tools for transitions as the Storyboard:

- Select all the clips on track 1 and take a look at the junctions of the clips. Each junction, and the beginning and end of the movie has a transition icon tool that works in the same way as the ones we saw in Storyboard mode.
- Click on clip 2 to select it. Notice that all the other Transition icons disappear.
- Click on the remaining icon and from the menu select crossfade.

Crossfade added to the start of clip 2

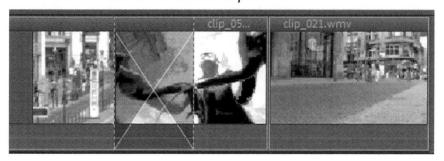

The first thing to notice after the transition has b e e n automatically previewed is that the movie has shrunk in duration. If you remember back to when we

looked at adding transitions in Storyboard view, although I explained why this happens, there wasn't any visual representation of it happening. In Timeline view there is.

The area of the crossfade is marked with a thin white cross and some shading at the point it occurs in the movie. Whatever transition you choose it will be marked this way.

- Click on the transition icon.
- Select the transition Change from the menu.
- The transition icon changes, but the transition markings on the Timeline track stay the same.
- Open the menu again and select Cut (no fade).
- The overlap is removed and the movie reverts to its original duration.

We can also control the duration of the transition with the transition menu option Set transition length, but the menu isn't the only way of adding transitions, or changing the duration. We will be seeing a good deal of that white cross shortly!

Track object mouse cursors.

If you now deselect the clips (clicking on the blank space in track 2 will do it) and hover your mouse over one of the clips again you will see that there are eight areas where you can have five different mouse cursors, These are a very powerful set of tools and I'm going to describe the function of each before we start to do anything significant with them.

Move a clip

The easiest cursor to generate is the move cursor, which looks like a hand. You use this tool to pick up and move any object.

- If the Timeline view isn't at 100% of the movie, press the F key
- Hover over the middle of clip 3 to generate the hand.
- Click and hold – the clip border turns yellow, and the hand actually closes a bit!
- Drag the clip right so it starts to go off the right of the track.

- Release the mouse button. The timescale should adjust so you can see the whole movie again, this time with a gap between clips two and three.

Moving a clip

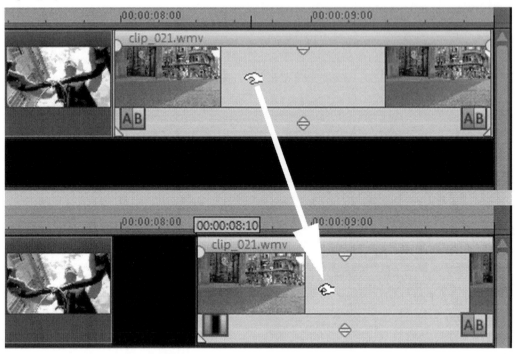

So that's how you move a clip. We can move it anywhere in the Arranger:

- Zoom the timescale out a bit more with the - (minus) button.

- Drag the clip left and right and notice a tooltip appears displaying timecode. This tells you where the In point would be if you dropped the clip.

- Drag the clip down and you can see how it can go on another track. The track numbering illuminates showing there is material on the track.

- Move it back up to the blank space on track 1 and then slide it slowly left.

- As it begins to overlap the second clip, the white cross appears in the overlap area.

- Slide it so that it about half overlapping and release the mouse button.

What we have done is automatically created a transition. Play the movie to see it in action. The white cross shows that there is a transition, and the Transition icon on the clip has changed from the cut "AB" symbol to the grey crossfade icon.

The next action may surprise you:

- Click and hold on the right section of the final clip again.

- Drag it further left., past clip 2. When what was clip 3 starts to overlap clip 1, that clip starts to get shorter.

- Carry on dragging until you have got to the start of the movie.

Now, what was the first clip has been completely overlapped by what was the third clip. Because we are creating a transition, that transition can only be as long as the shortest clip.

Let's now move the clip again, but before we do I need to check one thing:

- The middle group of tools on the toolbar has a magnet in the middle.

- If it doesn't have a light background indicating it is active, click on it so that it does.

The Magnet tool icon

- Now, click, hold and drag the first clip of the movie back to the end of the movie.

- In fact we only take the video clip_21 – the low wide shot. Clip_20 stays at the start.

- Drop clip_021 at the end of the middle clip, without it overlapping. It should snap into place.

- There is no transition showing anymore, but the high wide shot, which did have a duration of 6 seconds, is still only 2 seconds long.

How creating a transition can shorten a clip

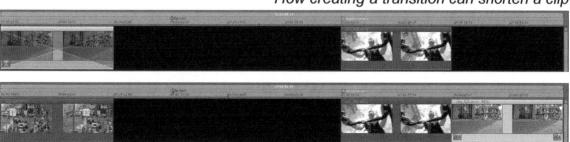

The first clip has been truncated during the creation of the transition. If we had changed our mind about what we had done, it would have been better to use Undo, but I'll show you how to repair clip_020 in a moment.

The creation rules for transitions generated in this manner can get quite complex. In most cases you can get feedback from the visual representation. In some circumstances you can generate two transitions, but before explaining that, I need to describe the other clip tools.

This behaviour can be a bit confusing if you have come from a simpler NLE program. How can you rearrange the clip order in Timeline mode if these transitions keep getting generated? How can you just switch it off? Why doesn't it behave like the Storyboard?

Well, if you want to drag and drop clips in Timeline mode, you have to live with the transitions, I'm afraid. Timeline mode is set up to deal with multiple tracks, and there are plenty of tools we will be able to use to rearrange the movie. If you haven't used more than one track, then simply switching back to Storyboard is a good option. I will show you easy ways to rearrange your movie in Timeline mode, but please be patient!

Trimming a clip

We have already noted that the width of an object on a Timeline track is relative to the duration of the object. Rescaling the Timeline view doesn't alter the duration – it just means we can fit more or less clips on the track. So, to alter the duration we move the In or Out points.

We saw that the Razor tool could be used shorten clips in Storyboard mode – split and discard - and this technique it can also be used on the Timeline, but it doesn't allow you to extend a clip that has already been trimmed.

There are two mouse cursors that can be used for trimming clips, and in some circumstances they do the same thing. At other times they differ. Let's start with the simple one:

- The first clip on the Timeline should now be clip_020. It's only 2 seconds long now, followed by a 4 second gap.

- Hover over the clip's bottom right corner. A horizontal double-headed arrow cursor should appear.

- Move the mouse up a little and the cursor turns to double vertical lines with small arrows either side – we DON'T want this cursor yet!

- Move the mouse down again to get the simple trimming cursor - a double-headed horizonal arrow.

- Click, hold and drag slowly to the right, observing the result.

As we drag, the clip extends to the right. The Program monitor shows the current frame at the Out point.

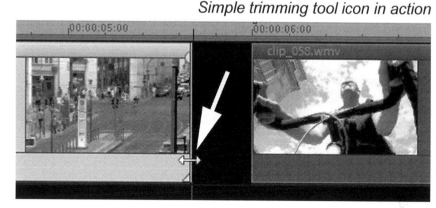

Simple trimming tool icon in action

- Drag further. Eventually the Out point will snap to the In point of the second clip.

- Release the mouse button.

Ok, that's the clip restored to its original duration and position!

Using this control, it's possible to set the In and Out points very accurately, but you can only extend a clip if there is material available:

- Generate the simple trimming cursor for the Out point of clip 1 again.

- Click and drag left and see if you can use just the mouse to find the point we used before with the cyclist in front of the white van – we put a marker there.

- Release the mouse to set the Out point.

- Now use the move cursor to drag the clip right so it snaps up to clip 2.

- Try to trim the In point. You will find you can move it later, but not earlier.

There is no more video available on the front of clip_020, so we can't move the In point left, only right.

- With the In point at the start of clip_020, drag the clip back to the start of the Timeline.

- Now extend the Outpoint again, but drag it past the start of clip_058.

- You will see the transition white cross again. Extending the Out point has created a transition, but don't release the mouse button.

- For now, drag it back to lose the transition and then release the mouse button.

So, this tool will create a transition when you try to overlap two objects. I'm going to show you how to modify transitions in a moment.

Rolling an edit point

This is a term that means adjusting an edit so that it happens earlier or later in time, but the two clips either side of the edit don't move on the Timeline. If the outgoing shot and incoming shot match – they might even be from two cameras recording the same event – then you don't want to change the relationship of the clips, you just want to cut from one to the other at a different point in the movie.

The Dual trim cursor

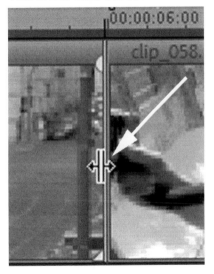

So, if you remove ten frames from the end of the outgoing video, you will need to add 10 frames to the start of the incoming video. This is where the next mouse cursor tool is useful:

- Hover over the end of the first clip in the movie, with the mouse around halfway up the height if the track.

- You should be able to generate the cursor I described before, double vertical lines with small arrows either side.

This is the Dual trim cursor. It will adjust both clips either side of it. It's a very important point that the cursor behaves differently, depending which Mouse Mode you are in. To roll an edit point, you need to be in the Mouse mode for single objects, which should already be engaged. I'll describe other operations you can do with the Dual trim cursor after describing the other Mouse modes.

- Generate the Dual Trim cursor and click, hold, then drag right. Notice both clips turn yellow. No transition markings appear – the boundary between the clips moves instead.

- You should be able to move only a certain distance. When you can't trim anymore, release the mouse button.

If you aren't convinced that the edit point has been "rolled", use the Playback cursor to check out the timecodes of the edit points. Clip 1 is now 7 seconds 12 frames, which is the full duration available – it was 6 seconds long, so it is 1 second 12 frames longer. The second clip ends at 7 seconds 24 frames, which means it is 12 frames long – 1 second 12 frames shorter than it was before.

Reverse the process:

Rolling clip 1 to it's maximum duration

- Generate the rolling trim cursor again between the first two clips.

- Trim the edit point as far back to the left as you can.

Because the second clip has only 1 second 12 "unused" frames at the start, that's as far as you can extend it. The movie should be back to its saved state.

The difference between the simple trim and dual trim modes is significant, but in certain circumstances they behave in the same way, which can be confusing until you realise it is happening.

When an object is not touching another object – there is a gap – then the dual trim cursor behaves in the same way as the simple trim cursor. However, if you carry on trimming and meet another object, instead of rolling the new edit point, the dual trim function behaves in the same manner as the simple trim and creates an overlap, and therefore a transition.

I must admit that I found this behaviour didn't help me while I was learning to use MEP, until I realised the significant thing to look for before you start trimming is if there are one or two clips selected. Rolling the edit point only occurs if the clips either side of the cursor are both highlighted in yellow. If only one clip is highlighted to begin with, either type of cursor could end up generating a transition. To show when the dual trim cursor can create a transition, try the following:

- Create a simple trim point at the end of the first clip and shorten it to create a gap in the Timeline.

- Generate a dual trim cursor for the now Out point and start to lengthen the clip again. Only the first clip turns yellow.

- Pull the Out point back to the left so it snaps to the start of the second clip.

Frame accurate trimming

Having discovered this much about trimming Timeline objects, you might be expecting the next thing on the agenda to be frame accurate trimming, particularly if you have moved to Magix from another powerful editing program.

I'm talking about not having to rely on mouse operation to accurately alter such things as the In and Out points. Of course, many things are possible with the mouse, but for example if you wanted to simply move an edit point by exactly four frames, you would probably need to rescale your view to do it.

Keyboard shortcuts or trim buttons are what are required here, and I want to make sure you are aware that Movie Edit Pro has these features in abundance. You can not only accurately trim edit points, you can adjust the content of clips or the timing of transitions. To do this you use the Object Trimmer and the Edit Trimmer.

However, these tools are best described with a bit more knowledge than I have imparted so far. In particular, how they affect other tracks, gaps and transitions will all be better demonstrated with a more complex project to play with after I've covered more topics.

So, for now, I'm going to just ask you to make do with the tools we have for trimming. I promise you that everything you need to know will be explained later in the book!

Controlling slopes

We are getting quite used to seeing the sloping white lines that indicate that a transition in in place. They can also indicate a simple fade in or out of the video, photo, audio or title, if there is only one of them.

What's more, by controlling the angle of the slope, we can alter the duration of the fade, and there is a special mouse cursor for this purpose:

- Hover your mouse over the first clip.

- In the left corner just below the title there is a white dot.

- Move your mouse over it and you get a diagonal double-headed arrow.

- Click, hold and drag right to create a sloping white line and shading. Drag to about half way through the clip and release the mouse button.

Using the slope cursor

So we have manually created a fade from black. Play the clip and you will see that where the slope finally ends is where the fade finishes.

If we want to adjust the duration or the fade up, it's just a matter if dragging the slope left or right, and now the handle is easier to see. What's more, the Program monitor will show the frame at the point the fade finishes, allowing you to set it with great accuracy relative to the source video. For artistic reasons, it would be good if the fade finished before the camera started to pan left:

- Hover over the clip again and a full white dot will appear where the fade up ends.

- Place your mouse over it and you will get the diagonal cursor again.

- Drag left to shorten the duration of the fade.

- Use the mouse to find a frame just before the camera pan starts by dragging left and right.

Adjusting the Out point of the transition (left) and the chosen frame (right)

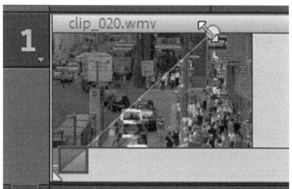 

- Once you have settled on that point, release the mouse button.

If you play the opening now, I hope you will agree that the fade up looks well timed, allowing us to see the scene properly before the panning shot starts to distract us.

When we want to create a fade up we use a cursor that slopes from bottom left to top right. Logically, to create a fade down we need a cursor that slopes the other way. That is what is generated by the white hotspot at the end of a clip.

- Hover over the last clip of the movie.

- Find the white dot at the end of the clip and generate a fade out cursor.

- Drag the fade left so that the cyclist is in the middle of the frame displayed in the Program monitor.

- Release the mouse button.

Our movie now starts and ends with tasteful fades in and out. Let's save it again:

- Use the File menu to save the movie as My Test Project rough cut 2.

Slopes and transitions

Now you've seen how we can control the duration of a fade with the mouse, you might be wondering if we can use this mouse cursor to control transitions. Well, yes indeed, we can:

- Drag clip _058, the middle clip of the movie, about half of its own width to the left.

- It will overlap the first clip and automatically create a crossfade transition.

- You might want to adjust your view of the Timeline to make the transition easier to see.

- Hover over the white dot at the top right of the transition area so as to generate a sloping arrow cursor.

- Click, hold and drag right.

- You will find that the program will let you lengthen the transition to the full duration of the second clip.

- Release the mouse and play the movie.

We have extended the duration of the transition so it takes longer to cross fade from the wide shot to the close up. If we had overlapped the clips less we might have run out of outgoing video to create the longer overlap. In this example, though, all was well.

- Regenerate the sloping cursor and drag it to the left.

- As you approach the start of the clip, the transition reduces in duration.

- When you reach the very start, the transition is set to a duration of zero –it becomes a cut.

- Don't let go of the cursor but start to drag it right again.

- Instead of the transition returning, it becomes a fade up from black.

- Now let go of the mouse button.

This behaviour is a little annoying if it's not what you intended to do, but it's easily rectified:

- Use CTRL-Z to undo your last action.

So, to control where a transition starts, you need to drag the incoming clip. To control its duration, you use the sloping arrow mouse cursor. Play with these two controls to see how they interact:

- Drag the second clip further to the left.

- The In point of the transition starts earlier.

- Drag the slope to the left.

- The transition gets shorter.

- Now drag the second clip back to its right so that it docks with the third clip.

- A gap has appeared in the Timeline because we forced the Out point of the first clip to shorten.

- Trim the Out point of the first clip back to the right so it clicks into place with the second clip.

- Our movie should be restored to its original format before we began working with the crossfade transition. Use Undos or reload rough cut 2.

Transparency

There is one mouse cursor tool left for video, photo and title objects:

- Hover over the top centre of the first clip and you will see a down arrow, where your mouse cursor turns into a vertical double-headed arrow.

- Click, hold and drag it down to about half the height of the track.

- Release the mouse button

Adjusting the clip transparency

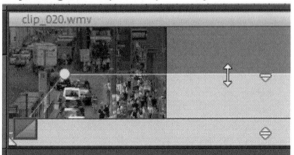

Play the movie and you will see that the clip never reaches more than half the brightness that it should be.

In fact this controls the transparency of the clip, not it's brightness, it's just that there is nothing underneath the video to show through, only black. To demonstrate this properly, we need to understand how tracks are superimposed over one another.

Track order

When you have audio as a source, it doesn't really matter which track it is on – all the audio tracks that aren't muted or faded out in some other way are added to the mix of sounds coming out of your speakers. Visual objects are different though. Most of the time these objects won't be semi-transparent like the one we have just created. They will be solid and if there is another visual object "behind" them, you won't see it in the final movie.

So which track is in front - the one that obscures all the others? The answer normally is that the track with the highest number is nearer the front, so an object on track 2 will cover up an object on track 1. Place a new object on track 3 and it will obscure both of them:

Two track arrangement to show transparency at work

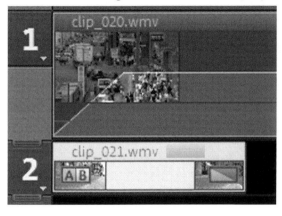

- Drag the third clip down to track two and slide it left so that the In point lines up with the start of the movie.

- Play the movie and watch what happens.

The low angle wide shot completely obscures the wide shot until the fade out begins. When that happens, instead of revealing "black level", we begin to see the shot underneath – on track 1.

If the above demonstration isn't working for you, check to see that you don't have any of the S or M keys lit in the track headers.

Let's just look at the transparency of clip 1:

- Drag clip 1 from track 1 down to track 3.

- Select the clip remaining on track 1 and drag it left to line up with the end of clip_021.

When you play the movie now you can see the effect of the transparency of clip_020. It never completely obscures the clips on tracks 1 and 2.

Three track arrangement

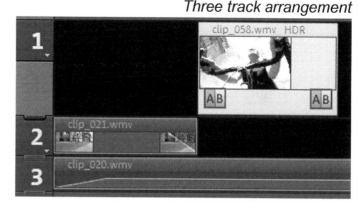

- Reset the transparency level of clip_020 to the top of the track by using the vertical double-headed arrow cursor.

- Play again and the wide shot on track three does fade up to completely obscure the cyclist's close shot.

Solo and mute revisited

I can now clearly demonstrate the functions of Solo and mute with this movie layout:

- Drag the clip on track 1 to the start of the movie as well.

- Play the movie. It starts with the low angle shot, then the high angle shot fades up to obscure it.

- Click on the M icon for track 2

- When you play the movie now, the movie starts off with the clip on track 1, because track 2 is muted.

- Click on the S icon for track 2.

- When you play the movie now, all you see is the clip on track 2 because you have selected Solo. Solo overrides Mute

- Click on the S icon for track 3.

- Now we see clips only on tracks 2 and 3 because they are both set to Solo.

So in fact, Solo doesn't actually mean "play just this track". It means "once any Solo button is pressed, play only the tracks that are soloed".

Backgrounds and track order

Track 1 of any movie is where the designers of MEP expect you to put your main video source. We will shortly see that certain editing operations work with that in mind. However, what if our main video is a green screen shot of someone talking and we want to chromakey a background behind them?

Obviously placing the background on track 1 and the foreground on track 2 will work, and obeys the track order rules. Unfortunately you won't be able to take advantage of the multi-track editing rules that make track 1 special. So MEP offers an alternative.

The context menu for any picture object on the Timeline has an option Background design/Set as background. Checking this option sends the object to the back of the track order, regardless of which track it is placed on. To demonstrate this, we need to re-arrange the movie:

- Either restore the rough cut 2 project, or re-assemble the clips into the order 020, 058 then 021 on track 1.

- Make sure that you have deselected all the Mute and Solo buttons.

- Drag the middle clip down to track 2 and then to the beginning of the movie.

- Play the movie.

As you would expect, the close shot of the cyclist is in the foreground at the start of the movie.

- Right click on the close shot of the cyclist to bring up the context menu.

- Open Background design and click on Set as background.

- Play the movie.

Setting track 2 as background

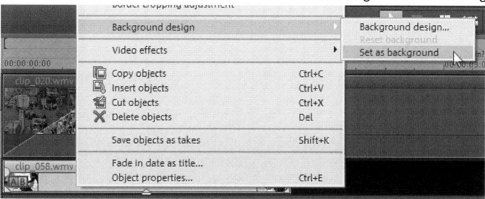

Now, although the movie starts with the close shot of the cyclist, the wide shot fades up in front of it. The close shot of the cyclist has been sent to the back because the Set as background option has been checked. In the context menu there are further tools which automate the process of adding backgrounds.

The potential confusion caused by setting an object as a background can be partially alleviated by changing the clip colour. If you get into the habit of doing this you will be able to see instantly if a clip is set to be a background when you look at the Timeline.

Duplicating a clip or clips

In Storyboard mode, Duplicate is in the Edit menu, where it replicates the currently selected clip, or clips, and places the copies in front of the originals. You can also use the D keyboard shortcut.

In Timeline mode it behaves somewhat differently, because it places the duplicated clips over the top of the originals, displaced 30 frames later. You are then expected to drag them to the required destination.

Now that we know about dragging, I can show you a far better way to create duplicates in Timeline mode:

- Highlight a clip or selection of clips on the Timeline.

- Hold down the CTRL key.

- Click, hold and drag the selection to a blank area of the Timeline.

So, by holding down CTRL, you can leave the original clips in place and drag a copy to any new destination. This is a really handy tool and a good alternative to copy and paste.

CTRL-Dragging a duplicate of the selected clips

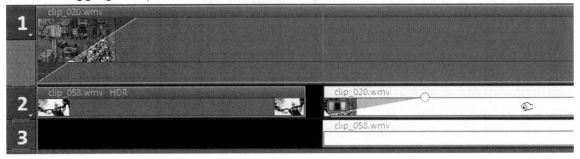

The Timeline toolbar

There are a number of new tools available on the tool bar of the Timeline mode, and some of the tools you have already seen work a little differently. The layout is also slightly different from early versions, so if you are using MEP 2013, for example, all the mouse modes will be in one drop-down.

The new tools on the Timeline toolbar

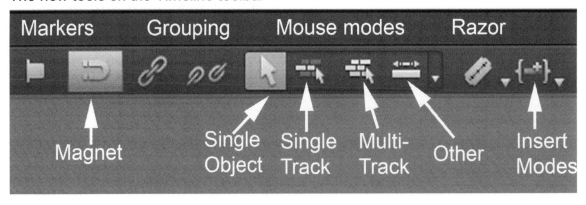

The left and right hand groups are the same – viewing options and Sound options respectively – but there are 14 tools in the central group. In comparison to the toolbar in Storyboard mode there are some missing as well, as there are no tools for Cut, Copy and Paste. Don't let that fool you into thinking that you can't use these tools in the Timeline mode, though. They are still available in the Edit menu, the clip context menu and also from the keyboard using standard Windows shortcuts.

The first new tool is Set Chapter marker. I've already introduced markers and briefly explained what chapter markers do and will look at them again in conjunction with menus.

The Magnet and snapping

With the Magnet tool on, objects tend to snap into place. We have been working with it on up until now and it makes lining up clips quite easy. The tooltip for the Magnet tool is a bit vague, in my opinion. There isn't a grid as such that objects can snap to – they click into place with the In and Out points of objects. You have probably noticed that they work across the whole range of tracks as well:

- Reload (or reassemble) our rough cut 2.

- Grab the middle clip from track one and drag it down to track 2.

- Dragging it left and right you can snap it into a number of places.

- The In or Out points of clip_020 and clip_058.

- The In point of clip_058 with the Out point of clip _020.

- The In and Out points of clip_058 and clip_021

- The In point of clip_058 with the Out point of clip_021.

However, what if you wanted to align the In point of clip_058 just a few frames before the Out point of clip_021? It's really quite tricky unless you zoom in the Timeline view.

Snapping works when you are using the mouse to trim the In and Out points of objects as well:

- Drag the clip on track 2 so that it's In point is in the middle of the last clip on track 1.

- Generate a mouse cursor to trim the Out point – the horizontal double headed arrow.

- Drag the Out point of clip_058 left and you will find it snaps into line with the Out point of clip_021 on the track above.

- Repair the project with Undo, or reload it.

There will be occasions where the snapping is forcing a clip or trim point to where you don't want it go, hence the ability to turn off snapping by clicking the Magnet tool or using SHIFT-U to toggle its state.

The Playback cursor as a snap point

The orange line of the playback cursor can act as a snap point as well. I discussed that the default behaviour of Movie Edit Pro is to leave the playback cursor where it is when selecting objects, but this can be overridden in Settings/Program/System/Other so that it behaves like some other editing programs and moves the cursor to the start of any object you select.

If you chose to change the setting, you can't use the cursor as a temporary snap point, and it was this that persuaded me to get used to the default behaviour.

Having this facility has many uses. For example, if you have spent some time finding a point in a clip, leaving the cursor there will allow you to drag another clip to that point, whether it is on the same or a different track.

Also, while there are many circumstances where the Program monitor will give you a guide as to where you are moving a clip, if you are trying to align to the Out point of a clip it is of no help. If you are trimming an In or Out point you can use the Playback cursor to mark the spot on the hidden track you wish to align it to as well.

The final advantage of using the Playback cursor is that the Magnet tool doesn't affect snapping – if you only want to have one snap point then use the playback cursor and switch off the magnet. Clips will still snap to the cursor!

Setting a snap point

There is also the facility to assign a third snap point to every object on the Timeline, in addition to the In and Out point.

This isn't a toolbar option but it is available from the object context menu:

- Use the playback cursor or the Q and W keys to find the point at 3 seconds we marked before with a Timeline marker.

- Right-click on clip_020 on the Timeline and select Edit snap point/Set snap point.

- Now it's very easy to align the In or the Out point of the clip on track 2 with the moment when the cyclist is in front of the white van.

If you move the playback cursor, you will see that a white vertical line remains on the video object. The snap point is anchored to the object, not the Timeline, so it remains in the same place in the object even if you move the object's position in the movie.

Removing a snap point is also achieved via the context menu.

Adding a snap point to a clip

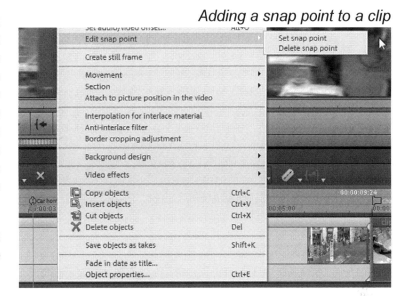

Constraining drag operations with SHIFT

Now I've explained snapping I can demonstrate another useful control for accurate object movement. Often you will want to move an object or group of objects to a different track but you won't want to move them laterally – they are in the right place in relation to the timescale, you just want to put them on another track.

If you use CTRL-drag to create a copy and then drag it vertically, it will normally click into place with its original version which is still in place on the original track – the In points will snap into place. You can then delete the original and your object is on a different track.

However, there is a tool which will stop the object moving horizontally when you drag it – all you need to do is hold down the SHIFT key before you start to drag:

- Click and hold on the middle clip and drag it down to track two.

- It will snap into the same horizontal position as it occupied on track 1 because it's In point aligns with the Out point of the first clip on track 1.

- Now click on the Magnet tool to switch off snapping.

- Try to move the clip on track 2 back into the gap on track 1.

- Even if you think you have succeeded, you may not have been frame accurate, so press CTRL-Z to put the clip back onto track 2.

- Now hold down the SHIFT key and perform the same dragging operation.

- You will find you can only place it in the correct place!

- Switch the magnet back on.

You will find the SHIFT modifier useful in a number of situations. If you find clips snapping into positions you don't want it to then it will override any tendency to snap if you leave the magnet on. Also, if an object has been accurately aligned but has no reference points to snap to, you can use SHIFT-drag rather than CTRL-drag and then delete the original.

Group and Ungroup

The ability to link two or more objects on the Timeline together so that they behave as one object is called Grouping. Not only can grouping be achieved using the toolbar, there is a keyboard shortcut (G) and an entry in the Edit menu.

To form a group is just a matter of using multi-selection, and then the tool:

- Use CTRL-Click to select clips 1 and 3. Click on the chain link icon to form a group.

- Click on clip 2 to select it. Now click on clip 1.

- Both clips 1 and 3 are selected – they are a group.

- Drag them down to track 2 and they keep their relationship to each other.

- CTRL-click on the remaining clip on track 1 and use the G key to group the items.

- Clicking on any clip doesn't break the grouping – select one and you select them all.

- Click on the broken chain link to ungroup the clips, then click on clip 1.

- The first level of grouping is still in place between clips 1 and 3. Drag them back into place on track 1.

- Break this link by using the SHIFT-G keyboard shortcut.

- From this you can see that Grouping is nested.

Grouping is a very useful tool when re-arranging your movie. For example, you can multi-select a section of your movie spanning a number of tracks and group all the objects together. Now, anytime that you select one object in the group you select the whole section, and there is no danger of you leaving a component behind when you move that section.

Ungrouping

Mouse Modes for selection

There are six possible modes in which the mouse can operate. The first three have their own tool icon and you select the others in the same manner as the Insert modes – either by selecting them from the drop-down menu or using keyboard shortcut keys.

The first three modes operate in the same manner when just clicking to select objects, but differ when you come to Drag and Drop mode.

Mouse mode for single objects means that the mouse will normally select one object. When you click on an object it becomes the only selected object. You can use the Windows multi-selection modifiers to add more objects to the selection, but when you click and hold down the mouse key in order to drag you will only move the selected items. As well as using the drop down menu, you can force the mouse cursor into Object mode by pressing the 6 key on the main part of your keyboard.

Mouse mode for a track has the same selection properties as single object mode, but if you click and hold down the mouse button, all the objects to the right of the selected object on the same track are highlighted, and when you drag, they all move. So they behave as if you had multi-selected them. The keyboard shortcut for one track is 8.

Mouse mode for all tracks is just as useful. It includes all the objects to the right of the current object on all the tracks in any dragging operations. The shortcut key is 7.

Let's compare the modes:

- With the movie in the state we saved as rough cut 2, press the 6 key to ensure the Object mode is selected.

- Click on the middle clip and it highlights yellow. After a brief pause so that you aren't double-clicking, click again and hold down the mouse key. No other clips should change colour.

- Drag right. You should see the expected behaviour – the clip overlaps clip 3 as you move past it, and then ends up as a clean clip at the end of the movie. Drag it back to where it started.

One Track Mouse cursor

- Press 8 on the main keyboard. We are now in One Track mode. When you hover over a clip you will get a different mouse cursor.

- Try to move the middle clip as you did before. When you click on clip 2, clip 3 is also selected.

- Clip 3 is moved along with clip 2 even though it wasn't initially selected. Move them both right and leave a gap in the movie.

- Now select clip 1 and move it right.

- All three clips move. After experimenting, put them back to the start of the movie. There will still be a gap.

Three clips selected even though you have clicked on just clip 1

- Select the second clip again. You can now close up the gap by moving clips 2 and 3, but instead, drag them to track 2 and line up the start of clip 2 with the end of clip 1.

- Try to move clip 1 on track 1. The clips on track 2 are completely unaffected. Slide it so that the In point of clip 1 lines up with the middle of clip 2 on the track below.

So that demonstrates the One track mode. It should now be easy to predict how the All tracks mode operates:

- Press the 7 key or use the drop-down menu to select All tracks.

- Hover over a clip to see the new All Tracks cursor

- Click on the close shot of the cyclist on track 2 and slide it left to the start of the movie

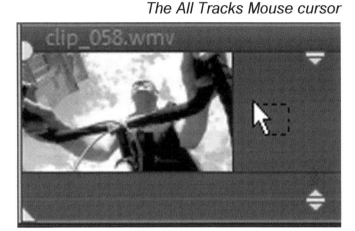

The All Tracks Mouse cursor

- All the clips are later than this one, so they all move, keeping their relationship to each other.

- Click and drag the wide shot on track 1 to the right. The other wide shot on track 2 moves with it. But the close shot of the cyclist stays where it is, because it starts before the clip above it.

- Now move the low angle wide shot on track 2. It moves independently because no clips are later than it on the Timeline. Slide it right on to track 1 so that you leave a gap large enough to drop the close shot of the cyclist into.

- Now grab the cyclist's close shot and try to move it onto track 1. Because there isn't room to move the clips on track 1 up to another track, you can't.

- Switch to One track mode. Now move the clip on track 2 into the gap between the other two clips on track 1.

- Staying in One track mode, you can slide clip 3 up to the end of clip 2, then clips 2 and 3 up to the end of clip 1.

- Finally, selecting clip 1 allows you to move all three clips to the start of the movie.

- When you have finished experimenting, press the 6 key to return to Object mode.

You can see that these three mouse modes can be used to help you rearrange your movie in Timeline mode. I'll look at some strategies for this when we have looked at all the other tools.

While this tool is called mouse mode, the choice of Single or All tracks also has an effect on another tool in addition to mouse operations. We will see this when we investigate the Object and Edit trimmers.

Mouse modes and Dual trimming

Earlier in this chapter I described how you can roll and edit with the Dual trim mouse cursor when the Mouse mode for single objects is selected. Now we have a good idea of how the other two modes work, I want to describe how we can trim a clip without disturbing the other objects after the clip, either on the same track, or on all the tracks.

To best demonstrate the differences, we need a multi-track project, so let's simulate one based on our simple movie:

- Restore rough cut 2 and switch to Mouse mode for single objects.
- Select all the clips, hold down CTRL and drag them down to track 2.
- Repeat the operation to clone track 2 onto track 3.

Adjust the view so that you can see all three tracks clearly, then save the movie as My Test Project multitrack.

Multi-track simulation movie

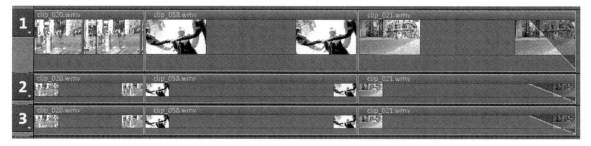

First of all, let's see what happens when we roll an edit point as before.

- Select Mouse mode for single objects.
- Generate the Dual trim cursor over the junction between the first and second clips on track 1.

- Click and try to drag left. You can't roll the edit point that way because there is no spare footage after the In point of the first clip.

- Try to drag right. You can, because there is spare video after the current Out point of the second clip. You can roll the edit until you run out of video at the end of the first clip.

- Drag back to the left to reset the edit to its original condition.

Ok, If we use the next mouse mode we should see the following clips treated differently:

- Select Mouse mode for a track.

- Generate the Dual trim cursor as before.

- Try to drag left. This time it works!

Dual trimming left in single track mode

- The second clip is being moved, not trimmed. What is more, the third clip is also keeping station.

- Drag back right. Again the second and third clips stay attached to the changing Out point of clip 1.

Dual trimming right in single track mode

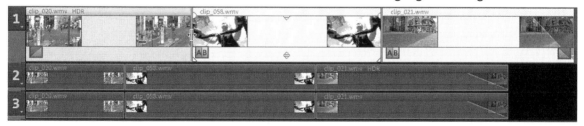

- Drag back left to snap the edit point to its original position in line with the other clips.

This is a very useful feature. If there were more objects to the right on track 1, they too would move.

Hopefully, if I've made myself clear when describing the mouse modes up until now, you should be able to predict what the third mode will do:

- Select Mouse mode for all tracks.

- Generate the dual trim cursor as before.

- Drag left a few seconds, and then release the mouse button.

Dual trimming left in all tracks mode

Take a while to to study the Timeline here. The clips in the track we have selected behaved in exactly the same way as before, but the other tracks have followed suit – almost. Instead of overwriting the outgoing video of the first clips on tracks 2 and 3, though, they have overlapped – and created transitions.

- Generate the Dual trim cursor over the same edit point.

- Drag right as far as you can and release the mouse button.

Dual trimming right in all track mode

Now the following clips have been pushed right, but although the Out point of clip 1 on track 1 has been extended, the other tracks have a gap. The first clips on tracks 2 and 3 have not had their Out points altered at all.

This behaviour isn't limited to track 1 – any of the tracks can be trimmed in this way, with the other tracks compensating for the movement without destroying the In and Out points. Sure, the transitions that are created might not be what you want to happen, but they do indicate that there is a clash, which you can then fix.

This mode of operation – dual trim and all tracks - is a very important one to understand and use. When we make a multi-track project it will allow us to keep all the elements in sync while adjusting our main video.

Mouse Mode Drop-down menu

The remaining mouse modes need to be accessed via a drop-down menu, unless you use the keyboard shortcuts.

Click on the small arrow to the left of the razor and it will reveal three choices.

Mouse mode drop-down menu

Stretching

Changing the speed of playback of an audio or video clip is often used as a creative effect. In particular, slow motion allows you to see action more clearly – for example, analysing a sporting moment. Fast motion can make a boring shot interesting. Additionally, if you find yourself with a gap to fill in a movie and the shot you want to use isn't quite the right length, then a small change of playback speed might go unnoticed and alter the duration of the clip to solve the issue.

To alter the speed at which a clip plays back requires the addition of a Speed effect, and this can be done using the Effects tab in the Media pool. You select the clip and then set the playback speed. This automatically changes the duration of the clip.

However, the Timeline has a special trimming mode that works the other way around. You set the duration by trimming with Stretch activated, and instead of the In or Out points changing, the Speed effect is added automatically, using the correct factor to achieve the required change in duration.

To see this in action, try the following:

- Revert to the single track project My Test Project rough cut 2.
- Drag clip 3 on the Timeline right to create a gap of around 2 seconds between clips 2 and 3.
- Select the Stretch mouse mode from the drop-down, or use the 0 number key.
- Hover the mouse over the right edge of clip 2. In the two areas where you would normally generate trimming cursors you will get a new cursor style – a tiny film strip with arrows at each end.

- Click, hold and drag right so that clip 2 fills the gap in the movie. Don't let it overlap; let it click into place.

Stretching clip 2

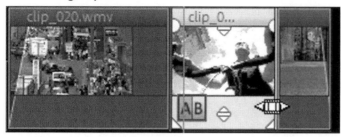

Play the Timeline. Notice that the middle clip has slowed down to around half speed.

Now that the clips are touching, we can investigate the trimming modes. Unfortunately there is only one cursor in Stretch mode, so you have to differentiate between normal trimming and Rolling trim by looking at the clip selection:

- Hover the mouse cursor in the middle of the right edge of clip 2 and click.

- Clip 3 will also highlight in the paler yellow colour. Dragging right will now roll the edit point into clip 3.

- Drag right to reduce the duration of clip 3 by about half.

Rolling edit in stretch mode

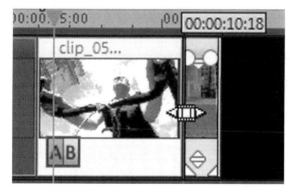

Playing the movie now reveals that clip 2 has been slowed down a bit more and clip 3 has been speeded up.

So, what about the normal trimming mode? Well, we know that the hotspot to generate that is at the bottom of the clip, but you won't get any indication until you have pressed the mouse button:

- Hover your mouse over the junction of clips 2 and 3 to generate the stretch cursor.

- Move the cursor down so it is as close to the bottom of the clip as it can be.

- Move it slightly left to ensure it will be clip 2 that you trim. Press the mouse button.

- If clips 2 and 3 both highlight then you haven't got the correct mode. If only clip 2 turns yellow, drag left.

- The clip will shorten. Just reduce it to about half of its length and release the mouse button.

We now have a gap in the Timeline.

You might be wondering how you can tell that a speed effect is in place on the clips, without having to play the movie. Even then, if there were just a small variation from real-time playback, you might not be able to spot it. At the top of each stretched or shrunken clip, after the file name, should be the letters TS – which I assume stands for Time Shift. If you can't see this, then adjust the timescale and Timeline view so that it can be read.

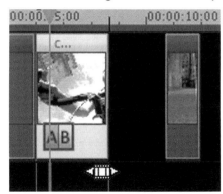
Trimming a stretched clip

When we come to add other effects to clips they will be listed in this area. To see this briefly we can add an effect from the clip context menu. This isn't where you will find most effects but one in particular is available:

- Right-click on clip 2 and select Border cropping adjustment from the context menu.

- The words Anti-cropping will be added to the effects list after the filename.

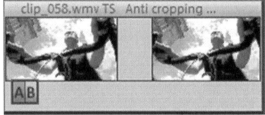
Clip labelled with effects settings

- Play the movie to see that the default crop settings from the Master effects panel have been added to clip 2.

- Right-click on clip 2 again and deselect Border cropping adjustment.

OK, now we know how effects are indicated, we can use this as a way of removing the speed effect:

- Generate the Stretch cursor on the Out point of clip 2 and adjust the length by dragging to about 2 seconds.

Slowly adjust the length left and right – at one point, the TS label will disappear. When it does, release the mouse button.

Of course, you could see what is in the context menu:

- Right-click on clip 3.

- Select Video effects/Reset video effects.

- Clip 3 reverts to its original duration.

- Slide it left to lose the gap in the movie.

Resetting video effects using the clip context menu

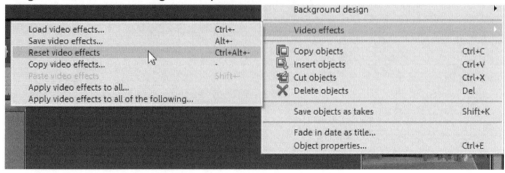

The Curve mouse mode

Where the Curve mode is particularly useful - and why it is named as such - becomes obvious when we start to use Track and Object curves. These are audio and effects tools which we will explore later.

As a byproduct of this behaviour, Curve mode actually disables clip selection when you click on them. This makes it easier to draw a rectangle around objects to select them. I showed you how to use the lasso/marquee tool when multi-selecting clips, but we could only do it when there was a blank space to start the selection rectangle off. If you want to draw a lasso and need to start on a clip, the standard modes will select the clip when you click. Switching to Curve overcomes this problem:

- Check you are in Object mode. Click and hold on the blank space in track 2 below clip 1.

- Drag up and right to form a rectangle with the dotted line that includes parts of all three clips on the track above. When you release the mouse key, they are all selected.

- If there were objects on track two, you would not be able to do this. Try clicking on clip one and you can't begin to draw the rectangle.

- Switch to Curve mode using the drop-downs or by pressing 9.

- Now if you click and hold on the inside of clip 1, it doesn't become selected.

- Drag a box to touch all three clips and release the mouse button.

- You have used a lasso to select all the clips.

Using Curve as a selection method is also useful if you want to select objects that overlap completely. A normal selection will only highlight the "upper" object, but if you use a selection rectangle it will select both objects.

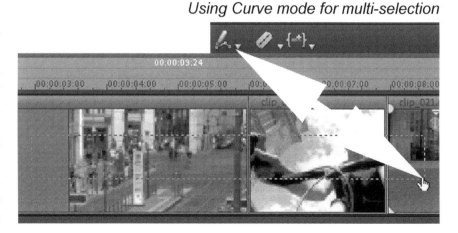

Using Curve mode for multi-selection

Audio preview

This is a slightly oddball option. I can't demonstrate it at the moment because we don't have any audio on the Timeline. When selected, the cursor changes to an arrow and speaker. When you click and hold on a clip, if that clip has audio it plays over the speakers. If it has video, it plays in the Program monitor as well. When you release the mouse button, the clip stops playing.

It's the sort of feature you are more likely to find in an advanced audio editing package than a video editing program.

The Razor options

We have looked at the Razor option when we studied the Storyboard, but there are differences and further enhancements when working in Timeline mode that need to be understood.

The Split Razor tool, that splits an object at the point of the Playback cursor, does exactly that in Timeline mode, but which clip it splits depends on what is selected.

The Razor tool modes

If none of the Timeline clips are selected at the point at which the cursor is sitting when you use the razor, all of the clips at that point get split.

If any objects under the cursor are selected then only objects that are under the cursor and selected get split.

Let's simulate a multi-track project with our simple movie:

- With the three clips of our movie on track 1, select all the clips, hold down CTRL and drag them down to track 2.

- Repeat the operation to clone track 2 onto track 3.

- Adjust the view so that you can see all three tracks clearly, then save the movie as My Test Project multitrack.

The Multitrack test project

Now we can run through the way the razor works:

- Click on a blank area of the Timeline so nothing is selected.

- Place the playback cursor in the middle of the first clip.

- Make sure the simple razor tool is selected, then click on the tool.

- The clips on all three tracks are split.

- Use Undo or CTRL-Z to repair the split.

- Highlight the first clip on track 1.

- Now use the razor tool again – only the highlighted clip is split.

- Use CTRL-Z, and then try the same thing with two clips selected.

- Repair with CTRL-Z for the next demo.

The Remove Start and Remove End razor tools can be thought of as working in two stages. As we saw earlier, when working in the Storyboard mode on a single track, the object is split and then the section before or after the split point is removed, with all the following clips moved up to fill the gap.

In Timeline mode we need to consider what happens to all the tracks that contain objects. Not only does the splitting action vary with what is selected, but the behaviour of the second part of the action varies as well – and in order to explain this I first want to tell you about another razor tool, Delete Scene.

Track 1 is special

In Timeline mode, different behaviour applies to objects on track 1 – which is the master track and the one we would normally put our main video on. When we use the Delete scene tool (or its keyboard shortcut CTRL-Delete) on an object on track 1, it behaves as it does in Storyboard mode. The gap is removed and the objects to the right are moved to the left.

However, what if there are objects on the other tracks? Well, these keep their relationship to the objects above, even if it means overlapping other objects and creating transitions:

- With the multi-track movie loaded, highlight the middle clip on track 1.
- Press the Delete tool or the Delete key and the clip disappears, leaving a gap.
- Use CTRL-Z to bring the clip back.
- Highlight the clip again and use the Remove Scene tool from the razor drop-down (or you can use CTRL-Delete).

The result of removing a scene from track 1

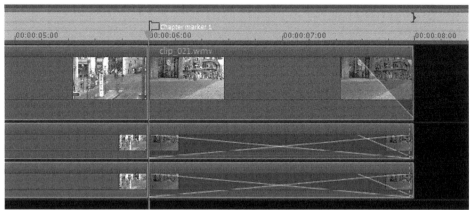

Now the clip on track 1 has been removed. The clips that were underneath on tracks 2 and 3 are still there. What has happened to the clips that followed though? They have be pulled to the left so that they are still in line with what was clip 3 on track 1 – they have stayed "in sync". Because we have created overlapping objects, the program has added a transition.

Incidentally, you don't actually have to select a clip for Delete Scene to work. It takes the object underneath the Playback cursor on Track one as the target, and behaves in exactly the same way.

So, what if we haven't selected an object on track 1? Basically, the ripple effect – moving objects left to remove the gap – doesn't happen when you remove the object. Track 1 takes precedence and won't be disturbed:

- Use CTRL-Z to restore the movie.

- Highlight the middle clip of track 2 and use Remove Scene or CTRL-Delete.

- A gap appears in track 2 and nothing else moves.

Removing a scene from track 2

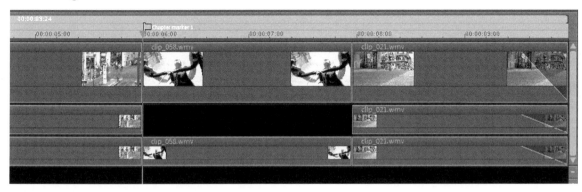

Remove Start and End

Now that we know that objects on tracks other than track 1 don't ripple when you use the remove scene function, we can extend this knowledge to using the compound tools. If we apply one of them to track 2, for example, we will leave a gap.

When you remove the start or end of a clip on track 1 you will not leave a gap on that track, but what happens to any other tracks? In fact, the behaviour depends on what is selected. If you don't have any objects selected at all, then all the objects on all the tracks are split at the Playback cursor, the gap in track 1 is closed up and the objects on the other tracks are rippled left to maintain sync:

- Use CTRL-Z to restore the movie.

- Highlight clip 1 on track 1 but place the playback cursor halfway through clip 2.

- Select the Remove Start tool from the drop-down razor tool menu.

Removing the start of all the clips

Because none of the clips underneath the cursor were selected, we get the same behaviour as we did when we used the simple razor tool – all three clips are split. Then the gap is removed and the two other tracks are rippled to keep the sync. However, you might not want to ripple the other tracks:

- Use CTRL-Z to restore the movie.

- Highlight clip 2 on track 1

- Position the cursor half way through the clip.

- Use the Remove start tool (it has the keyboard shortcut Z)

Removing the start of clip 2 on track 1

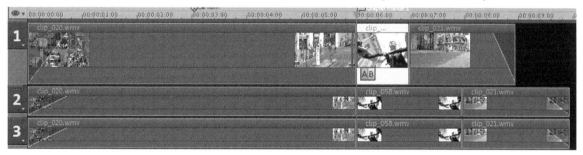

Ah – that's different! In this case you might expect the lower tracks to still be rippled, causing an overlap, but that doesn't happen – the objects on tracks 2 and 3 aren't rippled. So by using selection you can control if rippling is, or is not, applied.

Split Movie

This works in the same way as it does in Storyboard mode – creating two separate movies in two different tabs. All the tracks are split and the objects to the right of the cursor are placed in the newly created second movie.

Insert mode and the Timeline

The additional tracks in Timeline mode mean the Insert options are more powerful than they are in Storyboard mode. Just to remind you, the Insert options dictates how the movie layout responds to having objects sent or dragged from the Media pool or the Program monitor – where the objects may have been pre-trimmed.

The Insert modes again

These tools do not affect what happens when you drag objects from one position to another on the Timeline.

Additionally, in Timeline mode there is a significantly different behaviour between using the Insert tool or V key, and what happens when you Drag and Drop from the Program monitor or Media pool.

Automatic Insert Mode

In Storyboard mode, Automatic always appended anything you tried to insert into to the movie to the end. When dragging and dropping it behaved as if you had Multi-track ripple selected. With the Timeline view selected, Automatic has the same behaviour when using Insert:

- Use CTRL-Z or load the saved version to restore the multi-track test project.
- Place the cursor at the start of the movie.
- In the Media pool, click on clip_058 to highlight it.
- The Insert tool should now highlight on the toolbar to show it is available.
- Hover over the tool to check it says Automatic insertion. If it doesn't, select the correct behaviour from the drop down menu.
- Click on the Insert tool.

So, regardless of the fact that the cursor was at the start of the movie, an additional copy of clip_058 has been placed at the end of track 1. This happens regardless of where the cursor is placed or whatever clip is selected. Even if you have another track selected, the inserted clip is sent to the end of track 1 where it causes the least disturbance.

Automatic drag and drop

When you use drag and drop it is possible to define the destination, but again, Automatic mode is very protective of your movie layout:

- Delete the additional copies of clip_058 you have placed on the end of the movie.

- Click and hold on clip_020 in the Media pool and drag it to hover over the middle of the clips on track 1.

- Release the mouse key and w a t c h where the new clip goes.

Where you intend to put the new clip

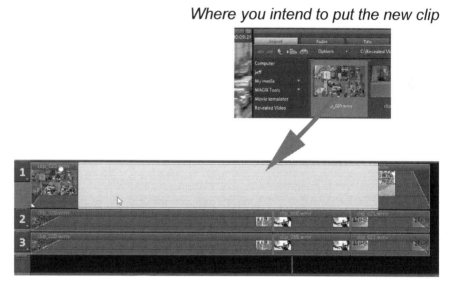

You may not even see it at first. It certainly hasn't inserted itself into track 1, and it's not at the end of the Timeline. It's actually been

Where the new clip goes when in Auto mode

placed on track 4, and you might need to shrink your vertical Timeline view or adjust the screen layout to see it.

It has been put in the correct position horizontally, but on a track where it won't disturb or overlap any other objects.

It's also worth investigating if the new clip always goes to the last track:

- Multi-select clips 2 and 3 from tracks 2 and 3 and drag them right so that the In points of clip_058 align with the Out point of the last clip on track 1.

- Now try to drag and drop a copy of clip _058 into the gap.

- Success! The gap is small enough and the new clip slots into the gap.

- Finally try to drag and drop another copy of the same clip over the clips on track 1 above the gap on track 3.

- There isn't room on track 1, but there is on track 3, so that's where it goes.

So, it doesn't always go on the last track. It goes into the first available gap further down the track order. Only if there is nowhere to put it without causing an overlap does the program resort to putting it on the final track.

Single track Ripple

I glossed over this in Storyboard mode because we couldn't see the effect, but now all can be revealed. If you want to insert an object into a track and move all the subsequent objects on that track – and only on that track – to the right so that nothing overlaps, then you should use Single-track ripple mode.

Using the Insert tool in this mode (and Multi-track ripple) always puts the object you are inserting into track 1, at the position of the playback cursor:

- Restore the multi-track test movie to its original layout.

- Just to see what happens, highlight clip 1 on track 2.

- Drag the cursor to the middle of clip 1.

- In the Media pool, click to highlight clip_020.

- Press the key for number 2 on the main keyboard (not the number pad).

- The Insert icon turns to the symbol for Single-track ripple.

- Clip_020 is inserted into track 1 at the point of the cursor, splitting the original copy of clip_020 into two parts. The second part and all the subsequent objects move right to accommodate the new clip.

- The other tracks aren't affected at all.

Single track ripple and Insert

Remember that Insert can also be used on a trimmed clip in the Program monitor if you make that the active window.

It's time we revisited some of the Timeline tools I've already described as we restore our movie:

- Select the new clip on track 1 and press CTRL-Delete.

- Because we are dealing with the master track, the ripple effect is reversed, moving the clips that were displaced back to their original positions.

- The first copy of clip_020 has been split however.

- Hover your mouse over the junction between the two parts of the clip and generate a rolling trim handle.

- Click, hold and drag right. When you reach the end of the second part of clip_020, you won't be able to trim any more.

- Release the mouse button. Clip_020 has been restored to its original duration in the movie.

If you use Drag and Drop from the Media pool or Program monitor you can choose your destination more accurately. In the examples above, all our work on track 1 can't be seen because tracks 2 and 3 are superimposed over the top, so let's try to add a trimmed clip to track 3.

- Check that the magnet tool is active.

- In the Media pool, click and hold on clip_020 and drag and drop it into the Program monitor window.

- Set the Program monitor range to the last 1 second of the clip.

- Drag the clip in the program monitor down to track 3 and align the start of it with the cut between the second and third clips. It should snap into position.

- Release the mouse button to drop the new clip into place.

Play the movie and you will be watching track 3 (unless you have activated some of the mute or solo buttons). We have added a new shot to our movie.

It works, sort of, although there is a degree of "double action" because we have only cut away from the high wide shot for 11 frames of real time, while the close shot of the cyclist is 38 frames longer.

The resulting movie

Multi-track ripple

As the name implies, when you switch to this mode and Insert an object into track 1 on the Timeline, all the other tracks are adjusted. Again, the Insert tool always puts objects on track 1, so everything on all of the tracks will shift to compensate for the intrusion:

- Park the Playback cursor at the start of clip 3 on track 1. You can be sure it is on the start by navigating there with the ALT-Q and ALT-W keys.

- Drag clip_020 from the Media pool to the Program monitor. If the trim range isn't still set as the last second of the clip, reset it.

- Click on the Program monitor preview to give the focus to the window – the thin blue line at the top will indicate this.

- Press the 3 key on the main keyboard. The Insert mode switches to Multi-track ripple and the clip in the Program monitor is inserted into the movie.

Regardless of which track might have contained a highlighted clip, the inserted second of video will have gone to track 1. One second gaps will have been created on the other tracks underneath so that all the clips to the right remain in sync.

If you decide to use drag and drop to track 1, you won't get any surprises. However, if you target another track, something will happen that you might not expect. Only tracks with a higher number will be rippled:

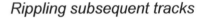
Multi-track ripple to track 1

- Drag the 1 second clip that should still be in the Program monitor and drop it at the end of clip 2 on track 2.

- The clips and the gaps to the right on tracks 2 and 3 get shifted right.

- Drag the trimmed clip in the Program monitor again, this time dropping it after clip 2 on track 3.

- In this case, only track 3 is rippled right.

Rippling subsequent tracks

Ripple respects gaps

You can see from the previous example that when you insert or drag and drop when you have a ripple mode selected, the duration of any gaps are preserved. This is integral to maintaining the synchronisation of clips between tracks. At the moment this may not seem an important point, but when we come to work with audio clips that are lip-synced to video clips but on a separate tracks you will appreciate the importance of this principle!

Grouping affects rippling

If two objects are grouped together, then they are treated as one object. Select one and both get selected, for example. The Grouping effect is enhanced when the grouped clips are on separate tracks – for the purposes of the ripple action, the tracks that contain the grouped clips are treated as one track:

- Reload the saved multi-track project.
- Multi-select the first clips on tracks 1 and 3 and use the Group tool to make them a group.
- Select Single-track ripple as the Insert mode.
- Drag and drop clip_058 from the media pool to the middle of the first clip on track 3.

Notice that track 1 has also been rippled right, with a gap the same duration as the the inserted clip added to track 1 above the new clip. Because track 1 has a clip that was after the insert point grouped with the affected clip on track 3, the gap has been inserted to maintain the relationship between the grouped tracks.

Grouped clips acting as one clip

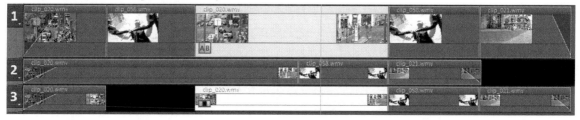

Again, the introduction of audio to our projects will show how important this behaviour is. Grouping allows us to move synchronous audio to another track but still ensure that the relationship between the clips remains unchanged, even when inserting new objects into the clips themselves.

Exchange

This tool works exactly the same way in Timeline view as it does in Storyboard – the item that you are inserting replaces the target. If the duration of the new object differs from the old, the duration of the movie is adjusted.

The operation is carried out with multi-track ripple engaged, with further enhancements to handle the shortening of the Timeline. The attempts to keep everything in sync can get confusing in complex projects. In relatively simple cases, though, the tool can be very useful.

In the version I'm using to write this book there is also some unexpected behaviour when exchanging trimmed clips that have clips with the same Out point on other tracks. An extra gap gets added. This has been acknowledged as a bug by Magix and by the time you read this it should be fixed. Just in case it isn't, or you are working with an older version of the program, then the following demo bypasses the problem:

- Reload the saved multi-track project.

- Highlight clip 2 on track 2.

- In the Media pool, highlight clip_020.

- Select the Exchange mode from the drop-down menu of the Insert tool.

- Click the Exchange tool or press the V key.

Notice how the all three tracks are rippled – it doesn't matter which track is the target.

Exchanging a short clip with a long clip

The process works when exchanging long clips for short clips:

- Highlight the new clip 2 on track 2 –the long clip.

- Highlight clip_058 in the Meda pool.

- Press the V key.

- The project should be back to how it was before – the gaps in all the tracks are closed up.

Drag and drop operations in the Exchange mode don't require you to accurately line up the clip you are bringing from the Media pool over the target clip, but this behaviour can sometimes lead you to performing an exchange on the wrong clip:

- Try to drag and drop clip_020 from the Media pool to clip 2 on track 1.

- However I place the clip, it always jumps to either clip 1 or clip 3.

- Restore the project with CTRL-Z, then place clip_020 in the Program monitor and trim it down to around 4 seconds.

- Now a drag and drop operation should be fairly easy to achieve.

It may be that this behaviour is related to the other bug I mentioned and you will have less difficulty than I do when the bug is fixed. If so, this would make Exchange more useful, but you still need to take care. For example:

- Switch to Mouse mode for single objects.

- With clip 2 on track 2 having been replaced with clip_020 from the Media Pool there should be a gap after the second clips on tracks 2 and 3.

- Multi-select these clips on tracks 2 and 3 and drag them right so that they start at around eight seconds into the movie.

- Now Exchange the second clip on track one with clip_058 in the media pool.

The Timeline is a bit of a mess now, I think you will agree. The original copies of clip_058 that were on tracks 2 and 3 had nowhere logical to go, because the space they occupied on the Timeline no longer exists. So, Magix has left them where they were. However, the copies of clip 3 on track 2 and 3 have been moved left so that they keep sync with track 1.

Unwanted overlaps

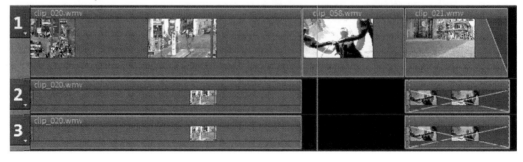

This has led to the clips trying to occupy the same place on the tracks, resulting in an overlap which shows itself as a transition.

These last two examples show that you need to use exchange with care!

Overwrite

This is a much more straight talking kind of tool. It just barges in and cuts out a hole for itself on the target track, removing the material that was there. It doesn't disturb any other tracks either:

- Restore the multi-track test movie with undo or reloading.

- Place the playback cursor at around 5 seconds.

- Make sure nothing is selected on the Timeline.

- In the Media pool, highlight clip_021.

- Press the 5 key on your main keyboard.

- This switches to Overwrite mode and performs an overwrite operation.

Notice the clip has gone to track 1 and starts where the cursor was placed. It also straddles the edit point, so it has overwritten the end of clip 1 and the start of clip 2.

Overwrite in action

Track 1 is always the destination of an overwrite operation using the tool or the V key, even if you have a clip on a different track selected. If track 1 is locked, nothing happens at all. So, as you might guess, Overwrite is more powerful if you use Drag and Drop:

- Make sure that snapping is turned on – the magnet tool is highlighted.

- Leaving the movie as is, highlight clip_058 in the Media pool, then click, hold and drag it to the Timeline.

- If you hover it over track 1 you will be able to get the Out point of the clip you are dragging to snap into place with the Out point of the remainder of the original version on the Timeline.

- Drop it into place and clip_58 will be restored to its original duration.

- Use the clip trimming tool to roll the Out point of clip 1 on track 1 to the right so that it obliterates the current clip 2.

- The movie should be back to its original form.

Multi-track workflows

There are a number of features when working with multiple tracks in Timeline view which aren't immediately obvious, but once you are familiar with them, they can speed up the way you work. We will explore how to work with multiple tracks in the context of a real project shortly, but there are some principles you should be aware off.

If you have come from a different video editing package, you might also find some of the principles a bit alien to you. I'd urge you not to resort to saying "I wish it worked the way I'm used to" but take some time to learn the new principles, because they will make you a more accomplished editor in the long run. It's a little like learning to swim quickly – breast stroke or doggie paddle is easier to get started with; when you start using front crawl it seems very challenging at first, but with practice you will become a better swimmer. If you are making simple movies or perhaps slideshows, with little in the way of multi-track objects, then you might want to start your projects in the Storyboard mode where changing your mind about the order of clips is nice and simple to achieve.

Multi-track trimming

If you want to trim a number of clips at the same time, it's possible to do this if the clips are grouped or have been multi-selected. You can only work on In or Out points, not a combination. However, the In or Out points need to be aligned before multi-track trimming will work, although you can start a trimming operation and the additional clips will be picked up and added to the trim when the In or Out points are aligned. This is probably easier to demonstrate than explain:

- Use the trim tool on the Out point of clip 1 on track 2 to make it around 3 seconds long.

- Use multi-selection to highlight clip 1 on both tracks 1 and 2.

- Generate a simple trim tool – the horizontal arrow – on the Out point of clip 1 on track 1.

- Click hold and slide the Out point to the left by just a second or so.

- The Out point of clip 1 on track 2 is unaffected.

The second Out point is picked up as the first one gets in line

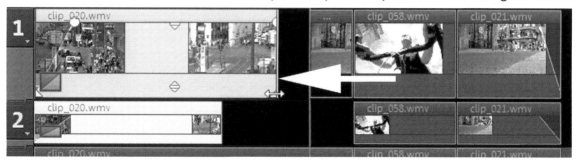

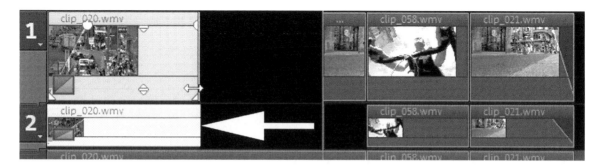

- Now slide the trim further left until it passes the Out point on track 2.

- The two clips now become synchronised.

- Slide the trim back to the right so it snaps back to the In point of clip 2.

If you want to test the same function by grouping clips on different tracks, you will find it works in the same way.

Multi-track and Multi-object snapping

One important principle that is worth getting your head around is how snapping works when you have more than one object selected. It took me some time to realise what I was doing wrong when I encountered what at first I thought was a problem.

When a group of objects is selected, the "secondary" objects are shaded a paler yellow than the "primary object", which will normally be the last object selected. If you already have a group of objects multi-selected and you wish to change the primary object, hover, click and hold on the object you want to snap into place.

The important point here is that the snapping action only happens between the In and Out or Snapping points of the primary clip, so if the objects aren't clicking into the place you are expecting, you probably have hold of the wrong clip:

- Click on clip 2 on track 2. It will highlighted in the strong yellow colour.

- Hover over clip 3 on track 3 to generate the hand icon.

- Hold down CTRL , click and hold, then release the CTRL key. The clip on track 3 will become highlighted, while the clip on track 2 becomes a paler yellow colour.

- Slide the group of two clips around the Timeline. At no point will you be able to snap the In point of clip_058 into position with any other snapping points.

- Drop the pair of clips in the blank area at the end of the Timeline.

In this arrangement, you can't get clip_058 to snap with anything

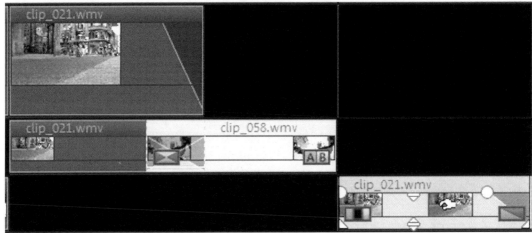

- With them still highlighted, hover over clip_058 to generate the hand icon, click and hold.

- The colouring of the clips swaps over.

- Now dragging the clips allows you to snap the In point of clip_058 with objects on the Timeline.

- Put the clips back where they were.

Multi-track copy and paste

Cut or Copy and Paste aren't a good way of re-arranging a multi-track project, in my opinion. Not only do you have no choice of which track is the destination of the paste, but also any overlaps will become transitions should you paste over an object that is already in place. Furthermore, the transition that occurs is limited to the duration of the shortest clip.

So, unless you are pasting into a gap that is larger than the objects you are pasting, things aren't going to go smoothly! Having said that, if you make the gaps beforehand, copy and paste can be a useful addition to a workflow.

Re-arranging a movie in Timeline mode

Have you ever played one of those tile sliding games? With eight numbered squares trapped in a 3x3 frame with one space in which to slide them you can have hours of amusement or frustration trying to put the number in sequence.

The basic principle applies to the workflow I'm going to demonstrate. I'm going to show you how to swap clips 1 and 2 around on the Timeline. The main tool is the use of the Mouse mode, switching between Object and All Tracks, so it's worthwhile getting familiar with the keyboard shortcuts to switch between modes. The number key 6 on the main keyboard engages Object mode, the number key 7 swaps to All Tracks:

- Restore the multi-track project
- Press 7 on the man keyboard, or select the All track mode.
- Hover over clip 1 on track 1 to generate the All Tracks mouse icon.
- Click hold and drag right. All the clips on the Timeline move.
- Create a gap of about 3 seconds at the front of the movie.
- Switch to Object mode or press 6 on the main keyboard.
- Multi-select clip 2 on all three tracks – you can probably draw a bounding box if track 4 is in view.
- Drag the three clips to the start of the movie.

- Press 7 to switch back to All tracks.

Shuffling clips

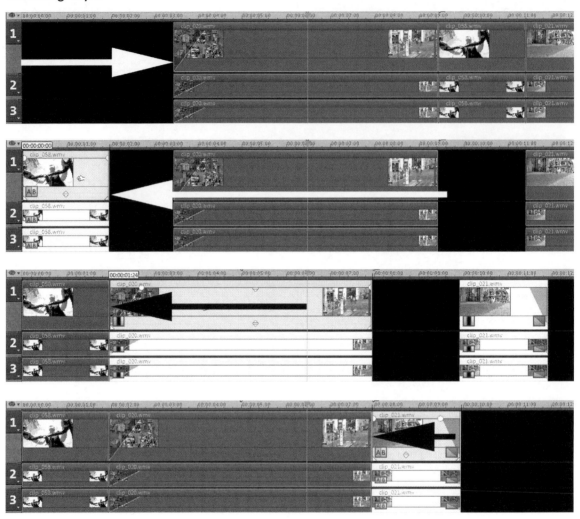

- Hover over what is now clip 2 on track 1 to generate the All Tracks icon.

- Click and hold. Everything in line and to the right on all tracks is selected.

- Drag left so that the In point of clip 2 snaps to the Out point of clip 1.

- Repeat the above three steps on clip 3, to close the gap left when we moved the clips to the start of the movie.

At first sight, that might all seem a bit overcomplicated. With everything in view, it might seem simpler to just multi-select clips as required rather than using the All track mode. But be warned – when your projects get longer, the end of the movie may well not be in view, or if it is, the scale might be so reduced that you don't see small objects on the lower tracks. The lower tracks might not be in view either once your track count gets above 4. So, using All Tracks makes the process as near to fool-proof as possible.

As I mentioned in the previous section, you might want to consider using Cut and Paste instead of Drag and Drop once your movie gets longer and the objects you are moving are from the far end of the Timeline. Just remember to make large gaps!

Takes

The purpose of a *Take* is to allow you to create a new object in the Media Pool that describes a modified clip on the timeline, including any trims or effects, so you can use it within a movie rather than re-creating the modified clip again.

A Take is a small file that holds data, not video or audio. The data describes the location on the computer of the clip and it also has information about any In or Out points that have been set and any effects that have be added. We haven't looked at effects yet, but we have certainly pre-trimmed objects – that is, defined a new Out point for a video clip.

So a Take is a shortcut to a video or audio file. Video Takes also contain a thumbnail so that you can visually recognise that it is a video clip. However, it's important to recognise that it isn't a copy of the source file. Take files typically consist of just a few Kilobytes, even if they represent source files many Gigabytes in size.

In previous versions of MEP, the Take flies had the suffix .TAK. With the introduction of Proxy files in MEP 2014, the files type .TK2 from VEX has been adopted. There is a slightly lower level of functionality with the .TK2 files in that they don't show a red dot when included in a movie.

How do you create Take files? It's done in the Movie editor, in any of the viewing modes, and there are two ways. Any clip, or selection of clips, can be re-created aa a take by using the right-click context menu and selecting the option to Save objects as Takes. There is also a keyboard short cut to accomplish this – SHIFT-K. Using this option will create Take files of all of the selected objects and place them either in the default Takes directory or a Takes directory in the custom project folder.

There is a more interesting way of creating Takes, however. You can simply Drag and Drop clips from the Movie editor to the Media Pool. If you want to make a copy, you can hold down the CTRL key as you Drag and Drop:

- Repair the project by reloading.

- Right click on the second clip on track 1 and add the Border cropping effect from the context menu.

- Trim the Out point of the clip so it is only about 1 second long.

- Switch the Mouse mode back to Object.

- Check that the Media Pool is open at Import/Revealed Videos.

- Hover over the trimmed version of Clip_058 with the effect added.

- Generate the Hand icon, then click hold and drag the clip up to the Media pool.

- Release the mouse button.

- The chosen clip is removed from the Timeline, but a TK2 file has appeared in the Media pool.

Creating a Take

Neat, eh? The Take object has a different icon to other objects – a star – so you know it is a Take.

If you switch to Large Icon view you can see the thumbnail as well - note it is a different quality to the other thumbnails.

Now you can rename the TAK shortcut to something more obvious:

- Right-click on the TAK file and from the context menu select Rename.

- In the white box change the first part of the name from clip_058 to CU Cyclist.

- DON'T delete or change the .TAK extension. If you do, the media pool won't list the file.

- Press enter to complete the renaming.

Renamed TK2 file in the Media pool

Moving Takes

You might be wondering what all this has to do with re-arranging movies on the Timeline. The great thing is that when we add the new Take to the movie it will be coming from the Media pool, so the Insert modes will be obeyed:

- Select Multi-track ripple.

- Drag and Drop CU Cyclist.TK2 from the Media Pool to the very start of the Timeline.

- The whole movie moves right to accommodate the new object, with tracks 2 and 3 all staying in sync.

- The new object is a trimmed version of clip_058.

- It even has the Border cropping effect added!

This is potentially a very useful feature for moving single objects and retaining sync. It's not as useful for multiple objects, where you are probably better off using the "sliding tiles" approach outlined earlier.

You can use Takes in any movie, not just the one that created the Takes, so that opens up all sorts of workflows. For example, you might use Takes to pre-trim sections of a long recording rather than use scene detection. And don't forget that any effects added are stored with the Take as well.

The TK2 file inserted into the start of the movie

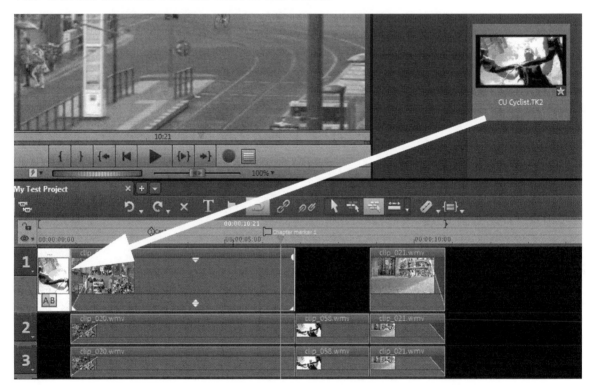

Multicam View

Yes, there is another Edit view mode, I know! If you think I've missed it out, then I haven't. Like the Object/Edit trimmer, it needs a special project to explore it properly, though, and I will return to the subject later.

…and now for more Movie Making

Up until now, I've just been working with some demo clips. I hope you feel we have covered the basics of putting a movie together. There are a lot of features still to cover in Movie Edit Pro, including some pretty exciting ones - and we haven't even looked at using audio yet! I will be describing most of them in the context of demonstration movies. Feel free to skip ahead to find an answer to a question you might have, or use the Contents and Index, but I'd like to encourage you to make the movies with me, as I'll be making comments on best practice and workflows as we go through the demos.

The Flight Movie Rough Cut

The next few sections of this book can be used in two ways. I'm going to use sample projects to demonstrate workflows using features already covered and then use those projects to demonstrate features not yet explained. Where I introduce a new feature of Movie Edit Pro, as well as using it for the purposes of the project, I'm going to describe it in greater detail for reference.

So if you just want to work through the projects, you can skip the full details of a feature and jump to the next section, making sure not to skip any of the text marked with bullet points. You can then return to the skipped section when you want to learn more. You can also learn about how each feature works without actually building the project yourself – for example, if you are familiar with most of the functions but want a detailed description of the Title Editor, then use the Index or sub-headings to skip straight to the section about the titler.

I'd hope that you would make the projects, because you will get a better view of the features in action and it should give you some ideas about the best way to approach your editing. I will make it possible for you to skip ahead, though, by providing the projects in pre-made form at the end of each chapter so you can start the next chapter without working through the preceding material.

The first project is a holiday movie of a flight in a light aircraft over Mount Snowdon in North Wales. The second project demonstrates how to use slow motion. I'll combine the first two two projects to enable me to show you how to create a disc project.

If you have used one of my earlier editing software books for Pinnacle Studio you will be familiar with the flight source material, but I'm making a slightly different movie to show off different functions. You will have the main source file you need, though.

If you don't have the source files, you should be able to download them if you have a reasonable Internet connection. I realised that my service provider was not providing a fast service to some parts of the world in the past and you will find alternatives links for the bigger files. If all else fails I can send the files to you on a Demo DVD at what I hope you will find a reasonable cost. The complexities of small scale book publishing means it is very hard to include a disc inside a book. If you have the Demo DVD, you will find all the files for the Flight project in the Flight Over Snowdon files and clips folder.

A Flight over Snowdon

This chapter is concerned with ways of using the elements of MEP that I've already covered, but in greater depth.

For the first project you only need one video file. It is called Project1mp2.mpg and is a bit over 10 minutes long. You can download it from the website **www.Dtvpro.co.uk**. Follow the instructions and use a browser to put it in the Windows Downloads location. If your Internet connection is too slow you may need to get someone else to download it for you or send off for the Demo DVD.

When you have the file, take a look at it using media playing software such as Windows Media Player. The first few shots are exteriors, with the remaining video being taken from inside the Cessna as it takes a pleasure flight to view Mount Snowdon – the highest peak in England and Wales.

It's a great memory for me. I can watch it and remember the day clearly. The family was on holiday in Wales, and we all had ideas for days out. My wife wanted to climb up Snowdon, my daughter wanted to take a boat trip to see the seals and dolphins, but I really fancied a pleasure flight from Caernarfon Airpark to see Snowdon from the air. I got my wish on the clearest day, although there was a bitingly chilly wind.

While we waited for our flight, I took some shots with my handheld DV camera. I was really just checking the camera, but once aboard the aircraft, decided I had enough battery power and tape to let it run for the whole 30 minutes. Some of it is very wobbly, the camera is mostly set to automatic, and although my camera has a fairly good zoom lens, bouncing around in a light aircraft makes it hard to get decent tight shots. You might also be surprised if I told you that in the past I was a professional broadcast TV cameraman, but my excuse is that I was on holiday to enjoy the day with my family, not to make a documentary!

There is about 30 minutes on the original tape. I've trimmed it down to under 11 minutes, and burnt in a timecode top right to help us locate precise parts of the file to the nearest frame. I think we should be able to make a short movie that could hold a detached viewer's interest.

Setting up a project

To begin, I want to look in detail at the choices you can make when you first start a new project and changes you can make once a project has been started. We skimmed through this at the start of the book, and you will find some screenshoots there if you haven't read from the beginning.

Opening the program or using the File menu to start a New project normally opens the "What do you want to do?" box over the main program window and for now I'm going to use that approach.

Let's begin by starting a project and giving it a unique name:

- Run the program, or if it already open use the *File* menu and select *New Project*.

- If the *What do you want to do?* dialogue box does not appear you have probably disabled it. Use the *File/Settings/Program* option, select the *System* tab and then under *Program interface* click on *Reactivate dialogues. Select File/New project* again.

- Check that the first option, *Create new project,* has its radio button selected.

- Click on the text box below and enter *Flight Over Snowdon* as the new project name, but don't press Enter just yet.

- Beneath the new project name is a checkbox to *Automatically create proxy files*. The video source for this project isn't so heavily compressed nor is it high resolution, so it should not require the use of proxies. Therefore make sure that the box to create proxies is unchecked.

- Now, to look at some further options,click on the drop-down arrow for the blue *Options* box. Some new choices appear.

- Don't press *OK* yet!

Using a Project Folder

We now have revealed some additional choices that need further explanation.

Create a new project folder where all imported media will be copied to is possibly a good idea from a housekeeping point of view. However, I find that Movie Edit Pro gives me two issues when using this approach.

One issue is that the program isn't entirely consistent when you import files or use takes and you may experience error messages that are confusing, if not actually wrong. The other problem is that you end up with lots of duplicate files unless you specifically ignore some of the warnings, and if you do that you aren't creating a proper project folder.

In the fully professional version (not covered in this book) the project folder can be displayed as a separate program window, which makes it more powerful, but in MEP my personal opinion is that the added complications aren't always worth the benefits, particularly as one major result – having all your assets in one place for backup – can be achieved using the Backup Copy file menu option instead.

If you decide you do want to use the project folder option, then you can choose any hard disc location for the project folder, and if you have more than one hard disc I would recommend that you consider using a disc other than your Operating System drive. However, in this case let's stick with the default behaviour:

- Make sure that the box for *Create a new project folder* is unchecked.

This doesn't mean I will be taking an irresponsible approach to media management, but I'm going to do it manually, in particular when I use the Recording options.

Movie settings

Movie Settings preset choices

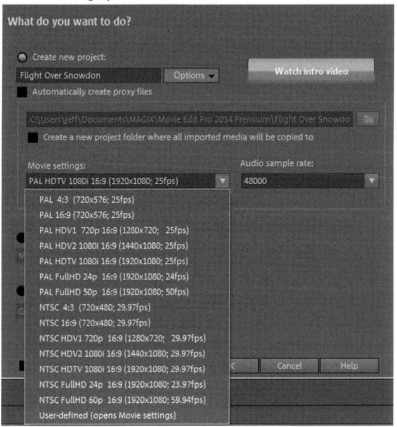

Here you will find a drop down box which allows you to choose the video standards that the editing program will work to.

The best way to decide what setting you need to use is to consider the source material as well as how you are going to "publish" your final masterpiece. If you are considering publishing at a higher standard than the source footage, then any titles or photos you add might benefit but the original video isn't going to look any better. On the other hand, if you have some

High Definition video but are only going to send the movie to people who don't have a Blu-ray player, then you are adding a lot of extra stress on the computer by working in HD when you don't need to.

However, in Movie Edit Pro, when you choose your Movie settings they aren't set in stone; you can change them at a later date without having to remake your movie, so it's not the end of the world if you choose the wrong settings.

PAL vs NTSC

In the project we are about to make the source footage is PAL standard definition widescreen video and we are going to end up by making a DVD, which can only reproduce standard definition material. (If you are in North America you might not be able to play a PAL standard DVD, but I'll show you how to get round that later on).

For standard definition video, PAL and NTSC differ with slightly different resolution and a more significantly a difference in frame rates. When we move up to high definition video, then the only difference is the frame rates. Converting resolutions is relatively easy – you just resample the pixels to resize the picture. Converting frame rates is far harder to achieve – in fact, it's impossible to do without some form of degradation or altering the duration of the shots. At its simplest, converting a 25 frames per second movie to 30 frames a second involves repeating every fifth frame, resulting in a slight stutter. Converting 30 frames to 25 involves removing every fifth frame, giving a skipping effect. More complex conversions try to interpolate (which is just a nice way of saying guess) what the missing information might be, but this can't be done perfectly. Otherwise, to avoid skipping or stuttering, you are stuck with slowing down or speeding up the material so that many actions will look unnatural.

30fps or 29.97?

NTSC has a little extra confusion. For reasons to do with colour encoding that are too complex to bore you with, the NTSC frame rate is actually a tiny bit less that 30fps – 29.97 in fact. This minor difference is often ignored and for the sake of simplicity people talk and write about 30fps. Sadly, there are also a very small minority of cameras that actually shoot at a true 30fps, causing a few anomalies. When you double the frame rate of NTSC to progressive (non-interlaced) scanning, it is actually 59.94fps, but most people call that 60p.

Aspect ratio

Standard definition video comes in two aspect ratios – the 4:3 shape of old TV sets (and roughly the "Academy" ratio of classic cinema), and the newer widescreen aspect of 16:9. The ratio is expressed as the width:height. However, for standard definition the actual pixel resolution is the same – the pixel widths are stretched or shrunk to make them fit the screen. HD works the other way round – displays are always 16:9, but HD video with a vertical resolution of 1080 can be 1440 or 1920 pixels. In the case of 1440, the pixels are stretched to fill the width of the display.

SD vs HD

Open the drop down box and compare the settings available as presets. One of these should be suitable for any project you want to publish for display on a TV set.

There are 4 SD project formats. PAL 4:3 and 16:9 at 720 horizontal pixels by 576 vertical pixels formats have a frame rate of 25 frames a second, and by definition this is an interlaced format (see Chapter 1 for an explanation of interlace). NTSC has 30 interlaced frames a second and a lower vertical resolution of 480 pixels – but again, the horizontal resolution is 720 pixels and this is stretched or shrunk to achieve the desired aspect ratio.

If you are only using video from a DV camera or older analogue video from a VHS or 8mm type of camera then these are the best settings for you to use.

In all there are 10 HD settings. Three resolutions exist and they are defined by the vertical resolution. 720p is 720 pixels high and has a horizontal resolution of 1280 and if you do the maths you can see that has a ratio of 16:9 – the pixels are displayed as squares, not rectangles. HDV2 has a vertical resolution of 1080 but is a non-square pixel format because although the aspect ratio is 16:9 the horizontal resolution is only 1440 pixels – if the pixels were displayed as squares the aspect ratio would be 4:3! This format is the norm for most HDV cameras, and perhaps surprisingly is used by some broadcast quality cameras as well.

"Full" HD is 1920 by 1080 with square pixels, but there is further confusion caused by the various frame rates and scanning options, because Magix defines "Full" HD as being 50p (PAL) or 60p (NTSC).

In addition, a further frame rate is possible – 24fps (actually 23.97). Because film cameras shoot at this rate some video cameras can also shoot at this rate.

So, which should I choose?

The best thing to be guided by is the highest quality video you are going to include in your movie as source footage. In our case this is only 720 by 576 pixels, 16:9 aspect ratio, shot at 25fps. So:

- In the *Movie settings* drop down box select PAL 16:9 (720x576; 25fps).

- Click on *OK* and the dialogue box will close.

You will notice that I didn't bother to alter the audio setting. The 48000 matches that of the source material and we might as well use the highest quality possible.

Another option that you may also have noticed in the drop-down box for Movie settings is User Defined. This option opens a further settings box for you to alter the video standards and a number of other parameters. You would use this option to choose video standards that aren't provided as a pre-set. We are going to explore the setting box now anyway.

More Movie settings

Once you have used the New project dialogue, there are still things that you might want to alter or enhance. Also, if you change your mind about a project some of the initial parameters can also be changed. One choice that can't be altered is the allocation of a project folder, but I've advised you against doing that.

When you alter the settings, you don't lose any content that you have already added to your movie. Let's look at what can be changed:

- In the *File* menu, select *Setting/Movie*.

Project/movie settings

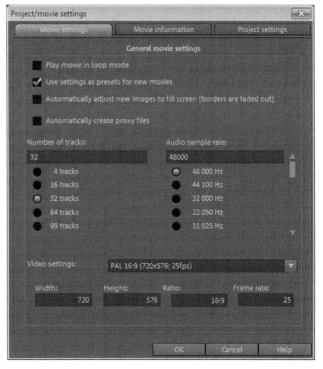

- A box with three tabs opens. Make sure that the first tab, *Movie settings*, is selected.

There are four check boxes at the top of the box.

Play movie in loop mode forces the Program monitor to return to the start of a clip or movie and play it again when it reaches the end. This may have some uses, but I don't use the option – in particular because the current view of the Storyboard or Timeline is played, even if much of it contains no video.

Use settings as presets for new movies is more helpful. If you always want a particular number of tracks or a particular video standard then you can force the currently displayed setting to become the default when you chose to create a new project.

Automatically adjust new images to fill screen works on photos only. If you enable this option and then try to use a still picture that has an aspect ratio that doesn't match the project, it will be automatically cropped to hide the black/transparent bars that would result. This means you will lose some of the information in the picture off of the sides of the screen. Initially a dialogue box warns you what is about to happen to the picture, but that can be disabled (and re-enabled using the Reactivate dialogs control).

When this option is active, you don't get any choice of exactly how the cropping is achieved, so don't expect the results to have any artistic merit. Neither is there any indication on the Timeline clips that an effect has been added. If you want to modify the effect, you will find it has been added as a *Movement effects/section*, and if you attempt to remove the cropping you will see a warning message. Movie Edit Pro doesn't attempt to crop pictures it detects to be shot in portrait mode – that is with the height greater than the width.

Automatically create proxy files give you another chance to enable proxy editing. I'll discuss this later in the book.

Changing the number of tracks

We have already seen this control in action, where we reduced the number of tracks to make the edit screen display easier to navigate. It is unlikely that we are going to need more than 4 tracks for the Flight project, and if we decide we do, we can always add more, so:

- In *Movie settings/Number of tracks*, click on the *4 tracks* radio button.

Custom video and audio settings

I've already pointed out that we may as well leave the audio sample rate a 48,000 Hz, but if there were a problem with that setting, you could change it in the settings box as well.

What is more interesting is that not only can you select a new set of video standards from the drop down box, but there are boxes in which you can type in "non-standard" settings as well. So, if you want to use a resolution, frame rate or even an aspect ratio for your movie that isn't one of the "normal" TV standards, you can enter them here. Mind you, you are unlikely to need to do this for any movie you expect to be played on a conventional TV – you will probably confuse it no end. Where the feature might be useful is custom files for Internet or other forms of playback – creating movies to fit into odd shaped boxes on websites, advertising displays or within other programs such as Powerpoint. Bear in mind that if you want to preserve the final movie in the customised format you will probably have to also customise the export files settings as well.

One interesting thing to note – although MEP 2014 doesn't have any presets for the emerging 4K video standard, it's possible to use custom settings to create a project and export a file with those settings. I can't really predict how well these will work though. MEPs handling of the 4K format is currently designed so you can use the footage in other projects, probably with the aid of proxy file management.

- Click on the OK button to close the Movie settings dialogue.

- Adjust the screen layout so that you can see just the four tracks in the Arranger.

Recording Video – an introduction

In the Media Pool chapter I showed you how to use the Import tab of the Media Pool. We located the Demo video clips and moved them into a custom location for use in the First Project demonstrations. You might want to simply use the same techniques to acquire the video file we need for this project and skip this section. However, I thought I'd

The Recording button

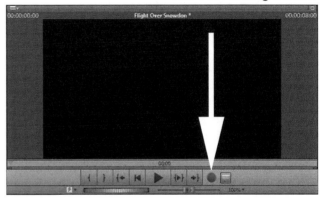

use this as an opportunity to introduce you to the Recording function.

Beneath the preview window, the penultimate button on the left is a red Video or Audio recording tool. You can also access this function via the *Record audio/image/video* entry in the File menu. Click on the red button now and it should reveal the recording source selection dialogue.

Now, you might be thinking that Recording is the wrong term for what we currently want to do, and you would be right. However, in six of the seven available options, Recording is the right word.

The Recording source selection box

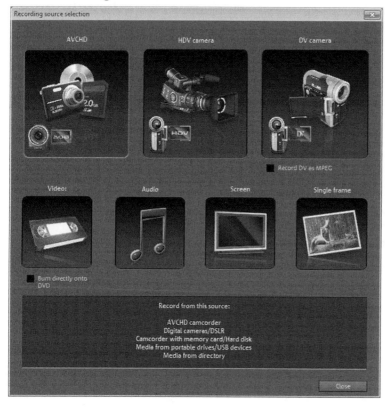

Ignoring the first option labelled AVCHD the other sources are:

HDV camera – for transferring HDV video from a camera tape to your hard drive via a firewire port.

DV camera – the same but for Standard Definition DV tapes.

Video – to capture analogue video in real time from a webcam, analogue capture device or TV tuner.

Audio – to capture analogue audio in real time from a microphone or other audio source connected to your computer.

Screen – for capturing the screen of your computer while using programs.

Single frame – for grabbing a single frame from an analogue video source.

Now, all those options are for some form of real time capture, and until a few years ago, most of your source material would have to be brought into the computer in this manner. Any other source would have been as a file, created by another computer or another program on your computer. As we have already seen, there are ways and means of getting video files to appear in the Import section of the Media pool so we can use them in our projects.

However, with the advent of cameras that record straight to a file, an efficient way of transferring the footage from the camera or memory device is now a necessity. You might want to transfer many files at a time, changing the names and specifying the location they are moved to. Movie Edit Pro has such a function with the AVCHD import option. It's been given that name because the majority of cameras that need this feature are AVCHD format, but in fact any valid video, audio or still picture file can be brought onto MEP using the feature.

As we only want to import one single file, which might already be somewhere on our computer, this feature is a bit of a sledgehammer to crack a nut. However, it is worth learning to use because it will save you a lot of work in the future.

First, you need to get hold of a copy of the file in question - Project1mp2.mpg - using one of the means I mentioned earlier. Hopefully it's now in the Download location of Windows. It may be on a DVD disk, or it could be on a removable memory card or hard disc location. Wherever it is, you will be able to "record" it so that it appears somewhere convenient in the Media pool

The AVCHD Import Window

Select the top left option in the Recording source selection. You will now see the media management screen. The top left section deals with source and destination:

- In the drop down box under *Video source* there will be a list of places you might want to look, but also the option to *Select own folder*.

- Cick on this option and a *Browse for Folder* dialogue box opens.

- If you have downloaded the file, select Your User Name (in my case, the screenshots show *jeff*) and look in *Downloads*.

- If the file is on a DVD, select the DVD drive.

- If it is elsewhere on your computer, select the folder where you have placed it.

- Click *OK*.

Recording from my Downloads location

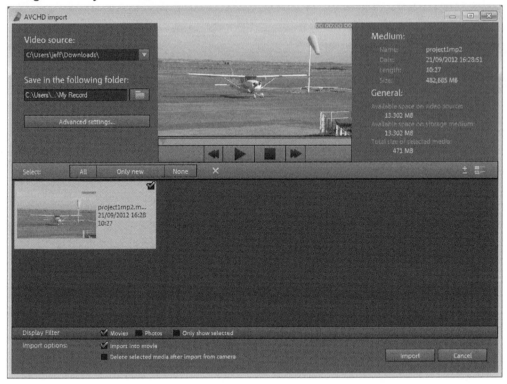

Depending on the location you specified, a single file, or a number of files, will now appear in the main window in the centre of the box. We want to select one file for import, but if you were working with a camera you might want to select a whole group of files. There are a number of tools to help you find exactly what you want.

At the top right of the display window an icon allows you to chose a Details or a Large icons display. You can change the size of the icon display with the +/- slider to the left. The Details display can be sorted by Name, Type, Size or the time it was modified or created. You do this by clicking on the labels at the tops of the columns, and usefully, when you return to the Large icons display, the sort order is retained.

Selection is achieved by clicking on the icons or details or by using the usual Windows multi-selection tricks, and there are also All and None buttons at the top of the window. Notice that there is also an Only New button for filtering out files that were on the camera the previous time you used the import function.

A display filter at the bottom of the window also allows you to exclude Photos or Video from the display, and remove any files from view if you haven't selected them.

- Click on the file *project1mp2.mpg.*

- It will turn a pale blue colour, and the small checkbox top right will show a tick.

The video will now appear in the import preview window. You can use the playback tools to explore the file. Alternatively, double click on the file just to play it (if it's on DVD, this might be a bit sluggish).

With these tools, it's easy to investigate the files, selecting the ones you want to import. If you were choosing files from a camera, you would probably use CTRL-click to add all the files you were interested in to the selection.

To the right of the preview window you get further information about the currently highlighted file, and underneath the sizes of the source and target destinations and the current size of your selections are shown, so you can tell if you are going to run into space issues.

Using the advanced AVCHD Import functions

There are still a few things we need to attend to before clicking the Import button.

Save to the Following Folder allows you to choose the target destination of the import – where the files are going to be copied to. In this instance I want you to put a copy of the project video in the default location:

- Check that the *Save in…* location is still *C:\Users\….\My Record*.

- If it has been changed, use the Browse for Folder tool to set it to *Your user name/My Documents/Magix Projects/Movie Edit Pro 2014 (version)/My Record*.

If you were recording from camera memory you might want to choose a folder in *My Videos* and add a date or identifier to the folder name so that the files could be found easily by other programs or Windows.

Advanced settings needs looking at as well. Here we can rename the files as they are copied across, specify what date to associate with the file and deal with duplicate names.

- Click on the *Advanced settings* button to open the dialogue.

- Select the *Save as* radio button.

- Enter "Flight" in the box above the text + *Running number*.

- Check *Keep creation date* and *Automatically rename new clips* buttons.

- Click on OK.

Advanced recording settings

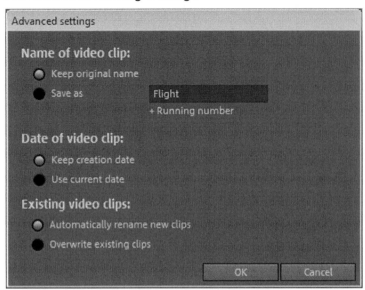

This will preserve as much information as possible. By renaming the clip we are making things clearer. Keeping the creation date and not overwriting old files is also a good idea, but if you were re-importing lots of camera files you might chose to do things differently.

We still aren't quite ready to press the *Import* button. The bottom of the window has some import option checkboxes. *Import into movie* will place our imports into the movie as well as the Media Pool, and in this case, it does no harm to leave it checked.

The *Delete selected media after import from camera* option is more drastic. It's important to note the wording – the files will only be deleted **after** they have been successfully copied, so if you want to clear space on your camera memory automatically, it's very unlikely to cause you to lose files. On the other hand, you might prefer to use the camera controls or Windows to do this at a later date, when you are sure that you have finished with the rushes.

In our case it will do no harm to check this box – the file isn't irreplaceable – although if you are importing from a DVD disc it's not going to work anyway because the disc is read-only!

- Check *Import into Movie*.

- Check *Delete selected media…*

- Finally, click the *Import* button.

When the process completes, you will be returned to the edit screen, with a file called *Flight* placed on the Timeline. The number of the "+ running number" function would have been added if we had selected two files - the next one would have been *Flight1*.

In this introduction to the Recording process, we have only looked at one of the seven functions. Somewhat oddly, although it is called the AVCHD function, we have used it to import MPEG-2 video, and we could use it for any other recognised format, or indeed, for photos. I hope you will now consider using it instead of the methods described earlier in the book, particularly for bulk imports.

The other Recording functions all feature some form of real time capture. If you want to use these, then you will need to check out the Importing Media chapter later in the book.

Time to look at the media

So now we have the source footage on the Timeline. You might also wonder where you can find it in the Media Pool:

- Click on the *Import tab* of the Media Pool.

- If you have a complex tree view displayed in the side bar, click on the Folder view tool to return to the simple view.

- Click on *My Media* to reveal the sub-locations.

- Click on *Recordings*.

The Flight file should be on view on the Timeline, along with any other recording you may have made. So, if you hadn't asked the Recording feature to put the imported files on the Timeline, they would be nice and easy to find.

The Flight footage loaded onto the Timeline

Let's play through the footage again. You might not want to watch it all in detail, but at least scrub through it to get an idea of what material we have to play with.

Here is a list of my highlights:

1. The take off

2. Passing the Nantlle Ridge

3. Recognising the peak of Snowdon

4. Seeing the construction work at the top of Snowdon

5. Following the Mountain Railway back down

6. View of Caernarfon and its Castle

7. The landing.

What about the Audio? The soundtrack is virtually useless. On the ground it's all wind noise and in the air, apart from the take-off and landing, it's just a drone. We could record a voice-over, but there isn't much to say that cannot be covered with a few well-placed titles. However, some uplifting music might go down well.

It's a simple story. Plane takes off, flies over some spectacular scenery, and lands (safely!). Let's start work.

Using Scene detection

Before we start re-arranging and trimming our video, it would be quite handy to split it up into sections. There are some cuts in the footage where I've pre-edited it, and Movie Edit Pro has a feature that will detect these changes of video content and divide up the shots for us.

If you've skipped some of the earlier stuff, you might still be working with multiple thumbnails for your Timeline clips. The next section will be easier to understand if you switch to the Simple mode. In File/Settings/Program/Video/Audio/Timeline check the box for Simple video object display (first and last image). This might not normally be your preference, but maybe I can change your mind!

- To open up the tool for detection, right click on the Flight clip on the Timeline and select the third option from the top – *Scene detection*.

A box opens with the title *Scene recognition*. The first stage is to detect the changes, and we only need to deal with two choices before doing so.

The checkbox with the shaded text Apply DV Timecode.... would be available if we were dealing with DV footage. A break in the embedded timecode would indicate that the user had stopped and restarted the camera, indicating a scene break. We are dealing with analogue Mpeg-2 video, so the box is inactive.

Search from beginning of range has no effect unless we have set a range above the Timeline. If we had, the search could be confined to the range by checking the box.

Let's start the detection going:

- Make sure both check boxes under the *Start search* are unchecked.

- Click on Start search.

- Wait for the progress bar to travel fully to the right.

Scene detection in the Clip context menu

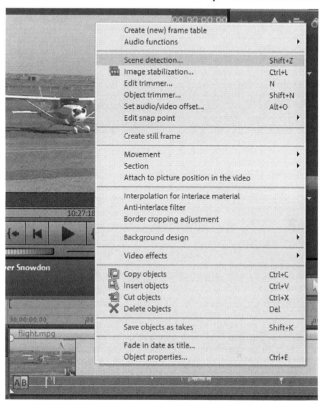

Now we can take a look at the second section – Scene control. Hopefully there are 19 Found scenes, and they are listed in the table below. If you haven't got 19 scenes, then adjust the sensitivity slider at the bottom to 5.0.

Highlight Scene 1 in the list – you will see a number of things change. The two thumbnails to the right will show the last

Scene recognition after searching

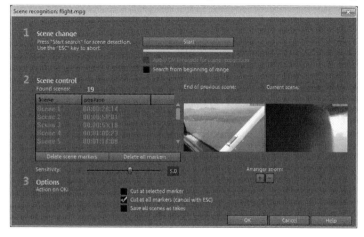

frame before the detection and the first frame after it. The end of the previous scene is a parked white plane, the start of the next scene a military plane on display. If you can't see the marker bar above the Timeline because it is covered by the Scene detection dialogue box, drag the box up so that you can. You should see a string of orange Scene markers on the strip above the timescale, and the first one on the left should have a white highlight around it. This indicates the position of the currently selected break.

If you scroll through the list of detected scene breaks by clicking on them, or using the Up/Down arrows, you will see the thumbnails change and the arranger view change to display the currently selected marker. If you want to zoom the arranger view, two small controls are provided under the scene thumbnails.

- Select Scene break 13 in the *Found scenes* table.

- If required, move the Scene recognition box away from the Arranger Timeline.

- Use the + tool to zoom the view right in. Eventually you will see that there are two markers just one frame apart.

- The timecodes in the list confirm that Scene 13 is only 1 frame in duration.

Single frame scene

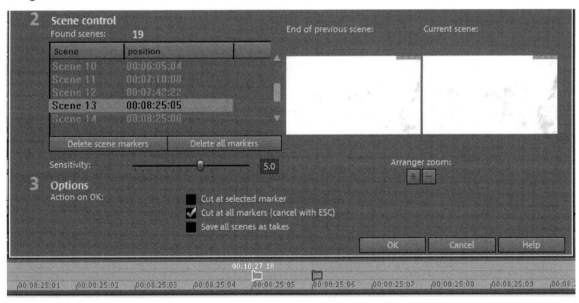

You can see from the above that there are quite a number of "false" detections. Very bumpy camerawork and fast changes of video level have caused some of them.

There are a number of strategies you can use to eliminate the false detections. The first choice is to adjust the sensitivity slider – and very conveniently, there is no need to rescan the file.

- Drag the slider fully to the right so the value reads 8.0.
- The number of detections goes all the way up to 86.
- Highlight Scene 1 in the list of detections.
- Reduce the sensitivity to 3.0.
- The setting isn't sensitive enough now – we have lost the obvious cut at 28 seconds.
- Adjust the slider again to 4.0 – there are now 14 detections.

We have lost some of the false positives, but not all of them. We will find later that we have also missed some obvious cuts, but I'll show you how to deal with that too.

Let's delete the obviously wrong ones. Sadly, there is a typo on the left-hand button and you can only delete one marker at a time. So it's quickest to use the keyboard.

I'm going to start at the end of the list, so we don't keep changing the numbering:

- Highlight the last scene – 14 – in the list.
- The End and Current frames look sufficiently different.
- Use the up arrow to select Scene 13. That looks like a false detection.
- Press the Delete key.
- Notice that Scene 14 has now been renumbered as Scene 13. We have already deleted the original, so leave this one alone!
- Use the up arrow to select Scene 12. Press Delete.
- Repeat for Scenes 11 and 10.
- Leave Scenes 9, 8, 7 and 6.
- Delete Scenes 5 and 4.
- Leave Scene 3.

- Although Scene 2 looks like a false detection, leave it so I can show how to repair an unwanted cut.

- Leave Scene 1.

We now have 8 scene breaks. The next stage is to decide how we want to divide the original clip. We could just leave the markers above the timescale, return to the Timeline and make the cuts manually having studied them in more detail. However there are two other options. You can chose just to have the currently selected marker position translated into a cut, or all the markers. By choosing all the markers we won't be doing any permanent damage as it very easy to re-join the clips together. This option also will rename the clips so that the object name that appears in the Timeline clip or Storyboard thumbnail are sequentially numbered – becoming Flight001, Flight 002 and so on.

The final checkbox allows us to specify if the program automatically generates Takes of the cut scenes. We looked at these earlier, but I'm not going to generate them automatically because at the time of writing the 2014 version of MEP doesn't implement takes quite as well as the 2013 version. If you do want to turn your scene detected clips into Takes you can do it using this option, or you can do so by using the clip context menu.

Let's make the cuts:

- Click on the *Cut at all markers* checkbox to select it.

- Make sure the *Save all scenes as takes* box is unchecked.

- Click on OK.

Nine Scenes on the Timeline

Eight scene breaks means nine Scenes, and the clip should now be divided up into nine clips, so hopefully track 1 of the Timeline will now have the original Flight video clip divided up into nine parts.

Repairing a cut by rolling an edit point

Because I deliberately got you to leave in a false detection, I can now show you how to remove an unwanted cut between two continuous clips. We have looked at the various trimming tools previously, so here is a summary

- Check that you are in Timeline mode.

- If it isn't already highlighted, select *Mouse mode for Single objects* by clicking on the tool on the Timeline toolbar that looks like a normal mouse pointer.

- Zoom in the Timeline and scrub the Playback marker across the junction of the second and third clips – Flight002 and Flight003.

- Notice that the video is in fact continuous. Flight003 is just over 3 seconds long.

A rolling trim point cursor

Rolling the cut right

- Hover your mouse over the middle of the junction between the clips.

- This should generate a mouse cursor of two arrows and two vertical lines.

- If you are too high or low you will get double-headed arrows.

- With the double-line cursor visible, click and hold.

- Both clips should be highlighted.

- Drag right so that Flight002 overwrites Flight003.

- When the third clip is completely overwritten the cursor will snap into place.

So, that's how easy it is to repair a false detection if you let one slip through onto the Timeline.

Manual Splitting

So, what if you have missed a cut by making the scene detection too insensitive? I've done that (deliberately) which meant you didn't have to delete too many false detections. If you have a look at 00:09:01.09 on the Timeline you will see a very obvious cut that the detection missed – it's probably something to do with the "bad" frame just before.

Let's fix with the simple use of the razor tool:

- Play, scrub and jog using one of the many methods available so that the Playback marker is parked exactly on the first frame of the wideshot looking out to sea.

- Check that the simple Split function is selected as the razor tool by hovering over the fourth tool from the right on the Timeline toolbar and checking the tooltip.

- If it isn't use the small dropdown arrow to reveal the options.

- Click on the *Split* tool. (You could also use the T key).

Splitting a clip

Now we have added another cut. The labelling of the objects has gone a little awry – there are two Flight008 clips and no Flight003, but we could rename them manually.

However, I'm going to do some more work on the clips and give them "real" names, so we can do that then.

If you look in detail at the first Flight008 clip, you will see that there are a number of other cuts we have missed. I'm going to use other techniques for extracting the parts we need from those shots, so don't bother to repair them now.

Storyboarding the movie

Stories are most often told in chronological order – *In a land far, far away a sad Princess...* at the beginning and *They all lived happily ever after* at the end. Sometimes the story might be made more interesting with flashbacks or even flash forwards – *Citizen Kane* starts with his death.

However, you don't always shoot in the same order as the story. A TV programme or a feature film will almost always be shot in the order that is most cost-effective for the production. If you are making a documentary you may be shooting material without necessarily knowing the order in which the final piece will be put together. The sort of movie I'm asking you to make now might appear to have been shot chronologically, but we could swap around the order in which we visit the landmarks if it made the movie more interesting. More fundamentally, I have a shot of a plane taking off which isn't embarking on the trip I shot from inside the plane. However, it's my intention to make the viewer believe that it is the same plane taking off at the same time.

If you are interested in a longer discussion about **Continuity editing** – making events appear to be occurring in real time even though they aren't – there are many books on the subject. I have discussed this in another book "Videomaking - The Grammar Revealed" which covers many topics including continuity editing.

Given that the shooting and story order of the clips can be very different, and the story order isn't necessarily set in stone, it's very handy to have a simple way of experimenting with the order of the clips. Hence the Storyboard.

Let's switch to it now:

- Click on the Storyboard icon furthest left on the Arranger toolbar.
- Adjust the windows layout to optimise the display – the Storyboard icons are a fixed height and probably don't need as much space to display as the Timeline tracks.
- Click on the second clip of the movie, labelled flight002.

When you perform the last action, the playback cursor moves to the start of the clip selected, and it is displayed in the program monitor. When we investigated the behaviour of the Playback cursor in Timeline mode, I mentioned you could choose how it behaved in the settings dialogue. However, even if you have set it not to move when you select clips, it will in Storyboard mode. So, if you want to see a clip in the monitor, you just have to click on the Storyboard thumbnail.

Storyboard display, showing clip 2 in the Program monitor

Play the clip. I don't think it's going to be of much use in the movie, but you never know. Let's get it off the Storyboard, but in a way that means we don't completely forget about it:

- Right click on the thumbnail and select Object properties at the bottom of the menu.

- Click on the text box for Object name and edit the text to read *Hangers*.

- Select *OK* to close the properties dialogue.

- Check that the Recordings window is still open in the Media pool.

- Drag and drop the newly renamed *Hangers* clip up into the media pool window alongside *flight.mpg*.

Right, it's gone, but not forgotten! We could have used the context menu to *Save objects as takes*, but this would not have removed the clip from the movie, and it would have been stored in the default Takes directory.

By dragging and dropping, we've saved time, and the *Hangers – 0001.TK2* file serves as a reminder in the Recording location we are using as a quick form of project folder.

Clip 2 removed to the media pool as a Take

Let's look at the remaining clips, renaming them as we go:

- Rename *flight001* to *Taxiing*.

Wobbly, as I said before, but potentially the first shot of the movie.

- Rename *flight004* to *Ext Take Off*.

We will probably want to cut the rather wild zoom in off the front of this.

- Rename *flight005* to *Int Take Off*.

Some very useful parts here, particularly the turn on to the runway and acceleration.

- Rename *flight006* to *Nantlle Ridge*.

Attractive shot we could use out of position unless all our viewers are very familiar with the geography of the area!

- Rename *flight007* to *Approaching Snowdon*.

Some rather wild moments, but we can just pick out the shape of the summit.

- Rename the first clip called *flight008* to *Peak and Railway*.

Many shots of use here – the close-up of the summit, and following the mountain railway down the mountain, plus the shot of Carmarthen and the Menai straits, and the very wobbly close-up of the castle.

- Rename the second clip called flight008 to *Turn to Finals*.

A nice shot of preparing to land.

- Rename flight009 to *Touchdown*.

We probably don't need all of this final shot, but the moment of landing is rather good.

A Rough cut

What we are about to embark on is a Rough Cut – in fact it's a very "rough" cut. I'm going to get you to chop up the clips rather crudely and rearrange them. The aim is to show you how to try out some ideas in the Storyboard. If they work, you can then switch to the Timeline view to finesse them.

So, what's the first shot we have? While the first shot on the Storyboard is the first thing I shot, if we are going to pretend that the interior and exterior shots were recorded at the same time, the Int Take Off shot begins before the Taxiing shot becomes live

Now, we might not actually start the movie with Int Take Off, but if we want to use the very start of it, and also the start of Taxiing, then Int Take Off has to come first in the movie. Why? Well there would be a great deal of double-action as the plane passed the very obvious bright orange windsock twice.

So, let's swap the order of the first 3 shots:

- Click, Hold and drag *Int Take Off* to the left.
- When the red line indicating the drop position is at the start of the movie, release the mouse button.

Now let's use our imagination. Play the first 30 seconds or so of the first shot, then stop playback, click on the second clip and press play again. If we were to use just the first part of the very long interior shot we could then cut to the start of the second shot and the windsock would be behind the plane.

We don't want to abandon the remainder of the *Int Take Off* shot, but we can split it so that it becomes two shots:

- Play the movie from the start, and then stop playback at around 25 seconds.

- I want you to park the Playback scrubber on a shot of the control tower. The frame I have in mind is at exactly 23 seconds in the current movie – the timecode top left of the playback monitor.

- It's also at 00:02:02:17 on the timecode I have burned into the top right of the video.

- You can try to drag the Playback marker in the Storyboard, but you will find it too coarse.

- Use the Shuttle control under the playback monitor to get it close.

- To get the actual frame, use the jog wheel.

- Use the Razor tool to split the clip, or press the T key.

You may find the jog wheel behaviour confusing. Depending on the settings of the program, you are likely to see not just single frames as you jog, but two fields. You will jog forward, the program monitor will show a slightly different picture, but the timecode won't change.

The flight clip is interlaced, and if you have *Automatic interlace processing* checked in *Settings/Program/Video/Audio/Other* the monitor displays subsequent fields as you jog. The program won't let you split a clip or perform any other kind of trimming on a field boundary though – it will cut on a frame boundary.

This does mean that if you are just looking at the pictures as you jog the video, rather than checking the timecode as well, you might not be cutting on the exact field that you think you are. In Timeline mode, you can use the left and right arrows to jog a single frame at a time – my preferred method – but in Storyboard, this takes you to the next or previous clip unless you have the Program monitor selected.

So, you can either turn off automatic interlace processing (which I'm loath to recommend because it won't give you the best preview) or just bear the issue in mind. In Storyboard mode you are unlikely to be working to frame accuracy anyway.

Look at the Storyboard now. There are two clips called *Int Take Off*. The first has a duration of 23 seconds, the second over three minutes.

Our next task is to rearrange the clips. We need to move the *Taxiing* clip in between the first two clips:

- Click, hold and drag clip 3 left.

- When the red line is between the first two clips, release the mouse button.

First four shots of the Flight rough cut

Play the edit. The continuity is roughly right. We could work on it a bit more, but as I said, this is a rough cut.

Highlight clip two so that the cursor jumps to the start, and play the movie. When we get to the cutting point to what is now clip 3, there is a huge amount of double action – the plane returns to the grass and taxis past the control tower again. We need to trim the start of clip 3. However, there are a lot of reference points in the outgoing of clip 2 – the other planes parked on the stand. Instead of waiting until our plane – the Cessna – has past both the military and the twin engine plane, I'm going to suggest editing when the twin engine plane is in both the outgoing and incoming shots. Firstly, trim the end of the *Taxiing* shot:

- Select clip 2 so that the playback cursor moves to the start of the clip.

- Let's use the playback marker timescale as described in the Program Monitor chapter to reduce the sensitivity of the scrubbing.

- Drag one handle on the thin grey timescale above the program monitor transport controls and make the bar about 10% of the width of the video display.

- Drag the bar left or right to locate the orange marker above.

- Now drag the marker – you will find it far more sensitive.

- Park the marker on a movie timecode of 00:00:43:00, a burnt in timecode of 00:00:20:00.

- The twin engine plane should be clearly in view on the left of frame.

- Split the clip.

We are now indulging in a form of editing not dissimilar to editing actual film – Split, remove and rejoin!

- Highlight the third clip – *Taxiing* duration 8 seconds 14 frames.

- Click on the Delete tool on the toolbar – it's got a cross as an icon.

We are back to having 9 clips in the movie. Play the movie again and you will see clip 2 finish just as the twin engine plane is established in shot. We now need to trim the start of clip 3:

Preparing to delete the end of the Taxiing shot

- Use the technique of your choice to park the scrubber at 1 minute 11 seconds movie timecode, 00:02:30:17 burnt-in timecode.

- I'm going to get you to use one of the more efficient razor tools this time. Click on the small down arrow to the right of the razor tool.

- In the drop-down menu, click on the second tool, *Remove Start*.

Play the first three shots. I hope you will agree that although it's a bit slow, and the

Remove Start tool

edits are a bit rough, we have created a coherent sequence. You might even believe that the shots are of the same event!

This would be a good time to save your project. As things get more complex you might appreciate the chance to go back to a checkpoint should things go wrong. Use the File/Save as command to save the project with a new name, Flight Over Snowdon rough cut 1.

Editing on the Timeline

Splitting and trimming clips in Storyboard mode is a bit clumsy and we will have more control of this part of the process if we switch to Timeline mode. With careful screen arrangement, we will also be able to see thumbnails for both the In and Out points of clips, helping us to visualise the edit.

At this stage in the process, though, where we are still editing with just one track, there is no reason why we can't switch between modes to make our life a little easier.

We need to trim down the rest of the Int Take Off shot, and intercut it with the Ext Take Off shot.

- Use the Timeline mode icon to switch to Timeline view.
- Hover your mouse over the border between tracks 1 and 2 in the track header area.
- When you generate a vertical double-headed arrow, click, hold and drag down to increase the height of track 1. Release the mouse button.
- Use the view controls and scrollbar to zoom in and fill the Timeline with the Int Take Off clip.

When you create a view of the clip similar to the next screenshot, you will find it easy to scrub up and down the video looking for ideas and edit points.

My thinking was to cut down the length of time it takes to get the plane onto the main runway. However, we haven't got any other to shots to cut away to so we need to find some parts of the shot that will cut together. There is a section at just past 3 minutes on the burnt-in timecode top right of the source video where the camera is looking at the pilot and passenger. For brevity, I'm going to use the abbreviation BITC from now on to indicate when I'm referring to this Burnt In TimeCode.

Let's isolate this interior cockpit section by splitting the clip:

- Scrub to exactly 00:03:05:00 BITC. You can now use the left and right keyboard arrows for single frame jogging because we are in Timeline mode.

- Split the clip with the razor tool or the T key.

- Move the Playback marker to 00:03:12:00 BITC.

- Split the clip again.

Now that we have a shot that isn't linked to what we can see out of the side windows, we can cut a big chunk out of the journey to the runway:

- Find a frame at 00:02:49:00 BITC where we have a clear view of a small plane.

- Split the clip at this point.

- Click on the section after the split we have just made to highlight it.

- You might want to adjust the view to check that you have highlighted the fourth clip on the Timeline.

- Click on the Delete tool, or press the Delete key.

Oh dear – not what we want. There is a hole in the Timeline now and instead of some (boring) taxiing footage, we have 16 seconds of black level!

Even when we are editing on track 1 – the "special" track for syncing purposes – some Timeline functions aren't always as convenient as working in Storyboard mode. If we had performed the same Delete operation in the Storyboard the gap would have been removed automatically.

However, we don't want to be switching between modes just to be able to perform a task as simple as removing a clip without leaving a gap. Let's repair the damage and use the correct tool:

- Press CTRL-Z or use *Undo* in the *Edit* menu to bring back the deleted clip.

- Highlight it again.

- Use the drop-down arrow alongside the razor tool to open up the submenu of razor tools.

- Hover over the fourth entry – *Remove Scene*. The tool tip tells us that the keyboard shortcut is CTRL-Delete.

- Either click on the tool or press CTRL-Delete.

The clip should now disappear as before, but all the clips to the right will be moved left to eliminate the gap. Remember CTRL-Delete – you will use it often.

Play the movie from the third clip. I hope you will agree we have removed 16 seconds without the viewer realising the jump in time continuity.

Let's now trim off the rest of the interior shot before the plane turns onto the proper runway:

- Locate a frame at 00:03:37:00 BITC in the fifth clip.

- With the playback cursor parked at this point, Use the *Remove scene start* tool from the razor dropdown list, or press the Z key.

This is a powerful tool. Not only does it split the clip, it then removes the first part of the split and moves up all the subsequent clips. We've removed another 25 seconds.

Although I'm not going to demonstrate it now, the *Remove scene end* tool can be just as useful when working on the Out point of a clip.

My next idea is to show the moment of take-off using the exterior view. That shot happens to be just one clip further down the Timeline at the moment. The process I intend to use is to choose a rough Out point where we will cut away from the view from the cockpit and split the shot there, then chose a rough In point when we start to use the view of the (other) plane taking off. We will then move the exterior shot to butt up to the interior shot:

- On the fifth clip, about 1 minute 30 into the movie, find the point where the runway markings have left shot.

- Set the scrubber to 00:04:00:00 BITC and spilt the clip here.

- On what is now the seventh clip in the movie, Ext Take Off, set the scrubber to 00:01:00:00 BITC.

- Because we are very unlikely to want to use the wild zoom in, use the *Remove scene start* tool to set a new In point for the clip.

We are now going to attempt to move Ext Take Off one clip to the left using drag and drop:

- Make sure the Magnet tool is active.

- On the toolbar, select *Mouse mode for single objects* (or press the 6 key).

- Click, hold and drag clip 7 left, then release the mouse button.

Well, that's nothing like what happens when you drag and drop a clip in Storyboard mode, is it? The two clips have been overlapped and a transition generated. In order to drag and drop to re-order clips, we need to make a gap:

- Use CTRL-Z to undo the previous action.

- Select *Mouse mode for a track* (or use the 8 key).

- Click and hold on clip 6. It and all of the subsequent clips are highlighted.

- Drag them all right to create a gap that looks bigger than clip 7.

- Release the mouse button. We have made a gap.

- Select *Mouse mode for single objects* (the 6 key).

- Click, hold and drag *Ext Take Off* (clip 7) left until it's In point snaps up to the Out point of clip 5.

- Hopefully you made the gap big enough so the end of the Ext Take Off clip doesn't overlap the next clip. If you didn't, use Undo and start again.

- Reselect *Mouse mode for a track*.

- Drag clip 7 left to click into place with the end of clip 6. This closes up the first Timeline gap.

- Drag clip 8 left to close up the remaining gap. All the subsequent clips move with it.

Now you can see why Storyboard might have been quicker to use to do the re-arranging!

We are losing a nice shot by hanging on to the exterior of the plane for the rest of the take off. I think it would be good to cut back inside the plane for some of the rise into the air. There are a number of ways we can achieve this. We could bring a new trimmed version of the shot from the Media pool and take advantage of the Overwrite mode, but I'm concentrating on editing on the Timeline at the moment – I'll look at using the media pool as a source shortly.

(Coincidently, you may see some anomalies with the BITC around this section; it sometimes doesn't increment on the correct field. I've taken this into account in the text.)

Let's begin by selecting a section of the interior shot just after the plane has lifted off:

- Search the seventh clip for a point where the plane has clearly left the ground.

- I have chosen 00:04:13:00 BITC. Use the *Remove start* tool.

- Chose an Out point of 00:04:20:00 BITC. Use the *Split* tool.

We now have a clip which we need to insert into the previous shot. We could make a gap by cutting a hole in Ext Take Off and dragging the new shot into the gap. However, it may be that we want to insert the new shot into a gap that is exactly the same duration, therefore maintaining the correct time continuity. In this case it's not strictly important to maintain the continuity, but in other cases it will be, so let's at least start with the right edit, even if we decide to cheat it afterwards.

Using more than one track – B roll

I'm not going to get into a major description of multi-track editing in this section. For now, I'm just going to show you how to take advantage of one aspect of it. You may know this as B roll editing, or using an overlay track. Whatever it's called, it's a useful tool.

Any video or photo object placed on track 2 will be overlaid on track 1. If the object has transparent areas track 1 will show through, but if the object is solid – another video clip, for example – then you will only see what is on track 2 for the object duration.

Before embarking on the next operation, let me warn you that I'll be asking you to undo all of this so I can demonstrate an alternative to using track 2. If you haven't set the number of possible Undos to 30 or more (in File/Settings/Program/System /Undo/Redo) then do so now, or save a new version of the project - Flight Over Snowdon rough cut 2.

I'm going to move the newly trimmed section for the Int Take Off shot to track 2 so we can see the effect:

- Right-click on the Track 1 header and set the *Track height* to *Big*.

- Do the same for Track 2, then adjust the screen layout so you can see just the two tracks in the Arranger area.

- Set *Mouse mode for a single object*.

- Drag the newly trimmed *Int Take Off* clip down to track 2, then left so that it goes underneath the *Ext Take Off* clip.

- As you drag left and right, look at the Program monitor. This is previewing the point on track 1 at which the new clip would start if you dropped

Dropping a clip down to the B roll track

it there – so it is showing you the first frame of the track 1 video that would be overwritten.

- Find a point where the plane's wheels are just clear of the ground in the background.

- The BITC will be about 00:01:07:00. You might find it hard to be frame accurate, but get close.

- Drop the clip on track 2.

You can see that this is a pretty efficient way of inserting the clip, because we get a live preview of where it is going to go. What's more, we don't have to guess on the size of gap needed.

Getting frame accuracy might have been a problem for you. That can be addressed in at least one of three ways.

If you are using the default Playback marker behaviour, (by not having *Move play cursor when object is selected* checked in File/Settings/Program/System/Other) You could have placed the scrubber at the desired In point, and the clip on track 2 would have snapped to the scrubber.

If you prefer working with the play cursor following clip selection, then you can add a marker at the chose Timeline position with CTRL-Enter, and then let the clip snap to that.

Perhaps the best way is to adjust the Timeline view so that you can drag the clip more accurately. I'm going to use the last method:

- Place the scrubber roughly near the start of clip 6.

- Use CTRL Up and DOWN arrows to adjust the view so that the clip on track 2 occupies about half the width of the arranger window.

- Drag the clip on track 2 slowly left or right. You should be able to do this to frame accuracy.

- Line the start of the clip up with the BITC 00:01:07:00 on the program monitor view of the plane on the air.

Integrating tracks

Putting a clip on track two is very convenient, but what if we aren't ready to make this into a multi-track project yet? We can't really use the Storyboard now, and if we start editing an earlier part of the movie we will need to tread carefully to avoid destroying the relative positions of the clips in tracks 1 and 2.

While I think understanding how to work with multiple tracks is essential, particularly once we start to add titles and separate audio, there will be times that you wish you could integrate a clip one track into another:

- Jog the playback marker around the first frame on the clip on track 2 so that it lines up with the first frame. You can watch the program monitor to be sure.

- Highlight the clip on track 1 and split it.

- Move the playback marker to the first frame after the clip on track 2.

- Split again.

- Highlight the clip you have created on track 1.

- Delete the clip. Because we are working on the Timeline, a gap is left behind.

- With the magnet tool on, drag the clip on track 2 up into the gap. It will snap perfectly into position.

So, our movie is all on one track again!

Moving the B roll clip up into the gap

Inserting from the Media Pool

There are two fundamental approaches to putting a movie together. You can throw everything you think you will need into the Arranger, and then arrange it, or you can carefully build it up from the source material a bit at a time.

If you work by having put all your sources on the Storyboard, you can work quickly, but not always that accurately, and you can only work with one track.

If you apply the same approach with the Timeline, there will be times that moving clips around is clumsy. You might think you could use Cut and Paste instead of Drag and Drop on the Timeline, but you can't.

You have much more power if you bring your sources from the Media pool or the Program monitor – we have seen how to use insert and overwrite in the first section of the book. I'm going to expand on that way of working shortly.

However, there is one way of taking advantage of the working from the Media pool that will help us out in the current situation. If we go via the Media pool we can use the Overwrite mode. How? By putting the clip we want to move into the Media pool as a Take, then moving it back to the Timeline:

- Restore the project to how it was before we moved clip 7, either with Undos or by reloading *Flight over Snowdon rough cut 2*.

- Ensure that the Recordings location is open in the Media pool - There should be our original source file and the *Hangers* take there.

- Drag and Drop clip 7 from the Timeline up to the Media pool.

Dragging a Take from the Media pool in Insert mode

- It will appear in the Media poll as *Int Take Off – 0001.TK2*.

- Because we are in Timeline mode, although the clip disappears from the Timeline, it leaves a gap.

- Select *Mouse mode for a single track* and drag what is now clip 7 left to close the gap. The subsequent clips will follow suit. You don't have to do this, but I'm trying to make the subsequent operations clearer.

- Adjust the view so that clip 6 occupies most of the Timeline.

- Use the drop-down menu for the Insert Object tool – the last on the right of the centre group on the toolbar – and select Overwrite.

- Drag the *Int Take Off* take from the Media pool down to hover over clip 6 on track 1.

- Move it left or right so that the start lines up with 00:01:07:00 BITC on the *Ext Take Off* shot, which you can see displayed in the Program monitor.

- Drop the clip. It will overwrite itself over the underlying clip.

Using overwrite doesn't move the following clips

There are a couple of small problems here – if you don't quite get the clip where you want it, you will have to use undo and try again, or delve into another feature we haven't used yet – the Edit/Object trimmer. You slightly cluttered up the Media pool with a temporary file, but it's easy enough to delete. Apart from that, it's a pretty efficient way of working.

However, a further issue rears its head when you try to work on the clips either side of the inserted clips. They have been Grouped together. This doesn't happen if you use Insert rather than overwrite, and I have to say that it seems like a bug to me. Unfortunately, if you try to ungroup the clips, the audio gets separated out. That can be repaired, but it's not something I want to get into just yet, so I'll show you how to work round this grouping it in just a moment.

Tightening up the story

The next couple of minutes are interesting, but not so interesting that they couldn't be tightened up.

Look at the shot following on from the clip we have just inserted. The plane is in limbo, and shortly after we cut back to it, the shot goes badly out of focus. We could easily cut to this shot later because the viewer has no reference to know how high the plane has climbed.

From now on, I'll use MTC as the abbreviation of Movie TimeCode, the scrubber position shown top left above the preview window. Remember that BITC is the timecode on the footage itself, top right.

- Scrub to 00:01:51:00 MTC, 00:01:19:17 BITC.

- Split the clip.

- Click on clip 8, the newly created clip that includes the out of focus section.

- Assuming you used the Overwrite method (and the bug hasn't been fixed), two clips will be highlighted, clips 6 and 8.

- We can't just delete clip 8, so instead we will trim it out.

- Hover over the bottom right corner of clip 8 to generate the double-headed horizontal cursor for trimming.

- If you have control of the correct clip, the white hotspots will show up on the clip.

- Click, hold and drag the Out point of clip 8 to the left until it disappears completely.

Trimming out a clip

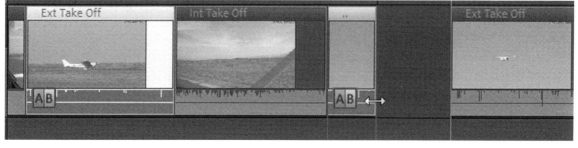

- Set the Mouse mode to single or multi-track.

- Drag and Drop what is now clip 8 left to close up the gap. All the subsequent clips will follow suit.

Phew! That was a bit of a palaver, all caused by what may, or may not be a bug. When we start working with a separate audio track the bug won't affect us anywhere nearly as much, as we can just *Ungroup* the clips.

I'm now going to give you a series of cuts, but not list exactly how you should go about removing them – you can try going back to the Storyboard, or use any of the tools on the Timeline. You can judge which you prefer, and which is more efficient (which isn't always the same thing!).

If you were to sit through the movie, making notes before tackling all the cuts in one go, it would be better to work backwards as each time you make a cut it will alter the movie timecodes after, but not before, the change. In the following list, though, I'm expecting you to work forwards, so you need to make the changes in the order I've given them.

Remove sections of the movie using the following timecodes. The first pair of codes indicate the first frame to remove, the second pair the first frame after the edit.

- 00:01:53:23 MTC, 00:01:28:07 BITC to the end of the clip.
- The start of the next clip, 00:01:53:23 MTC, 00:04:20:00 to 00:02:25:14 MTC, 00:04:51:16 BITC.
- From the start of the Nantlle Ridge clip to 00:02:26:07 MTC, 00:05:24:00 BITC.
- From 00:02:41:12 MTC, 00:05:46:00 BITC to the end of the Nantlle Ridge clip.

If you move the scrubber to the end of the movie now, the duration should be 00:07:04:01.

Trimming rather than cutting

As you get more confident about what you are looking for, you can save time by looking for an In or Out point at the same time as trimming a clip. You can take advantage of the feature that what is shown in the program monitor is the currently selected In or Out point.

We've just performed this type of operation – out of necessity – to trim out a complete clip, but now I want you to try working to more accuracy. The next clip on the Timeline is Approaching Snowdon. I'm intending to put a title over this, indicating where the peak actually is, so we want the most stable section of the shot:

- We want the best mouse sensitivity possible, so place the scrubber roughly in the middle of the clip and use the CTRL-Up/Down arrows too adjust the timescale so the clip fills most of the Timeline display.

- Generate an In Point trim handle and drag right. You should be able to do so smoothly enough to gauge how the shot is moving about.

Trimming the In point

- After a change of exposure, the shot settles down for a while around about 00:06:32:00 BITC. In most cases you will be looking at the content, but in this case, find that exact frame and release the mouse button.

- Now the clip is shorter, you can probably optimise the view again. If you were a few frames out, you can probably readjust the In point more accurately.

- Turn to the Out Point. I want you to set it to 00:06:44:00 BITC, making the clip a frame of 12 seconds and 1 frame long.

In order to review the edits, we need to close up the gaps. It's a good idea to rescale the display again:

- Press the F key on the keyboard, and you will be able to see the whole project.
- With *Mouse mode for a track* selected, drag the *Approching Snowdon* clip left to dock with the previous clip.
- Repeat the action on the *Peak and Railway* clip to close the other gap.

Adding pre-trimmed material

The next clip on the Timeline contains four sections I'd like to use:

A close shot of the peak.

A wide shot of the mountain railway

A wide shot of Carmarthon.

A close shot of the castle.

The rest of the clip isn't needed, and the two close shots will require very careful selection because they are so wobbly. I'm hoping to slow them down but we still haven't got much.

We could carry on using the Timeline as a source, but using the Program monitor for In and Out point marking is more flexible, and we can also use Insert. This section should give you an idea about how you would build up a movie from the Media pool as well.

It would be possible to revert to using the original Flight footage but we have already used much of that; if we drag a Take of the clip up to the Media pool we will have less material to sift through:

- Select *Mouse mode for single objects*.
- Ensure the Import window is open at the Recording location.
- Drag the Peak and Railway clip up to the Media pool.
- Close up the gap in the Timeline as I've shown above.

We didn't need to do this last action, but it will allow me to show off the Insert ripple mode later!

- Select *Single track ripple* for the Insert mode.

- Rearrange the layout to increase the program monitor size as much as possible without losing sight of track 1.

- Adjust the track timescale so that we can see the whole movie and just a little bit of space at the end.

- Drag and Drop the take we have just created – Peak and Railway 0001.TK2 – to the Program monitor.

Now scrub through the source take in the Program monitor using the scrubber under the window, the transport controls or keyboard shortcuts. Firstly, I'm looking for the best section of my attempts to get a close-up of the peak. At around 00:07:20:00 BITC there are a few frames, but there is a better section around 00:07:36:20. I'm going to attempt to do a freeze-frame, so I've chosen the last frame with care. We can't make the shot too short, so from that point I'll work backwards at least a couple of seconds looking for a relatively stable few frames:

Setting the first pair of In and Out points

- Find the frame 00:07:38:12 BITC and set an Out point.

- Jog backwards until the shot starts to widen. Keep going until the shot steadies for a while.

- Set the In point to 00:07:35:12 BITC.

- Drag the trimmed clip down to track 1. As you drag it left and right, you will see the first frame of what it will replace in the Program monitor.

- Find the start of the *Turn to Finals* shot – the wide shot looking out to sea. The dragged clip should snap into place. When it does, release the mouse button to drop the clip.

About to insert the trimmed clip into the Timeline

You should see the whole movie increase in duration in order to accommodate the new clip. If something has gone wrong, or perhaps you dropped the clip in the wrong place, use Undo then try again. You won't need to reset the In and Out points if you drag the take from the Media pool and drop it into the Program monitor again – they will be preserved.

Play the resulting edit and you'll see that the clip is very short and ends abruptly, but try to imagine what it will look like with a freeze frame on the end. I'll attend to that later. Let's continue extracting material from the Peak and Railway shot for now:

- Drag and drop the pre-trimmed take from the Media Pool again to make it active, then play the next part.

- The shot of the railway is badly over exposed, but we should be able to cure that.

- Set the In point to 00:07:49:00 BITC.

- Set the Out point to 00:08:02:00 BITC.

- Drag and drop the trimmed clip onto track 1, placing it immediately after the peak shot we have just added.

Next, we want a good few seconds overlooking the town of Carmarthen and the Menai Straits:

- Repeat the above, setting the In point to 00:08:29:24 BITC and the Out point to 00:08:37:10 and dropping the trimmed clip after the railway shot.

Finally, we want the close-up of the castle from the Take in the Media pool. Again it will need to be slowed down and still-framed:

- Repeat again, setting the In point to 00:08:51:05 BITC and the Out point to 00:08:52:09 and dropping the trimmed clip after the wide shot of Carmarthen.

Three more trims

We still need to tighten things up a bit at the end:

- Remove the end of the *Turn to Finals* shot, ending on the pilot, by locating 00:09:13:00 BITC and using the *Remove scene end* tool.

- Slice off the start of the *Touchdown* shot by setting the scrubber to 00:09:51:00 BITC and using *Remove scene start*.

- Tighten up the end of the last shot – 00:10:24:00 BITC and *Remove scene end*.

Now, there is still a huge amount of work to do on the movie. I'll use the chance to show you many of the other features of the program, along with suggested workflows. But for now, we have a trimmed movie, which from a video point of view, is quite compact. If you look at the duration (press the end key and look at the timecode top left of the program monitor) it should be 4 minutes 02 seconds and 21 frames.

- Save your movie as *Flight Over Snowdon rough cut 3*.

At this point, even if you have been meticulous with following me operation by operation, you might not have ended up with quite the same movie as me, simply because of minor mistakes or ambiguities in my writing. In fact, if your duration matches mine you should be pleased! However, if you have understood the principles, don't keep going back over the project looking for the discrepancies. We can synchronise our projects. First off, have a look on the **DTVPro.co.uk** website and compare your video with the streaming version, or download the rendered file for comparison. That may well help you spot the differences and you can change your project to match mine.

Loading projects and the File not found error

If you still can't spot and fix the differences, or don't want to mess around, then download my project file – Flight Over Snowdon rough cut 3.MVP – and open it in Movie Edit Pro. (You will also find these files on the DVD Data disc).

Unless your name is jeff, The project isn't going to be able find the source file Flight.mpg and you will get a File not found error message. You will need to select the Folder button, then browse to the actual location of the video file – C:\Users\Your User Name\Documents\Magix\Movie Edit (your version)\My Record. Select this location, click OK and the project will load.

The File not found dialogue

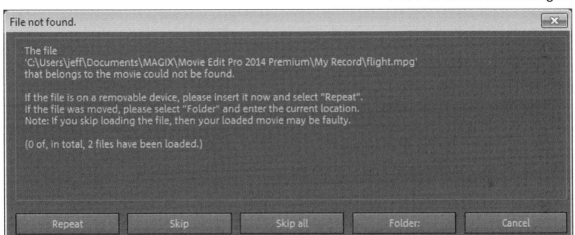

Now save the project again as Flight Over Snowdon rough cut 3, and we should be in sync with each other!

Audio Editing

This chapter will introduce you to using audio in your projects. There are some fundamental ground rules that apply to Movie Edit Pro that need to be explained before we can return to the Flight project and work on the the sound. We will also add some music to the movie.

If you have been working on the flight project, you will probably have turned your speakers right down by now – the plane effects, and in particular the wind noise over the first few shots, are particularly irritating after a while. Every vision cut is accompanied by a sharp change in the audio, even when we are trying to fool the viewer into thinking this is continuous time.

Audio monitoring

Before you start making any judgments regarding the quality and levels of audio, it's a good idea to calibrate how you listen to your sound. I'm hoping you have a reasonable pair of stereo speakers attached to your computer, and that the left channel comes out of the left speaker and the right channel comes out of the right one! If you have to use your computer in a noisy environment (or need to keep the noise down out of respect for others) then consider using a pair of headphones.

Play some music with Windows Media Player or get Windows to make some noises and set the volume of your speakers fairly high. Click on the small speaker icon you should have at the bottom of your Windows task bar and make sure that playback levels are high – at 80%, not flat out. In Vista, Windows 7 and 8, each open application has its own volume setting that you can reach by right clicking on the speaker icon at the right of the Windows taskbar and opening the Volume mixer.

Next, start a new project and locate some video that contains audio onto the Timeline. I've provided a short clip on the website (and Demo DVD) called Bars_and_Tone. You will need to import this via the Record feature or at least move it into a new location (such as the Revealed Video location we created earlier) using the copy and paste controls in the Import tab of the Media pool. If you just try to use it straight – "stumble upon" it – then it is possible that you may not get the option to create a waveform.

The default behaviour is for MEP to put the Video and Audio on one track. You can change this default in *File/Settings/Program/Video/Audio/Timeline*. Open that settings box now and you will also see a few other options. *Half* waveform display is a setting that simplifies the waveform we will generate. In the Import box you can see an option to automatically generate a waveform on import – normally unchecked. Import video with sound should normally be checked.

Audio settings

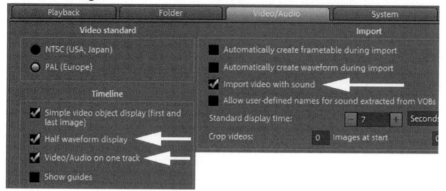

Having checked the settings and closed the dialogue box, make sure you are in Timeline mode. Drag the *Bars_and_Tone* clip to the start of track 1 and set the height of the track to *Big*. You can now discern that underneath the video thumbnail is a small space where the audio should be. Unfortunately, making the track height greater doesn't increase the space allocated to the audio.

Play the clip. An annoying whistle should emanate from the speakers - this is test tone and you should hear it very clearly. If you can't hear anything just yet, bear with me.

Muting

There are two places that you can mute the audio. One is on the track itself - the M button that Mutes the video also turns off the audio. If you can't see the Colour Bars picture in the Program monitor as well, then that's almost certainly the issue.

Next check that the overall Mute control isn't activated on the Timeline toolbar - its the small speaker icon third from the right. It should not have a line drawn through it.

There are three ways of "looking" at how loud an audio source is – a waveform shown on the Timeline, the small track meters in Timeline view, and the large meters available in a tool we have yet to look at yet – the Mixer panel.

Creating waveforms

If the audio area of the clip is all the same dark colour, you haven't generated a waveform yet. Right click on the clip and in the context menu select *Audio functions/Create waveform.* If the option isn't there, you may have to go back and import the clip via the Recording function.

Once the waveform is generated, you will just see a solid light blue area with a couple of gaps in it. Zoom the display in and with a magnified view you can see the individual waves making up the

The audio waveform below the video thumbnail

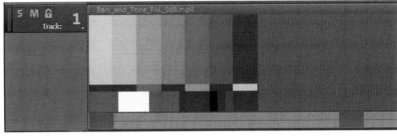

tone. Most audio isn't this constant and will have a far more obvious form, even when not zoomed in, but all audio is made up of waves.

If we had selected not to have the Half waveform display in the settings panel, the waveforms would be symmetrical and you would see the correct shape of the waves. Selecting the half waveform option lets us see more information, even though it isn't a true picture.

Half waveform tone, zoomed into frame level

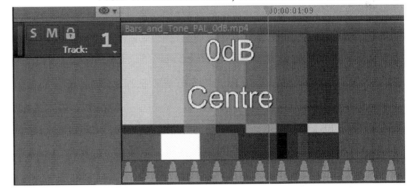

Track volume meters

Optimise the display view and play the clip again. If you can't hear anything you may have the mute control selected in the track header. With a waveform in place and the track playing, the small meter at the very left of the track header should bounce up and down where there are gaps in the audio.

If you can see the waveform but the meter isn't registering, then you should skip ahead to the audio level options then return to the Mixer section when you have the meter moving.

Track meter registering a high level

The Mixer

The final place to check the audio is the Mixer. Open this by clicking on the icon furthest right of the Timeline toolbar.

This is a pretty impressive tool. Depending on the number of tracks in your project, it might be quite big, as it has one fader for every track. To make things easier to display, go into the Movie settings and reduce the number of tracks to 4. Now you can drag the Mixer by one of its "dead" areas (if in doubt use the Master label area bottom right) so that it doesn't obscure the Timeline - place it over the Media pool for now.

The Mixer Panel registering tone on track 1

Play the clip again. Three more meters should be registering the levels – the meter beside the track 1 fader, and the two meters between the master faders. If you still have no audio, are the faders set to zero? Click the reset button top right to normalize the settings or double click on the fader buttons to set them to zero. No luck? Skip ahead to audio level options and return when the meters are working.

With audio showing up on the Master meters, if you still can't hear audio, recheck you can hear sound from other applications, and the volume control for MEP isn't turned down or muted. If that fails, you may need to re-install your software.

With sound playing, the clip I have provided should allow you to check your speakers are wired up correctly. If the tone comes from the left when the caption says right, you need to swap them over.

If you can't really tell that there is a difference when the tone is panned left or right, there may be a wiring fault, or you may have a problem similar to one that I encountered. My current laptop has a control called SRS which is supposed to enhance the audio that you hear from the tiny speakers. In doing so, it destroys the true stereo image. Search you laptop for special audio enhancement modes, and then turn them off!

OK – now the waveform and the meters should be the same as the screenshots. Beneath the master faders the values should be peaking at -0dB. If this still isn't the case, refer to the audio level options then return here.

Finally, we have a reference level! You should now adjust the volume control for your speakers to a decent setting – not painful, but not quiet either. That's the level you are going to monitor your audio at. If you want to adjust the volume when using other applications, mark any physical controls and make a note of software settings so that you restore your monitoring levels when editing.

When creating the audio for your movie, the meters shouldn't ever go into the red – or if they do, only on the rarest of occasions. Neither should you let the meters bump along at the bottom, and compensate by turning up your speakers. Over the course of the movie there may be sections that are very quiet, or very loud, but it's important that you use your ears as well as the meters to judge the levels.

In the past, making your levels too high would cause distortion very easily. It's not so much of a problem now we aren't trying to record to tape and audio electronics have got better. But if you produce movies that are significantly louder than anyone else (or quieter, for that matter) it really annoys the viewers, who have to keep changing the volume that they listen at.

Now you've revealed the mixer, it's easy to get carried away with it. My recommendation is that you don't use the mixer panel for anything until you are in the final stages of making a movie, and even then it may not be needed.

So why is it there then? It's a powerful real time tool. You can use the faders to make live changes to the track volumes, control the overall level of the sum of the tracks, add effects to any one or all of the tracks – compress and limit the output so that it doesn't vary too much and much more. What's more, the track faders can be automated, so when you play back, they follow the settings you have already given them.

However, its design is from the time when you would do a "layback" of all the audio in real time, re-recording the final mix back onto the the video master tape, but nowadays most consumer output is to file and therefore isn't done in real time.

But for me, the main problem is that it affects the tracks, not the clips on the tracks. If you make a volume (or any other sort of) adjustment and then move the clips that the adjustment relates to, the adjustment does not move with the clip, but stays locked to the track position.

Therefore, you must be sure you have made all the changes to the movie (called Picture Lock) before using the mixer panel, or you may have to redo at least some of the track settings.

The output faders are useful, as are the mastering tools, because you can treat the whole audio output at the same time. Unfortunately, they are not automated, so you can't vary the master volume when mixing down to a file, only when playing back in real time. (Actually, you can, but as you can't monitor the file output, it's of no use).

If you are mixing down multi-track music recording then you might use the Mixer in the way it was intended, but for movies with relatively simple audio, it's probably better to get the sound correct at the clip level.

So, for now, make sure you understand that there is a clear distinction between Track curves (which use the mixer) and Volume or Effects curves (which are clip based). Although I will discuss the Mixer again, I won't be using Track curves in any of the projects.

One track or two?

You have seen in the setting panel that it's possible to put the audio onto a separate track, although by default video and audio are on the same track. There are certain advantages in the early stages of making your movie for keeping the sources together. They take up less space on the screen, it's impossible to move one without moving the other and therefore losing the synchronisation, and any transitions you add will automatically crossfade the audio as well as transition the video. So that you don't have to separate the tracks too soon, there are also many audio functions that are possible on audio within a combined track.

The disadvantages of keeping the tracks together start with you being unable to edit at a different point in the sound to the vision. This is a very important technique, particularly when editing dialogue. You can't use transitions without affecting the audio. There is also a programming limitation that means you can't alter the level or effects on audio over time – apply a small fade up or down during the clip, for example.

Splitting the tracks is easy, and opens up many more possibilities. Before we do so, though, let's look at what can be done with the audio still attached to the video.

Clip audio levels and fades

Before we look at the specialised audio tools, hover your mouse over the clip and take a close look at the thin area displaying the waveform. When we looked at the video only clips there was one control in the centre of the clip which altered the transparency of the video. Now, you will see that a similar hotspot exists on the audio portion of the clip – in this case a double headed version. A line extends the width of the clip, showing the audio level.

Dragging this hotspot up and down raises and lowers the line, and hence level at which the clip is played. Because of the height of the track, the sensitivity is very coarse, but this is still a reasonably good way to make quick adjustments – or at least just to mute the clip. Hovering over the clip reveals the icons and the line at which the level is set, so you know the level has been tampered with.

The "normal" position for the line is mid-way, representing a level of zero dB. To restore the clip to normal, just double click on it.

The additional audio hotspot controls audio level

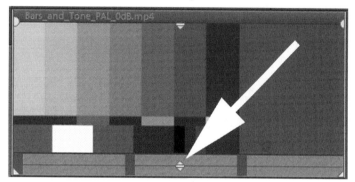

So, if you can't see any reading on the track meter, the level setting is the first thing to investigate.

We can also set the levels more accurately with the context menu or with the use of an audio effect, but before we turn to that, you might want to also experiment with the hot spots we used to add a fade out to the video. Use one of these with audio attached and you will hear the audio fade out at the same time as the video does.

These hotspots – level and fade – will also be available to use on audio only clips, but will be much easier to use because of the greater height of the track.

Audio level menu settings

All the important audio functions on combined clips can be accessed via right-clicking to access the Clip context menu and opening up the Audio functions sub-menu. I'm going to describe the functions that affect levels first, rather that sticking to the same order as the menu.

The Audio sub-menu

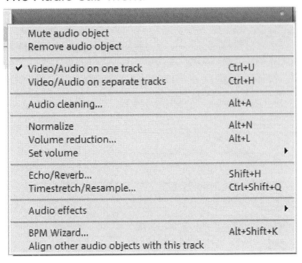

At the top, *Mute audio object* does just that – it switched off the audio, even though it leaves the waveform in place. Because there is no indication that you have muted the audio, the potential for confusion is very great. If for some reason you have muted the audio, the entry in the menu will instead say *Restore audio object* – your only clue as to why you can't hear anything! However, using this option to turn the audio on and off for troubleshooting has its uses, particularly as volume changes and other effects are preserved.

I would normally prefer to use *Remove audio object*. If you don't want to use the audio, then this option will remove the waveform from the track, allowing an increase in size of the video thumbnails. It's obvious just by looking at the clip why you can't hear the audio. If you decide you want the audio back having removed it, a new entry allows you to Restore original sound. The one downside is that removing and then restoring the audio loses any level changes you may have made.

The fourth group of sub-menu entries affect the level of the playback, but it's the last in the list that is most likely to be useful when first working on the audio.

Set volume opens another sub-menu with a range of settings. Selecting any of these alters the playback level, and you will see it affects the line and hotspot on the audio section of the clip. So here is a way to set the playback levels of a clip, or series of clips, quite accurately, rather than the rather coarse freehand dragging when using the mouse.

The Set volume sub-menu

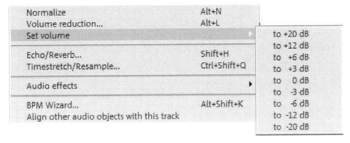

The scale used in audio measurements is decibels, which is logarithmic, matching the way we perceive audio. So although the steps available – from +20, +12, +6, +3 and zero and so on down - don't look linear, they fit the scale better.

The other two entries in this group above also deal with level control, but are much more sophisticated.

Volume reduction could confuse you. It actually performs a function similar to a DJs microphone "voice over" function – so when the audio on one track begins (a voice over, perhaps), the audio on a linked track (the background music?) drops in level. When the audio stops on the dominant track, the other track returns to its previous setting. The feature uses Track curves, so you can't move the clips after you have applied the effect.

Normalize is a function that analyses an audio clip and sets its level according to the peaks. This is more useful on longer clips. If you try to use it to "equal out" a series of short clips the results can sometimes be worse rather the better.

Splitting the tracks

There are two entries in the Audio sub-menu for splitting and restoring the audio tracks. They are a little more powerful than they initially seem.

If you highlight a clip, then use the context menu option *Audio functions/Video/Audio* on separate tracks the video track will lose its audio content (as if you had used *Remove audio object*). Immediately below the video a new clip will be created containing only the audio. If there is anything in the way, the remaining tracks will be pushed down, and if required a new track added to the bottom of the Timeline.

The video and audio might be now separated, but they are grouped together. While in this state you can't split one without splitting the other. When you move or trim one, the other is affected as well.

The result of splitting tracks and optimising the track heights

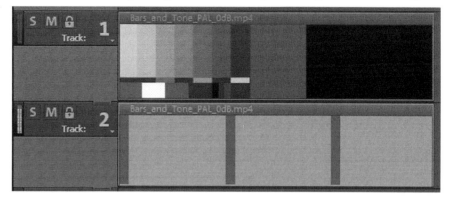

Without ungrouping them, however, there are still advantages. The audio track can be expanded to make it easier to see and manipulate. Most usefully, you can now add variable audio effects, and in particularly you can alter the volume over time within the clip – so that brief fade up and down is now possible without using the track curves (the ones that don't move with the clip!).

Once you have made changes that would be difficult – or impossible – to achieve with the audio on the same track, the clever feature is that by selecting *Video/audio on one track* the modified audio gets integrated back onto the video clip.

There is one proviso to doing this. If you ungrouped the audio and trimmed or moved it separately from the video you must restore it to its original length and position before you ungrouped it. You also need to Group the clips together before the function becomes available.

With the audio and video separated and ungrouped, you can do anything with the audio you want – trim it so that the In and Out points don't coincide with its video parent, move it vertically to a different track and move it horizontally so it isn't locked to the sync of the video. This is very powerful and I'll show you how it lets you be creative in a moment.

You should not worry too much about ungrouping the audio and video so that you can move or trim the audio separately. You can still group the clips back together again so that you can keep them in sync or retain any offset you have generated. If you change your mind and you want to restore the original audio to the video you can also use the *Restore original sound* command.

Back to the project It's time to put some of what I've described into action.

- Load up the *Flight over Snowdon rough cut 3* project.

- Check that you are in Timeline mode, with the magnet switched on and *Mouse mode for single objects* selected.

- Open up the mixer panel and place it over the Media pool so that you can see it clearly, but still work on the Timeline.

- Play the project from the beginning and watch the Master meters.

Unless you've altered the audio levels, the meters will be reaching into the yellow area, but not the red. This is fine if the sound of the plane was all we were going to use, but it's my intention to add some music. When we do the levels would start going into the red and cause distortion. Also the plane audio isn't particularly attractive to listen to at high volumes, and listeners will probably start reaching for the volume controls. So let's begin by pulling down the level of all the clips.

- Multi-select all the clips in the project, right-click on one clip then select *Audio functions/Set volume/-6dB*.

Now play the project again and you will see that the meters aren't getting out of the green area. We have created some headroom so that when we add the music, the whole project can get louder without running into the danger of distortion.

OK, the first clip has some useable audio. Although it's not particularly attractive, it's going to be better than silence. What about clip 2? Well, that sounds dreadful because of the wind noise hitting the camera microphone.

If you are expecting me to apply a wonderful effect to make the audio usable, I'm afraid I'm going to disappoint you. Yes, minor improvements are possible, but wind noise is really hard to eliminate without destroying the quality. We could spend hours treating the clip (I've tried), but the pragmatic approach is to replace it.

What with? Well, all of the video shot from outside the plane is affected in some way. We could use a sound effect if we could find one. There are some good free resources available on the Internet, but you will probably not find "Cessna taxiing" in a hurry. My plan is to use the interior audio and modify it sufficiently so it is believable.

So that we don't use the exterior audio, even in error, let's remove it from the clips:

- Multi-select clips 2, 6 and 8, Taxiing and Ext Take off.

- From the Context menu select *Audio functions/Remove audio object*.

- The waveforms will disappear and the video thumbnail will now occupy the whole height of the track.

We can always restore the audio if we change out mind, but now it is clear that the clips are silent. You could just pull down the level, or use the option to mute the audio, but I'm really sure I don't want to use the poor audio.

Play clip 5. This has a great bit of audio as the plane turns onto the runway and accelerates. I'm going to try to use that as the basic background audio track.

We have nearly run out of options while we keep the audio on the same track as the video, so the time has come to split the tracks:

- Right click on clip 5 and select *Audio functions/Video and audio on separate tracks*.

- The audio disappears from the clip on track 1 and appears as a grouped clip on track 2.

- With both the clips still highlighted in yellow, click on the Ungroup tool on the Timeline tool bar.

- Alter the track heights to make track 2 easy to work with.

- Now trim the Out point of the audio clip on track 2 to the right so it extends and snaps into place with the end of clip 8 on track 1.

Play from clip 4. That's not too bad, is it? The original audio is still being heard during clip 7 and the small change of volume when we cut to and away from the Ext shots without audio helps the deceit. What does it sound like when we remove the audio from clip 7?

- Use the context menu to remove the audio from clip 7.

Clip 5 audio extended to clip 8

Play the section again. Its not so convincing now, is it? However, if I were to just change the level at the cutting points, it might work. We could start splitting the audio clip and adjust the levels, but there is a better way which I'll show you shortly.

First, let's look at the beginning of the movie:

- Remove the audio from clips 3 and 4.

- Extend the audio clip on track 2 so it starts at the beginning of video clip 2.

For me, that doesn't really work, because there is no change of engine note as the pilot turns onto the taxiway and the prop changes speed. Let's have a listen to the other possible source:

- Drag the In point of the audio on track 2 back to the start of video clip 5.

- Detach and ungroup the audio from clip 1 onto track 2.

- Extend the Out point to snap to the second audio clip.

Clip 1 audio extended to clip 4

Still not quite right. There is a change in engine pitch, but it happens too late. I'm going to slip the audio clip forward:

- Listen for the change of pitch in the first audio clip. I make it at 00:00:38:08 MTC.

- Trim the In point of the audio to that timecode on the top left of the Program monitor.

- Find the point on clip 1 on the video track where the prop starts to change speed.

- That's 00:00:27:10 MTC or 00:00:04:10 BITC.

- Mark that point with a marker or the Playback cursor.

Trimming the audio and marking the video

- Drag the first audio clip left so it's new In point lines up with the marked video position.

Repositioning the audio

- Extend the In and Out point of the audio to fill the gaps in the Timeline.

Audio extended to cover video clips 1 to 4

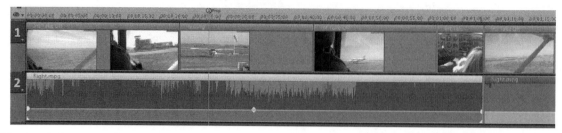

That might sound wrong when you play it back, but if you were to play the original, it's what happens in real life!

There is now an issue at the cutting point between audio clips 1 and 2. There is a definite click on the cut. This doesn't always happen, but if you zoom the Timeline view in, you will see a very abrupt change in the audio wave forms. We could mess around with trying to match the levels perfectly or trimming the audio to a different point, but the viewer is happy to accept a level change on a video cut – it's just the click that is disturbing. The quickest way to fix this is with an audio crossfade:

- Centre your view in the cut and zoom the timescale right in so you are looking at frames rather than seconds.

- The easiest way to set the timescale is with a right click on the timescale and select *Zoom 1 frame*.

- Generate an Out point trim cursor on the first clip.

- Drag it right just two frames.

- An overlap will be created.

Generating a 2 frame crossfade

Play the edit and you will have softened the click.

If you make an error doing this you can't just drag the new Out point back. You will have to use CTRL-Z or deconstruct the overlap by moving the second clips In point right so that you can get at the first clip's In point, then reset the edit to its original position.

In fact, what I've done is make the crossfade happen after the cut instead of either side of the cut. If you wanted to, you could rebuild or move the transition so it happens "correctly", but I'm happy with how it is for now.

Using Fades

Having used a transition, you have probably realised that you can also use the fade handles as well. We can quickly add a fade up or down to a clip without getting involved with the Volume curve tool. Let's add a short fade up at the very beginning of the movie so our audiences aren't startled by the opening:

- Adjust the view of the movie so the timescale is showing seconds.

- Hover over clip 1 on track 2 in order to generate the hot spots, then drag the fade in hot spot just a short distance right.

- Play the opening and see if you think it is too sudden or too gradual. It's very easy to adjust.

- I've made my fade in about one second in duration, but it's not critical.

- For the beginning and ends of movies this might be all you need to do – and you

Adding a simple audio fade up

can do this without detaching the audio from the video as well, although it can be a bit of a fiddle.

Volume keyframing

If you want to vary the levels of a clip in a more complex manner, you are better off using volume keyframes. Let me just remind you that these aren't the same as **Track curves** as controlled by the mixer – the alterations you make with **Volume curves** activated stay with the clip as you move it around.

What exactly is a keyframe? It's a point in the video or audio clip where a particular video or audio effect parameter is specified. So, if you have defined a value – a *key value* – for the volume to be 50% at *frame* 0 of an audio clip, that will be the first keyframe, instructing the program to set the volume to 50%. You can define another keyframe at 1 second into the clip setting the volume to 100%. The program will then interpret this data. In the one second during which the audio clip is played, the volume steadily increases from 50% to 100%. The values aren't stored for all the intermediate frames, only for the keyframes – the significant positions. Every frame can have a value for every parameter that can be controlled by a keyframable effect.

Curves or keyframes?

If you just have a few keyframes then, in general, the parameters will change in a linear manner between each keyframe. However, if you use enough keyframes, you can in effect draw curves. Movie Edit Pro even has a special mouse mode – Curve – that plots a series of keyframes so close together that complex shapes can be drawn.

Even if your keyframe points are just joined together with straight lines the resulting set of keyframes are referred to as a Curve in MEP.

There are two ways of setting keyframes. In the Effects tab of the Media pool, Keyframes can be created and edited on a small Timeline. It is also possible to display the resulting curve on a clip. In the case of some audio effects – most notably Volume – you can actually create or edit the curves on the clip itself.

For all the audio in this chapter, we will use the second method as it's much easier to see what is happening.

The mouse cursor for setting keyframes

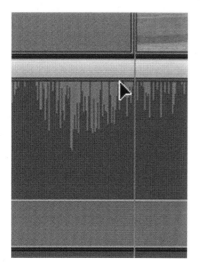

The first thing I'm going to get you to do is to drop the volume of the audio while the video of the *Taxiing* clip is playing:

• Adjust the Timeline view so that it is mostly occupied with the second video clip and the audio below.

• Use the context menu on the audio clip on track an enable *Volume curve*.

• A thin green line will appear at the top of the waveform. It might be quite hard to see, so expand the track height.

• To set a keyframe, make sure the mouse mode is set to Single or Track mode.

- Hover over the green line in line with the video cut to clip 2 above.

- The mouse cursor will change to a black arrowhead as in the screenshot.

- Click once on the line. A very small green box will appear at the point. This is your first keyframe.

The first keyframe with new cursor

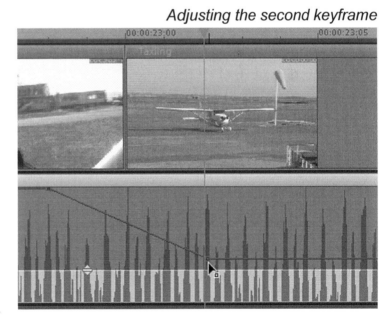

- Hover over the keyframe. The mouse cursor shows a small box beneath it when you are over the keyframe.

- Click, hold and drag the keyframe around. You will see the whole green line moving with the keyframe. You can also drag it left or right along the line, repositioning it in the time dimension. Make sure the line is at the top of the available space – maximum volume – and just before the cut above.

- Create a second keyframe just to the right of the first. Drag this down to about 25%, just above the yellow shading. The line will connect the two keyframes.

Adjusting the second keyframe

- Now rescale the view to 5 frames using the timescale Context menu.

- Adjust the two keyframes so that they are around two frames either side of the cut above.

Play the clip. You should hear a sudden drop in audio level. Now we want to bring the level back up when we cut back to the interior shot:

- Scroll the Timeline to the next cut.

- Place a new keyframe on the green line and drag it to the top, just after the edit away from the exterior shot on the track above.

- Generate a fourth keyframe on the slopping green line to the left.

- Drag it down and right so the line is horizontal and then slopes sharply up just before the second edit.

How the first audio curve should look

Now when you play back the movie, the level should drop as we cut to the exterior shot and return to its previous level when we cut back to the interior shot.

Editing Volume curves

Editing volume curves requires patience and good eyesight – even if you enlarge the track sufficiently the keyframe nodes are hard to see. When the centre of the square is black, the node isn't selected. Clicking directly on the node will select it and the centre gets filled in as the same colour as the node. You can constrain the direction of adjustment by holding down keys while dragging. The SHIFT key restrains the moves to vertical – you can alter the volume without adjusting the position horizontally. The CTRL key confines the movement to the horizontal – you can adjust the time position without altering the volume.

If you want to edit keyframes even more accurately, then you can to use the keyframe editing options in the effects editor. I'll describe these in detail later.

Deleting Volume curves

You should be able to delete a volume keyframe by selecting it and hitting the delete key, but it can be tricky. In early builds of 2014 it didn't always work and I'm not convinced that it is consistent - the whole clip sometimes disappears. Until you are familiar with the effects editor, take care and use CTRL-Z to remove unwanted additions.

- Now repeat the above procedure to lower the audio level for the first *Ext Take Off* shot.

- As the camera, and therefore the viewer, is further away, drop the level lower – under the yellow shaded area.

It's not just simple drops in level that we can accomplish with keyframing. When we cut to the final exterior shot, I want to initially drop the level, but then fade it out completely as the camera widens:

- Place a keyframe on the second audio clip just before the final *Ext Take Off* shot.

- Use another keyframe just after the video cut to drop the level to around 50%.

- About a quarter of the way through the remaining audio, use another keyframe to drop the level to 25%.

- Finally use a keyframe to pull the level down to nothing at the end of the clip.

The second and third volume curves

- You should end up with a dog-leg shape as shown in the screenshot.

Subjectively, I think this last effect is more pleasing than a straight fade out.

Having faded out the audio of the plane, I'm going to let the music take over for a while, and just return to the real audio for the landing:

- Multi-select video clips 9 to 16 (the penultimate clip)

- Remove the audio objects from the clips.

Drawing Volume curves.

Although not an essential tool, I think this next feature is very neat. It involves the use of the Curves mouse mode and allows you to draw a freehand curve of Volume (and other Audio effect) keyframes.

We have left the audio on the last clip of the movie so that I can demonstrate the Curves tool. My aim is to gradually fade up the sync audio as the plane approaches the runway to land, so that it when it hits the tarmac we clearly hear the bump, then to fade the audio out. Yes, this could be done with a few keyframes, but we might get a better subjective result using a proper curve:

- Split the audio and video for the last clip.

- Rearrange the Timeline view to look at just the last clip.

- Mark the point at which the plane hits the tarmac – either with a marker or by leaving the playback marker there.

- Adjust the height of track 1 to Small and customise the height of track 2 to be as big as you can.

- Enable Volume Curves on the audio clip.

- Select the Curve mode for the mouse – you may have to use the drop-down to find it.

- The trick now is to click, hold and drag across the clip.

- You can go in any direction, leaving a trail of keyframes behind you.

- As you can only have one keyframe per frame, those that were there before get erased.

- Once you've understood the principle, draw an asymmetrical Bell curve centring in the moment of touchdown – see my screenshot.

My effort isn't exactly a model of perfection, and yours need not be either. When you listen back, I hope you will agree that the audio sneaks and out in a more natural way that if we had used a few simple straight lines.

Volume curve produced with the Curve mouse tool

Panorama – altering the stereo balance

Movie Edit Pro can work with surround sound, which I'll discuss later. Unless your viewers have the playback equipment, though, most people who watch your movies are likely to hear the audio in Stereo at best – two channels, one left and one right, yielding a two dimensional audio image across the screen.

I'm going to add a sound effect of the tyres of the plane squealing when it lands, and then enhance it by adding stereo positioning to show the basic method of controlling what Magix call Panorama using clip keyframe curves:

- Get hold of the audio file tyre_squeal.wav by downloading or copying from the DVD, and using Wndows to put it in the same *Recordings* location as flight.mpg.

- Arrange the Timeline view so that you can see track 3

- Mark the point in the video clip on track 1 where the plane hits the tarmac – 00:10:10:08 BITC.

- Switch the mouse mode back to Single object.

- Drag the tyre_squeal clip from the Import window to track 3 and line up the start with the marked position.

- You may need to force the audio clip to show a waveform, using the context menu.

- Zoom the Timeline view right into frame level and you will see the audio doesn't really peak until a frame later.

- In the interests of accuracy, drag the audio clip a frame to the left!

The tyre squeal in position

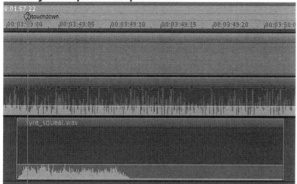

Because the right side of the plane touches down first, I'm going to start the squeal panned over to the right, and then swap it to the left as the second wheel makes contact. So first of all we want to get the clip to display a panorama curve:

- Right click on the new audio clip on track 3 and select *Audio effects curve/Panorama*.

- Mark the point where the plane becomes about level at 00:10:10:15 BITC.

Plotting the Panorama curve

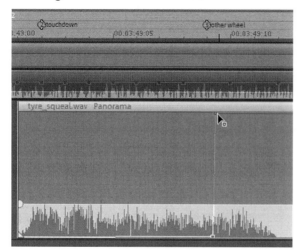

- Increase the height of track three to give you more control.

- Use three keyframes to start the white panorama curve at the bottom of the clip, and then switch it to the top of the clip at the marked point.

- Play that back and I think you will agree it could be louder.

- Set the volume of the clip to +6dB.

Open the Master mixer panel if you closed it and play the section again to check we are still a bit short of going into the red. We might need to check this section carefully when we add the music.

I have to admit that every time I play this tweaked effect, it makes me smile!

Audio/video sync

Although we cannot integrate any of the modified audio back onto the video track, we can take steps to ensure that it stays with the video clip it is mostly associated with. While with a bit of care it is quite possible to make changes to a multi-track project without destroying the sync between tracks, grouping the audio to its associated video is a wise precaution. It also has the added bonus of reminding you where the sync is most important if you come to re-visit a project at a later date.

- Multi-select the second video clip and the first audio clip and click on the *Group* tool.

- Do the same for the fifth video clip and the second audio clip.

- Now select the last clips on tracks 1, 2 and 3. *Group* them together as well.

Sometimes you may come across a video clip which is out of sync – people's lip movement not matching the audio track being the most obvious example. It may have been recorded like this, or the sync destroyed by a video editing program. Acquiring video from recorded DVDs is a process I find particularly prone to this issue. While you can accidentally knock a clip out of sync once the video and audio have been put on separate tracks, it's also easy to avoid by taking care or re-grouping them.

You can use split tracks to repair out-of-sync clips, but there is another option in the main clip context menu, Set audio/Video offset. It's a fairly straight-forward tool – you specify the offset you want to test in frames and play the clip from within the tool until you are happy with your fix. Applying the offset isn't destructive – you can return to the clip and re-adjust or reset it at any time.

The advantage of this is that you can keep the audio on the same track as the video. One small disadvantage is that it's not clear from the Timeline what you have done as there is no label added to the clip in the manner that is done with most effects.

Soundtrack Maker

Although I will be describing the remaining audio effects, I'm going to skip ahead so that we can finish off the audio elements of the project so far. I want to add some music to fill the gap in the middle.

We could just chose some music from the Slideshow music folder, other copyright free music, or if the video was for private use, just add some commercial music. We would find something of a suitable duration and drag it down to track 4. It's unlikely that the music will be the perfect length although it's not that hard to cut out a few bits and get it close. You will probably find once you add the music you will want to re-edit the video so that edits are more sympathetic with the pace – not always cutting on the beats, perhaps, but at least avoiding cutting just off the beat!

However, I'm going to use the Soundtrack Maker wizard to generate a background music track for us. It still won't be the perfect length, but we can use it as a guide for further trims and the transitions I intend to add. Another feature of the wizard is that it can generate "mood changes" within the score, adding more variety and perhaps matching the content more accurately.

To get the most from this wizard, you have to put in a bit of time experimenting with the options. I'm not claiming that I've used it to build the best possible soundtrack, and with more effort you could improve on it a good deal. However, we haven't finished editing the video yet, and I want you to be able to match my later demonstrations.

The duration of the soundtrack created is normally set to the length of the movie on the Timeline and the resulting music will be of the full duration, or at least thereabouts. Given the structure of the music, the shorter the duration the less likely that your music is going to be an exact match. If you only want a section of the movie to have a soundtrack made for it, you need to set a range and depending on the style and emotion, you can't make the range too short. Most emotions have to last around 20 seconds. You can always physically edit down the creation after it has be generated. When I first began developing this project (in the 2013 version) The music was placed on track 4, but for some reason it has changed to track 5, so first we need to add another track to the project:

- Open *Files/Settings/Movie*.

- Alter the number of tracks to 5 and click *OK*.

- Adjust the layout to show all tracks.

- Now create a blue range above the Timeline with the In point at the start of clip 8 and a duration of 2 minutes.

- In the *Edit* menu, select *Wizards/Soundtrack Maker*.

- A new dialogue box will appear.

- In the first section, select *Relaxed (EasyListening)* from the drop down box.

- Ensure that *Apply style to selected range* is checked.

- Highlight *Jazzy* in the box of emotions on the right.

- Make sure the *Automatic cut adjustment* is unchecked.

Soundtrack maker Wizard with range set below

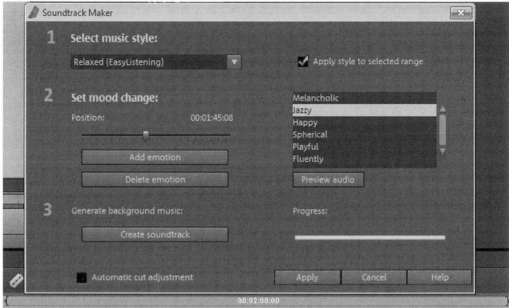

This last step is important, because if you apply the soundtrack to the movie with it checked, Magix will mess about with your cuts to make them match the music. If you've not put a lot of effort into choosing the In and Out points of your clips you might want that to happen. We don't!

First we are going to generate a sample soundtrack. I've asked you to uncheck the Automatic cut button just in case you clicked on Apply in error, which would complete the wizard:

- Click on *Create soundtrack*.

- The emotions are added in a new strip that has appeared above the timescale.

- Wait as new audio clips are placed on track 5.

- Adjust the view if you can't see track 5.

Without closing the Soundtrack maker dialogue box, play the movie from the take off.

You will hear where, after about 90 seconds, the program has got bored with Jazzy and switched to Happy. You can also see that it hasn't quite made a track of the specified duration.

The soundtrack ready to be applied

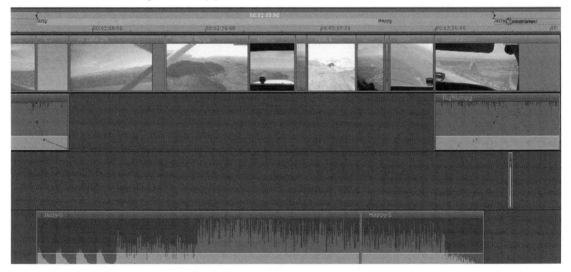

Neither of these things are critical for the project - in fact the change to the Happy emotion works quite well – so I'm going to live with what has been made for us:

- Double check that *Automatic cut adjustment* is unchecked.
- Click on the Apply button.
- The wizard closes and the new music track remains on track 5.
- Select both the music objects and use Shift-Drag and drop to move them up to track 4.
- Save the project as *Flight over Snowdon rough cut 4*.

We've done with the project for now, and the rest of this chapter ties up the audio loose ends. If you are keen to get on with making the movie, feel free to skip ahead and come back when you want to know more about the other audio options.

Manipulating the Soundtrack maker emotions

It's quite possible to remap and alter the emotions used, although you can't normally perform a mood change precisely when you want to. You can preview what they sound like with the Preview button below the list – which then turns into a stop start button. Don't rely on the descriptions, because they aren't that good - listen instead.

The first thing you might want to do, particularly on a shorter piece, is use the Delete emotion button to get rid of the changes, or if you start again, put the cursor at the start, add a single emotion and *Create variation*. From there you can add more emotions starting at points in your movie. You will see that the music is made up of individual clips and in many cases you can reorder them and the edits will still work – some better than others!

The *Vary only selected emotion* will only appear after your first creation, and you have to select the clip or clips on the Timeline that you want to regenerate. Sometimes it's hard to tell the difference!

However hard you try, you are unlikely to get a sound track that is ideal for your first video cut. You can consider using a time stretch effect for small alterations in duration, but with the music in place, you may want to start matching the video editing to the music. This is what you would have to do if you used pre-composed music anyway. MEP even offers an automatic tool in the Edit menu – *Musical Editing Adjustment* – to fine tune your edits to match the tempo of a music track.

If you use the adjustment feature, you will also come across a tool for detecting the tempo of a piece of music - the BPM wizard. You can access this via the context menus directly, and you can use it to assess cutting points. However, I find I often have to resort to tapping the tempo key manually. If you like to cut to the beat, and want to place markers, you can add them on the fly by pressing CTRL-Enter on each beat as the music is playing, then press again to clear the name box.

More Audio effects

In the context menu where we found the Panorama curve setting, you will have noticed there were five other possibilities for adding curves.

The first two – Aux 1 and Aux 2 – send a signal to the mixer to be fed to a separate effects channel. Remember how I said that anything we do with the mixer is track based and is likely to confuse both you and me at the early stages of making a project? Well the same applies to the Aux feeds. I haven't found an audio effect that can't be added to a clip in some way, so we don't need to use the track based mixer yet.

Sharpening boosts or lowers the low frequencies, but attempts to leave the higher frequencies untouched. If your audio has a muddled bass sound, you can set this to a high value.

Smoothing reduces the high frequency components while trying to retain the low frequencies.

Neither of these controls have quite the same effect as using simple Bass and Treble controls, although when you try them on music they may sound similar. You are most likely going to find them useful for cleaning out unwanted noises or improving poor recordings.

Distortion is just that – it squares off the signals. If you wanted to give the effect of dialogue coming through a cheap intercom this is the tool for you!

All of these effects can be keyframed. There are nine more adjustable effects that can't be keyframed, all of them powerful. You can add them to an audio clip using the context menu, and four of them are accessed through the general Audio cleaning dialogue, which can also be accessed by double clicking on an audio clip as well as through the context menu.

Audio cleaning dialogue with 4 tabs

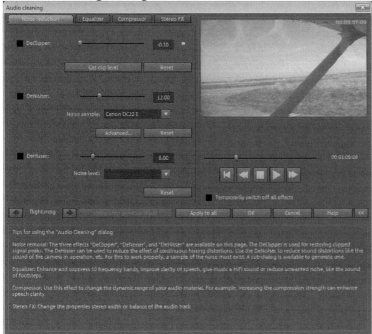

The audio cleaning box has four tabs, and at the the bottom of the window a Tips section which does a pretty good job of describing what all the effects can do.

A preview window and transport controls allows you to test the changes you are making to the audio without returning to the editor. Also note that you need to enable each effect with a checkbox before it does anything!

How you use these tools will depend on the original source material and often you will need to experiment. Make use of the *Temporarily switch off all effects* checkbox often, to make sure that you are actually making things better, not worse and bear in mind that there is no magic solution to poorly recorded audio before you spend too much time adjusting parameters.

The first tab is *Noise reduction*, and contains 3 effects. *DeClipper* repairs peaks that have gone into distortion. I've found the *Denoiser* can be quite effective if you have a constant background noise, but the wider the frequency band of the noise, the more of the audio you want to preserve is going to be lost as well. *DeHisser* would be most useful when using poor quality tape recording

Another tab leads to the *Equaliser*, where you can modify the gain of 10 separate bands. Perhaps most useful are the presets available from the drop down box where you can perform common functions without having to set up the bands yourself.

The next tab is for a *Compressor* which limits the dynamic range of an audio signal – the difference between the quietest and the loudest parts of an audio clip. Again, the presets are probably the best way to use this tool.

The fourth tab - *Stereo FX* - can be used for some interesting stereo adjustments, but the list of presets reveals some essential tools if you've got a bit technical with your audio recording techniques. For example, on one of my cameras I can record the camera mic on the right channel, and an external mic on the left. I also sometimes use a separate digital recorder that can have different sources fed to the left and right channels – for example taking a high level and lower level feed from a PA mixing desk, avoiding the danger of just ending up with distorted audio. (If you are wondering how I sync up the audio from the recorder with the video, I use the wonderful option *Align other audio objects with this track* in the audio context menu.)

If you use these techniques, you will find the list of audio presets here invaluable. You can separate out the right and left channels and put copies of the audio on different tracks, then chose which audio you need to use. They can even compensate for incorrectly wired up microphones that are "out of phase". Many of the presets can't be created just using the adjustable parameters, as the Note points out.

Two more audio effects are available directly from the context menu. *Echo/Reverb* opens a fully functioning plug-in that will allow you to add echo or delay to achieve anything from slightly sweeting a singer's voice, through mimicking the acoustic of a large room to making the most impressive of Science fiction style sound effects. Again, the presets will save you a lot of time here.

Finally *Timestretch/resample* will change the tempo – and therefore the duration – of music or any other audio to make it fit a duration. You can also change the pitch and bring that rather flat singer's bad notes back into tune, should you have the time!

Audio effect presets

Once you have created a particular effect, it's a shame to lose it. To this end it's very easy to Save an effect. It wouldn't be much use if you couldn't Load it back, so both these options are available via the context menu. Saving involves you choosing a location, and if you use the default, the effect will be place in a location that can be accessed via the Media Pool.

If you visit the Media pool effects tab and expand the Audio effects location, you will see there are two possibilities. I've avoided the General tab so far because I'm going to show you how to use the keyframes there with a Video effect. If you open that location you will find version of all the effects I've talked about.

Opening up Presets shows you a range of pre-made effects that you can drag onto audio clips on the Timeline. If you save any effects of your own, they will appear here as well, showing a different icon to the other presets.

Preset effects in the Media pool

Clicking on any of the presets plays a short sample, so you can get some idea of what they do without having to apply them.

Scrubbing

When we move the Playback marker across a video clip, the frame at the current location shows up in the Program monitor, and this is a very useful tool. If the audio also played each time the marker moved, it would be quite irritating for most of the time, but on occasions may be helpful.

To this end, you can choose what sort of behaviour you get using the drop-down dialogue in the second tool from the right on the toolbar.

There are four options. *No scrubbing* is the default. *Scrubbing (1 frame)* plays just one frames worth of audio, so if you are moving very slowly it can be quite hard to comprehend, while *Scrubbing (long)* plays a much larger chunk of audio, but can keep playing long after you to have stopped moving the cursor.

Scrubbing options

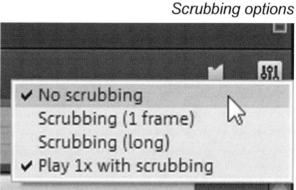

The final option, Play 1x with scrubbing should normally be checked, in my opinion, switching it off means the last sample gets played over and over again even when you stop moving the scrubber. It may have it's uses, but I haven't found any yet, and it's very irritating!

Audio mixdown

If you are sure that you are happy with your audio tracks, you can use the Edit menu option to mixdown the tracks to one new track. This option uses a very high quality audio compression scheme, so you won't notice any difference. However, with the number of tracks available to you in Plus and Premium, and the ability to group clips together, I don't ever find a need for this feature. Perhaps if you are mixing down a Symphony Orchestra with a microphone on every instrument, you might be more likely to need it!

Using the Mixer panel channels

Despite my advice to leave it alone, you are probably curious as to what can be done with the mixer panel. To experiment, you might want to use the music we have added to track 4, or start another project and put some other music of your choice in the Timeline.

Each track has a mixer channel allocated to it. If you want to add an Audio effect to the entire output of the channel, and therefore the track, you can use the FX button top left of the channel.

Mixer with the FX channels revealed

This opens up a composite effect box that includes the reverb panel we can use on clips, and two graphically different but functionally similar versions of the compressor and graphic EQ effects contained in Audio cleaning.

If you want to use these effects at a clip level but put them on every clip, you would have to use a method such as *Apply to all* in the effects dialogue, or save and load effects. Making a global change to everything on the track is a bit clumsy. By using track effects you can make changes easier.

The Channel FX tool

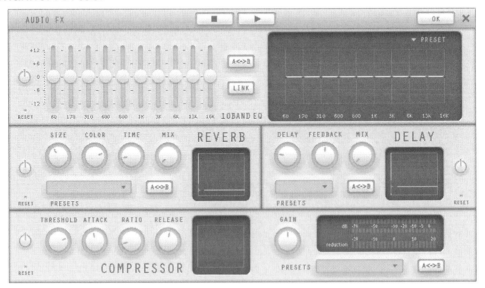

Because these effects can't be keyframed – altered over time – it's safe to use them via the mixer even if you have further changes to make. When any of the effects are turned on, (via the on/off icon buttons) then the FX button light shows on the mixer channel panel. There is no legend on the clips themselves, though, and if you move the clip to another track, the effect doesn't go with it.

The other button at the top of each mixer channel is the Auto button – short for automation. This control is linked to the track curves display.

When auto isn't engaged and track curves aren't displayed, the fader controls the level of the track, but nothing is remembered. This is fine if you want to adjust the overall level of a track, but not alter it over time.

When you switch on automation, you also enable the display of track curves, consisting of a green line at the top of the track, indicating volume, and a white line in the middle indicating balance – or panorama, as Magix calls it elsewhere.

You can't edit these curves with the mouse, whatever mouse mode you are in. You have to use the faders, clicking and holding then dragging the fader. With Auto lit, any movements you make of the track fader is remembered and displayed as a track curve.

Display Track curves is a context menu option on the Timeline, which is even available on an empty track. If Auto is off and you switch on Track curves, the fader behaves as if Auto has been pressed even if the button isn't lit up. There seems to be a disconnect here and my advice is to always use the Auto button to be sure of what is going on.

Track curves displayed - on an empty track!

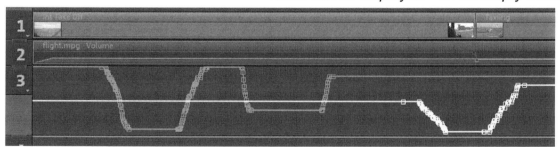

I began with a serious problem with using the fades in real time (the only way that they work) because of the latency of my system. I would move the fader and hear the change over a second later. Admittedly the changes I made were recorded when I made them, but it meant that I couldn't properly hear what I was doing.

Solving this was a case (for me) of going into the Settings/Program panel and switching the Audio playback settings to Direct, rather than use the Wave driver. There is still the odd lag, but doing so made the system useable. I'm sure that with a high quality audio set-up and some tweaking of the wave driver parameters you can set up a system suitable for proper real-time mixing.

If you are unhappy with your live mixing attempts, you can go back and readjust the fader position, recording over the top of the previous settings. Alternatively you can use the Context menu to Reset track curves/Volume and try again.

Two horizontal sliders marked FX 1+2 send a proportion of the post-faded channel to a new channel on the mixer. As soon as you alter the slider the new channel appears to the right of the track channels but before the Master channels - see the screenshot at the top of this section. An FX channel can then have an additional effect added via the FX button, the overall level of which is added to the master mix by the FX channel fader. This isn't automated. We are getting into serious music mix-down territory here, but the tools are there if you want them.

The left/right pan knob behaves it the same way as the fader for the channel, controlling, and controlled by, the Balance track curve when Auto is engaged.

Finally, each channel has a Solo and Mute button, mimicking the same controls on the track headers.

The Master mixer controls

The mastering suite

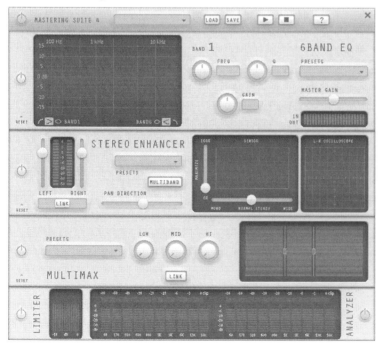

I've already mentioned these, but it's important to remember that there is no automation – and therefore no overall "Master" track curve.

Yes, you can add an effect to the master output, via the FX button. The Reset button is a very useful addition if you just want to be sure you left nothing turned on. Beneath these controls is a Mastering button, which opens up a new set of effects optimised for modifying your final output.

Perhaps the most important of this is the *Limiter*. Engaging this will ensure that you never inadvertently overload the output channel. If you have mixed your audio a bit too high in general, the Limiter will flatten the dynamic range. If you have set your levels a bit on the low side, then you might be able to push them a bit higher and let the limiter guard against causing distortion.

Notice that the limiter is frequency based, so it won't push down the overall level if there is just a particularly loud peak just in one frequency band.

Six band EQ and *Multi-Max* both work on frequency response and have some presets you might find useful, particularly for music. The *Stereo Enhancer* can do the same things as the Stereo FX panel does to individual tracks.

5.1 Surround sound

If you have a surround sound system, a way of monitoring it on your computer, a version of MEP Plus or Premium and the desire to make movies with 5.1 Dolby surround, then the final button is for you!

Engaging it warns if you don't have the requisite audio monitoring, but then changes the simple Panning controls on the channels into more complex displays. Clicking on them opens up the positioning editor. What's more, you can automate the positioning in the same way as levels and panning.

If you have imported recordings made in 5.1 surround from Mpeg-2 files, they will have been imported as discreet channels or you can extract them using the context menu on the Timeline. Any other effects or music you might want to move around will need to be given their own tracks as well. You have six target channels to work with, including the LFE (bass channel) and the potential is vast.

The 5.1 Surround Editor

One thing to bear in mind – even with just "simple" stereo movies, is that the professionals hardly ever put dialogue anywhere other than in the centre of the audio "image" – and that's why there is a centre speaker as part of the surround system. By all means be as bold as you like with the music, background and spot sound effects, but if you start to try and place voices in positions that match the characters position on the screen, every edit will be a huge amount of work for you, and probably a source of confusion for the audience.

Making Titles

The aim of this chapter is to explore the title features in Movie Edit Pro. We will be creating a few titles along the way to use in the Flight project, but if you want to be getting on with it, you can skim through keeping an eye out for the bullet point lists that indicate what you need to do to move on to the next stage.

The aim of the title editor is to create text to be read off the screen. At its most basic you can create a title card using any of the fonts available. Quite often, you will want to overlay your text on a video background, and this is also handled easily. Another thing you are likely to want to create is a moving title such as the roller captions at the end of the movie. Again, there are simple ways to do this.

If you want to create complex, professional looking titles quickly, there are lots of premade templates available, but it is also possible to build then from scratch once you understand the concepts of adding layers and movements. You will need to understand how to use movement keyframes for the more complex moves, which I will cover in the next chapter.

Adding a title

If you are still working with the Flight movie, it's time to take a break so you can experiment with titles. Make sure your current project is saved, and start a new blank project.

The Title Editor

Titles aren't easy to see unless you are in Timeline mode, so be sure to select that as well, and also make sure the Timeline marker is at the start of the movie.

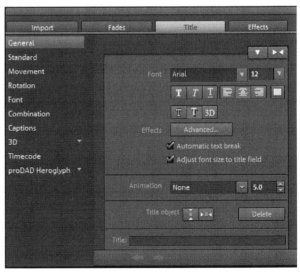

The easiest way to create a new title is to use the toolbar icon "T". When you click on it a number of things happen. Make sure the Import tab is selected in the Media pool and click on the "T" tool now. The Media pool tab changes to the Title tab, a small text place holder appears in the Playback Monitor, and when you move your mouse down to the Timeline over track three, an object appears on the track.

The default title in text editing mode

We now have a title which, if you still have the default options set, is quite small and in the centre of the screen. If you are using the first release of 2014 the text will initially say "Titel" because the translations from German haven't been completed.

To the right and above the text are two clickable symbols – the "no Entry" sign will remove the text object, the "tick" will accept it.

When the text first appears it will be highlighted, meaning that if you begin typing, the text will be replaced. Type "Test" and click on the checkmark. The text will change to having a dotted box with orange handles around it – this is called the Title Field.

A small Title Field

We could start to reposition or resize now if we wanted to, but let's just leave it where it is and click on the Timeline to accept the title. You can do anything that switches the focus away - press Play, change to another Media pool tab – to stop editing the title.

Now we have a title object on track 3. If that track was occupied at the point where the scrubber was, it will be on a lower track. If you check the duration it will be, by default, 5 seconds.

Another way of creating a title is possible once the Title editor is open in the Media pool. Click on another area of the Program monitor and you will get a new title, positioned where you clicked. Another text layer has been added, and you can see it on the Timeline as well, sitting one track below.

In Movie Edit Pro, each text layer is assigned its own track, and you use the normal Timeline controls to manipulate the duration and temporal position of the layers relative to each other. You can group the various elements together so that the title acts as a single object and also include objects that aren't text – graphics with transparency for example This is the key to producing very complex titles. Let's get back to basics for now though.

You can delete the second layer in a number of ways. If you haven't yet accepted it, just clicking the No Entry tool will make it go away. If it is in positioning mode, you can press Delete on the keyboard. If it is no longer in any edit mode, just delete the object on the Timeline below.

Ignore the fact that the original title is a bit small for the moment. What if we wanted to change the text? The quickest way to reopen the title editing functions is click on the text in the Player window. Click once and you return to the re-positioning mode. Double-click and you can re-edit the text. Double-click now, and instead of typing straight away, use the forward arrow to deselect the text and add "Text" to the end of the title. Now re-position the text cursor between the two words and press Enter. Text gets moved to a new line – which is why we can't use the Enter key to exit from the text editing mode! Click on the Timeline to accept the title.

Before we start repositioning and resizing the text, there are two important controls I want to introduce you to.

Text breaks

When you are editing a title, the Title editor showing all the adjustable parameters should automatically appear in the Media Pool window. If you want to open the editor manually, you need to open the Title tab and select General option in the list on the left.

Checkboxes in the titler

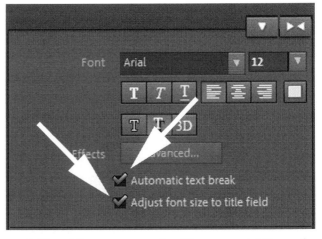

In the middle of the Title editor, just below the Advanced button, is a checkbox for *Automatic text break*. With this enabled MEP won't let you type off the screen area - it will add carriage returns so that the text fits the width of the screen. It will even add them in the middle of a word if it has to. This is the mode you are most likely to want to use

– after all, there is normally no point in having text that can't be seen. However, you might be trying to create a title that you will animate or one where you want to control the text breaks themselves. Unchecking this box will let you do that.

As you start to enter text into a new title, the Automatic text breaks are selected by default. You can override them and continue to work. If you end up with text flowing off the sides of screen that is hard to see, then in addition to scroll bars, MEP provides you with a handy text entry/editing box at the bottom of the editor that you can use as an alternative.

It's important to know about the effect of automatic text breaks, particularly if you are going to be resizing the text once you have entered it. You might find that the breaks defeat your efforts to create a particular text layout, in which case you should consider turning this feature off and adding your own breaks.

Font Size and Title Fields

The second checkbox is *Adjust font size to title field*. It is also on by default, and generally this is a good option. The Title field is the box containing the text defined by the dotted lines in positioning mode. If you resize the box, then the text's font size will be reduced or expanded to ensure the text continues to fill the box.

However, there may be times that you don't want the font to vary. You might want to be lining up title fields for various text layers but need the text sizes to be consistent. You could also be prone to accidentally resizing the title field when all you want to do is move it. With the option unchecked, the text font size remains constant.

Repositioning title fields

Now we know what those checkboxes are for, make sure they are both on, and click once on the *Test Title* to take us back to the repositioning mode. There are handles at the sides and corners of the title field and dragging any of them makes the field bigger. Do so now and you will see that you will also enlarge the text font. Once you have finished adjustment check out the value of the font size in the Title editor and see what you have changed it to. With a bit more adjustment, set it to about 30pt.

Hover in the centre area of the title field and you get a familiar four-way cursor – and you can drag the title anywhere on the screen. Move it bottom right.

Now that the Title Field is larger, another handle has appeared above the box which rotates the text, so grab it and move it left so that the title is tilted to around 45 degrees.

OK, that's a bit radical but it proves the principle! Use CTRL-Z to straighten it up, then click on the title again to display the Title field.

What about the handles at the sides? They normally let you change the width or height of a box, but currently they behave in the same way as the corner handles. This is because we have the second checkbox selected. Uncheck *Adjust font sizes to title field* and then you can use the side handles to make the box wider without it affecting the font size or the height of the title field. Adjust it so that it's about twice the width of the text. Because the text is currently centre justified, the title will move to the centre of the Title field.

The re-positioning, rotating or resizing of a title field once you have set it up initially is controlled by

Moving a Title Field with rotate handle arrowed

adding further video effects, although this process is invisible to us when we manipulate the title field using the handles. You will be able to see parameters in the effects editor, and I'll introduce you to that in the next chapter.

Fonts

Above the Advanced button are a whole host of tools for altering the text font. You have already seen the font size box in action. You can click on the drop-down arrow to reveal a slider to adjust the size gradually, or type a new font size into the box. It's quite easy to confuse yourself and the program by manually adjusting the title field size and then adjusting the font size when the automatic adjustment is disabled. The program will adjust field height to accommodate large text. With the Adjust font size to title field box re-enabled, the title field will revert to maintaining its aspect ratio. As a general rule, I only adjust the font size manually on a current title if I've got this box checked.

The font typeface can be selected in the main font box. If you are just browsing for something suitable you can use the dropdown box and preview the styles. If you know what you want, begin to type the name of the font into the textbox until you've typed enough letters for it to be the only possible choice!

Selecting a font

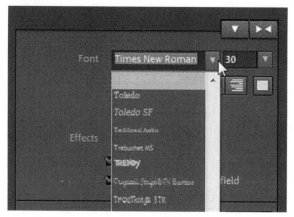

In order to change the typeface of an existing title you need to be in the text editing mode. Double click on the Test Text title and then select the font name (by default Arial) in the font selection box. Begin to type Times New Roman and watch the text change its font style as the styles are offered to you. It may depend on you having extra fonts installed, but on my computer I get Times.. offered to me after just two letters. When it is offered to you, just press enter to select it.

Text attributes

Immediately below the Font controls are a number of buttons for setting the text attributes. Select the text so that you can see the title field, and then click on the first button on the left – Bold. The text takes on a bold appearance and the title field lines disappear but don't worry – as long as you don't click away, you can continue to experiment by clicking on Italic and Underline. Notice how the buttons are additive, so you end up with all three attributes. Click again to switch them off in any order you like to see the attributes removed one at a time until you are back the normal text.

Text attribute controls

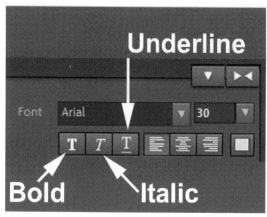

If you want to apply one or more of these attributes to a section of text, you need to get into the text editing mode, highlight the section you want to change with CTRL-arrow left or right, and then click on the attribute.

If you try that now with just the word Text, you will see that de-selection of the partially applied attribute is just a matter of clicking on the attribute button.

Justifying the text

The next three buttons justify the text. How it behaves will depend on if you have adjusted the field size without adjusting the text size (or vice versa). In the previous examples I've asked you to create a title where the text doesn't fill the title field. Click on the three attributes in turn and you can make the text left, centre or right justified within the title field. Return it to centre justified.

Where a title has been created without additional space, the justification controls will position the title field across the width of the screen. You can see this in action if you click on the monitor to create a new temporary title and then apply the justification buttons. This is a useful feature for achieving consistency in your title placement, although it doesn't address the problem of vertical placement. There are additional controls for that.

Justification controls

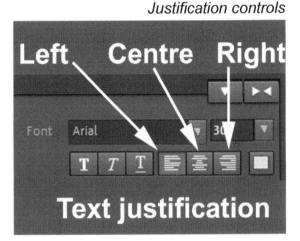

Centring

Let's break off from the Text attributes for a moment to look at the controls for positioning text objects. Often you want your titles to be in the middle of the screen, at least horizontally if not vertically. Two buttons in the lower part of the editor after the label Title object can do this accurately for you, even if you have set the field width differently to the title width.

With the title field selected, click on the left-hand button with the vertical arrowheads. The title will move up to the vertical centre of the screen. The field will cease to appear to be selected, but if you try the other button it will put the title in the horizontal centre as well.

The centring buttons and text entry box

Incidentally, if you ensure these buttons are highlighted before you create a title with the T tool, the title will end up centred. They get switched off when you move a title.

Text colour

You aren't always going to want white titles. The face colour of the titles can be edited using the furthest right button under the Font boxes – Change text color. Select the text and click on it now to reveal the Color picker.

Changing the text colour

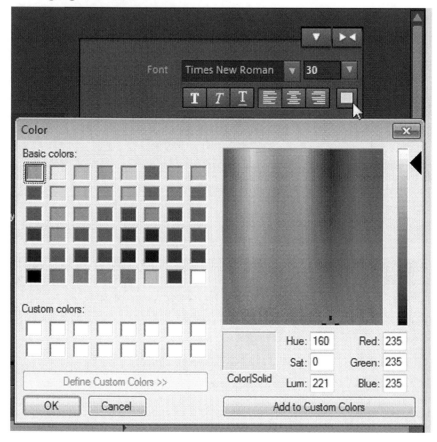

This is a fairly standard windows type of control. If you aren't familiar with its use you should find it easy to understand. The top left area gives you an array of standard colours which you just need to click on to select.

If these colours don't give you what you want, to the right is a spectrum where you can select a hue (the actual colour) and a saturation (the strength of the colour).

On the far right a slider to select the brightness. The colour you create is shown in the box below. You can even type in values if you want to match a colour in another program.

Having created your own colour you can add it to the custom colour list so you can carry it over to other uses. Try it out now – create a light blue colour and add it to the custom palette, then click OK to apply the new colour to the titles. Keeping it as a light colour means it still shows up against the black background.

Text effects

Three more effects can be added to your text. An outline puts a different coloured edge all around the letters, and a shadow is a displaced copy of the letters that give the impression of a shadow. The third effect gives your text a 3D appearance – but it's not a stereoscopic effect.

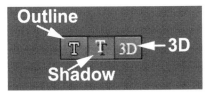

Three Text effects

In order to explore them, we need to open up the Advanced dialogue.

Advanced Effects

Clicking on the button reveals three further boxes. Top left is a checkbox to constrain your titles to the title safe area. I discussed this idea earlier in the book. Top right is a choice of background colour. It's important to realise that this is just the default background – what is displayed instead of the transparent areas of a title if there is nothing on any lower layers. Normally this is black, but if you are working with dark titles you might want to change this to white. Do it now and you should see that the title you have created has a black drop shadow. If it doesn't, then we can set it up so that does have.

The lower area controls the text effects and has checkboxes for switching them on and off. Check *Shadow* and uncheck *Outline* and *3D*. To the right of the checkboxes are buttons for setting the colour of the effect. Click on the box for Shadow and you will see the colour picker we saw earlier. Choose a dark blue colour and select OK.

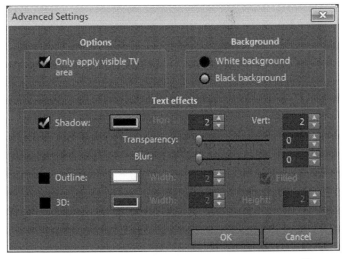

The box for Advanced text effects

Back in *Advanced settings*, you can use the Hori and Vert boxes to set the offset of the shadow – negative values are possible, so set the offset to -5 hori and 5 vert and you will see the shadow cast below and to the left – as if the source of light is above and to the right.

Transparency only affects the "shadow". Set it to 50% and you will see some of the underlying video through the shadow. Blur gives the shadow softer edges, as if the light source isn't a spotlight but a softer light source. Set it to 50% for a more natural look.

Outline adds a border around the text. If you are going to superimpose your title over video, you can't really control what will be behind the title. If you chose a light colour, it might be over a bright spot, if you chose a dark colour it might be over a dark patch. One possibility is to choose a strong primary colour, but this will often look "cheap". Adding an outline that contrasts with the face colour solves this issue, because if the edge can't be seen, you can be sure that the face can!

So, let's add a border to the text – choose the same colour as the shadow, a dark blue, and set the width right down to 1. You might want to experiment with the Filled checkbox – it removes the face colour in the centre so you have "hollow" titles. Check it again to fill the hole.

3D is a text effect that isn't related to making movies in 3D. It creates a solid block behind the text to give a three-dimensional look. It works best if the colour of the "sides" of the blocks is the same hue as the face colour, but slightly darker (or perhaps lighter). To experiment with this, switch off the Shadow and Edge, turn on 3D, increase the offset values in the Width and Height boxes and select a slightly darker blue for the colour.

Now return to the main title editor by clicking on OK and check what affect the three buttons have now – we have customised what they do!

Resetting the text settings

The next feature applies to many of the effects editing boxes we will encounter later in the book. Having spent ages experimenting, you might want to just clear all the parameters and return to the default settings.

The Text attributes reset button and the drop down menu

Each edit box, including the title editor, has a pair of icons at the top right. The furthest right has two opposed arrowheads and is the reset button.

I hope you don't feel I've cheated you by making you go through all the above and not left you with a set of parameters we are going to use, but there are a couple of reasons I want you to reset the titles settings. Firstly, you should have got the idea, but you may not have followed me parameter by parameter, so you might not match my settings. Secondly, at least on my computer, I find the text settings can get a bit cranky after repeated use. And thirdly, some readers might be skipping through the text looking for bullet points so that they can continue with the Flight project!

So, please reset the text settings, delete the titles on the Timeline and then ensure that both checkboxes are checked for auto text breaks and linked font size.

Additional options

The other icon at the top right is a downward pointing arrowhead which opens up a submenu. This is one control I now always check the tooltip for before opening it, because on a number of occasions I have accidentally used the reset button and lost all my work. You might want to be as cautious as me on future occasions.

Click on the icon to reveal a new menu. *Load title template*, the first entry, indicates that it's possible to load a preset template. These templates have the file type .TFX. A simple template can define fonts and font sizes, text colours and effects as well as justification. The checkboxes and centring options aren't remembered.

The title position can also be part of a template, as well as other features we have yet to look at - animation and keyframed movement. Even more impressive is that any transitions you add to the beginning or end of the title are saved as well – from a simple fade in or out to the most complex available.

To create a template, you simply apply all the parameters you wish to the current title then use the menu option Save as title template. Then to retrieve the template, start a new title then use the menu to load the template. You can edit the text either before or after you apply the template.

It took me a little while to work out why some of the templates already available were so complex. The next menu option, *Save as special effect* also creates a title template with the same file type as a simple title template, but can contain multiple layers. To create a special effect, you first group all the tracks you want to be part of the complex title template and use *Save as special effect* instead. Until we have looked at special effects in general, masks and transparency, you should stick with grouping just titles together for now.

So, if you have created a title with a background to aid visibility on a track below the title, you can bundle this graphic file along with the title styles and so on as a title special effect. When it comes to loading the more complex title style, you simply load it using the same dialogue as you would for a single track template – *Load title template*.

The next two options can save you a lot of time. If you have already added titles to your movie, and decide that you want to change them all to a different style, then change just one of the titles and use *Apply title settings* to all. Every title in the movie will have the attributes of the currently selected title applied to them, regardless of which track they are on.

You can be a bit more selective about what you change by using *Apply title settings to all following*, where only the titles to the right are affected. If you want to be even more selective, use Windows multi-selection before applying the changes or applying a title template.

Standard Presets

In the left pane of the Media pool/title tab, we have up until now been working with the *General* entry – opening up the title editor on the right. If you select *Standard* instead, a range of presets are loaded up in the right hand pane. These are the same title templates available from the drop-down menu in the title editor that I have just been describing, so if you create any new templates they will also become available here.

Standard templates with an additional flight titles custom template

The workflow here is easier. Templates that you have created have a generic thumbnail, but those supplied with the program have thumbnails that give you some idea of how they will appear when applied. You can double-click on the template to open up the default text in the editor, then accept the edited title as normal. Alternatively, you might want to drag a template onto a title that is already on the Timeline, when the new look will be applied to the existing title.

Further presets

If you work your way through the other categorises, you will find some pretty complex titles. Many are locked while others are multi-layered. The text itself can always be edited, however. You should get some good ideas and hints looking at the ones that can be edited as well. If you have the Magix 3D Maker program, you can re-edit the 3D titles, by the way.

Timecode

A series of presets are available in the Timecode section that enables you to superimpose date and time information. Some of the title effects use information from the video file if it exists. For example, *Recordtime* will use the timestamp from a MTS file, or will actually pick up the rolling record time from DV-AVI files and *Rec. date&Time* includes the shooting date. *Timecode* shows the movie time. If you wanted to send someone a video file asking them for comments, this could be added so that they can reference precise points in the movie.

Back to the Flight project

Let's return to the flight project now, and create a text template to use for the titles we are going to use:

- Open Flight over Snowdon rough cut 4.

- Place the scrubber at the start of the movie.

- Click on the T Timeline tool to create a new title. The Title editor will open in the media pool.

- Make sure the two checkboxes *Automatic text…* and *Adjust font…* are ticked.

- Select *Arial* as the font and 48 as the font size.

- Click in the *Bold* text effect button.

- Click on the title colour selection tool to open the colour picker.

- Choose the lightest blue available in the basic colours – fifth on the top row.

- Make it an even lighter shade of blue by increasing the luminance slider to give a value of 212 and save this as a custom colour. Click OK to close the colour picker.

- Open the *Advanced* box, uncheck *Shadow* and *3D* and check *Outline*.

- Select the Outline colour selection box to open the colour picker again.

- Use the custom colour as a basis, then slide the luminance down to 20.

- Select an empty Custom colour box with the arrow keys, click *Add to Custom Colours*, then close the colour picker again.

- Change the width of the outline to 4 and make sure the *Filled* box is checked.

- Make sure that *Only apply to visible TV area* is checked in the *Options* box.

- Close the *Advanced* box with the *OK* button.

So far, so good. The parameters I'm giving aren't particularly critical if you want to tweak them – as long as the face is a light colour and the edges dark. We now want to position our title:

- Click on the check mark above the title in the Program monitor. The text editing box is replaced with the orange title field.

- Drag the title down to the bottom of the screen. When you release the field, it will jump back up to stay just within the visible TV area.

- Click on the horizontal centring button.

Now all that is left to do is save this as a title template:

- Use the dropdown menu in the titler to select *Save as title template* and use the save dialogue to store your new template as *Flight Titles*.

OK, we have our template so that we can match this look and placement in later titles. Now let's change the text and other parameters so that it becomes the title for the movie:

- Double click on the title object that has been placed on track 3 at the beginning of the movie.

- Change the text to *A Flight over Snowdon*. It should automatically split over two lines. If it isn't centre-justified use the centre justification button underneath the font selection area.

- Click on the check mark to accept the changes.

- Put the scrubber at 14 seconds from the start of the movie, just before a particularly large bump in the shot. If you have changed the default scrubber behaviour to *Move play cursor when object is selected* then you will need to drop a marker here.

- Extend the Out point of the title to the 14 second mark.

- Create a fade up of 1 second at the beginning and a fade out of 1 second at the end by dragging the transition handles of the title object.

So now we have an opening title for our movie! I'm going to make some more changes to this title later, but let's move on and add some more titles:

The opening title

- At 2 minutes 20 seconds into the movie create an 8 second title *The Nantlle Ridge*, using the Flight titles template.

- Add 1 second fades to the beginning and end.

- At 2 minutes 42 seconds create an 8 second title with fades - *Approaching the peak*. The title template parameters should still be loaded. Break the title with a line break between *Approaching* and *the* and centre justify the text to give it a more balanced look.

- This title will look better at the top of the screen. Drag it up to the top so it goes as high as the cropping control will allow, then re-centre the title with the horizontal centring control.

Notice how the edges we have created allows the title to be just as easily read over the sky as it was over the ground.

Simple animation – Rolls and Crawls

We still haven't used the animation section of the title editor, so I'm going to create a simple example now. In the title editor there is an animation box containing four possible styles. Because of the way we read, in the western world at least, you are most likely to want to scroll text from right to left across the screen (known as a crawl) or from bottom to top (a roll). The options to create these effects in the other direction also exist.

The menu for simple text animation

I'm going to put a text crawl over the second *Peak and Railway – 0001* clip (the long one showing the Mountain railway) so that I can show more information than would be possible without obliterating what I'm expecting the viewer to be looking at. (I know that the shot is overexposed, but I'm going to sort that out later.)

- Select the second *Peak and Railway* clip (the twelfth on on track 1) and place the scrubber at about 3 minutes into the movie.

- Click on the Title tool and enter the following – *The mountain railway was opened in 1896 and carries tourists to the 3,560ft summit.*

- Don't worry about formatting, but apply the Flight titles template.

- In the Animation drop-down, select *From right to left.*

- Accept the title by clicking the checkbox.

A couple of things will happen. Firstly, the text becomes a single line, and secondly it will assume the same duration of the last title you made. On the Timeline, if you alter the duration of the title object down to a few seconds you will see the title wizz through frame with barely time to read it.

Roll and Crawl durations

To adjust the duration of these sorts of animations, you can use the duration box on the right of the animation section. Getting the duration correct is quite important.

- Align the beginning of the title with the start of the *Peak and Railway* clip.

- Enter 20 seconds into the box.

- Play the movie from the start of the title.

Notice how the length of the title object has automatically adjusted. Now, while the title seems much better in terms of readability, it is still crawling through frame after we cut away from the railway. We could carry on adjusting the duration using the box, but if we trim the clip on the Timeline it will automatically adjust the animation:

- Adjust the Out point of the clip so it aligns with the Out point of the *Peak and Railway* clip.

- Notice that the duration box now reads 13 seconds.

Now when you play the title, I think you will agree that it is just a little too fast. We have three alternatives. We can lengthen the shot of the railway so we can make the title longer in duration – but we may have chosen the In and Out point with care. We could apply a slow motion effect, but this tends to be noticeable. Or, in this case, I'm going to use less words!

- Edit the title to read *The mountain railway (1896) carries tourists to the 3.560 summit.*

That's a good compromise, I hope you will agree.

That's all the titles I want to you add to the movie, although feel free to add more if you wish – perhaps a closing roller caption with some credits?

- Save the movie as *Flight over Snowdon rough cut 5.*

In the next chapter I'm going to introduce you to some video effects, and the all-important topic of keyframing effects.

Working with Effects

There are a number of reasons for wanting to add effects to video, photo or audio sources in your movie. The most obvious one is to make corrections to objects that don't quite match the other objects in the movie – perhaps one video clip is a slightly different colour temperature to all the others. Even altering the volume of an audio clip can be achieved by adding an audio effect – although I've shown you how to do this without opening up the effects toolbox in an earlier chapter.

These sorts of effects can often be used to make improvements to video clips so that you can include them in your movie even if they are substandard. One example of that is the badly overexposed shot of the mountain railway at around 3 minutes into the Flight movie. I'll tackle that in a moment.

Other types of corrections include stabilisation to smooth out wobbly shots, or framing adjustments such as levelling up the horizon on a wonky photograph.

Effects can also be used for creative reasons – you could deliberately tilt a photo to give it a zany look, or apply an artistic filter to a video clip to make it look like an old film. There is also an array of tools for resizing and moving video and photos to make montages.

Most of these features are accessed in the same manner – using the Effects tab in the Media pool. When you open the tab, the browser tree on the left offers an array of categories and these fall into two types – presets that you drag from the media pool to the clip you want to modify, or effects that offer you a range of parameters that will be applied to the currently selected clip. We looked briefly at adding presets to audio objects in the audio chapter. The parameter method of working is fairly similar to the manner in which we edited titles.

A simple correction – exposure

To familiarise you with applying video effects let's run through the workflow to correct the second Peak and Railway clip that shows the Mountain railway.

- If the Flight project isn't open, load Flight over Snowdon rough cut 5.

- Drag the scrubber to roughly 3 minutes into the movie and click on a blank part of the Timeline so that no clips are selected.

- In the Media pool, select the Effects tab, and then in the tree view on the left, open the Video effects choices with the small selection arrow.

- Now select the first effect, Brightness/Contrast.

Opening an effect without a clip selected

At this point, the window on the right should just be displaying the message "Please select a photo or video object to be able to apply the effect". The point of showing you this is to make it clear that the effects are applied to the currently selected clip, or clips, and not the object where the scrubber is positioned. It's important to remember this – I still sometimes begin to make adjustments and wonder why I'm not seeing the results, and it's because the scrubber isn't displaying the selected clip.

- Click on the second *Peak and Railway* clip (showing the Mountain railway) to select it.

- The parameters for Brightness/Contrast appear on the right of the Media pool.

The parameters for Brightness/Contrast

If you are working on a reasonably-sized screen, the next feature may not seem that useful, but some adjustments you may want to make are best achieved with as large a preview monitor as possible. To lose the tree view window, you can click on the double arrow before the title of the effect above the parameters.

Now it's possible to make the monitor window wider and still see the entire parameter box.

A hidden navigation bar

A further enhancement is the small downward pointing arrow to the right of the effect name that now appears. Clicking this restores the tree view but now it is overlapping the parameter box. Click the downward arrow again and the tree disappears.

This function allows you to switch between effects quickly, even though the Media pool is minimised in size.

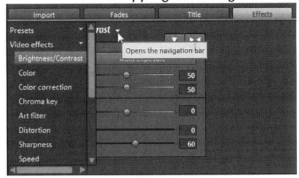
Overlapping the navigation bar

To restore the Media pool to the two window layout, click on the double arrows to the left of the effect name again.

Auto exposure

The first control is a simple on/off tool that optimises the video levels. If you use it on a reasonably well exposed clip you might well wonder what it does. This will be particularly true of a video shot with automatic exposure – it's going to try to do much the same thing as the camera's electronics do, spreading out the minimum and maximum levels in the frame to match the upper and lower limits of the video level. What both systems are bad at is any form of intelligent compensation for a strong backlight or a bright foreground object and therefore making the intended subject correctly exposed.

With the clips we currently have on the Timeline it's hard to demonstrate how powerful the auto exposure tool can be because it doesn't seem to do a great deal. Even with the Mountain railway clip it's not very effective. There is also one feature of the function that isn't immediately obvious and can be demonstrated much more easily with a specially prepared sample clip I have made.

Please locate and import the video file *variable.mp4* from the website or DVD if you want to try out this experiment. Place it at the end of the current movie and examine it by playing it. It starts too dark, but the exposure is about right by 4 seconds in, then it gets too bright.

Place the cursor at the start of the clip and make sure the new clip is selected. Now return to the effects tab in the Media pool and click on the *Autoexposure* button. Wow! That's better. If you examine the video closely you will see the picture is quite "noisy" because electronic gain has been added, but never the less the exposure looks much better.

Now play the clip. Ah, not so good. The new settings are fixed, and as soon as the exposure starts to increase, the new settings cause the clip to become vastly overexposed.

Using auto exposure on a test clip

Resetting effect parameters

Having applied an effect, there are many ways of clearing it. If you decide immediately that you don't want to use what you have done, you can of course use Undo or CTRL-Z. In the case of Auto exposure it's just as easy to click on the button again – one click adds it and another removes the effect. If you expand the Timeline view of the clip you will see the effect description (Auto lighting) added and removed from the clip as you do so.

For many other effects the easiest way is to return a clip to normal is to use the reset button top right of the parameter box. We saw this when working on titles. Click on the button with the two small opposing arrowheads and all the parameters for the currently selected effect will be normalised. If you want to remove all the effects on a clip, you can do so using the either the effects menu available to the left of the reset tool or the clip context menu, both of which contain a Reset video effects command. It's also possible to selectively switch effects on or off or remove them individually and I'll show you how to do that shortly.

For now, reset the Auto exposure by any of the above means, set the scrubber to the end of the clip and try again.

Now the end of the clip has been reduced in level so it looks OK, but I expect you can guess what the earlier parts look like without even scrubbing down to them – indeed, they are all now underexposed. Delete the effect, set the scrubber to the middle of the clip and try again. This time nothing appears to change, even though the effect can be seen to have been applied because the Auto exposure tool is highlighted.

The manual is a bit vague on the topic, but hopefully now you can see that the levels applied by Auto exposure are decided upon by looking at the current frame displayed in Preview – in other words where the scrubber is parked. So you will get different results for different positions. You can just about see this if you also work on the first or last frames of the Mountain railway clip, but there is nowhere throughout the clip where Auto exposure works well.

A radical exposure repair

Unfortunately, Auto exposure isn't an effect that can be Keyframed – we can't vary it over time. However, it can be applied in a rather painstaking manner to shots that vary in exposure and this sometimes might help you out in a spot. It's unlikely to work on video shot on a camera set to auto exposure, though. You might want to try this out with the test clip we have just loaded.

Zoom the Timeline view in close, set the scrubber to the second frame of the clip, press the T key to split the first frame from the top and then press the forward arrow key to move to the start of the next frame. Repeat this 50 times (I said it was painstaking!) until the first two seconds of the clip is subdivided up into 50 individual frames. Now park the scrubber at the beginning and select all of the subsequent frames. Return to the Effects tab and select Auto exposure again.

When you examine the result you will see each individual frame has been set to its optimum level, and with such accuracy that the exposure now appears to be fixed – and at the correct setting. Look closely and you will see the "noise" of the video gain is very noticeable at the start of the clip, and reduces as the correction becomes less.

Splitting a clip into individual frames to repair the exposure

I've used this technique to rescue what would otherwise be unusable shots – a lot of work but worth the effort.

Brightness/Contrast

Let's return to the project.

- Delete the test clip from the end of the movie.

- Scrub to the mid-point of the Mountain railway clip and select it.

- Click on the M icon on the track 3 header to hide the title and give us a clear view of the problem.

- Open up the *Brightness/Contrast* effect as described earlier.

I'm not quite sure what when wrong with the exposure at this point in the shoot. I had pressed the backlight compensation control at some point, but must have set it too high. The result is a shot that has its highlights burned out. Some of the detail can be recovered, but not much. The basic Brightness and Contrast controls can do most of what we need.

Brightness affects the overall level of the picture and contrast is the amount of variation between the bright and dark parts. To complicate matters, the eye registers these values in a non-linear way. Even further complications are added by the reproduction systems – cameras and video displays aren't capable of reproducing as a wide range as the eye can detect – and by the viewing environment – it's easier to see details on a screen if the ambient light is lower. There is one more complication – our eyes require a higher contrast to resolve both high and low frequency changes in brightness - fine details and subtle variations are harder to see than those in a mid-range of around 6 cycles per degree of view. And that's before our eyesight starts to deteriorate with age!

The practical upshot of this is that for a good result, if we adjust one of the parameters, we generally need to adjust the other.

Play with the two sliders to see what I mean. Decrease the brightness down to 30 by dragging the slider, we can see a little more detail in the mountains behind Snowdon, but the picture begins to look washed out.

Resetting individual parameters

A tip – although you can alter a parameter by dragging or by double-clicking and entering numbers in the value box on the right, if you want to quickly return a slider to its default setting, you can double click on the button of the slider itself. Do this now on the Brightness slider button and it will return to the value it begins at, which is 50.

Now adjust the contrast. Decreasing the value means the differences in level get smaller – eventually you can't see any details at all. Increasing the contrast makes the whites lighter and the blacks darker – but most the intermediate shades of grey are still too bright.

- Set the contrast to 70.

Now the dark parts are better, but the overall picture is too bright and we are unable to see any detail in them.

- Slide the brightness down to 30.

We seem to have brought most of the levels back into a range where both the display and our eyes can perceive them.

You might want to experiment a bit more with these values. I think what we have is pretty good. Some details just simply are not recorded in the file and we can never get them back. To do anything better we need more powerful tools other than just globally altering the brightness and contrast.

Adjusting the levels makes a reasonable improvement

Effects overview window

I want to explain the rest of the features of the Effects tabs before we explore more effects. At the very bottom of the Media pool is a bar that contains three icons and the currently selected file name on the left, and a duration box and clock icon on the right. The first tool on the right is an arrow that opens the Effects overview above –

if it isn't open as shown in the screenshot, click on it now. The next two arrow tools let you navigate to the previous or next clip on the Timeline, and the box gives the duration of the current clip. The clock tool opens up a dialogue that allows you to change the duration of the selected clip, but only works with photos.

You might still not be seeing all the information depicted in the screenshot, as the area above has a variable height. Hover over the black bar to generate a vertical double headed arrow, click and drag to expand and contract contract the window below. There should be two effects in the list, so adjust the view so you can see both of them.

We are revealing more and more complexity here, much of which is concerned with keyframing, but just for now let's concentrate on the list of effects, and in particular, the left side.

The Effects overview

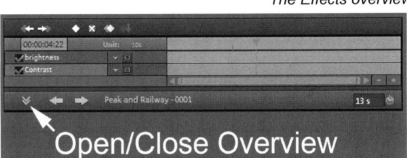

There are two labels for the two currently applied effects, brightness and contrast. To the left of the labels are check boxes and these turn the individual effects on and off, without changing the parameter values. Click in the brightness checkbox and the clip reverts to the default setting of 50. Click on the contrast box as well, and the clip is now in its original condition. Check both boxes and we have our correction back.

These boxes are great for checking what the parameters are actually doing, or disabling a particular parameter temporarily will let you work on others more easily.

To the right of the labels are small drop-downs that offer you menu options for working on effects. Only one option concerns us at the moment – *Delete effects*. This removes the currently selected parameter from the list and the effect from the clip. You don't actually need to use this option, though because if you click on the label and press the Delete key, it has the same function. We will look at the other options in the menu when we look at keyframing.

Masks/Mattes

The next icon to the right opens up a whole new box of tricks. When it is highlighted it indicates that a mask has been applied to the effect. You may wonder what a mask does, and the easiest way to explain that is to apply one. First of all, I'm going to use an example, then apply it for a practical purpose.

The mask icon and it's tooltip

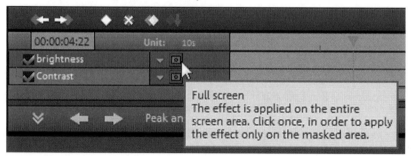

Click on the mask icon alongside the brightness parameter for our *Peak and Railway* clip. A windows style *Select effects mask* dialogue opens, pointing at the location where Magix has stored a set of pre-made mask files. You will see two folders; we are only working in standard definition, so open the SD folder and select the file Matte 10_0001.png. Make a mental note what it looks like before you open it.

By the way, if you have the standard version of MEP, you may not have a vast array of masks. I've included the two I've used here on the DVD and website.

Loading a mask

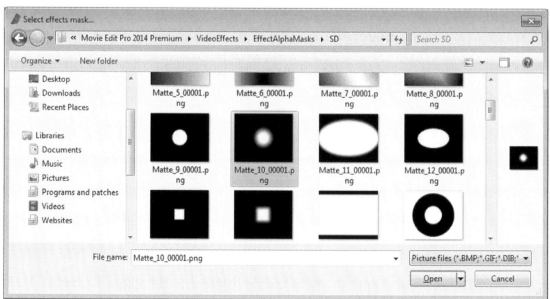

If this were an HD project, we would be best off using the files in the HD folder. Incidentally, Mask and Matte are more or less interchangeable terms – Matte being of French origin but widely used in the film industry thanks to the Lumière brothers. A Matte was a term for the plain backing to a picture. The term was also applied to the pieces of card placed in front of a lens to blank out sections of a film so that a double exposure could be used to create a different background. This also explains why professional lens shades and filter holders are often called Matte boxes, although these days they are hardly ever used to hold mattes.

When you load the mask, you should see a number of things change. In the program monitor, the centre of the picture is still being modified by the effect parameters, but outside the circle the effect isn't being applied. Also, a new clip has been added to the Timeline beneath the selected clip. This is the mask file.

Let's talk about the way the mask works first. It is a .png file, a type of still picture that can hold transparency information. The centre circle is solid, so all the effect is applied. The outer part is transparent, so none of the effect is being applied.

If you look carefully you can see the parameters are faded out around the edges of the circle. Remembering back to the appearance of the mask, the edges of the circle were blurred; it faded out around the edges as well. So the effect follows the level of transparency of the mask – as it becomes more "see-through", less of the effect is applied. If I had asked you to use a mask with a sharply defined edge, the effect would have abruptly stopped.

The mask added to the Timeline and the effect it has

There is a slight anomaly the first time you add a mask. The parameter that you loaded the mask to is affected and the icon turns red, showing it is active. However, so are other parameters – in our case, contrast has been affected, but it's mask icon isn't highlighted even though it should be. Click on the mask icon for that parameter and you won't get offered the chance to load a mask – the effects for that clip already has a mask loaded and it is already in use. Click on it again and the icon ceases to be active and so does the effect. Click on it again and the mask come back into play.

In my opinion this is a bug, albeit a minor one. After adding a mask, if you refresh the Effects overview by selecting another clip and then returning, all the mask icons are lit up.

You are only allowed one mask per clip. If you want more complexity you will have to use more tracks.

The mask object added to the Timeline is placed on the first free track beneath the clip it is associated with. It's also grouped to the clip, so any time you try to move or edit the clip, the mask sticks with it. Normally the mask object will be the same duration as the clip, but you can confuse the program by having an object on a track below that doesn't start at the beginning of the target clip – the mask won't overwrite the other object and therefore may not extend the full length of the target clip. Because of this, and the possibility of confusing both yourself and the program, I'd recommend that you consider creating a clear track specifically for masks if there is any question about where the mask might go, or what duration it might end up.

The mask control

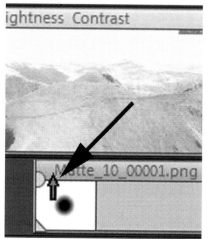

An object that is being used as a mask has a special icon added to it when you hover over it – a downward pointing arrow near the start of the mask. If you click on this, the effect is inverted. So, if you can find the correctly shaped mask for what you are trying to achieve, but it is black where it should be white, you can flip the "polarity" using the arrow.

If you want to change the mask, you have to delete it – and that may mean ungrouping it. Click on our mask and use the Ungroup tool above the Timeline then delete the mask clip using the Clip context menu or the Delete key. The mask effect disappears, but the original parameters are still applied to the clip.

Let's do something practical with masking. I would have like to have made the sky brighter in the Mountain railway clip but found it difficult with just brightness and contrast. With other effects it is possible, but I'm going to use a mask. If you have been following the above demonstration, delete the mask we have just created if you haven't done so already.

- Select the *Peak and Railway* clip, open the effects tab at the Brightness/contrast effect and check the settings are still 30/70

- Click on the mask icon after the brightness label in the Effects overview

- In the dialogue box, open the SD folder

Scroll down the list of matte files. We have effectively darkened the sky with the effect in place and we are looking for a mask that will apply the effect to the lower part of the picture, but not the top. We also want the effect to fade out gradually. With masks, the white area is where the effect is going to be applied fully, the grey areas less and the black area not at all. Although we can further manipulate the mask once it is loaded, it would be great if there was one that fitted the bill quite closely. There are two files that are the correct layout – numbers 3 and 48 – and the way the gradient is arranged, I think the best bet is the file matte_3_00001.png. I tried the other one and it only just lightened the very top of the picture.

- Select file *matte_3_00001.png* and click on *OK*.

- If the scrubber isn't parked on the Mountain railway clip move it there so we can examine the effect.

You can immediately see a problem. The project is widescreen, but the matte obviously isn't – it's 4:3 and we are seeing the effect not being applied to the sides of the video. This does at least give us a good idea of how the matte is affecting the video. To fix the problem, we need to change the properties of the mask.

Changing the object properties

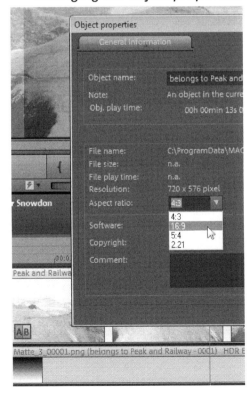

- Right click on the mask object on the Timeline.

- Select the bottom command from the context menu – *Object properties*.

- In the File Information box, use the drop-down to change Aspect ratio from 4:3 to 16:9. Click *OK*.

- The next dialogue box asks us if we want to change the other objects selected, Click either box because the other object is already 16:9.

- The next dialogue box is redundant in this case as well – the project is already 16:9. Choose either.

The mask has made a pretty good job of keeping the sky bright, while the brightness/contrast effect has vastly improved the exposure of the mountain in the foreground.

In more complex situations you can reposition masks with the movement effects, animate them manually with keyframes or automatically with motion tracking. You can also create custom masks using an external photo editing program.

- Make an incremental save - rough cut 6 – if you are going to try out the next set of experiments.

Gamma

In photography and video reproduction, Gamma is used to describe the non-linear way in which luminance is displayed and perceived. The eye does not see a light which is theoretically twice as powerful as being twice as bright. Additionally, displays don't behave in a linear manner. If we adjust the Gamma of a picture, we affect the gradient between light and dark. Magix call the effect Selective brightness which describes it quite well.

In MEP, you can apply a different display curve in one of four ways. An overall adjustment is just labelled as Gamma. You can also selectively alter the curve in the Lows, Mid or Highs regions.

Using the test chart to experiment

Understanding gamma is made easier if you apply it to a test chart, rather than a picture. I've prepared one for you to experiment with which you can download or copy from the Demo DVD. It's called gamma test chart. I haven't included any further screenshots because I doubt if the book printing process will show the changes anywhere nearly as well as you can see them within the program. Put the photo at the end of the Timeline and apply the brightness/contrast effect, then try the following adjustments.

Set the section to Gamma and reduce the level. Everything but the peak whites get darker, but if you reduce the gamma too much you can't distinguish between 10% luminance and completely black. Reduce it even further and even the 15% band looks completely black. If you had a picture that didn't have any properly dark areas you could reduce the overall gamma to improve it. In fact, that's what we could have done to the overexposed Mountain railway shot. I wouldn't have been able to demonstrate brightness, contrast and masks, though!

Increasing the overall Gamma has the opposite effect – everything except true black gets brighter, but increase it too much and you burn out the white areas – you cannot distinguish between 95% and full white.

Switch to Lows and try again. The curve is now affecting just the dark areas, so increasing the value doesn't ever blend the 90% region into true white, but the difference between 10% and true black now looks huge – the 10% band looks more like it should be labelled 50%! Highs has the same sort of effect on the light areas.

Mid is even more interesting. The middle 48% and 52% bands are changed greatly as you adjust the gamma, but the effect is considerably less on both the black and white areas.

What you should notice most about any of these gamma adjustments it the true black (0%) and white (100%) are not altered at all. They are powerful tools that are best used by studying the picture you want to correct and deciding what you want to do to it before you apply gamma correction.

HDR

The Plus and Premium versions of MEP 2014 also have High Dynamic Range effects. Some cameras can make multiple exposures or record a wider range of levels and then the pictures can be manipulated by software so that all the detail is combined into one image that can be displayed within the limited dynamic range of the display medium – whether that is photographic paper or a TV screen.

Even normally shot photos and video have a little detail in them that will normally not be displayed. By selectively adjusting the gamma when adjacent picture areas are either predominantly light or dark, detail can be displayed that you wouldn't normally see.

This approach sometimes works really well, and at other times it looks rubbish. If you have the test chart still loaded, I can show you how it looks when it's not working well, then I'll show you doing a good job.

Reset the effects on the chart photo at the end of the Timeline, set the HDR blur to zero and then adjust the HDR gamma to 100%. It's not really doing anything that you can't do with normal gamma, although it is a bit more radical – the mid greys are actually blended in together – we are stretching out the white and black parts of the scale so much we have lost mid-range definition – because we can't have our cake and eat it something has to be sacrificed.

What about the Blur parameter? Slide that up to 100% and something very weird happens. Where there is a radical change of luminance there is a change of gamma, that then fades out. On a picture with lots of sharp changes and plain areas – such as our chart – the effect is very odd. The human eye can make out the blurred areas and isn't being fooled at all.

Let's try the effect on a different source. Scroll to the landing shot – the last clip of the flight movie proper - and also select it. Notice that the default setting for HDR blur is 60, then increase the HDR gamma to 50.

Notice that we can see detail on the dashboard. Admittedly it's very noisy detail, but you can make out the instruments. Look closely and you will see that the gamma has been tweaked, but only for the dark sections, and when we reach the windscreen although there is a bit of a halo on the edges it looks like a reflection.

HDR off (left) and on (right)

What's more, more detail is available in the sky – scrub through and you can see more cloud detail. The HDR effect is looking at small areas in order to extract as much detail as possible. A neat effect if you don't overdo it!

You can see where it isn't working too well – check out the bottom right corner where there is quite a bit of shading when we reach the runway. The blocky look of the sunshade is also somewhat objectionable, but remember this is MPEG-2 video at quite a low Bitrate – if you were applying this to high Bitrate HD video it would be much more effective.

Delete the test clips from the end of the movie and reset your experimental gamma effects, or if you are not sure what else you have changed, reload the rough cut 6 incremental save I suggested you made before the gamma experiments.

Colour

The Colour effect

There are a number of features within the Colour effect. You will mostly use these to correct problems, but it's also possible to use them for artistic effect as well.

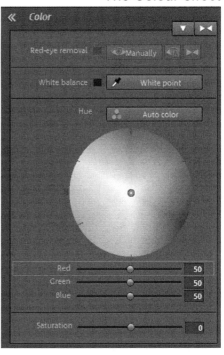

Red eye removal only works on photos and will attempt to reduce the red effect in people's eyes caused by camera flashes reflecting off the blood inside the eyeball. The auto mode will not always work, in which case you can use the manual mode which prompts you to draw a rectangle around the problem areas. You can reset the red-eye removal tool on its own with the reset icon.

White balance is a useful feature, particularly if you have been using incorrect camera settings.

A word about White balance

The human eye and brain adapts to recognise "white" as white. Daylight is blue relative to most artificial light while old style tungsten bulbs give out a much more noticeable yellow light. This variation is measured as a colour temperature – the temperature that an ideal "black body" radiator (such as the Sun) emits light of the same hue as the white light we are measuring. A candle might have a colour temperature of 2000 degrees Kelvin. It's light will look yellow if it isn't the only source of light. Normal daylight is around 6000 degrees K, but can climb much higher.

If you have lit a whole scene by candlelight, and used automatic colour balance, the picture won't look yellow. You actually might want to bring some of that yellow back into the picture for artistic effect. On the other hand, if you had the camera on a daylight setting, the video will look far too warm (yellow) and you may want to cool it down (blue).

White point is a tool that lets you choose what should be white. If you check the White balance box before you have set the white point you won't see any difference. Click on White point and a dialogue will open (unless you disabled it) explaining that you need to select the part of the picture you want to define as "white". Hover over the program monitor and the mouse cursor turns into an "eyedropper". Choose a section of the video that should be white, click, and that which become the reference point. You can then enable or disable the correction with the checkbox.

An ideal shot to experiment with is at 30 seconds into the Flight movie. Click on the white of the plane and nothing seems to change because the plane is, and should be, white. Click on the yellow stripe on the fire tender that is just coming into the foreground and you will see a very radical, and very wrong, change of colour balance!

Experimenting with the White point control

I've found this tool very useful, but sometimes it's only a starting point and you might need to use further corrections. The Hue parameters in the box below can be used in conjunction with or instead of applying the White point tool.

The Auto colour feature works in the same manner as the Auto exposure tool – it analyses the video at the current scrubber position and attempts to balance the colours and saturation. In the footage we currently have on the Timeline it is more likely to make the colours more vibrant than alter the balance significantly.

The colour wheel below has complementary colours on opposite sides of the wheel. If your picture is looking too red, dragging the dot that starts in the centre away from red area adds Cyan to the balance which neutralises the red. You may also need to increase the saturation – the amount of colour – to compensate. This is controlled by the slider at the bottom of the box. Above that are three sliders for more radical changes that control the Red, green and Blue elements – the three primary additive colours that together in equal amount make up White.

The colour wheel can be reset to having no effect by double clicking on the dot.

Colour correction

In my opinion this effect should really be called Secondary colour correction. It duplicates what you can do with the colour wheel in the normal Color effect tool, but also allows you to apply the effect to either a selected "foreground" or "background" area.

Again, a quick demonstration will give a clearer idea of how to use the effect, and then on this occasion I'm going to add it to our movie.

In the effects tab, open up *Design elements* in the tree view and click on *Test images*. Look for the SMPTE (PAL) set of colour bars and drag the image to the end of the Timeline. Select the object and park the scrubber over it so it is displayed in the program monitor, and then switch back to *Video effects/Color correction*.

The basic principle is that the video or photo source is split into foreground and background areas, and then you can adjust the colour settings of both areas, or the picture as a whole. Selection of the areas is controlled by the top box. Click in the Add radio button and then hover over the Program monitor; the mouse cursor changes to the eyedropper icon we saw when setting the White point earlier. Click on the Blue bar on the right and observe the grey hatching indicating the area we have set to be "foreground" – the thin blue area on the left is also hatched, and therefore selected.

Selecting a foreground area

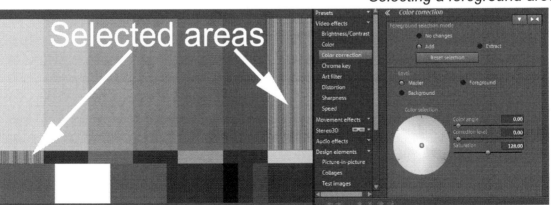

We aren't limited to one colour. Click on the Cyan bar third from the left and that too is added. In a real example, you would probably be selecting various shades of the same colour to build up a selection. OK, now that we have one range of colours added to the foreground, we can also remove sections. There isn't a definable "tolerance" level to selections so at some point you are going to possibly select a shade that has unwanted consequences – perhaps adding parts of the image that you don't want to included. Switch to the *Extract* radio button and click on the Blue bar. We are left with just the Cyan areas.

If we are unhappy with the selection, we can reset it with the dedicated button rather than resetting the whole effect. When we are happy we can lock the selection by using the *No Change* radio button to avoid unwanted changes. Let's do that now.

So, Cyan is our foreground. In the next box down click on the Foreground radio button, then adjust the colour wheel. You can turn Cyan (and anything else included as Foreground) into a completely different colour or just make subtle adjustments. If you want a greater range you can adjust the saturation slider, or if you want to make it monochrome you can set the saturation to zero.

You can't make the Cyan a primary Red, though, however hard you try. This is because we are adjusting the colour, not replacing it, and red is the complimentary colour to cyan. You would need to remove the Cyan completely, rather than add to it. To test this, switch back the Add selection mode and click on a Black area of the test chart, then adjust the colours again. With the saturation set to 255, the colour angle 0 and correction level 0, you can just make the pure black area underneath the red bar match – it's the area at the bottom of the frame below the left side of the bar.

None of the background has been affected. Switch to that radio button and pull down the saturation to see how it can be corrected completely independently of the foreground.

Finally, we can correct both areas together by switching to the *Master* radio button. As you can see, the scope for adjustment is huge. (It's not quite as huge as the range available with the tool in the professional version of Magix – VEP X5 - though, because there you can adjust the colours separately in three areas – low, mid and high luminance!)

Let's now put this tool to a practical purpose. If we look back at the Mountain railway clip, although we have made significant improvements I would have preferred to make the sky a little blue to match the other shots. Delete the experimental clips or restore our incrementally saved project, then follow these steps:

- Select the Mountain railway clip and park the scrubber in the middle of it.

- In the Media pool, select *Effects/Video effects/Color correction*.

- In the upper Foreground selection mode box, click on the *Add* radio button.

- Hover over the Program window to generate the eyedropper tool, then click on the sky very close to the top of frame.

- An upper area consisting mostly of sky should become grey and hatched. If you have generated a larger area, try resetting the selection and re selecting.

- When you are happy, select the *No Change* button, and then in the area below, the *Foreground* button.

Selecting the sky

- The hatched area may disappear. Don't worry. Adjust the color wheel to tint the sky area blue.

- I've settled on Color angle 215, Correction level 25 and Saturation 128. You may want to be more or less subtle!

- Unmute the title track if it is still muted.

- Save the movie again as *Flight over Snowdon, rough cut 7*.

A worthwhile improvement, don't you think? While this might seem a trivial use of the Color correction tool, I hope it shows you the principles.

More Video effects

Now I have established the principles of applying effects I'm just going to briefly mention the next few. I'll be using some of them in more advanced examples later on.

Chroma key automatically generates a matte so that you can substitute areas defined by brightly coloured area, black, white or transparency with other video or photo images. You most likely know this as Green Screen, where you place a subject in front of a green cloth and then electronically replace the green cloth with a false background. The tool has many more uses as well. I'll be using Chromakey later in the book.

Art Filter allows you to apply a whole range of effects on to a video or photo source. You should just run through the possibilities now to see what wild and wacky things you can do. Don't discount if as a tool you could use for more subtle adjustments, though – it's not just for making 70's pop videos!

Distortion contains another box of tricks which will provide hours of endless fun. One option you might find useful is the Mosaic effect, often seen when you want to scramble information of a sensitive nature – the number plate of a car, for example.

Sharpness can be particularly useful to add a bit of zing to poor quality video, but if you overdo things it can look awful as well! You will also find effects to blur your videos here too. Like all the effects I've mentioned, they can be applied via a mask so you can selectively blur parts of your video for artistic purposes. The Artistic blur feature is something you might consider adding with keyframes to enhance a transition.

Speed effects

The ability to speed up or slow down motion is a very useful tool. We have looked at the use of the Stretch tool in the Timeline Editing chapter, and that allows us to use slow and fast motion to create a clip that fits a required duration. We can also use it for "freehand" speed control, but the Effects/Speed tool allows you to do things by numbers – you can set a precise speed. You can also use it to reverse a motion so the action runs backwards. The other great feature about using the effect is that it is keyframable – so we can change the playback speed over time. I still haven't introduced keyframing yet and will do so with an effect that is easier to demonstrate.

The other thing we have to be wary about is that because the speed effect adjusts the duration of a clip, it will interact with other clips following the one you adjust. Let's start by looking at that issue in conjunction with the Flight project.

Remember – Track 1 is special

If we are altering the speed of a video clip on track 1, MEP assumes this is the master track and deals with the other tracks accordingly. It can deal with them in one of two ways. Note that the Insert mode has no bearing at all – leave it in Automatic if you like. In order to change the Timeline behaviour you use the Mouse selection mode.

If you have the Single object mode selected and a clip on track 1, none of the other clips on any tracks have their position changed when you use the speed effect. If you speed up a clip, therefore reducing the duration, a gap appears in the movie.

- Open the Flight over Snowdon rough cut 7 project.

- Locate the first Peak and Railway clip on track 1 at 00:02:53:13 and select it.

- Select the Mouse mode for single objects.

- Open the *Video effects/Speed effect* box.

- Alter the *Factor* slider to 4.

Speeding up a clip

The duration of the clip has shrunk to 18 frames, the frame rate is showing as 100 (4 times 25) and a gap has appeared on track 1 following the adjusted clip.

- Change the Factor to .25

The duration is now 12 seconds and the frame rate 6.25. Now the clip has been lengthened, it has extended itself into the next clip, and this is showing as a transition. This is a classic example of Overwrite that we have seen when trimming clips before.

Slowing a clip in Single object mode

We don't want the transition, though, and the only way to avoid it is either to re-trim the following clip, or move everything along to make room. This is when we use the alternative mouse mode. Both Mouse mode for a Track and Mouse mode for all tracks work in the same manner here – I'll use the former.

- Double click on the Factor slider button to reset the speed to 1.

- Select Mouse mode for a track.

- Change the factor to 0.25.

Using Mouse mode for a track

At first glance that seems perfect. The very snatched, wobbly, shot has been slowed down nicely. It could be a bit smoother but because we are working with interlaced footage this is a bit difficult to fix – the footage would need to be de-interlaced (reducing the resolution) before the Interpolate intermediate images checkbox would make things look smoother rather that actually worse.

There is a problem with the Timeline, though. Looking at track 4, the music beneath the extended clip has stayed in the same place, but where there is a cut (caused by using a different emotion) the second part of the music has moved down 9 seconds so that it is still in the same position relative to the video above.

If this was a title or sound effect that is exactly what we want to happen, but Movie Edit Pro can't double guess everything we might want it to do! Even if we had grouped the music clips together it would have broken the grouping in order to maintain sync. In this case it is simply a case of moving the second clip back to the left. Alternatively, assuming you have nothing else on the track other than the music, you can lock the track with the padlock tool before applying the speed effect.

Things are slightly worse when you shorten rather than lengthen a clip with the Speed effect:

- Change the speed factor to 4.00.

Now our clip has shrunk, everything has moved up to the left – no gap this time. However, the second music clip has also moved up, overwriting the first clip, and this time there isn't even an automatic transition generated because the music isn't on track 1. So in this case we might not notice a problem until we came to play the music. If you do that now you will notice a jump.

- Reset the effect again (or reload the project).

- Lock track 4 and check Mouse mode for a track is selected.

- Change the factor to 0.25.

- Unlock track 4, then save the movie as *Flight over Snowdon rough cut 8*.

By the way, it is possible to have a greater range of speed control than the slider allows. I'll show you how in a few pages time.

Speed on other tracks

The next section is a demonstration – I'm not making a further change yet, I just want to show the different behaviour when you aren't working with track 1.

Switch to Mouse mode for single objects, select the Approaching Snowdon clip, hold down CTRL and drag a copy to track 2 below. Now adjust the speed factor of the clip to 0.6. It increases in duration, but nothing else moves. However, this isn't because there is a gap following it, it's because of the mouse mode. Set the speed factor to 0.25 and the gap is filled completely, but if you play the clip, it is truncated – the Length should be 48 seconds, but it's only occupying 24 seconds on the Timeline. It hasn't overwritten the following clip in any way, even with a transition. Shorten the clip to a factor of 4.0 and nothing else moves either. This is the safest way to alter the speed of overlays or animated titles.

Switching to Mouse mode for a Track, and then altering the duration via the speed effect will cause objects on other tracks to move, but when overlaps are about to occur, they do so differently. If you lengthen the clip, it makes a gap in all the other tracks where required. If you shorten it, however, instead of the truncation we get when working on track 1 we get transitions.

So, you can see that you need to choose the mouse mode with care when applying speed effects on multi-track projects. If in doubt, use the track mode because you will be warned of any possible problems by the appearance of new transitions.

Converting frame rates

One issue that may confront you when you work with a variety of video sources is the mismatch of frame rates. You may be working with a PAL project but need to include some 30fps video from a NTSC source, perhaps, or the other way around. When you play a clip with a frame rate that differs from the project settings you will see jerky movement caused either by duplicate or missing frames.

If you are willing to put up with a change in speed and duration then changing the frame rate of the incorrect clip to that of the project by using the drop down *Frame rate* box in the speed effect will ensure that at least the movement is smooth.

Changing the frame rate

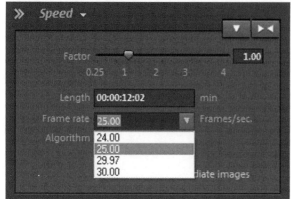

If you apply it to real world video of, for example, a car driving down the road, the car may be travelling a little faster or slower than reality, though!

Where this tool will be most helpful is where you are trying to use motion backgrounds or other stock footage which isn't available at 25 fps. You can even compensate for video shot at a true 30fps, rather than the more strictly accurate NTSC rate of 29.97 fps.

Audio algorithm

You can't apply the Speed effect to audio clips on their own - there is a tool for that in the audio effects. When audio is linked to video, however, you need to choose how the audio is treated. The Algorithm drop down box offers *Timestretching*, which attempts to keep the pitch unchanged, or *Resampling*, which does change the pitch. Changing the pitch may not always be very successful, particularly with large changes (and sometimes quite small ones). Resampling often can be distracting, if not downright comic. You need to choose, but sometimes it might be best not to include the audio at all.

Reversing video

When you engage the *Reversed* checkbox, MEP writes out a temporary file with the frame rearranged backwards and uses that. You see the effect as you scrub through the video as well as when you play it. Unchecking the box reverts to the original source file, but if you re-apply the effect it should be able to find the temporary file again, saving you a little time.

If you want to experiment, try the second clip of the flight movie!

Adding a freeze frame

There is another shot that I said needed work – the close up of the castle. Let's begin by slowing it down:

- Reload rough cut 8 if you need to.

- Select the clip on track 1 starting at 00:03:26:01.

- Set Mouse mode for a track.

- Open the speed effect and change the factor to 0.25.

Not very good, really. It's still not long enough, and the framing goes way off. What I'd like to do is freeze the shot after a few seconds, and there is a tool for this. Unfortunately, the tool doesn't work reliably on video that has already been slowed down, so we need to reset the effects:

- With the Mouse mode still set to a track, reset the speed *Factor* to 1.

- Jog the clip to 00:03:26:05 MTC, 00:08:51:09 BITC (the grey code burnt into the clip).

- Right click on the clip and select *Create still frame* from the context menu.

Selecting the still frame function

The clip gets split into two parts at the scrubber. The first part plays as normal, and the part after the scrubber is frozen. Notice it is still a video clip; it hasn't been converted to a still photo, so the quality should match the previous shot.

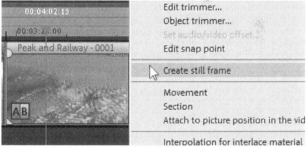

We can now trim the clip and the video will still remain frozen. So if your frame of choice were, for example, the very last frame, you could create a freeze and although it was only one frame long, you could then increase the duration.

I'm going to adjust the duration of the freeze anyway:

- Switch to Mouse mode for ALL tracks.

- Hover over the edit at the end of the frozen shot to generate dual trim cursor.

- Drag right. As you do so, a tooltip should appear showing the current movie time.

- Adjust it to 00:03:29:05 and release the mouse button.

The clip is now 3 seconds long. Everything on the Timeline to the right should have shifted to accommodate the trim.

Our effect still isn't long enough, though, so let's slow down the first part before the freeze.

- Select the clip before the frozen frame.

- In the Speed effect, you can see it is only 4 frames long.

- Slow it down to 0.25.

Now, this is a little better, but it could still be longer/slower. We have run out of range on the adjustment slider though. Fortunately, we aren't just limited to using it!

Entering a value for greater speed range

- In the Length box, currently reading 16 frames, I want you to change the value to 00:00:03:00 (three seconds).

- You will need to click on the individual units to alter them – click on the seconds so just they are highlighted and type 03.

- The highlight moves to the frames units. Type 00.

- Press Enter.

That's a very handy thing to know – typing in a duration allows you a far greater range of slow or fast motion. It only allows a greater range if you don't have audio included in the effect, so you may have to move audio to a separate track.

You may think that the durations of these slowed down shots are a bit long, but I'll be adding some transitions later in the book.

- Before we make any more changes, please save the movie as rough cut 9.

Movement effects

The next entry in the tree view is for Movement effects. Close the Video effects branch and open the Movement effects branch with the small arrows to the left.

Now you can see there is quite an array of choices. They are presented in the order in which you are most likely to use them, but what isn't immediately clear is that many of the options have overlapping functions. They are also applied in different ways. Before we examine them in detail, I think it would be helpful to summarise what they do.

The Movement effects

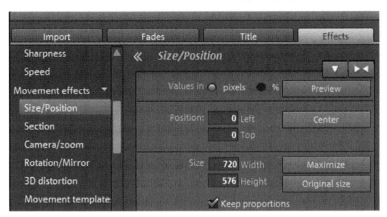

Size/Position controls the two dimensional size and position of the current video or photo relative to the display screen. All these parameters can be keyframed - altered over time.

Section selects a part of the video or photo and discards the rest – it's a crop tool. You can choose to leave the cropped source at its new size, or blow it up to the full size of the screen. You would use this to isolate a part of the source before applying other effects. Section can't be keyframed.

Camera/Zoom is another tool. It makes it easy to add simple animated two dimensional moves to a clip. It doesn't do anything that could not be achieved with the Size/Position parameters in conjunction with keyframing.

Rotation/Mirror allows you spin the picture about an axis. At its simplest it works on the Z axis – treating the source as a 2 dimensional object that you can rotate. Special tools are provided for levelling a wonky horizon, flipping a picture that was shot Portrait mode or making a reflected image. You can also rotate about the three dimensional X and Y axis.

3D distortion isn't a stereoscopic effect. It's a warping effect that lets you move the corner points of the source so that isn't rectangular, with the picture content being distorted to suit.

So, of the five effects, Section and Camera/Zoom are tools, while the other three give us total control of how the source is displayed relative to the display screen.

Using the Program monitor to adjust a source

If you have read the Titles chapter, you will already know that we can manipulate an object's position by using handles. This is also the main method which you use for adding movement effects to photos and videos. You can type in parameters as well.

Let's use the Flight movie to demonstrate. Select the first clip on track 1, place the scrubber at the start of the movie and open the *Effects/Movement effects/Size/Position* effect.

There may not initially be any handles or dotted lines visible. At the top of the Size/Position parameters boxes are two radio buttons and a Preview/Edit button. Click on the Edit button and nine dots should appear connected by dotted lines in the Program monitor. Now you should be able to reposition the clip.

Hover over the program monitor and in most places you will generate a four-way cursor. Click, hold and then drag down and left; the dots and lines move, but the picture doesn't. Release the mouse button. Ah, the picture has moved to be contained within the lines. Checking the parameter boxes shows that the new position is marked by new values for Left and Top. Toggling to the "%" (percent) radio button shows the parameters in different values. Click on the *Center* button and the picture returns to its normal position.

Program monitor in edit mode

Adjusting the handles around the edges alters the size, but unless you uncheck the *Keep proportions* box, the side handles work on both height and width. The *Original size* button restores the picture to its opening settings while the Maximise button also centres it.

Making the picture smaller with the handles is easy, but although zooming in is possible; it is easier to use the slider in the parameter box.

Zooming into a picture

It's worth bearing in mind that if you zoom into a video source it will be degraded unless the movie resolution is less than the source video. If you have included some HD footage in a Movie destined to be burned to a SD DVD then you can reframe quite a bit, but normally you can't zoom in more than around 10% before the video starts to look jagged or blocky.

Photos are a different matter – most digital stills camera have more than HD resolution, and the very best DSLRs have even higher resolution than 4K video. It's simply a matter of dividing the horizontal resolution of the source with that of the movie to work out how much you can tighten.

With pictures, you may find that the range of the zoom slider isn't enough, but you can either use manual parameter entry, or make use of the different interface of the Camera/zoom tool I'll show you shortly.

2D Rotation

The ninth handle in the Program monitor is either above or below the top centre handle, depending on the current size of the box. With this control you can drag the picture around it's Z axis, even when you don't have the Rotation/mirror effect open. Do that now and tilt the picture to about 45 degrees. That isn't showing anywhere in the parameters in the effects tab. Switch to the Rotation/Mirror tab and there you will see that the value is shown in the third box. You can still reposition and resize the video, and if you switch back to the Size/Position effect you will see the new values recorded there.

Rotating a picture

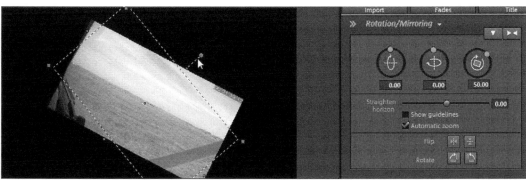

So with either of these effects open you can still use the other one via the handles.

While we are looking at the parameters in Rotate/Mirror, check out the other two rotation tools that spin the image about its horizontal (X) or vertical (Y) axis. Perspective distortion is added to objects that don't have stereoscopic properties.

There are also a couple of handy tools. *Straighten horizon* can compensate for a titled picture, and using the checkboxes allows you to superimpose a grid to do this accurately, and to apply an automatic zoom so you don't shoot off the sides of the photo or video as you straighten it up. *Flip* transforms the image so that it looks like a mirror image, both vertically or horizontally. *Rotate* lets you correct for photos that were shot in portrait mode or even upside down. Note that this last tool can't be reset with some of the usual controls – you actually have to switch it off or delete if from the effects overview.

3D distortion

Clear all your experiments from the current clip and switch to the 3D distortion effect. Now you should see eight handles. Dragging any of them warps the picture.

Using 3D distortion

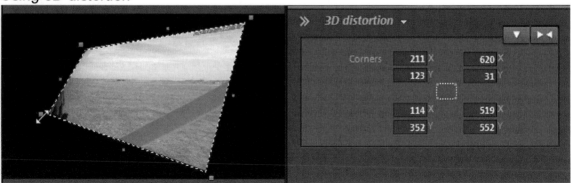

Apart from using this for fun or artistic reasons, it's handy for things such as overlaying a picture on a TV screen because used with care it can add a 3D perspective look to an object. Notice that when you adjust the corner handles, only one set of parameters is affected. Adjusting the handles at the sides adjust two corners simultaneously.

Section

Clear any distortion effects, switch to the *Section* effect and make sure clip 1 on track 1 is highlighted and showing the program monitor. I mentioned earlier that this tool uses a slightly different interface. The two important controls here are the Edit/Preview button and the Fill Screen checkbox. Although you can generate handles in the Preview mode, they do nothing. (I think this is a minor bug in the program.)

Click on the Edit button – it will show the label *Preview* which means you can now edit.

Defining a section in Edit mode

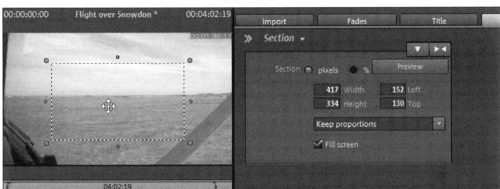

Ensure the default drop-down *Keep proportions* is displayed and then try dragging the top left handle. You can only move it in or out from the centre of the screen. The bounding box that joins the handles shrinks or expands, maintaining the same aspect ratio at all times. You are adjusting the size of the section. Drag so that it is about quarter size and release the mouse button, then hover over the middle to generate a four-way arrow, click and drag the bounding box to the centre of the screen then release the button.

Previewing the selection in Fit screen mode

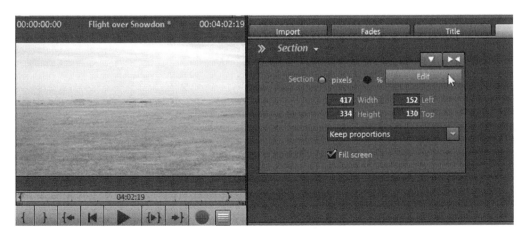

We have now defined a section that we wish to display. Ensure that *Fill screen* is checked and click on the *Preview* button. There – we have effectively zoomed into a section of the video, showing us a reduced resolution picture. If this were a decent quality photo the resolution would not be degraded.

Disabling the Fit screen function

Now uncheck the *Fill screen* box. Ah, now we are seeing the selection we defined! This is the most likely mode we would use for video sources. If you wanted to move the cropped image to another part of the screen we would need to switch to the Size/Position effect.

You don't have to shrink the bounding box and then move it – you can just draw a section by clicking and then dragging when you see the box drawing mouse cursor. This a great way to create a selection, particularly if you select Free proportions in the dropdown box. Other options allow you to choose fixed aspect ratios, and portrait or landscape layouts.

As I said earlier, you cannot use keyframes with the section tool. However, the next tool I'm going to describe is designed for the sole purpose of setting keyframes..

Camera/Zoom – an introduction to keyframing video

The *Camera/zoom* effect uses similar controls to the *Section* effect, in that Edit/Preview switches between two distinct views in the Program monitor, making zooming in easier. I'm going to jump straight to the second section of parameters and add an effect to another part of the Flight movie:

- Reload the *Flight over Snowdon rough cut 9* movie.

- Scrub to and select the Approaching Snowdon clip on track 1 (00:02:41:12 MTC).

- Open Effects>Movement effects>Camera/zoom in the Media pool.

- Open the Effects overview panel at the bottom of the Media pool.

- Click on the *Edit* button (it then switches to say *Preview*). The handles and bounding box should appear in the Program monitor.

- Click on the *To section* icon on the right of the parameter box.

- The bounding box shrinks. Readjust it to make it smaller and centred on the peak as shown in the screenshot.

- Click on Preview and play the clip.

Setting the To section

You should see a number of things. As the clip plays, the picture slowly zooms into the peak, making it clearer which one is the actual summit. In the list of effects, there is now an entry for *Image size/position*. You might have expected to see *Camera/zoom* as the name of the effect, but it just uses the size and position parameters.

The most significant addition, though, is the presences of keyframe markers. To the far right of the effect label is miniature Timeline display. Click on the top grey bar and a playback marker will appear which you drag and scrub. As you do so the timecode in the box above the Effect name changes, showing you the position relative to the duration of the clip. Under the scrubbing bar another track contains two diamond shaped icons. These are the keyframe markers. One is at the very start of the track. Click on it and it highlights blue. A timecode appears showing the position of the keyframe relative to the original source file. The other keyframe is at the very end of the Timeline.

Selecting the first keyframe

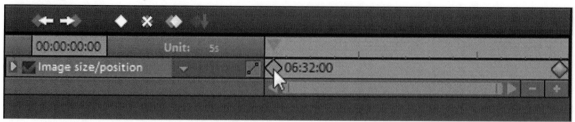

So, the Camera/zoom tool has created an animated effect by adding two keyframes with different parameters.

The *Direction of movement* section at the top of the parameter box creates another sort of keyframed movement – a pan across the image, in the direction of the arrow you click on. This is a useful tool for adding a little movement to photos.

Incidentally, at the very bottom of the effects list Timeline, there is a scroll bar that we can use to adjust the view. If you are working on long clips and putting keyframes close together, you can use this in the same manner as the one underneath the main Timeline to adjust the view.

In the *Camera movements* effect, there are a number of radio buttons in the *Duration* box. These can be used to alter the positions of the keyframes.

- Click on *2 second edge*. Notice that the keyframes are moved inwards.

- Click on *30% in center* and they move further in.

- Play the clip. You will see that the move starts later – when the Timeline playback marker reaches the first keyframe.

- Unfortunately, using these buttons often changes the positions back to the defaults, so when you play the effect, we may have lost the position we programmed in for the end.

- Press CTRL-Z twice to restore the effect to the way we set it up.

- Click, hold and drag the first keyframe to the right. Watch the Program monitor for the title to fade out.

- Position the keyframe so that the clip BITC timecode shows as 00:06:40:00 and release the mouse button.

Now play the clip. The effect doesn't start zooming into the peak until the title has faded out. This time our framing should be intact. Notice that in the *Duration* box, the *Custom fit* radio button has been automatically selected.

Adjusting the start position of the zoom in

There are two shortcomings with the effect we have created. One is that the video appears to go out of focus as we zoom in to the peak. There isn't anything that we can do about this, because we are zooming into video and effectively reducing the resolution. The other thing is that the zoom starts and ends very suddenly.

Hard and soft curves

We can address the speed at which keyframes are interpreted with the use of a small tool at the far right of the effects list. In the linear mode is shows as a box with a straight diagonal double-headed arrow. This indicates it is using straight interpolation.

- Click on the curves button.

- Play the effect.

Setting a soft curve

When the button is showing a curved symbol, the effect eases in and out. I'll be able to show you why these are called curves when we have explored a bit more of the keyframes interface. For now, I'm happy with the effect. It makes it clearer to the viewer which peak we are heading for. There are more keyframe features to explain, but I'm going to add a further effect to show you how these work.

Customising keyframes

For our next trick, we are going to create a picture-in picture effect from scratch. I want to show the moment of take-off from both the exterior and interior at the same time, with the exterior shot shrunk and displayed over the interior shot. What is more, I want the exterior shot to animate to its shrunken position. There may be a pre-made effect we could use for this in the many presets available, but that's not the point! In creating this effect, I'll be able to show you how to use the remaining keyframe features.

- Check the magnet tool is on, and you are in Mouse mode for single object.

- Locate the Ext Take off clip that starts at 00:01:31:08.

- Drag the clip down to track 3. It should click into the same position it was on track 1.

- Extend the Out point of the clip so that shows 00:01:09:00 on the burnt-in timecode. The plane is now just against sky with no foreground reference.

The Ext Take off shot moved and extended

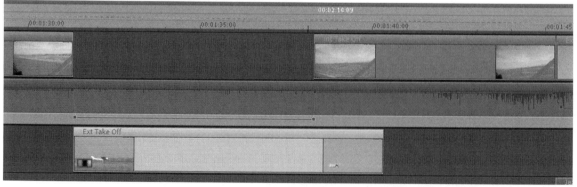

- Scrub to the first clean frame after the Cessna has passed the military jet – 00:01:04:04 BITC.

- Highlight the clip and then open Effects>Movement effects>Size/Position in the Media pool.

- Make sure the Effects overview area is showing at the bottom of the Media pool.

I now want to set my first keyframe – up until this point, I don't want to add any effects, so the first keyframe will still have the default parameters. We need to turn our attention to the small black keyframes toolbar at the top of the Effects overview area.

There are six tool icons here, as shown and labelled in the screenshot. If none of the tools in the toolbar are

The Keyframe tools

highlighted, it's because the currently selected effect isn't keyframeable. Switch to the section effect to see that, then switch back to *Size/Position* and the third tool from the left – a diamond the shape of the keyframes we have already seen – will highlight. This is the Set keyframe tool.

- Click in the Set keyframe tool.

- You may now need to scroll up the Effects overview area to see that *Image size/position* has been added to the effects list. It's currently not checked, as there are only default parameters set, but you can see the first keyframe we have added at the Playback Marker position to the right.

- Jog forward 12 frames so the BITC reads 00:01:04:16.

- If required, click on the Edit button in the parameter box to make the handles and bounding box appear.

- Drag from the bottom right handle to make the picture occupy the top left of the

The first keyframe

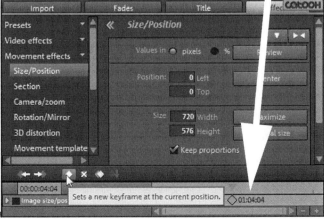

screen, looking at the Size parameters and setting them to 375 wide and 300 high.

- Drag the whole picture to the left of the screen and down a little, then fine tune the position to 15 Left and 5 Top using the arrow keys.

The parameters for the second keyframe

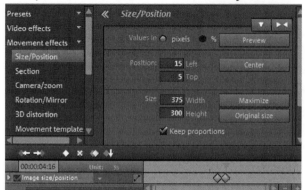

•Look at the keyframe Timeline – a new keyframe has appeared. Switch to Preview mode and play the clip.

OK, that's stage one. We have shrunk the picture into the top left corner. Now that we have a proper effect, most of the keyframe tools have become available. Clicking on the arrow tools navigates from keyframe to keyframe. We have already used the Set keyframe tool. The X tool would delete the current keyframe if we wanted to, while the last two tools are Copy and Paste.

Because I want to hold the picture in this position for a period of time, I'm going to set another keyframe at the point I want the second move to begin. In the current circumstances we could just create a new keyframe, but at other times we might need to copy and paste, so let's do that now:

- Use the arrow keys to move the scrubber to the second keyframe.

- Click on the Copy tool. Notice now that the Paste tool has become available.

- Move the scrubber to the end of the clip, then jog back 12 frames.

- Click on the Paste tool.

Pasting the third keyframe

If you were to play the Timeline nothing will have changed yet . We need to set one more keyframe to make the picture disappear altogether.

- Drag the keyframe Timeline scrubber to the end of the clip.

- In the parameter box, click on Edit and set both Size parameters to the value of 1.

Now when you play the clip you will see the full effect. We aren't finished yet, though. I want to show you where all the values are stored.

- Click on the small arrow at the front of the Image size/position label in the effects list. This opens the Movement effects tree.

- Adjust the Effects overview window to see all the parameters.

The sub parameters for Image size/position

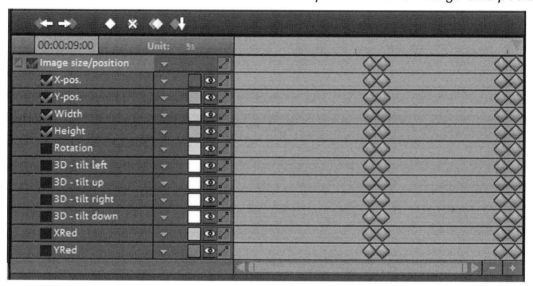

There is an individual label and a keyframe Timeline for all four parameters we have changed. There is also one for each parameter we might have potentially changed – the distortion and rotation values. If we wanted to, we could adjust, by dragging or copy and pasting, the individual timing of each value.

You will also see two new icons next to the Curves button. The eye symbol controls whether the curves are displayed on the clip. Click on the one for the X-pos parameter. A line appears on the clip showing how the parameter changes over time. You can change the display colour with the box to the left, which opens up a colour picker when you click on it.

This is a good opportunity for me to show you the effect of the Curves button. Click the curves button for the X-pos on and off and see how the shape of the curve changes on the display. When you have finished experimenting, switch to linear curves but don't remove the line just yet.

Linear (top) and Bezier Interpolation (bottom)

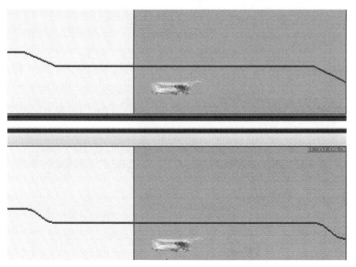

I'm going to enhance the effect a bit more before we sort out the background:

• Use the keyframe navigation arrows to move to the second keyframe.

• Open the Rotation/Mirror effect and adjust the X rotation (the left hand parameter) to 35 degrees so that the picture looks like it is tilting towards the viewer.

The Xred rotation parameter in action

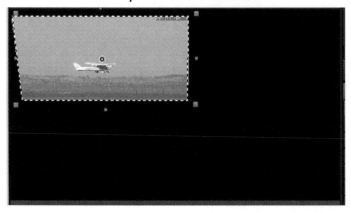

Play the effect and you will see that we also need to adjust the third keyframe to stop the picture straightening itself out. We can do this with the keyframe tools alone:

• Click on the second XRed keyframe to highlight it and click on the copy button.

• Select the third XRed keyframe and click on the delete tool, then click on paste.

• Select the fourth keyframe and set the value to 90 degrees.

Right, let's now sort out the background. We can simply extend the In point of the next clip on track one:

• Generate a double-headed trim cursor at the beginning of the Int Take Off shot to the right of the gap.

• Drag the In point to the left until it clicks into place at the end of the gap.

Now when you play the section in context, the picture in picture seems to disappear rather quickly. Let's see what happens if we extend the clip. You could normally do this by eye, but I want you to match my numbers:

- Move the main Timeline scrubber to 00:01:42:00 MTC.

- Trim the Out point of the effects shot on track 3 to click into place with the scrubber.

An important principle is demonstrated here. Although we have adjusted the duration of the clip, the keyframes haven't been adjusted. The picture still flies up to the top left corner at the same point in time, as you can see from the curve view that we left in place. This is the default behaviour, but it can be changed. In this case we could just move the keyframes, but I want to show you another way to adjust them.

The extended clips and fixed audio

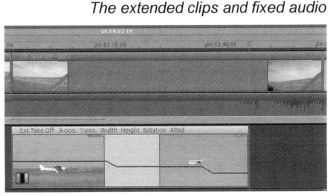

- One small thing - adjust the audio keyframes so that we return to the louder volume as the exterior clip zooms back.

Effects curves menu

Click on the drop-down arrow after the Image size/position label to take a look at the options available. Bear in mind that these are special commands for dealing with keyframes. The clip context menu holds the commands for effects in general.

Delete effects will remove the effect and remove it from the list.

Delete effects curve will remove the keyframes.

Copy effects curve will place the the current set of keyframes onto the clipboard.

The Effects curves menu

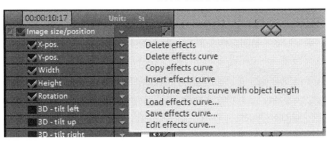

Insert effect curve deletes the current set of keyframes (if any) and then pastes the keyframes from the clipboard to the clip.

Combine effects curve with object length will match the keyframe spacing to the length of the clip. This won't have any effect when you first create a keyframed curve, but it will come into play if you then trim the clip, or paste the curve to a different clip. This isn't just a command, though. Once you have activated it, the keyframes will automatically adjust to the duration of the clip. You can switch it off again to revert to the default behaviour.

The keyframe curves associated with the Ext take off clip are currently set to positions related to the original duration of the clip. Let's see what happens if we adjust them with the Combine tool:

- Highlight the effects shot and open the Effects curve menu using the drop-down after the *Image size/Position* label in the effects lists.

- With your eyes fixed on the display curve, select Combine effects curve with object length.

- The pair of keyframes are moved to the end of the clip, but the first pair are also moved right a little so that it hasn't completely fixed the issue – but then again, the timing of the first pair may not be that critical.

The effect of the Combine command

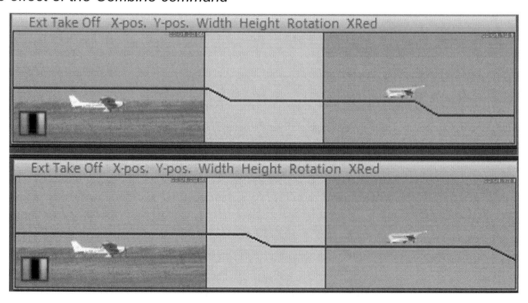

- You may notice the keyframe timelines haven't refreshed. Click away to another clip and back and you will see them in the new positions.

We will now manually put the first pair back to where they were:

- Click on the first keyframe in the Image size/position Timeline.

- Drag it left while watching the Program monitor. Find the point where the foreground plane's tail just disappears out of frame, and release the keyframe.

- Now drag the second keyframe left so that the gap between and the first frame looks the same as between keyframes 3 and 4.

- Please save the movie as *Flight over Snowdon rough cut 10*.

I was hoping to show you how we can multi-select keyframes by using the CTRL key, but it seems it is always the furthest right keyframe that is monitored. In many circumstances, though, multi-selection will be a useful tool.

Back to the Effects curve menu. *Load effects curve* won't do anything until we have saved an effect, so use the next option, *Save effects curve*. You will be prompted for a file name (use fly_back_top_left), and the effect will be saved in a *UserVideoEffects* directory.

If you now select the last clip of the movie – the landing shot – and add a keyframes, you will be able to load your newly saved effects curve onto another clip. You may be surprised to see that there are 11 files with the name you chose. The file you want will have no numbers at the end. The others have a number before the *.moc*.

The Effects curve tree

The Movement effects were all revealed when we opened the tree, and each effect has an effects curve menu. When you use this on individual items, only the keyframe data for that item is acted on. So it is possible to save a set of keyframes for Width and save them to Height, for example. There may be times when this could be a useful tool but more often than not you will get confused – I do!

Most of the other effects available for keyframing aren't arranged in this tree structure. If you want to save, load, copy and paste effects as a whole, you are far better off using the Effects clip context menu, more of which shortly.

Manual editing

The final entry in the Effects curve menu is *Edit curves*. This is a somewhat cumbersome tool, although it does have a few neat tricks. If you wanted to completely reverse the order of the keyframes this would be the tool to use. If you just wanted to adjust a few values, it's far better to stick with the methods I've already described. We still have the loaded effect on the last clip of the movie if you want to try out the editor. Select the Edit effect from the Effects curve menu for Image size position and a new, undocked parameter box will appear.

Editing curves with the edit tool

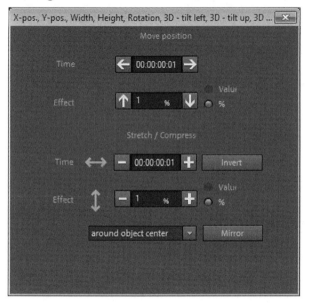

In the title bar is a list the curves you are editing. Each parameter has two arrows to increment the value, while the box between the arrows allows you to set the size of the increment. So, changing the timecode in the Move position/Time box to 00:00:01:00 means that each time you click on the left or right arrows, the curves are moved 1 second left or right. Moving the Effect up or down adds an offset to all the effect parameters. Stretch/Compress alters the duration and amplitude of the curve.

The most helpful tool is the Mirror button, and of the options available in the drop-down box, *only around curve center* has a useful effect on our complex set of curves – effectively reversing the parameters and reversing the effect so that the picture flies in. You will have better success with single parameter curves.

Context effect commands

I need to make it clear that the best way to deal with effects as a whole is with the Effects branch of the Clip context menu. If you haven't done so already, you should remove our experiments on the last clip by right clicking on it and selecting *Video effects/Reset video effects*.

The Effects section of the Clip context menu

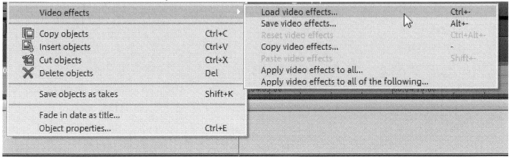

The Video effects submenu doesn't just apply to the effects listed under Video effects in the Effects tab, but all the others, including Movement effects.

Not only can you *Load*, *Save* (in another special folder) and *Reset* effects, you can *Copy* selectively, where a dialogue box appears allowing you to choose which parameters to put on the clipboard. When you come to Paste you can do so to a multiple selection of clips. Two further menu options automate this process more – You can apply all the effects attached to the current clip – or a selection of them –to all the subsequent clips on the Timeline.

Design Elements

The effects tab also has a huge array of pre-designed effects and other assets in the Design elements section.

The Design elements and Picture-in-picture

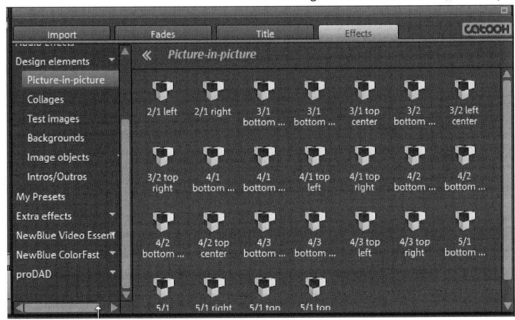

Picture-in-Picture holds premade effects like the one we have just created. You can preview the effect in the Program monitor, and then just drag and drop it to a clip, or use the Send to Timeline to apply it the the currently highlighted clip.

Collages are more complex, perhaps requiring the addition of extra tracks. To use a collage, you put all the elements you want to use consecutively on the same track. Then dragging the Collage effect to the first item causes the collage to be built up using the subsequent objects, adding them to lower tracks as required and removing them from the original track.

Test Images contains not just the colour bar images you can use at the front of your movies to line up your playback equipment, but a collection of preset and customisable colours. If you use the User-defined icon, a Colour picker opens up for you to choose any colour you like, but you will also need to use the Object properties tool to set the aspect ratio to that of your movie. All the assets in this tab are flagged up as backgrounds in MEP, and if you use the Send to Timeline command they will be automatically Set as background to the highlighted clip as discussed earlier. If no clip is selected, Magix will open up a dialogue box to help you choose. Using drag and drop on this set of assets places them cleanly on the Timeline.

Backgrounds are another set of assets for use as backgrounds. If you drag and drop these, you will still enter into a dialogue. Included here are motion videos that can look very impressive if used with care.

Image objects are pre-prepared foregrounds that you can drag onto clips on the Timeline. Some of them are simple static objects, others are animated video clips – and some even have audio associated with them. It's not possible to put these objects on the Timeline on their own.

When you superimpose these objects onto a video or photo source, they behave in the same was as a title would, so it is easy to resize or move them. The superimposition is carried out in a variety of ways, depending on the object, with video objects sometimes using chromakey. This part of the process is all handled automatically when you drag and drop or Send to Timeline.

Intros/Outros take the pre-made assets to a higher level. They are effectively mini-movies that you can apply to the first or last shot of your work to give a very polished appearance.

They normally consist of a number of objects. Foreground graphics or video may have chromakey build in so that they become transitions between your footage and the effect. They often contain a title, which you can subsequently edit to suit your own movie.

My Presets has its own category, but it's just a collection of the effects that you have built and saved yourself. You can drag these from the Media poll to any clip on the Timeline.

Additional effects

Magix supply a number of additional effects with Movie Edit Pro. Some of them are downloadable; others are supplied with the more expensive versions of MEP. A plug-in manager is available, when you select Extra effects/Plug ins, where it's possible to control and add third-party effects. Sometimes the interface will be very basic, at other times advanced, but very different from the standard Magix interface. The plug-in manager also allows you to build up a template of effects and save it for future use.

Using the plug-ins manager

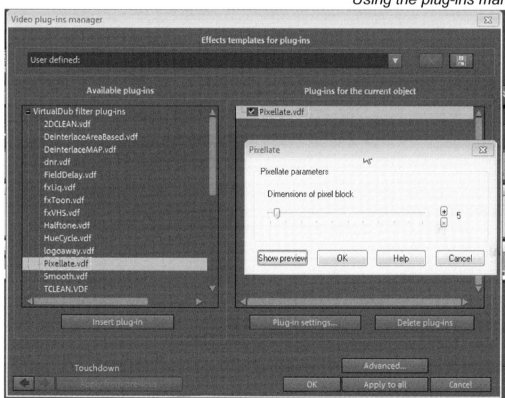

If you don't know if you have all the possible plug-ins available for your version of Movie Edit Pro, then check two entries in the Help menu – *Install extra programs and Download video effect plug-in*s. I've also searched the Internet, found some free filters originally written for the VirtualDub program, placed the .vdf file in the same location as other effects as shown in the Video plug-ins manager, and after rebooting MEP the filter has appeared in the list of available plug-ins. This is unlikely to provide you with a vast array of additional effects but there may be some unusual filters that fulfil a particular task you need to perform.

Image Stabilisation

One effect that we haven't been able to apply within the effect section of the Media pool is Video stabilisation. It is available via the Clip context menu, along with a number of other effects. Most of them are there for convenience, but Stabilise is, in effect, a Wizard.

What all stabilising filters do is to reframe the video in order to reduce shaking. To this end Magix uses keyframes to re-adjust the position of subsequent frames. It can also zoom in a small amount so that we don't see the edges of the video frame.

The hard part of stabilising a video source is analysing it in a way that allows the program to differentiate between movement that you want, and movement that you don't want. If you are simply hand-holding a camera pointing at a relatively static scene then eliminating any wobble is a relatively easy task. However, if the cameraman starts to deliberately move the camera the program has to allow the framing to change. The increasingly popular action camera shots – where you strap a small camera to yourself and then do something brave (or stupid) such as skateboarding - are harder to process because almost all the video content is changing frame by frame.

Some shots are beyond automatic repair – you could try a frame by frame analysis and set your keyframes manually if the shot was vital, but normally this would be far too time-consuming. Letting Magix do the work sometimes makes things a lot better by just using the default settings, but to use the tool properly you need to understand what the parameters do, and be willing to also use trial and error.

- Open the effect tab in the Media pool at the Size position tab and ensure the Effect overview is showing.

- Highlight the second clip of the Flight movie, the Taxiing shot, right-click and select Image stabilization.

The dialogue box you are presented with has a number of areas, with the preview on the right and three numbered sections on the left. Let's leave everything at the defaults to begin with.

Firstly, we need to analyse the clip.

- Click on the *Perform stabilisation* button bottom left.

- Dismiss the warning message that this will take a long time – the clip is quite short.

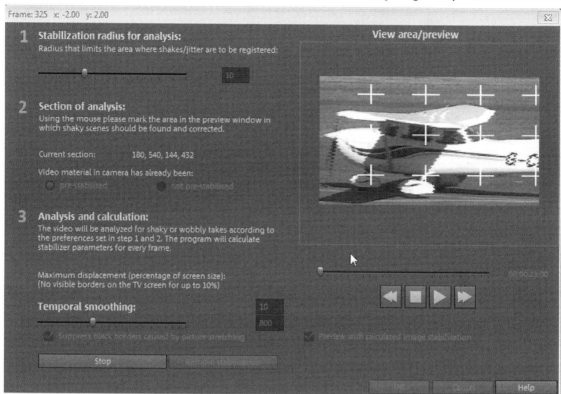

Watch as a section of the clip plays in preview with a number of white crosshairs superimposed. They jog about trying to track the same point in the video. Next, the progress bar runs across the message area at the bottom of the program as the data is analysed. Finally, if you have arranged the media pool correctly you will see a series of keyframes placed along the keyframe timelines, four for each frame of the clip.

You can now play the clip in the small preview window, to save you returning to the Timeline. To clearly see how much work the stabilisation is doing you can watch the burnt in timecode bobbing in and out of frame. To watch the clip without the stabilisation you can uncheck the box Preview with calculated image stabilisation.

- Click on the *OK* box to return to the Timeline.

- Save the project as *Flight over Snowdon rough cut 11*.

Study the result. That's a pretty good job, really. To try and improve it we need to adjust the settings. The settings are to a large part interactive, though, making it difficult to appreciate the full scope of the parameters.

Stabilization radius for analysis is the setting that affects the range over which the crosshairs are allowed to move in an attempt to detect movement. A low setting here will mean that only small movements will be tracked. A high setting will cause the crosshairs to try and look on over a greater range, so it might try to smooth out a deliberate pan, only to have to give up and flick back to the start position. So a shot that has a constant vibration would work best with a low setting. Too high a setting and you are likely to make the shot worse.

Section for analysis allows you to define which part of the picture is scanned. It's simply a matter of drawing a box with the mouse around the section you want to stabilise. So, in the case of our panning shot of the plane, the default area is pretty good, including as it does most of what we want to stabilise. If you select a smaller area, the process is more prone to errors. Choosing an area with little in the way of detail is even worse, and choosing a large area can confuse the program, particularly when there is fixed foreground – the handlebars of a bike, for example.

Changing any of the above parameters will normally require the footage to be re-scanned, while the following may sometimes only require the regeneration of keyframes.

Two radio buttons allows you to choose if the footage has been pre-stabilised in the camera. The analysis appears be a little more sensitive if the footage has not already been stabilised.

Maximum displacement determines how far from the central position the picture can be moved. It can have a value of between 1 and 50. The effect of this is best seen with the checkbox for suppressing borders turned off. A value of 1 will only remove the smallest of shaking, and value of 50 allows very big borders to be generated. However, if you haven't detected a great deal of shaking – perhaps you have set the radius to a low value – then increasing this value will have no effect above a particular value.

A message here is a little confusing in my opinion. *No visible borders on the TV screen for up to 10%* is nothing to do with the checkbox for suppressing borders. It's telling you that on a TV with average overscan (discussed earlier), setting the value to 10 should result in the viewer not being aware of the borders. You will see the borders on a computer though, unless you use the suppression checkbox.

Temporal smoothing affects how swiftly the stabilisation reacts to detected shakiness. You can use this setting to dampen out the stabilisation, and a low setting will preserve camera movements that might be deliberate. Set it high and you will clearly see panning movement being suppressed, and then the picture drifting back to the central position. Set it low and slow moves will not be stabilised as much.

I'd suggest that you experiment with the *Suppress black borders caused by picture stretching* box unchecked, even if you intend to suppress them eventually. This control will apply a variable zoom factor to the shot so that it always fills the frame, and the downside of this is that you will lose resolution should the effect need to zoom in too much. It's harder to see the extent of the zooming than the size of the borders. When you do check the box you probably won't need to re-analyse the shot again. You may find too much zooming can be more distracting that a few wobbles, so you might decide to re-adjust the displacement value to a lower setting.

If you fancy experimenting more with the stabiliser, you can try working on the first clip in the movie. This is quite tricky, as it contains both low level vibration and really big bumps. What is more, not only was the image stabiliser already switched on in the camera, but there is not much detail in the centre of frame to latch on to. The Magix stabiliser doesn't attempt to rotate the picture, so the tilting horizon will never be fixed. Given those clues, you might be able to improve the shot, but I've failed to make any significant improvements in one section of the shot that don't make another part worse.

Other Context menu effects

There are a number of effects available when you right click on a clip. *Movement* is another route to applying the Camera/zoom wizard presets. *Section* allows quick access to the section tool. *Attach to picture position in the Timeline* is in fact a very powerful effect that is a form of motion tracking. It requires careful setting up, and we will look at it in detail later in the book. You can also add interlace correction and border cropping via the context menu.

This chapter may not have covered every possible requirement you might have for effects, but it has covered the principles of applying them. Don't forget that there may already be a pre-built effect in the Design elements section that could be modified rather than building something from scratch, but with an understanding of masks, keyframes and the use of multiple track you should only be limited by your imagination, not the program itself.

Advanced Transitions

We have looked at transitions previously and you should have a general idea of the principles, but I'm going to summarise them before expanding on the subject and adding them to the Flight project.

What is a transition?

When one shot is immediately followed by another, the junction between them is called a cut. The last frame of the outgoing shot is followed by the first frame of the incoming shot. This is such an obvious way of jointing two shots together that the term transition isn't normally applied. Any other way of replacing one shot with another is termed as a transition. In the early days of film, fading down the outgoing shot by closing the aperture of the lens so that eventually all you could see was blackness was probably the first transition. Fading up the next shot by reversing the process resulted in a fade through black. A crossfade could be achieved "in camera" by winding back the film and double exposing the film.

A transition can tell the audience something that a cut doesn't - most noticeably that time has passed between two two shots. Once they began creating transitions during the editing of the film they became more complex, with increased artistic effect.

With video it's very easy to create transitions. In fact, it's so easy, they tend to get overused. However, they are an important tool in the story telling process.

The transition icon

In Movie Edit Pro transitions are indicated in Storyboard mode by an icon between each clip. In Timeline mode the transition icon appears only on video or photo objects that have been highlighted by selection, at the front of the incoming clip. If the object happens to be the very last object on any particular track,

The transition icon for a cut

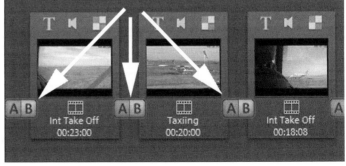

an icon is also present at the end of the object so you can transition to black at the end of the movie.

346 - Advanced Transitions

Last video clip of a movie

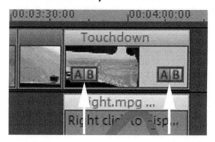

If this icon displays A/B as shown in the screenshot, there is no transition over time, the Out point of the clip on the left is followed immediately by the In point of the clip on the right. This is a cut.

If the icon shows as three bars – orange, black then blue – there is a fade up, a fade down, both, or a gap in the movie.

If the icon is a white diagonal cross, then the outgoing video crossfades into the incoming video.

If the icon shows a more complex pattern, then a more complex transition is in place. From the icon you may or may not be able to tell what the transition might be.

A gap, a crossfade and a "flying" transition

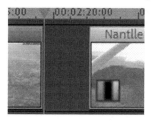  

Transition menu

The transition menu

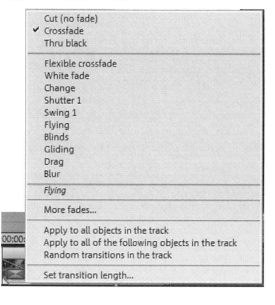

If you click on the transition icon, a menu is revealed that allows you to control the transition. You can change a simple cut to another type of transition, or remove a transition by changing it back to a cut.

The menu also allows you to replicate the transition so that it is applied to other junctions between objects either on the whole track or to all the objects that follow the current one. There is also an option to add random transitions to every junction.

The final option opens a parameter box so that you can change the duration of the current transition, or if you have selected a group of objects, the duration of all the transitions in the group.

Timeline transitions

In Timeline mode, if you drag one object so that it overlaps another, a crossfade is automatically created. This is represented by a white diagonal cross spanning the duration of the crossfade. The transition icon will also change to a crossfade. Fades up and down are represented with the slopes at the start or end of a clip. Transitions can be generated automatically when making adjustments to movies and there is a conflict between objects.

The duration of transitions and fades can be manipulated on the Timeline by using the handles on the slopes.

Overlapping video

I made the point earlier that for the duration of a transition, there needs to be two sources of video. When you use the transition icon to generate a crossfade, the incoming video is moved earlier to create the overlap.

If you adjust the duration of the crossfade within the transition menu, the incoming video's position on the Timeline is altered so that the original In point of the incoming video is at the start of the transition and the original Out point of the outgoing video is at the end of the transition.

Automatically adding a crossfade

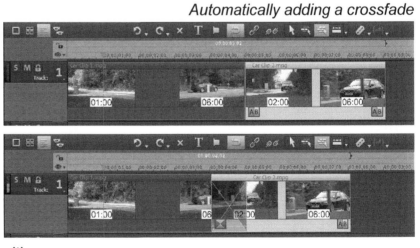

This automatic behaviour has implications for other objects on the Timeline which we will look at shortly. We will also look at when and how you might want to override this behaviour. I'm now going to demonstrate the use of transitions as we add them to the Flight movie.

Transitions and multiple tracks

Let's load up our Flight movie and begin to add some transitions:

- Open *Flight over Snowdon rough cut 11*.

- Select the Nantlle ridge clip starting at 00:02:19:12 MTC.

- Adjust the Timeline view so that you can see tracks 1 to 4 and as far right as the *Happy-1* music clip on track 4.

- Check track 4 isn't locked.

- Click on the transition icon for the Nantlle ridge clip and select *Crossfade*.

A number of things will happen. The Program monitor will play the transition you have just added. I find this behaviour a bit irritating, and if you do as well, you can turn it off in *Settings/Program/System/Other*.

The transition icon will have changed to a crossfade, and the white cross will have appeared at the start of the clip. The Nantlle ridge clip will have been moved one second to its left, creating the overlap required. All the other clips that followed the target clip will have also been moved to the left, maintaining the sync of the tracks and shortening the movie by one second.

There is a problem though. We saw this before – the music track, which is in two sections, has been overlapped with an audio crossfade at around 3 minutes 10 seconds, ruining the audio edit. MEP had a conflict and rather than overwrite anything, it created a transition.

Overlap created on the music track

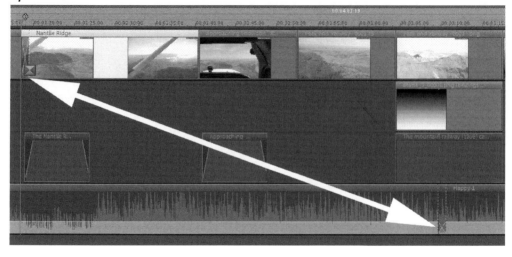

- Open the transition menu again and select *Cut*.

Everything will be back to normal. MEP reverses the process, shifting everything back to where it was before. Even if the transition hadn't been created via the menu, removing a transition keeps everything in sync.

Notice that I didn't specify which mouse mode we needed to be in for this behaviour to occur. The rippling of objects happens on all the tracks, regardless of the mouse mode. What's more, the "track 1 is special" rule doesn't apply. Adding or removing a transition using the menu should be fairly foolproof in most circumstances. The Flight movie at this point is an exception. If the transition had been added before or after both music clips we would not have a problem. It *should* be easy enough to solve:

- Use the padlock in the track 4 header to lock the music track.
- Use the transition icon menu to change the Cut to a Crossfade again.

Argh! Look closely and you will see that the only track that has rippled is track 1. Because the program can't move some of the clips it thinks that it should, it has chosen to move none of them. So you need to be very aware that when adding or removing transitions in this way locking tracks isn't a solution.

- Use CTRL-Z to undo the transition – don't use the transition menu.
- Unlock the music track.
- Add the crossfade back in with the transition menu.
- Make sure you are in *Mouse mode for single objects*.
- Drag the second music clip to the right to undo the overlap.

Transition duration and the transition menu

It's unlikely that a 1 second transition will be perfect for every occasion. A slow paced movie might want a two or three second transition. If you want to alter the duration accurately you can use a slider or number entry box after you have added the transition:

- Select the *Approaching Snowdo*n clip beginning at 00:02:40:12 MTC.
- Use the transition icon to change the Cut to a Crossfade.
- Use the transition menu again to select *Set transition length*.

- Adjust the slider to set the duration to around 4 seconds.

- Click on *OK*.

Adjusting the transition duration

We will take care of the music shortly. We now have two transitions of very dissimilar durations, one probably too short, one too long. We can make changes to groups of transitions providing that they are on track 1. Currently we only have two, so we can use the option to apply the changes to all the transitions:

- Open the transition icon menu for either of the transitions and select *Set transition length*.

- Use the number entry box to set the duration accurately to 2 seconds.

- Click on *Apply to all*.

You will notice that there is also a checkbox available to *Apply to selected range*. This doesn't work according to clip selection, but operates on a range you set as a blue bar above the Timeline – another function of the range feature we looked at earlier.

Using something other than crossfades

There are many types of transitions other than simple crossfades. If we wanted something more complex, there are two workflows possible. We can create other types of transitions from scratch using the Media pool, or we can create a crossfade and then change it. There are also two ways of changing a crossfade, and you will have already seen a list of alternatives in the transitions menu. This is the simple way of changing a transition quickly. The list isn't very long, but it is possible to add more and I'll show you how to do that later. For now, let's use something a little more dynamic for the second transition:

- Click on the Transition icon at the beginning of the *Approaching Snowdon* clip.

- From the menu, select *Swing 1*.

- Move the Playback marker to the end of the transition.

- Make sure that the Magnet is on and that the mouse mode is for single objects.

- Drag the *Approaching the peak* title on track 3 to the right so it clicks into place at the end of the transition.

- Move the *Happy-1* segment of music on track 4 left to remove the overlap.

So, now we have two transitions that have been created with automatic overlaps.

Manual transition creation

Let's look at the next edit point. I'm going to show you how to manually create a "normal" overlapped transition first, the sort we get with the Transition icon menu. You might well want to do this for speed, or if you wanted the start of the transition to line up with a particular point.

Swing 1 transition and relocated title

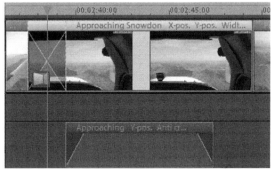

- Make sure the Magnet is on and no tracks are locked.

- Select Mouse mode for all tracks.

- Locate the first *Peak and Railway* clip at 00:02:49:14 MTS.

- Adjust the Timeline view to give a clear view of the area – I suggest *Zoom 1 second*.

Manual transition creation

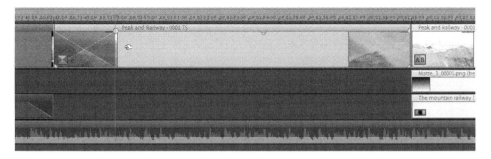

- Click on the clip on track 1 and drag it left. It will begin to overlap the previous clip and bring all the other objects to the right with it.

- It will snap into place with the end of the title on track 3. Release the mouse button.

That's a neat job. We can produce a transition quickly, and choose the duration easily – rather than think about numbers we can gauge the space they take up on the Timeline, making artistic decisions, or lining them up with other events on the Timeline.

There is a problem with the new transition though. We have already created an effect where the framing zooms into the peak and we are masking some of that move under the crossfade. The overlap – automatic or otherwise – has destroyed all of the thought that has gone into the editing.

You might wonder what would happen if we dragged the *Approaching Snowdon* clip right in *Mouse mode for single object*s. This is a perfectly valid way of creating a transition but we won't solve the problem that way, and will end up with a gap in track 1.

So, what we want to do is extend the Out point of the Approaching Snowdon sufficiently after the effects zoom has finished allowing time for a transition. Fortunately, we can do this in one step:

- Use the Transition icon menu to change the new crossfade back to a Cut.

- Adjust and enlarge the Timeline view to fill show the transition at the start of the *Approaching Snowdon* clip as well as the end.

- Hover over the lower part of the end of the *Approaching* Snowdon clip to generate a horizontal double-headed arrow mouse cursor.

- Click and drag right to generate a transition of roughly the same duration as the transition to the left.

Extending the outgoing video to create a transition

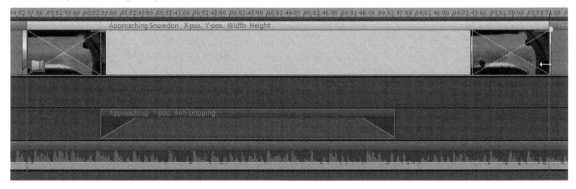

We have extended the Out point of the outgoing video and created a transition in overwrite mode – notice that the clips to the right haven't moved position. Play the clip and you will see that the effects zoom stops before the crossfade begins. At least – it should!

If you worked through the effects chapter, you will be aware of the function that allows you to combine the length of an effects curve with the duration of the object it is applied to. We didn't use this feature on the Approaching Snowdon effect. If we had have done so, the zoom would still end on the last frame of our extended shot. If you find that your effect keyframes are moving about when you trim a clip, and don't want them to, check out the Effects curves menu for the clip in question.

You might want to create a transition where the outgoing video isn't important, but you want to see the current In point of the incoming video clearly, without being overlapped. In these circumstances you would use the double headed trim cursor on the In point of the incoming video, extending it to the left – the mirror image of what we have just done.

Adjusting transitions manually

Once a transition is in place, you can adjust its duration manually by simply dragging the node at the top right corner that appears when you hover over it. This adjustment happens in overwrite mode – you will be moving the Out point of the outgoing video.

- Hover your mouse over the transition we have just created. A white hotspot will appear at the end of the transition.

- Click, hold and drag right to extend the transition to about two thirds of the duration of the clip.

Play the section and you will see some rather nasty wobbling about showing through the last stages of the crossfade. We are showing the viewer parts of the video we didn't want them to see when we chose the shots. Worse still, extending a transition could mean our source footage might switch to something else entirely. If you find that the program won't let you drag at all, or only by a small amount, it means you have actually run out of source video to extend.

If you want to move the point at which a transition begins, you can use the rolling trim cursor:

- Hover halfway up the the start of the transition to generate the double line cursor.

- Click, hold and drag left.

We have now shifted the start of the transition, but maintained the duration. We are seeing less of the wobble, but now we have masked the end of the effects zoom, swapping one issue for another.

- Press CTRL-Z twice.

So – all alterations of a transition on the Timeline other that dragging the clips themselves results in overwrite behaviour. If we wanted to set our new transition to a specific duration using the tool in the Transition menu however, we would be working in insert mode, altering the overlap and moving the incoming clips. It's possible to get in a bit of a muddle if you don't have a clear idea of these different behaviours, particularly if there are conflicting aims. If you want to make very accurate changes to a transition you should consider using the Edit trimmer – the subject of the next chapter.

Photos and transitions

It's worth mentioning that although all the above descriptions are demonstrated with video sources, if you are using still photos exactly the same behaviour occurs. Some more simplistic editors treat photos differently because unless you have added a movement effect there are some advantages in extending a photo rather than overlapping the sources.

If you have come from one of these editors you may not even be aware of the different handling of sources, but just to be clear, transition behaviour is identical regardless of the picture source.

Transitions in the Media pool

If you use the transition menu option *More fades* nothing happens other than the Medial pool changing to the fades tab. From there you are expected to drag and drop transition. You don't have to use the Transition menu to get to the fades in the Media pool:

- Click on the Fades tab in the Media pool.

- In the tree on the left, select *Standard*.

- Drag the first object – *Alpha magic* – down to track 1. When you hover it in the area of a transition icon you get an icon that looks like a film frame, anywhere else a *No entry* icon.

- Drop the transition on the start of the first Peak and Railway clip, where there is already a crossfade.

We have changed the transition, and it has inherited the duration of the previous transition. Open the transition menu by clicking on the icon and you will see that *Alpha magic* has been added to the list of transitions available so we can now add it from the menu if we wish.

If you drag a transition from the Media pool to a position on the Timeline that just has a cut, a one second fade is added, overlapping the sources just as if you had switched from a cut to a crossfade in the transition menu. This workflow is very efficient way of adding transitions other than crossfades to your movie.

Dragging a transition from the Media pool

- Drag the same transition – Alpha magic – to the next cutting point, the start of the second Peak and Railway shot we have added the mask to.

- A one second transition is added, overlapping the video sources.

- Make sure you are in the correct mouse mode and readjust the second music clip on track four again to lose the overlap.

Editing transitions

There is a huge range of transitions available if you explore the various options in the tree. Some of them have Stereoscopic properties. Others require additional tracks. There is even the option for you to create your own transitions with the *Export as transition* option in the file menu. If you have the Ultimate version of the program you also have access the Adorage plug-in with its own interface.

Even most of the basic transitions can be edited, though. The scope for editing varies with the type of transition.

- Select the second Peak and Railway clip and click on the transition icon.

- You may need to adjust the window sizes in the Media pool to reveal the editing functions for the Alpha magic transition.

- Choose another pattern and click the small play button to preview view it.

The player doesn't play just the transition, but the run up to it as well, but it's quicker than going back to the Timeline.

If you check out all those available, you might come to the conclusion that they are all a bit fussy. What if the fade were shorter?

- In the small time parameter box at the bottom of the edit window, enter 0.5 seconds.

You can also open the *Set transition duration* box with the tool icon to the right. I'm still not happy though. Let's look at some other choices. Select as many different types as you have time for, checking out the various parameters that you can change. I've ended up with something that isn't too fussy, even when played fast:

- Drag *Zooming* from the Standard selection to the new transition.

- Play it to see how it works with the default settings.

- Select *Enlarge from one corner* from the drop down box.

- Check the *Reverse A/B* box.

- Select the downward point arrow for *Direction*.

- Leave *Springs* at zero – it only works well for longer durations.

- Reset the second music clip one final time!

Editing the Zooming transition

I'm now going to demonstrate adding multiple transitions for the rest of the movie. As long as you leave the durations the same you can experiment further by replacing the crossfades with the vast array of possibilities available.

Rippling transitions

- Select the third Peak and Railway clip and add a one second crossfade to the start using the Transition menu icon.

- Use the menu again to *Apply to all the following objects in the track*.

This has added crossfades to the rest of the movie. We are past the point where the music clip will try, incorrectly, to stay in sync so we don't need to adjust that. There is one unfortunate consequence, though. The point where we added a freeze frame has also acquired a crossfade.

- Select the Transition icon for the freeze frame of the castle - and change the crossfade to a cut.

You will notice a fade has also been added to the end of the movie as well. Let's match that at the beginning.

- Scroll to the start of the movie, select the first clip and use the Transition icon menu to change the cut to a *Fade in*.

- Drag the slope on the title below to match.

- Save the movie as Flight over Snowdon Directors cut.

Adding a Fade up to clip 1

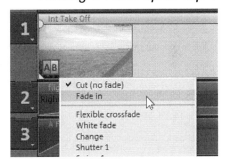

I've finished with the movie now. It's got a duration of 4 minutes 8 seconds and 5 frames. I'm going to show it to my Producer!

If your movie is just a few frames out I'm sure it's fine, as dealing with transitions and trimming points can sometimes be a little variable. If things are very different, you can always load my version for the next stage.

Fine Tuning with the Trimmers

Well, I've had my viewing, and the Producer has given me a bunch of notes:

- The bump on the first shot is very disturbing. Can we start the movie after it?

- The bump at the end of shot two is disturbing.

- Taxiing down the runway takes too long – lose some of the journey.

- The first cut after the exterior take off shot seems to jar.

- Can we reduce the rest of the movie to get it to a duration of less than four minutes?

- Don't lose the music so early.

I could attempt these changes with the functions we have already used, but I'm going to use the Object and Edit trimmers. These might not be the best tools for some of the things I'm going to do, but I'll be able to explain the power, and the pitfalls, of using them.

The trimmers

Movie Edit Pro has a pair of trim tools which seem like they were specially designed to work with the Storyboard. With them you can alter the position, duration, content and In and Out points of objects and transitions. They allow very precise control because the editing is parameter based.

The tools have some useful features even when used in a Timeline environment. Because they have two monitors you can study the In and Out points of an edit while still adjusting them. They make it very easy to adjust the In and Out points of an object simultaneously, allowing you to slip the content of an object without affecting its duration or position.

The disadvantages of using the trimmers in a multi-track environment are that the behaviour with regard to trying to keep the Timeline in sync is complex, particularly with grouped audio. Also, on-going changes are only shown on the chosen track – it looks like the objects on the other tracks aren't keeping sync, whereas they will move when you select OK - sometimes!

The trimmers are accessed via the clip context menu. If you right clip on a clip it highlights, and when the context menu opens, you can chose to open either the Object or the Edit trimmer. Once you have one of the trimmers open its very easy to move between the two types of trimmer, and between target objects and edits, without returning to the Timeline.

Opening the trimmers

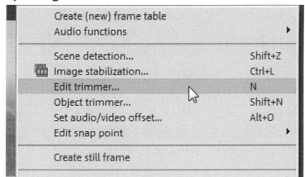

Each trimmer consists of a pop-up window which is fixed in size but can be moved for convenience. No controls other than those in the trimmer will work until you close the window. The trimmers look quite similar, with two preview monitors left and right. Other than the small label, they are distinguished by the central areas between the two monitors.

Open the Object trimmer on any clip to see the visual difference between the two tools. The Object trimmer shows a pink representation of the current object between the monitors. Even if there is no fade in at the beginning, there are slopes for both the In and Out points.

If you click on the arrow icons below the monitors the next or previous object on the track gets loaded into the Object trimmer - which is how you navigate along the clips on the Timeline without going back to the Timeline.

The Trimmer navigation controls

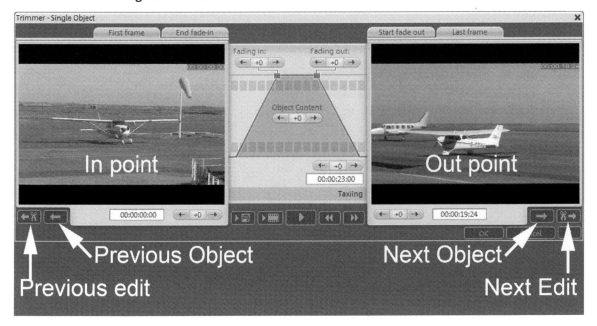

Clicking on the scissors icons below the monitors switches to the Edit trimmer mode, selecting the junction at the beginning of the highlighted clip.

The Edit trimmer showing a different central area.

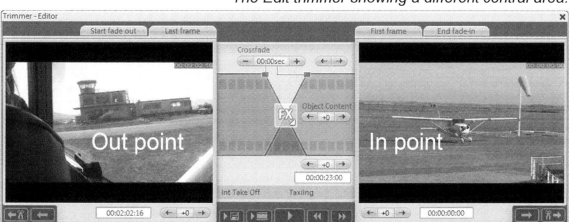

The central area in the Edit trimmer shows a cross with a FX icon in the middle (even if there is a cut here). So, it's easy to navigate up and down the movie, switching between objects and between the edit points, with the navigation buttons under the two monitors.

Transport controls

The other set of controls that are common to both types of trimmer are the transport buttons located at the bottom of the central area.

The three play tools have slightly different functions. They all cause the area of the video indicated by the blue range to be played in the left monitor, The range is set when you open a trimmer and is, by

The common trimmer transport controls

default, centred around the beginning of the object or across the edit point.

If the computer is low powered and the transition complex, you may have to render the transition. In this case the furthest left play button would play just the rendered section. The second button plays the range a frame at a time even if it needs to slow down playback so that you see each frame, while the third "normal" playback button plays the range in real time even if that requires frames to be skipped. You will probably only be able to use the third button on an reasonably up to date computer.

The scrubbing buttons move the scrubber, and the blue range, so that you can preview other parts of the clip. However, if you move the range so far that it no longer contains the In point of the object, it will skip back to the default position when you use the Play button.

Left and right monitors and tabs

From the screenshot on the previous page, you can see that the left and right monitors display different video thumbnails depending on which trimmer you are using. In the Object trimmer the left monitor shows the object's In point, or the first frame of the video after any fade up that might be applied has been completed. Which of these two points you see is controlled by the tabs above the monitor.

So, if the object had a 12 frame fade up applied to it, then selecting the *First frame* tab would show you black level, and the switching to the *End fade up* tab would show you frame 12. Even if there is actually a crossfade the Object trimmer treats the part of the object used in the overlap as a fade up. If there is any other transition, or a simple cut, then the two tabs show the same frame - frame 0.

Looking at the right monitor, the same two tabs exist but are labelled *Start fade out* and *Last frame*.

For the Edit trimmer, the left monitor shows the Out point of the preceding clip. If there is a transition, the tabs select if you see the frame of the outgoing when the transition starts - *Start fade out* - or ends - *Last frame*. The right monitor shows the In point of the highlighted clip, and the tabs are *First frame* and *End fade in*. You don't see the transition unless you play or jog using the transport controls.

Object trimmer parameter controls

The rest of the controls for each trimmer are parameter based. They are small and unlabeled, so for clarity I'm going to label them in my screenshots. Starting with the Object trimmer, I've label the controls from A to Q. The brief description below is only a start - I will also demonstrate the functions and how they affect other clips later in the chapter. You might want to bookmark the pages with the labelled screenshots to refer back to quickly. Some of the parameters have keyboard shortcuts as well.

A - Shortens a fade-in at the start of an object (shortcut E).

B - Lengthens a fade-in at the start of an object (shortcut R).

C - Shortens a fade out at the end of an object (shortcut U).

The parameters labelled in the Object trimmer

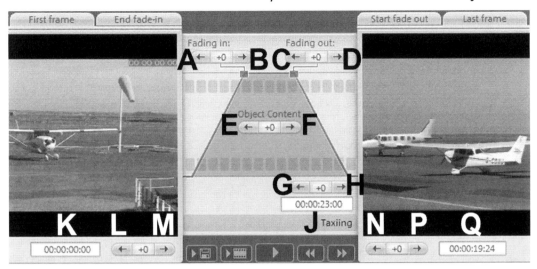

D - Lengthens a fade out at the end of an object (shortcut I).

E - Moves both the In and Out points earlier, slipping the content of a clip without changing it's position or duration on the Timeline.

F - Moves both the In and Out point later, slipping the content in the reverse direction to arrow E.

G - Moves the object earlier on the Timeline.

H - Moves the object later on the Timeline.

J - Timecode entry box to change the position on the Timeline where the object begins.

K - Timecode entry box to change the In point of the object. The duration and position are both affected.

L - Moves the In point of the object earlier on the Timeline, increasing the duration.

M - Moves the In point of the object later on the Timeline, reducing the duration.

N - Moves the Out point of the object earlier on the Timeline, reducing the duration.

P - Moves the Out point of the object later on the Timeline, increasing the duration.

Q - Timecode entry box to change the Out point of the object. The duration and position are both affected.

The Object trimmer In and Out points

Object trimming In point behaviour

When you aren't playing or using the scrubbing controls, The left monitor shows the In point of the object. Beneath the monitor the timecode (label K) shows position of the In point relative to the whole clip. If the In point has not been trimmed, this will show zero. You can type a timecode in here and alter the In point of the clip, or use the offset controls L and M to adjust the In point a frame at a time.

When you adjust the In point of an object, the behaviour of the preceding clip is to automatically trim it's own In point in sympathy.

Therefore if you move the In point of clip 2 earlier (using L), the Out point of clip 1 is moved earlier by the same amount. Earlier in the book I called this Rolling the edit.

← 50 Frames back

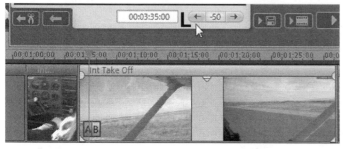

If you make the In point of clip 2 later (using M), the Out point of clip 1 will be extended if possible. If there is no material to extend, a gap is created. The clips are never overlapped.

50 Frames forward →

The monitor on the right of the Object trimmer shows the Out point of the object.

When you adjust the Out point of an object, the following clip remains attached. It's the subsequent clip that is affected.

So if you shorten clip 1 by moving the Out point earlier, (the arrow labelled N) clip 2 moves in its entirety in sympathy and a gap is created between clips 2 and 3. If you lengthen clip 1 by moving the Out point later (the arrow labelled P), clip 2 is moved to the right by the same amount, but it is not shortened. Instead of overwriting clip 3, it overlaps it, creating a transition.

As an aside, I find this behaviour somewhat confusing. My tactic is to avoid adjusting Out points in Object mode, but use the Edit trimmer instead.

Object trimming Out point behaviour

50 Frames back

50 Frames forward

Moving Object Content

Sliding the content of a clip

If you have a clip in a position that you don't want to move, of a duration that you don't want to alter, you can still shift the In and Out points simultaneously to slide the content of the clip backwards or forwards. The value in the Object content box shows the current In point from the start of the clip in frames. If you use the offset boxes (labelled E and F) you can slide the content back and forth, choosing suitable In and Out points. You can also adjust the Object content in the Edit trimmer, where the same control works on the incoming video.

Moving Object position in the Object trimmer

In object mode, this control has almost the same effect as if you use the rolling trim cursor on the In point of the selected object. It works in Mouse mode for all tracks as well. If you use the left increment control labelled G, the whole clip moves to the left, overwriting the outgoing video to its left.

If you move the object to its right using the control labelled H, the Out point of the preceding clip is extended to line up with the In point of the object you are moving.

Up until the point where the outgoing video runs out of material this is the same as rolling the edit point, but whereas if you do so on the Timeline you can't roll any further when there is no more outgoing video, you can use the Object trimmer to move the clip further, creating a gap.

Moving an object and it's effect on other tracks

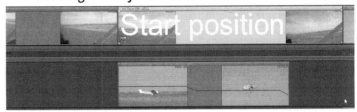

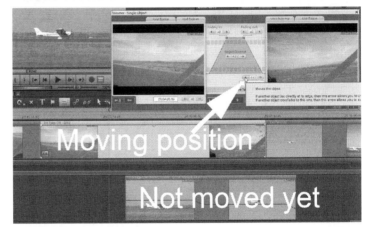

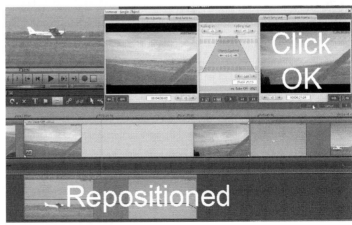

What is a great cause of confusion is that the Timeline as a whole only updates the current track smoothly. You may not see objects on other tracks move at all, or if they do it will be in jerky steps. Only when you accept the changes with the OK button will the other tracks move to the correct positions. This is illustrated by the screenshot, but will be easier to understand if you try it out!

If you are using this feature to move a clip within a complex multi-track project, particularly with grouped objects, it's important to only make one movement at a time, otherwise it's possible to knock some of the objects out of sync, particularly if gaps are being created. Unless you really need frame accuracy, I'd suggest using the Timeline tools for this.

Editing fades

You can create or adjust fade in and outs very easily with the Fading in (labelled A and B) and Fading out (labelled C and D) controls. Using the view selection tabs above the monitors allows you to judge to perfection where a fade ends or begins. This is an example where the trimmer is superior to the Timeline tools!

The Edit trimmer parameter controls

I need to add labels to the Edit trimmer as well. I've reused labels that have the same function, or the mirror image of that function, caused by the monitors being swapped.

The parameter labels for the Edit trimmer

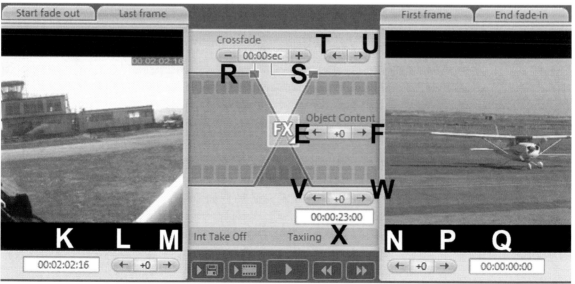

K - Timecode entry box to change the Out point of the outgoing object. The duration and position are both affected.

L - Moves the Out point of the outgoing object earlier on the Timeline, decreasing the duration.

M - Moves the Out point of the outgoing object later on the Timeline, increasing the duration.

N - Moves the In point of the incoming object earlier on the Timeline, increasing the duration.

P - Moves the In point of the incoming object later on the Timeline, decreasing the duration.

Q - Timecode entry box to change the In point of the incoming object. The duration and Out point position are affected.

R - Reduces the duration of any crossfade between the outgoing and incoming objects.

S - Increases the duration of any crossfade.

T - Moves the cut or transition to the left.

U - Moves the cut or transition to the right.

E - Moves both the In and Out points earlier, slipping the content of a clip without changing it's position or duration on the Timeline.

F - Moves both the In and Out point later, slipping the content in the reverse direction to arrow E.

V - Adds or increases the duration of a transition by moving the incoming object to the left.

W - Reduces the duration of a transition by moving the incoming object right.

X - Timecode value for the start of the incoming video.

Using the Edit trimmer

There are significant differences when you are using the trimmer in Edit mode. It's on the whole more useful, but it still has its quirks.

The left monitor shows the Out point of the preceding clip. If you change this all the content to the right moves to hold position. Again, it won't be clear where objects on other tracks will end up until you click on OK.

The right monitor shows the In point of the selected clip. If you change this the duration of the selected clip is altered, with objects to the right holding position.

What is really useful, is that you have an instant preview of what the edit is going to look like. You don't even have to use the Play button, you just glance between the two monitors and you will get a fair idea, particularly if you are looking for continuity errors.

Edit trimming and Object content

The Edit trimmer controls

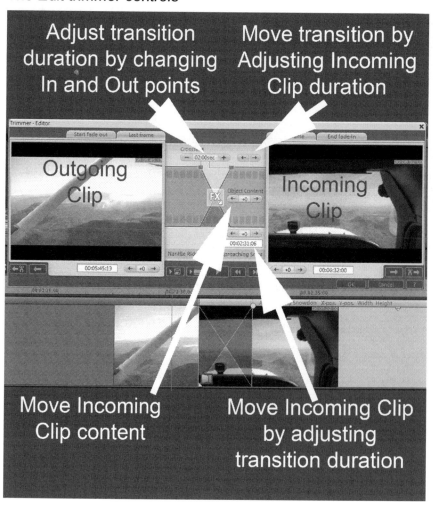

I've already described what moving the object does, and how useful it can be. In the Edit trimmer you can do this on the selected clip - to the right of the edit you are monitoring.

The function behaves in the same way as it does in the Object trimmer using the arrows labelled E and F. It even works if there is a transition instead of a cut,

Trimming Transitions

The edit trimmer is centred on the junction of two objects. You can move the transition even if it is a cut. Unlike the Object editor, you cannot do so if there isn't sufficient material – no gaps are ever created. This means that the Edit trimmer is a more useful way of rolling an edit point than using the Object trimmer, as other Timeline objects are more likely to hold sync.

Moving the transition (or cut) between clips 1 and 2 to the left (labelled T) reduces the duration of clip 1 and increases the duration of clip 2. The point at which the transition occurs becomes earlier in the Timeline.

Moving a transition

Moving the same transition to the right (label U) increases the duration of clip 1 and reduces the duration of clip 2. The point at which the transition occurs becomes later in the Timeline.

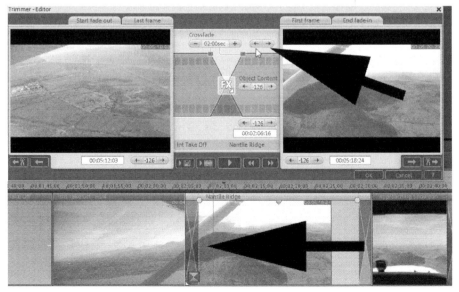

You can change a cut into a crossfade by one of two methods. Increasing the duration from zero (label 3) builds a crossfade centred on the original cut – both the incoming and outgoing video is extended by equal amounts, which is clear when you click on the tools – each click is for 2 frames, one each from both sources.

When you create a transition using the Transition menu, moving the Incoming clip to the left or dropping a transition from the Media pool onto a cut, neither source is extended; instead, the Timeline duration shortens because of the overlap. To achieve this in the Edit trimmer you need to move the incoming video using the buttons labelled V and W

With the four tools – crossfade duration (R and S) , moving the transition (T and U), moving the incoming object (V and W) and moving the content of the incoming object (E and F) you have total control of the transition.

Changing crossfades

The FX menu

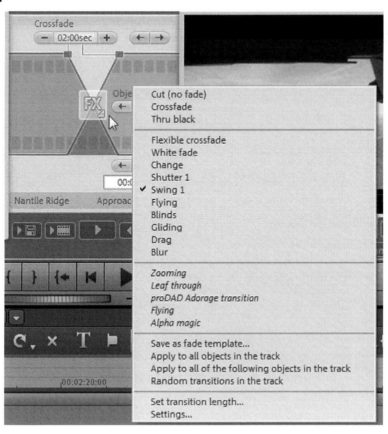

In the middle of the Edit trimmer is an FX icon. Clicking on this brings up the transition menu, from where you can perform all the functions previously described.

So from the above descriptions, you can see I have more reservations about using the Object trimmer than the Edit trimmer. Apart from adding fades to objects, I'd recommend you use the Edit trimmer by choice. There are still some potential traps awaiting you, but less of them!

Fine cutting the Flight project

With the Director's cut open. let's return to the list of notes we have to address for our Flight project. If you've skipped straight here from the end of the last chapter, the bold label letters (such as M) refer to the earlier screenshots of the Object trimmer on page 361 and Edit trimmer on page 366..

The first task is to come into the opening shot later, after the bump:

- On the Timeline, trim the In point of the opening shot to the right so that it clicks into place with the end of the title on track 2. This gets us in the ball park – we have trimmed off the first 14 seconds and the bump is about to happen.

- Right click on the first shot and open the Object trimmer.

- Click on the End fade in tab above the left monitor so we are seeing the shot as the fade ends.

- Use the right pointing increment arrow below (M) to jog through the bump.

Trimming the In point of the first clip

- I've settled on +50 frames as being stable enough. Use the trimmer's play button to preview the fade up.

- I think we can lengthen the fade. Use the Fading in box B to set the duration to +50 frames.

- Click on *OK* to accept the trims and return to the Timeline.

When you play the opening section, don't worry about the title or audio for now, we will sort them out when we have a few more changes. The next thing to adjust is the first edit. The plane jumps from the grass to very close to the tarmac, giving a poor continuity edit:

- Right click on the second shot and select the Edit trimmer.

- Under the left monitor, click on the Right pointing increment arrow (M) a couple of times.

- This is the wrong direction, and because there is no more incoming video a gap is created.

- This won't usually happen – there will normally be some source material, but you need to know how to fix the problem

- Try to fix the gap by using the other arrow the same number of times so the offset returns to zero.

- Unfortunately the gap will remain!

- Look in the "move Incoming clip" offset box between V and W and it still says the number of frames you moved the In point in the wrong direction

- Use the left pointing arrow V just once.

- The gap disappears! This neat trick closes up the gap and the offsets have all returned to zero.

If the above hasn't worked for you, you can always abandon trimming by clicking on Cancel - a handy strategy while you are unfamiliar with using the trimmers. Then open the edit trimmer and carry on:

- Now use the left pointing Out point increment arrow L to loosen the Out point.

- We are aiming to match the continuity between the left and right monitors.

- At +200, the plane is just about to leave the grassed area. This matches the In point on the right.

- Click on *OK* and the all the objects to the right will jump to their correct positions.

Review the edit. The continuity is great. Unfortunately, the next bump on the start of the incoming shot is still there. To fix this we can roll the edit to the right and the continuity should still be good:

- Open the Edit trimmer for clip 2 again.

- Move the transition with the upper buttons to the right- T and U. You can check the cut by using the play button. You can even adjust the position while the edit is playing in loop mode.

- I've settled on +75 frames. Set your offset to that and click OK.

The new edit to shot 2

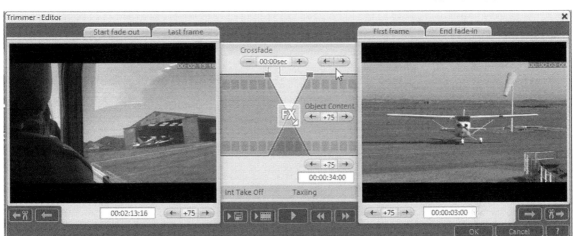

Our next task is to shorten the taxi run. I'm going to leave the second shot before the twin-engine plane appears, losing another wobble, and start the next shot after we have past it:

- Open clip 3 in the Edit trimmer.

- Trim the Out point of clip 2 in the left monitor back using the M arrow.

- We are looking for a point where the twin-engine plane is just about to appear, but we haven't seen it yet.

- You can trim back if you go too far by using using the L arrow.

- I've settled on -50 frames.

- Now we can cut out the the twin-engined plane from shot 3.

- Trim the In point of clip 3 in the right monitor using N and P to +145 frames, so the twin engine plane has loft chot and we are starting to see the next plane.

- Click on OK.

Shortening the taxi run

You will notice that there is a big overlap on the audio track now, and the audio keyframes are no longer lined up with the shot changes, but the rest if the Timeline is in sync. We will fix these issues in Timeline mode:

- Switch to Mouse mode for single objects.

- Drag the first title on track 3 and line up the end of the title with the end of clip 1.

- Trim the first audio clip to line up with the start of video clip 1.

- Zoom the Timeline in sufficiently, then reduce the audio cross fade between audio clips 1 and 2 to a few frames by dragging the duration handle left.

- Use the CTRL key while dragging the audio keyframes to line up with the cuts in the video above. That way you won't inadvertently change the levels, just the horizontal positions.

- Press the F key to see the whole movie.

- Select Mouse mode for all tracks.

- Drag the whole movie to the left to lose the gap at the start.

Losing the gap at the start of the movie

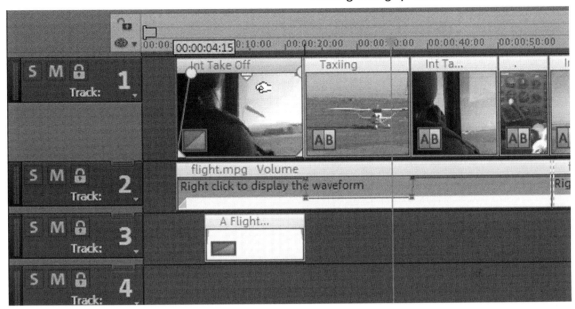

I'm going to add a new transition after the last take-off shot. If we added this conventionally the zoom out won't get a chance to settle and if we add it in overwrite mode we might see the reframe at the end of the zoom, so lets fine tune the transition by using the Edit trimmer:

- Click on clip 8, the first clip after we faded out the audio, and select the Edit trimmer.
- Using R and S, change the crossfade duration to 12 frames.

You can see from In and Out point offsets that we have grabbed 6 frames from each side of the edit.

- Play the transition using the play button in the trimmer to study the transition.

Let it play once to get itself up to speed properly. It seems to jar a little as we see the abrupt halt to the zoom. We don't need to stop playback for the next change:

- As the transition plays in loop mode, keep incrementing the duration.
- By the time you reach 24 frames, the jarring is virtually unnoticeable.
- Stop the replay and switch to viewing the Start fade out and End fade in using the tabs above the monitors.

The new crossfade with the Start fade out and End fade in selected for viewing.

- Your trimmer should match the screenshot. If it does, click on *OK* to accept the changes.

There are now just two more notes to address.

- Can we reduce the rest of the movie to get it to a duration of less than four minutes?

- Don't lose the music so early.

In fact, the movie is now already under 4 minutes, but not by much. If we can find a suitable section to lose, the second note will take care of itself, not starting to fade out until we cut to the touchdown shot.

When you have to edit a project down to a certain length, you often have to sacrifice something you quite like. I've decided that the pan back to the airfield could be removed:

- Open the Edit trimmer for clip 9, the Nantlle ridge.

- Select the *Start fade out* and *End fade in* tabs above the monitors

- Adjust the Out point in the left monitor by clicking in the right pointing increment arrow labelled M.

- Keep the button pressed and you will see the shot run backwards until it is looking at the mountain range and not the airfield.

- Stop at an offset of -350 frames.

- Use the play button to check the new position of the transition.

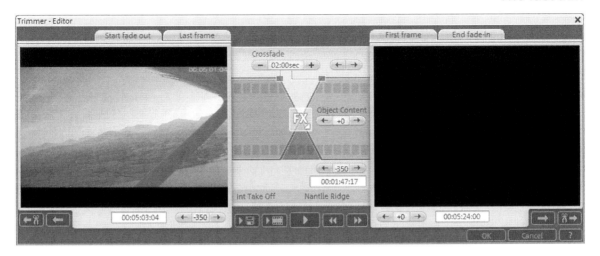

- It seems OK to me - select OK.

- Switch to Mouse mode for single object.

- Adjust the second part of the music track to lose the overlap.

Well, the movie is well under 4 minutes now, and if you listen to the music, it is still running as we bring up the atmosphere for the landing. I think we can say we have addressed all the Producer's notes.

- Save your project as *Flight over Snowdon Final cut*.

Let's hope they like it!

Advanced Techniques

This chapter explores a number of editing concepts that may have been touched on in the earlier chapters, but not demonstrated. To make it easier to study them individually, I'm going to use smaller, standalone, projects rather than shoehorn them into the Flight movie. The first two projects we make will be used in the final DVD project, although as usual you will be able to load the projects from the website or Demo DVD if you want to skip ahead. The source files and projects are in the Advanced techniques folder on the DVD.

Variable Speed

Some editing programs only allow speed to be added as a constant effect so if you want a video clip to gradually speed up or slow down, that's not possible to do, at least without complex workrounds. Movie Edit Pro does have this capability, even though it doesn't publicise it very well! Other editing programs may call it dynamic timewarp or variable fast or slow motion.

Let's take a simple clip and show basic principles. Start a new empty project and load the file *Car Clip 1.mpg* onto the Timeline. Depending on your project settings you may be prompted to match the settings to the clip. If you are asked, do so. If not, check the movie settings in *File/Settings/Movie* are set to 720*576, ratio 16:9 and frame rate 25. If they aren't, change them to match.

The clip is 8 seconds long and has timecode burned into the bottom of frame. Highlight the clip and scrub to 3 seconds exactly into the clip. The car is now properly into frame and the camera has started to pan with it.

Open the Effects tab of the Media pool, select *Video effects/Speed* and ensure the Effects overview is open at the bottom of the Media pool so that you can see the keyframe Timeline. Click on the diamond icon to set the first keyframe.

You should now see *Play Speed* in the effects list, with one keyframe located at 3 seconds on the keyframe Timeline. Scrub to exactly 4 seconds and alter the Speed Factor slider to 0.25 – the slowest we can go without removing the audio. Another keyframe appears, and the duration of the clip changes to 20 seconds 15 frames. Before we examine the effect ensure that the *Interpolate intermediate images* checkbox is clear.

Play the clip. It plays at normal speed for 3 second, then over the next second of burnt in timecode, but 1 second 15 frames of real time, slows down to quarter speed. The remainder of the clip takes 16 seconds of real time to play 4 seconds of video.

Keyframing the Speed effect

Locate the scrubber at the start of the clip and jog with the left and right keyboard arrows. You will see that the content changes every frame. Now scrub through the next section between the two keyframes. You will begin to notice that some of the frames are repeated. By the time you reach the third keyframe each frame appears to be repeated twice. You might have expected each frame to be repeated four times – quarter speed after all. If this demonstration used Progressive rather than Interlaced video that would have been the case.

Slowmotion and interlacing

In the opening chapter I explained the interlacing scheme – each frame of video consists of two fields, with each field made of either the odd or even scan lines.

Interlacing dates from the days of cathode ray tube sensors and displays, and really isn't needed any more, but there are still many systems that retain interlacing for backward compatibility. It therefore can't be ignored. It's also not just a simple case of "de-interlacing" interlaced sources before applying a slowmotion, because however well it is done, there is always some loss of information.

In order to display frames of interlaced video on a computer monitor or a modern flat panel TV, de-interlacing often happens automatically. Some editing programs hide this process, but in Magix Movie Editor Pro you can switch the processing off. Open *File/Settings/Program/Video/Audio/Other* and uncheck *Automatic interlace processing*. Now examine the clip. To begin with, the static video looks the same. Once the car appears, though, you can see the moving areas of the pictures have jagged lines around them. Once the camera starts to pan, the background and the wheels of the car are moving and these parts of the frame have the lines, while the car itself has less because it is relatively static – I'm panning with the car at roughly the same speed. When the black car goes through the foreground it's just a mess of lines as it's moving through the frame twice as fast.

As you jog through the second half of the clip, you will see that there is only one change of frame for every four steps – Quarter speed. The slow motion looks much jerkier – in fact, twice as jerky.

Close up of automatic interlace processing turned off (left) and on (right)

So interlaced video – when processed properly – makes for smoother slow-motion because it is recording 50 or 60 images a second, even though those images aren't of the whole frame. The interlace processing carried out by Movie Edit Pro isn't just a case of throwing half of the information away though – De-interlacing can be area based, so parts of the picture that aren't changing between fields can be shown full resolution.

We can leave the Program monitor's interlace compensation turned off, and apply it to just the current clip if we wish. In the clip context menu is an option for *Interpolation for interlace material.* However, if you check the box and play the clip you won't see any improvement initially. This interpolation needs to be calculated, so we have to render the section.

Set a blue range for the whole clip by setting the scrubber to the start of the Timeline and pressing the I key, then pressing End to send the scrubber to the end of the Timeline and finally pressing the O key.

Now click on the small dropdown arrow next to the eye symbol above the Timeline and select *Start preview rendering.* In the dialogue box that opens up, select Range. A red line appears above track 1 and the information bar at the bottom of the program window shows a progress bar. When complete, the red bar turns green, showing the range has been rendered.

Preview rendering menu

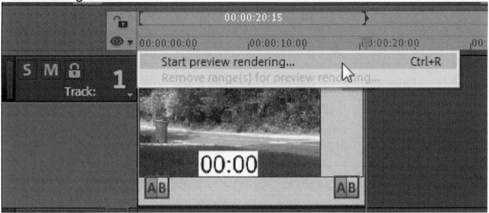

When you play back now, you will see the de-interlacing has actually worked. So there are two methods of de-interlacing, one using the computer hardware and the other software.

Interpolate intermediate images

When you select this checkbox in the Speed effect, the software will attempt to smooth out the jerkiness caused by slowing down the video.

Let's try it now. Switch the Program monitor interlace processing back on. Use the render menu and select Remove ranges for preview rendering. Confirm your choice and the green bar will disappear. Now check the Interpolate intermediate images checkbox and play the Timeline. What you see will look horrible! The car actually appears to go four steps forward then travel backwards! However, this is a quirk of the Program monitor and would not be what you see when the clip is exported. It seems that the automatic interlace processing is clashing with the interpolation attempts in real time

You can fix this in one of two ways. Firstly try rendering the section. Follow the steps above and you will see the intended effect of using the Interpolate checkbox. When you study the individual frames after the speed has dropped to 25%, each frame is different, with the frames that were duplicated before a mix of the frames either side – every fourth frame even shows the last digit of the timecode with two values!

Alternatively, you can switch off the automatic interlace processing and set the clip to Interpolation for interlaced material. However, you will still need to render the section to see the result, and to my eyes I can see no difference in quality between the two methods.

So a couple of important points here:

The Automatic interlace processing isn't foolproof. If you are slowing down interlaced material and using the Interpolate intermediate frames option you need to render the section to see the effect properly even if scanning the Timeline tells you nothing needs rendering.

Interlaced material can result in smoother slow motion - 50i is better that 25p for smoothness even before you try to interpolate. 25p is better for detail.

Speeding up

Let's add a few more keyframes to the car clip. At 05:00 seconds on the Burnt-in timecode, 00:00:08:15 Movie timecode, add another keyframe with the value still at 0.25, then at 06:00 BITC, 00:00:12:15 change the Speed value to Factor 4. Make sure Interpolate intermediate images is turned off.

Notice that as you alter the speed factor using the Effects toolbox, the clip not only changes duration but the display attempts to fill the width of the Timeline window with the clip. This can be confusing at first, particularly as we are working with just one clip and have no reference points.

Interpolated image (middle)

Jog through the last few seconds of the clip. Once you pass the third keyframe the car starts to speed up. Once it has reached "normal" speed there is one frame of video for each frame of Timeline, but that only lasts briefly as the effect drops more and more frames until we see only every fourth frame. If you try to interpolate speeded up video it will attempt to get the spacing between frames correct by blending images together, but the effect is lost within a blur of fast motion.

Effect curves

Click on the small "eye" icon after the effect label Play Speed and the effects curve will be superimposed on the clip.

Enabling the Speed curve view

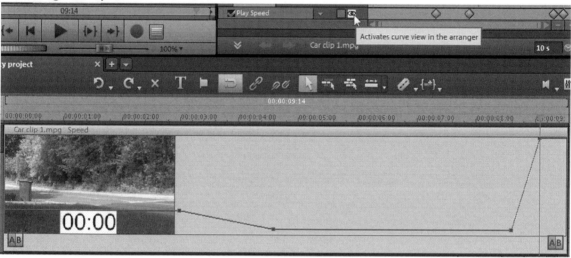

You can see that it consists of straight lines, and there is no option to impose Bezier curves in the way we can with other effects, but remember that the speed effect ramps up over time anyway, so the changes tend not to look that linear anyway – notice how the car appears to slow down gradually.

A big word of warning. The features of the effects curves menu do work after a fashion, but because the data was created for a clip that was changing duration as you entered the parameters, if you try to use the curves on another clip the results are totally unpredictable. The Combine effect curve with object length option has even odder results – you can end up with the curves going back in time!. So, my advice regarding the use of these functions is – don't even think about it!

However, revealing the curve does alert us to a major possibility – they can be edited in the same way as volume curves, using the mouse on the nodes on the curves themselves. The problem is that every time you make a change, the clip changes duration! You can even use the Curves tool to make non-linear curves, but you have to be very careful indeed.

"Real" slow motion

If you want to slow down movement properly, interpolation is not normally going to give you good results. There are special software tools that will analyse video on a frame by frame basis and only work on the areas that should be moving. For these methods to work, you need to choose the source footage very carefully so that the software can differentiate between what should, and should not, be treated. For example, a skateboarder flying through the air in a locked off shot might be a good source, but panning with him while he is on the ground is unlikely to work well. One commercial product is called Twixtor, which plugs into some editing programs (but not Magix), while a free standalone program called SlowmoVideo is also available for you to pre-treat clips and include them in your movies.

The real solution to getting smooth slow motion is to use a camera that captures at a higher frame rate than the standard you are using for your movie. The higher the framerate, the more discrete frames you get and the more you can slow the video down without getting jerky motion. While professional cameras that do this are expensive, the latest models of GoPro cameras can record video at as high a frame rate as 240 frames per second if you are willing to lower the resolution. One downside of using high frame rates is that by necessity you have to use a high shutter speed, so the footage can look quite jerky when played back normally.

The Bird slow motion project

For this movie, I've shot some GoPro video at a rate of 100 progressive frames a second with a resolution of 1280 by 720. We will be able to slow this down significantly without the judder becoming noticeable.

The original file is very long. I have rendered two versions for you to use. The MP4 file *Bird slomo compact.mp4* is small (9MB) and of reasonable quality. If you have the Demo DVD or a fast Internet connection you might want to download the very large (139Mb) high quality Cineform rendered file – *Bird slomo cineform.AVI*.

Movie Edit Pro and codecs

Movie Edit Pro doesn't come with the codec required to use the Cineform AVI. Fortunately, if you install the codec on your computer, its presence will be picked up and MEP will be able to use it. If you download and install the free GoPro Studio 2.0 program (or a later version) from www.gopro.com you will get the codec required.

- Copy the file of your choice from the DVD or Download folder to the Video Library/Your User Name Videos

High frame rates and Project settings

I want to start a 100 frames a second movie project, but there isn't a preset for that. Normally, if you add a clip to an empty project and the settings don't match, a dialogue box will warn you and offer to change the movie settings. However, if you happen to have the correct resolution already selected, unusual frame rates seem to be ignored. The safest thing to do is set the movie parameters manually:

- Start a new Project and in the opening dialogue select *Create new project* and enter the name *Bird slowmo*.

- Open the options box and in the movie settings select *User Defined*, then click on OK

- In the Project/Movie settings that appear next, choose NTSC or PAL HDV1 1280x720, and then change the frame rate to 100.

- Click on *OK*.

- Open the Import tab of the Media pool, locate the Bird feeding video file and drag it to the beginning of track 1.

OK, we are ready to review the source video now. Play the Timeline and you'll see how short the clip is. Jog through a few sections and you will see that the timecode shows 100 frames for every second.

Here's the plan: Start at quarter speed as the bird waits in the bushes. As it takes off, slow the video even more to see it in flight. When it lands I want to speed it up as it takes the food, slow it back down for the first few flaps of take-off, then bring it back up to normal speed.

I'm going to show you how to generate most of these speed effects using the curves on the clip itself, but first we need to get into the correct mode:

- Open the Effects tab in the Media pool and select *Video effects/Speed*.

- Adjust the height of track 1 so that it occupies about 25% of the available screen, then adjust the other areas to suit.

- Highlight the clip and place the scrubber at the start.

- Click on the Add keyframe tool and then pull the *Speed Factor* slider down to 0.25.

- Click on the eye icon to the right of the *Play Speed* effect label (see the illustration on page 386) to activate the curve view in the arranger.

- Save the project.

Play the clip. You can see that the speed effect is very pleasing. The 100 frames a second slowed down to 25 frames still looks smooth to the human eye even though each frame is being repeated 4 times. If we rendered this out to a 25fps file there would be no repeated frames.

We can now see the red line and if you look closely you can just make out the single keyframe superimposed on the start of the clip. For the next step I'm going to choose a point in the bird's first flight where I want to begin to slow the motion down even more.

- Use the timescale context menu to set the view to Zoom 1 second.

- Scrub to 00:00:02:50, where the bird has just left the bush. Leave the cursor there as we will use it as a guide.

- Click on the intersection of the red speed effect "curve" and the cursor. A new keyframe appears.

- Scrub along to exactly 6 seconds where the bird is just about the land.

- Use the same technique as above to set a new keyframe.

- Hold down the Shift key to restrain movement to the vertical and try to drag the keyframe lower – you will find that you can't.

- If you move it upwards, the keyframe also travels to the left, because the clip is getting shorter.

- Pull it back down to the minimum value and release the mouse button.

Speed restrictions

If you want to alter the speed factor outside the range of 0.25 to 4.00 you have to detach the audio.

- Right click on the clip and use *Audio functions/Remove audio object*.

Now, I could just let you drag the keyframe down to zero, but if you do so you will cause MEP all sorts of problems. You can touch zero, but need to come back up again or otherwise you get a freeze frame and the program doesn't know what duration to set the clip to – theoretically it should be infinity.

- Set a new keyframe at 7 seconds exactly – still with a value of 0.25.

- Adjust the Timeline view to Zoom 10 Seconds.

- Now, hold down Shift, pull the third keyframe – the one current at the 6 second mark – down to zero.

If you play the Timeline now you will see how the bird almost freezes. Let's set a few more keyframes for the second take-off:

- Set keyframes at 15, 16, 17 and 18 seconds exactly.

We could use the parameter box to set the last keyframe to Factor 1 exactly, but here is another way:

- Make sure that the factor value can be seen in the Media pool.

- Place the scrubber at the end of the clip.

- Use SHIFT drag to raise the level of the last keyframe.

- You can adjust it to exactly a "normal" speed value of 1 by watching the value change in the Factor box.

It's not possible to use that trick in every circumstance, though, because the video clip may be changing duration at the point you want to monitor. If you didn't have to match my numbers you could just adjust by trial and error, but I need you to set the sixth keyframe, currently at 16 seconds, to a value of 0.10:

- Locate the keyframe in the Effect keyframe Timeline and click to select it. It will turn blue.

- Enter the value 0.10 into the Factor box.

- Make a safety copy of the movie so far - *Bird slomo 1*.

Bird slomo 1 with keyframes arrowed

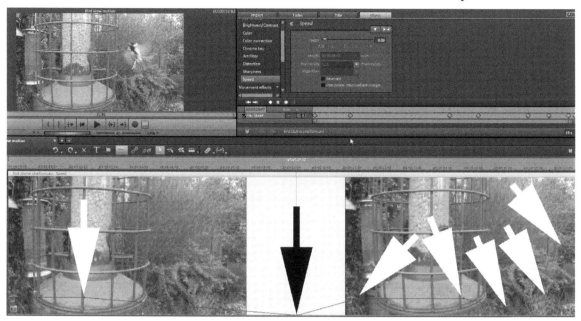

Creating Bezier curves manually

We could just leave it there, but you might want to experiment with smoothing out the curves and seeing if they make a difference. In the process you are bound to end up with a different duration to me, but that won't matter too much.

Take a look at the screenshot below - I've enhanced the keyframes and lines to make it clearer. I've adjusted the first curve for the landing by adding another 7 keyframes to the 7 we had already. I've only adjusted the first and last frames horizontally using the CTRL key to limit the dragging, and I've not changed the central keyframe at all. Using freehand dragging I've created a reasonable curve with the additional frames. There may be a certain amount of flickering when adjusting low values, but if you are having issues, use the SHIFT key when dragging.

Manual curves

A warning – as it is possible to set the value right down to zero, if you create two such keyframes next to each other Magix will get very confused, as I mentioned before.

So, with care, try to create a curve similar, or better, than mine. Play the modified effect and I think you will agree the new curve does make an improvement to change of speeds, albeit a small one.

You could attempt to draw a curve with the Curves mouse tool, but it requires patience and a steady hand because the duration of the clip keeps changing under the cursor. Even when I achieved a good looking curve, the end result wasn't significantly better enough to warrant the hard work!

- Save the movie as *Bird slowo final cut*.

Audio sync

Some people shoot events with more than one camera. One camera might hold a wide shot and one or more of the other camera closer shots of the event. They then put the recorded footage on separate tracks and line them up so that they are all showing the same moment in time. Even if you then don't use any special editing modes this is a very efficient way of making a cut movie.

Movie Edit Pro Plus and Premium do in fact have a special editing mode for using two cameras, more of which later, but the first problem you will have is getting the video clips from more than one camera lined up so that the audio and action match on the separate tracks.

The major issues with using consumer or semi-professional cameras to do this are that they don't employ proper timecode. If you have a DV or HDV camera it is possible to extract a tape time or even a time of day but it's very tricky to set two cameras up so that their timecodes match. Other cameras don't even have this feature.

It's actually not that hard to get the clips lined up physically. You can normally identify a visual point that all the cameras can see and use this as a reference point. If you plan ahead, you can use a device such as a clapper board or flashgun to create an accurate reference point before the event starts, but then you have to keep all the cameras rolling for the duration of the event.

Better still is if all the cameras have an audio track. You can put clips on two tracks, study the waveforms and drag to get the clips in the ball park, and then use the Object trimmer to adjust the positions on a frame accurate basis until they sound correct when played at the same time. On-board microphones are normally good enough for this even if one camera might be using an external microphone, or you use an external digital audio recorder for high quality sound.

Movie Edit Pro has a really useful feature to help you line up audio sources. Even with quite variable quality sources it has a high success rate. To show you how it works, I'm going to use some sample footage:

- Find the clips *camera 1.mpg*, *camera 2.mpg* and *camera 3.mpg* on the website or Demo DVD and copy them to a suitable location.

- Start a new project, calling it *Multi Camera*.

- Drag and drop the three camera clips to the start of tracks 1, 2 and 3.

- Select all the clips using CTRL-A.

The tool is going to attempt to sync up all the selected clips. You need to nominate one clip to be the target that the other clips sync up to, although that is no guarantee that the target clip won't be moved to make space for the others. Normally you would choose the source with the best quality audio, or the longest duration. Let's arbitrarily choose the camera 3 clip:

The audio sync function

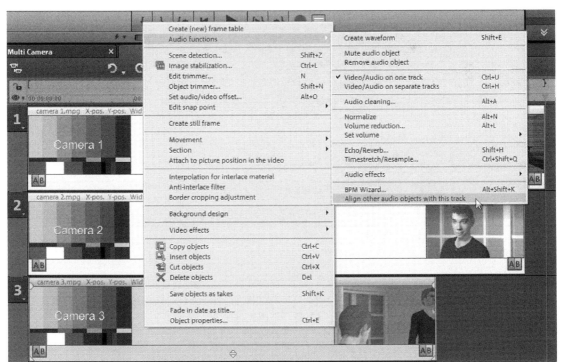

- Right click on the camera 3 object on track 3.

- It will be highlighted deep yellow, the other two clips pale yellow.

- From the clip context menu select Audio functions and in the sub-menu right at the bottom you will see *Align other audio objects with this track*.

- Select it.

To begin with, the action occurs in the Information bar at the bottom of the screen. Waveforms will be created for the audio tracks if they don't already exist. Then the waveforms are scanned and compared, and finally the clips will be aligned on the tracks. Notice that although we chose track 3, the clip has been moved because the clips on the other tracks need to start earlier.

Play the Timeline and you will hear the audio is slightly odd – because the audio isn't exactly frame accurate between the clips there is a certain amount of phasing and echo. This is likely to be an issue with most consumer camera sources because they aren't locked together, but the audio is never going to be more than half a frame out, and the program can cope with this. What's more, the human viewer will find a sync error that small very hard to detect as long as you don't try to mix together two audio sources that are slightly out of sync.

The three clips aligned

Obviously I have made the job quite an easy one because all three clips have the same quality audio, but I can assure you that I've had great success even with syncing up three cameras, one of which was fitted with a high quality external microphone. I can also normally sync up a footage for a DSLR that records audio with an onboard microphone to an audio file recorded by Digital audio recorder using a tie clip mike.

Sometime it does go wrong, and when it does the sync is normally way out, so you know straight away that it's wrong. If the program keeps latching on to the wrong waveform you can try trimming the clips to shorter sections and trying again, which sometimes gets a result. Even with a 90% success rate, however, you save a huge amount of time!

Save the current project as *Multi Camera aligned*.

Multi-camera editing

With three cameras now synced up on the Timeline you can see how it's possible to edit your event very quickly. One option is to use the Mute buttons for monitoring, splitting the clips with the razor and dragging the chosen shots down to track 4. You can choose the best audio track as the source and split this off onto a further track, then disable the audio on the other clips. Fine adjustments can be made with rolling trims and if you decided to cut out a whole section, all you need to do is cut all three tracks, select the unwanted sections for all the tracks and use CTRL-Delete.

Movie Edit Pro Plus and Premium offer a further enhancement – Multicam. In this mode you can automate the selection of the live video source, either in real time or as you work your way along the Timeline. Unfortunately the multi-cam tool in Movie Edit Pro can only handle two cameras at a time (Video Edit Pro can handle 9 sources). It's quite possible to stop and start the process, though, so you can drop additional cameras in by changing the selection.

Multi-camera works by nominating track 1 for the final video and track 2 for the final audio. By default track 3 is used as one source, track 4, the other. When you are in Multi-camera mode, the Program monitor displays a split screen with the two potential sources on the left and the output on the right. When you click on your chosen source on the left, it is copied up to the top tracks at that point on the Timeline. You can make these choices either during live playback, or with the scrubber stationary. During live playback the Timeline and right preview will lag a little behind your choices, but when you stop playback you can review your work and the cutting points will relate to the exact moment you clicked on the mouse button.

You can see that we need to do a bit of housekeeping before we can try this in action.

- If required, add tracks to bring the number up to 8.
- Select all the Timeline objects and drag them down to tracks 3, 4 and 5, leaving tracks 1 and 2 clear.
- Click on the Multicam icon alongside the Timeline view icon.

- Set the Playback marker to the beginning of the Timeline.

In the top left of the Program monitor you will see Camera 1's output. Camera 2 has yet to have a picture, and there is nothing either on the right or on the top two tracks.

Multicam mode ready to roll

- In the Program monitor, click on the picture from camera 1.

- It will appear on the right, and the video and audio from track 3 will appear on tracks 1 and 2.

- Save the project as *Multi Camera setup*.

You can now try a little bit of "live" vision mixing. Let me describe what I want you to do first:

- Switch the Program monitor to full screen.

- Play the Timeline and watch the wideshot.

- After the interviewer says "Hi" he turns his head to look at camera 2. That will be the first cut, where you click on the camera 2 feed in the program monitor.

- Now listen to the dialogue, and prepare to cut back to camera 1.

- The moment he finished talking, the camera starts to reframe, so you want to cut back to the wide shot.

When you have played the Timeline a couple of times and are ready, have a go:

- Set the scrubber back to the start of the Timeline, play the video and perform the two cuts as described.

- Switch the Program monitor back to normal and examine the Timeline.

- Switch off the Multi-cam icon and tracks 3, 4 and 5 will become muted and the Program monitor returns to normal. Play the movie.

Now, if you got it right first time, well done. If you didn't, then you can either select all the clips on tracks 1 and 2 and delete them and try again, or switch back to Multi-cam, scrub to the point where you cut late and adjust the edit by clicking again.

The first cutting point

Choosing audio

You will see that the audio clip under each video clip comes from the same camera, but if you had very good audio on one source and just guide audio on the other you can change that audio source. Click on the drop-down arrow just after the track head number and there is a small menu – we have used the track size options already, but under Multicam you can nominate which track is used as the source audio.

The Multicam menus

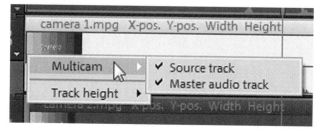

•Delete the clips on tracks 1 and 2.

•Use the Multicam menu on track 3 to select it as the Master audio track.

•You don't have to switch to Full screen preview if you are confident.

•Switch on the Multicam mode.

• Repeat your vision mixing task again.

Now if you look at the audio on track 2, although it is still split at the cutting points, it is all from Camera 1.

Choosing source tracks

You will have spotted that the Multicam menu also allows you to nominate which tracks are shown as sources, but you can only have two, so you need to deselect one track before you can add another:

• Use the Multicam menus to deselect track 4 and select track 5 as sources.

• Notice the coloured bars on the Timeline after the clips that indicate the source tracks have changed.

• Now play the Timeline and attempt to cut to camera 3 before the Interview stops speaking.

When you look at the Timeline, you may be puzzled. You didn't cut back to Camera 1, but the program has. The reason is because we run out of material on Camera 3. Let's do the job again.

• Play the Timeline yet again.

- This time cut to Camera 1 once the interviewee has finished standing.

Obviously there are limitations with only being able to have two sources and wanting to edit on the fly. You will always be undoing any edits you have already created to the right of the scrubber. If you work in a linear manner and are happy to stop and start, though, you can use more than two sources.

Multicam performance issues.

I have deliberately supplied standard definition MPEG-2 video for this demo so as not to put too much of a strain on your computer. The program is having to calculate three resizing operations as well as monitoring your editing and attempting to update the Timeline, all during real time playback. Working with HD sources, particularly H.264 video, will probably be quite difficult on most hardware. If that's the case, then you should consider using Proxy editing if you want to do Multicam efficiently. How to do that, and the pros and cons of doing so, are discussed later.

When you have finished your Multicam edit, you will need to switch back to the normal Timeline mode to view it. When you do so, all the sources on the lower tracks will be muted so you get a clean output to view and to export

Split Audio Video edits

Cutting the video and audio at different times is a very useful technique. Editors often call this type of edit a Split AV. We have alluded to the principle in the Flight project when we extended audio from our interior shots to cover the exterior shots.

There are many other reasons why you might want to edit audio and video at different points. Artistically, reaction shots may have more value than the shot of the person saying the words that are being reacted to. Splitting an edit can also make it look more natural or fix a continuity issue.

Movie Edit Pro shows Video and Audio on one track by default, so to perform a Split AV edit the first thing to do is separate the audio and video onto separate tracks using the clip context menu. Even then the clips will be grouped together, so you need to break the grouping so that you can achieve split AVs. If you made the Flight movie you should know how to do this, but I'm going to give another example now using dialogue clips.

We will be using the three camera clips from the previous Multicam demo. If you haven't loaded them from the Demo disc or Internet, do so following the instructions above. It's not relevant that these are from a multi-camera setup – even if you had shot them sequentially we could still use the same principle although they would be likely to have more continuity errors, making split AV techniques even more useful.

- Start a new PAL SD 16:9 project – *Split AV edit*.

- Drag the Camera 1 clip to the beginning of track 1.

- Scrub to 00:00:05:00 on the Timeline and use *Remove Start* or the Z key to chop off the beginning.

- Use the Insert Object mode tool to select overwrite mode.

- Set the Timeline scrubber one frame before the interviewer's head turn begins – 00:00:01:13.

- In the Media pool, locate the Camera 2 clip and either use the toolbar braces or dragging to place it in the Program monitor.

- In the Program monitor find the frame before the head turn - 00:00:06:10.

- Set this as the In point by using the Program monitor controls or pressing I.

- If you need to, go to the end of the clip and set an Out point so that the blue range covers the part of the shot we need.

- Drag the clip in the Program monitor down to track 1 so that it clicks into place where the Timeline scrubber is.

Review the first edit. It could be improved by rolling it to the right a few frames so that the cut is motivated by the head turn, We could do this on the Timeline, but let's use the Edit trimmer:

- Right click on clip 2 and select Edit trimmer using the context menu.

- Use the Move transition arrows to the right of the crossfade duration box to move the cut right by 5 frames.

- Use the Play button to preview the edit. It should look more natural now.

- Click *OK* to exit the trimmer.

The aim now is to cut away from Camera 2 after the Interviewer has said "Hi, I want to keep all of the first phrase, and" and then cut to Camera 3 when he says "keep the third phrase in the sentence as well." We then lose the middle of the speech which has a minor fluff – "cut out the second phrase, but". We will do this on the Timeline:

- Scrub the Timeline to find the gap between "and" and "cut". It should be at 00:00:05:00 MTC. Park the scrubber there as a marker, or place a marker.

- Put the Camera 3 clip in the Program monitor and find the gap between "but and "keep". It's at 00:00:11:10.

You might find this a bit tricky to do in the Program monitor. In other circumstances you might want to do this trim on the Timeline where you can see the waveform. I've given you the numbers here to speed up the demo.

- In the Program monitor set the In point to the gap in the words and Out point to the end of the clip.

- Drag the clip down to the Timeline so that it locks into position after the scrubber or marker, overwriting Camera 2's shot.

Review the edit now. The audio is great, I think you will agree. We could soften the audio cut with a brief mix if it wasn't working too well but in this case I think it is best left as it is. The third edit now doesn't work, but we will fix that later.

What about the second edit?

Very poor continuity for the second edit

If you look at the drink can in the interviewer's hand, there is very bad continuity – it jumps from his lap to his mouth over the edit. This is where we need to use a split AV:

- Select the whole Timeline with CTRL-A.

- Right click on any clip and select Audio functions/Video/Audio on separate tracks.

- The audio is moved to track 2.

- With all the clips still selected, click on the Ungroup tool.

Because camera 3 is behind the interviewer we can't see his mouth moving and therefore we have no audio sync issues. I'm going to get you to roll the edit to the left until the can is out of Camera 3's shot. We could use the Edit trimmer, but it will move the audio as well. If we perform the edit on the Timeline we can use the clip thumbnails:

- I'm using Tool tips to make the demo frame accurate. Switch them on in the *Help* menu if they are off.

- Adjust the height of track 1 to big and the zoom view to 1 second. If you have a smaller monitor you may have to enlarge the Timeline scaling even more to ensure you see the detail.

- Ensure that you are in Mouse mode for single objects so that the edit point rolls rather than overwrites.

- Hover over the middle of the edit between clips 2 and 3 to generate the double line rolling trim cursor.

Rolling the edit back to fix the continuity

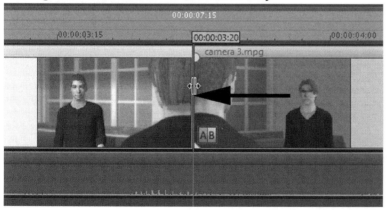

- Click and drag slowly left and the thumbnails will update as the edit moves.

- When the drink can completely disappears in the incoming shot the tooltip should say 03:20.

- Release the mouse button, and then review the edit.

I think we've fixed it, don't you? Now we need to tidy up the rest of the movie by cutting back to the interviewer's eyeline. I'm going to try to do that after the word "phrase":

- On the Timeline look for the Out edit point. Park the scrubber at 00:00:06:03.

- Put the Camera 2 clip into the program monitor and find the In edit point. I make it 00:00:13:06.

- Set the In and Out points and drag it down to the Timeline to click into place with the scrubber or marker.

When you play this edit you can currently hear both audio tracks and they are clearly a little bit out of sync. If we weren't editing multi-camera shots this would be academic – we would judge the edit on its own merits and adjust it accordingly. However, we might as well get it spot on!

- Open up the Edit trimmer for the cut between clips 3 and 4.

- Play the edit using the trimmer play button. As it loops, adjust the In point of the incoming clip on the right with the arrow adjusters under the right monitor.

- Listening, you can fine tune the audio so that it is in sync – the offset is -2.

- Click OK to accept the adjustment.

- Split both tracks at 00:00:07:14 and remove all the clips to the right.

- Right click on the last Camera 2 clip and select *Audio functions/Remove audio object*.

You may wish to cut back to the wide shot, but as I finished demonstrating a split AV edit, I'll leave that up to you.

Some editing software uses the terminology L-cuts and J-cuts to describe split AV edits. When you look at the shape of the Timeline around the split edit the camera 2 video and audio clips could be said to look a little like the letter L. If the edit had been performed by leading the audio it can look like the letter J. Another term you may hear is "leading the audio" (a J cut) or "extending the audio" (an L cut). Leading or delaying the video are other valid terms, but the result doesn't look like a letter!

Chromakey

This may be a familiar trick to you – it's been around for a long time now. It is sometimes called Green Screen. In the UK, the BBC called it Colour Separation Overlay, which helps explain it a little better. Before colour TV, the trick was attempted in monochrome – Luminance Overlay or Luma key

What basically happens is that a key signal is independently generated from a strong colour, deepest black or peak white, and this signal (or channel), like the "transparent" background of a title file, is used as a Key to determine if the background is shown, or the foreground picture is overlaid at any particular point on the screen. This process is sometimes called clipping. In Movie Edit Pro you can even use Alpha – (transparency) information if it is available in the source file – most likely a graphic, but possible with some video file types - as a clipping signal.

Chromakeying in principle

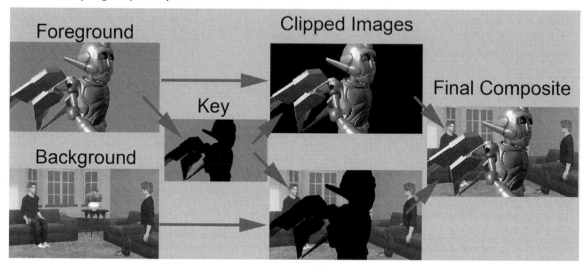

The real secret to achieving a decent overlay is getting the original shot as good as possible, and the most important factor is the lighting. If you are shooting your own material to use for Chromakey, place the foreground subject as far away from the background cloth as you can, as well as lighting the background as evenly as possible. It also helps if you can back or rim light the foreground with separate light sources if you have any. If you are going to do the whole thing in natural light, then a cloudy day is best, so you can avoid shadows from the foreground falling onto on the backing.

I've created two clips for you to try. Because they come from an animation program called iClone, the lighting is perfect, so we can explore what is possible with ideal material.

- Start a new PAL widescreen project called Chromakey and place the camera 1 clip on track 1.

- Trim the clip so it starts 5 seconds in and lasts for 10 seconds.

- Locate and copy a new video file called *Green Chromakey test.mpg* and copy it to your Video location.

- Drag it from the Media pool to the start of track 2.

- Highlight the clip on track 2, open the effects panel and select Video effects/Chroma key.

- Place the scrubber at 7 seconds.

You will just be seeing the foreground object – out fantasy figure (I'm going to call him Robbie) surrounded by green. By default the Chroma key setting is *Stamp* – which effectively does nothing unless the foreground contains transparency information. If we shrank the foreground we would be able to see off the sides, but it's not doing anything that wouldn't happen without the effect in place. You can treat it as an Off button!

I'll come to the other two tabs alongside Stamp in a moment, but underneath are some handy presets. The obvious one for the current clip is *Green*:

- In the lower section where it says *Colors to be hidden*, click on *Green*.

- Some of our character Robbie has now been superimposed on the background video, but it's nowhere near perfect.

- Play the video to see the effect.

The Chromakey effect

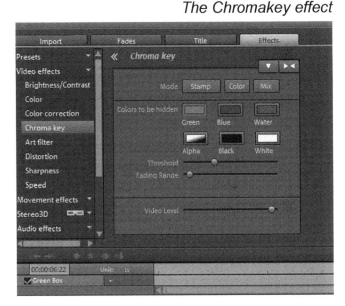

Three sliders have appeared. *Threshold* controls the level of the hard clipping while *Fading Range* softens the clipping. You might want to try adjusting these two faders to see more of Robbie, but you either end up with some parts of him looking transparent or green fringing.

The third slider, *Video level*, only affects the level of the foreground that has actually been inserted – you can make the bits of Robbie that we can see semi-transparent if you wish.

So why can't you get a perfect clip? Well, to start with, I have deliberately created a green background that isn't a pure colour – it is slightly off and somewhat desaturated. This is much more like you would get in a real studio, putting actors in front of a green cloth.

Before we refine the clip, a word about the other presets. *Blue* is an alternative primary colour, while *Water* used blue as a base, but modified with a broader range and transparency to give an artistic effect. *Alpha* uses any masking information available in the photo or video source, while *Black* and *White* offer keying on luminance, rather than colour.

Bad clipping with the Green preset

Let's return to the upper buttons. *Mix* is a preset that just adds the two sources together, but the one that will really help is *Color*, which allows us to sample the background to give us a more accurate key signal to clip on:

•Click on the *Color* tab.

•A dialogue box will open telling what to do next, so read it and select *OK*.

•The Program monitor will show the foreground video only, and when you hover over it, the eyedropper cursor appears.

•Draw a bounding box around a purely green area and release the mouse button.

Selecting the clipping colour

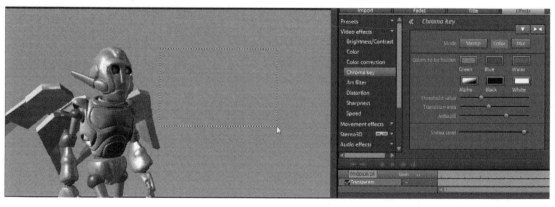

OK, that a bit better! The clip is more in tune with the actual color of the "green screen" I've created. If there were shading on a real backcloth you could chose an area with the eyedropper to include some of the shading.

Experiment with the controls again. While *Threshold* seems to be about right, reducing *Transition area* a a little makes a great improvement. It's still not possible to get a perfect clip, though.

A third control has also appeared – *Anti-Spill*. This can be used to reduce the key colour from the foreground source. In a real studio you are likely to get the colour of the backdrop bouncing off the foreground object, particularly around the edges. This is know as *Spill*. Increase the level of the slider and watch Robbie become less green!

But we still can't get a good clip, and the reason for that is because Robbie is the wrong colour for Green screen – he is mostly yellow, which is next to green in the colour spectrum.

Let's try Blue screen instead. It's easy for us, but if you had to re-dress an entire studio, you might suggest a different coloured robot.

- Locate the file *Blue Chromakey test* and replace the green shot with it.
- Highlight the clip and apply Chromakey.
- Select the Blue preset.

Well, that's significantly better already by just using the preset. The blue backing is also not a pure primary, though.

- Click on the *Color* tab and select a section of the blue background.
- The program has chosen some good values, but lowering the *Transition area* improves the clipping even more

When you switch to full screen preview there is a small blue fringe, but we are working in SD for speed, which makes the flaws more obvious. Hopefully you now have an understanding of the tools available, and more importantly, the need to choose your background and foreground colours with care.

- When you have achieved the best clip you can, save the project as *Chromakey final*.

Foreground and background in Chromakey

It's not always required to put the foreground on a track below the background. You may want to put your foreground on track 1 to take advantage of the way track 1 is treated by some editing actions. You may have skipped here and not be aware of the *Set as background option* in the Background design section of the clip context menu. We could put Robbie on track 1, the Camera 1 clip on track 2, set the track 2 clip as background, and Chromakey would still work. We will need to do that in a moment anyway.

Motion tracking

Movie Edit Pro has a tool which can help you move foreground objects – titles, graphics, masks, photos and even videos – so that they hold their position relative to a moving object in the background. Real life examples might be blanking out the number plate on a car, or the "witness protection" effect where you give someone a pixelated head. When the car or the person moves, then so does the area you are adding the effect to.

Don't expect miracles here. While the tool works, it does struggle to track objects that are moving violently or those that are just trembling a little. If the object you want to track is not that clearly defined or changes size, the tracking will often fail. However, because it uses keyframing, you can use the tracking information as a basis for further editing of the keyframes to improve matters.

I'm going to add a brief title to the previous project that will move with Robbie as he walks across the screen. If you haven't made the project, you can load it from the website or Demo DVD:

- With the project *Chromakey* open, create a new title on track 3 saying "Hello!"

- Change the font to 48 point and change the drop shadow to an edge.

- Move the title object on the Timeline so that it starts at 7 seconds.

- Trim the Out point so that it is the same duration as the Blue Chromakey test clip.

- Place the scrubber at 7 seconds.

- Use the Program monitor to move the title so that it is superimposed over Robbie's chest.

What isn't immediately obvious when you use this function is that the video you are tracking must be on track 1. This might cause you an issue in some circumstances, but if you have read the previous section, you will know that we can arrange the tracks of the current project to work

- Drag the clip on track 1 down to track 4.

- Drag the clip on track 2 up to track 1.

- Drag the clip now on track 4 up to track 2.

- Right click on the Camera 1 clip on track 2 and select *Background design/Set as background*.

- Test the movie to check that the Chromakey still works.

- Save the project as *Motion tracking*.

Ready to use Motion tracking

Motion tracking is a clip context menu option, but it is a little oddly named. I had been using MEP for many months before I realised that it even existed!

- Right click on the Hello title clip and select *Attach to picture position in the video*.

- The next dialogue box warns you to position the object that is to be moved to the correct position relative to the video that is to be tracked. We have already done this, so click *Continue*.

- The next dialogue box tells to that you need to choose an area of high contrast. Click on *Continue*.

- The Program monitor switches to a clean view of

Where to find the Motion tracking tool

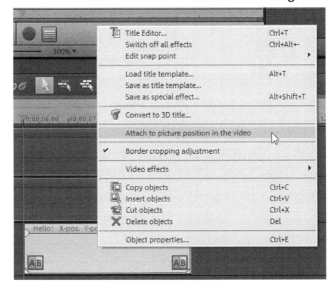

track 1, with the scrubber positioned at the start of the title.

Drawing the area to track

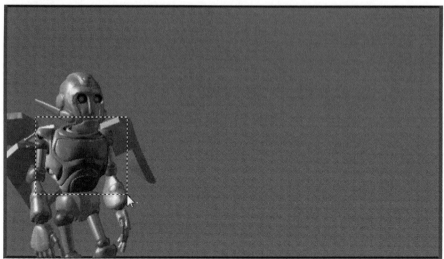

- Now draw a bounding box over Robbie's chest.

- When you release the mouse button, the tracking calculations begin.

Watch the process. The bounding box does well keeping up with Robbie until he gets too big, and when he leaves frame the tracking goes badly wrong, but we can cut that bit out.

- Play the movie and review the effect.

- If you don't get a decent result, try a slightly different tracking area. It doesn't need to be exactly where the title is to go, but if you try using his head the title will seem to drift upwards.

- When you are happy, trim the Out point of the title clip to 00:00:07:15.

- Save the movie as *Motion tracking final cut*.

If you open the *Movement/Size/position* effect, you can see the keyframes on the effects Timeline. It's here that you would edit the motion tracking to make improvements.

I've played for hours with this effect, and there are some video sources that just simply don't work – for example, I wanted to put an arrow that pointed at the peak of Mount Snowdon in the flight project but there isn't enough contrast and I think that the movements are too small.

One point I made briefly earlier was that you could use motion tracking on a mask. This is how you would apply a blur or pixilated effect to part of a video clip.

3D Stereoscopic video

The principle of 3D video is relatively simple. Humans get a sense of depth perception because they have two eyes, spaced apart. If we can record, edit and play back a separate picture for each eye then all we need to do is feed the viewer's left and right eyes with the separate videos and they will experience the depth perception.

Recording at a basic level is fairly easy. Two cameras placed side by side about the distance of the human eyes will give us the two channels we need. The details of the correct spacing, alignment, synchronisation and recording methods can get very complicated, but that hasn't stopped consumer video camcorder manufacturers, and you can buy 3D cameras relatively cheaply these days. They use special lenses and pickups so that 3D recording is achieved within one camera body and the scene recorded as one file.

The principle of editing 3D isn't that complex, either. The two video streams must be treated as one stream. That's about it really. The complex bit is how you feed the two eyes individually.

You can use head mounted displays to do that, but it's a pretty expensive and antisocial way of watching a movie. Cross-eyed is a format of two pictures side by side that may allow you to view 3D without any special equipment, if you can do the "cross-eyed" trick. I've never been able to achieve this form of 3D viewing, which requires you to go cross-eyed and stop focusing on the image. All I get is a blinding headache after a few minutes of trying. So this one isn't for everyone!

The first real commercial solution was the use of coloured filters in front of the eyes of each viewer. This is called anaglyph filtering. Normally 3D glasses for this method use Red (left eye) and Cyan (right eye) which are directly opposite each other in the colour triangle. When you view an image that has been coded as an anaglyph without the glasses you will see odd coloured fringing. Put the glasses on and a 3D image appears. It's not brilliant 3D, even in a darkened room.

There are three other practical methods of displaying 3D on a screen, but they all need complex hardware.

Light can be polarised – so that it vibrates in one plane only – by passing it through a filter. With a screen that transmits two images polarised at 90 degrees and two polarising filters at 90 degrees placed over each eye of the viewer, the eyes can receive two separate images.

Glasses with a shutter system can be used to switch between the left and right eye in synchronisation with a screen that is showing alternative left and right images.

Screens that use masks or lenses to display two images to a viewer whose head is in a certain position are called Autostereoscopic.

Although these three methods all require special hardware, that equipment simply needs to be fed the left and right video streams to work. In the past both streams were combined in a side-by-side view so that only one signal chain was required to connect up the viewing hardware. Formats are now being developed that combine the video signals in a way that is compatible with older equipment.

Apart from the requirement to be able to recognise the various 3D video formats and decode and recode them, editing 3D video is no different than 2D. MEP has a wide choice of methods to monitor 3D video, but unless you own a special 3D monitor or are willing to wear Red/Cyan glasses you won't actually see the 3D effect while editing.

Displaying 3D

The Program monitor display options menu

The Stereoscopic features in Movie Edit Pro Plus and Premium start with the Program monitor. The display modes can be changed using the small icon top left of the monitor.

It is possible to switch the display from a standard 2D view to seeing an Anaglyph picture for viewing with coloured glasses. If you don't have any special hardware then this is your only option to view 3D.

Row interlaced and *Side-by-side* displays are fairly meaningless to the naked eye. You are going to need a 3D equipped computer or external display to see the 3D effect. There doesn't seem to be a universal standard about which signal is supposed to feed which eye, so you have the choice of swapping the feeds over.

3D effects

The 3D properties toolbox

The effects tab holds a subgroup called Stereo3D.

Properties allows you to set up 3D clips so that they work in Magix, and even to create 3D images even if you don't have an integrated 3D camera. Select Standard (2D) for an object and you can give it some 3D depth by adjusting the slider. 3D Stereo pair allows you to flag two separate files on two tracks as being two components of a 3D pair. This way if you have shot video with two separate cameras you can combine the sources. The side-by-side options allow you to flag photos or videos that have been shot using side-by-side techniques so that MEP treats them as 3D.

If you import "proper" 3D video files using the MVC codec, you will have to active the feature over the Internet and pay a fee to do so.

The *Mix down* box will merge the objects into one single object.

The Aligning tools allow you to correct or adjust sources so that they work correctly. They are particularly valuable when creating your own 3D files from two camera sources. You can swap the left and right sources over and automatically or manually align the pictures. You can edit the positions manually with drag and drop using the Program monitor or by entering parameters. Corrections offer even more sophisticated alignment tools if your sources weren't positioned perfectly. You can even Shift frames in case the camera sources aren't synced up relative to each other time wise.

The Alignment tools

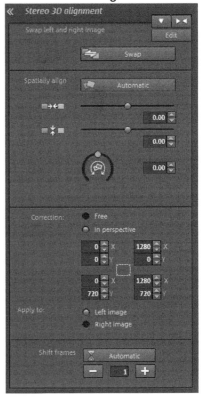

Exporting 3D files

When you enter any file or disc burning dialogue, you will find options for exporting to 3D formats. The options are a little harder to find when exporting to optical disc formats but I'll flag them up when we look at discs. There is a huge range of choices, as you can see from the screenshot.

So from my brief look at the features in MEP, you can see that working with 3D is very dependent on the source, monitoring and playback devices at your disposal. If you have a purpose made 3D camera and TV there are still many choices that you will need to make by referring to the documentation that comes with the equipment.

3D export options

Media Management

So far in this book we have been taking an ad hoc approach to where we get our source material from. I've only asked you to use files provided for you, and we have tended to "discover" them in the Import tab of the Media pool before bringing them into the project we are making, or use the AVCHD option in the recording screen. I describe the other methods of acquiring source material later.

Firstly though, I want to talk about where you might want to put the files you are going to use, and the role of the supplementary files that Movie Edit Pro can generate. Keeping your projects and their source files well organised may not seem like a major priority when you first start out working with movies, which is why I didn't start the book with this subject. However, the day that you re-open an old project to remake it and Movie Edit Pro tells you it can't find the source files will be the day you start to take more interest in managing your media!

Windows user profiles

Even if you are the only person who uses your computer, you will have a user account and profile. A shared computer may have more than one profile, or you could set up different user accounts for different tasks – a Video Editing profile, perhaps.

User account "jeff" in the Media pool

When you are logged into a particular profile, there are special locations for My Documents, My Video, My Photos and My Music for that user profile, and many programs default to those locations. Media Player will rip CDs to My Music, for example. If you use the standard Windows tools for importing photos from a digital stills camera they will end up by default in My Pictures. What's more, when you browse these locations in Windows explorer you will get extra functionality for the types of files in those folders.

Movie Edit Pro uses a set of default locations which only makes limited use of your user profile. It creates a location within the current user's My Documents called Magix\Movie Edit Pro 2014 (Plus or Premium). Within that location, subfolders are used to store recordings and other files.

You can see and also change the default locations by using Settings/Program and opening the folders tab.

Clicking on My Pictures Switches to the My Media section of the Import tree

If you only have one hard disc then these are arguably the best place to put the source files you are going to use in MEP. You can put items in sub-folders to help you stay organised, and what's more the locations are pre-programmed into the Media pool Import tree under your user name. Other programs may put potential source material into My Video, My Pictures or My Music, but these locations are easily browsed to within the Media pool – they too are automatically added to the Import tree.

If you are a very organised type, and have been using computers with operating systems earlier than Windows XP you might be used to creating your own folder structure and ignore the User locations. That's fine if you are used to working that way – you just need to divert the recording operations to your folders, which is pretty easy to do, and add shortcuts to those locations in the Media pool Import tree

However, even if you don't have your own folder structure, you might want easy access to the Video files that you load onto your computer with MEP. You might want to browse them in Windows, play them in Windows Media player, or you might even want to use another video program on occasions. So, the ideal location is My Videos, and I'd suggest you consider changing the default locations used by Magix. There are many other things to take into account though.

Additional hard drives

There are a number of reasons why you might want more than one hard drive:

1. Keeping large amounts of data in a separate location to your main working OS drive makes it easier to make system backups.

2. Keeping large video files separate can reduce the amount of fragmentation.

3. If you are a regular video user, you need a lot of storage space and adding extra drives is easier than changing the system drive.

4. Windows is a multi-tasking operating system and will be constantly using the main OS drive in the background, which can interfere with video playback, and in particular analogue recording.

Points 1 and 2 of the above list can be addressed by partioning your main hard drive – that is, dividing up one physical hard drive into two or more virtual drives. It's possible your computer is configured like that anyway, with the C: drive holding the OS and the D: drive the data. How you can do this yourself is outside the scope of this book, but you will find plenty of guides on the Internet, and specialist software that can make it easier to do.

Point 3 is perhaps the most obvious. The current maximum drive size seems to be 2TB, and if you have a large amount of video to store you can fill that up quite quickly. The problem is made worse if you are running a Solid State Drive as the C: drive. These are very fast, but large drives are hugely expensive and the speed isn't needed for most video work.

Point 4 used to be very important, but now technology has moved on it's not essential. Most hard drives can cope unless you are using lightly compressed files and therefore the files are too large to be read quickly, as discussed in the first chapter of the book.

Types of hard drive connection

If you have a desktop computer, adding a drive inside the case gives the fastest connection possible, but makes it hard to swap drives around unless you have some sort of caddy system. If you have a laptop, then only top of the range models will have space for a second drive, so you will probably need to use an external drive.

Hard drives connected by USB 3.0 or Thunderbolt boast such a fast connection that in the real world they are as good an internal drives. Even if your computer can only use USB 2.0, then the transfer speeds aren't so much slower than the internal drives that you will notice a difference – in most cases the CPU will be the bottleneck for Video editing and rendering (again, refer back to Chapter 1 for a deeper discussion).

Accessing and storing source files on external drives

Once you have one or more external drives, then you need Movie Edit Pro to use them. This is very easy. The *Settings/Program/Folder* option available from the File menu lets you change the default locations.

Customised default folder locations

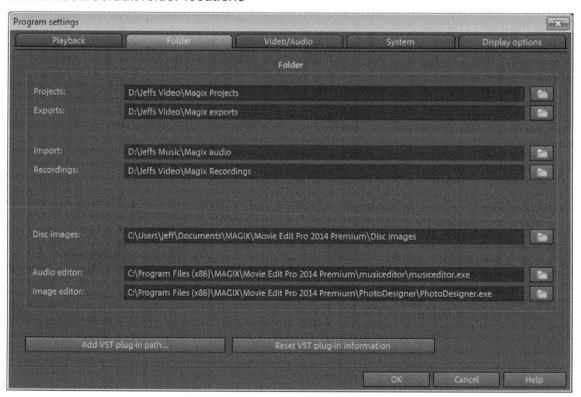

As a matter of course I would change my Recordings destination to my external drive. This means that I can access them in the Media pool in My Media/Recordings. Any other default locations that I decide to divert to my hard drive can be added to the tree view in the Media pool by creating a Link, as described in the Media pool chapter. OK, it requires a little housekeeping, but won't fill up the C: drive with potentially large files that I might have to move anyway.

It seems a shame that we can't take advantage of the User profile that is hard coded into the tree view. It is actually possible to move your profile to a drive other than C: and if you are confident of your computer skills you can do that, but the Microsoft approved way of doing so doesn't help us because Magix have hard-wired the user location to where it *should* be, not where you have moved it to. There may be a way of doing this that involves NTFS junction points that Movie Edit Pro would understand, but there are a lot of potential pitfalls. While Magix may behave itself, when the User profile is on an external drive, and if that drive is easy to disconnect, you may get into all sorts of trouble.

Windows Libraries

If you have been a computer user from many years you may take little notice of those Johnny-come lately Windows Libraries. If you are still using an operating system prior to Windows 7 then you won't have them anyway. However, they take the concept of User profiles and improve on it.

There are still specialist folders for documents, music, pictures and videos, but they aren't just confined to the user profile – you can **add** other locations to your libraries even if they are located on other hard discs.

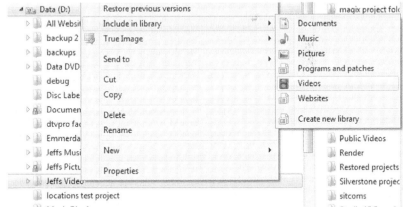

Adding a folder on D: to a Windows Library

Unfortunately, Movie Edit Pro doesn't show Libraries in the media pool by default but as we have already discussed, it's easy enough to link to them. So, if you are running Windows 7 or above, you can integrate your new locations into the Windows Libraries without the complications of moving your User profile. A win-win situation!

The Project folder

There is another place to put your files – a specific folder for all the assets in your current project. The advantage is that everything is in one place, even all those pesky little files that MEP keeps cluttering up your regular folders with. By the way, the .H0 files are the graphics data for the audio waveforms and the .HDP files hold data about them. If you delete these files, the program just recreates them when required.

MEP behaves differently if you tick the *Create a project folder...* box before you start a new project.

Creating a Project folder

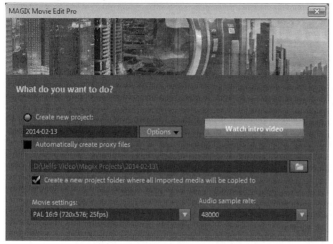

By default it creates a folder in the location specified in in the settings box for Magix projects to be stored, so we can divert the project file to any hard disc we like. You could override this choice if you wish, but it's not a bad one anyway. The differences don't stop their either.

Any recordings you make while working on the project are placed in a further sub-folder – *Specified Project locations/Project folder for current project/Recordings* – unless you override the setting in the Import module you use..

Now, this might all sound like a bit too much work. After all, you might be making a new project but using files that are already on one of your hard drives. Again, there is special behaviour when a project folder has been specified, because if you can browse any location in the Media pool, drag a file to the Timeline and then MEP intervenes – do you want to copy a new version of this file into the projects folder, or use the original? If you have plenty of disc space and the file isn't too huge, you might as well copy the file – the copy has a unique hexadecimal number added to the end of the file name so you know it's a copy.

If the file is very large you can elect not to make a copy. There are still tools for you to make a backup of your entire project, so just bear what you have done in mind. So, with a project folder in place, you can choose.

Once you start using project folders, you aren't stuck with them. If you are importing media specifically for a project, and just that project, import it once the project is open. On the other hand, you have just got back from holiday and want to load the video and photos onto your computer for general use, you can either use Windows, the tools that came with your cameras, or the Magix import routine from a project that doesn't have a project folder specified.

Incidentally, if you specify a project folder and then end up not using it, when you quit the project if MEP detects the folder is empty it will ask you if you want to delete it.

There are other advantages to using project folders as well – they can help you keep your hard discs less cluttered.

Preview files

We have already taken a brief look at using preview files. In Plus and Ultimate you can force the creation of files to replace a complex part of the Timeline so you can play it smoothly. These files are normally placed in a folder called *PerfBounce* in the current location you are using to store project files. If you have specified that the current project should use its own project folder, then a PerfBounce folder is created within that location. So instead of having a whole bunch of preview files lumped together and you not knowing which project they relate to, the project files are a bit more organised.

The Eye icon and ranges detected by auto calculation

We only used Range settings to help use preview slow motion and interlace optimisation, but there is more to it than that. If you build up a complex sequence and your computer is struggling to play it back smoothly then you can ask for help.

Auto-calculation can be invoked with the eye icon top left of the Timeline. Clicking on it will automatically start a scan of the movie Timeline and if there are any areas that could benefit from preview rendering that are marked with a red bar and you are asked if you want to create files for the marked areas. Clicking *Yes* starts a process of creating the files in the *PerfBounce* folder, and when completed, the red bar turns green. The Timeline should now play back smoothly, using the preview render files, but when you finally export the movie the original source files will be used so that there will be no unnecessary drop in quality.

If you try to use this feature when the Playback cursor is within a green rendered range you will be warned of what you are trying to do, but offered the chance to remake the render files or search the rest of the Timeline for time-critical areas. If there are green areas somewhere other than under the Playback cursor you can opt not to re-render these and just do an automatic search.

Preview render dialogue when the cursor is within a rendered range

If you make a change to areas that have been Preview rendered then the green area will turn back to red. It's possible you might want to leave that area alone but search for others because rendering is taking up a lot of time. When you use the eye tool in these circumstances you are offered the chance for it do that, or re-render everything.

As we saw earlier, there is a further small menu for preview rendering available from the drop down arrow alongside the eye icon, or the options can be reached from the Range context menu. You can force a section of the Timeline marked as a blue range to be preview rendered even if MEP doesn't think it is required (as discussed during the Slow motion project). You can also delete all the rendered ranges.

Proxy files

This feature, also only available in Plus and Ultimate (and not introduced until the 2014 edition of MEP) takes preview rendering a stage further. If you have enabled *Automatically create proxy files* in the *New project* dialogue (or turned it on in Movie settings), then whenever you add a video file to the project Movie Edit Pro will consider generating an entire preview quality file for the source file you are trying to add.

If the program thinks a proxy file is a requirement for smooth playback it will make one. It will place it in the same folder as the source file, use the file for playback, but replace it with the source file at the time of render. That's the same process as using Preview render, but carried out earlier in the workflow. Once you are using a proxy file, adding effects or transitions may not require further preview rendering because the proxy file is easier for the program to process in real time.

Notice that I said "consider". If the program *doesn't* consider you need a proxy file, it won't make one. However, in the build I'm using to write this book, it also throws up a warning message which is, in my opinion, very confusing. It tells you that there has been an error, whereas it has made a deliberate decision not to create the file. So, when you see

If you see this message, don't panic!

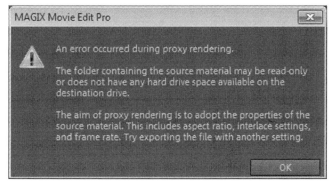

the warning but are confident that the settings are correct, don't think you have a problem, just carry on!

Proxy files are likely to be useful when working with high Bitrate, complex codec or 4K video files, for example the Cineform 100fps file that you may have used in the slow motion project.

As you might guess, proxy files can be large – you sometimes will double the amount of space required to store the source files for a project. So, specifying a project folder, particularly one which isn't on a small OS hard drive, is a very good idea.

Preview and Proxy formats

Magix uses – by default – its own video format for preview and proxy files – MXV. It's so unique, that I can't find a program that isn't made by Magix that will play or analyse the files – or at least, if I don't change the file extension. However, although I can't be sure, it seems that the files use a high Bitrate Mjpeg intraframe codec – a format not dissimilar to DV-AVI. If you change the file extension to *.mjpeg* you can play the files in VLC player. When generating these files the program will also often reduce the resolution. HD files with a resolution of 1920*1080 are reduced to 960*540 – a quarter of pixel count, half the vertical and horizontal resolution.

This is a robust, good quality alternative which can be decoded quickly, requiring less computing power to play back smoothly.

You do have a choice of other preview and proxy formats though. If you wish to use Mpeg you can – either DVD or HD format. These options are available from the *Settings/Preview and Proxy rendering* entry in the *File* menu.

The Preview and Proxy settings

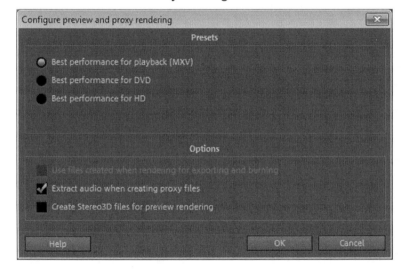

If your computer is up to it – and it most likely is - then these files will still be OK for playback. The resolution will also match the original files. There is an added advantage as well. You can force the program to use these files when making DVDs or HDV video files, saving you quite a bit of rendering time. If you are considering this, though, you might want to consider some of the information I discuss when we look at Smart rendering in the Exporting Files chapter.

Archiving projects

It's great to keep all your stuff organised with project folders, and if you want to move your project to another hard drive for storage it's easy because you know where all the assets are – in the project folder - and what's more you won't need to regenerate preview or proxy files. If you aren't confident that you have allowed the program to copy source files into the project folder you can find a list by opening the Movie settings and switching to the Movie information tab.

However, if you haven't got all your assets in one folder you can still make a backup using one of the options in the *Backup copy* entry in the File menu. Here you can get MEP to copy all the assets required into a folder for either the currently selected Movie or the whole Project.

Backup copy menu

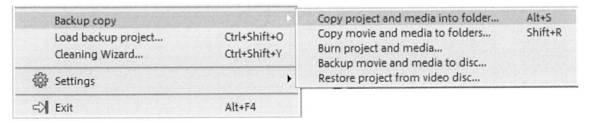

The next two options do the same thing - with a twist. The files are prepared for burning to an optical disc with the supplied program Speed 3.

The subprogram creating a project backup disc

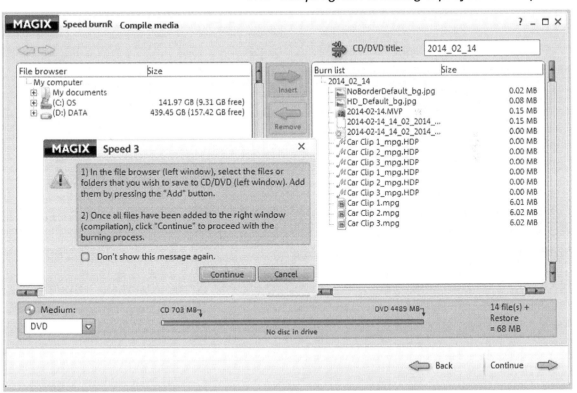

This process is totally automatic, and results in a disc that will autorun on insertion into an optical drive and offer to restore the project to a folder for you. The problem with these options is that the disc is limited to CDs or DVDs, so any project of a significant size isn't going to fit on the disc. Perhaps Blu-ray will be added to this feature at a later date.

The final option isn't designed for reloading the disc backup made using the above process. It's also possible to add backup files to an optical disc project when you are in the Burn workspace so that your final product can also be used as a backup for re-editing the project. Backup copy/Restore project from video disc looks in your optical disc drive and if it finds an archived project on the Video DVD it will restore it for you.

Looking in the File menu, you can also see an option to *Load backup project*. To clear up any misunderstandings this option doesn't restore any archives created by any of the methods I've just mentioned, but looks for automatic projects created at timed intervals, as detailed in the second chapter of the book.

Cleaning Wizard

This was also mentioned earlier, but we can look at it in a bit more detail now. The first option, *Delete specific files* allows you to specify a specific file – probably a project file – and finds all the other files that relate to that file so if you have safely archived a project you can delete all the components. The second option *Search and delete superfluous files* scans for all Magix related files. If you have moved your default project location and want to do a proper clean up, it's a good idea to add your hard discs to the list using the advanced tab.

The Cleaning Wizard with the Advanced tab open

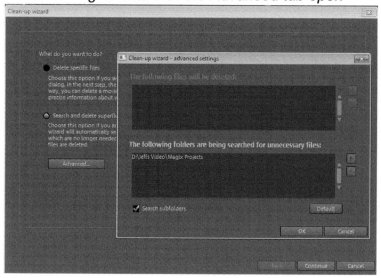

After running either option a list is presented to you. Files that Movie Edit Pro consider safe for deletion are checked, and other files are marked with a comment explaining why you might want to keep the file. Hopefully now you have the information above about file types you will be able to differentiate between those that can be recreated and those that can't.

Movie settings and information

I mentioned earlier that each movie has a list of its assets available in the *Movie information* tab of the *Settings/Movie* File menu option. The list is just for the currently selected movie, so you need to switch tabs if you have more than one movie loaded into your project.

There is also an opportunity to be more organised in the *Project settings* tab, because you can add a description which will appear as a tooltip when you hover over the project in the Media pool. This feature works even with tooltips turned off.

You can also specify a different thumbnail for the project file in the Media pool – either a JPEG file of your choice or a custom selected frame from your movie.

How you decide to organise your computer, media and projects is entirely up to you. Movie Edit Pro has tools for both the highly organised or the chaotically creative. Putting just a little thought into things before you start a project is worth the effort, though. Is this something that might benefit from using Proxy files? Is there a danger of running out of hard disc space? What do I want to do with the source files when I have finished using them in this project? Think about the answers to those question first and you might save yourself a lot of work.

Asset list in the Movie information tab

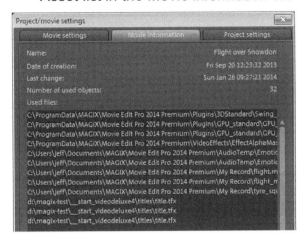

The Project settings tab

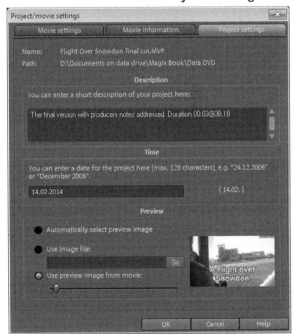

Importing Media

Now I've covered where you might want to put source files it's time to return to the additional ways of importing them. We took a look at recording methods starting on page 193, and I have covered in detail how you can bring in files from external devices such as cameras, memory cards and even external hard drives that might only be attached to the computer on a temporary basis. In these cases we have transferred the files into a more permanent location on your computer's hard drive. For this we used the AVCHD option offered when we selected *Record* from the file menu or the Program monitor. I described how the AVCHD option is for much more than just AVCHD video – it's a way of getting any file based video or photo onto your hard drives, or moved to new locations between drives or even folders. There are many other potential sources other than files, though, and Movie Edit Pro has options for all of them.

DV and HDV

Two video formats that have been popular for years with consumers and prosumers are the original DV and later HDV tape-based formats for standard and high definition cameras. While they are no longer sold, many people still use them.

These cameras normally record on Digital Tape. Importing from tape is often called *ingesting*. Video information stored on a tape is of no use to a computer, but a relatively simple digital transfer can be used to ingest the data without degrading it in any way and place it in a file suitable for editing.

One disadvantage of this form of storage is that you can only play back from the tape in real time; another is that mechanical issues can cause poor tracking, leading to data that is incomplete. However, in comparison to analogue formats such as VHS it is far superior.

DV and HDV cameras normally connect via Firewire (otherwise called an IEEE 1394 port) even if your camera also has a USB port. If your computer doesn't have FireWire built in, expansion cards for desktop computers and PC slot adaptors for laptops are available. Some analogue capture hardware also includes a FireWire port. (There are a few rare DV cameras that can pass video via USB, but you will need to use the software supplied with the camera to import from those).

If you are a Windows 7 or 8 user, you may have some issues with generic FireWire devices. If you are having trouble getting your computer to see your camera, you need to investigate if you need to install a Legacy device driver. You can find details on the Microsoft website.

If you find that the camera is detected and you can use the remote transport controls but you don't see any video signal, try replacing the cable – I once bought a cheap one that developed a fault and caused exactly this sort of problem.

DV capture interface

For DV capture a checkbox on the Record screen gives you a choice to record the files as Mpeg-2 video, rather than the native AVI format,saving space but reducing quality a little. If your project is going to end up on DVD and you don't intend to add effects or many transitions, the quality loss will be avoided if you use Smart Rendering to make your movie, but this can bring other problems. Smart render is discussed in the next chapter. My recommendation is to record AVI files unless you really are short of hard disk space. HDV cameras produce Mpeg-2 files anyway, so you don't get the choice with them.

When selecting *DV or HDV camera* you should see the interface shown in the screenshot.

The DV ingest interface

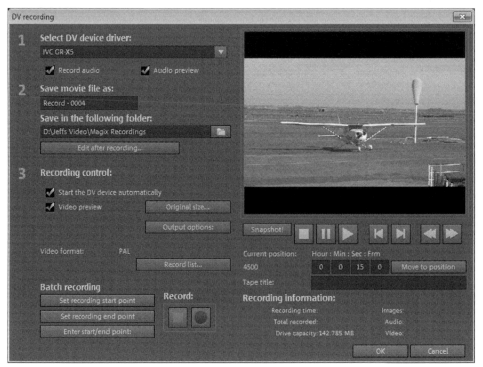

If your firewire connection doesn't exist you will get an error dialogue, so set up your camera first – connect it to your firewire port and switch it on and into Play mode. If it doesn't appear in Windows in the Device Manager than it won't appear in Movie Edit Pro.

Once the device is successfully connected, using the DV capture mode brings up the following options:

1: Select DV device driver: Lets you choose if you happen to have more than one device connected. You can disable Audio recording and preview here if you need to – although I can't think why you would disable audio.

*2: Save video file a*s is where you specify a filename, and optionally a destination folder.

Edit after recording opens a setting box with a number of choices to help you automate your capture sessions. For now leave them unchecked, but make a note of what is possible – scene detection, chapter marking and immediate export to disc or file.

3: Recording control. Because Firewire is a bi-directional connection you not only have controls for recording, but also for the camera. Checking *Start the DV device automatically* will start the camera rolling when you click on the Record button and stop it when you press Stop. If you don't check *Video Preview* you can't see what you are capturing, but you might want to use this control if you are dropping frames because of a slow computer.

Original size opens a larger preview window which gives a better preview but consumes more resources. *Output options* seems misnamed to me – on my camera it opens controls that are duplicated underneath the preview window, with just a little added info. This may differ with other devices.

I find that my DV camera (which has seen better days!) doesn't give me a very good preview, but don't forget that you can always use the camera's viewfinder. I can still capture without dropping frames, so if your preview doesn't update properly either, don't worry.

The Recording list button opens a window that holds a set of recording stop and start times that you can set with the options below – either by marking the current tape position or entering numbers. If you logged your recording you can enter the numbers for the parts you want to digitise directly here. This mimics the workflow of a professional – where only the useful parts of the tape were loaded, perhaps from a list produced by a script supervisor or a data logger. You can enter a whole list of numbers, then set batch recording going and leave the process to happen automatically.

Manual timecode entry and the record list

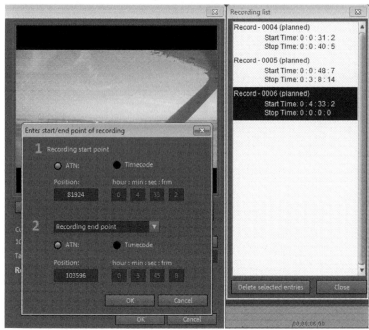

When you do finally get round to capturing, the *Recording information* below holds amongst other things the all-important *Dropped frames* information.

Logging

Incidentally, MEP keeps a list of the timecodes of DV clips for each project. If you close a project and delete one or more of the source files that you captured from tape (to save space or in error) then when you reload the project MEP will prompt you to connect up your camera, load up the correct tape and recapture the video files it needs. This all happens automatically and seems to work very reliably. However, if you can spare the storage space, the clips are probably safer on a hard disc than on a fragile tape.

Hard disc data rates – a capture bottleneck?

Let's presume you have a solid, working FireWire connection to your camera, which is playing the DV tape successfully. You are capturing in the DV-AVI format, so no fancy processor work is involved. However, after a few seconds of successful capture, the Dropped frames counter starts to register losses. This is a Very Bad Thing.

If you remember back to Chapter 1, I explained how either the CPU or the hard disc drive could be a bottleneck when working with video, depending on the Bitrate and complexity of the format.

The ingest process is pretty straightforward. When I perform DV capture the CPU usage in the Task Manager/Performance tab hardly gets into double figures. The other time-critical task is storing the file onto hard disc. It doesn't go straight there –

it is buffered through the computer's random access memory to start with – but the disc needs to be able to keep up in the long term.

Consider the DV-AVI file size. It consists of 3,600KBytes for every second of video, so even on the most well equipped computer it won't take long to fill up the spare RAM. That data needs to be written to the hard disc at the same speed it is being generated from the DV tape – over 3 and a half million bytes a second.

Modern hard discs can achieve this with ease. Real life drives can peak at over 20 times that data rate. What can possibly go wrong?

I've stated that one of the recommendations for video work is to use a separate drive for storing files. The main reason for this is that the operating system which occupies the C: drive (in most circumstances) is never really idle. Having a separate drive for video means it isn't being constantly interrupted by other access demands. This could affect playback and capture.

What if you do only have one drive? Well, capture should still be easily possible if the drive is in good shape. Windows stores files in an increasingly random pattern as the drive fills up. If a large number of small files are deleted, the OS may decide to fill up the empty space with one large file split into smaller parts. The process is called *Fragmentation*. It occurs on all systems and lowers the performance of the computer.

Basic defragmentation tools are available in Windows. Others are available that do a better job, but you don't need to go over the top – if a drive is reported to have less than 10% fragmentation it's highly unlikely that it is causing dropped frames.

It's not just the Operating System that may be accessing the main drive – other background programs can be using it as well. Some programs could even be scanning or indexing other drives, so it pays to keep a check on what is going on behind your back.

It's possible to automatically compress hard disc drives in some circumstances. Newer operating systems have introduced automatic indexing to speed up searching. Both processes can disrupt smooth data transfer. I'd recommend you turn both off on any drive you wish to capture to. You will find check boxes for these function in Windows/My Computer, right-clicking on the icon for the particular drive and select properties.

On older XP computer systems the next thing to check would be what transfer mode your capture drive is working in. It isn't likely that your hard drive is working in a mode called PIO, but DVD drives can be put into this mode by a bad disc, while for hard drives it is normally the sign of an internal fault in the drive.

You might want to check the speed your drive achieves. In Windows 7 and 8 you can find the **Resource Monitor** in Windows *Start/All Programs/Accessories/System Tools/*. It provides a running graph of disc activity and the transfer speeds achieved. The screenshot shows the graphs generated by recording DV-AVI video to an external drive.

The Resource Monitor

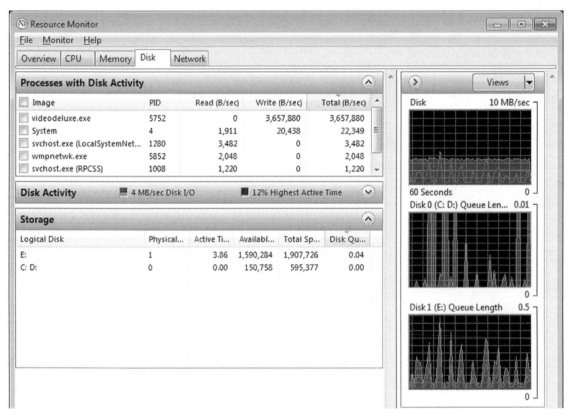

If you have an external hard disc connected by FireWire 400, or more likely USB 2.0, another source of problems can be that the external connection is clashing with other devices. Check the data rates and make sure that they aren't sharing a hub connection. The best way to do this is to plug them directly into the back panel sockets of the computer.

One final thing that can affect disc performance is power management software. This is unlikely to be affecting the hard disc of a desktop machine, but a laptop, particularly running on battery power, could be affected by general slow running, including the disc drives.

In the "bad old days" trying to capture to a hard disc using DMA mode 1 access, I could cause a dropped frame just by moving the mouse. Modern discs should be absolutely fine, even if you only have one, but a culmination of factors might still lead to dropped frames.

These aren't the only causes of poor capture, but the others are more likely to cause problems with analogue video, so let's move on to that.

Analogue capture

Ah, those crumbling VHS, Betamax and 8mm tapes in the loft, mocking your promise to transfer them to DVDs. One day, one day…

If you have decided to bite the bullet, you are going to need some hardware to convert the analogue signals sent out by the tape player to a digital file. This process is often called *Digitising*.

If you are familiar with analogue video principles and what digital actually means, you can skip the next few sections, but if you're not really sure how an audio or video picture can be passed down a single wire, take a deep breath. I'm going to go quite a long way back…..

An analogue video primer

Let's start with Audio and how an electrical signal can represent it. Before I can explain that, I had better define what sound actually is.

It's a variation of air pressure. A bell passes its mechanical vibration to the surrounding air. The sound of my voice is created by my vocal chords by vibrating the air as it passes through them. When that air vibration reaches your ears, it moves your eardrum, which translates to signal into nerve pulses that are deciphered by your brain.

The human ear can hear vibrations of varying speeds. A slow vibration – let's say 50 times a second – will be heard as a very low note, and a fast vibration – perhaps 16000 times a second - as a very high note. If that vibration is pure and at one frequency, it will be a clear sound like the tone of a tuning fork. All other sounds are a mixture of frequencies.

In order that we pass sounds down wires, over the airwaves or record them onto a mechanical or electronic device, we first convert them into an electrical signal that consists of electrons moving around a circuit. They can do that at all the frequencies we can hear, as well as very much higher ones.

So, a graph of a sound wave against time will look the same as the voltage present in an audio circuit. Both will look similar (but with more detail) to the full waveforms that Movie Edit Pro draws on its audio timelines.

For high quality sound, the components of any system need to carry nearly all the frequencies humans perceive as sound equally – and you may have heard of the term Frequency Response as a measure of how good an audio system is.

OK, I need to define vision next. The human eye sees light reflected off objects around us. This light – a very high frequency radio wave – enters our eyes through a lens and hits light sensitive cells at the back of the eyeball where it is converted into nerve signals. These signals are sent to the brain and deciphered. The slightly different frequencies of the light waves are what we perceive as colour.

When we look at a TV set, the "trick" that fools us into believing we are seeing a true moving image is the same today as it was hundreds of years ago when people made novelty devices such as zoetropes or a set of flick cards . A series of still pictures displayed in rapid succession will appear to the human brain as fluid motion. This is often called the *persistence of vision*, but in fact more recent research shows it is a brain function known as the *Beta Movement Phenomena*. Whatever you want to call it, a flip book of drawings or 16 photographs projected within a second is seen to be smooth movement and this led to the invention of film. Even with further advances, the standard for film projection is still only 24 frames per second.

Television *(from the Greek **Tele** (far) and Latin **Viso** (to see))* needed a way of turning this fast succession of pictures into an electrical signal that could be passed down wires, or transmitted over the airwaves. The solution is still with us today, and involves scanning an image to create an analogue Video signal.

A frame is divided up into a series of lines, and these are scanned, starting at the top, from left to right. To produce a monochrome signal, the brightness would be measured along the scanned line and represented as a variable electrical signal. At the end of the line, a new one is scanned from slightly lower, and the process repeated until the whole frame is scanned. Then the next frame is scanned, and so on. Negative pulses are added to the signal to indicate the start of a new line, and larger ones for the start of a new frame.

Ah, but that's only black and white, I hear you say. A colour TV picture is made by mixing the three (additive) primary colours – Red, Green and Blue. If you can get those colours pure enough, then by mixing them, you can reproduce any other colour. The original cathode ray tubes fired electrons at phosphors. LCD displays use liquid crystals to filter light. Plasma displays contain tiny fluorescent light sources. All of them mix the three primary colours – and a full dose of each will produce white.

Three signals can give us the full colour range, and some Video connections are indeed **component**. A two wire system (**S-Video**) consists of a luminance (black and white) signal, and another which encodes the hue (colour) and saturation (how much) into one signal know as chrominance. Finally, a **composite** video signal needs only one wire, as the **chrominance** signal is modulated onto the luminance signal in a similar manner to radio signals.

The single composite video signal also has to have audio modulated onto it in order to be transmitted through the airwaves on a single transmission frequency. The result is the complex, fragile signal that has been used to transmit and receive analogue television pictures since the introduction of colour TV in the 1950s. It has only just been phased out in some parts of the world, and will be around for many years to come in other parts. What's more, it's what comes out of the back of a VHS machine!

Interlacing, frame rates and digital compression.

Having described the complexities of analogue signals, I can now refer you to the first chapter of the book where you should find the rest of the information you need, starting at page 13, to understand the process of how video is manipulated and stored in the digital realm. Once we get the fragile analogue signals converted to digital files, the biggest threat to the quality is over-compressing the files.

Capture hardware for Movie Edit Pro

The Videowandler 2

Magix have used an industry standard to interface with capture hardware, so you aren't limited to devices that they sell. Having said that, you will need patience to get many devices to work. My experiences are limited to two devices, the Magix USB Videowandler 2 (red and white) device, and a Pinnacle 510 USB Moviebox. I have used the former on a 32-bit XP computer, and the latter device works in 64-bit Windows 7

and 8. But it's vital that I do things in the correct order to ensure that it appears in MEP. If all else fails, any capture device you buy *should* come with capture software of its own, and while it's not as convenient, you can always use that software to transfer your analogue sources to digital files.

The most common forms of capture devices connect by USB 2.0. Internal PCI cards are rare now – the one I used to own was not 64-bit compatible. Grass Valley, formally Canopus, make a range of devices that connect via Firewire, but you would use these with the DV camera interface, which leads me to another alternative.

A neat Analogue Capture alternative

If you own a DV camcorder that you can connect via FireWire, you might be able to use it to capture an analogue signal. This will depend on the model – it's a feature that is more likely to be provided on high-end camcorders.

Check the manual to see if it has Analogue In and is capable of DV pass-through. Some models of camera may have this feature in the North American versions, but have it disabled on the European version to comply with import quota restrictions. You might be able to get a "crippled" European model modified to work.

If you have the correct equipment, you can use the DV capture mode to capture the analogue signal plugged into the camera. One stumbling block could appear to be that when you click capture, the camera starts playing its DV tape. The answer to this is to remove the tape and close the tape housing door.

Sometimes, this method may require a long run up time – the camera needs to obtain a stable signal before the capture routine is ready – so recording the first few seconds of an analogue tape may be problematic. Once working, though, the quality should be as good as any other capture device and you are capturing straight to DV-AVI.

HD capture

There are a number of devices around that can capture HD. They fall into two categories. They may contain memory storage of their own, so you use them as a standalone device and just import the files as normal. Others connect via USB 3.0 or Thunderbolt. For these, you will again need to use the supplied software. If you are interested in video, rather than capturing games play, it's far better to use the files from a video camera rather than try to digitize its output.

A brief word about connections

You need cables of some sort to connect your tape player to your capture device, and this may not be entirely straightforward. At the basic level, you should be able to use an RCA/Phono set of leads, yellow for video and white/red for audio. However, there are other possibilities.

S-video uses a four-pin connector carrying two analogue video signals, chrominance and luminance, down two separate wires. This offers better quality as the final combination of colour and luminance is not required. If your analogue source has an output socket providing S-video it is better to connect up to your capture device using this if you have suitable cables.

One important warning – the front panel RCA sockets on VCRs, DVD recorders and TV sets are almost always for input only – you won't get a signal out of them to feed your capture device. Some TV sets may have output RCA sockets at the back. If you look closely, sometimes a tiny arrow pointing in to the socket indicates it is an Input; when it is pointing away the socket is for Output.

In Europe, you will be used to the presence of SCART sockets on VCRs, TVs and DVD machines. These connectors are normally bi-directional, but if you have a SCART plug with only one set of leads, there is a 50/50 chance the leads are for input **to** the SCART. If you need to buy a SCART lead or adaptor, I'd recommend you get one with an input/output switch.

Another word of warning about SCARTs – the sockets of a particular machine may not necessarily output a S-Video signal. If it is capable of doing so, you may have to operate a switch on the back panel, or a menu option on the machine itself. If in doubt, consult the manual. A muddle in this area is a major cause of only getting a black and white picture.

Getting Magix to recognise your capture device.

Having installed the device using the manufacturer's drivers, it should appear in the computers Device manager when it is plugged in. Having got that far, these are the steps I take to ensure I can see my capture device – they might not be required every time, but it's a good troubleshooting workflow.

Close down the computer, connect the device to the computer and the video source to the device using composite cables, and then start up the computer again.

Open Movie Edit Pro and then open the Recording dialogue. Ensure that the (direct to disc) box is unchecked and select *Video:* to open the Video recording dialogue.

The analogue digitising interface

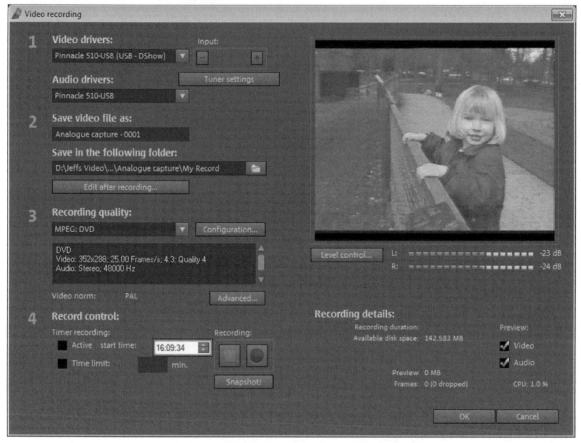

In *1 Video and Audio drivers:* select the device you have connected. If you don't see video in the preview monitor after 10 seconds, *Tuner settings* may give you some options if you have the right sort of capture device. Failing that, use the *Advanced* setting button in section 3 to access the drivers for your device. Here you should be able to control the Input, Video standards and settings, cropping and more, depending on the device. It might sound like a cop out if I say you may need to tinker with the settings, but there are so many variables! On my Moviebox, for example, I can't switch the input to S-video within Magix, but I can change a vast array of other settings. Fortunately it defaults to composite input after a restart.

*2: Save video file a*s is where you specify a filename, and optionally a destination folder.

Edit after recording opens a setting box with a number of choices to help you automate your capture sessions. For now leave them unchecked, but make a note of what is possible – scene detection, chapter marking and immediate export to disc or file.

3: Recording quality gives you a choice of codec – MXV or MPEG-2 – and resolutions. Recording at less than 720*526/480 resolution seems pointless to me unless you are having problems – and recording Standard Definition analogue video at any higher resolution is also a waste of file space. By choice I would record using *MPEG: DVD* because it possible that you will be able to Smartrender when making DVDs.

You can also set the actual aspect ratio here, or change it later. The monitor will always show as 4:3.

4: Recording control allows you to set an automatic start time in case you are using a TV tuner. You can also set a recording duration, which can be useful if you want to capture a long tape but not have to watch it!

The *Snapshot* button creates a JPEG still and places it in the Recording folder, but only works when you aren't actually capturing video.

It's important to set the audio volume before you start capturing. The meters below the video preview show the levels. Clicking on the *Level control* button opens Windows controls, but for most capture devices you are probably going to have to use the device controls via the *Advanced* button.

When you are finally ready to record, first do a test by starting the tape or other source and using the simple Record button. You should be able to preview both Video and Audio without issues, but be warned – the video isn't going to look good. Interlace decoding isn't carried out properly and you may see bad combing on movement. Don't be alarmed, the files aren't going to look like that!

This is where you should keep an eye on the levels making sure they are healthy but don't go into the red, but more importantly the Frames counter and the figure for the number dropped. You might get a few frames dropped at the beginning of a tape as it stabilises, but the figure should be very low – if you get into tens or hundreds, you have a problem. If you don't have problems, stop the recording with the Stop button, and close the Video box with *OK*. You will now have the test recording placed on the Timeline and you can check the quality. If you don't think it's very good, review the settings, but don't forget that analogue, and in particular VHS, isn't a very good format!

Even if you are happy with what you see, it's worth reading the next section before embarking on a long capture session as it has some useful tips.

Analogue Capture issues.

Obviously dropped frames mean a bump in the recording, but a more disconcerting consequence is that the Video and audio streams can get out of sync, so you end up having to correct the audio positioning on the Timeline. Worse still, you might not notice it until you show the movie all the way through.

One possible cause of dropping frames is the Hard Disc bottleneck described earlier in the DV section. It is far less likely to affect MPEG-2 capture but it's easy to check for, so it should be the first thing on the list when troubleshooting capture issues. If that doesn't solve your dropped frames, let us start looking for the problem at the start of the signal chain.

Most analogue capture is likely to be from domestic video recordings – VHS or Betamax VCRs or analogue camcorders. I'd wager that the tapes you are trying to record from aren't fresh either. To eliminate the cause of the dropped frames being unstable playback from tape, try recording a more stable video signal - the video picture from a camcorder, the off air signal from a TV or the output from a DVD player should all be very stable. If you drop frames with these, then the next section about tape playback can be skipped.

If you can, use the same VCR or camcorder to play back the tape that recorded it. That may not be possible, particularly if you are doing a favour for someone else! The next best bet is a VCR with a timebase correction feature, although some of the simpler ones can cause "flash" frames (a single frame in an incorrect place) when used in conjunction with the top end capture devices. My VCR has a "Video Stabilizer" feature that has exactly that effect. It is good to have the choice, though.

I have boxes of VHS tapes which I'm still supposed to be digitising, and I have to admit to not storing them in ideal conditions. It is worth spending a little time making sure you are getting the most stable playback you can. If the tape has been stored somewhere like a basement or loft (or particularly a garage!), leave it in the house for a least a few hours to let it acclimatise - preferably longer. Then put it in the playback machine and spool it (fast forward and rewind, as opposed to play) up and down its entire length a couple of times to even up the tension. Finally, run a cleaning tape through the playback machine.

When you start playback to set the audio levels, either let the machine automatically adjust its tracking, or if you have manual control, adjust it for best playback. This is best done on a TV if you can connect to one. If you still see disturbances on playback, it is likely to cause dropped frames, particularly with the simpler capture devices. The newer upmarket capture hardware incorporates more sophisticated electronics.

If you still experience dropped frames, the next suspect to investigate is another computer process interfering with the stream of data. The cheaper devices use software and the computer's CPU for capture. Open up the task manager at the performance tab and have a look at CPU usage when capture is running. If it's peaking over 50%, check for background processes. Disconnect your Internet connection and shut down all the anti-virus, anti-spam security clutter which clobbers the performance of your computer.

Another possible culprit is the interface between the capture device and the computer. I assume you didn't get any error messages when following the install procedure - if you did you will need to follow them up. If you are using an internal capture device, PCI cards may, in rare circumstances, clash with other PCI devices, and one solution in the past was to switch the capture card to another slot, but I've rarely heard this reported in recent years. If you have a choice, put the card in the first slot.

USB (Universal Serial Bus) is another matter, though. There are 3 standards, but USB 2,0 is the most common. It can transfer at data rates up to 480Mbits a second – more than enough – but USB 1.1 has a maximum data transfer rate of 12Mbits a second. That's not very good – the standard is obsolete. Most high speed devices will complain if they are connected via this standard, but you also need to be suspicious if don't find the word *Enhanced* in the Hardware Manager/Universal Serial Bus Controllers entry in the Device Manager.

Connection via a USB hub can cause conflicts, and for capture devices that take their power via USB, be warned that some USB ports are limited in the amount of power they can provide.

So, eliminate all unneeded USB devices, and plug your capture device into a back panel USB socket on your desktop or tower computer. If you are using a laptop, don't use a socket on the front edge, and make sure you are running on mains power.

If you think you have tried everything, see if you can try another computer – there is always the possibility that the device itself is faulty!

Burning analogue straight to disc

If you check the *Direct to disc* box before entering the Video recording dialogue, a series of events occur that automates the making of DVD from an analogue source without creating a file – or giving you the opportunity to make any edits. If you can reliably digitise analogue and burn DVDs all will be well, but if you are troubled by dropped frames or poor burning you could just end up with coasters.

The sequence first opens the Burn workflow and prompts you to set up a DVD for burning, then switches to the Video recording section. Once you are happy with all the settings, pressing the record button starts the Direct to disc process. When the DVD is full or you have recorded enough, pressing Stop, you are returned to the Burn dialogue where the disc is finalised and ejected.

So, it's possible to make DVDs from tapes or other sources in virtually real time. I've successfully copied tapes and DVDs this way very quickly, without having to pay much attention to what is going on.

Audio capture

Recording from a microphone is something many applications can do – you will have one in Windows (sound recorder) and can download free programs such as Audacity. However, the Audio capture feature in Movie Edit Pro integrates with video playback so that you can record a real time voice over while looking at the pictures, and that recording is then placed on the Timeline in the correct position.

I've always found the hardest part of using these features in all editing programs is getting the microphone to work properly. Many PCs have poor quality microphone input circuits that aren't shielded from interference. In addition, recent PC sound hardware is more sophisticated, but that means that if the microphone isn't already up and working before you launch MEP, it might not be detected.

So, get the microphone working in Windows first. The Windows taskbar at the bottom of the screen should contain a small speaker icon. Right clicking on that will allow you to open the Sound panel, and opening the Recording tabs. A correctly connected microphone will be flagged with a green tick, and if you click on the Properties tab you can choose to *Listen* to the microphone and set the levels to test it.

In Windows you will probably have to turn your speakers down, but if you can listen on headphones, so much the better as you will be able to set the levels without worrying about the howl-round you get when the speakers feed back into the microphone.

Because the feature is designed to let you watch the screen and also record your commentary, you are going to be near your PC. Make sure the microphone is as close to you as it can be without "popping" (where your breathing causes distortion) and as far from the noise of the PC as possible.

Some microphones will sound low level – even with the Windows fader pushed up to full level. You may be able to address this with Windows settings - look for a Boost setting. If you are going to do a lot of voice-overs I suggest you consider buying a small external audio mixer to feed your microphone into. You can then feed the mixer's output into a line level socket and avoid all the hazards of interference floating around inside your PC case. You can also ride the level of the microphone manually, fading it out if you don't intend speaking for more than a few seconds. Another alternative is to use the line output of a Digital Audio Recorder, either using it's built in microphone or plugging in one of better quality.

Selecting and setting up a microphone in Windows 7

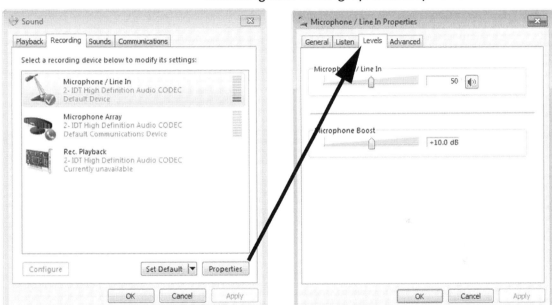

Once you have achieved a reasonable quality of microphone recording you need to check that MEP has selected the correct source.

1 – Audio driver should be set to match the microphone you have set up. The *Normalize after recording* box will adjust the level of the recorded file once it is placed on the Timeline using the normalise features, but this shouldn't be used as a substitute for setting up the microphone properly.

2 is the usual box for giving the voice over file a name and location – I'd suggest you stick with the defaults.

3- Recording quality: – I see no reason to use anything other than CD quality here. If you don't want to record in sync with video playback, uncheck the *Play while recording* box. The *Display volume* control box enables the meters to the right and the Record Level opens the Windows volume control we have already seen.

The *Advanced* button opens another dialogue box. You might want to use *Mono recording* to prevent your microphone only appearing on one channel. The *Real-time resample* box will match the recording to the project's current sample rate.

The Audio record interface

Automatic volume reduction isn't quite what you might expect. It works on the Track curves of the other sources and puts an automatic fade down on them before the voice-over starts, and fade up when it ends so the new recording isn't drown out. The parameters of this effect are controlled by the characteristics in the box below – it doesn't monitor if you are actually talking, like the V/O feature on a DJ's mixer. Because this feature works on Track curves and doesn't react to the voice, I think it has limited use and would generally remix the audio afterwards. You can chose to only alter the video tracks.

Using the feature is quite simple once it is set up. Place the Timeline scrubber at a point just before you want to start adding commentary, click on the *Record* button and perform the voiceover. When you press *Stop* you have some options. You can have another go (the current take is saved in case it turns out to be the best one), delete the last take and return to the record screen, or to keep it and add it to the Timeline. Accepting it places it on the first free track in line with where you began recording, and if you chose to use the ducking feature track volume curves are added to the other tracks.

You can still shift the recording after it has be placed; you can split it up and shift just parts of it or remove fluffs and the like, but it makes sense to get as good a recording as you can in the first place.

Screen capture

This option isn't present in the basic version of MEP. It allows you to record activity on your PC screen accompanied by audio from your microphone or other device.

Selecting it brings up an initial dialogue with a number of settings:

The initial screen capture interface

1 – *Audio drivers:* lets you choose the audio source. In the drop down box are the audio sources available and you most likely will want to choose a microphone to record a commentary, or *Rec Playback* for the output from your PC. This may be called something slightly different depending on your OS and audio hardware.

2: *Save video file* as and *Edit after recording* behave the same as DV and analogue capture.

3 – *Recording quality:* gives a choice of codecs and quality settings. Because you will be asking the computer to multitask, it's probably best to choose the low compression MXV option, although various levels of Mpeg-2 are also available. If you want high quality, low lag captures you might need to experiment with the *Configurations* settings, particularly with regard to frame rate.

The *User defined* options for both MXV and Mpeg-2 records only part of the screen. If you select this you can choose an area of the display you wish to capture by resizing a bounding box that appears on the monitor just before you record.

4- Record control: shows you the current audio levels and offers you a button that lets you change them in Windows. In Windows 7/8 you may have to drill down through Properties/Level to reach the volume sliders. The message in the text box about recording PC audio currently seems badly translated – check out my instructions for Audio drivers above.

A checkbox allows you to preview audio – perhaps not a good idea if you are using a microphone and not wearing headphones as you might get feedback. Finally, the *Record* button doesn't actually start recording, but takes you to the next stage. Pressing it replaces the MEP window with a much smaller record control with further options.

The second screen record interface

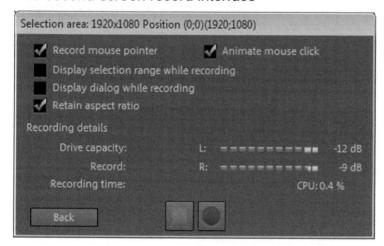

Record Mouse pointer does just that, and *Animate mouse click* adds a small animation whenever you use the mouse button. If you *Display selection range while recording* you can choose and resize the screen area you are capturing, and Retain aspect ratio locks the recording area to the aspect ratio selected when you defined the capture area.

The other active control – *Display dialogue while recording* - controls if the box that I'm currently describing stays on screen when you click on the record button. That's fine if you are just recording an area, but intrusive if you want to capture the whole display. Uncheck it before recording and the box minimises when you hit *Record*. Clicking on it in the task bar stops recording. In some circumstances I've had to open the Hidden tasks box to find it though.

This tool is useful for capturing software demos, gameplay and even videos from your screen. You may have to be very selective with the settings if you want to capture fast gameplay, and if you want to capture yourself working with Movie Edit Pro you will have to run a second instance of it from the Start menu!

Still frame capture

This feature uses your analogue capture device to create photos from video sources. The only difference in the feature is that JPEG files are created, with various choices of quality available. There is also a timer feature so that you can take a whole set of snapshots from the video – perhaps useful for creating timelapse movies.

Ripping CDs

The CD ripping interface

This is a file menu option that allows you to rip your CD music to your hard disc and include them in your project. By default it uses the *Import* location. You can rip whole CDs, individual tracks or even sections of tracks by using the *Read Start* and *Read End* option. It converts the file to the .WAV format – the best quality

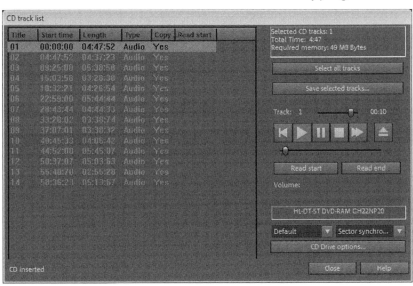

available. What's more, if you are connected to the Internet it will try to find the title of the track and use in on the Timeline if possible.

The alternative is to use Windows Media Player, so that the music is available more widely for all your applications. There is an option in WMP that allows you to specify ripping to the .WAV format

Scanning photos

This is also a File menu option. It firstly allows you to select a scanner that you may have connected to your computer, then by using *Start scanning* invokes the scanning interface supplied with the device. Once you have imported your scan you are asked for a filename, location and if you want to store the picture as a bitmap or a JPEG –

the JPEG option will create a smaller file. Finally the file is place in the specified location and on the Timeline.

Importing DVDs or Blu-rays

Movie Edit Pro doesn't have a specific command for getting the video content from a DVD or Blu-Ray disk into your computer. However, it will automatically recognise a DVD, AVCHD or Blu-ray disc and act accordingly. It won't let you import copy protected material from commercial discs.

Before you begin working with discs as a source, it's a good idea to stop them automatically beginning to play in Windows. Doing this isn't essential, but you will be constantly fighting with Windows Media Player or whatever playback software you have installed. You achieve this in the Windows control panel under *Hardware and Sound/Autoplay*, changing the default behaviour for DVDs and Blu-rays to either *Take no action* or *Ask me every time*.

DVD video discs

The first step is to insert a disc into an optical drive. MEP normally will detect this and switch the Media pool Import tab to view the drive. You may need to wait a while as it works out what is on the disc. When it has detected the material it will only display useable source files.

DVD Media view in the Media pool Import tab

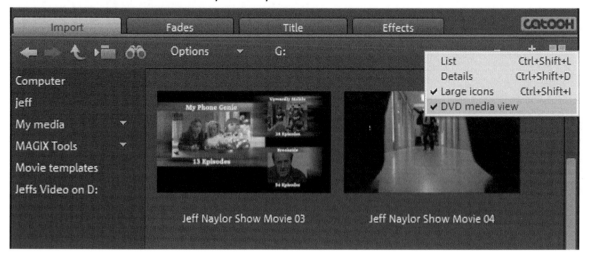

Jeff Naylor Show Movie 03   Jeff Naylor Show Movie 04

If you click on the Display Options icon top right of the Media pool you will see a fourth item has been added to the list - *DVD Media view*. Sometimes this option doesn't appear straight away, so if it hasn't, switch away to another location in Computer and then return to the optical drive. You can still chose if you want to look at *List*, *Details* or *Large Icons* (the latter is the most useful) but you don't actually see the true contents of the drive.

When switched to DVD Media view you are seeing **Titles** on the disc. Some DVDs may contain only one but most will contain many titles. On a commercial DVD this might be the "extra features" such as the "making of" documentary. In Movie Edit Pro each movie tab in a project will produce a separate title when you create a DVD.

Don't confuse titles with **Chapters** – these are markers within each title to aid navigation. They are most likely to be used to enable scene selection within a movie. MEP can't import specific chapters – it has to import the whole title.

Switching off *DVD Media view* reveals the actual files on the disc. There will always be a Video_TS folder (TS stands for Title Set). If there are other files imbedded on the disc you can find them this way. Often there is an Audio_TS folder but unless your DVD doubles as an Audio DVD it will be empty.

Opening the Video_TS folder will display a series of files. Some will be information or backup files, but the important ones will have the file type .*VOB* (standing for **V**ideo **Ob**jects). They are Mpeg-2 files but with additional information. VOBs files have be be less than 1GB in size because of the disc file structure used, so titles over a certain duration will consist of more than one VOB. During the import process MEP will automatically join all the VOB files for a title together as one VOB file.

If you try to drag a raw VOB file to the Timeline, Magix will interrupt the process and tell you that the file is part of a DVD and guide you through. If you are working in DVD Media view the next part of the process is semi-automatic.

So, in the vast majority of circumstances when you are working with discs you should use the DVD Media View, but it's important to realise that you are in that mode and not seeing the actual content of the disc, just a list of the titles available.

These titles can be dragged straight to the Timeline, but MEP will need to copy the VOBs to a folder so you can work quickly, and also allow you to remove the disc. The default destination is the *Magix Exports* folder as defined in *Program settings/Folder*. You can specify another location each time you start the process of importing a DVD title, but a better idea is to set up the project to use a Project folder because the DVD content will be copied into a sub-folder within it.

If you try to drag a title to the Timeline and get an error message saying the item is empty, what Magix are *really* saying is that you are trying to use copy-protected material, and it will have nothing to do with what you are doing!

Once the copying has happened – and this can be quite slow – the title will appear on the Timeline as a single VOB file, even if it originally consisted of more than one. You can remove the disc, and if you put titles into a Project folder you will be able to find them easily.

AVCHD and Blu-ray discs

Blu-ray or AVCHD format discs use a folder called BDMV to store the disc structure, and inside this video is stored as M2TS files. This stands for Mpeg-2 Transport Stream but these files can contain either Mpeg-2 or H.264 video. The video files are normally stored in the *Stream* folder of the disc.

As most video playback software can handle M2TS files directly, it isn't such a problem to extract non-protected video from the disc. Additionally, HD disc formats aren't limited to files sizes under 1GB, so having to use multiple video files for long titles is not a necessity, removing another complication

However, Movie Edit Pro still provides the same workflow when dealing with HD discs – even to the point of using the same name for the DVD Media view. The only difference for the user is that even static menus will appear in the list of media available for import.

Disc Images and ISO files

I mentioned earlier that DVDs need not be on an actual disc – the Video_TS folder can exist on a hard drive and you can treat like a disc and play it in Media playing software. The same thing works in MEP – navigate to the location of the Video_TS folder and it will be seen as a disc and treated as such. This saves you a lot of time actually feeding the discs into your computer, and the images can be read at a greater speed. For AVHD and Blu-ray discs the BDMV folder serves the same purpose.

ISO files are a format that holds an exact image of the disc structure and contents in one file. Movie Edit Pro will not work natively with ISOs for import.

How well ISO files will work for you may depend on the operating system you use. In Windows 8 and above you can automatically "mount" an image as a virtual drive with ease and MEP will see the drive just as if it were a real drive. In earlier operating systems you may have to use special software so it appears as a virtual drive to

Windows and other programs. In Windows 7 I have to report I get a lot of crashes when I use this technique with Movie Edit Pro. Perhaps the mounting software I use is at fault.

You shouldn't dismiss ISO files completely even if you aren't running Windows 8 though. If you want to store a DVD image for later burning with third party software it's a very neat way of doing so, and MEP is capable of saving a DVD movie in ISO format. I store all my important DVDs as ISOs on a hard drive in case the discs ever become unreadable.

Magix Tools

Other potential sources of material lie in the Import folder Tree view. *Downloads* will hold any files you have downloaded from Magix sites, *Database* points to media that has been stored by other Magix programs, the *Online Album* is an Internet location where you may store media

Internet media opens a version of Windows Explorer with tools that let you load photos, take screenshots or record from your screen. There isn't anything in this option that you can't do with an external browser, but you may want to carry out the tasks from within MEP. *Travel route* is where you will find the output from any route animations you may have created with the Travel route Wizard supplied with the Ultimate version of Movie Edit Pro.

Exporting Files

One question that I often see asked on editing forums is "What's the best format and settings to use for export to (xxxx)?"

It's not a surprising one when you consider the vast array of options that are possible. The answer to the question really depends on what you want to use the file for. Most programs offer presets that indicate they are suitable for a certain task. However, sometimes people think that by using the presets they are being cheated out of the "best possible quality" and look for something better.

Movie Edit Pro not only offers presets, it has a very wide array of choices to cater for legacy users – people who need the file to be in a particular format to suit another application or to meet a request. Further to that, many of the choices can be customised further.

Even more complications are added with the use of Containers and Wrappers. Two apparently identical file types can contain completely different types of video and audio. Conversely, two files that don't seem to match at all may actually hold identically encoded content.

Before I go any further, if you haven't read pages 12 to 16 at the start of the book please do so now. I'm going to assume that you know the differences between resolution and bitrates, Intraframe and Interframe encoding, and also are aware that video codecs have been evolving over time and still continue to do so. If you are unsure about frame rates and the differences between interlaced and progressive video, you should read pages 9 to 11 as well. Additional information about these subjects is available in the later section about slow motion video.

The Export tab

Let's start with the Export workspace, because everything here is a safe choice. Click on the tab at the top right of the main program window and you will be presented with the screen we looked at briefly on page 29. It contains 6 choices.

Output as a video file

This simple dialogue gives you four choices of resolution: Web (640*480), DVD (720x576 for PAL, 720x480 for NTSC), HD 1 (1280x720) and HD 2 (1920x1080). There are three possible encoding methods: Windows Media Video (WMV), Mpeg-2 (mpg) and Mpeg-4 (MP4). However, you can't use MPEG-2 and MPEG-4 for all the resolutions.

Output to file

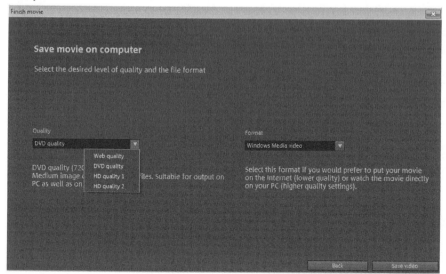

The *Windows Media Video* format allows you to create files in all four quality settings. WMV has been around for a long time but it has kept up with technology and the current version 9, used by MEP, is comparable with MP4 video using the H.264 codec. So its advantage is great quality for low file size. The downside is that you need fairly powerful hardware to play the file, and even more power to edit it. WMV is not a completely universal codec and Apple devices might need some persuading to play the files. Another disadvantage seems to be that if you use the Web or DVD settings and try to upload to YouTube, 16:9 video is transcoded to 4:3.

The bitrates for the four WMV settings are approximately 1, 1.3, 2.5 and 5 Mbps.

The *Mpeg-2* format only has presets for HD 1 and HD 2 resolutions. These files are comparable with the output of a HDV camera. The Mpeg-2 format is of a lower complexity than WMV or MP4, so doesn't require powerful playback hardware, but it does result in large file sizes making it unsuitable for Internet use.

There may be circumstances where you might want to produce DVD resolution Mpeg-2 files – they are after all the native format for DVDs and it's possible to use them for smart rendering which will be quick and preserve the original quality. If you want to do this, you will have to use the export options in the file menu.

The Bitrate for Mpeg-2 HD 1 is 26Mbps, for HD 2 it's 27Mbps.

The *Mpeg-4* format allows only three resolutions, so you can't use Web quality. While the MP4 file format can contain older codecs such as *Simple* or H.263, MEP uses the latest H.264 codec for these presets. However, the bitrates used aren't very high, so the resulting should be considered suitable for viewing and Internet use but not for archiving material.

The bitrates are: DVD quality 2.7Mbps, HD 1 4.2Mbps and HD 2 10Mbs. When you consider that even the cheapest AVCHD cameras use bitrates of 17Mpbps for HD 1 you can see why you might want to use another setting if you aren't preparing files to share on the Internet..

Output to device

This simple export interface has a long list of potential target devices from Apple, Android and Microsoft. The resolution, codec and Bitrate are preprogrammed and should be the most suitable for the chosen device.

Once you have chosen your device, the file is rendered to a temporary location. You don't get a choice of file name as the Project name is used. When the file has successfully rendered you are prompted to move it to the device which should be connected to your PC. You can also put it in a regular folder on your hard drive if you wish.

I haven't tested all of these presets, but the ones that match devices that I own seem to be a very good choice. However, if you suspect you might get better quality by upping the Bitrate, you can examine the file using a freely downloadable program such MediaInfo. and use the basic settings as a starting point for you to create your own preset using the File menu export options.

Export as Media Player

If you want to create a file to use on a website, this option with create not only the file (fixed at HD 1 quality) but the other component files to allow you to embed the video within a website for use with a media player. The MP4 file has a higher Bitrate than the normal MP4 preset. All the files are all placed within a folder named after the movie from which the file was created. How you go about using the components will depend on the website creation software you want to use.

Export 3D movie

If you have made a 3D stereoscopic project, this option allows you to export a WMV 3D side-by-side or anaglyph file.

Load into the Magix Online Album

You will need to have set up your Magix Online Album before this option will function. It is duplicated in the next section, and also in the Share menu.

Upload to Internet

This last option interfaces with various online video sharing sites: Facebook, Vimeo, Magix Online and YouTube.

The interface allows you to choose the target site with the Community drop-down at the top. Selecting the Magix option goes straight to file render, but for the other options you need to fill out the form – and if you leave some boxes empty you can't proceed to the next stage. You can choose between Private or Public uploads but for more choices you will need to use the website in question to change things after the video has been posted.

The export setting determines the file quality, and therefore size, of the upload. There is little point in exporting a file using settings much higher than the original source file and in fact Magix seems to limit the output to match the project settings – so even if you ask to upload a HD file from a SD project, it will just create a SD file for upload

The file exports are all H.264 MP4 files with the following resolutions and bitrates:

- Preview – 480x272 0.9Mbps

- SD – 640x360 1.7Mbps

- 720p – 1280x720 3Mbps

- Full HD - 1920x1080 8Mbps

These files are placed in the default Export folder, and they are not deleted after they have been used, so beware that you might find your hard disc filling up if you don't do some housekeeping! They will have the same name as the Movie from which they were exported, with incremental numbers for each upload file.

You can track progress of the render in the message area at the bottom of the main program window. Once the file has been made you may be asked to log-in to the appropriate website if you haven't already, after which the upload begins. Again, progress can be monitored in the Information bar. When completed, when you click on OK in the final dialogue the website is opened in a browser window.

Manual uploading

Now, here's a thing – while you are uploading the video file (sometimes a very long process) you can't use Movie Edit Pro to do anything else! So, unless the movie is small, I tend to make an MP4 file of slightly higher quality and upload it manually using a web browser. Although this is a little more work, it frees up the editing program for me to carry on working during the upload time.

If you do want to try higher quality uploads of your movie you will have to use manual uploading. It is unlikely that you will make much difference to the final quality of the video on the Internet, though. The sites try to keep the files as small as possible and use very powerful encoding tools to do so. One exception is Vimeo, which will allow certain types of account holders to make the original upload available for re-downloading.

The final reason for manually uploading is that all the sites occasionally change the API – the interface that allows Magix to write the upload routines into their program. So, for a period of time, automatic uploading may not work until Magix do some work at their end.

Export Movie

This File menu option is far more comprehensive than the Export tab. Some of the options are purely there for backwards compatibility, some are highly customisable. You can also create your own presets so that once you have found a bunch of setting that suit

Export options in the File menu

File	Edit	Effects	Window	Share	Help		
New project...				Ctrl+N			
Open...				Ctrl+O			
Last opened disc projects:					▶		
Save project				Ctrl+S			
Save project as...				Shift+S			
Manage movies					▶		
Export movie					▶		

Video as AVI... — Ctrl+Alt+A
Video as DV-AVI... — Ctrl+Alt+D
Video as MPEG... — Ctrl+Alt+P
Video as MAGIX video... — Ctrl+Alt+M
Video as QuickTime movie... — Ctrl+Alt+Q
Video as uncompressed video... — Ctrl+Alt+U
Video as Motion JPEG AVI... — Ctrl+Alt+O
Video as a series of single frames... — Ctrl+Alt+E
Windows Media export... — Ctrl+Alt+V
Video as MPEG-4... — Ctrl+Alt+G

Audio as MP3...
Audio as wave... — Ctrl+Alt+W
Export as transition... — Ctrl+Alt+T

Single frame as BMP... — Ctrl+Alt+B
Single frame as JPEG... — Ctrl+Alt+J
Animated GIF... — Ctrl+Alt+F

your purpose you can recall them when you want to make more files to the same standard.

A typical File export box

A big word of warning: There are so many possibilities with the customisation options that it would be impossible to test them all, and I've found many combinations that can crash MEP or p r o d u c e unreadable files. You should test your output thoroughly after exporting with custom settings.

You reach each format through the *File/Export Movie* sub menu, and in the next few sections I'll be describing the *Video as AVI* options, but most of the other formats have the same interface

File Export Presets

The top dropdown box holds a few limited choices. In many formats you can extend the choice by ticking *Show all* – without this checked you are normally limited to the presets that match your TV standard – NTSC or PAL.

To the right are *Delete* and *Save* buttons. As soon as you change any of the parameters in Export settings the preset description changes to *User defined:* and the Save button becomes available – clicking it gives you the chance to name the current settings and save them as a new preset that will appear in the drop-down list. The Delete button will destroy a saved preset, without you having a chance to change your mind, so use it with care. If you click in error, the preset won't disappear until you open the drop-down box, so you can re-save it if you realise what you have done.

File Export settings

When you enter the file export box, Magix will attempt to match the export settings to the project settings. You don't have to match the settings and can override them – you might want to make a SD file from an HD project, perhaps. If the selected codec can't match the project, or you change the settings before exporting, you will be warned and given a chance to do so, either by altering the project or the settings.

Resolution: offers all the common video resolution standards. The new 4K standard isn't yet pre-programmed into MEP 2014, but you can chose a completely custom resolution by using the **More...** button alongside. This opens a box for numerical entry. I would advise you not to make up non-broadcast resolutions unless you have a very good reason, and test the output very carefully.

Frame rate: holds all the normal rates – and a few more – for the format specified. Again, you can enter your own value.

Ratio: allows you to change the ratio of the width to the height, not by altering the pixel count, but defining the pixel display ratio. Some formats won't be able to hold this data within the file header. The normal choices are 16:9 and 4:3. 2.21 – a cinema wide screen aspect ratio is also possible. You can enter your own value as well.

Interlace: You can choose *Progressive*, *Top field first* or *Bottom field first*. Every time you interlace or de-interlace video there is a possible loss of quality, and getting the field order swapped over once is bad. Doing it twice is disastrous!

Media: allows you to exclude the audio from a video file if you wish – it will save a little space

Stereo3D: numerous 3D encoding options are available here.

Format description: shows the main details of the settings you are about to use for export including the audio settings. Changing these, and other settings require you to open the *Advanced* tab, which varies between codecs.

File name and storage location

The box here shows you the default target location, and the file name will be based on the movie name. You can change the folder and the name by using the small icon on the right to open a Windows style *Export movie* dialogue.

Underneath, a checkbox allows you to overwrite any file that has a duplicate name. This is a dangerous option, but if you are experimenting with export settings it can be useful

Other settings for export

Export selected range only is a very handy tool – you set In and Out points for the blue range above the Timeline and only that portion of the movie gets made. It's great for selective export or just testing the options.

Applying the anti-interlace filter will be most useful when making slideshows, but you may want to apply it when you have a Timeline of mixed sources or are converting interlaced to progressive output.

Shut down PC… will come in handy for long renders. You can leave the computer on and got to bed – or even on holiday!

Calculate video effects on GPU will use the graphics card to render some effects and transitions. I say "some" because the effects need to be written with this in mind. You also need to have a decent graphics card to make a difference. Importantly, it's a good troubleshooting device – if you are having poorly rendered effects or even getting crashes, make sure this checkbox is turned off.

Play after export: will be useful if you have a device connected to make a recording of the rendered file, such as a firewire connected digital tape machine or camcorder capable of DV recording. You will need to export to the correct codec for this feature to be available – to export to my DV camcorder, for example I need to be using the DV-AVI export function.

When you have selected your chosen settings, making the files is just a case of selecting *OK*. A further window appears with progress information and the chance to open a preview window to watch the file being made. It will slightly slow down the export process, but you may spot errors here, so it's worth keeping it open most of the time, although some custom settings don't produce a picture - in particular, files that are being Smartrendered.

When the export is complete, the file will be played in WMP or your default media player if the checkbox *Automatically preview exported clips* is selected in *Settings/ Video/Audio/ Export* in the File menu.

AVI formats

Saying that a file is an AVI means very little. Most video formats can vary, but AVI is one of the most variable of them all. AVI stands for Audio Video Interleave. That's it. The audio and Video data are interwoven in the same file, but there is no further standards we can guarantee and the data can be encoded in a multitude of ways. So you should never assume that all AVIs are the same.

Advanced codec selection

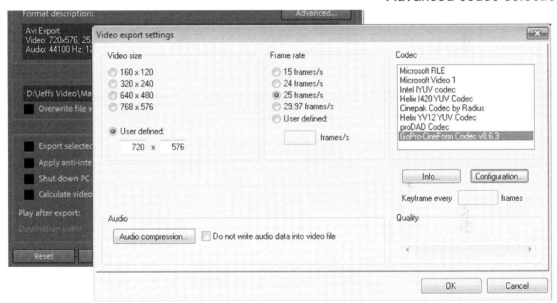

There are four Export options that produce AVIs. Let's open the first one and examine the *Advanced* options. Most of the choices you see can be set in the main Export settings panel, but at the bottom of the box is a button for *Audio compression*. It is rare that you would want to change the default options, but you can do so here.

On the right is a list of codecs. Your list may be shorter or longer than mine, as some of these codecs will have been installed by Magix, and others picked up from your other programs. I'd consider all of the standard codecs provided by Magix to be "legacy". You might use the Intel IYUV in some high quality archive situations but it uses a very high Bitrate.

As you select them, the *Info* and *Configuration* buttons highlight if there is more information available or additional settings are possible.

If you have installed the GoPro Studio software, as suggested when we were working with timewarp, you should see the GoPro Cineform codec in the list. For this codec, selecting *Configurations* offers a good deal of choice, but even just leaving the defaults as they are gives you access to a very high Bitrate, high quality archive format.

From the Export menu, **DV-AVI** is a much more tightly specified format, and you will get very few options to change settings, even in the Advanced box. There are options for Smartrender, which can speed up export by around 5 times for DV-AVI on my computer given the right circumstances. We will discuss Smartrender later.

Uncompressed video also uses the AVI suffix. If you really want lossless video, this is the option to use, at the expense of massive file size. The files are so big for a given duration that they hit the HDD speed bottleneck and you are unlikely to be able to play them back smoothly even if you have Solid State Drives. The animations I've used are exported from iClone software using this format. You might also want to use uncompressed video if you are exporting to some high end post production software.

Motion jpeg AVI is an Intraframe codec similar to DV-AVI - in fact it pre-dates DV-AVI a little. The Bitrate can often be varied, but not in Movie Edit Pro, where it is fixed at 12Mbps for SD video 75Mbps for full HD.

Magix MXV video

It's my theory that Magix uses Motion JPEG for its internal files format. Change the file extension of a MXV file to *.mjpeg* and you can examine it in some programs such as MediaCoder. We have already seen it in action when used for preview and proxy files. It's easy to edit and when using the default setting the files appear to have the same Bitrate as the Motion JPEG AVI setting.

By comparison, DV-AVI has a higher Bitrate than mjpeg but can't be used for HD resolutions. Mjpeg can, but has a fixed, lower, Bitrate. In the Advanced box for MXV video, though, you can increase the default quality from 85% to 100%, which trebles the Bitrate. These files are OK for SD but unwieldy for HD.

Remember that Intraframe compression isn't very efficient, and DV-AVI and Mjpeg don't use the latest techniques even for single frames, so the potentially massive file sizes don't mean that these make them ideal for archiving. There are newer intraframe codecs that would be a better choice, although they aren't part of Movie Edit Pro's standard set of codecs. For consumer purposes, we need to take advantage of **Interframe** compression.

MPEG-2

Until recently, MPEG-2 was the most important video codec for the consumer video market; it is used by DVD video discs and many digital transmission systems. Recently with the introduction of web streaming and Blu-ray, other more compressed formats have become just as important, but MPEG-2 is still with us in many forms.

It's an Interframe compression method, and I've described the basic principles in the first chapter.

Let's make an MPEG-2 file of the Flight project and compare the effect of Bitrate. I'll also be using the resultant files when we look at Smartrender later.

- Open the *Flight over Snowdon final cut* project.

- Open *File/Export Movie/Video as Mpeg*.

- In the dropdown box select *Standard DVD PAL widescreen*. If you have a NTSC installation of MEP you may need to check the Display all in order to find this setting.

- Set your export location to somewhere convenient where you can find it later – *My Videos* will do - and click on *OK*.

The next process takes under 2 minutes on my computer. You should end up with a good quality file that matches the DVD video specification. You could increase the Bitrate slightly and still put it on a DVD, but sometimes burned DVDs struggle to play back higher Bitrate files.

- Return to the same export dialogue and click on the Advanced button.

What opens is multi-tabbed settings box with so many options it's almost frightening.

I'm not even going to stray into most of the boxes. Suffice it to say that you have plenty of scope for experiment! Lets just change one parameter in the General setting tab.

- Notice that the preset value for the Video Bitrate is 6000 - alter it to 1000 and close the advanced settings box with OK.

- Change the filename to *Flight over Snowdon low Bitrate*.

The Video Bitrate set to 6000

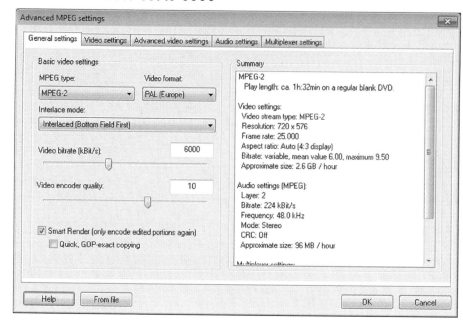

• Click on OK to start a new render. The second render will take about the same time.

Now compare the two files using Windows Explorer. Firstly the sizes are 164MB v. 34MB. That's not quite a 6 to 1 ratio, but remember that we didn't change the audio Bitrate – and that's rolled up in the same file.

Now look at the quality. You can use Windows Media Player, or drag both files to the Timeline and monitor full screen.

I don't think that the low Bitrate version is six times worse, do you? I suppose it's how you qualify it, but the titles seem about the same. Where it really shows is on fine, moving detail. Look at the background as the plane taxies – if you look closely you can even see the detail level jump back up every time that there is an i-frame.

I've created a pretty extreme comparison there, and it shows you what to look for when assessing if you have used a high enough Bitrate.

What about the other obvious setting – Quality? In other codecs, this will control the amount of time is spent refining the encoding, but for SD MPEG-2 there seems little difference in both the time taken and the end result.

Variable Bitrate

You will notice that in the Summary box of the Advanced settings, the Bitrate is described as "variable, mean value 6.00 maximum 9.5". This means that over a reasonable timescale the file will maintain the average of 6, but if there are bursts of fast motion it might use more bits to describe the motion. It's also possible to use a

Constant Bit Rate (CBR as opposed to VBR) but this is less efficient. Most hardware now can cope with added complexity of VBR without issues.

Bitrate control in Video settings

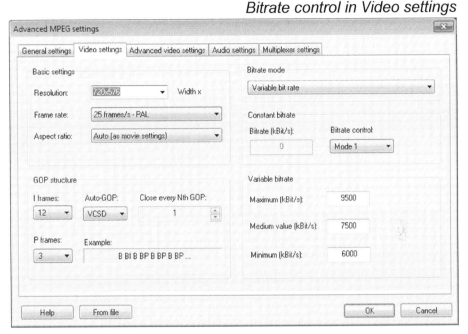

In reality, you might be wondering if it's worth creating 7Mbps video for your DVDs. To be honest, you may struggle to see the difference, particularly if the source video was an analogue capture from VHS. But if you were to turn up the rate, you would have to take into account that the peaks could go over the maximum recommended for reading back from DVD discs. You would need to check *Video settings* where, with VBR selected, you can define the maximum and minimum values as well as the average.

Mpeg-2 presets

There are a range of presets for SD video that show without the *Display all* box checked. The DVD quality presets have an average Bitrate of 6Mbps and offer choices of aspect ratio and audio encoding – AC3 is Dolby and can hold 5.1 surround sound. The Cahoot setting is very high Bitrate of 40Mbps and you can consider this as a potential high quality archive format. Long Play averages 3Mbps.

Revealing the full list shows that there are plenty of HD settings too. HDV cameras use the MPEG-2 codec so there are settings for those, and there are archive formats similar to the Cahoot settings as well. However, if you are working in HD, even with HDV camera footage, you probably will want to use the more efficient H.264 codec.

Mpeg-4 Export

The Advanced MP4 export options

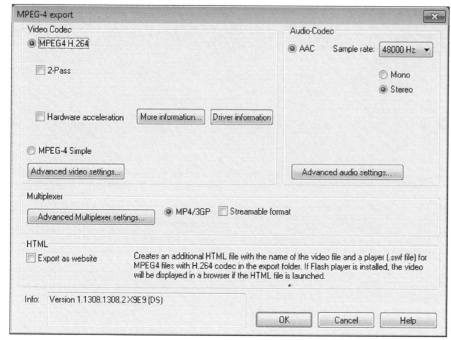

There is an intermediate MP4 *Simple* codec that you can access in the Advanced settings should you need it, but all of the presets in MEP use the H.264 codec.

Just to confuse us even more, you can export H.264 video in a MPEG-2 **TS** wrapper with the file extension M2TS – used for Blu-ray - from the Mpeg-4 interface.

At the time of writing this really is the codec of choice for HD video – it's the staple of AVCHD cameras and discs which may use an MTS wrapper (just a renamed M2TS file). GoPro action cameras put their H.264 video in an MP4 wrapper. Other recent cameras might use the .Mov container, or even AVI. However, the video is encoded with H.264.

Selecting the various presets shows a remarkable range of bitrates displayed in the format description box. For general use and uploading to the Internet the HDTV or PC settings are OK, but for good quality you will probably want to use the Transport stream settings. It's possible to change the various settings but in doing so I've often ended up with files that won't play on Windows, so test any custom setting properly.

Encoding H.264 options

Open up the Advanced tab and you will see some interesting options.

2-pass takes two goes at scanning the Timeline to optimise the variable Bitrate settings, and obviously takes twice as long. Enabling hardware acceleration can speed up render considerably but you need to check the chosen Bitrate isn't lowered automatically when you select it.

Using the Advanced video settings button takes you to even more options.

More Video codec options

Movie Edit Pro can use a number of methods for encoding H.264 but will normally select the software method. Intel Quicksync and Cuda are supported but you need to select them. Quicksync specifically can use Intel GPUs built into the latest CPUs, while Cuda can take advantage of high powered nVidia graphic cards. Again, check the Bitrate hasn't been lowered when you select these options.

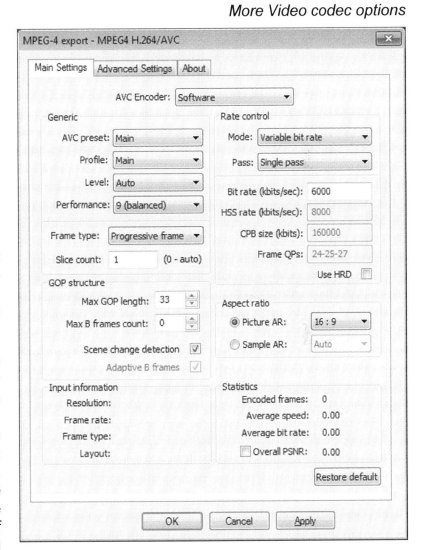

There is a further choice of encoding –the quality settings under the heading *Performance*. You can speed up rendering with a reduction in fine details, but slowing down the rendering doesn't make a huge amount of difference to perceived quality.

After days of testing, I found many settings that would make things worse or slower, and some that would refuse to work at all. Others resulted in unusable video files. I found no settings that had any significant advantages over those already offered as presets. So my advice is that unless you know what you want to change, and the side effects of changing it, leave well alone and trust the programmers!

Smart Rendering

Movie Edit Pro can save you a good deal of time making files or discs by using a technique called "Smartrendering", otherwise known as Direct Stream Copy. This saves time and also avoids introducing further errors to the video because it hasn't got to reprocess it.

In order for Smart render to work on any particular section of a movie, a number of criteria need to be met:

- The source video needs to be encoded with the same codec as the target format.

- The compression level of the source material must be the same or lower than the target for the final file.

- For MPEG-2 and H.264 the section needs to start and end at a Group of Pictures boundary. If the first frame of the exported section isn't an i-frame at the start of a GOP, a "short" GOP needs to be re-rendered, and then smart rendering can continue from the next GOP boundary.

- No video effects, titles or transitions have been added or, if they have, that section of the movie has been preview rendered with a codec that matches the output format.

The codecs that allow Smartrendering are DV-AVI, Mpeg-2 and H.264, but for export of DV-AVI you need to dive into the Advanced settings to enable Smartrender.

For the other codecs, if Smartrender is a possibility an additional box will be present at the bottom of the Export video interface – *Smart render info*.

Here is a little demo:

- Start a new project.

- Locate the *Flight over Snowdon final cut.mpg* normal Bitrate file that we made earlier in the chapter and place it on the Timeline.

- Create a simple title and place it over the first half of the movie.

- Open the *Video as mpeg* interface and click on the Smart render info button.

- Read the message – it should indicate that the second half of the movie will Smartrendered.

- Close the info box and output the file, watching the progress.

The Smartrender information

The obvious sign that Smart rending is happening is the speed of render - at least twice that of normal file rendering. Half way through the export there will be a dramatic increase in the progress - you will find that often the speed of rending is limited by the transfer rates of your hard disc.

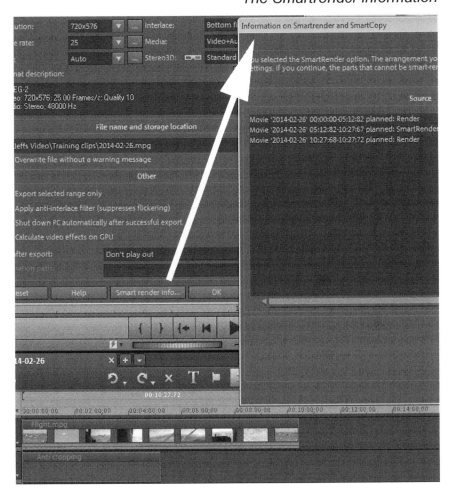

In the case of Mpeg-2, you have to disable Smart render if you don't want it to occur. It's possible that it can malfunction and make a mess of the audio sync or create flash frames at the junction of GOPs. That's my experience in other editing programs, but be warned – it could happen in MEP, so check your exports carefully.

So, what about H.264? DV and Mpeg-2 will generally be in the same container format, but H.264 could be in many formats. Smart render is feasible with mixed file types as long as the target format is M2TS, but it's somewhat unreliable.

Magix are clearly not as happy with H.264 Smart render and so it isn't the default. When you try to export, if the Smart render info button isn't present, you've not chosen the correct preset or Smart render just isn't possible. If the button is there but there is no information in the info box when you open it, you need to set the Smart render checkbox in the Advanced settings.

There is a further checkbox that enables *Smart copy*. This function will allow you to include video with different properties, but they have to be whole GOPs, and if your edits don't coincide then they will be changed. Not really my idea of creative editing!

I've noticed another issue with Smartrender – even when it seems to work OK, the difference between re-encoded and Smart sections is quite noticeable – the video levels don't match. This may only happen on certain clips or types of source files, but it's very distracting and not really acceptable when it happens.

So – to Smartrender or not? DV and MPEG-2 is OK, but those files are quick to render anyway. H.264? In my opinion only for trimming and copying video – cutting out the good bits from a rushes file and saving it to a new, shorter file quickly and without loss. For a proper movie, I don't think it it works well enough. By the way, this opinion isn't just restricted to Movie Edit Pro – other software I've worked with fails at the same tasks.

Quicktime

This is "native" Apple video format, with the files ending in .MOV. It's a wrapper, and a very versatile one at that. Movie Edit Pro renders .Mov files with the simple MP4 codec by default, which isn't ideal, and the default bitrates are rather low, but you can modify the quality to increase it.

Other codecs are available via the advanced button, but oddly, I can't get H.264 to work on my system. However, the Quicktime encoder does work with some interesting third party codecs including Avid's free LE codec pack which includes the professional DNxHD codec.

Windows Media export

We looked at this codec earlier, and within the Export Movie interface it's highly customisable via the Advanced button.

Series of Single frames

Some applications may accept video as a series of bitmaps and this option will allow you to export them from the Timeline. Because bitmaps are uncompressed, you end up with big files – Full HD images are 6Mbytes each!

Gifs

This format was developed as a low bandwidth way of putting pictures on the Internet, and as well as displaying single frames, Gif graphics can be animated, playing back a series of frames. They are most suitable for lower quality pictures and logos. MEP can create an animated GIF from the Timeline which you can then imbed in websites.

Single frames

These options allow you to export the image at the scrubber position as either an uncompressed bitmap or a lightly compressed JPEG. When exporting from a Standard Definition widescreen project, the horizontal resolution is increased from 720 to 1024 so the image isn't squashed when displayed with a 1:1 pixel aspect ratio.

Export as a Transition

Using this feature, you can create your own transition on the Timeline. At its simplest, the transition will consist of your movie and a crossfade between the incoming and outgoing video. The level of the incoming video is controlled by the brightness level of the video. If you create an animated matte and check the *Set brightness gradient manually* checkbox, you can generate wipes instead of imposing a crossfade.

The file is saved as a MXV file in the Standard transition location, where you can use it just like any other transition.

Audio Export

You can also chose to output the audio from the movie as a WAV or MP3 file, with control of the sample rates.

Export to device

This file menu option extends the range of devices offered in the Export tab and lets you customise the presets - and save them in the list – before creating a file and then exporting the file to the target. It includes the option to record your movie back to a DV camcorder if your model can handle external input.

Batch conversion

This is a very handy wizard that automates making files. You can define a list of movies (including the one on the Timeline) and files on your computer, define a target format, and then let the process run without you having to attend to it. One reason you might need to use it is for the conversion of source files that MEP has difficulty editing, another would be to archive source files for convenient storage.

I'm going to describe how to use this wizard by processing the three .mxv files we used near the beginning of the book, converting them to .wmv files – this will work around the bug in some builds of MEP that causes issues with .mxv file thumbnails.

- Start a new empty project. This means that the wizard takes it settings from the source files rather than the project settings.

- Select *File/Batch conversion*.

If you did have a project loaded when you opened the wizard you would get a dialogue asking you if you wished to work just with the video on track 1 of the current movie (*Objects in the movie*) or all the movie in the project (*Multiple movies),* and files and projects would automatically be added to the list.

- When the Wizard appears, check the queue is empty, then click on *Add files.*

- In the Import Windows dialogue that opens, browse to the **C:/Revealed Video** location where we copied the .mxv files.

- Select all three files and click on *Open.* The dialogue will close and the three selected files will appear in *Queued entries...* section of the Wizard.

- In the *Format settings...* section, the Windows Media setting should be selected by default, and the resolution set to the same as the .mxv files, 512 x 228.

- Click on *Advanced settings*, and another dialogue box will ask you about the renaming scheme you wish to use. We are going to use the original names, so click on *Specify folder*.

- Change the destination path by using the folder icon in the Specify destination path area and using the Windows dialogue to choose C:\Revealed Video\.

- We now have the chance to use different parameters should we wish to do so. In this case we don't. Click *OK* to return to the Wizard.

- Now all you need to do is click on *Start processing* and wait. Before very long a dialogue box will tell you the results of the conversion. Close that and you return to the main program.

- As you are now going to use the wmv files during the opening chapters, I suggest you delete the copied mxv files – you can do that in the Media pool Import window by selection and the use of the *Delete* key.

The Advanced settings

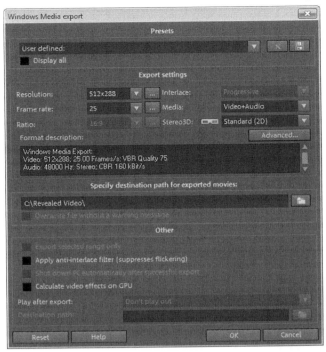

The wizard ready to start converting.

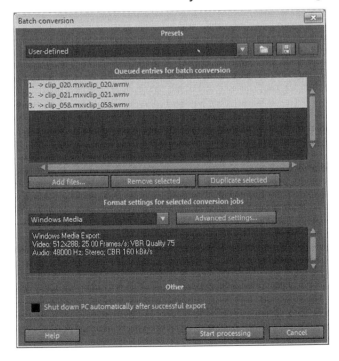

Menus and Discs

For many people, the final stage of making a movie will be creating an optical disc to play at home and perhaps distribute to other people. It's possible to burn a rendered movie file to a data disc so it can be played on a computer, but in order to be able to use the discs on standalone players they normally have to be authored to a set of standards - DVD-Video for SD, AVCHD or Blu-ray for HD.

Although simply using the default settings in Movie Edit Pro will normally result in a perfectly useable disc, if you want your discs to be widely compatible with the most of the players out there, it's a good idea to plan ahead.

The first thing to consider is the duration of the material. Trying to squeeze too much video on a disc means you have to use a lower Bitrate. You can consider using Dual layer discs to double the capacity, but they tend to be a bit more fragile, and you have the added complication of the "layer break" which may cause problems.

At the other extreme, don't get too obsessed with quality. Using the highest Bitrate that is technically possible may be fine for "pressed" discs, but home produced burned discs tend to have a lot more errors due the nature of the technology. These errors are usually covered up by digital error correction, but the faster you have to read the data from the disc, the more likely it is that the correction will get overwhelmed. If you can really see the difference between SD MPEG-2 video at 6 and 8 Mbps on a domestic TV you have got good eyesight!

Think about the navigational structure before you start. There are two navigation elements – **Titles** and **Chapters**. Title menus (which MEP calls Film menus) can be used to play a whole movie – and you might have more than one movie – while chapters are typically used for Scene selection within a movie.

Consider how elaborate you want to make the Menu. Yes, you can have moving backgrounds and thumbnails and accompany each menu with music clips, but the more complex the menu, the more likely it is confuse the firmware of some, perhaps all, players. Movie Edit Pro has some pretty smart looking templates that scale neatly to the size of a project and they will be reliable. By all means add your own personal touches, but bear in mind how little time is spent looking at a menu, and how irritating a constantly looping sound bite can be!

Make your discs with care – I'll detail a workflow later that might not appeal to the more impatient amongst you, but could save you a good deal of frustration in the long run.

I'm going to walk through the making of a disc project using most of the common features and pointing you in the direction of others. The plan is to make a Video DVD that holds two titles, one of which will have a chapter menu, and for the movies we will use projects made earlier in the book. If you haven't made them, you can cheat by downloading them or copying them from the Demo DVD.

The Burn workspace

- Start a brand new empty 16:9 project, and then switch to the *Burn* tab.

We looked at this briefly on page 28. The layout is quite different to the Edit workspace. I'm showing screen shots from a 1920*1080 display, but if your monitor is smaller you will have a slightly different layout with a smaller Menu preview area and the right panel divided into two columns. The Burn screen workspace isn't adjustable in the same way as the Edit workspace.

The Menu bar at the top of the screen is very similar to the Edit workspace, but with far few items in the menus. You can do project management and adjust the Program, but not the Movie, settings. You can switch back to the edit screen with the tabs on the right.

Left side in Edit mode

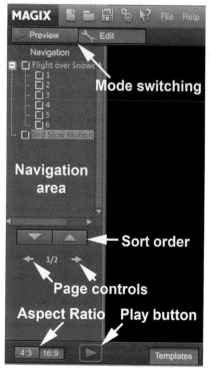

Beneath the Menu bar is a toolbar. Two controls are always present – Preview and Edit. When you click on the Edit button the Burn screen switches to Edit mode which offers another 6 tool icons on the toolbar. In the centre of the workspace is the Menu preview screen. When in Edit mode you can select and adjust the elements of the menu with the mouse, in Preview mode they are locked. Switch to Preview if you aren't already in that mode using the button in the toolbar. There are no bounding boxes for the objects.

Switch to Edit mode. On the left is a navigation tree showing you the current structure of the project, on the right a series of controls that lets you alter the behaviour of the menu structure and its appearance. Now return to Preview mode. The space on the left contains a remote control for previewing the Project behaviour while on the right is a large icon to move to the next stage of the creation of the disc.

Beneath what is currently the DVD controller are buttons that are also present in Edit mode. The Play button to the right will preview any animations that have been added to the current menu – and it works in Edit mode as well, so you don't need to switch to Preview mode to check. The aspect ratio buttons don't control the current menu, only the style of templates on offer below. On the far right a printer icon opens a sub program for creating disc labels.

In the middle there is always an *Apply* tab, which works with the templates below – you can apply whole templates to a menu while still in Preview mode.

The Template area in Preview mode

Switch back to Edit mode and study the template preview area at the bottom of the screen. To the left a tree view lets you explore the templates available in your particular version of MEP. The tabs that have now appeared let you choose just specific elements of a template – button types, fonts and order – which really means the maximum number of buttons and their layout. The *Apply* tab lets you apply the highlighted template, or template element, to the whole disc, all the menus of one branch of the navigation, or just the menu in the preview window.

If you have the basic version of MEP, you will only have a couple of items in the template area. You can still make some good looking menus, but you'll have to put in a bit more work.

The default menu template

When you first go to the burn screen with a new project, a specific way of generating menus is applied. This is what I'm calling the default design. In the template area there are a few other templates called *Defaults* but the specific one that is used when you first switch to the Burn screen is under Static/General - shown in the screenshot above.

My workflow is to create the whole navigation structure of the disc using this template before customising the look or applying a new template. Adding more titles or chapters is handled automatically, scaling the layout to make sense. The number of buttons is limited to sensible numbers, adding extra menus as required instead of creating a crowded layout.

At the moment we only have one title and no chapters. It's worth experimenting a little at this stage as it should make the principles clearer. Return to the Edit screen and use the movie + tab to add seven new movies to the project – they will automatically have numerical suffixes added to the name, so the last one will be *Empty project – 07* (or whatever is the name of the open project).

Switch back to the Burn screen and take a look at the new layout. At the top of the menu is a text field currently showing the Project file name, and each of the eight movies are represented by a button each, with the movie name and a black thumbnail for each movie. In the navigation panel on the left there are now eight entries, one for each button.

A disc structure with 8 Titles

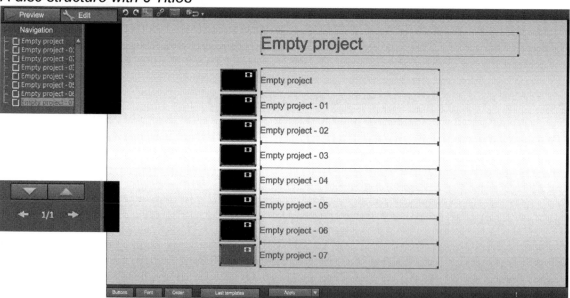

Multi page menus

Let's assume you don't want to make the buttons any smaller for now. What happens if we add another movie to the project? Switch back to Edit and do so, then return to Burn.

You will be seeing a different menu – it's only got one button for the ninth movie because the maximum allowed on a film menu in the default template is eight. There is also a new button top left of the screen. It's a back button, and when the menu is live, it will take us back to the previous menu

A disc structure with 9 titles, page 2 of 2 selected

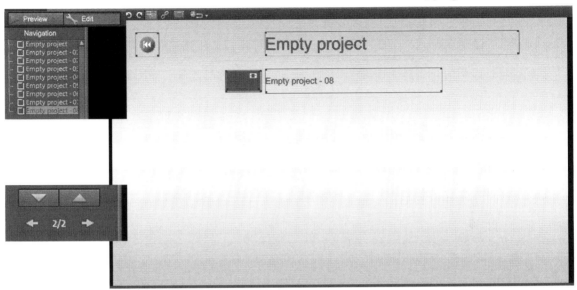

Selecting menus

So where is the first menu? On the left under the navigation panel are four arrow buttons. The two horizontal ones should have the number 2/2 between them – we are looking at the second menu out of a total of two, so click on the left pointing arrow to reveal the first menu, which you see has now acquired a forward arrow top right. You are now looking at **Page 1 of 2**.

An important concept here is that there could be more menus at this top level, and you won't see that in the navigation bar – you see a list of individual titles and chapters. Currently all our title buttons are on two pages. If there were 3 pages then we could click through 3 levels with the page selection arrows. This becomes even more important if you manually add additional pages that aren't part of the automatic structure.

There are a number of other ways of making your way round the various menus. In the navigation panel you can click on any button entry and the menu containing that button will open in preview. By right clicking on any object in the menu preview a context menu appears, and if the object is a navigation button the first option is *Simulate DVD action*. With any button selected, a yellow jump button in the right hand pane lets you *Jump to linked page*. You can even switch to Preview mode and use the DVD simulator.

Menu order

You will have noticed that the titles are displayed in the same order as the movies in the edit screen tabs. You might expect that this would be the way to re-order to titles – return to the edit screen and use *Sort Movies* tools. This *doesn't* work – in fact, if we had re-ordered the tabs after loading the movies but before switching to Burn, the titles in the menu would have been in the original order which we loaded the movies into the project.

The way to reorder buttons is therefore to click to highlight them and then use the up and down arrows below. You can only do this with titles, not with chapters.

Automatic inclusion and exclusion

Each element in the navigation pane has a small checkbox before its name, currently with a red checkmark. If you don't want the automatic menu creation system to include some of the titles (or chapters) you can also choose to exclude them by unchecking the red tick boxes. This this doesn't mean those elements aren't reachable in some other way. The red check marks only indicate what has been included in the structure automatically, and if you manually add more pages and link to them, the checkboxes will stay unchecked.

Movie and Title names

Changes in the Navigation bar

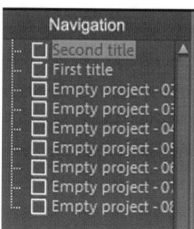

You will notice that each title button has a text field using a name which is initially generated by the movie title in the Timeline in the Edit workspace. Unlike the order of the titles, editing the names of Movies does result in a change to the text used to label the titles. This happens both in the navigation sidebar and within the buttons themselves. However it's important to realise that this is a one-way process. If you edit the button text within the Burn workspace (we will see how on page 490) it isn't reflected in the Movie titles. What's more, the automatic behaviour ceases and any further changes to the Movie titles won't show up in the menus.

Chapters

If a movie only has one chapter mark then selecting that button plays the movie. In order to create more chapters we have to return to the Edit screen. Do that now. We also can't add them to a blank movies, so switch to the first movie, locate the flight footage we used (or any other video with cuts in it) and drag it to the Timeline. Right click on the clip, select *Scene detection* and with the sensitivity set to 5, click on *Start search*. We did this earlier as well (*Using Scene detection*, page 202), so it's possible the detection data has already been created if you made the Flight project. You should have 19 scenes, or if you are using another clip, adjust the sensitivity so you have around this number. Now select *Cut at all markers* and click *OK*.

It's time now to look at a new command. Right click on the timescale above track 1 and select *Markers/Set chapter markers automatically*.

Auto chapter marking

The dialogue box has some very useful options. I'm going to suggest you use *At the beginning of object in track:* and make sure track 1 is selected in the box alongside.

In other circumstances you could use another track, title objects (we will later), time intervals or just say how many chapters you want. This is just the Automatic mode; you can set them on the Timeline manually, with Shift-Enter, drag them with the mouse, or delete spurious ones.

Create chapter marker for first title.MVD

Note: A maximum of 99 chapters is possible; the minimum length of a chapter is 1 second.

Automatically create chapter marker

● At beginning of movie
○ At beginning of object in track: 1
● At beginning of title object
● Specified interval (minutes):   5   results in 3 Chapter
● Specified amount: 6   fits every chapter: 1m 44s

Naming chapter markers

○ No marker name
● User defined: Chapter   + Marker number
● Apply object name

Options

■ Delete existing chapter markers
■ Only take the selected range into account

OK   Cancel

There are naming options and you can choose to remove the existing markers before applying the automatic ones, or just working with a specific range.

So, with the second option selected, click on OK, and then return to the Burn screen.

The initial result of adding chapters

The first title button will now have a button to the right, and the entry in the navigation panel will have a plus symbol beside it – click to see the full list of chapters. If you navigate to the first chapter menu, you can see that there are 16 chapters on the page, with a button to lead you to a second page, which has the remaining 3.

Let's just return to the concept of automatic inclusion for a moment. We currently have two pages at the title level because there are nine titles and only eight allowed on each page. We also have two pages at the chapter level because there are 19 chapters and only 16 allowed per page.

Click on the first chapter link to display page 1 of the chapter menu but note that the message below indicates 1 of 2 pages. Now exclude 3 of the chapters by unchecking their red check boxes. The chapters all fit on one page now. The chapter menu navigation buttons have disappeared and the message indicates 1 of 1 pages. There is only one page to the chapter menu at this level.

Click on the Empty project navigation link above. The message indicated 1 of 2 pages. There are two pages to the title menu at this level.

Disc options

In the right hand pane are options to change the menu behaviour and appearance. They start with the global options at the top under the heading *Disc options valid for the entire DVD*.

The Disc options

If you are considering applying a template to your work, then do so before you start making any further changes, because they won't survive. If you are happy to modify the default menu, though, you can save your work in the Last templates tab.

The first choice, *Intro Video* is for you to specify a file to play when the disc is first loaded. On a commercial disc this would often be the copyright message or trailers for other movies, and to that end, you can also specify that the video can't be skipped. The "…" button opens a windows dialogue for you to select a file. You can't chose a movie project, so if you want something elaborate you will have to render out a file for this purpose.

Film Menu allows you disable the top level menus to simplify your structure. If you only have one title, you can disable the automatic creation of a titles menu that would only have one entry (although it still makes a good "Play whole movie option"). If you want to use this option, you can't have an Intro video clip.

Chapter Menu allows you to disable chapter menus as well. If you also disable Film menus you end up with a DVD that has no menus at all – when you load it the movie plays automatically.

Buttons may have a number of elements, depending on their purpose; the next three options allow you to choose if those elements appear globally in your menus. *Preview images* are the thumbnails that are normally the first frame that the button refers to (although this can be edited). *Numbering* controls the appearance of numbers on buttons that tell the user what numbers to enter in the DVD remote control to navigate to that link. *Border* switched on and off the highlight borders that indicate to the user which button is currently selected.

Design page options

Design page options

Adding and deleting pages is handled by the plus and minus buttons at the top of this section. The ability to add new pages (and buttons) is not possible in the standard version of Movie Edit Pro.

New pages are added to the current menu, so you will see the page count increase over on the left when you add one. When you click on the plus button a small dialogue allows you to change the text label for the new page. There is also a *Sort as first menu page* checkbox to help you define where the new page is located.

With the checkbox clear, clicking on OK in the dialogue causes a new button to be placed on the **currently displayed menu page**. That new button links you to the new page which is added as the last page for that menu. The new page only consists of two items – the text label and a back button that returns you to the page that sent you here.

If you add a new page with the *Sort as first menu page* checkbox set, **a new page appears as page 1 for that menu**. It has a text label and a button that links you to the next page. Once you have created your new page the links can be customised and new ones added. The minus button deletes pages, but will only allow you to do so to pages you have created yourself.

Background design

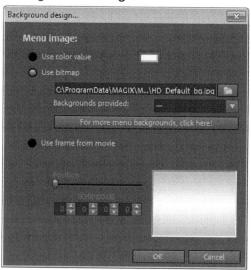

The page **Edit** button lets you change the background of the current page, opening the Background design sub-menu. You can just set a colour, browse for a graphic file or select a still frame from a movie. Magix also provides a link to use an external graphics editor and by default that opens up their own program Photo Designer, provided free, or available to download. You can use the graphics editing program of your choice by specifying a different target in the *Setting/Program/Folder* dialogue.

If you want to add a music clip to play in the background of the menu, you can check the *Sound/Music* box, and select an audio clip from your computer.

Setting a background video

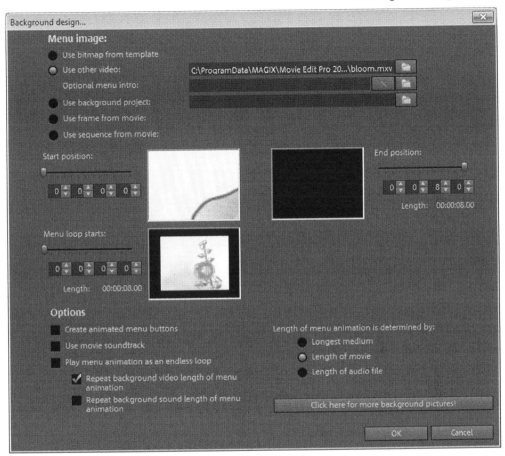

Video is a bit more complex. Not only can you add a motion clip, you have extensive control of the start and where it loops. You can use Background templates or movies within the current project, and it's even possible to use one video when the menu first opens and then cut to a looping video (*Option menu intro*). At the bottom of the box are many options for adjusting the length of the menu and the video and audio sources.

What's even more complicated is the ability to set all the video thumbnails on the menu page into motion – *Create animated menu buttons*. I'm not a big fan of most of these options – and in particular animating the thumbnails because it can make the menus very fussy indeed. What's more, you are beginning to push the menu system to its limits and I don't always get reliable results. In particular, menus for

AVCHD or Blu-ray discs can be a problem for some players. If you do want to use these features, start small and test frequently on a player itself.

Which brings me to another point – the DVD simulator isn't capable of previewing menu animations. You can play the individual menus or the audio or video elements with the various play buttons, but even then you won't see the thumbnails animate until you burn an image and test that.

One puzzle for me is the *Apply to all pages* button. On my installation it doesn't seem to work so I have to modify the pages one at a time.

Button Design options

Button design

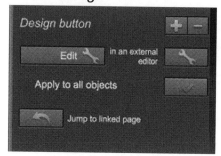

The button options start with the plus and minus buttons for creating new buttons, or deleting ones that you have added. Creating a button opens a dialogue with the text options on the left (discussed in moment) a choice of graphic on the top right and a complete choice of where the button will link to below that.

Clicking the *Edit* button brings up a number of options, some of which aren't available for some types of button.

Menu Text will be the one you want to customise most of all. Some buttons consist of only text – the titles of menu pages – and other don't appear to have text. The default Chapter thumbnails are set to a point size of zero, but if you increase that, a label will appear below the thumbnails. There are very extensive controls for justifying and formatting text.

The External editor button allows you access to the border graphic for the selected button, should you wish to alter it.

Menu image lets you define a thumbnail if the button is allowed to have one. You don't have to use the start of the chapter or title that the button links to – you can set a new In point or chose a graphic.

If you are editing an automatically generated Title menu button you have an extensive choice of what happens at the end of the movie, including making it loop and play again.

Menu properties options

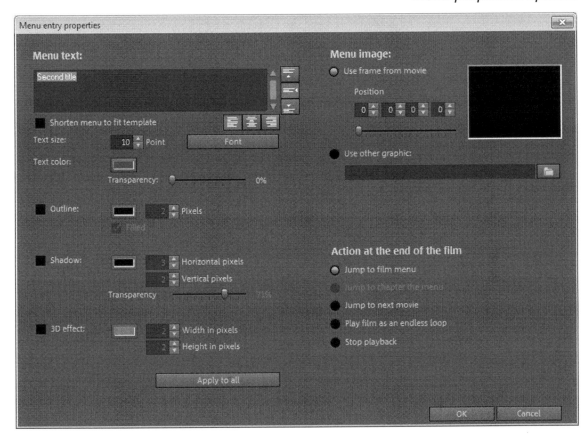

Working in the preview area

There are a number of functions that you can perform in the preview area in the middle of the Burn workspace. Let's begin with the context menus that appear when you right click.

The background context menu allows you to save the menu in the *Last templates* space in the tabbed area below. If you have the Plus or Premium versions you can also add

Preview area context menu

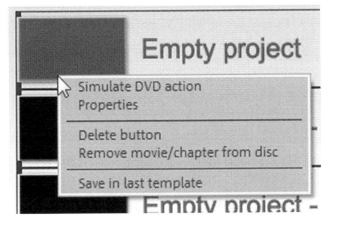

new pages or buttons to the current menu.

Properties opens up the edit dialogue for the selected object – as does double clicking on the button itself. You will be offered the chance to delete the object and also remove the target that the button links to – which won't work if there isn't a link set. If a link is set, then you can simulate the action from the context menu, as I showed earlier.

Once you get a good structure, you may want to alter the appearance or layout of the menus more accurately, and for this you can drag and resize them with the mouse. Above the preview area a short row of tool icons offer you help with this.

The Preview mode tools

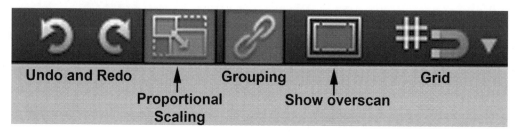

Undo and Redo   **Grouping**   **Grid**
Proportional   **Show overscan**
Scaling

After the Undo and Redo buttons is a *Proportional scaling mode* tool. It should help you make sure you maintain the aspect ratio of objects, but have to use the corner nodes. The *Grouping* tool breaks up the selected button into its component parts so that you can resize the thumbnails, text and border separately. Clicking it again re-groups the parts once you have made your required changes. The fifth tool simply switches on a guide that helps you keep items within the overscanning area recommended for graphics – if you set a button too close the the edge of frame it may not show up on some TV sets.

Grid options

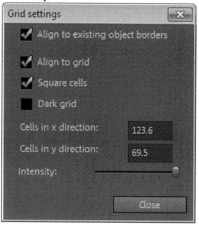

The final tool offers you a *Grid* to help with alignment. I think there is nothing that makes a menu look amateurish than it not being properly aligned. The drop down arrow opens options for the grid tool, and you might want to at least have *Align to existing object borders* checked, even if you turn the sensitivity down.

One very important point about positioning of buttons is that if you aren't completely accurate - to the nearest pixel - then when you navigate around the screen with a DVD remote control and it's buttons you may experience unwanted effects. For example, pressing the down arrow may look like it should take you to the next item below, but if the left edges aren't lined up, you could find yourself selecting an item further down the page. It's therefore very useful to use the grid tool for perfect alignment.

We have nearly finished using the current example, so if you fancy realigning the menu buttons so that they stagger across the screen, you will see what I mean when you test the buttons with the DVD remote simulator. You can also explore how the grid options can help to make a neat job of it. We will use it as an example in the next section.

Using template features

If you are working with the basic version of MEP you still have a couple of useful templates, and you can save your work in the *Last templates* tab so that you can retrieve it later.

It's important to remember that applying a full template to a menu structure will reset it almost completely. If you have made any modifications to the test project (and don't want to keep them) you can see this in action by locating the default template and double clicking on it. It should return to the starting point it was at when we finished adding the movies and chapter points to the project. This is what all the templates do.

You may want to look at some of the choices available to give you an idea of what is possible. Don't forget to play the pages to see what the motion backgrounds look like. Then having chosen something suitable for a particular disc project, you can make further customizations.

There are more than just templates though. The other tabs allow you to apply a global change to a complete set of menus but they only change one aspect – Buttons, Fonts or Order.

Controlling the number of items on a page

This last option is somewhat misnamed; *Order* controls the maximum number of linked buttons on a page, which has a major effect on the number of multi-pages in any menu but doesn't actually alter the order.

Of all the template options, it is by far the most powerful. If you want to build up your own menu from the basic template, its the only way to control the number of items on each page. By default, you will automatically get up to eight titles or 16 chapters.

Some Order options in Plus and Premium

Applying one of the Order options can reduce this number right down to just one object per page.

A Chapter menu page with a 6/1 composition order applied

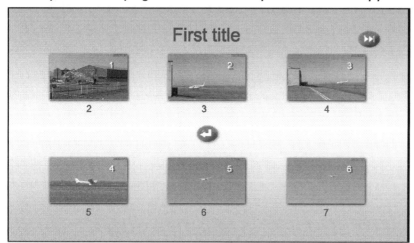

It's worth checking out what a major difference using these templates can make. They will re-align any buttons you have modified, so the random positioning I encouraged you to create earlier will be fixed, and the DVD arrow movements will work as they indicate that they should.

Depending on your chosen design and the size of your disc project, you may achieve a far more elegant structure with smaller number of items arranged in one of the patterns available to Plus and Premium users without you having to begin resizing and re-arranging the items on a page.

Making the Demo disc menus

I'm now going to talk you through the creation of a project to use in the next section of the chapter. It won't be that complex, but you can follow the workflow to create your own more complex disc structure.

- Open the *Flight over Snowdon final cut* project.

- Use the file menu to open the *Bird slow motion final cut* project, but when the dialogue box appears asking if you want to close the current project, select instead the option to add the new movie to the current project.

You should now have a project with two movies. The left-hand tab will read *Flight over Snowdon* and the second tab will be named *Bird slow motion*. If you dive into the Settings/Movie file menu option you should find that the first movie is 720*568 25fps, the second 1280*720 100fps.

The next task is to add chapter markers to the first movie:

- Select the Flight over Snowdon movie tab.

- Right click on the scale above the Timeline and select *Markers/Set chapters markers automatically*.

- In the Create chapter marker dialogue select the *At beginning of title object*, *No Marker name* and *Delete existing chapter markers* and click on OK.

- Looking at the timescale, we've got four markers. I want two more – for the Castle and the final approach. Set the scrubber to 00:02:44:09, press *SHIFT-Enter*, move along to 00:03:06:16 and do the same again.

- The first chapter marker isn't at the start of the movie, and it needs to be. Use the mouse to drag it to the start of the Timeline.

- Save this as a new project with the name *Disc Project.*

OK, we've got two titles and six chapters.

- Switch to the Burn workspace. Make sure you are in Preview mode and check all the links go where you would expect by clicking on them.

The title page looks OK for layout. However, in one version a made, it seemed to have picked the name of a previous saved version of the Flight movie. I'm also not happy with the automatic naming and think we can choose better images.

- Switch to Edit mode and double click on the Disc project text button to open the Properties.

- Change the text to *Magix Movie Edit Pro Revealed* and click OK.

- Use the same technique to change the first thumbnail button text to *A Flight over Snowdon* but while the properties box is still open adjust the *Menu Image* to a more interesting frame. I've chosen position 00:02:09:11. Click *OK*.

- Edit the second button to read *Bird Slow Motion* and adjust the image to 00:00:13:00.

Let's also tweak the page colour.

- Under the Design page options on the right, click on the *Edit* button.

- In the Background design box that opens, select the *Use color value* radio button, then use the colour swatch alongside to open the colour picker.

- Select the lightest grey – values 192, 192, 192. Close both boxes with OK.

The button numbering seems a bit unnecessary on such a simple menu.

- Turn off *Numbering* in *Disc options*.

- Right-click on the Arrow button to the right of the first thumbnail button and select *Simulate DVD action*.

- The preview should switch to the Chapter menu. I'm just going to adjust one chapter thumbnail.

- Thumbnail 5 might look better as a shot of the Castle. Open the properties for the button and set the Menu image to 00:02:53:20. Click *OK*.

Sometimes when you adjust thumbnails they may have some patterning or distortion on them. This appears to be just a sampling error and doesn't always show on the final disc. In some circumstances you might not want to take the risk, so use a frame that doesn't show the distortion.

I think it might be good to have something a bit more elaborate for the background to the Chapter menu. We could chose a pre-made graphic, or even create our own, but I think there is a suitable still frame for the movie:

- Click on the Design page *Edit* button and in the Background design dialogue select the *Use frame from movie* radio button.

- Use the scrubber to find a suitable frame. Choose one of your own by all means. I've settled on the image at 00:01:45:00. When you are happy, click *OK*.

- You might change your mind when to see the buttons drawn over the frame you have chosen, so you might want to open the dialogue again and experiment.

- For my chosen frame, the Flight title at the top of frame overlaps the plane's wing on the left. I switched on the grid and dragged it right.

- With *Align to other other objects* switched on it snapped into place nicely with the return button, leaving the text clear and looking quite balanced, if not quite centred.

How about an opening video? I've added one from the Demo project that we used as a source for the very first movie in the book. It's not very long, so if you have a intro of your own you could use that, but just to establish the principle I've done the following:

- If you don't have the _Demo project installed on your computer, copy the file *magix_logo* from the Demo DVD or the website and place it in the place you normally put your project video.

- Click on the Disc options Intro video checkbox.

- A *Windows Open…* style dialogue appears. Browse to the location of the file, or if you have the project installed *C:UsersProgramData/MAGIX/Movie Edit Pro 2014 (version)/_Demo*.

- Select the file and click on *Open*.

You won't see this video when you use the disc simulator, so you will have to wait to see the effect.

If you are the owner of a basic version of MEP, then your work is done – the next feature isn't available to you. For the rest of you, I'm going to add an additional menu page. It's possible to add files to DVD that aren't actually part of the structure, so in this case I'm making the very disc that you would receive if you ordered one, with the source files. You may not actually want to do this yourself, but even if you skip that stage later, I want to put a message on the Video DVD so that if it plays automatically when inserted into a computer, the user knows how to find the files.

- Switch back to the Title menu.

- Click on the + button alongside *Design page*.

- In the box that opens accept the default text and make sure that the *Sort as first menu page* box is unchecked, then click *OK*.

- A new button has appeared on the page and the page count reads 1 of 2.

- Double click on the new button, and in the dialogue box change the text to *File Info*.

- Click *OK* to close the box.

- Switch on the Grid Aspect ratio and overscan indication tools. Grab a corner node and shrink the box so that it is a small as possible keeping the text on one line.

- Move the button over to the bottom right, positioning it just inside the cut off area.

- Right click on the new button and select *Simulate DVD action*.

- We are now looking at the new page and need to create a text button.

- Click on the + tool alongside the *Design button* label.

- In the text box enter *This DVD contains files that can be accessed on a PC by browsing with Windows Explorer.*

- Select a font size of 24, centre justification, change the font colour to black, then click *OK*.

- Adjust the box and text position to centre it on the page.

- Change the Back button to read *Back to Main Menu*, then adjust the box to place it centrally on one line under the other two buttons.

The added button to page 1 and the new page 2

 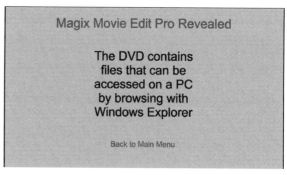

Testing the Menu

Switch to the Preview mode and explore how all the buttons behave. Don't just click on the screen – use the arrow keys on the remote control. As I mentioned earlier, if you have a complex button layout you can see unusual behaviour if they aren't aligned carefully.

Be sure to test all the chapter points. Sometimes what seems like a good place to start a chapter can be a bit jarring. For example, the Mountain railway scene starts with a transition. In this case we have to choose between seeing the transition or being able to see the start of the rolling title. You may want to adjust chapter points when you see how they behave be returning to the Edit screen.

Double check the layout and text as well. It's very annoying to have to remake a disc for a simple error.

Disc Selection

We are ready to move to the next stage, where we choose what type of disc we want to make.

Click on the Burn tool on the right to open up the Disc selection dialogue. There are three choices:

DVD creates DVD-Video discs with a resolution of 720*568 (PAL) or 720*480 (NTSC). They will play on your computer, or in most circumstances on standalone DVD players. Most Blu-ray players will play them.

The disc choice options

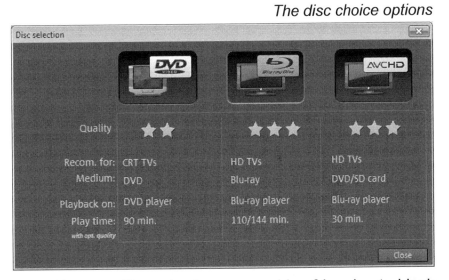

Blu-ray produces High Definition discs. For this you will need a burner capable of burning to blank burnable Blu-ray discs. You need a Blu-ray player to watch the discs on your TV – you can't use a DVD player. You can play them on your computer, but will only see the menus if you have Blu-ray playing software installed – Windows Media Player is not enough, at least at the time of writing.

AVCHD is a halfway house. It too will produce High Definition discs, but you only need a standard DVD burner and burnable DVDs. You still need a Blu-ray player for playback of the disc. However, the AVCHD standard allows you to use memory cards as the target medium, so if you have an HDTV with a memory slot you may be able to play the "disc" image you create on the TV. One limitation with this technology is that a few models of Blu-ray player (older, cheaper, and lesser known brands) may not recognise the discs. The other limitation is a drastic reduction in the amount of material that you can put on a disc.

The sample durations shown in the *Disc selection* box for each format are the optimal movie sizes. Within certain limits you can put less video on the disc and get better quality or squeeze more on and get reduced quality. The mechanism used for this is to adapt the Bitrate of the rendered video objects that are burned to disc. The lower the Bitrate the less the quality but the smaller the files for any given Bitrate. The size of the image you make is also influenced to a lesser degree by the choice of audio codecs you use, but in my opinion these are best left at the default settings for compatibility. I'll discuss the limits for each type shortly.

DVD Burning dialogue

DVD Burning options

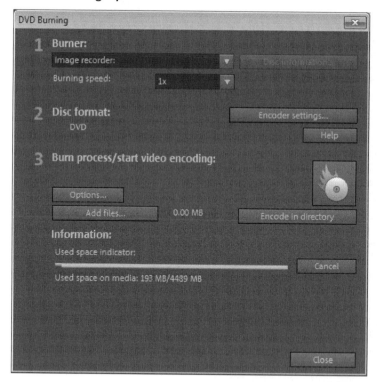

When you select DVD as the disc option, you get the dialogue shown in the screenshot. The top section 1 Burner: is entirely concerned with disc and burner selection – if you have more than one burner you can select which you use, and also discover the disc information of whatever is inserted into the burner.

If you choose *Image recorder* then the program will make an ISO file of the disc for burning later.

Burning speed will normally be set to the maximum that the burner/disc combination is capable, but there are times when you may want to experiment. I read conflicting advice about this - some burners don't actually work well at their maximum speed, others may not perform properly if you slow them down. As a basic rule, if you are experiencing issues with bad disc burns lowering the speed of burning may well help, although having to do so is a sign that the discs are of poor quality (or fakes) or the burner has past its prime.

Disc types

What exactly is a DVD disc? Like the CD that came before, it is a plastic disc sandwiching a layer of material that has a variable reflectivity. By bouncing a laser light beam off the disc onto a photo-sensitive cell, the playing device can read a series of bits of data - the basis of all digitally stored information. Huge amounts of data can be stored on the disc, but sometimes not all that accurately, so error correction is built into any playback system – something that digital storage achieves quite easily.

The critical difference between DVD and CD is the wavelength of the laser used to read the disc. A shorter wavelength enables a smaller area to represent one bit of data, and therefore more data can be squeezed on a disc. Incidentally, the same applies to Blu-ray - even more data can fit on a disc because the system uses a shorter wavelength still (a blue laser, not a red laser, hence the name Blu-ray).

Two more facts about DVDs – DVD doesn't stand for Digital Video Disc, but Digital Versatile Disc (they can be used to store other forms of data, including audio only), and the data is written from the inside of the disc outwards, unlike vinyl records.

There are 2 sizes of disc – 12cm and 8cm, although 12cm disc are far more common. Discs can also be double sided – they need to be read from both sides - and Dual layer, where the laser focuses on different layers at different depths in the disc. I've mentioned earlier that I'm not a fan of Dual layer discs as they seem to be more fragile and prone to problems than single layer. Then again, I don't make long movies. All the examples I give later are based on single layer discs. With Dual layer you have double the capacity to play with, so twice the potential duration. At the other end of the scale, you might want to choose D/L discs so that you can increase the quality to maximum and not run out of space. Read my comments about Bitrate and perceived quality and make some test discs, rather than just looking at the numbers.

Optical DVD discs fall into three categories:

Read only discs that are pressed from a glass master. These are used for mass distribution and have a type of *DVD-ROM*.

Writable discs that contain an organic dye which can have its reflectivity changed when a high powered laser beam is fired at it. A pattern of 1's and 0's is burned on the disc – hence the name burner. A low powered beam doesn't affect the dye, so the disc can be read using the same laser with adjustable power settings.

Re-writable discs that use an alloy instead of the dye, so that the writing process can be reversed – the disc is therefore capable of being erased and reused.

Writable and re-writable discs come in a number of formats. There are three basic standards - DVD+R, DVD-R and DVD RAM. DVD RAM is a more flexible format, but only a limited number of stand alone players can read the discs.

The first few times you make a DVD, I'd recommend using a rewritable DVD as a test. You will want to eventually make the disc using –R or +R discs that can't be re-used. They are much less expensive nowadays, but it's still a shame to waste them on experiments.

This leaves +R and –R. A very common question is "What's the best type of DVD to use in order to ensure maximum compatibility?"

The quick answer is to send people one –R and one +R. The obvious (and unhelpful) answer is to get them pressed for you by a "Glass House". These will be proper DVD-ROM discs, but the process is far too expensive for anything other than a major commercial operation.

A less obvious answer is to disguise the discs as DVD-ROMs. At least then the DVD player won't reject them out of hand. The process required to do this is called Bit setting and involves altering the Book Type.

The first few sections of a DVD can't be written to. This is where commercial DVDs hold the encryption information that is supposed to protect them from being pirated. Just after that comes data that tells the DVD player what specification the DVD is – its Book Type. On DVD +R discs, with *some* DVD burners installed with *some* firmware and using *some* burning programs, you can set this book type to DVD-ROM!

There are far too many "somes" in that last sentence for me to go into greater detail, but all you need to know is out there on the Internet. I've bought a DVD burner that can do Bit setting when I use ImgBurn (a free third party burning program), and a player belonging to a family member that couldn't play anything I burned now plays everything I burn.

If you don't want to go to any of those extremes, then anecdotal evidence points to –R being the best choice.

Disc Quality

I suggest you don't follow my example when I first embarked on making DVDs in quantity. I went into the local electronics store and bought a great big spindle of "top value" discs. I didn't want all that packaging, and I wasn't interested in brand names. That caused me weeks of frustration as I tried to make DVDs that didn't either fail completely or skip about on playback.

I'm sorry to say that brand names are not always a guarantee of quality either. There are only a few disc manufacturers in the world, some with much higher standards (and prices) than others, and a number of the "name" brands buy their discs in from subcontractors – and not always from the same source each time. Another issue is that there are even some fakes around – very poor discs pretending to be made by one of the top names.

For me the good guys are Taiyo Yuden (hard to find except online and now using the JVC brand name) and Mitsubishi Verbatim. To avoid any lawyer's letters, I'll avoid naming brands that haven't worked – after all, they could have been fakes – but I suggest you do some Internet research if you are unsure.

Encoder settings

Back to the *2 Disc Format:* section of the DVD Burning dialogue. It shows you the disc format selected – in this case DVD – but the important button alongside is *Encoder settings*. It has a Selection drop-down at the top, with the icons to allow you to save your own presets.

Bit rate in kbit/sec will be set appropriately for the chosen preset when you enter this dialogue. The Longplay setting aims for acceptable quality and increased duration, while the Standard setting is about halfway between Longplay and maximum. I've already mentioned the issues that going for maximum quality can bring –
even good quality burns may

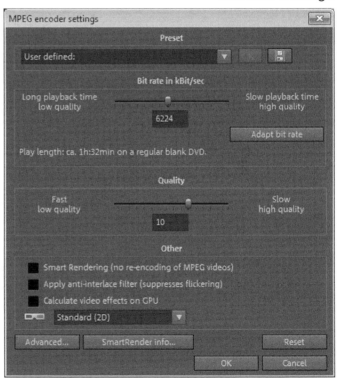

overwhelm the player's error correction. So, for maximum compatibility, the Standard setting may be a good choice, even if you don't use all the disc space.

So what's the subjective difference as you increase the Bitrate? Well it certainly isn't linear, as I've discussed in the Export chapter. In particular, if the source footage isn't in tiptop condition – anything less than DV-AVI for SD DVDs, I'd argue that the effects of increased compression will be masked by defects in the original source material, particularly in the case of video that has been captured from VHS tape

Obviously, if you think you might be using the DVD as source footage in other movies then you want to use the maximum Bitrate possible, MEP will allow you to adjust the Bitrate without exceeding the DVD limits when using VBR and you might consider using the Advanced settings to switch to CBR. If you are archiving precious material, however, I don't think DVD-Video is the best medium anyway. (In case you are wondering what I think is, then I'd suggest high Bitrate AVCHD stored on a hard disc or the Cloud).

Adapting the Bitrate

At this point, you may need to drag the Encoded setting box out of the way to see the predicted disc usage for the current movie at the current Bitrate with the disc you have chosen. At the bottom of the DVD burning box the *Information:* area shows you the situation with a bar and some numbers. If the first size figure exceeds the second, your movie isn't going to fit. You could plough on, and MEP would attempt to help you split up the movie and burn it to individual discs, but that's not going to result in a well laid out Box Set!

Disc usage information - top for the current movie, below for an oversize project

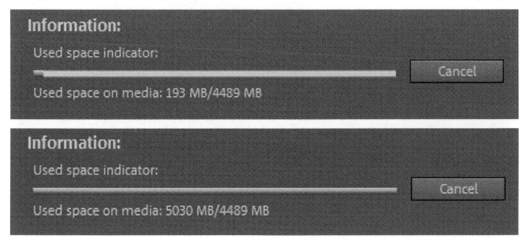

Returning to the *Encoded settings* box you can manually adjust the Bitrate. By adjusting the slider you can see that the most you will get on a single layer disc is around three hours. If you want to burn at best quality, then it's about an hour.

If you adjust the slider you won't see if your guess was good enough to fit the duration onto the disc until you click on OK, when the Information box will update. A better alternative is to use the *Adapt Bitrate* button, which will calculate the required rate needed to fit the project onto the current disc.

So, if your project is too big for your disc, this is the best option. It doesn't work the other way, however – it will only lower the Bitrate. It won't increase the Bitrate to take advantage of all the space on the disc.

Encoding Quality

In the Export chapter we looked at what is accessible via the *Advanced* button at the bottom of the encoder settings dialogue box.

Advanced encoder options

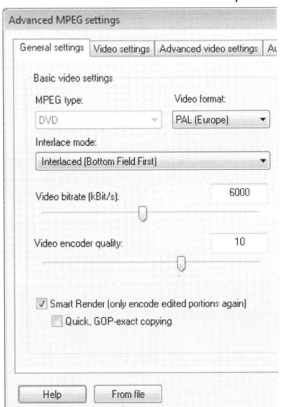

The default for Quality is a value of 10 and seems a good compromise. There is very little speed saving if you lower the setting to 1, at least on my system. Raising if from 10 to 15 does impact the speed of making the movie – about 10%. The quality of the 1 setting is noticeably blockier – in particular on moving fine detail. The difference between 10 and 15 requires taking a close look at the same detail, but I think it may be worth the extra time on good footage and in particular, if you are going to multiple copies a disc that requires only one render session.

Other Encoding options

This box is where you can enable of disable **Smart Rendering**. We have discussed this in detail in the Export section. It can save a good deal of time but my recommendation is that if you use it, check the final disc carefully. *SmartRender info* in the previous dialogue box tells you what the program is planning to do about direct stream copying.

The anti-interlace filter can have negative effects if you use it when it isn't required, while *Calculate video effects on GPU* is a good idea if you have a decent video card, but if you experience crashing or odd artefacts on transitions and other affects you may want to disable it.

Encoding in a directory

Return to the DVD burning dialogue and take a look at the third area of the dialogue. The button *Encode in directory* is a very useful tool and I'm going to suggest that we use in now. Why? Well the steps of making a disc fall into two parts even if you aren't using the option. First, all the required files are created and placed within the correct folder structure which is created in the default *Disc Images* folder defined in the program settings. The next step if to carry out the actually burning process where the folder structure is recreated on the disc.

If you use the *Encode in directory* option the process stops before the burning starts. You can then use Windows Media Player or other software to test the DVD. You can check for any problems that may occur during the render. If all is well then it is possible to proceed to the next step of burning without having to re-render the files – which is often the most time consuming part of the process. (But read the workround at the end of this section first.)

You can also use the *Encode in directory* method to create a disc image that you can burn using another program. I'm a big fan of the free program ImgBurn, although MEPs burning options are comprehensive and seems to work just as well. There are still times I use ImgBurn, though – for the bitsetting I mentioned earlier, and the making of large batches of discs. When you encode to a directory you can specify a different destination for the target directory, making it easy to find. The only downside of this is that Magix won't find the image if you ask it to perform the burn for you.

Let's actually do some work now.

- With the Disc project open in the Burn workspace, click on the Burn icon then open the DVD Burning dialogue.

- Don't worry about inserting a disc yet. The program should assume you will be using a single layer disc.

- The *Information* area should indicate no issues with our small project as it will take less than 200Mb at the default settings.

- Go into the Encoder settings and crank the Bitrate up to maximum and the quality to 15. We may as well go for the best for testing purposes because your disc isn't for distribution. (Mine is, so the Demo DVD uses the default settings.)

- Click on the *Encode in directory* button.

- In the Browse for folder dialogue, create a folder called *Test disc* in a location that is easy to find – *My Videos* will do. Click on *OK*.

- Unless you have tried to make the image before, creation will now commence. If there are files in the chosen location you will be asked if you want to reuse them. Chose to remake all the files.

- When the rendering process is complete, You should see a Burning successfully completed dialgue box. Click on *OK*.

- Switch to Windows and open Windows Media Player. Use the *Open file* option (you may have to right-click on the top toolbar to find it depending on your settings)

- In the Open box, browse to the location we put the image and click on the *Video_TS.INF* file.

- WMP should open the DVD in a window and you can test it by clicking on the buttons.

Switch to full screen to test the quality but remember this is only a SD project and your monitor has more resolution than that. Happy? Then let's move on!

By the way, a workround is needed if you want to encode to a directory, test the image and then use the files for burning if the image is good. It is possible to rename and copy the image to a place where it will be used, but it's longwinded and prone to errors. What you would need to do is have a burner selected but not insert a disc. MEP will encode to the default directory when you click on the Burn icon, and then stop and ask you for a disc. If you cancel, the Image can be found in the default location.

I haven't used this method because our render times are so short and I wanted you to locate the image somewhere convenient so you could find it in WEP.

Burning options

Now we are ready to actually make the disc, we should look at the burning options.

Click on the *Options* button. *Simulate first* runs a dummy pass of the burn operation to check your disc will burn – without actually turning on the laser. This will weed out problems with the burner and the data rates without wasting a disc. You shouldn't need to use this with a well set up system. *Activate buffer underrun protection* keeps the burner alive if it runs out of data from the computer rather than create a bad disc. There appears to be no downside to this, so I always check it.

Format entire DVD/CD-RW media does a full, rather than a partial, reformat of a rewriteable disc. This also checks the disc's integrity so that you don't end up with a bad disc, but takes a long time. If you are going to verify the disc it's a duplication of effort.

The burning options

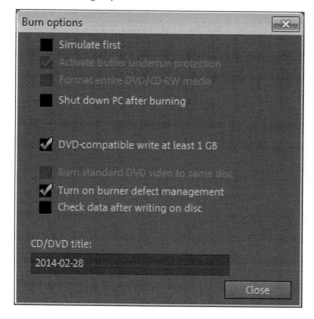

Shut down PC after burning is for projects that you want to leave unattended but not leave the computer running afterwards. *Burn standard DVD video to same disc* is an HD disc option and won't be available here. It makes some types of HD discs playable on standard DVD players by adding SD DVD compatible files.

Some DVD players will reject discs if they don't have enough data on them, so short projects won't play. *The DVD-compatible write at least 1GB* option fixes this. *Turn on burner defect management* is burner specific, and may be worth checking if you are getting bad burns.

The important setting is *Check data after writing on disc*. This verifies the burnt disc against the disc image and shows up obvious burn errors. I almost always use this option even though it takes a bit longer. Even if you are using high quality media there are sometimes the odd bad discs in the middle of a batch.

The last option allows you to change the title of the disc.

- Open the *Burn options* box.
- Check that fifth and the eight options are set.
- Change the title if you wish.

- Close the box.

Adding files

This option back in the DVD burning options allows the addition of files that aren't part of the DVD Video structure to the disc. There is a possibility that it could affect disc compatibility. I've used it on the Demo disc to add a whole folder containing the source files. As you can see from the options available you can back up the entire project's source files if there is room. This is really useful should you ever want to re-edt the disc and have lost the original project and it's files.

- Click on *Add files* and select the Project backup.

- Over 600MB of files get added to the disc layout. Click *Close*.

If you live in a PAL country, you are now ready to burn, so skip the next section.

Making an NTSC disc

All the way up until this point, we have been working with PAL, or 50Hz based, video footage. If you are a NTSC user you have not been working with the native frame rate for your TV system, which is 60Hz. This should not have caused you too many issues – you might have had to look a little harder for some presets in the Export dialogues, but computer playback of any files you have made will be fine. Uploading to the Internet won't be an issue, either.

Now we have an issue, though. Most PAL standard DVD and Blu-ray players will handle a NTSC format DVD. Unfortunately, it's not true the other way round, so to ensure that you will be able to play the disc on your standalone player you need to change some settings.

Although the program has settings that will change the defaults from PAL to

Changed setting for NTSC users

Advanced MPEG settings

General settings | Video settings | Advanced video settings | Audi

Basic video settings

MPEG type: Video format:

DVD   NTSC (USA, Japan ▼

Interlace mode:

Interlaced (Bottom Field First)   ▼

Video bitrate (kBit/s):   6000

Video encoder quality: 10

☑ Smart Render (only encode edited portions again)
☐ Quick, GOP-exact copying

Help   From file

NTSC and vice versa, we have PAL video on the Timeline. Even the HD movie is 100fps – while in the NTSC world this would be 120fps.

Fortunately, we don't need to change either of the above settings to force MEP to create a NTSC disc – the one that needs to be changed is the Mpeg-2 encoding preset.

- So, **for NTSC users only**, click on Encoder settings and then Advanced.

- In the first tab, General settings, in the Basic video settings area there is a drop down box labelled Video format. It will currently be set the PAL.

- If you are an NTSC user, select NTSC.

- Close the boxes and proceed to the burn stage.

This isn't a silver bullet to the conversion problem, because all the encoder does is insert a repeat frame every fifth of a second. The resulting conversion looks a little jittery, but it will play reasonably well for out testing purposes.

Making the disc

- Put a RW or R disc in the drive, wait for it to be recognised, and then click on the Burn icon.

- If required, select the DVD drive in the drop-down *Burner:* box.

- Now click on the Burn icon in the Burn process area.

- If you inserted a re-writeable disc that was not blank, you will be asked if it is OK to delete it. Click *Yes*.

If this isn't the first time you have tried to burn the current project, it's likely that files have been already created that may be useful. In these circumstances MEP opens a dialogue box offering the chance to keep or overwrite files. If you haven't made any changes then it's a great timesaver to use the old render files. If you have just made a few small changes and were confident that some of your files could be reused you have the chance to keep them. For example, if all you have done is correct a spelling mistake on a menu it seems a shame to have to re-render all the long VOB files. In the case of the current project, though, I suggest you re-encode everything, including checking the tick boxes

You will now need to wait for the video encoding process to occur. A disc image is created in a folder with the name *DVD Image Disc_Project*. When this is complete, the burner kicks into action, writing the image to the disc. It will then write the lead-out of the disc, and that may take quite some time as well.

Finally, you should get a completion message, and when you click on *OK*, the burner should open. Job done – or is it?

Testing the disc in Windows

The first thing to do is close the burner tray again. Depending on your auto run settings, it may run in Windows Media Player, or you may have to choose the option. If that fails, try using Windows Explorer to *Play* the disc or use the method of opening an image we used with WMP earlier.

I would be very surprised if your disc doesn't play, because we have tested the image already and computers are much more tolerant of disc errors.

If you have a problem, there is one possibility at this stage other than a burner or disc failure – the software has got confused by disc names. If this isn't the first time you have played a DVD with exactly this name it may be getting confused to find different information on the disc. Try clearing the cache in the privacy settings of WMP.

When you check the disc, unless something very out of the ordinary has happened, the menus should work identically to the images you tested. The only possible issue might be with dual layer discs and the placing of the layer break affecting the menu navigation, but I've not seen that happen in MEP.

Check in particular for skipping of freezing. That would indicate a particularly bad disc or burn – if a disc won't play on your computer, it's highly unlikely to work in a player.

Why won't it play in a DVD player?

OK – let's assume now that the disc plays back OK on your computer. Put it into your stand alone DVD player. Does it play smoothly on the TV? If the answer is yes, a small smile should creep over your face. If you've got more than one player, a DVD recorder or a games console that plays DVDs, try them. If they all work, allow yourself a proper smile. Try the neighbours? How about the Electronics showroom? I'm sure if you search for long enough, you may find a player that either ignores your disc, or plays back in a jerky manner. Let's look at the problem of recognition first.

Why don't all burned DVDs play on all DVD players? A good question without a simple answer, I'm afraid. We can partly blame the DVD player manufacturers. Some of the oldest players just don't play burned DVDs – they aren't designed to. Others only play some types, +R or –R, rewritable or not. So there are a small group of players that are always going be a problem.

I've got an old DVD player that is very picky. Even though it can play some DVD-RW discs, it can't play every brand. It also doesn't like discs that have a duration of only a few minutes, although most burning programs including Movie Edit Pro now burn a longer lead-out sector to overcome this.

A flat refusal of a DVD player to play a disc – either with a "wrong disc" type of error message or by it just going into a sulk - has a few potential solutions:

- Double check you aren't trying to play a PAL DVD on an NTSC DVD player.

- Try a different disc type – rewritable discs are less likely to work, and more DVD players will play –R discs that +R.

For skipping or freezing discs:

- Burn at the lowest speed possible if you that option.

- Try a different brand of disc.

- Use a different burning program.

Having said that, there isn't one burning program I've tried that can make my old DVD player accept DVD-RW discs made by one particular manufacturer. I've tried quite a few NLE programs that burn DVDs, and they have all failed as well.

If you want to use a 3rd party burning program and don't have one, I'd suggest you download ImgBurn. It's free, and even Microsoft have been known to recommend it. It is pretty user friendly, if a bit chatty at times. You can make an ISO file in Magix and load it easily into ImgBurn. Alternatively, if you use the Video_TS folder, ImgBurn may point out what it considers to be an error.

Making an AVCHD disc

We can take advantage of our disc project to show off the AVCHD disc system. You will need a Blu-ray player to view the final result on a TV, unless it has a memory slot for playing files.

- With the disc project open in the Burn workspace, click on the *Burn* icon.

- In the next dialogue, choose the AVCHD option on the right.

- You are now presented with an AVCHD Burning dialogue, but it appears identical to the DVD dialogue.

- Open the Encoder settings.

You should see that a full resolution HD setting has been chosen, but if you drop down the choices you will see a few more of lower resolution. You will also see a choice between NTSC and PAL frame rates – to switch formats you don't need to go into the advanced settings box like we did with the DVD. There are also settings for Full HD at 50 and 60 progressive frame rates. In theory, these formats should only be allowed for memory cards, but because the Bitrate is lowered from the 28Mbps that 50/60p cameras shoot at, you are able to burn to disc.

The default Bitrate is set at around 18Mbps which allows about 30 minutes of playing time. Cranking the rate up to the maximum of 22Mbps only reduces the possible duration to 27 minutes, and on the Bird slow motion footage I think there is a noticeable difference.

Reducing the Bitrate allows you to squeeze up to two hours on a DVD, but the compression makes the pictures look quite poor. In fact, they look little better than a SD DVD, although the resolution is higher. What's more, the encoder seems a bit unreliable at these settings.

The point here is to make high quality HD. Most AVCHD cameras shoot 16-24Mbps, unless you are shooting 50/60p full HD, so it's a reasonable range. If you want to make long movies or get the most from DSLR cameras shooting HD video at higher bitrates, you should invest in a Blu-ray burner.

- Slide the Bitrate up to the maximum setting.

- There is room on the disc to back up the files using the Add files button, should you so wish.

If you want to test an image first, you can follow the same steps as before, but there are a few issues with testing AVCHD and Blu-ray images, more of which in a moment.

- Insert a new disc and click on the *Burn* icon.

A lot more video encoding has to be done of AVCHD, so expect a much longer wait.

Computer playback for HD discs

Windows Media Player doesn't do HD playback. You may own some other software that can play back HD discs and images as if they were a disc. There is one free player that claims do this – VLC media player, so it's worth downloading that just for this purpose.

If you just want to check the quality of the video, however, it's quite easy. The files are contained in M2TS or MTS wrappers, so you can play them in WMP anyway. First, though, you need to find them! In an AVCHD disc image, the video files are contained in the path *Private/AVCHD/BDMV/Stream*. In an Blu-ray image, you will find the M2TS files in *BMDV/Stream*.

If you play your disc on a decent HDTV via a Blu-ray player, you will see a vast improvement over the DVD when checking out the Bird movie, and even the titles overlaid on the SD Flight movie look far better, without the jagged edges that occur because of the rescaling of SD to HD.

Blu-ray

Choice of codecs for Blu-ray burning

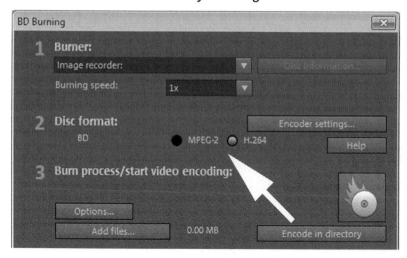

Making a Blu-ray disc follows virtually the same path as AVCHD. In the Burn dialogue you can choose between Mpeg-2 or H.264 encoding, because Mpeg-2 is allowed on Blu-ray discs for compatibly reasons – some older players may behave better with the simpler codec. If you aren't having any trouble playing back your discs, chose H.264 for better quality for a given file size.

Bitrates are limited to the same preset range as AVCHD, so a standard Blu-ray disc will hold 10 hours at a poor quality setting, 2 hours at best quality.

I say best quality, but the theoretical limit of Blu-ray is actually 40Mbps. However, I hear lots of reports of the burned media simply not being able to sustain that rate, and discs skip and freeze. If you are using footage that might warrant a higher Bitrate, you can customise the rate in the advanced settings. I've had reasonable success with this, although it is arguable that there is any point in doing so for the vast majority of consumer video footage. Commercial discs hardly ever approach the maximum Bitrate either, so it's often the quality of the original source material that shows through.

50/60p Full HD modes currently aren't available for Blu-ray, although some newer players can support that mode. I'm expecting to see this added as a preset to Movie Edit Pro in the not too distant future.

Writing to a memory device

Most of the latest TV set and Blu-ray players have memory slots, and it's easier, quicker, and less prone to errors for you to just encode you movies to solid state memory rather than disc. The only issue is the cost of memory that can sustain the required bit rates and if a particular player can support menus from memory cards. With home streaming another alternative, and 4K video becoming a real possibility in the next few years, I'd suggest that the days of optical discs are numbered.

In conclusion…

I've written this book as a narrative – with you launching the program for the first time in Chapter 2, to burning a completed movie to a DVD at the end. We have had plenty of diversions on the way, and I doubt if many of you have used a linear approach to reading the book and making the projects, but if you have, then you deserve a word of congratulations!

When I began writing, Movie Edit Pro was my second editing program. I bought it because it had features I needed, such as Proxy editing and Multi-cam. As I've learned to use the program properly, I've liked it more and more, and now it has become the editing program of choice for me. I hope I've showed you why!

Index

29635258R00307

Made in the USA
Charleston, SC
18 May 2014

LATENT
STATE

Ben Winter

Please visit me online and follow me on Twitter for updates.

www.benwinter.co.uk
@TheBenWinter

JRH

STATE 00

I ran past abandoned buildings – a drizzle-soaked nightmare of corrugated metal roofs. They reflected the garish discotheque of Neo-London across the river.

I was in the heart of the old city – broken and knackered, a remnant of the mobile revolution that had swept before it. The Thames embankment a dividing line where the wealth had fractured.

A homeless man hunkered beneath a holo-display. *Biggest explosion since 2052; links to terrorists suspected,* the floating neon text read.

He muttered something under his breath. It was mostly incoherent. Surprised irritation mixed with a reflexive request for a handout – wild, bloodshot eyes peeking out beneath a filthy scarf.

I ignored him; it was easy to ignore the mad. There were too many of them – castaways who didn't fit the new infrastructure or were driven to despair because of it.

The night sky was black. Dank pollution blocking out the stars and bouncing neon haze to Camden. We ran past the ancient, dried-up lock. A muddy bed filled with acidic rain and ramshackle tents. A place for tramps to take refuge.

Onwards. We could con drugs from the homeless, or steal from their unconscious bodies, but tonight we had more lucrative errands.

"You still with me, Daryl?" Sebastian called back to me, his feet splashing on rain-soaked paving.

I wheezed an affirmative. He knew I was there, but he was checking if I was out of breath. I wasn't as fit as Seb, and keeping up was a chore, sometimes to the point of puking. We didn't have time for that; we were on a schedule and running behind.

Would his tip pan out? He had a habit of exaggerating, but to hear him talk, it was rock solid.

Between alchovials at the sim-shop, Limbo, Seb's dim-witted mate, had let it slip. His sister worked as a dispatcher for a security firm supplying night guards. One abandoned building in Camden had been given strict instructions: never deviate from prescribed routes.

That left much of the place unmonitored. Limbo thought that was weird. Weird enough to mention it to Seb, who'd picked up a reputation for poking into things. It was our speciality.

Seb had played it down, telling Limbo the buildings in Camden were old and dilapidated and the guards kept to safe routes for insurance reasons. There might have been truth in that, but he'd held back – he knew something else. Camden, before removing state welfare, contained treatment centres for homeless addicts. Places where half-dead, brainless freakers could try to get off their habits. That, along with social funding, was a thing of the past, but Seb's hunch was some drugs may have been left behind. He'd mentioned something called *morphine* and thought it was worth getting our hands on. Nothing like the intense delirium of SP1N, our beloved Synthetic Psycholoid #1N, but it would have niche appeal, and that meant we could sell it.

Why would anyone leave valuable drugs lying around? I'd challenged, and Seb agreed; it was a long shot. But why keep guards so carefully on their routes unless there was something worth hiding, let alone guarding? I had no answer to that, but we both knew it wasn't for their safety. Limbo was a dumbass.

Rounding a corner, we skidded to a halt in front of an alleyway stained with graffiti. "This is the place," Seb whispered. His face was soaked, hair plastered to a stubble-coated cheek. Eyes open and sharp.

"You sure?" I laboured between breaths, eyeing where the alley led. It didn't look much. A random collection of squat, grey buildings, huddled together in disrepair. A wry smile from Seb and a glance upwards. I followed his gaze. At the top of the alley, embossed on a rusty sign, hung a three-dimensional cube symbol. Beneath it, faded but readable: *Hive Ltd*. It was the name of the company Limbo's sister supplied security to. Yeah, this was it.

I looked around cautiously. I wasn't sure about this place; it looked like a rathole, but Seb seemed confident. He had instincts for spotting things, intuitions that saw us right more often than wrong. When things were at their worst, he'd turn up with two tabs of SP1N and an hour's credit at the sim-shop. If a dealer was breathing down our necks for money, he'd scrounge it together in the nick of time. And when I'd told him I needed steady income, he'd pulled some strings and got me a job at the Vault.

I considered the thick steel door and large double locks – the building was sealed up tight.

"How do we get inside this tin can, Seb? And what makes you sure security won't turn up?"

"Don't worry about that, Daryl-lad." He grinned, unconcerned. "Limbo says the security firm isn't exactly shipshape. The day guard always knocks off an hour early and the night shift starts at midnight. And hey, look at this ..." He tapped the watch tattoo on his left index finger. It was 10.54 pm.

We hunkered down behind one of the bins lining the alley, out of sight of the security door. My rain-soaked jeans clung to me, clawing at the hairs on my legs.

Seb leaned back, stroking his jawline, a considered look replacing the grin. "How's the Vault going, Daryl?"

Really? He wanted to discuss that now? I suppose I wasn't surprised. Seb never wasted an opportunity to chitchat. I shrugged and pulled a *not bothered* face. "Okay ... I guess."

He inspected the back of his fingernails, then continued raking them across his stubble, dissatisfied with the answer. "Only okay? I used a charm offensive on Pete to get you in there. How about a bit more detail for your brother?"

I forced back the creeping annoyance. Seb could small talk any time, even right before a job; it was part of his nature. I was different. My heart was in my throat and I could feel pinpricks of cold, anxious sweat breaking out over my head and armpits. I took a breath. He'd keep asking, so I'd better say something. I forced a smile. "Sorry, Seb, just preoccupied, you know ... But yeah, job's okay. Steady work. Good for keeping alchovials in the fridge and a tab of SP1N ready to go."

Seb nodded, but a frown appeared. "And good for keeping real food in you too, I hope?"

My face went hot. "Oh, yeah, course." I lied. I'd barely eaten more than rehydrated pasta for two weeks.

"Remember …" Seb continued, parental. I wanted to groan; he'd activated *lecture mode*. "… You're eighteen now. You can't survive on just that rehydrated junk. Gotta keep proper stuff in you or you'll get sloppy." He stopped stroking his stubble. "That's how the folks screwed up. They didn't take care of the basics. That's why they got taken. But we won't let that happen to us. We take care of the basics. Right, Daryl?"

It was a rhetorical question, but I answered anyway, unsure if he'd seen through me or guessed. "Yeah, okay, Seb. I got it."

He grinned, and the mood was reset. "Good lad. Anyway, it's been five minutes. Time to get going."

At last. I didn't know which was worse. The mini-lecture or the anxiety waiting to do the job.

A few moments later, on time (or rather, an hour early, as predicted), a security guard appeared from behind the door. Sebastian put a finger to his lips, pointing to the floor; indicating I wait behind the bin. He slipped something from his pocket, sneaking out and sticking to the shadows.

"Seb!" I whispered after him. What was he up to?

The guard turned as he tried to secure the door, fumbling with the locks. He was oblivious to the shape creeping down the alley. A moment later, Sebastian was on him, and seconds after, the guard collapsed, motionless.

I jumped up and ran over, slipping on the rain-soaked floor as I came to a stop. "What the hell did you do to him, Seb?"

He winked, showing me the skin-gun, its porous, high-pressure nozzle still hissing. "SP1N – Full tab. He'll have an awesome time but won't be vertical for at least an hour."

My jaw dropped. The attack or losing the SP1N – I couldn't tell which was more shocking. "Crap, Seb, a full tab? We could have used that!"

Running his thumb over the top of the device, he removed the leftover residue. "Don't worry, we've got a score coming. Besides, it was my tab." He licked his thumb, savouring the chemical flavour. Then looking around, he scooped up a broken bottle-end lying on the ground. Fit for purpose; he jammed it in the door's hinge, preventing it closing.

I couldn't believe he'd jumped that guy. Too big a risk. It might draw the attention of Neo-Guards. And a whole tab? What a waste!

Unless ... he'd scored extra without telling me? The thought crept in from nowhere, unjustified. I shook my head; it was post-SP1N paranoia. It had been a few days, and seeing the dose vaporised into the guard had brought on my withdrawal. Seb wouldn't do that. He'd banked big, expecting a decent haul. I hoped his enthusiasm was justified; it had been a while since we'd had a break. Was tonight the night? It really needed to be.

Anxiety in check, I stepped over the guard. He lay curled on the wet paving, face twisted in ecstasy. A pang of longing washed over me. It was unusual to use that much in one go; it rendered you immobile – the guard would experience a huge, hot rush.

Eyeing his thin, short-sleeved shirt rewarded me with a follow up dose of guilt – it was a cold night. SP1N made you feel hot because blood got pushed to the outside, sucking warmth away from the core. It wasn't uncommon to die of hypothermia if you took it in the wrong place. Somewhere like here.

I groaned. Seb was already gone, eyes on the prize, but I'd feel bad if this guy died, and it would definitely create a Neo-Guard investigation, which wasn't good either. I'd have to move him on my own.

I grabbed his wrist, warm to the touch as the SP1N worked its chemical magic. Straining, I yanked him behind a bin, fishing out some dry cardboard to cover him up. If Sebastian asked, I'd say I was keeping him out of sight. Seb considered all forms of security 'conformists' – even private guards. His annoyance would be clear if he thought I'd expressed any concern.

I hurried inside. The building was dark and smelled of mould. Medical beds were strewn about, mattresses long since removed, leaving rusty, metal husks. Defunct monitors and drips hung from walls, wet where the ceiling had leaked.

"Seb," I called, my voice echoing.

Somewhere in the distance, out of sight, I heard a reply. "Look around, dipshit. We've only got an hour before the next guard comes on duty."

I gritted my teeth. If he hadn't left the guard, I would have been looking already!

I switched my ARO to illumination mode, thankful as always for the multi-functional device attached to my left shoulder. Sebastian had shown me the old style of com used decades ago – phones. Flat black rectangles, made mostly of glass. Silly handheld things, stowed loosely in bags or pockets where they rattled around and picked up scratches. They looked so fragile, and the battery only lasted a day.

In contrast, the *Anterior Retracting Omnicom* locked to the shoulder. Robust and with a vast array of functions, its screen folded discreetly against the body to keep it protected. And the housing was mostly battery – it would run for weeks.

An analogy to a quiver of arrows had been made, and the acronym-come-abbreviation ARO was soon ubiquitous.

We were better for it. I couldn't imagine retrieving a delicate glass square from my pocket every time I wanted to access information or call someone. What a hassle.

The light illuminated the corridor. Reflecting off the cracked, mirrored cabinets and scattered shards.

I poked through anything that wasn't completely in bits, trying not to slice my hands on jagged edges.

The anxiety that had abated was back in force. But it was worse now, mixed with a sense of dread. This place didn't feel right. I'd been in plenty of dilapidated buildings, but something was off. It was colder than it should be – the darkness more resistant to light. Hunching my shoulders, I kept moving, trying not to imagine movements in the shadows I knew couldn't be there.

My head twitched, the atmosphere prompting my withdrawal again. I'd get the shakes soon and that would make everything twice as hard. I had to keep it together.

Reaching a T-junction, I listened out in both directions. I could hear Seb rummaging through lockers somewhere on my right, grunting and muttering to himself. I took the left, heading deeper into the darkness.

I swore under my breath as I stumbled on debris. The ceiling had crumbled, leaving lumps of plasterboard all over the floor.

I must be on the right path. If the guards had come this way, they would have cleared the obstacles. I was in unexplored territory.

I wandered down the corridor, flanked with rooms. I checked them as I went, but I soon gave up. Aside from the odd bedpan or useless piece of medical paraphernalia, they were barren.

I felt sure I could hear rats nibbling – gnawing at imagined corpses left behind, unseen in the darkness. I swallowed with a dry mouth and kept moving. Stick to the corridor. Wherever it was leading was likely what the guards were warned away from.

After what felt like an eternity of stumbling, but was probably less than a minute, my ARO reflected something back at me. It hovered out in space, yellow and white, criss-crossing my path. It was reflective tape, cordoning off the area ahead. A metal sign hung from it: *HAZARD – keep out*.

I shouted out to Sebastian, but the corridor had narrowed and the sound didn't carry. I flipped out the screen on my ARO and punched up his speed dial.

A second later his voice crackled over the connection. "Yea, bro ...-wha ... need?"

I frowned, my anxiety intensifying. Why was the signal weak? Something must be interfering. "I've found a restricted area." I hoped the crackle hid the wobble in my voice.

"Can't hear ... restric? ... Cool ... foun ... freezer ... checkin ..."

Freezer? That made sense. Drugs often needed refrigeration. It was a good place to look. "Okay, come this way when you're done. I'll turn my geolocation on."

"... kay." Seb crackled and vanished.

I was relieved to hear it go off. The sound of a weak signal was worse than the imagined sound of rats any day. I switched my ARO's geolocator to DISCOVERABLE and tried to push thoughts of disconnection aside. If we lost coverage, we were a few hundred metres from the outside where it would re-establish. And it wasn't like it was gone altogether, just weak. It'll be okay, I told myself; a silent dribble of sweat ran down my face, confirming my doubt.

A shiver passed over me as I pushed through the tape. The psychological effect of a hazard warning more powerful than the security doors. The tape came away easily, the glue holding it long since rotted.

The conjoining corridor was no different to the preceding one, but it *felt* different, like the temperature had lowered again. Surely my imagination? I turned my collar up and pushed on. There had to be something down here worth seeing.

There were no more side rooms to investigate, only featureless grey corridor. Then, abruptly, it ended, and I was confronted with a large symbol nailed to a closed door. It took a moment to interpret what the fan shape meant. I recalled holovids of decaying nuclear plants, the sort that still powered much of England.

I put my hands in front of my groin, as if the sign itself would cause my balls to shrivel up. *Radiation*. It was showing there was a source of radiation nearby.

But why? An old X-ray machine? Used for treating injuries on-site rather than sending patients to hospital? Possible, but did X-ray machines hold value? They were old tech but still in use, so yeah, they probably did.

Every part of me wanted to get away from the door. The sign held a promise of sickness and death, but if I left now, I'd never hear the end of it. I could practically hear Seb's voice: "Don't be daft, Daryl! It's a warning to stay back when the X-ray machine's on. There's no power to the building, let alone the machine!"

Sighing, I steeled myself against the panic and pulled my hands away from my groin. The handle rattled loosely. Locked and defiant.

I kicked myself for leaving my lazeblade at home. It would have sliced through the flimsy lock in no time. And annoyingly, the door opened outwards, so any attempt to kick it in would be futile. Not that I was capable of such a feat of strength anyway.

My breathing had become heavy. A raspy sound, echoing in the narrow space, mingling with the occasional drip of moisture. I had to stay calm. There must be something that would get the door open.

Scanning the corridor, I spied an abandoned metal bed leaning against the wall. One of the crossbars was rusty. It might be encouraged out with a bit of force.

I readied my steel toe capped boot and took aim, directing a hard kick squarely at the most rusted section. It connected cleanly, the crossbar clanging free in a burst of rust and dirt. It coated the air with mist smelling vaguely of blood.

Nice one. I picked up the bar and inspected it. It was jagged at both ends where it had shattered, but the centre looked strong. I pulled it against my knee. It didn't give in any direction – a satisfactory tool for the job. I thrust one of the broken ends between the handle and the frame where the lock should be and heaved. The wood groaned, splintered, and finally popped – the handle and lock wrenching from the frame. They landed on the floor with a satisfying thunk.

I stepped back to survey my handiwork, allowing a small amount of smugness. Moreover, I was relieved. There'd be progress to show when my brother arrived.

I peered inside. The light from my shoulder cam illuminating the dark interior.

It was empty. A featureless box. No different to the ones lining the corridor but without even the rusty furniture. If anything, it had been cleaned – no debris or dust at all. I could even make out the original white walls rather than moisture-stained grey that had been so pervasive up until now.

All that for nothing! I hated this place, but I couldn't mask the disappointment of finding nothing. I hoped Seb had found something in his freezer or this whole trip would be a waste. And worse, we'd have burned that tab for nothing!

I turned to report the anticlimax, stopped, and looked back, a nagging thought pulling at me. Why a locked room with nothing in? What was the point? If there'd been a source of radiation, an X-ray machine or something else, it was no longer there, so why bother taping off the area? Had I missed something?

The air wheezed out of me. I was sick of this misadventure. I wanted to be outside again, where the signal was strong, but Seb would grill me on the details, catch me out. One last check, then I'd head back.

I stepped inside and cried out in pain – assaulted by blinding light. It was coming from everywhere, filling my head with hot, white brilliance – a furnace behind my eyes! I dropped to my knees, feeling them crack on the concrete. What was this? Images cascaded through my mind, each one a painful blur.

I saw myself speaking to Sebastian by the collapsed guard. A third party to the scene that had unfolded earlier. Not part of it, but watching. The image switched. He was rummaging through the freezer, still muttering to himself – something I'd imagined but not seen. The picture changed again. I was eight years old, prodding a dead frog. Sebastian, thirteen, laughing along beside me – a decade old memory I was watching from the outside.

The images kept coming. Erratic memories from my life but also things I couldn't know. People I'd never met. Places I'd never been. An avalanche of the unknown. Each hitting me harder and faster, until I could no longer make them out individually. A river of white hot sensations. It was overwhelming, maddening. I wanted to look away, retreat from the onslaught, but I couldn't. I was trapped and slipping, falling back into my mind, retreating into an abyss of madness!

Then, a voice ... from out of sight. It was far off, but like a beacon, something to distract from the raging insanity. Closer now. Was it Sebastian? It might be. I couldn't tell. A feeling of pulling, urgently dragging, directing me away from the pain and the heat.

When I came to, my head was pounding harder than any hangover I'd ever experienced, a living drumbeat in my brain. It took a few moments to realise it wasn't a headache. I was being slapped roughly. A red-faced guard loomed over me, shouting words like "who" and "why", but the rest struggled to penetrate – my brain was mush.

His words weren't making much sense, but they didn't need to; he was pissed, that much was obvious, but where was Seb? He must be here somewhere. I couldn't see him.

The mist cleared and a feeling of dread knotted in my gut. Where was Sebastian? I leaned up on my shoulder and called out for him, ignoring the guard still shouting at me. I felt sick to my stomach, sweat pouring out of me. I had to find my brother!

I stumbled as I stood up but focused enough to stay on my feet. I was still in the corridor; the radiation-labelled door was ahead of me. The feeling of dread became a tornado of fear. I could see Sebastian; he was lying halfway through the door, face down. He'd fallen forward after dragging me free!

I pushed the guard aside in a panicked stumble of arms and legs, grasping for my brother's foot. Taking hold, I heaved him clear. The guard was screaming more commands, but they didn't register. I dragged Seb over the filthy floor to the corner and turned over his limp body. His face said everything. His eyes were open, and he was breathing, but there was nothing there. Nothing behind the eyes at all. No recognition, no reaction, just a sickening, motionless catatonia.

I puked, acrid stomach acid coating my teeth. "Sebastian! Wake up, Sebastian!" I sobbed, but there was nothing. I wasn't sure how long I'd been unconscious, but however long it was, he'd spent that time in the room, feeling the pain I'd only experienced for a few moments. All I could do was grasp and rock his vacant body in a mess of bile and tears.

STATE 01

They discharged me from police custody in the early hours. I felt empty and desperate, but I'd gotten lucky. Seeing the state of Sebastian, the guard had taken pity and reported us as trespassers rather than thieves. A criminal downgrade that only required a warning.

It wasn't free though. He'd demanded more of the stuff we'd shot him with, hands twitching in anticipation. I was envious – the first SP1N-cycle was always the best.

I burned some street cred and gave him a contact. It was a good deal; his discretion kept the Neo-Guards out of our business. I couldn't be sure what would happen if they got involved – it was common for suspects to vanish if they investigated. The nihilist in me wanted to disappear, but not like that.

Sebastian hadn't recovered. They moved him to hospital, where he lay, dead behind the eyes, breathing in and out, catatonic. I knew he wouldn't get better. I'd seen what he'd seen for a few moments – felt the tendrils of madness closing. He'd been there almost an hour.

The doctors identified SP1N in his system and diagnosed acute overdose. That was bollocks. It had been days since our last hit. But it didn't matter; they wouldn't listen, wouldn't go back and check the facility. Why should they? I was a rambling, delusional junkie. A gutter rat at best, a criminal at worst.

Without health insurance, the outcome was inevitable. A doctor strode in and delivered the news, detached and unemotional. They were moving Sebastian to Brixton Asylum. The last state-funded mental facility.

My heart sank. The asylum was a holding pen for crazies. It freed up beds in the main hospital, but it only dispensed basic care, if you could even call it that. Holo-feed scandals were common – patients starving in their beds or rented out for gang rape. He wouldn't last a year.

Spinning on a heel, the doctor walked out, dropping a scribbled release note on the bed. He didn't even bother with some contrived words of comfort. I scooped it up – they'd move Sebastian to the asylum the next day.

Blundering from the hospital, I ran into the rain. Purple signage reflected on puddles like neon bruises. Shit. We'd screwed up. I wanted to cry but couldn't; my eyes were dry, replaced with withering desperation. I ran until my lungs heaved, heart on the edge of exploding – the pain was good; it replaced the hollow feeling.

I stopped when the lightheadedness became overwhelming, stars speckling my vision. I was back in Camden, where everything had gone wrong. I'd followed my subconscious; blindly looking for answers, but there were none. The building was in lockdown. Cordoned off with every door and window welded shut. The Hive Ltd sign had been taken down and replaced with a demolition warning.

No one else was around. It could have been like this for years. Had I ever even been here? Perhaps the doctors were right. Nothing but a SP1N-fuelled bender – a hallucination. Sinking to my knees, existential fear gripped me. What if I couldn't distinguish between reality and illusion anymore! It was hard to breathe.

As I canted onto all fours, something glinted beneath me. It twinkled in the neon wash from the street lamps, staring back at me – an evil, knowing eye on the wet concrete.

It was the broken bottle-end Sebastian had used to wedge the door open. The existential malaise receded. I wasn't going mad. We'd stumbled onto something, and it was being covered up – quickly and efficiently. Why, though? I had no idea.

I leaned back and stood up, breath returning, hands shaking. I thrust them into my pockets to keep them still. It was cold and drizzling, but that wasn't what was causing the shake. It had been days since my last SP1N-cycle. It reaffirmed what I already knew. I was a worthless addict. But at least I wasn't out of my mind – not yet.

This place was a dead end. I'd uncover nothing new here. Anguish welled harder, like a pickaxe in my sternum. There was only one place left I could think to go.

Camden Town Underground (the Tube) was close. It was early morning, and the area was empty. Just a few beggars and SP1N wasters littering the streets. The station sat amongst a collection of boarded-up buildings. Someone had selectively smashed the red neon lettering: – – D – R – – OUND. Seemed about right.

A dark ticket office lurked at the bottom of a crumbled staircase. It was in a gross state of repair. Rubbish coating the floors, gates rusted open, a single fluorescent light, throwing long, intermittent shadows.

Like welfare, the Administration had cut funding to public transport, leaving the Tube to rot. There was only enough cash to run a couple of trains an hour.

Down the rusted and seized escalator, bodies huddled together. With no station staff, the platform had become infested with the homeless and criminal. The whole place stank of urine and the tangy body odour of vagrancy.

Using the Underground was always a risk. A train could take thirty minutes to arrive – an eternity in a place like this. The longer you hung about, the greater the chance a violent or inebriated occupant would mug you.

Palming my lazeblade in my pocket (newly stolen from a hospital vending machine), I sneered at the closest shape – a body sitting slumped in a metal seat. My thumb hovered over the activation switch, its metallic weight reassuring as the vagrant's bloodshot eyes watched.

I made certain everyone could see I was holding something hidden. The mystery was an extra deterrent. If they didn't know what I had, they couldn't tell how to counter it.

I recalled the last time I'd been attacked. A freaker had gone for me when I wasn't paying attention – my mind wandering in a post-SP1N afterglow. Seb had given him a good slice. But he wasn't here now. This was on me.

A few tense minutes passed until the train arrived. It rattled into the station in a state of broken windows and graffiti. I boarded quickly, taking a seat on the ripped upholstery. The carriage was mostly empty, just a couple of *low-riskers* – normal people. I relaxed as the doors closed and the train progressed. It moved along the Northern Line, creaking and clacking on the chipped tracks. The Northern Line bisected the city from north to south. I needed to go south.

After nine stops, the doors cranked open. The tramps here were as nasty as those in Camden – I beelined for the exit, repeating the faked bravado.

Topside, Elephant & Castle bustled. One of the few areas the public had free access to roads. Most were electronically tolled – fares only the rich could afford.

E-bikes hummed past – neon under-lighting streaking in multi-coloured blurs, LED side panels flashing catchphrases and kanji symbols. They were the personal transport of the masses, favoured by gang members and low-riskers alike. Seb and I used to have a petrol scooter, but it became useless when oil reserves dried up. We couldn't afford an electric conversion, let alone a new model.

I made the death run across the dual carriageway. The bikes barely slowed for each other, and definitely not for pedestrians. Someone swore loudly and something hissed past my head. A bottle. It shattered across the road, driving a rider onto the pavement. He wobbled, regained control, and made his way back, the LED panel flashing UNTOUCHABLE. Onlookers cheered and groaned in equal measures. I hurried on before more road rage spilled my way.

The sim-shop was in a low, flat building, hunkering beneath a bridge stretching across the Elephant & Castle intersection. It had been a famous dance club once: *The Ministry of Sound* – closed down after a string of drug-related deaths. Ironically, it was now a space for the desperate and drug addled to live out their virtual fantasies. Fitting into both those categories, I knew it well.

I nodded at the bouncer. His scarred face the product of hauling out a thousand drunkards. He attempted something approaching sympathy. "Supp, Daryl. Heard about your brother. Sorry, I guess." News had travelled quickly it seemed.

"Yeah, me too," I mumbled, not bothering to look up.

Inside snaked a long corridor lined with erotic holograms. They gyrated and rutted, advertising the virtual pleasures within. I'd seen them many times; they were practically invisible now.

An alchovial bar perched in the main room, positioned to kill the minutes between sessions while they cleaned the booths. A few locals drank here; it was quieter than places outside, and cheaper. It attracted a bottom rung of wasters pushing for an early grave. I liked it; people at the bottom couldn't look down on you.

Grimey was working, and he looked the part. He was probably cleanish, but a combination of synthetic tan and deep wrinkles made the troughs on his face appear dirt filled.

"Hey." I sidled up to the bar.

Grimey didn't reply. He didn't talk much, but he cracked an alchovial and slid it over, nodding towards the main office. *On the house.* I guess he'd heard about Sebastian too.

"Thanks." I grasped the vial. The beer wasn't brilliant, but it was the first I'd had since the incident. It barely hit the sides on the way down.

I drained the last drop and placed the half-glass/half-metal container on the bar with a thunk. I sighed as the momentary relief of alcohol took hold. It would pass in a second, but for a few moments, I felt better.

"Grimey."

He'd turned his back and was refilling an optic of vodka. He turned around, wrinkles deepening as his brows raised.

"Has Limbo been in?"

Nothing as useful as words came out, but he made a wanking motion towards the VR booths. Limbo was getting his rocks off. Grimey tapped his watch – and he'd be out soon.

I nodded and slumped over the bar, hoping the show would prompt another freebie. None arrived. Begrudgingly, I jammed a thumb on the bar-mounted fingerprint reader and ordered one. Not as good as the first, but it didn't need to be – I needed this one to last.

Fifteen minutes later, Limbo appeared from the booth. A bundle of animated chicken limbs, his shaved head sweaty and red, and a big smile on his face – the tell-tale signs of a good session.

A rake-thin arm, bare to the shoulder and covered with tattoos, waved furiously. His mouth was half open, ready to launch into a barrage of questions.

I interjected before he could derail me. "Limbo, why the hell you tell Sebastian about that damn place! He's seriously messed up now!"

Limbo's face dropped, eyes pained, arms less animated, though not exactly still. He fidgeted and stuttered as he tried to explain, hopping from foot to foot. "Yeah, Daryl ... not my fault. See ... was jus chat, ya know. Nuffin serious." Limbo didn't have an education, and it showed. His high-pitched sentences tumbled out clipped and half-witted. "How'd I know he'd go there? He tole me it was nuffin worf checkin, so why'd he go?"

He had me there. Sebastian had conned him out of the tip. It was a rare moment of clarity for Limbo. I changed direction. I needed something to go on. "Look, it's just as well you didn't go – it could be you lying brain-dead in hospital." Instead of only *half* brain-dead, I added silently.

Limbo's smile was gone, his eyes darting to the bar, looking for an exit. "Howdya figure? Sebastian overfilled on SP1N, that's all – prob found it in da place and got greedy. Should've bin more bloody careful I'd say."

This wasn't going how I'd hoped. Limbo was an idiot, but he wasn't bad natured; we'd sunk hundreds of alchovials together. I needed a different tack, and all I had left was the truth. I gripped Limbo's arms earnestly, briefly preventing him twitching.

"Had nothing to do with SP1N, Limbo. Seb burned his only tab drugging the guard so we could get in. Look at my hands ..." I released him and unfurled a hand, holding it out straight. It jittered, an unmistakable sign of SP1N withdrawal. "I haven't had a tab in over a week! Do you think if we'd found stuff I'd be like this?"

Limbo ignored the outstretched hand and leaned in close, inspecting my face. I knew what he was doing – it was easy to fake a shake, but the eyes never lied.

I kept talking as he peered into my irises. "It was something in the building that messed him up. So you see. I need more information. I know Sebastian lied, but nothing bad enough for the state he's in now."

Limbo pulled back, arms twitching again as he reconsidered. "Yeah, 'kay, Daryl. You don't look so gud – I seen eyes like yours before. You gunna feel the pain soon."

Wasn't that the truth. SP1N withdrawal got worse over time. The shake would progress to a headache, then sickness a thousand times worse than a hangover.

"I guess it weren't your fault what happened," Limbo continued. "Whadya need?"

Progress. I took the lead, trying to sound assertive. Seb always said you had to ask for things with authority or you'd be ignored. Limbo had reengaged, but he had the attention span of an insect and his eyes were still wandering to the bar. "Tell me more about how you got the tip, Limbo. I need details."

Limbo dragged his eyes away from the bar and focussed his attention. He squeaked out the best reply he could muster. "It was like what I said to Seb. The info came from mi sis, Lou. She tole me bout the place cos she tort it were odd da guards weren't allowed to patrol there."

I knew this already. I needed something new. "But what is Hive, Limbo? Who are they?"

"Dunno." He licked his lips. "Lou dunno either. She's jus a dispatcher. Lowest level in the comp. Jus chats to guards from da office. Never sees 'em."

I'd met Louise before. Nice girl, not as dim as Limbo, but hardly a bright spark either. I believed him when he said she wouldn't know anything. I sighed. Limbo was too simple-minded to hold things back. If he knew more, he'd tell me.

"Daryl." He interrupted my chain of thought. "I dunno anyfing, really. Barely remember to begin wiv. But I'm soz bout what happened ..." He licked his lips again. "Buy you a beer?"

That was a big gesture from Limbo; he struggled to make ends meet as much as anyone. I'd gotten a taste for beer now. It was a poor substitute for SP1N, but the two I'd had were pushing back thoughts of Seb. It wasn't like this conversation was going anywhere anyway.

Realisation struck. I hadn't come here for information at all. Limbo and Louise were about as low down the knowledge ladder as humans got. I knew that. I'd come here for something basic. I wanted to get smashed.

"Oh, and, Daryl ..." Limbo leaned in conspiratorially, slipping something into my hand.

I knew what it was but looked anyway. A glossy pink square stared back up at me. SP1N – full tab.

He winked. "I owed it to Seb. You ave it."

The urge to find out what happened became distant. The pressing need to put the little pink square into my system overriding it.

If a pal shared his stash, you had to drink with them for a while. We retreated and slammed more vials. The booze turned my withdrawal into anticipation. Once Limbo was suitably drunk, head lolling on the bar, I stumbled over to one of the VR booths. You could take SP1N on its own, but mixed with VR it was something else, and tonight I needed the works. It would cost me all my remaining creds, but I didn't care.

The 'booth' was a small cubicle behind a lockable door. A battered leather recliner and a ceiling full of equipment were contained inside. On the wall hung a cellophane sleeve dispenser. They expected customers to slide them over the recliner, although it was clear from the stains many hadn't. I yanked one out and placed it over the chair, elastic bindings snapping secure.

Taking a seat, I inserted the tab in my skin-gun and pressed it against my forearm, wincing as the trigger pulled. The high-pressure device hissed, vaporising the tab at high velocity. I could feel the chemicals passing into my blood.

Years of use had given me a high resistance. It would take a few minutes to feel the effects.

I pushed a button on the side of the recliner, and a touch sensitive panel dropped from the ceiling. It hung in front of me, a crack running vertically through it, warping the image, but it was still readable.

Relishing the pseudo-high before the real one kicked in, I flicked through the options. There were non-sexual VR experiences, but no one used them. I swore they were there for show. I filtered them out and pulled up the menus everyone came here for – erotic fantasies. The interface displayed options for the model I would interact with. Sliders for adjusting body shape, hair style, and skin colour, or pre-selects categorised by race and body type. A good selection of locales was on offer too. Beaches, swanky hotels, even yachts. The Elephant & Castle sim-shop was far from high-class, but they kept their software up to date.

I punched in my picks. Tall, blonde, and large-chested. Clichéd as hell and bottom of the barrel, but that's what I wanted – needed; every time a mixture of excitement and shame. I didn't care about the locale, so the computer selected something appropriate.

Choices locked, the control panel retracted. Out of the ceiling, the VR helmet and groin attachment descended. These were the most expensive parts of installing and maintaining a sim-shop – the law required cleansing systems to keep them disinfected.

I shrugged out of my trousers and pulled the rubber gasket over my groin. There was a pleasing rush of air as the system created a light vacuum, sealing the unit in place. Above me, the VR helmet floated on an articulated arm. I reached up and pulled it over my head. It blocked the outside world from view, immersing me in the virtual environment.

The helmet provided an ultrahigh resolution, three-dimensional image with realistic sound. Not indistinguishable from real life but convincing. It auto-detected I'd put the helmet on and launched the programme. I was standing by a beat-up American pickup truck on a dusty Texas plain. The sun was setting on the horizon.

I'd never seen these things in real life; they were relics from the past – extinct from overuse of resources and pollution. But they were consistent with what I'd seen in holovids of the period.

The blonde was leaning against the truck, convincing in every detail – white knotted t-shirt above daisy dukes. Belly button piercing on a flat, tanned stomach. The room had fans to simulate a breeze, though the smell of stale beer and sweat persisted. Perversely, I'd grown to associate the smell with the sim-shop experience. I almost liked it.

I could have programmed a conversation, but like the non-sexual options, most never bothered. You rented the booth by the minute.

The SP1N began to work. A warm glow spreading through my body. The colour in the images grew deeper, lines sharper, and the sounds of the virtual world more real.

Old-timers said SP1N was like a combination of Ecstasy and LSD, but orders of magnitude better. It created the heightened emotional state and warm buzz of the former, and the synaesthesia of the latter. The combination was potent. It not only heightened the experience but also tricked the brain. A complete sense of touch being replicated, fully transporting the body and mind into the virtual environment. A perfect melding of chemical and technological entertainment.

The SP1N peaked, and I was immersed, unable to distinguish the virtual from the real. The dusty plain was real, the pickup truck was real, and the girl in front of me was real. I knew none of it *was* real, but for the time being, it was more real than the real world itself. A sigh eased out of me. I'd feel terrible tomorrow, and disgusted with myself in an hour, but it was an escape from the nightmare outside. And that was good enough.

STATE 02

The sim-shop was the end of my investigation. I had no resources, no means of pursuing the truth, and no creds.

True to their threat, they moved Sebastian to Brixton Asylum. I told myself it wouldn't be so bad, and it was the best place for him.

I was delusional. It was a slow death sentence and I knew it. If one of the inmates didn't get him, neglect would. There were no other options though. All I could do was suppress the guilt into an acidic ball in the pit of my stomach and let it happen.

Two months passed. My routine degraded into a cycle of apathy and self-destruction. I worked enough between SP1N-cycles to avoid being fired. Ate enough not to starve. And slept enough to remain sane, although nightmares kept that on a knife edge – every night reliving the moment I lost my brother.

The anger and despair persisted, but it wasn't motivating me to find answers. It was fuelling laziness, and a need for oblivion.

My SP1N addiction was rampant. Worse than when Sebastian was with me. And it was costing me a fortune. I'd been in debt before, but Seb's side projects had covered the difference. That was gone now. I'd been forced to make shadier deals with more dangerous people, and with deeper lines of credit.

One of those lines would be getting deeper tonight, and I was dreading it. I'd exhausted all the low-end dealers – the safe fish. Only the sharks would deal with me now.

I wished Seb were with me. When he stood straight and drew his shoulders back, it was like a cobra unfurling its hood. A trick he could back up with natural strength – assets I didn't have. He'd made me feel okay about it: "Don't worry, Daryl-lad," he'd say. "You're the smart one."

That wasn't true. I'd picked up some hacking knowhow and had made it further in the state-schooling system than most, but I had none of Seb's guile or street smarts. He had a way with people; he knew when to be charming and when to be aggressive. A born player. God, I missed him.

Holding my nerve, I walked into the building and rode the escalator.

Situated in Soho, central Neo-London, the Trocadero Centre was an ancient, multi-floored entertainment arcade – most of the shops had closed down and been replaced with low-rent machine gambling.

I checked my ARO as I surveyed the atrium from the second-floor balcony. It was 10.57 pm.

I had a clear view into most of the levels, each one crammed with gaming devices of different shapes and designs. They blared as visitors jammed their thumbs on the panels, awaiting a miracle to befall them – the random number generators finishing tantalising close to a win, but seldom doing so. Vapour rose from hundreds of e-cigarettes as patrons sucked on different flavours of pseudo-tobacco. They mingled in the space above to create a ubiquitous *all-smell* that hung in the air.

The noise and chaos made it the perfect place for cutting deals. Each machine was a self-contained vault with safeguards – security systems that would electrocute tamperers. There was little need for human security.

I turned around and stared down the escalator. Encased in electro-plastic tubing, it displayed never ending swirls of bright graphics. A dalliance to entertain customers. Few appreciated the effort, keen to hurry to the next machine where they'd hope for better luck.

Feeling tense to my core, shoulders hunched, I stared trancelike at the colours and patterns. The surrounding noise both deafening and far away.

My ARO pinged, snapping me back to reality. I flicked out the screen and read the message. *From: Led. Msg: Be there in two minutes. Two for two hundred.*

My earlobes let go of my shoulders. I retracted the screen into its shoulder housing. Led was extending my credit. Thank God.

The sights and sounds of the Trocadero became crisper as my anxiety eased. A freaker across the room had lost patience with his machine. He was shouting and shaking his head in fury, spiked hair swaying, piercings jingling. He kicked it, which was a step too far. It buzzed, flashing blue. The freaker yelped, pulling his hand back from where it had been resting. Only a warning buzz. A stronger one could render unconsciousness. The freaker backed away to a safe distance – it wasn't unusual for victims to slump forward, receiving enough shocks to kill.

I yelled as a rough hand landed on my shoulder, flicking me around like a spinning top. I stared into Led's face, or more accurately, his teeth. A frightening grill of sharp metal stakes. He snapped them in front of my eyes with a loud click. A favourite intimidation trick. And it worked. I squirmed under a shower of spittle and tried to back up, but there was nowhere to go. I was at the edge of the balcony.

"Daryl ..." Led's tongue snaked around the metal-filled hole. "Where's my money, Daryl?"

Panic descended. "Er, Led, we agreed credit right? Two hundred for two tabs, yeah?"

"No, mate," Led hissed, teeth grazing my nose. "You misunderstand me. You can *buy* the two tabs after you've *paid* me the two hundred from last month."

Shit. I was in trouble. I had nowhere near that. I had ten creds to my name. Not enough for a beer and a tin of beans.

"You know what it means if you don't got the money ..."

It wasn't a question, everyone knew. It was a warning. If I'd crossed a line, he'd make an example of me. Led was a freaker general – his loyalty secured through fear. His recruits had to know he'd follow through on his threats.

I could feel my heels against the railing. My eyes darted left and right. The electrocuted freaker from earlier was looking at Led, as was one sitting on a bench, peering over his ARO. Their shark tattoos matched. All part of the same gang under Led. God damn it! I should've recognised them. I was trapped!

"Nothing to say, squirt!" Led grabbed my left hand, his powerful arms overpowering my toothpicks.

The freakers closed the distance, growling at anyone close enough to consider interfering. No one would interfere.

In a few moments, I was surrounded – Led in front, flanked by his henchmen. One turned his back to keep a lookout, and the other grabbed my free hand and whipped out his lazeblade. He held it in a reverse grip, his forearm hiding the red glow from onlookers, but I could see it – smell it burning my jacket.

Sneering, Led uncurled my little finger, yanking it towards his gaping maw.

"Please, no!" I pulled at the iron grip.

No one paid attention to my cries. They pretended not to notice, refocusing on their gambling. This was a regular occurrence, so no help would come. Led forced the tip of my finger between his jaws and squeezed down, drawing blood. He paused, savouring the moment before crunching into bone.

I shut my eyes and screamed, waiting for the agony of my missing finger to register. It would happen any moment, probably already had. I hadn't felt the pain yet – shock was covering it up.

The seconds ticked by, but the pain didn't arrive. Everything was quiet – silent, in fact. The pressure that had pierced my skin was still there. I could feel it, but the final act hadn't been delivered.

Fear held my eyes closed, but after a few long seconds they fluttered open irresistibly. Something was wrong. Led was there. Devil grin painted across his brutish face, but the expression was different – unmoving, lifeless. Like looking at a vicious holo-statue. And it wasn't only Led, everything was different. The world was still. I didn't understand.

"L-Led." He was frozen, eyes glassy like a waxwork. What the hell was going on!

The freaker on my right was statuesque, grip around my arm vice-like and static. My heart was thumping. Fear of mutilation transformed into something else – supernatural dread! None of this was right.

The dread gave way to a bigger problem – I couldn't breathe! I was gasping like a fish out of water. The air was thin and hard to draw in.

Fear of suffocation dominated all others. I tugged my left hand, but Led's teeth, clamped around my finger, held it firm. I didn't care; the urge to breathe was paramount. I yanked harder, ripping it free and tearing a messy gash, but at least it was still attached. I wiggled hard against Led's henchman, twisting my arm free and stumbling away to the side, landing on the floor in a heap. The air flowed again, allowing a few precious gasps, but no sooner had I sat up, it retreated again, blackness threatening the edges of my vision. I didn't understand what was going on, but the act of breaking away helped. I scrambled to my feet like a beleaguered diver searching for the surface and paced. The oxygen came with movement; it was still thin but enough to drive unconsciousness back.

The risk of suffocation faded, but the strangeness of the situation, temporarily put on hold, demanded my attention. I looked over the balcony. Everything was frozen in place. The people, the machines-, until recently a cacophony of sound and light, lay deathly silent. Even the e-cig vapour hung in the air, motionless like mist. A surreal quality enveloped the arcade. A dead, flat light coating the surfaces. Even walking was strange, more difficult, like wading through water or pushing against a heavy wind.

Were we under attack?

We were on good terms with China and Russia ...

Had America resurfaced? They'd turned tyrannical after disarming their citizens and collapsing their republic a decade ago. They'd been quiet a long time, but that could have changed. Had they developed something to pacify us? Was there going to be a follow up attack – troops marching through the streets, murdering people where they stood!

My mouth ran dry. They planned for us to starve! Trapped motionless and wasting away. But if any of that were right, why wasn't I affected? None of this made sense!

Then I saw it, and thoughts of state invasions vanished. A few metres away, a freaker kid had tripped over. Fresh faced with a few piercings, arm tattoos recently inked and still scabby. His oversized trousers, hanging below his arse, had slipped beneath his boots, tangling up his feet. He'd been holding a plastic vial of green fluid – a confection drink from the vending machines.

The scene was at its most dramatic – like a well-placed holo-snap. But his body wasn't frozen in space; it was frozen in the moment – hanging forward at a physics-defying angle. The vial had left his grip but hadn't dropped; it hung there, at least thirty centimetres from his hand, with nothing above or below. It was open and most of its contents had spilled out – green goo smearing across the open space.

Sauntering over, hand shaking, I reached out to touch the floating liquid. It didn't move. The composition a collage of levitated globs. Like Led, the freakers, and everything else, it was rocklike – unyielding. I passed my hands over, below, and all around like a magician. It was completely suspended.

Realisation dawned, along with an unexpected rush of relief. The reason for all this absurdity was clear. It was a hallucination! Nothing like this could exist in the real world. This was all imaginary; a construct brought on by SP1N withdrawal and stress. I was dreaming – probably in an alleyway somewhere, beaten to a pulp and missing a finger. My mind had trapped me here to spare me the pain.

I relaxed. It was good to have an explanation; it was the only thing that made sense – I was going mad! You've finally popped your lid, Daryl – it was only a matter of time. I felt remarkably calm at the realisation.

Nihilistic acceptance washed over me. They'd arrange a space next to Sebastian when they found me, dribbling and catatonic.

I looked at Led, no longer dangerous but still intimidating. It felt weird to stay so close to him. If this were a dream, it could still become a nightmare – prudent to put some distance between me and the Trocadero.

"See you later, sucker." I chided with fantasy confidence, then I moved away as quickly as I could, just in case.

Pushing against the headwind, I descended the stationary escalator and picked my way through the frozen throngs. Freakers and low-riskers, all stopped dead in their tracks – a human diorama of drinking, smoking, and gambling.

Movement was manageable but difficult – like a dream where you can't run or are stuck in glue. But this was worse. My imagination was layering on months of drug abuse, replicating exhaustion. By the time I reached the exit, I was completely worn out, sweating, and wheezing.

The weirdness continued outside. Soho, normally crowded and bustling, was still crowded, but the bustle was gone. Immobile shoppers, buskers, and homeless bodies filled the streets. Ghostly still, semi-transparent holographic billboards projected down from the Piccadilly Circus intersection, displaying half drawn ads. Even the rubbish, normally whipping around ankles, was stuck to the floor. It looked like an art installation. I expected to see pretentious, bearded arseholes wandering around. "Mmm ... Arr ..." I could hear them pretending to understand.

The roads in this part of the city were subject to heavy taxes. Wealthy low-riskers travelled in large, security-enforced vehicles with strengthened external cages. Carjacking was common, so they drove at high speed – the momentum an extra deterrent. Not so now; they looked parked and vulnerable. Any normal day, the freakers would have run riot.

The detail of the hallucination was amazing. It was like no dream I'd had before; I felt in control, lucid. It was as close to reality as anything I could recall. The odd spectacle of a deranged mind.

I could feel the weight of the thick atmosphere, the difficulty sucking in breath, even discomfort where Led had bitten me. I inspected the gash, a frown forming. The blood wasn't dripping; it was pooling around my finger like a fitted glove. A skintight barrier between my body and the hallucination. What significance this held, I couldn't tell. A deranged mind indeed.

The panic of earlier had given way to bemused acceptance. I was clearly losing my mind, but at least it was relatively painless and quiet. I closed my eyes and took a struggled breath. Is this how others experience madness? A strange dreamscape to be wandered eternally?

My eyes snapped open to the sound of a startled scream. The world was moving again. Disoriented, I tried to locate the commotion. It was coming from a woman a few metres away; she was pointing and shaking a finger. Other onlookers were also staring, confused or startled expressions on their faces.

I stumbled back, feeling like a sleepwalker ripped from a deep slumber, landing in a puddle. The cold wetness soaked through my jeans, bringing me back to my senses.

Somewhere behind me, I could hear Led roaring.

"Where is he? What's going on?" he bellowed from within the Trocadero Centre. "Quickly, find that little runt! He owes me a finger!"

That didn't sound like a hallucination anymore. I'd gotten away, but if he found me, he'd want more than a finger – he'd bite off my entire hand!

Forgetting the madness, instinct kicked in. I scrambled off the pavement, shouldering past onlookers.

It was a relief to be breathing freely again, and there was something reassuring about the fleshy, normal bodies I was pushing past. But why were they staring at me?

Clearing the crowd, I ran for the Underground, hoping Led hadn't seen me. I doubted it. I'd moved a sufficient distance, but there was still a chance.

I made the call to run the extra five minutes to Leicester Square. It was further than the Piccadilly Circus entrance outside Trocadero, but Led was less likely to grab me there.

At the station, for once I was glad to be on the homeless-filled platform. Its relative danger safer than being near Led and his goons. I'd escaped, but I didn't know how. Something had happened in the arcade.

I looked at my finger. Blood was flowing from the cut, covering my jacket and jeans. The mess was enough to deter the platform dwellers – too much hassle. I wrapped it in the bottom of my shirt and boarded the next train. The most important thing was putting distance between Led and me. I'd figure the rest out later. Either my mind was playing an elaborate trick on me or something far weirder was going on.

STATE 03

I lay partially conscious on the futon. Sunlight slanted in through horizontal blinds, the dusty beams bisecting the room and cutting across my face. I cracked an eye open, momentarily dazzled as light flared painfully in my vision.

For a few blissful moments, my mind was empty, rebooting from sleeping to waking. Then the memories seeped back. First the dull ache of my brother, who so often would have slept the night slumped in the chair opposite after a binge of SP1N and video games. For a moment, I saw him and I bolted upright. But as my eyes adjusted, I realised it was my jacket. It had formed a vaguely human shape over the old alchovials and pizza boxes where I'd slung it.

I leaned back, heart aching, head thumping, trying to pull myself together. The rest was coming back. The deal gone wrong; the unexplained madness.

I groaned and blinked a few times. My head was killing me. I was gripping an alchovial of vodka, had been all night. It was half empty, but it wasn't a hangover. It was worse – SP1N withdrawal. There'd be a pneumatic drill in my head until I scored another tab or rode it out far enough. It had been months since I'd abstained long enough to let the headaches recede naturally.

I glanced at the holo-clock. The arctic blue numbers hovering above read 8.30 am. What day though? I'd completely lost track. It clicked. It was Monday – a work day. I didn't have enough creds for my mobile plan or next rent, let alone dealer debt or fresh tabs. Groaning, I pushed aside thoughts of yesterday, struggled up, and staggered over to the bathroom, picking my way past discarded food packaging strewn across the tiny studio flat. I couldn't afford to lose my job.

I was scared to look in the mirror, knowing I'd barely recognise what confronted me. I looked anyway. A dead-eyed stranger was behind the glass. Cheeks pale and gaunt, and eyes dilated like saucepans. The corners of my mouth were down-turned in a perpetual sad face. It wasn't emotion; it was withdrawal – a chemical relaxing of the facial muscles. It would stay that way until I got my next hit or enough time passed.

I looked at my finger; it had stopped hurting, just a mild throb, but it was a mess. The blood had dried into a deep, stiff scab. At least it was still connected to my hand. I should be thankful for that.

Using water as hot as I could manage, I did my best to wash some colour back into my face and tame the mess of auburn hair. It was sticking up at irregular angles all over my head.

I re-inspected myself. Better. The dilated eyes were still a giveaway, but I had tinted glasses for that. I forced a grin; it looked ridiculous, maniacal, but it would hide my mouth. I'd choose mania over addiction – one would get me fired, the other may not.

I grabbed some clothes from the in-use pile. They were dirty by most people's standards but good enough to get me through the day. I sprayed them down with deodorant to make sure.

After pulling on my jacket, I grabbed my ARO from a charging alcove, slapping it to the magnetic shoulder plate. It made a satisfying beep as it thunked on, generating an endorphin rush – the pleasure of being connected to technology, and by extension, everything else.

It was state-of-the art, the one thing of value I owned, and connected with the best data plan I could afford – a greater expense than food or drugs. I pulled up my messages. Led's old text was still there, but a new one had arrived. I opened it. *From: Led. Msg: I'll find you.* Well, that confirmed parts of yesterday had happened – I'd gone to the Trocadero to score SP1N. It was everything afterwards that concerned me. My memory was unreliable; it was too outlandish. All I could be sure of was my damaged finger and lack of drugs. Whatever happened, it hadn't gone to plan.

Outside, the sun shone dimly through polluted clouds, washing Neo-London in a dull, silvery complexion. It was as good as the weather got. It lifted my spirits a notch.

My decrepit block of flats dominated the Battersea skyline – a grey, crumbling heap casting an intimidating silhouette. One of the cheapest places to rent in Neo-London.

My domicile was part of ten floors bolted atop the existing structure. A renovation that turned the thirty-floor council estate into a forty-floor super-tenement. The Administration dubbed them *extraplexes* – grand sounding but little more than modern day vertical slums. Tiny and lightweight to not upset the foundations, the domiciles were fragile and unstable – the extra floors listing a metre to the side, visible from the ground. Mine was on the penultimate floor, teetering close to the most precarious point. I couldn't complain. It was cheap and it kept the rain out.

Donning a pair of orange-tinted specs to shield my dilated pupils from the glare (and everyone else), I shuffled in the direction of the nearest tube.

Embedded in the busy commercial district, the Vault was a run-down mobile tech store off Oxford Street. *Fiercely independent since 2022*, its purple neon sign stated. Independent was a joke. Like every tech shop, the Vault took kickbacks from networks and ARO providers. It just didn't brandish their names on the door. That also meant it didn't enjoy national or global advertising. That was a mistake, but it wasn't my shop, and I wasn't planning to question Pete on his advertising strategy.

Entering via the back door, I used the thumb reader and punched in my security code. It was 9.20 am – ten minutes before opening time. With some staff yet to arrive, they might even consider me early. A miracle considering how late I'd slept.

Inside, they were setting up for the day. The Vault stocked a selection of AROs, ranging from budget-conscious Wingmates to high-end Shoulder Saracens like mine. The black blade logo promised cutting edge performance.

The Vault would connect AROs to any of the Telcom networks advertised around the shop. Redwave, Diecast, and Limelight were the key providers, competing aggressively in the saturated market.

Limelight was drawing ahead in speed. Their recently launched quantum broadcasting technology a huge step up. They didn't have brilliant coverage yet, but the improvements were significant. Limelight was now the premium service, leaving Redwave and Diecast to fight it out on extras and better subsidised AROs. A Limelight connection was outside what I could afford; I'd made do with Redwave. It was middle of the road but okay.

My Saracen was from the Vault too. A return inflicted with a minor cosmetic scrape. Pete had been generous – given it to me discounted. I'd still eaten beans for a month to cover the cost.

In the stockroom, sales targets were up on the holoboard, or the *board of doom*. I knew I was behind, but I hadn't checked in a while. I scanned the list of salespeople – down, down, all the way to the bottom. I was last, a solid fifteen per cent off my target.

It was my fault, but it still hurt my pride. Before Sebastian's accident – before the switch from casual user to hopeless addict – I'd been good at this job. I knew more about mobile tech than anyone here, including the owner. But over the past few months, my game had been utterly thrown off. A persistent bleariness dulling my instincts and recall. Others in the stockroom nodded, said hi, but wouldn't meet my gaze. They all knew what it meant to be fifteen per cent behind.

From public facing to back-office, Neo-Londonites served the Telcom networks or ARO manufacturers, and the corporations kept track – sharing employee records between them. Illegal, but the Administration didn't care; most of their income came from business tax. If I screwed up, I'd struggle to get a job emptying bins, and even those were in high demand.

Pete came in via the front door. He was stiff and unassuming but not a bad guy. He'd sold me the Saracen at cost. He didn't have to do that. I tried to avoid him, unpacking new stock, but he collared me immediately.

"Daryl."

My back arched like a cat disturbed – I wanted to bolt for the nearest shadowy corner. Reluctantly, I straightened, turning to face him. Might as well; there was no avoiding him now. "Oh, hi, Pete." It sounded exactly as evasive as it was. "Everything okay?"

I knew full well it wasn't. Pete's face was stern, although not unsympathetic – grey skin matching his grey hair. He'd known Sebastian; they'd been colleagues, of sorts. Seb had worked as one of the Vault's unofficial hawkers – customers for kickbacks.

"Orange sunglasses again?"

Shit. I went to make an excuse, but he cut me off; the words jammed in my throat.

"Look, Daryl, I know you've had it rough. Sebastian was a good man, but you're ..." He searched for the right word, not willing to commit to screwing up. "... flagging, and you're fifteen per cent down. That's a lot."

I dropped the fake smile, showcasing my down-turned mouth, making things worse. I couldn't help it; no one can smile while being torn a new one.

"It's not even me, Daryl. The Telcoms have already noticed I'm further behind than normal. That's a dangerous place for me to be in."

I stared at my boots, prickles of tears welling behind the shades. "So what's the deal, boss? You booting me out?"

I held my breath, waiting for the reply.

Pete went to say something then stopped, the words held behind pursed lips. He let them out in a puff, not ready to deliver the killing blow. "Okay, Daryl, look, I can give you to the end of the month to pull things back. You'll need to produce something special, but if you can, I'll put this behind us."

Holy crap, I wasn't being fired! My smile returned, although more from relief. I had a chance, a tiny one, but a chance. I took it with open arms. "Thanks, Pete, I won't let you down." It was all I could manage.

I went to get on with unpacking stock, but Pete wasn't finished; he rested a hand on my shoulder. "And, Daryl, you need to clean yourself up, if you know what I mean."

I did.

"You used to be this place's best salesman. That's still in there somewhere, but this ..." He looked me up and down. "... won't do. I need the old Daryl back."

I nodded, head pounding from withdrawal. It unsubtly underlined what Pete was inferring.

Pete squeezed my shoulder before leaving. It went on longer than an encouraging one would. There was a finality to it. A warning. I couldn't blame him. I was dead weight in this operation. I didn't think I had much hope of making up the sales, but I'd have to try, or everything would get worse.

The rest of the morning was slow, but if I wasn't making sales, I could at least appear busy. I restocked the Diecom area and caught up on the latest tech via the holo-feed. Limelight was expanding their coverage again. It was up to seventy per cent of Neo-London now.

It was around midday when things picked up. I was cleaning a display ARO when she walked in. Medium height, slender, and dressed like a freaker, although not really. The faux leather was high quality and well fitted – it was a style choice; she wasn't part of a gang.

Her hair was electric pink and shaved on one side, revealing an ear full of silver piercings. Not classically beautiful, features somewhat severe, but still engaging and attractive. She had the rare look of someone not completely in the Telcom's pocket. A public relations rep or holo-vlogger? The ARO on her shoulder looked beaten up. It needed an upgrade. I was good at selling upgrades.

I wasn't the only one who'd noticed. Jay had spotted her – the other sales rep on duty. We were friends, but that counted for little when targets were down.

I shot him a glance: *Back off. I need this.*

He ignored me, retrieving a middle finger from his pocket. He knew my situation, but sales were sales. We both went to intercept her. He got there first. It worked to my advantage. Jay was good at upselling, but his cold openings were dreadful.

"Welcome to the Vault," he declared enthusiastically. "Can I help?"

Amateur! One day, he must learn how to open. I held back for a second, awaiting the inevitable.

"No, I'm just browsing."

There it was. Jay's approach went down in flames, his dopey face suitably crestfallen.

I waited a beat. Long enough not to appear rude, but before Jay could try again.

"Looks like your TripLite's seen some action," I remarked casually, pretending not to look at her. "The V2's far more durable you know."

She squared her attention on me, eyes furrowed, quizzical, but interested. "Yeah, I suppose it is a bit tatty. I've had it for years."

I pretended to take more notice. "And for good reason. It's a great device, but the updated models have really moved things on." I pointed to the TripLite section of the shop and she wandered over in that direction. I followed behind at a respectful distance, smirking back at Jay. I made a cranking motion against my hand – winding up a middle finger, returning the one he'd given me earlier. Beaten, he slinked off.

I didn't feel guilty. It was survival of the fittest at the Vault. Anyway, with me off my game for so long, he'd made decent progress on the board of doom.

My head still felt like a hammer was attacking it, but seeing off Jay had put me in the zone. I was proud of my encyclopaedic knowledge of devices, providers, and plans. And I had a good eye for what people needed, even when they weren't sure themselves. I hoped I could hold it together long enough to close the sale.

I ran my new customer through the specs of the TripLite V2, explaining its updated operating system and features. But after a few minutes, I became distracted. Something strange was happening. She wasn't listening. She was nodding along, but it felt more like she was evaluating me rather than the device. Must be my imagination. I continued detailing options, but the feeling persisted; her eyes were on me rather than the display.

Maybe she'd seen through the orange specs and fake smile. She didn't look the sort who'd know, but SP1N found itself in all corners. No, it's paranoia.

"... So you see, its up-rated, flip-out screen can be converted to show a holographic interface or ultra-high resolution. It depends what you're after—"

"What's your name?"

The question confused me until I remembered I hadn't affixed my holo-badge. "Er, it's Daryl," I replied over my arm, where I'd been showcasing the ARO.

She was looking at me intently, eyes dark and wide. I'd noticed she was attractive, but I'd been preoccupied with the sale. As she gazed at me, I felt a knot tie in my stomach.

An uncomfortable amount of time passed. "Er, nice to meet you?" I said uncertainly – a stark contrast to the confident salesman I'd been presenting a moment earlier.

She smiled, studying and nodding. She held her hand out. "I'm Karin."

I took it and shook. A little out of sorts, but I couldn't refuse. Her hand felt soft, nails painted black and filed to subtle points – feline. They raked my skin as I retracted my arm, sending an electric tingle through me.

I tried to pick up where I'd left off, but I was hopelessly flustered, mind racing. It had been a long time since a girl had taken interest. A real one.

My mind switched from selling AROs; raw biology had taken over. But I had a new problem. Did I have the courage to do something about it? The idea sent shivers of fear and excitement through me.

Clumsily, I continued showing her the models, fumbling opportunities to develop the conversation.

Somehow, I still closed the sale, and she took out a Limelight contract too. A high-margin option. Pete would be pleased. She was definitely no freaker if she had the creds for a quantum connection.

I brought over the payment pad ready for a thumb scan. My last chance to make a move. I rehearsed it in my head: Hey? Perhaps we should exchange connection codes in case you need help with the new TripLite? – It sounded terrible.

I felt sick. No wonder people stuck to virtual girls.

She handed the pad back.

I opened my mouth to deliver the line.

Beep. Her ARO chirped. She turned away, checking a new message. Then, seemingly annoyed at the news and with little more than a nod of thanks, she grabbed the new ARO and walked out.

Damn. I'd flubbed it. I'd had at least a dozen chances to get her code over the forty minutes she'd been in the Vault. Why had I left it to the last minute!

Jay walked over. "Smooth operator."

Had it been that obvious? Disappointment surged as I realised I could still feel the tingle in my hand. "Get lost. How many Limelight connections have you sold today?"

"I'm two per cent over my quarterly. I don't even need to come in." He shrugged.

That brought me back to earth. The sale had helped, but not much. I'd need thirty more like that to get me on target. And it was a hollow victory. I felt like I'd missed out on something.

There were no more customers in the store; the lunchtime rush was over. Jay flipped the conversation. "You coming around tonight? I've made some upgrades to my rig. Fridge is full of vials too."

More beer. I wanted something stronger, but I couldn't think about that. I didn't have creds for tabs and the conversation with Pete was still fresh in my mind.

Something had changed today though. I'd felt like my old self for a few minutes. The missed opportunity was disappointing, but it was healthy disappointment – a normal disappointment. This was a chance to get back on track. Another clear night would get me over the worst of the withdrawal.

I thought of Sebastian, rotting in the asylum. I still didn't know what had happened or made a plan to get him out. I was a disgrace. He never would have abandoned me like that.

Pete's warning. The hallucinations. The girl. They were all signs I'd reached rock-bottom.

Jay was looking at me expectantly. "I've got a new action simulator …"

I didn't need more encouragement. I'd made my decision to clean up, but Jay's offer helped, and it would be a good distraction.

"Sure," I stated with a firmness that raised his eyebrows. "See you there."

STATE 04

C lapham was in a part of Neo-London that might be called ad-
equate. Not good; only a fraction could afford places that were
good.

Mostly pedestrianised, it was full of mid-range outlets and reasonably appointed domiciles. For sure, it was still grotty. Half broken
street lamps bathed the stained pavements in hazy green neon. But it
was less overtly filthy, and with fewer homeless or open acts of violence.

Jay's income was as meagre as mine, but his parents had been well off
– leaving him creds after they'd passed. The Administration had taken
its eighty per cent inheritance cut but left enough for him to buy his
domicile outright. That left food, utilities, and an ARO connection to
worry about, with no need to resort to criminal activities as I did. The
rest went into fuelling a serious virtual reality addiction. Different to
mine. His preference was for violent gaming. Retro action sims – the
new fad.

Retro sims were a reaction to dipping VR sales. Creatively bankrupt
developers had re-imagined old film and TV shows – turning them
into virtual experiences. Functionally, there was little difference to
modern games. But what's old is new; they *felt* more authentic and
there was an anachronistic novelty to living out past fantasies.

We were six games into the most recent release: *Commando 1985*.
I'd seen the film years ago, converted into holo-format. It was dumb,
but irresistibly of its time, and with a hilarious ending. The antag-
onist Bennet, the maniacal, chain-mail wearing ex-marine, had been
impaled through the chest with a steam pipe. This was still possible
in-game, along with new ways for players to dispatch each other.

Re-enacting the final scene, a cat-and-mouse battle inside a sprawl-ing, industrial basement, I was playing Bennett – armed with a peri-od-appropriate 9mm pistol. Jay had picked John Matrix, the epony-mous muscle-bound commando of the original film. He'd found the grenade launcher too. I was hopelessly outgunned.

Steam sizzled from valves, obscuring our vision as we ran around the underground complex, fighting for position. It was a maze of metal staircases, creating opportunities for stealth.

I paused on a walkway. I had to move slowly or the game would register my feet clanging, giving me away. The simulation was suitably lifelike – video-realistic graphics and convincing sound design. But it was still a game.

SP1N would change that. A quarter tab and I'd feel the heat of the steam and even smell the musty odours in the basement. It would also kill my damn headache.

Jay preferred not to use SP1N. He claimed it reduced his perfor-mance. That was an excuse – the reverse was true. Jay was paranoid; he only left his domicile to work. Putting something with an unknown supply chain into his system would be abhorrent to him.

He didn't care if I did though, and normally I would, but I was trying to stretch another night, and for once it made sense to be around someone who wasn't interested.

A grenade burst to my left, sending me careening against a wall. The game simulated an injury, reducing my mobility and causing me to stagger. I wasn't prone to VR nausea, but the sudden jolt still produced an unpleasant twinge.

"Daryl, I'm gonna KILL you, Daryl!" Jay loosed off another couple of grenades from across the basement. They exploded against a nearby railing, but the game now had me registered in cover. They boomed noisily overhead, causing my vision to blur, but were otherwise harm-less.

"Wrong film!" I yelled back.

Jay was confusing his '80s action thrillers. That line was from *Total Recall*. Same leading man though.

"Doesn't matter. You're still dead."

I could hear the smirk in his voice. I was good at VR games, but this one was about the race for the best weapon. Jay had memorised the spawn points before I'd arrived. I was at a huge disadvantage.

Pinned down, I snuck a look around the railing. Jay was out in the open, waiting for me to break cover. His body glowed blue – showing he'd found the body armour power-up. With my reduced mobility and underpowered sidearm, I was screwed. He'd soak up more ammo than I had in the 9mm.

More grenades burst and insults hurled. I considered rushing him, going out in a blaze of glory, but pride held me back. He'd won the first five games. I didn't want to hand him another victory.

I looked again. Tactically, he was in the weakest position on the map, metres from any cover, but he was so overpowered that it was starting to feel hopeless. Then something caught my eye. Something interesting.

Above Jay's position was an environmental feature he hadn't seen, or if he had, he hadn't realised its significance.

I couldn't be sure, but it appeared the game designers had put something in place to prevent this situation. A trick to stop overpowered opponents controlling the central zone. And if I was right, it was also an Easter egg; a reference to another film from the same era, and again, with the same leading man. If this worked, Jay wouldn't know what hit him!

"Hey!" I shouted out between grenade launches. It wasn't necessary to raise my voice, the game would cancel background noise, but it was difficult to remember that over the explosions. "Hey, Jay!" I said again, waiting for a pause in the bombardment. "What's the third rule in a crisis situation?"

Jay went silent for a moment before replying. "What the hell does that mean?"

I leaned out and fired the 9mm into what I'd spotted – a ball of chain above him. It unspooled with frightening speed. Jay yelled and swore, but it was too late. A ton of chain crushed his avatar, the simulation reporting him disabled.

"Duck!" I laughed, walking over to where he lay, buried in rusty metal. "I take it you haven't seen *Twins*?"

"Oh shut the hell up!" Jay sounded as indignant as he looked, one eye visible deep within the pile.

The game ended, darkening my screen. I removed the helmet and blinked a few times, eyes adjusting. Jay shoved his helmet onto his forehead, throwing his controller across the room. The glowing bundle of buttons and sticks shattered against the far wall. He had a box of spares to replace it, but being a sore loser cost him creds every month. He slumped back in his seat to sulk.

I yawned, looking around awkwardly – mentally adjusting to the real world. Exiting VR was always disorientating, no matter how accustomed you were. It left a surreal quality on surfaces – questioning whether the helmet was still down. It was just as well Jay's flat was such a slice of reality then. A quintessential bachelor pad. Modern, disorganised, covered with man-toys. A fake, Vietnam era M16 rifle was mounted on one wall, a nude holographic of a pole-dancer on the other. The whole place smelled of beer and the rubber gaskets used to seal VR helmets.

I picked up an alchovial and swigged hard. My headache still throbbed behind my eyes and the grenades hadn't helped, but it was a distraction, something to turn my mind off. The beer was helping too. Beer always helped.

"Better luck next time." I reached across and punched Jay on the arm. He recoiled. It was too soon.

"Piss off and die, Romeo."

It was a spiteful call back to my failed attempt with Karin earlier. I should have left him to cool off, but that was a low blow, and I wasn't in the mood to give it a pass. I let out a long sigh. More than required.

There was a minor delay, but after a few seconds, Jay straightened up. "I'm sorry, Daryl. I shouldn't have said that. I know things have been bad since Sebastian. I'm an arsehole. Ignore me."

Jay was a soft touch – easy to manipulate. I leaned back, using the moisture on the outside of the glass to rub against my head where the helmet had built up a funk. "Forget it."

I wished I could forget about it. Considering my more immediate problems, I'd thought about Karin more than I should.

Jay put his feet on the table, grabbing some crisps from an open bag between us. He continued to talk while chewing, crumbs flying everywhere. "You know ... Pink hair means she's an Administration agent anyway."

I groaned. Here we go. Jay, paranoid conspiracy theorist, had been activated. It was his main hobby outside VR. "Any more vials?" I attempted to change the subject before he got going.

"Yeah, by your leg."

I looked down. There was a pack sitting right there. The self-cooling wrap cold against my combat trousers.

"Anyway," he continued, not missing a beat. "All those PR girls are linked up with the Telcoms, and the Telcoms control the Administration."

"Uh-huh." I humoured him. "And what has that got to do with pink hair, exactly?"

"I'm getting to that." Jay reached to scratch under his helmet where it perched, then thinking better of it, removed it entirely. He was getting comfortable; I was in for the long haul. No escape until he'd said his piece.

I listened for the next ten minutes. According to Jay, network employees are all injected with an undetectable serum. It altered their DNA code to access Administration installations with blood-scan readers. It also turned their hair white, encouraging them to dye it garish colours.

"So yeah," he finished, hands behind his head. "You can't trust people with dyed hair. It's a well-known fact."

I nodded and took another sip, trying not to pay too much attention – this was one of Jay's less endearing qualities.

The holo-display in the room's corner flashed up a newscast. Jay had set it to alert him if anything of note happened. More paranoia. He was convinced the world was scheming against him.

There'd been a large fire in a commercial district of HK1. The image showed a low building blazing against the night sky. "At least five casualties confirmed," the electronic newscaster stated robotically.

I missed real reporters. The virtual ones were okay, but there had been something great about watching actual people stumble over words or swear on camera.

"Damn world's gone to crap," Jay remarked.

I slumped deeper in my chair, the words registering harder than normal. The world *had* gone to crap. It could be the withdrawal or the bad day at the Vault (or both), but everything felt worse right now. I thought of Sebastian and the events at Camden, a poisonous wave of guilt following. It started in my chest, working its way down my arms and fingers. I'd made no progress getting him out of the asylum, and what was I doing? Playing games and drinking beer. I'd had an excuse when I was deep in a SP1N-cycle, but what was my reason now?

Realisation struck. This bad feeling wasn't going away on its own. And I'd committed to staying clean so there'd be no help from that direction either. I could already feel the tendrils of depression pulling at me. I had to deal with this or I'd slip backwards, undoing my progress.

I got up from the sofa, unsteady as the beer worked through me. "Hey, Jay, I gotta go."

Jay bolted upright. "What the hell, man? We've only played a few games! Why you quitting so soon?"

"Sorry, I've got some things to take care of."

Jay gave me a disappointed look before leaning back in resignation. "Fine, I'll join up with some guys online." And then suspiciously. "You're not going to get high are you? There's almost some colour in your face for once."

I shook my head. It was a possibility, one I'd fight every inch of the way, but it wouldn't happen right now.

I saw myself out of Jay's block of flats and walked south. The customary Neo-London drizzle had recommenced. It was incredible it had held off this long.

Brixton wasn't far, only a couple of miles. No point risking the Underground; it was safer to walk. I had no overcoat; the rain soaked my hair and ran down my neck. Good. It felt miserable. I should feel miserable. I'd wasted so much time since the accident.

I passed a gang of freakers fighting, lazeblades flashing. It was a mock battle, blades set blue, voltage low – they'd burn rather than slice each other. Practise fights marked out the leaders, the most experienced building up patinas of burns across their hands and faces. I heard a yelp as a blade came in low under his opponent's guard, hitting his flank – the material of his jacket left smouldering. It was a mistake; the tattoos and scars of the aggrieved fighter marked him out as a general. The attacker had almost none – a low level grunt. It wasn't a good idea to make your general look bad in front of the troops.

"That's my favourite jacket, runt!" he remarked, licking his lips. I hurried past as his lazeblade switched to red.

On the other side of Clapham, Brixton Asylum was a converted indoor market. The shops and bars long abandoned – put out of business by freaker protection rackets. Sprawling and dilapidated, the old units were well apportioned for wards and holding cells though. Or so the local municipality thought.

I arrived at the barbed wire enshrined entrance past visiting hours. No one cared when people came in; the crazies had no concept of time. The asylum was more concerned with people getting out, but even then, not really. Locals found confused gown-wearing patients wandering the streets all the time.

The guard behind the security station barely registered me, buzzing the gate open disinterestedly.

Sebastian was on the public ward – a hangar-sized creation of knocked through shops. It housed patients deemed safe or catatonic enough to live together. I walked along until I found his bed, past row after row of vacant, dribbling, and muttering bodies. Seb was at the end, staring out a barred window, seemingly transfixed by the rain. I liked to imagine he was daydreaming, but I knew it was just the way his head was orientated.

I took a seat in front of the metal cot. The whole ward was a disaster. More like a homeless shelter than a hospital. Patients swearing at each other, rocking, or staring off into space. It was only operational because of volunteers but threatened with closure every year. Seb looked gaunt and his hair seemed thinner. His strong, good-looking features receding. Guilt welled heavier than ever, a deep pain in my chest seeing him so vulnerable.

Tears welled. "I'm sorry you're here, Seb." I hoped he might hear me. "I've been clean for three days now though. I'm trying to change."

A commotion was beginning at the end of the ward, but the floodgates were open, and I had to get this out.

"And I met a girl today. Believe that? A real one. I messed it up, but I came close to getting her code."

I paused, unsure how to continue. I'd held off saying the thing I'd come to say, knowing uttering it out loud would commit me and make it real.

Voice trembling, I took a breath, fumbling the words. "... Look, Seb, I'm ... I'm getting you out of here ... I swear it."

Tears descended as the commotion intensified. I looked up. A wild-haired man had become enraged. Volunteers went to restrain him, but as they closed in he reached into his pants, flinging handfuls of faeces – stockpiled for such an event. We were at least fifteen metres away, but the stench was immediate – thick and overpowering.

The volunteers held him down, chaining his writhing body to his shit-stained bed. He'd stay that way until the morning, when he'd be re-medicated and his bed sheets changed. In theory at least. That was anything but guaranteed.

I'd said what I needed to, so it was time to go. "Goodbye, Seb, I'll see you soon."

On the way out, I tried to impress on the volunteers how important he was, imploring they show him better care than the others. They nodded and said they understood, but their cold tones said otherwise.

As I left, I made a silent declaration. I was no clearer on what I would do, but that hadn't been the reason for coming. Out of sight was out of mind, and the temptation to slip into delirium too easy. I'd needed to strengthen my resolve, force myself to look at him – feel the pain. This would be my turning point. I'd wasted enough time. I just had to hold on a few more days to get out of the SP1N-cycle.

STATE 05

That night was restless. Cold shivers of withdrawal removing all hope of sleep. And itching uncertainties – the hallucinations at the Trocadero, rationalised but not forgotten, plagued me. Questions reverberated endlessly. What could I do to help Sebastian? Could I stay clean long enough? Was I losing my grip on reality? A milieu of thoughts, intermingled with uncomfortable, abstract dreams. Shadows chasing me, a girl laughing at me, the world folding in on itself – collapsing like a neon edged house of cards.

I woke with a jolt, covered in sweat. Had I been screaming? I wasn't sure. My throat was sore so I could have been. The holo-clock read 6.06 am.

I groaned, grabbing a crumpled t-shirt lying by the futon. I used it to wipe clammy moisture from my face, breathing in and out, trying to pull myself together.

The evening had been tough. Seeing Sebastian had been a double-edged sword. It had reignited my guilt but reminded me why I'd retreated into SP1N in the first place. Even with the promise to stay clean, I'd had to suppress the fresh urge to get high. Unwelcome thoughts kept breaking in: Hey, Daryl, you could trade your ARO for a cheaper model – that would cover some tabs for sure.

I'd held on, sleep fighting me all the way, and when it did finally take me, the dreams had fought me too.

There was no getting back to sleep; it had ejected me like vomit. Might as well get moving.

I went to wash. Properly this time, not just a face scrub. The cubicle was disgusting, with black mould, but the water was clean – or so I reasoned. I turned the temperature up to the severe side of uncomfortable. It caused pinpricks of pain as it hit my cold flesh – a poor man's acupuncture. I tried to imagine the heat burning the sins away from me. When I stepped out, I was a solid shade of pink and tingling all over.

I forced myself to look in the mirror. The gaunt figure was still there, but my mouth and eyes had returned to normal. That was good. No fake grin or shades needed today.

I held out my hand; it still shook, but it wasn't so obvious. My head still ached, but it was more of a dull background pain than the sledgehammer it had been before. I recognised the guy in the mirror. He wasn't especially wonderful to behold, but at least he was familiar. Not the maniac that had stared back the day before.

I rummaged around the flat, finding some genuinely clean clothes buried beneath the mess. Putting them on made me feel better. Not great, but human. I could imagine I was just another low-risker, worse for wear after a heavy night.

It was silly early, but moping around my filthy flat wouldn't help. I could open the Vault and do some re-stocking. It wouldn't help my sales target, but it might earn me some points with Pete.

Moreover, I was starving and there was nothing in the flat to eat. It was a normal, ravenous hunger, not the desperate post-SP1N craving for sugar. It felt good. A decent breakfast was in order. It would cost all the creds I had left, but it would be worthwhile. I had no idea how I'd pay for my next meal, but it wasn't worth worrying about. If the worst came to the worst, I would trade my ARO as my evil imagination had prompted me, but I wasn't there yet.

It was cold and dark outside. Street vendors were just opening. The owner of the burrito stall was Middle Eastern, speaking with a thick accent. He'd been among the last immigrants to get into Neo-London before the wall went up around the old M25 ring-road. He assured me his brand of meat protein was the best. It tasted like any other beef flavoured tofu, but it went down in big satisfying mouthfuls all the same.

I couldn't remember what actual beef tasted like. The last cows had died when I was six. Put down by a particularly infectious strand of mad cow disease. You could still get poultry and some red meat imports like lamb and kangaroo, but losing beef had driven up the value of remaining sources. The price of quality meat approached that of precious spices – elevated to a luxury good. The masses ate flavoured vegetable protein.

Finishing the burrito, I went to wipe my hands on my jeans, thought better of it, and grabbed a napkin from the stall instead. This was the cleanest I'd been in months, let's try to keep it that way. I lobbed the tissue into an overflowing rubbish bin and made my way to Soho.

I arrived at the Vault, and a new shipment had arrived, so there was plenty to do. Pete turned up an hour later. He thanked me for getting in early, but it was clear the conditions he'd laid out yesterday hadn't changed. *Hit your target, or hit the road*. What else did I expect? He was running a business, not a charity.

The rest of the day was uneventful. I made a couple of small sales. A sim-only contract to an older couple who wanted something 'no-nonsense', and a camera module to a freaker kid. He was pale and skinny, a bit younger than me. I suspected SP1N and VR addiction. They were starting younger and younger, but who the hell was I to judge?

Things picked up around 3 pm. I was showing a group of time-wasting kids the latest Saracen models when the door chimed and Karin walked in.

She'd braided her hair, striping her head pink on one side, and she'd swapped the dangling piercings for subtle studs. She was wearing a black, fitted overcoat that came down to her knees and met translucent boots at the hem.

She saw me and waved. My jaw dropped slack for a moment, prompting laughter from the kids. Face red, I hurried to distance myself from them.

"Hey, Daryl," she said, walking across the shop.

I met her halfway, trying to think of something to say. "Hi, it was Karin, wasn't it?" I answered, pretending I hadn't scribed her name on my brain.

She stopped in front of me, an appraising expression on her face. "You look different."

Oh crap, had my mouth turned down again? I held my breath as I waited for her to point it out.

"Oh, right, you're not wearing those silly orange glasses. You look better without them, you know."

I breathed a sigh of relief but couldn't help being offended. First Pete, now her. Those were my favourite damn shades!

"Anyway," she continued, "I need to return this."

She handed me a plastic bag branded with the Vault's logo. I noticed her old TripLite was back on her shoulder.

"Oh." I struggled to hide the disappointment. She'd come back for a return. Worse, I'd have to minus the sale off my beleaguered target. "Was something wrong with it?"

Karin shrugged, curling a finger around a braid. "No, not really. I just realised my old one had life in it." She patted the beaten ARO affectionately. "And anyway, I really can't afford this right now. You're a good salesman for getting me to buy it!"

"Oh, okay." I appreciated the compliment but still felt downtrodden. She'd purchased it on loan terms, which came with a cooldown period. As long as it was unused and in saleable condition, the Vault had to accept the return.

"But I'd like to keep the Limelight connection," she went on. "It's much faster than my old Diecast service."

Not all loss then. I'd refund the cost of the ARO and switch her to a sim-only contract. That was still a high-margin sale.

I nodded glumly. "Sure. I'll sort that out for you right away." I pulled out my scanner to refund the difference.

"Thanks ..." She paused, as if nervous or thinking before continuing cautiously. "Daryl ... I wanted to see if you'd meet me later tonight?"

I dropped the scanner, causing another burst of laughter from the teens who'd moved in closer to watch the exchange. Heart racing, I stooped to pick it up. I couldn't believe it. I was getting another chance, but how to reply without looking even more foolish?

"Sure, I mean, I guess – what did you have in mind?" I replied clumsily, standing upright again, fumbling as I processed the refund.

Her face lit up. "Well, I've got a friend who's having problems with his ARO. You know about this stuff, so I wondered if you'd come along and help."

Just like that, my heart dropped through my shoes. My body slumped and I could feel the blood rush to my ears.

She mistook my disappointment for rejection. "Oh please, Daryl, it would be a big favour. Look, here's my connection code." She aimed her ARO at mine, beaming the code over. It materialised on my screen, sourcing her photo and public profile from the Cloud.

I nodded, afraid my feelings would show if I spoke – unwilling to make things awkward by saying no.

"Great! We're meeting by the Shard at eight o'clock."

"Cool." I managed.

"Cool!" She spun neatly on her heel. "See you there!"

I sighed as she left, glancing over her profile, still displayed on-screen. She had thousands of followers, a busy feed of upcoming events, and loads of upvoted public messages. She was out of my league. My followers were drug dealers, VR merchants, and a couple of less-violent freakers (although I hid all that on my public profile). I was out of my mind to think she'd be interested.

I shook my head and did a mental check, trying to get some perspective. It didn't matter. It was more important to stay clean so I could help Sebastian. Even if it went nowhere, meeting Karin would be an excuse to avoid going home or obsess over SP1N. It was a blessing in disguise, even if it didn't feel like it. The teens were continuing to laugh, overtly now, pointing and ridiculing – like a pack of hyenas picking over a carcass.

I turned on them. Enough was enough. "Hey, you arseholes gonna buy something or not?" They left the shop giggling, but at least they were gone.

The rest of the day eked out as I continued to rationalise my disappointment. This was a good thing. My life had been on a downward spiral for so long. The only people I knew were addicts and perverts. Hanging out with regular people would be beneficial. I hoped l could remember how.

STATE 06

The screen on my ancient Casio, set in scuffed gold plastic, ticked past 7 pm. It was closing time at the Vault; an hour before I was due to meet Karin.

No one needed watches. The clock on my ARO was perfectly accurate, but it was quicker to glance at a wrist than flip out a screen. I was glad I'd found clean clothes this morning – I wouldn't have had time to go home and change.

I sent a message to check it was still happening. The reply came back promptly: *Yes, we'll be standing outside, opposite the tube station :)*

No backing out. I knew it was best to go, but it would be easier to go home and drink my last two alchovials. That wasn't a choice now.

I locked up and assessed my options. It was a few miles to the Shard. I could risk the Tube, but it wasn't raining for once. There'd be less hassle if I walked.

I headed out of Tottenham Court Road, taking a route hugging the north side of the Thames.

As in Camden, it was a stream, but here the homeless weren't permitted to squat around the banks. I liked the way its dark, mirrored surface reflected the bright parts of Neo-London. It hid the twisted nightmare of brick and metal that was there.

I stared at its surface, hands thrust in my pockets – reflective. If only I could step through to a place where the neon lights were decorations on a better city – one made of neat, towering glass. Clean and uncluttered. One free of gang members and addicts. Maybe there I'd have a chance.

On cue, my head jittered involuntarily, reminding me of my status. Junkie playing good boy for the night. I quickened my pace. If I could hold on a few more days, maybe that wouldn't be as true.

Forty-five minutes later, I reached London Bridge. A triple-layered mega-structure slathered across the river. Metal struts were affixed to its sides, reaching down like spider legs into the riverbed – bracing against the bulk.

The monstrous creation served as a metaphor for Neo-London's management. Rather than repair nearby bridges, they routed traffic here, building on extra ramps and levels. The collected vehicles could be tolled more efficiently that way.

The guards ignored me as I jumped the barrier. There was no point charging pedestrians; they'd just wade through the ankle-deep sludge of the river instead. Only those unable to leap the bar had to pay – the old or disabled mostly.

I could see the Shard peeking through London Bridge's oily surface. Its slender pyramid shape coming to a point in the grey clouds. Once the tallest building in Europe – a monument of glass – that had changed when the Administration transferred its headquarters there. A move fuelled with corrupt Telcom money.

The decision had been a step too far, attracting an army of low-skilled protestors. Rage of their out-phased skills ignited by the globalised Telcom agenda.

They'd gather on nearby roofs, launching rocks with homemade slings and compressed gas mortars – the highest and widest holes in the Shard's mirrored surface scoring the most points. Unable to defend such a soft target, the Administration had retreated to Whitehall and Westminster, the traditional seats of power.

The dissidents celebrated a victory against oppression, but a deeper strategy had been at play.

Unable to prevent the uprising, Neo-London's management had seen an opportunity. They replaced their vacated luxury offices with subsidised retailers and bars. Re-skinning the damaged outer glass with steel coating, striped white with neon to distinguish it from the skyline.

How quickly the protestors vanished in exchange for cheap goods and booze meted out by the Administration under a symbolically black and impenetrable surface. Control through consumerism.

I arrived and scanned the area. There was normally an event, something to distract from city drudgery, to get people in a spending mood. Today was no different. Outside the main entrance, artists gathered in the courtyard, displaying their works. The theme was forests and flowers.

The exhibition was drawing a significant crowd. Overdevelopment had all but obliterated parks and green spaces in Neo-London, but the human urge to experience them was very much intact.

On one side, a laser sculpture was on display. Hundreds of yellow and green beams intermingling to create an abstract, yet identifiable, Japanese bamboo forest. The artist had left space to walk through – providing the illusion of being enveloped. Opposite, a flower and rock garden had been created – a real one. I could make out the blue shimmer of an electrified dome surrounding it; two guards were patrolling its perimeter.

Flowers were a premium commodity. Each bloom poking through the decorative rocks attracted as much as high-end AROs. Sebastian would have had me searching for the power while he distracted the guards. I shook my head, ridding myself of the melancholy. I'd come here to be normal. To *try* to be normal. It was important to put the emotional baggage to one side. At least for tonight.

I spotted Karin. She was sitting on a bench near the rock garden, staring through the flickering field. She appeared to be alone.

"Nice, aren't they?" I wandered over, attempting to sound casual.

"Beautiful," she replied absently, not turning around. Then as if shocked from internal thoughts. "Oh, Daryl! Glad you could make it."

I couldn't tell if she was happy to see me or surprised I'd turned up. My nervousness intensified a notch. "Yeah, no worries." Then on a whim. "I'm meeting up with friends later. I had to come this way anyway."

I immediately regretted how contrived it sounded, but Karin took it at face value, eyes wide and curious. "Oh cool, where are you going?"

Damn, I hadn't thought that far ahead! I scrambled for an answer, hands fidgeting in front of me. "Oh, we haven't figured that out yet."

Her eyes narrowed in suspicion.

"So, where's your friend?" I changed the subject quickly.

Karin jumped up and straightened her jacket, the plastic crinkling. "Oh, he flaked out on me. Stuck at work, apparently, but that's cool. You're here now, so we can hang out if you like?"

So her friend had ditched her. At least she hadn't cancelled on me. The offer felt like charity – guilt driven for making me come all this way. What the hell. I'd take what I could get.

"Do you want to check out the art?" I shrugged, pretending to be sophisticated. I knew nothing about art.

"Have you walked through the bamboo forest yet?"

"Er, no."

"Me neither. Let's do it now."

She was enthusiastic, relaxed, and smiling. Maybe this wouldn't be too bad.

We walked over to the laser forest. The beams cut up to where the pollution hung overhead, casting dapples of colours in the grey. Admirers crowded the installation. Each jostling for a slice of beauty so out of place.

"Wow," I heard myself say, as I stared up. I had to admit, it was stunning. The sheer height and brightness. It was enough to blot out the dank blanket of clouds. "It's really something."

She paused, inspecting the sight. "Yeah, it is, I guess."

"You don't sound convinced?"

"I think I prefer the rock garden. This is too ... artificial."

I suppose she was right, but I'd never seen a real forest. Maybe VR addiction made synthetic experiences more appealing to me.

"Look at that!" Karin tapped me on the shoulder, sending a seismic shiver through me. It was a powerful contradiction to my last thought – perhaps some things were still better in real life.

I followed her finger. Nestled amongst the beams, a plinth was raised, topped with a sculpture of a bipedal cargo robot.

I recognised it. They were a mainstay of the construction industry. Its interchangeable limbs functioning as combination forklift truck and digger. The ground had grown up around its legs – foliage poking through its gears and pistons. It couldn't adopt an expression, but its posture was accepting rather than resisting its return to nature. I couldn't fathom any deeper meaning.

Karin twirled on her foot. "Daryl, can you take a vid of me by that statue? My followers will eat it up!"

She was off before I could reply, sprinting through the crowds. She reached the robot in a few seconds, clambering up its root-like legs. Flagrantly ignoring the *Keep Off* sign; drawing equal scowls and smiles.

I shrugged and opened my ARO. It was just as well I'd upgraded its video software. It now rendered in holographic 3D as well as ultra HD. That would give her some thumbs ups for sure.

A forward facing light blinked, signalling I was recording – a legal requirement and one of the hardest functions to disable. Low-riskers were fine with government monitoring, but a random guy with a video camera – *that* was unacceptable.

I focussed the camera. Karin had scrambled to the top. She hung around the robot's neck, kissing its slab plated cheek. I gave her an okay sign in case she couldn't see the light from the dozen metres that separated us.

She waved back and struck a different pose. Swinging around the robot's limbs. She was so energised and well adjusted – nothing like the losers I hung about with.

I looked through the viewfinder, making sure she was in frame. The forest lasers were washing her out. I adjusted the exposure to compensate.

I was good at making videos. It was part of my job to use ARO features, but it was more than that; I understood how to frame a shot and compose a scene. If I'd applied myself, I could have been a holo-editor. I sighed. Another missed opportunity lost to the SP1N-cycle.

The crowds parted for a moment. I dropped to one knee for a more dramatic angle, widening the lens to include the Shard, towering over Karin. Let's see what her followers thought of that!

Who was I kidding? It was her approval I was after.

The composition was ideal – very artsy. Light from the forest highlighted Karin as she continued posing. Her slim, fit body contrasted with the robot's stockiness – her plastic jacket casting interesting shapes and shadows. Flashes of thigh above her boots made her movements sexy, but without being obscene.

My heart quickened as I watched, but then something distracted me, dragging my eyes from where they wanted to be. It was a light – high on the Shard. It sparked in the display, breaking my concentration. What was that?

The explosion that followed was deafening. It ripped from the side of the Shard, beginning as a small flash before blossoming out and consuming the sky. I tried to look away, but it was too late; the piercing light blinded me, washing out the camera display.

Blinking, I tried to clear my vision, the world murky and spotted with orange. Shielding my eyes with my hand, I could make out a jagged hole in the building – bellowing out fiery slabs of metal and neon. Huge chunks were arcing through the sky, gathering height in our direction.

The shock caused Karin to lose her grip and slip off the statue, tumbling towards the ground.

I scrambled, looking for an escape, but there wasn't any – just walls of panicked, screaming people.

Instinct took over, forcing me to the ground in a defensive crouch, head buried in my arms. I tensed as I awaited the crash of wreckage.

Seconds ticked past. Enough to wonder what death might feel like. Would I even notice? Was the speed of being crushed faster than human cognition?

I continued to wait, but nothing happened. No pain. No sensation. Things should have concluded themselves, but they hadn't.

I opened my eyes. Everything was still and silent. It was like after my encounter with Led. But this was no hallucination. It was a nightmare. Everywhere, people were frozen in moments of terror. Women's mouths open in silent screams. Wild- and glassy-eyed men staring up – ropes of neck muscle tensed as they prepared to duck.

I'd seen holovids of catastrophes, but nothing could prepare me for seeing it in person. Raw and unstaged, perfectly captured.

I doubled over in a heave, feeling vomit in my throat. Then remembering the Trocadero, I grabbed my mouth and swallowed hard, sputtering to regain control. I looked at my finger where Led had bitten me. It had scabbed over, but at the time the blood had pooled around my hand like a glove. What would happen if I were sick? Suffocation seemed likely.

Gasping in the thin air (another returning and unwelcome sensation), I caught sight of Karin through the crowds. She hung precariously in midair.

Seeing her vulnerable refocused me. I couldn't count on this being a hallucination anymore. I'd been off SP1N for days. This felt all too real – too consistent with before. Something had let me get away from Led and it was happening again.

Understanding flowed over me like a wave. This had all started with that damn room in Camden! The suspicion had been growing for days – ever since the first time-freezing incident. It was too much of a coincidence. I'd thought it was deranging me, like it had deranged Sebastian, but that wasn't everything. It had done something else – something deeper and much scarier. My promise to Seb came rushing back like a haunting echo. That room was the key to everything! I couldn't ignore it anymore.

I shook my head and blinked, remembering my situation. The importance of the revelation was paramount, but at this moment, there were bigger concerns. The phenomenon was an opportunity to escape, and before I could help my brother, I had to help Karin. She hadn't intended to make an impact on me, but that was hardly the point – she'd managed it, and I felt the way I did. I spurred myself into action, wading forward.

The air was heavier than ever as I closed the distance. Karin was suspended, shoulder height above the crowd, surrounded by terrified faces, captured in their latent states of death. A lump rose in my throat as I peered at them in turn.

I grappled with my guilt. It was irrational to prioritise someone I'd just met. Should I try to help someone else? Or leave altogether? I didn't owe Karin anything.

I set my jaw. That wasn't true. I did owe her something. For a few moments today, she'd made me feel like a normal person. I was no hero, but I wasn't an arsehole either. We'd entered this nightmare together, and we were leaving together.

I tested Karin's arm. It was solid; a perfect manikin in a terrible magic show – the backdrop a sky peppered with chunks of steel and neon. Anxiety gripped me like a kick in the balls. It would take seconds for the lumps to crash down on us in real time. I had to hurry.

I looked around for anything I could use. We were in open ground with nothing sturdy to shelter beneath. Even if there had been, I doubted much would withstand the weight of falling steel. If we were to live through this, it wouldn't be by hiding – we'd have to leave. But how?

I scanned the sky again. The explosion had sent debris out in a semi-regular pattern. Larger lumps were thrust furthest forward, hanging over us imminently, but the ones nearer the building, where the blast had originated, were smaller and higher up.

My mind whirled, thinking through options. The Shard's stability didn't seem compromised. The hole was large, but it was only in a small part of the building. If time resumed, we could run, and with foreknowledge of where debris was falling, avoid it and take refuge in the Shard's lobby. That was if the pattern was predictable and we could plan the perfect run. And of course, there'd only be one attempt.

I shook my head. Absolute madness, but there was no other way.

It was about thirty metres to the lobby entrance, a marathon given the circumstances. At least the doors to the sheltered area were open with no obstructions. There were security guards, but they appeared as panicked as everyone else.

I estimated the first chunks would land in a few seconds, then roughly every second following. The later ones would be smaller, but just as deadly. In all cases, debris would smash at our heels all the way to the Shard.

About halfway between us and safety was a short, wide run of steps. Ten in total. Never had something so innocent appeared such an obstacle. I'd been considering carrying Karin. I wouldn't have time to right her, explain the situation, and get moving – but that plan was scrapped now. Karin was small but not insubstantial. Worse, the incline of the stairs would kill our momentum and create an unfavourable angle to the debris.

She'd need to be on her feet before the steps or we were dead in the water. There must be a better way.

Biting my lip, I re-examined the spread of debris. It appeared less dense and higher on the left. If we could make it the first few metres in that direction, I'd have a moment, maybe two seconds, to rouse Karin, then we could run up the stairs together. I puffed my cheeks and breathed out, incredulous at what I was considering.

I racked my brains. Had I missed something? I couldn't think of anything.

Another wave of doubt blindsided me. It was a complicated and dangerous plan. Why not just leave? Stroll out of this disaster and never look back.

An image appeared behind my eyes, burned there since I'd seen it. Sebastian face down in the treatment centre. The guilt that had dulled since seeing him in the asylum welled up.

This wasn't the same, but the effect would be. This time it would be worse. I had a chance to do something, to act with agency. I'd just stepped back from the brink. If I left Karin now, her death on my conscious would drive me over it.

Resolved, I moved to position myself beneath her, bending my knees in anticipation.

I didn't know how long I'd have to wait. At the Trocadero, time had resumed when I'd stepped outside, but I didn't know what triggered it. I'd been sure I'd imagined the whole episode – I hadn't tried to retain any details. All I could recall was the world restarting when I was out of immediate peril, away from danger.

Distance could be a factor then – moving away from the epicentre. But if that were true, we were screwed. If I left the area now, I wouldn't make it back to help Karin.

What else? Come on, Daryl!

The only additional detail I could remember was feeling calmer. Not safe, but in control, able to think. What if the frozen state was brought on by stress? Something that receded when I was less panicked?

Seemed like a long shot, but nothing else was coming to mind. It was worth a try, although I'd have to reduce the thumping in my chest first. Far from calm, it felt like I was having a mini heart attack!

I closed my eyes and breathed. I imagined myself and Sebastian at my flat, drinking vials. His drunken face grinning. He reached over and clapped me on the shoulder. "You know, Daryl, you're the smart one. You just haven't had your moment yet."

I couldn't remember if that had happened, but it was the sort of thing he'd say. The words drifted over me along with a brief wave of contentment.

Something changed. I could feel it. The world winding back up – the start of a breeze and a rise in temperature.

Eyes open, I paid attention this time. Events didn't just recommence; it took a few moments, like a video starting at half speed. Karin's body floated downwards a few centimetres before dropping suddenly.

I let out an "Ooph!" as she landed in my arms. "I've got you." I grunted under the weight, time returning to full speed against the roar of the explosion. She turned to look at me, expression unreadable. I'd feared she'd resist, but she didn't; she was compliant.

I started my (slow) sprint to the left of the stairs. Karin wasn't heavy, but I wasn't in good shape. Every step was difficult. "Be ready ... when I stop." I managed between wobbly strides.

I detected a nod as I heard the first of the steel slabs crash down. It boomed behind us, showering us with debris. The shock caused me to stumble forward, but I kept my footing. I tried not to think about the people crushed to a pulp behind us.

The crowds were reacting on instinct, feeling the paralysis I'd felt. Most were crouching, some running – all panicked. Free of indecision, we were the only ones attempting an escape.

Another crash, closer this time. This piece must have been on fire. A shower of sparks rained down from behind us.

Feeling the breath ebb out of me, I closed the remaining metres to the stairs. I wouldn't last much longer carrying Karin like this.

"At the stairs ..." I wheezed. "... Get ready to run." Again, I detected a nod.

As we arrived at the spot, I didn't so much drop Karin as let her slip, my arms giving in. She responded with surprising speed, sprinting up the stairs as her feet touched down. My lungs were burning, but there was no time to pause. I followed, labouring up each stair.

I looked ahead. The run to the lobby appeared clear. No ... not clear – damn it! A man in a green jacket was bolting to the lobby on a path that would intersect with Karin. He was young, fit, and moving with purpose. She'd be crushed if she changed course but would collide with him if she didn't. Another near crash, enough to make my ears pop as the shock wave flowed over me. I had to concentrate.

Mind racing, I looked for options. At the top of the stairs, a rubbish receptacle was in reach. A shoulder-high, metallic cylinder sitting idly. I was upon it before I had time to consider the consequences. Reacting more from desperation than sound judgement, I altered my course, considered the angle, and barged into it – aiming squarely for Green Jacket. It was a huge risk. I'd no idea if it was freestanding or welded to the ground. The consequences if it hadn't moved would have been dire.

It rocked off its stand, thankfully with little resistance. The thin metal deformed around my shoulder, and it was propelled into Green Jacket's path. Seeing it would impact him, he took a wider route, enough so he would no longer collide with Karin.

There was no time to celebrate or mentally applaud my dumb luck; we were in the home straight now. There were no more obstacles and the sounds of crashes were thinning.

Then out of nowhere, a lump of steel landed in front of Karin, not a big piece, but jagged, with enough of an edge to catch her toe. She tumbled forward, landing heavily on her side.

Within a second I was by her side, yanking her to her feet, but she was stunned and moving slowly, too slowly. All our momentum was gone – we weren't going to make it!

A green-sleeved arm reached down and grabbed Karin's other hand. It was Green Jacket; he'd caught up to us again. His extra pull was enough to resume our momentum, and with a few more steps we all tumbled into the lobby, the remaining debris crashing down behind us, blocking the door, and blasting smoke and dust in.

I gasped for breath, vision blurred from exhaustion. I wanted to say something to Green Jacket but had nothing in my lungs. He was already on the move, further into the building. Shame welled. My callousness almost killed him. I'd assumed he'd collide with us; I'd never considered he may help. I closed my eyes, the exertion pushing me close to unconsciousness. The new stab of guilt made me want to retreat into it.

Dimly, I was aware of someone calling my name, revoking permission to escape reality. Hands grasped my shirt, shaking me.

The world faded back into blurry existence. It was Karin. She was saying something. "Daryl, we've gotta get out of here!" She was serious and commanding, but calm. "Daryl! On your feet. We're leaving!"

Who was this? I didn't remember her being like this.

My head cleared. A few seconds had passed, although it felt like longer. Karin was tugging me to my feet with surprising strength. I pulled back against her hand and rose, head throbbing.

"Daryl, can you walk?"

"Yes." I tried to steady my voice.

She gave my hand a squeeze. "Good. You did great back there, guiding me out, but it's time to move."

I wasn't comprehending this. How did she know I'd guided her out? She should be terrified, completely disoriented, but she wasn't; she was composed.

"Come on, Daryl," she urged. "There's no time to lose. We have to go!"

Still confused, I allowed Karin to tug at my hand, leading me through the building – the way Green Jacket had gone. I felt bad for nearly killing him, but what about those left behind, crushed or dying under the wreckage? I suspected their memory would surface later, but I couldn't become paralysed with emotion now.

We made our way through the Shard's reception area, exiting on the far side. The area outside was unaffected by the carnage but still a scene of chaos. People gasping, proclaiming, and pointing. It had been less than a minute since the initial explosion tore through the opposing wall.

Once we were clear, I tried to get Karin's attention. I couldn't understand why I was the scared and confused one.

"Karin—"

She spun and grabbed both my shoulders, face serious. "Daryl, thank you, but you have to follow me now. There's more going on than you think."

"What—"

"I'm sorry, there's no time to explain. Are you injured?"

This conversation was happening in reverse. I should be asking her if she was injured! Bewildered, I shook my head from side to side like an obedient dog.

"Then follow me." She grabbed my hand again.

Not knowing what was going on or how to respond, I followed dumbly as she picked her way through the throngs of morbidly fascinated onlookers. The streets of Neo-London were bathed in the pink glow from the flames reflecting off the Shard's dark surface. If this was a hallucination, it had taken a turn for the worse. This was no longer a minor flight of fancy. It was a full-blown psychotic meltdown.

STATE 07

The following panic-stricken hours were a maze of running and hiding. I didn't know why. We hadn't done anything wrong, but Karin insisted we keep off the roads, directing us through every back alley and bad neighbourhood in Neo-London. I'd seen more unconscious bodies, spent skin-guns, and general filth than even I could cope with.

Every time we encountered a large group or busy area, she'd held us back. I couldn't tell if she was avoiding people or high-traffic areas – the shopping nexuses and arcades were given a wide berth.

Any attempt to broach the subject was shushed, making me feel like a naughty schoolboy. And like a petulant child, I'd felt the urge to throw a tantrum, demand she tell me what was going on. But I held my tongue, instinctive to the dangers of cornering a wild animal.

Karin was concentrating, brow a deep furrow, eyes narrowed like a hunting creature. Now and then, she'd freeze and listen. I couldn't hear anything, but she could, and armed with new insight, she'd decide our next move.

We were taking a circuitous route full of twists, but our direction was south-west, and we eventually arrived at the King's Road in Chelsea – a grim part of town.

Chelsea suffered hardest from the *Great British Backlash*. After a decade of resurgent Marxist movements, activists had convinced the poor that the rich were suppressing them. They'd revolted in a short-lived moment of madness. A purge. Armies of wound-up working class had swarmed the wealthiest areas to 'get their taxes back'.

It had been a night of chaos, with black clad anarchists torching, looting, and killing the rich, mostly elderly, population. The Backlash had caught authorities off guard – only mobilising after the damage was done.

Brief and ultra-violent, by the time it was over, the urban elites had learned their lesson, but not the one the anarchists wanted. Shocked at their vulnerability, they'd sold up and fled to the coastlines, taking their money with them.

With no disposable creds circulating, the area's economy collapsed. Chelsea turned from one of the most affluent areas to one of the poorest. Every previously lavish flat and townhouse was now packed with dissidents and thugs. It was a place the powerful preyed on the weak, far worse than the rich ever did. Made my extraplex look like a five-star hotel.

Karin stopped, nodding as if satisfied. She turned to face me, unbothered by the clusters of nearby gangs, tattoos close enough to read.

"All right, we'll be safe here for a moment."

"Safe!" I blurted out. "Safe from what?" I couldn't believe she'd stopped us here of all places.

Her eyes wandered to the rooftops. "Surveillance."

I followed her gaze. She was right. No cameras here. Police and Neo-Guards had given up monitoring this place. These people didn't pay their taxes, so why bother protecting them, but that explained nothing.

"Who are we hiding from?" I continued nervously. A gang of freakers was taking an interest – their bare chests and shaved heads menacing, even at a distance. One licked his lips in Karin's direction.

"I'll explain at your domicile. It's nearby isn't it?" she carried on, unconcerned.

My head snapped around to look at her. She wanted to go to my place? Sure, it was close, over the river, but I wasn't in a cooperating mood.

My fists found my hips as I stood my ground. "I'm not going anywhere until you tell me what's going on."

Karin's hands tensed at her sides, then relaxed, retracting like claws. She breathed out and her face softened. "I'm sorry, Daryl, there's too much to go over, and I don't know how I'll explain it yet. Besides ..." She glanced over my shoulder. "... As you've no doubt noticed, we're attracting unwanted attention."

The local freakers had decided we were worth investigating. A group was walking our way, thumping their chests – a tribal act of aggression. I could see lazeblades tucked in their combats. They made no effort to conceal them at all.

The need to be safe overrode my need for answers. I'd play along. "Yeah ... Okay, maybe we should leave." I mentally hopped from foot to foot as the gang approached. "But when we reach my place, I want answers ..." I trailed off – a panicked plea for us to get moving.

Karin smiled, replying meticulously, playing a deranged game of chicken. "You got it, Daryl. Lead the way."

I was already going, checking over my shoulder. Gang members were shouting and one had dropped his combats, exposing a large, excessively pierced penis, but they weren't pursuing. It was too early for violence; they'd have been asleep all day – probably hadn't eaten breakfast yet.

Rushing out of Chelsea on hot coals, we made our way to Battersea, my extraplex soon looming overhead.

We hurried inside and ascended to the penultimate floor. I clicked the lock and armed the security. I hadn't bothered turning on the electrified door in months. My only item of value was my ARO and that was always with me. Today it seemed worth the cost of electricity, although I still didn't know why.

I turned to face Karin, who was searching for a clean place to sit. My face flushed red. "Sorry," I mumbled, clearing away empty alchovials and convenience packages. I kicked a soiled pair of underpants under the bed, hoping she hadn't seen those too.

"Yeah, don't worry about it," she answered – the time between each word suggesting she was very-much worried about it.

Once the mess was concealed, a thought occurred. "Do you want a drink or something?"

Karin eyed the place sceptically, considering if there was anything she could consume that wouldn't kill her. She dithered for a few moments then finally settled on an answer. "Have you got a beer?"

I smiled. That was the one thing I did have. Freshest and safest thing in the flat. "Sure."

I fetched two beers from the kitchen. The fridge was broken and didn't chill well, but the vials were colder than room temperature. She cracked the seal and drained it in one go. I did the same.

We stood in awkward silence for a few minutes. Now the opportunity to ask questions had arrived, I was afraid to. I knew the Shard was no delusion, but what that meant was staggering. I wasn't sure I wanted it confirmed.

I stared at the top of my empty beer vial, like a tea-leaf reader, trying to divine answers from the suds gathered on the rim.

Karin broke the silence. "Daryl."

I looked up.

"I know this is confusing, but you should trust me."

I dropped the vial, frustration bubbling over like a shaken bottle. "What do you mean? Trust you! I don't know you at all. You're just some girl I sold an ARO to. How do I know you're not an agent or undercover Neo-Guard?"

Karin was unfazed, raising her hands in platitude. "Daryl, do I look like a Neo-Guard?" She pointed at the futon. "Look, sit down for a moment. You'll need your strength soon. We shouldn't be wasting energy."

Misdirection. Why shouldn't I be wasting energy?

Still, I collapsed on the futon anyway. I'd been desperate to since getting inside. I was physically and mentally exhausted.

"All right …" I continued, trying to calm myself, rubbing my hand across my forehead. A tension headache was building on top of the withdrawal that still hadn't departed. I wanted to sleep, but I needed to quiz Karin. "What, exactly, do you mean?"

She didn't answer right away, just cocked her head to one side, listening for something. "Nothing … yet, just a strong feeling."

This was ridiculous. I was being confronted with riddles. I was too tired to unpick the strange behaviour. I continued with her previous point. "Look, you said I should trust you. Why should I trust you? I have no idea who you are."

She dropped onto the futon beside me, hard enough it bounced me into a comfortable slump.

My body responded with a wave of fatigue, locking into a relaxed position.

She gave me a sidelong glance. "Look, Daryl, rest. I don't think you're capable of hearing this right now."

That should have triggered me into a soft rage, but tiredness was coming on like an avalanche. The explosion, the mad dash across

Neo-London, and my withdrawal. They were all taking their toll. My burnt-up adrenaline had created a hole only sleep would fill – imaginary weights tugged at my eyelids.

There was enough resentment to prompt again as my eyelids began to flicker. "You ... you didn't answer my question ..."

Through closing eyes I heard a faint response, left in the air. "Because ..." Her voice drifted further into the distance. "... I trust myself."

More riddles, but it was too late; the wave of exhaustion hit, taking me into unconsciousness. My frailty was pathetic. I couldn't even hang on long enough to finish the conversation.

STATE 08

S ebastian was with me, beer in hand. Eyes hazy with drunkenness. I couldn't tell where – some dive sim-shop. The walls were distant shadows, visible through swirls of vape smoke. It was hard to hear over the din, but he was telling one of his long-winded tales – I could tell from the way his hands animated. It didn't matter; the details weren't important.

Content he'd made his point, he leaned back, taking a swig of beer, but he left it there too long. The liquid ran over his chin and down his jacket.

I laughed out loud. Silly bastard. He was always doing that.

I expected him to pull the vial away and wipe his sheepish face, but he didn't. He'd stopped drinking and was letting the beer drain over him. Something wasn't right.

He was staring at his right hand where it grasped the vial. It was frozen in mid-air – pinned – his arm pivoting and yanking around it. He shouted as he grasped with his other hand, words muffled by the vial, still lodged in his mouth.

I jumped up, rounding the table, but slammed into something before I could reach him. A barrier, like a sheet of toughened glass, cutting me off. I pounded my fists on it, but the surface was impenetrable.

Sebastian's other hand froze to the vial, both arms straining, pulling like a mime against a door handle. His shoulders and head writhed as he silently screamed from across the barrier.

I thumped with no effect, feeling left and right, trying to find a way around. But there was no way through, just a smooth, impassable surface. All I could do was watch.

Sebastian's arms stopped moving as the freeze spread along them and through his body. Eventually only his head was moving, but then that, too, froze still. I could see he was shouting my name. Desperate for me to help him.

It spread to his mouth, locking it in a dumb look. Wild eyes, darting and terrified, turned glassy and still.

I'd seen that face before – a mask of vacant catatonia. The one he'd worn when I pulled him from the room in Camden. Where he'd sacrificed himself. Where he'd lost his mind.

I woke with a start. Cheeks wet. A mewling sound coming out of me like a dying animal. Karin was standing over me.

Disoriented, I tried to remember where I was. I sat up and sniffed, unable to hide the sobbing. "How long was I asleep?" I managed.

"Seven hours," Karin responded gently.

I sensed she wanted to ask if I was okay, but it was too awkward. I had to pull myself together. "Seven hours?" I replied more firmly, checking the clock – it was past 6 am. I couldn't believe so much time had passed. "Did you sleep too?"

She nodded. "A few hours."

She'd tied her hair into a ponytail on one side and removed her makeup. It matched her demeanour – serious and thoughtful. "It's good you're awake though; we've got a problem."

Shaking off the nightmare, I eyed her cautiously. "What do you mean?"

"We have to leave."

The words were ominous, but Karin said them with a detached, bored expression.

I was alert now, focussed on the situation, and aware I was still in the dark. I couldn't hide the frustration. "Just hold on a minute. You asked to come back here last night. You still owe me an explanation!"

"Yes, I know, but it has to wait. We're out of time." And with an air of genuine apology. "I'm sorry, Daryl."

I took a breath. Despite the fitful night, I felt better, more able to think. I forced myself to remain calm. I needed her to explain what she was on about. "Okay, Karin, what do you mean *out of time*? No one knows we're here."

She sat down on the futon. "Good, you're calm. You'll need to be for this next part, but you're wrong; people do know we're here."

"Who?"

"You'll see soon enough."

I tried to get up, stand so I could argue, but her next words stopped me dead.

"Daryl, I know you can stop time."

Hearing it out loud made me feel lightheaded, like I was still dreaming. I slumped back down.

"At least," she continued, "I do now. I wasn't sure before, but I am now." She looked around the room, voice wistful. "I can do things too. Not the same as you, difficult to explain, harder to demonstrate. You need to trust me a bit longer."

Karin was turning into a broken record. She'd said something similar last night. That I should trust her because she trusted herself. Whatever the hell that meant.

"Daryl, I know more about what's going on than you, but I didn't know things would escalate this quickly. They have though, and the danger has followed us here."

What danger? We were safe in my domicile. What was she talking about?

She glanced at the window. "Look for yourself."

Reluctant to move, I looked at her, then the window, and finally let out a sigh. I stood and opened the glass pane – it was too dirty to see through closed.

The view wasn't much from the thirty-ninth floor. Neo-London's pollution hung around at this level. I could make out the shadows of other extraplexes – shapeless neon tracing through the smog. "I don't see anything."

"Look down."

It was better lit at street level, lamps illuminating the foggy, drizzle-covered courtyard. It was empty save for some abandoned vehicles and overflowing bins. I was about to say so, then three black vans arrived. They had no markings, but they looked beefed up, with flared wheel arches and strong grills. I'd seen similar vehicles on holovids – at riots.

I swallowed dryly, anxiety building.

The rear doors opened and a dozen guards stormed out, making their way through the courtyard. Their black armour was accented blue – Neo-Guards. I spun and stared at Karin. "How'd you know they'd be coming?"

She stood purposefully. "Don't worry about that now. I can get us out of here, but you need to keep close and not question me." Her eyes were wide and intense. Her body had taken on that feral, cat-like quality again.

Indecision gripped me. I hadn't done anything wrong. Maybe if I explained myself they'd let me go?

I shook my head. Don't be an idiot. No visit from the Neo-Guards went well. Most people outright vanished. Karin was right. We had to leave – now!

"What do we do?"

Karin explained in short clear sentences. "Neo-Guards carry plasma stun-guns. Widespread, but no good at distance. We need to keep out of the ten-metre effective range. But that's not the biggest problem."

There was a bigger problem than that?

"They use their numbers to flank and corner, and they're augment-ed for strength. If they catch you, they'll take you down. So unless you're a martial artist ..." She looked me up and down. "... Well, let's say there's no defence if they catch us – we'll need to stay ahead of them."

She stopped to check if I was comprehending.

I nodded, dumbstruck. Apart from the bedrock of panic and in-creasing sense of surrealism, I understood what she was saying. I want-ed to know how she'd come by such detailed information though.

Karin turned to leave, then glanced back. "Can you follow orders without questioning me?"

I blinked, not understanding.

Her tone turned patronising – I needed it. "This is going to be tough, Daryl. I need to know I can rely on you."

For a moment she sounded like Sebastian. I nodded slowly, hating the imbalance of knowledge and power between us. I was in a video I had no script for, but the pressing urgency of the Neo-Guards was paramount. "Yes, I can follow orders." I acquiesced. "But I won't keep following blindly. You need to tell me what you know when we get away."

"*If* we get away." The sinister statement hung in the air as she strode across the room. "Unlock the door, please."

Lips pursed, I followed, unlocking the door. The security panel flashed green. "The lift's this way." I pointed to the left.

"I know, but they'll come up that way. They're already half-way up."

There was no way she could know that.

"Follow me," she whispered and moved in the opposite direction along the corridor, keeping low. I gritted my teeth and followed.

We emerged on the adjacent side, the walkways open to the elements. High railings, but no windows – not cost effective. There was a strong wind howling.

I took a second to lean over the railing, craning to see around the corner and down into the carpark. I could make out one van.

Two Neo-guards were waiting, stationed to check anyone exiting the building. I couldn't imagine how we'd get by.

We paused at the sound of voices. Official, military – the radio chatter carrying on the wind. "Check his room. Everyone else split up and cover the rest of the floor."

Karin was concentrating, head cocked – focussed rather than panicked. "This way," she urged.

I towed along, back scraping the wall until we were in front of a closed door.

"This one's unlocked." She rapped the composite material with a knuckle.

"How do you know that?" I whispered back.

She ignored me, twisting the handle – the door swung open.

I gagged at the offensive smell that greeted us, but I hurried in, closing the door behind us. I didn't need long to figure out why the place stank. I recognised a drug squat when I saw one. Rotten mattresses, rusty skin-guns, and discarded scraps of food – the stench of neglected, unwashed humans.

I'd been to places like this. Paid jobs to collect people who'd spun off the rails. Desperate family members willing to pay to find their loved ones. We'd never fallen this low, but I recognised similarities. I hadn't been far off.

Karin covered her mouth with her sleeve and crouched down, whispering urgently in a low voice. "Daryl! Get down."

We hunkered by the door, listening in tense silence. We could hear boots thumping outside and more military chatter.

"They're not in his room. Search the halls!"

The stomping got closer until it was right behind the door, then receded as they searched further along the corridor.

Karin leaned in close to my ear. "We can't stay here long. They'll lock the building down soon, search room by room." She cocked her head in that infuriatingly mysterious way.

I silently vowed to understand what she was doing.

This time, rather than declare our next move, she furrowed her brow. "Damn. I don't know where to go next. It looks like we're on our own for a while."

On our own? Was she receiving help? That would answer some questions, but who, and why had they left? This was maddening!

I didn't enjoy being kept in the dark, but Karin had been leading the way. With that sense of security ripped away, a blithering sense of panic descended.

"Daryl!" Karin grabbed my shoulders, breaking my mental paralysis. "This is your building. Is there another way down?"

Her voice was steady, but her nails were sinking in – a sign her confidence was slipping. I had to think.

The extraplex was forty floors high. We were on the thirty-ninth. There was a bank of three lifts, although only one of them worked. There was also an emergency stairwell running through the centre of the building. I relayed all this back to Karin.

"No good; all those will be covered." Her hands flexed back and forth as she thought. "What about rubbish chutes?"

There were rubbish chutes, but they were clogged and unusable. Most threw their trash out the windows.

"Sorry, they're blocked up and overflowing."

Karin leaned against the wall, eyes towards the ceiling. After a few seconds, she hit on a thought. "What about the roof? Anything we can use up there?"

I scratched my chin. I'd been on the roof a couple of times to smoke weed. My neighbours were thugs with a habit of shaking down residents. I didn't want to attract them with the smell.

There wasn't much up there. A flat expanse with some water tanks. Other extraplexes were around, but it was too far to jump. I did a mental walk around. A shape of something appeared in my mind. "You know, I think there might be something there that could help."

Karin set her jaw, reading something imperceptible, then sprung to her feet, heading for the window. "Okay, let's go."

"Wait! Don't you want me to tell you?" A mixture of confusion and fear swept through me as I second guessed myself. I wasn't sure I'd remembered correctly. I'd been high on weed the last time I was up there!

"No time." She examined the window. "We've gotta move, I can hear them searching rooms."

I stopped to listen. True enough. I could make out the sound of pounding on doors. I wasn't sure what was scarier – being caught or being wrong about the roof. Standing, I joined Karin, trying to avoid the human waste scattered over the floor.

"How are you at climbing?" Karin slid the window open, yanking away the safety mesh. Dim light flooded the room, casting a sad, stark reality on the scene. At least there was a breeze to hide the smell.

I was about to answer, protest the logic of climbing on a rickety extraplex, but before I could make my case, Karin had slipped out and shimmied out of sight. The lack of hesitation was remarkable.

I peered out, wind whipping around my head. I wasn't terrible with heights, but the thirty-ninth floor was enough to fill my throat with acid. It felt like I'd been kicked in the balls.

I craned my head to see where Karin had gone. She'd already reached the next floor – using a bunch of cables as a makeshift rope to clamber up. They were powering one of the neon advertisements affixed to the building.

"Move your arse, Daryl!" she shouted from above. "It's easygoing, the cable's strong."

It didn't look strong. I couldn't believe how quickly she'd moved. She may have lost whatever had been guiding her, but if she was afraid, she wasn't showing it. This was crazy – no way I was going out there!

Thump-thump-thump. The door rattled on its hinges. "We're coming in to search this domicile," a static-filled voice commanded. "Official Neo-Guard business!"

Holding my breath, I climbed out the window and around the ledge, just in time to hear the door burst open behind me.

Cold fear encased my chest as I faced the extraplex, fingers gripping like iron hooks to the window frame. I was standing on a ledge narrower than my feet, forcing me onto my toes, heels hanging into space. I was glad I couldn't see down from this angle.

Paralysis threatened as the wind howled, grabbing at my hair and clothes. Move yourself, Daryl. If I didn't get going now, I'd freeze up entirely.

I shimmied along awkwardly. A glance upwards showed Karin's foot disappearing over the top. "Hurry up!" she called down, barely audible over the wind.

Easy for her to say – I eyed the ancient electrical cables and decrepit staples holding them to the wall – she was much lighter than me.

There'd been no further commotion from the domicile. We hadn't been seen. The stink had probably done us a favour. Not even a Neo-Guard would want to inspect that place.

I reached the cables. They were a thumb-width wide, and the rubber was peeling off, revealing the shielding layer beneath. I hoped they were still insulated; dying from electrocution would be ironic. Karin was okay, but she may have gotten lucky.

I grabbed a fistful and tested my weight. They wiggled but felt secure.

Gingerly, I climbed, hand-over-hand, wedging my toes against the staples spaced every half metre.

On the third step, I looked down to check my footing and regretted it. The height was immense. It made my head swim. Anxiety dominated, but before it could take hold, a noise made my blood run cold. The sound of metal wrenching against concrete.

I stared up. The top staple, anchoring the cable to the wall, was crumbling in its hole. The bonding was struggling under my weight. Maybe Karin had disturbed it on her way up? Either way, it was going; I could feel the vibrations as the cable slipped through the slackening staple.

My heart was pounding in my chest, each beat a lightning bolt through my body. I looked for something to purchase on, but there was nothing. I was halfway between floors with nothing except featureless concrete on all sides.

The wrenching stopped. Its absence worse.

I looked again. Freed of its mortar, one side of the staple had come away and was bent at an angle, the metal turning white at the warped joint. The cables were hitched around the remaining side. If it were to hold, I might—

Pop! The other side came away with sickening finality, and with nothing left to support it, the cables went slack in my hands.

I let out a scream as I slid backwards into oblivion, gripping the cable with all my might.

It went tight again. My eyes were closed, but I knew what had happened. I was getting used to the sensation, and I was seeing a pattern. Peril brought on the time-frozen state. I'd never felt more grateful for it.

The wind died away, leaving the distorted drumbeat of my heart pounding in my head. Breathing was difficult, a weight on my chest. I cracked an eye open. I'd managed to keep my feet on a staple. I was hanging away from the building, suspended in midair.

The angle should have been difficult to hold, but it wasn't; it took barely any energy at all. The thick atmosphere was propping me up, reducing my weight. But I was running out of breath.

I couldn't get freaked out this time – lightheadedness would be fatal.

I continued climbing, thinking away the detached cable – the top end hanging out in space, half a metre from the building.

It was taxing, but only because of atmospheric resistance. Moving vertically was no harder than moving horizontally when time was frozen.

With the air around me acting like a safety harness, my paralysis receded. I was at the top and onto the roof in a few moments, coming face to back with Karin. She was frozen in a partial spin, a snarl on her face. Probably irritated at how long I was taking.

I wasn't sure if I was getting used to my abilities or the terror of recent experiences had desensitised me, but I was already feeling calmer. If the pattern held, that meant time would resume soon. I should use the chance while I could. I wanted to check if my memory of the roof was accurate. I couldn't believe how Karin had committed us, jumping out the window before I'd explained. She must be insane.

I swam past the water tanks that bisected the roof, a sigh escaping as I emerged between them. It was there. The extraplex had given up cleaning windows along with a bunch of other basic maintenance, but they'd left the cleaning crane. It sat, hunkered and rusted, on the far side of the building, but it was no figment of my imagination.

I stooped to get a closer look. It appeared usable, loaded with a spool of braided cable. Proper metal cable, not the rubbery, flakey stuff we'd used to climb up here. The crane lowered a platform to access the windows from the outside.

"Daryl!" Karin was calling from the other side as time resumed. "Where are you?"

"Over here!" I yelled back. The transition to real time had taken me by surprise. I needed to get better at noticing, or figure out how to resume it when I wanted.

Karin appeared between the water tanks. "How did you—" Her eyes widened. "Ah, you froze time didn't you? Are you okay?"

"Yes, when the cable came away from the building."

"That was lucky." Her tone was pragmatic, glossing over the near death. "Good for if you fall off a building, I guess."

"Or for surviving an explosion."

"Quite."

"Or avoiding having a finger bitten off."

Karin stared at me blankly.

"Don't worry."

"Fine. Well, back to business; they'll search the roof soon." She joined me by the crane. "Is this why you brought me up here?"

"Yeah ..."

She walked around, appraising the crane, nodding her approval. "Good idea." She did her listening thing and shook her head. "We're still on our own. Any thoughts on how to use this thing?"

The "on our own" comments were grating me. Did she have a hidden radio? Someone she was taking instructions from but was out of range? – Who? Why? I knew she wouldn't explain, so I answered her question instead. "I've seen window cleaners on other buildings use similar systems. We can use it to lower ourselves down."

Karin wrinkled her nose. "Know how to operate it?"

Damn, no, I didn't.

"Come on, tech boy." She encouraged. "How hard can it be?" She added a smile for good measure. It was manipulative but effective. I quietly added multiple personality disorder to the list of afflictions Karin seemed to suffer from.

I took another look. The neck was three metres long, attached to a platform for the cleaners to stand on. There were control panels on the crane itself and on the part that lowered. I climbed over the safety railing onto the platform. There were a few controls and they were intuitive. It had several functions. It could swing 360 degrees, orienting itself over the edge, and was mounted on a track running the roof's perimeter – allowing cleaners to access all sides. A separate control governed ascending and descending, and there was a manual hand brake connected to one of the pulleys. I could operate it, it was simple tech, but the problem was power. "It's dead."

"That's a killjoy."

"Wait a second." I eyed a lead running from the crane to an external box sitting aside on the roof. I ran over and yanked the cover off. It was the breaker unit for the crane. The security panel was red – showing the alarm was armed.

"Encrypted security," I explained as Karin joined me.

"Daryl, I don't mean to pressure you, but it's only a matter of time until the Neo-Guards find their way up here."

"I know. Don't worry. I've got this."

Minor equipment would only have low-level security to dissuade casual tampering. Sebastian and I had cracked more advanced systems, and customers at the Vault were always locking themselves out of their accounts.

I pulled out the touch screen on my ARO, booting up the de-cryption tool-set I'd cobbled together over the years. It connected wirelessly. As I suspected, the encryption was basic. It didn't need an algorithm. My ARO brute forced the lock with superior processing power, and the panel flashed green.

I couldn't hide the smug look as I faced Karin.

Her eyebrows popped up. "Okay. I'm impressed, but don't get cocky. We really have to go now." It had been a few minutes since we'd been in the drug squat, but they'd check the roof eventually.

We ran back to the crane; the control panel was lit up. I swung my legs over the safety rail onto the platform.

"We should descend on the other side." Karin jumped on board. "It's further away from where the vans are parked."

I nodded and manipulated the controls, hoping the crane wasn't rusted into position. It shuddered to life, grinding loudly as it made its way. I winced at the sound, hoping it wouldn't carry to the men looking for us.

After an eternity of agonised metallic screeching, we reached the far side. I input the command to swing the crane. It strained against the cables, lifting the platform.

Gripping the railing, knees shuddering, we slid into open space. Swaying in the wind, I held my breath as we hung, tentatively, forty floors up.

The platform had looked sturdy on the roof, but now it felt old and fragile, a rusted mesh of creaking metal. I winced, concentrating on the controls. I didn't want to bring on another episode of time-stopping.

"You ready?" Sweat was building on my hands where I was gripping the controls.

Karin gave me a thumbs up with both hands; she wasn't even bothering to hold on. Whatever biological process existed to assess risk was missing in this girl.

I pulled the lever downwards, beginning the descent.

It was rickety going. Gusts of wind swung the platform unnervingly.

Every few metres, slack in the cables unwound, dropping the platform a few centimetres. And each time, my heart jumped to my throat, but we made progress down the side of the extraplex.

There were blue flashes behind the windows. Neo-Guards searching the building. That was good; they hadn't converged on the roof yet. The windows hadn't been cleaned in years. We'd be unlucky to be spotted through them. Still, we kept low, moving around on the platform to avoid any that were open, or slightly cleaner.

The platform stopped with a jolt, controls reporting we were at maximum descent. Frowning, I looked down; there must be at least ten floors left.

I realised immediately what had happened, announcing it in disgust. "Damn! The crane must have been reused when they added the extra floors to convert it to an extraplex. They didn't upgrade the bloody cables – they're too short!"

Karin was straining to see around the corner. "We're sitting ducks out here, Daryl!"

I stared at the controls, trying to think. There'd be little point going back through a window. Our situation would be the same there as on the roof. And we were too high to jump – ten floors was as deadly as forty. My eyes settled on the emergency brake I'd noticed when I'd inspected the platform.

"I've got an idea. It's mental, but I've done something like it before."

Karin had taken a seat, legs splayed untidily. She leaned forward, placing an elbow on her knee.

"We need to cut the cable."

Karin's elbow slipped off her knee, causing both herself and the platform to lurch. "Cut the cable! Are you nuts?"

"Probably." I grunted, steadying myself. "Have you got a lazeblade on you?"

She stared incredulously. Whatever intuition she'd had before had abandoned her. She looked genuinely shocked, even a bit scared.

Despite myself, I felt the need to reassure her. "Look, I've trusted you up to now. That runs both ways. Believe it or not, this isn't the first time I've been in a situation like this."

It wasn't. A few years ago, Sebastian had caught himself in a lift shaft breaking into an arcade. It wasn't exactly the same, but we'd used a similar principle to get him out. Karin shook her head and reached into her jacket, producing a lazeblade. I wasn't surprised she had one.

I looked at the sleek metal device. "Okay, good. So here's the plan. If we cut the cable in the right place, it will unwind from the pulley at the top of the crane, doubling its length. But I can control the descent using the brake on the unspooling portion."

"But we'll go sideways!" Karin was aghast, lip curled in disbelief.

She was right. That wasn't something we'd dealt with in the lift shaft. Perversely, I was enjoying the reversal of our positions. "I guess we'll have to hold on." I shrugged.

Karin opened her mouth to speak, closed it, then finally spoke. "Well, you're full of surprises, Daryl, and we don't have much choice, do we?"

"Not unless you want to take your chances back in the building?"

Karin inspected the side of the building – flashes of blue through the murky windows. She shook her head.

"Okay, but we'll need to work together." I motioned for her to join me on the side of the platform facing the building. "If you cut the cable, I'll work the emergency brake."

Karin crouched next to me, looping her arm around the railing, nestling it in the crook of her elbow, her other hand ready with the lazeblade.

I did the same, only I gripped the emergency brake instead. A feeling of familiarity passed over me. Echoes of a previous life. At least if I checked out it would be eventful, and better than a sad overdose.

I took a breath to steady myself. "Do it."

Karin activated the lazeblade, its emitter telescoping from the handle, sparking as the beam arced, creating the blade. Laze was a colloquial term. The beam was focussed plasma. Most were blue, but expensive ones were customised – Karin's was violet.

She worked assertively, using the blade like a saw. The plasma made short work of the cable, the platform lurching as each steel thread pinged free on high tension. "Get ready," she shouted over the whine of tortured metal. "Last ... bit."

I wasn't prepared for the speed the platform listed and fell. It was like someone had removed the world from beneath us! We went sideways immediately, dangling from the railing as the cable unspooled at speed. I lost my grip on the emergency break, causing us to plummet three floors. Desperately stretching, my fingertips found the handle again. I re-grasped it and yanked hard.

At first there was no slowing, but as I applied more force, I could feel the metal-on-metal friction slowly scrubbing off speed, the handle becoming hot in my hand. Finally, two floors from the bottom, we juddered to a halt.

Breathing hard, I looked at Karin. Her face was flushed red, eyes wide. One side of her mouth upturned in a half smile. My heart was pounding in my chest, although not as bad as when the power lines had given out. That had been sheer terror, this was controlled fear – it hadn't brought on the frozen time-state.

I loosened the tension on the brake, letting us move at a manageable speed again, lowering us the rest of the way.

We jumped off as the platform touched down and righted itself.

"Hey, that wasn't too bad," Karin said chirpily, rubbing the crook of her elbow where she'd been holding on. Her reaction wasn't honest though. I could see a subtle shake as she popped the lazeblade back into her pocket. I'd already thrust my hands into my pockets; they were practically quivering.

She did her listening thing and grinned. Whatever disruption had occurred was now clear, not that I could see how it would help – the Neo-Guards would be covering all the exits.

Unperturbed, she walked to a large wheelie-bin parked against the curb. "Here, help me move this."

The bin squeaked out the way on rusted wheels, revealing an open manhole cover.

"Get in."

Of course. The sewer. Why not?

We dropped into the passage below, slipping out beyond the confines of the extraplex.

Our presence, by some miracle, had been undetected. The Neo-Guards would pick up our trail soon, but we had a head-start, and by God, before they did, I was going to find out what was going on.

STATE 09

Lazeblade held high, Karin cast violet light through the labyrinthine interior – our boots making luminescent ripples as they sloshed through the foul smelling, ankle deep wastewater.

Her guiding instincts back, Karin's turns were purposeful and informed.

Not so for me. Disconnected from line-of-sight to satellites, the GPS on my ARO blinked DISABLED. The pedometer function worked – we'd walked a kilometre, but that could have been a giant circle.

Natural light penetrated the interior, growing stronger until we emerged, draining into a Thames outlet. We dropped into the polluted trickle, mud sploshing up to our knees.

"What now?" I rubbed my eyes against the change in light. It was overcast and smoggy but enough to put spots in my vision compared to the blackness of the tunnel.

"We need to find somewhere to hide," Karin answered, nose wrinkled in disgust. Grime had travelled all the way up her translucent boots; they were effectively brown now. "I knew they'd chase us, but not so quickly. We're dealing with some serious people, Daryl."

"Any idea where we should go?" I said, sinking further into the slime. "You know, before we get stuck in this crap."

Karin thought for a moment, looking across the riverbed, then sighed. "Yes, there's one place we could try, but it depends if he wants to see me."

Before I could enquire, Karin was wading to the far bank. I guess I'd find out when I met him.

It was morning rush hour as we boarded the nearest tube. The carriages were full of scrubs – retail employees and sex workers. Those with money drove or connected to their offices in VR.

On cue, a group of tired-looking prostitutes boarded. Hair natty, lipsticks smeared. Street sex was bottom rung compared to sim-shops. Girls only made enough to feed themselves, and by the look of these, it still wasn't enough. Whatever, it was good to have people on the train; they kept the homeless at bay.

Leaving a slit open, I shut my eyes. The last few hours had been a surreal dream. The timeout was appreciated.

We rode in silence, Karin deep in thought, mouth twitching. For once she didn't bother checking her networks. Wherever we were going, it was playing on her mind big time.

We alighted at Farringdon, north of central Neo-London. The prostitutes got off with us.

Farringdon was the only place the bars didn't close – the 24-hour clubbing district. Despite their knackered appearance, the girls weren't done for the night. They'd come to pick up more business. I couldn't imagine they'd have much luck.

At street level, wasters and freakers lined the alleys, heads bobbing to bass-driven, electronic music seeping from doors and windows. The air was thick with sound. Deep vibrations you could feel in your chest. The floor was littered with alchovials and skin-guns.

Farringdon had been through a cycle of death and rebirth for years. The seedy bars and underground clubs a recent return to an old past.

At the end of the century, the commercial district had bought up the area. Investment banks gutting the sweaty buildings and turning them into sleek, modern offices. The new spaces had flourished until the property crash of the late 2020s when prices had gone into free-fall. Desperate to preserve their investment, landlords had fled for the hills, leaving a heap of modern, disused property.

Ex-clubbing patrons, sore at the loss of their dance mecca, saw an opportunity and formed a consortium, crowdsourcing funds and buying back the property at rock-bottom prices. They created a new super-clubbing district. *Music by the people, for the people* – with a policy to keep the party going 24/7.

The bars had reopened in the renovated buildings the city had left
– clubs cycling their opening hours, ensuring at least one was open at
all times.

With Neo-London's ten million residents, there was always enough
demand to keep the party going. But like any commune, it was sensitive to external influences.

Around the time the consortium was converting properties back
into nightclubs, SP1N had flooded the market. Pink tabs poured out
of state-sponsored labs in China, along with the skin-guns to shoot
them. It was a hit. More powerful than ecstasy, cheaper than speed
or cocaine. And music was a readily available sensory input. It didn't
create the immersion of VR, but the synaesthesia, the oneness with
the music, was almost as compelling – without the sim-shop fees.

SP1N destroyed the purity of the 24-hour party. Revellers came to
shoot-up and forget reality. Drugs had always been synonymous with
clubbing, but it had been an equal partnership – altered states of mind
adding to the music. In Farringdon, the relationship had reversed – it
was closer to a drug squat that played music now.

I'd spent a lot of nights here with Sebastian, but never sober. Seeing
it without a filter was unpleasant. People looked like ghosts. I knew
they felt good, but to onlookers they were at death's door. It was
another log for the pile of shame.

Karin knew the area too. She avoided the carnage, making a beeline for an alley. Neon signs hung from the walls, dripping rainwater
into reflective puddles. Mid-morning, the clubbers were thin on the
ground, but still present, and in various states of drink, drug, and sonic
based-delirium.

A skinny freaker leaned against the wall, blocking the narrow path.
Shirt off, nipples pierced, head bobbing to the pervasive beat. He
looked like he might be guarding what was beyond, but he made no
movement as we approached.

As we came closer, the reason was clear. His eyes were shut behind
his mirrored shades – lost in another world. He looked like he could
maintain the position indefinitely, nodding along as his skinny frame
wasted away.

He'd be slung to the outskirts of Farringdon if he dropped dead
from starvation or exhaustion – no one bothered investigating deaths
here.

We squeezed past unnoticed.

Karin stopped in front of a closed door. The neon sign above was broken, every other orange letter flashing intermittently, but I could still make it out: *The Pit*. It appeared closed – not enough of a crowd to open yet.

Karin tapped a message into her ARO and a few moments later the door opened and we hurried inside.

I hadn't been to this place before, but it was typical of the area. Dirty red faux-leather booths and a marred, potted dance floor. A concrete slab at the side served as a bar.

When open, it would be bathed in darkness, shot through with lasers and smoke, but with the fluorescents on it looked like an abandoned car park.

The place stank of sweat. Without patrons, there was no one puffing flavoured e-cigs to hide the smell.

A man was refilling optics at the bar. Something about him seemed off. He had a large forehead and strong features. The wrinkles around his mouth and eyes suggested he spent most of his time smiling, which he did as we approached – face crinkling into a friendly but suspicious grin.

"Karin." His voice pitched higher than I expected. "Didn't think I'd see you again so soon."

"Daryl, this is Emmett." Karin introduced us. She highlighted the 'm' sound in his name, as if she was saying M-et.

Emmett moved forward and vanished, like the ground had swallowed him, appearing a second later from around the bar. He was under a metre tall – a dwarf. The strange pronunciation of his name was now clear, the M insinuating a more derogatory term, although I couldn't tell if it was a true pejorative or a term of endearment.

Emmett looked up at Karin, eyes narrowing. "So, I'm guessing you must be in trouble." It was more a statement than a question.

"What makes you say a thing like that?" Karin sounded bored, like she knew this discussion would happen and wanted to be done with it. It was an act. I'd seen how agitated she'd been on the way over.

Emmett rolled his eyes in my direction, acknowledging Karin being difficult. It was a moment of unexpected but welcome solidarity.

I returned the eye roll, noting with satisfaction Karin's bored expression had become a frown.

Emmett continued. "Well, last time you were being chased for burglary, weren't you?"

I looked at Karin and she shrugged.

"And the time before you turned up barely coherent."

"I'd been drugged," she replied defensively.

"And what was the time before?" Emmett waved a hand in the air as he grasped for the memory, snapping his fingers as it returned to him. "Oh, that's right, it was a murderous boyfriend, wasn't it?"

"He wasn't a boyfriend," Karin whispered but didn't correct the 'murderous' part.

Emmett squared up to Karin, both hands on hips. An absurd gesture as she towered over him, but he was stocky around the gut – it lent him gravitas. "So what's it *this* time, young lady?"

Karin looked at me and then back to Emmett, her voice serious and apologetic. "You know, M, it's better I don't tell you."

Emmett relaxed his posture. Like Karin's fake boredom, it was a veiled attempt to hide his obvious affection for her. They were both playing games.

"That serious?"

Karin relaxed too. She hadn't been certain he'd be receptive, but things appeared back on track.

"Yes, but we only need a couple of hours and we'll be out of here. I swear."

Emmett held up his hands and let out a defeated groan. "Okay, but I'm trusting you're not dragging me into something."

"No, no!" Karin lied. "It's ... complicated – messy. It's best if you don't know the details, that's all."

I suppose that was true. If we explained, Emmett would think we were certifiable, and as a dwarf working in an underground nightclub, his tolerance for loons was probably low. And if he knew nothing, it might benefit him later if he was questioned.

"Okay." Emmett shrugged. "You know where to go."

"Yep, thanks, M." It was definitely a sign of endearment. Karin beckoned for me to follow.

We made our way to the back of the club and down a narrow corridor. It ended in a door with a *Staff Only* sign. Karin placed her thumb on the reader. The door lock flashed green and clicked open.

"I used to work here," Karin explained. "M likes me. When I kept coming back, he didn't revoke my security access."

Inside was a scruffy office. On one side, a desk strewn with paper records, and on the other, shelves full of ancient hard-copy binders. An old ink-jet printer sat on a stool in the corner. I didn't think they still made cartridges for them. Emmett had radically eschewed the trend of the paperless office.

Beneath the shelves hunkered a large beige sofa. It looked like it'd seen better days but also looked comfortable, covered with divots from a thousand backsides.

Karin dropped onto it with familiarity. "I think we better talk."

"Yeah, I think so too." I took the desk chair, trying to stay calm. I was raging with questions, but I'd learned my lesson with Karin; getting agitated just shut her down.

"Where do you want to start?"

Interlinking my hands to prevent them twitching, I took a breath. Before we discussed anything further, I had to know something. I'd accepted my episodes of time-freezing were no delusion, and Karin knew something about it.

"Why can I stop time?" I asked plainly. It still sounded ridiculous to hear out loud.

She fixed eyes with me for a moment before delivering the blunt answer. "It's complicated. I don't know precisely."

My jaw locked. I'd known the answer wouldn't satisfy or she'd have told me earlier. Holding my frustration at bay, I probed through gritted teeth. "Then why are you able to predict things? Who are you listening to? You must at least know that."

"That's two questions, and I don't have the whole answer to that either."

The cap on my frustration blew. I leapt from the chair, sending it careening into the desk in a mini explosion of office papers. "For Christ's sake, Karin! I want to know why the hell you've dragged me into this!"

She didn't react, just sat there, composed. It was infuriating.

Finally she replied. "Daryl, I know this is hard to understand, but at the moment you're asking the wrong questions. I don't know the 'whys' for much of this."

She paused, waiting for another outburst.

I held it back, biting my tongue.

"I know some things though," she offered. "For example, I knew to find you at the Vault."

I forced my mouth to relax, worried I'd scream the next words. They came out loud and strained all the same. "And how, exactly, did you know that?"

"I told you before at your domicile. Because I trust myself."

Throwing my hands up, I let out a frustrated growl and sat back down. I hadn't realised this conversation would be so exhausting! Breathing deeply, I leaned forward, hands on my knees. I wanted my next point to be crystal clear. "You'll have to do better, Karin, or I swear I'm walking out the door right now. I'll take my chances on my own if you can't give me some justification for the crap I've been through."

Karin wriggled uncomfortably. Something had gotten through. "Look, I'm not trying to be difficult, Daryl. It's hard to explain. I've never had to articulate it before."

"Try."

She paused to arrange her thoughts into something intelligible. "You're right, I *can* predict some things, but I can't tell you why I'm able to do it. I've never found that out. All I can tell you is *how* I'm able to do it."

I relaxed a little, this was a start. "Go on, begin with that."

"I'm ... connected to someone ... someone I trust very much. She guides me. She's the one who keeps me safe, but she's also the one who compels me to act."

So I'd been right – she *was* receiving messages. "So, what is it? Have you got a hidden communicator or something?"

"No, it's innate within me. A mental link."

I frowned. I hadn't been expecting that. Some sort of implant? "Okay, but who are you speaking with?"

Karin leaned forward, matching my posture and locking eyes. "Daryl, I'm not *speaking* with anyone. I only *receive* messages; it's a one-way street. I know this will sound insane, but I'm trusting you've seen enough weird things to accept it at face value."

I sighed and nodded, any explanation would be better than none.

"Okay, here it is ... the person I receive messages from is ... myself. A future version of myself, or it could be one from a different dimension. I'm not sure."

I blinked a few times. She delivered the information with conviction, but she was right; it sounded insane. I must not understand. "You mean you're acting like you'd expect your future self to act?"

"No, I'm literally receiving messages from the future."

She was acting like that cleared everything up. It's what a schizophrenic would say. I needed to be careful; I hadn't considered Karin might be crazy.

"How do you know it's yourself sending messages? Is it like a voice in your head?"

"I'm not mad, Daryl!" Karin reacted sharply, her cool breaking.

"I didn't say you were." I lied – I'd just been thinking it.

"But you thought it. I can tell, and not because what I'm saying sounds crazy. I felt and saw it. Sensed it. Like a psychic intuition."

"So you're perceptive?"

"No, you idiot! You think I could have found my way to you through perception alone. Could I have predicted the Neo-Guard attack at the extraplex? Wake up. This is real. As real as what you can do." She leaned back again, lips pursed. "You think this is easy to talk about? Imagine trying to explain how you stop time!"

This wasn't going well. Whether or not she was a lunatic, chances are I'd have to work with her – better to apologise and hear her out. "Okay, I'm sorry. I'm tired and this is confusing. Please, go on."

Karin continued, pressed back into the sofa, a scowl on her face. "Here's the thing. I don't have perfect clairvoyance. The messages I receive are vague and only relevant to the near future." She paused to see if I understood.

I didn't, but I nodded anyway.

"They're dreamlike and they vanish quickly."

I used my fingers to push away a confused frown that was developing.

"Look, I know it's hard to understand. Here's an example. If I walk past an alleyway, I might get a hot feeling and see an image of a lazeblade. That's enough to tell me there's a mugger nearby. But I wouldn't know who the mugger was, his specific location, or even that he would definitely mug me until I got much closer. It's like an early warning system."

"So at my extraplex, when we stopped and hid in the drug squat, you knew it was empty because ..."

"Because I felt cool and sensed an impression of an empty box."

I nodded thoughtfully. In an odd way, this was all lining up. Why was I so reluctant to believe her anyway? It was no stranger than what was happening to me. I needed to be cautious, but I resolved to listen more carefully.

"Okay, Karin, but if these messages are so vague, how can you be certain who's sending them?"

Karin's scowl started to lift. "Because they come to me in a shorthand I can understand. It's like knowing your own handwriting."

I was trying to understand but my bewilderment must have shown.

"Think about it," she continued. "Have you ever read something you didn't remember writing but were sure it was yours because of the way it was written?"

Not precisely, but I knew what she was getting at. While hacking, I'd come across code I couldn't recall, but I was sure was mine because of how it was annotated. So yes, I understood what she meant.

I moved my hand from my brow, nodding my comprehension, but her answers created more questions. I'd already spotted a big one. "Karin, if the messages are coming from yourself, why wouldn't you know for sure? You must send them back, right? Even now, aren't you having to send messages to your past self to warn of things to come?"

"No. I don't need to. It doesn't work like that."

"Well that doesn't make any sense."

"I know, but that part is complicated and I'm sure you've got more important questions right now?"

That was true. This conversation had derailed me from the most important thing I wanted to know. I tried to frame it; I needed a clear answer.

"Karin." I leaned forward further, almost to the point of falling out of the chair. "How did this happen to you? To us? How is the room in Camden connected, and what is Hive Ltd?"

Karin's eyes flickered as she sifted through what I'd said, answering simply. "Room? Hive? I'm not sure what you mean."

I lost my temper again, spittle flying. "The room, Karin! ... In Camden. Where I almost lost my mind!"

She sat for a moment, eyes unblinking, even under the shower of phlegm. "Stop shouting," she said firmly. "I'm afraid I don't know about a specific room, and I've never heard of Hive."

I could feel a pressure building behind my eyes and between my ears, a palpable rise in blood pressure. I couldn't believe it. This was crucial, and she had no information. A cold well of despair began to descend. How could I help Sebastian with nothing to go on!

Karin was still speaking, interrupting my self-pity. "... It happened to me on a sub-jet coming into Neo-London. We were flying low through the buildings when I felt like I was in many places at once. The next I knew, I was being woken by a hostess. I thought it was a weird dream, and later, when I started receiving messages, I was sure I was mad. But the visions came true. It was then I realised something had happened to me."

I caught the story mid-flow but learned enough to be grateful I'd tuned back in. It tied up with what happened to me and Sebastian. The locations were different, but the rest was the same.

As if in answer to my inner monologue, Karin said, "Daryl, I don't think what happened to us is connected by any specific place."

The pressure in my head calmed. "I see that. Some of your story is like what happened to me." I was still talking loudly, for no reason. I paused, regaining control before continuing. "I'm guessing none of your messages explain it any better?"

"I'm sorry, they're too vague, and whatever is going on is well hidden. I've not found out much on my own. Any time I get close to someone who might tell me something, they vanish, you know: *disappear* – with a flimsy official excuse logged in the system. Moved to another country, contracted an illness; typical cover-up bullshit."

I did know, recalling the speed the treatment centre in Camden had been locked down. I'd been lucky to escape unnoticed – I owed that guard a lot for keeping his mouth shut.

"Anyway," Karin continued. "That's when I stopped digging. It seemed obvious more prodding would only attract attention. Get me vanished too."

Okay, this was good. We were both speaking calmly again; maybe this wasn't completely fruitless. "But whose attention are you avoiding, Karin? Why are the Neo-Guards after us now?"

"Not sure. All I knew was I didn't want them finding out about me before I found out about them. That's irrelevant now, but I was right to be cautious. Whoever, or whatever, we're dealing with must be well connected if they can send Neo-Guards after us."

"Do you think it's the Administration?" It was a natural conclusion.

"Could be, but I doubt it. The Administration has no real power; they're just puppets of the tech corporations."

My mind hurt as I churned Karin's words. It sounded right though. The only entities with power were the Telcoms, although why they would take an interest I had no idea. I mentally filed the information. I didn't have the brainpower to untangle it. Besides, there was more I wanted to know. "You were going to say before how you found me?" I probed. "It couldn't have just been a coincidence?"

Karin yawned and rubbed her eyes before continuing. It was contagious. We were both getting tired. She carried on though; maybe she believed my threat to walk out. It wasn't entirely a bluff.

"All the leads I could safely pursue had ended," she explained. "I'd accepted that I needed to limit my search to passive observation, try to get on with my life. Then I walked past the Vault and in popped an urgent message – it compelled me to go in."

"Just like that?" I was genuinely interested. Karin's messages were intriguing if nothing else. "What did you see?"

"An image of a puzzle box, surrounded by black."

I stared at her blankly, prompting a better explanation.

"A puzzle, when solved, is shorthand for a solution – or answers. Black is like putting something in bold – it means very important."

"But what about me? The message told you to enter the Vault. It said nothing about meeting me."

"When you came over to serve me, I saw a green aura. That meant I was on the right track, but there was something else. I saw a silhouette of a person standing next to you. Male, bigger, but with similar proportions. So I assumed your brother was involved somehow."

She knew about Sebastian? "How could you possibly know that was my brother? That could have been anyone."

"It's my mental shorthand. If it was your father, the image would have been above you; a friend would have been standing further away." She paused. "It could have meant a lover, but I guessed that wasn't your thing."

A worried look crossed her face like a shadow.

"What is it?"

"Something about the image was unsettling to me. Silhouettes like those are normally solid, but the person standing next to you was different. It was an outline, not all there – hollow through the centre. I've seen nothing like that before, and I don't know what it means."

I knew what it meant. The image was hollow like my brother's mind. My voice wobbled as I explained. "Sebastian ... He pulled me out the way when I got hit with ... whatever I got hit with. I only experienced it for a few seconds, but he was in there much longer. It took his mind away. He's a vegetable in Brixton Asylum now."

"I'm sorry. I didn't know that."

"And you can't help him, can you?"

"Not right away. We don't have enough information, but there must be an answer. We found each other for a reason, Daryl."

Maybe, I pondered. A few days ago I'd been on my own. We were on some kind of path now, but I couldn't tell if it was any better. And I wasn't sure I trusted Karin, not yet. What was her motivation for this? She didn't seem under any special hardship – why not continue as normal with her new powers? They weren't obvious to other people – no one would know.

"Daryl." She interrupted my thoughts. "What's important is we've learned something new today. We're unusual."

I banked my concerns for another time and snorted. I couldn't help it; the comment was so absurd. "Of course we're unusual! You can predict the future and I can stop time. It doesn't get weirder than that!"

"No, you misunderstand me. I mean *rare*. We were only exposed to the effect for a short time. Me, because I was on a sub-jet. You, because you were pulled out the way. We were influenced for long enough to change us, but not enough to lose our minds. That's significant."

I wasn't sure why that was significant, but it did prompt another question. I asked it quickly while it was front of mind. "Hey, Karin, what about the others on the sub-jet? Wouldn't they have been affected like you?"

"Yes, I thought of that myself. I even got a flight manifesto and followed up on the people who had been travelling with me."

"And?"

"And nothing. They were unaffected, or exceptional liars. Not to mention, all the time I spent investigating, I was seeing red – literally.

My mental shorthand; it means stop or wrong. Anyway, my guess is there must be something physical about us that makes us susceptible. But that's just speculation."

"So that would make us even rarer."

"Yes."

There was a knock on the door; it was Emmett. He entered carrying a tray of rehydrated protein buns over his head. From where I was sitting, it completely obscured him, making the tray appear to float.

"Thought you'd be hungry," he said as the buns levitated to the office desk. White gelatinous exteriors steaming from the microwave. "There's a fridge under the desk with water and alchovials in."

"Thanks, M," Karin said.

I thanked him too, reaching for the buns. They were stuffed with synthetic beef, but it was good quality. I hadn't realised how hungry I was until I saw them; we'd not eaten in nearly two days.

Magic trick complete, Emmett faced us. "You two know how long you'll be holed up here? I can keep the club closed until nightfall, but after that I need to get back to work."

"We'll be gone by then, M," Karin replied sweetly. "I promise."

Emmett nodded. "Well, you both look tired. Why don't you rest for a while, but out by tonight, okay?"

Karin reached for a protein bun. "Definitely."

Emmett retreated. I wondered what sort of relationship they had. It was too close to be employer-employee – it must be paternalistic. I tried to imagine Pete putting me up in the Vault but couldn't. Thinking of that place was odd; it was distant now. I should contact him, let him know why I hadn't turned up today – make some attempt to preserve my job. It didn't seem important. I knew I was never going back.

I hunkered in my seat and closed my eyes. I wanted to know what was driving Karin, and we hadn't even discussed the explosion yet, but we'd spoken enough and were running on empty. Whatever was happening, it was in motion now. We were either going to sort it out or disappear, like the others. At least there were no decisions or regrets anymore. The inevitability was comforting in a way.

STATE 10

We slept for a few hours. Karin on the sofa, me on the floor. I'd made do by balling my jacket into a makeshift pillow and spreading some office papers over me.

It was around 6 pm when we rejoined the living, riddled with self-inflicted jet lag. I felt grim. My body no longer had any sense of day or night. I didn't need a lot of sleep, but these snatched hours were taking their toll. And the anxiety of our situation didn't help – it was an omnipresent tension between my temples.

There were a few hours left before we had to vacate Emmett's bar.

Karin stretched as she stood from the sofa. Some of her braids had come undone, leaving a tangled pink fuzz on one side, and a lack of make-up wasn't doing her any favours either. Still, dishevelled as she was, her eyes were bright and she looked energised. Non-junkies have better immune systems, I reasoned.

Speaking of which, the itch for SP1N had reared its head. A persistent, scratching need to use, responding to days of persistent, scratching pressure. I rubbed my face to try to clear it, grabbing some water from the desk fridge and drinking deeply.

"So what's our next move?" I asked, wiping the overspill with the back of my wrist.

"Can you pass me some water too?"

Leaning over, I retrieved another, wishing I'd gotten her one in the first place. Things were shitty, but I should avoid being an arsehole. I had to keep Karin on side. She was my only link for helping Sebastian, and myself.

I apologised, handing her the vial. She cracked it and drank thirstily, answering my question when finished. "We need a plan. A way forward."

"No clairvoyant hints?"

"No, it's like I said." She used some water to smooth down the escaped braids. "It doesn't work that way. It's situational – short term. If someone handed me a plan, I might see if it was worth trying, but I can't produce the plan itself."

"Right." I swilled water around my mouth, trying to clear the bad taste that had taken residence there. "I forgot. *Short-term* clairvoyance."

"Right," she answered, either not noticing the sarcasm or choosing to ignore it. I kicked myself. So much for not being an arsehole.

I thought hard. It had only been two days, but so much had happened. It was difficult to remember it all. The carnage at the Shard, the way the explosion had ripped through the building, and the mad dash to escape falling debris.

The details were fading like a dream. We needed something solid.

I crossed to the desk computer, opening my ARO. A memory surfacing.

"What is it?" Karin straightened, intrigued.

I connected to the monitor, streaming out the last video on memory. The picture faded to an angle among a crowd Karin centre frame climbing a statue; the Shard looming in the background. The footage was still there.

"Oh, right!" Karin snapped her fingers. "I forgot you'd been recording! Great thinking!"

I scrubbed through the images, checking what the ARO had captured. I'd gotten everything up to the hasty exit through the back of the Shard.

"Yeah, and it looks like we got a full account."

"Well, play it!" Karin fussed excitedly. "Let's see what happened."

Tense, leaning on the desk, I returned to the beginning, letting the video play out at normal speed. It was something to behold. The disorientation and terror harder to watch a second time around.

I'd caught the explosion as it blasted from the Shard, the shaky camera doubling over to the floor when I'd curled up. My hands gripped the desk as I remembered the sick taste of fear – waiting for a crushing death. A moment later I was catching Karin as she fell from the statue – the minutes I'd investigated jump-cut while time was frozen.

The next moments were like watching us star in our own action holovid. Darting in and out of debris with superhuman intuition.

The video captured details I hadn't noticed the first time around. Falling masonry crushing men and women on either side. Their bodies shredded like papier-mâché dolls. It was horrifying. I didn't want to watch, but I couldn't pull my eyes away either. My knuckles turned white as they held fast to the desk.

Worse was to come.

My face flushed hot as I watched my on-screen double barge the receptacle into Green Jacket's path – narrowly missing killing him as he swerved to avoid it. My intent was even more blatant watching it back.

I felt Karin's eyes on me. "I didn't know about that bit." She breathed.

I tried to stutter a response, but she interrupted me.

"Thank you. That's twice you've saved my life."

Shocked, I looked at her. She hadn't acknowledged Green Jacket whatsoever. "But ... I almost killed that man." I was pleading for forgiveness. I didn't want her to think I was a monster.

"It was me or him." Karin's expression was serious, but her body relaxed, unconcerned. "You chose me. Thank you."

Consternation fell away, replaced with confusion. Karin's reaction made me feel better, but it created questions. She had a hard edge and ruthlessness to her.

We watched the last moments as we made it to the Shard's reception area, the video ending with a static pop, breaking the tension. We both stood away from the desk.

"That was exciting." Karin stretched her arms over her head. "Like a movie or something."

"Yeah," I mumbled, distracted by the exchange we'd had. "But all those people ..."

"That's not your fault, Daryl. You couldn't save them."

"How did you know I'd save you?"

"I didn't exactly, but I knew I wasn't going to die. I was pretty sure something major was about to happen, something I needed to see. It's what took me there in the first place. But I was sure I'd be okay."

"Did you know *I'd* be okay?"

"We better double-check the footage for clues." Karin sidestepped the question.

I grimaced at the meaning.

We ran the video back at normal speed, then half speed, and finally frame-by-frame, examining every part.

We cross-checked against the newsfeeds. They were reporting the incident as an accident. Faulty wiring in a server room.

Was that the best they could do? When does a server room use enough power to rip up a building! We ignored the official reports; it was an obvious attempt to whitewash the event.

I didn't know what to look for. There was no mastermind in a black trench cloak. No suspicious flash showing a fired rocket. It was a lot of people going about their business, not knowing a terrible disaster was about to befall them. They'd been talking, pointing at the exhibition, or like I'd been, taking pictures and videos with their AROs.

"Wait a minute," I said, rewinding the video to the earliest point, when the image had been at its widest.

"What?" Karin stopped checking holovids and joined me at the monitor.

"I, er ... I don't know how important this is, but do you notice anything in common about the people in this picture?"

Karin leaned close to the screen, tangles of pink hair brushing my face. They smelled faintly of soap – amazing; seven hours ago we'd been walking through a sewer. She scanned the forty or so people in frame. "No, not really."

"Look again." I pointed to the woman closest, my finger hovering over her ARO.

After a few moments, Karin replied. "Huh, I think I see. A lot of people have a certain ARO right? They all have a green-yellow hue."

"Yeah, but it's not the device that's the same – the networks control the colour. Each of the Telcoms has custom external lighting to brand them. You can change it if you dig deep enough in the settings, but almost no one bothers." I pointed to my own Saracen – even I hadn't bothered adjusting the crimson glow Redwave used.

"Oh, right." Karin twigged. "That's Limelight's branding. I recognise it now. But why's that unusual? Limelight's pretty popular, isn't it?"

"Sure, but it's not *that* popular; it's too expensive. The only time you see that many is for family or corporate plans. This is weird."

"Do you think they all work for the same company?"

"They could do, I suppose, but look ..." I pointed at the clusters of people on screen. "Do these guys seem like they know each other?"

We stared at the display. The groups weren't acknowledging each other. They were getting on with their business. Elderly couples, professionals, even a few freakers loitering. All different, but all with Limelight connected AROs.

"You see – they're from all walks of life."

"Yeah, okay, I buy that, but so what?" Karin leaned back, snapping her ARO against her shoulder – its green light pulsing against the bracket.

"Whoa! Karin, I forgot you're connected to Limelight!"

A confused frown appeared at the urgency in my voice. "Oh, yeah, it's way better than my last provider."

"Quick, let me see your ARO."

"Why?"

"Just hand it over!"

Delicately, almost reverently, Karin disengaged the magnetic release and peeled it off, handing it to me gingerly. "Careful, I like that thing a lot."

I looked through the interface, searching for something specific, breathing a sigh when I found it.

"What?"

I turned the display to show her. The connection quality said *Non-Quantum*.

"What does that mean?"

"It means we're damn lucky. Limelight doesn't have a broadcast mast up around here. You've automatically switched to a conventional connection."

"So?"

"Think, Karin. If Limelight's involved, how do you think they've been tracking us?"

"Oh, shit!" Karin's eyes widened in realisation. "Turn it off!"

"I've already disabled it, and as I said, we're lucky – there's no direct signal around here, but ..."

"But what?"

"We travelled a long way to get here, and Limelight's signal penetrates the Underground. Even if we've lucked out in a dead zone, if they wanted to find us, they'd know our general direction."

My hands felt clammy, and looking at Karin, I could see she shared my anxiety.

"So they're following us?"

I nodded. "I think they could be. What about you? Any signals."

"No, they go dark when there's lots of randomness – like at your extraplex. Remember when I couldn't guide us? That was because there were too many outcomes."

"That's not very helpful."

"Actually, it is. The messages I receive are vague – directional rather than explicit. There's huge room for error if I do something wrong. If the margins are too slim, they shut off. It's better I don't receive messages at times like that."

"So you don't second guess yourself in a crisis?"

"Exactly."

I was beginning to wonder what good we were to each other. One of us couldn't control their ability and the other was horribly inconsistent. We'd been fortunate so far, but I wasn't sure that would hold if the pressure piled on again.

As if the idea of a crisis willed it into existence, a kerfuffle broke out inside the club. I froze, eyes glued to the door. In the distance, we could hear Emmett protesting. "LOOK, no one's HERE. Please stop disrupting things. I NEED to open the bar!"

He was being unnecessarily loud. He was warning us.

"Shit." My heart rate jumped. "What the hell are we going to do?"

"They don't know we're here, do they?"

"Probably not. They don't have a mast; they must be searching the whole area."

Karin leapt into action, tugging at the sofa. "Quickly, help me move this."

I joined her, pulling the heavy two-seater away from the wall. To my surprise, it moved easily, sliding on greased rails, and revealing a metal hatch beneath. I could make out *Service Tunnel* embossed on the rusty surface beneath.

"Future messages?"

"No." Karin hushed. "Hurry!"

I helped Karin pull up the hatch. Outside, we could hear boots thumping on the club's dance floor, reverberating into the office like a war drum. We jumped in, lowering the hatch, encasing us in a dark, musty crawl space.

"What about the sofa?" I whispered.

"Help me." Karin groped around on the floor, finding a rope end. It extended up through the top of the hatch.

I grabbed it and we heaved together, hearing the sofa slide above. Just as the rope ran out of slack, the door burst open to a familiar blast of radio chatter.

"No one here," came the distorted voice.

I covered my mouth, afraid my breathing might give us away.

The guard rummaged around.

I could hear things being tipped over and smashed. There was no need; the room was tiny – he was frustrated. How many clubs had they searched so far?

He left the room grumbling.

"What now?" I looked at Karin. She was centimetres away but I could only see the outline of her face. "We can't go back through the bar; they'll be swarming the area by now."

"Follow me." Karin switched her ARO light on, blinding me.

"Sorry." She pointed the light further into the hole we were crouched in.

The stars cleared. I could see a low tunnel beyond, leading away.

Tunnel was optimistic. Large pipe would be more descriptive; it was half a metre in diameter. Karin went down on her hands and knees, shimmying forward. With no choice but to follow, I did the same, flat on my stomach as I squeezed through the narrow space. The pitch blackness and closeness was suffocating. I bit back my fear, trying to remember how much worse getting caught by the Neo-Guards would be.

Mercifully, after twenty metres of crawling, the tunnel widened. We emerged in a chamber with grates in the ceiling, casting slats of light across the floor and curved walls. Underfoot was thick with dust and rubbish, but also the rusted remains of an old track. Overhead, footsteps of pedestrians intermittently broke the light.

I stood and brushed myself down. "What was that about?"

Karin answered as she forged ahead. "The subterranean clubs in Farringdon are built into old train tunnels. They were abandoned when the station was reconstructed – after the investment banks moved in. The tracks had service and maintenance access. Most were blocked up, or converted into storage areas for the nightclubs, but some were left open."

"What's with the secrecy of this one?"

"You have to ask? You've seen Emmett. He's not exactly the toughest guy. Places around here get shaken down by freaker gangs all the time, not to mention violent alcoholics and spun-up losers. It's dangerous. This is Emmett's emergency exit."

"Well, you and your friends are full of surprises." I sputtered, dust catching in my throat. I tried not to think about the nasties dropped down here over the years.

We arrived at a ladder and started climbing.

"Yeah, but I think I'm out of surprises." Karin called down between rungs. "We've exhausted my bolt holes and I've been in a dark zone for a while now. I don't suppose *you've* got any ideas?"

We emerged into an alley a good distance from Emmett's club, walking in the opposite direction, heads down, trying not to draw attention. Karin's inference was annoying but clear: *Pull your weight, Daryl, I can't do this on my own.* She was right, but I wasn't flush with ideas.

Thinking it through, I came to the sad conclusion there was only one person who might help, and he'd be even less happy to see us than Emmett had been.

Sighing, I changed direction.

"Where are we going?" Karin sounded surprised; shocked I did, in fact, have an idea.

"Clapham," I answered, hoping Jay was in the mood to accept visitors.

STATE 11

With Karin's Limelight connection severed, I was confident we could travel without being tracked. Freakers wrecked CCTVs cameras faster than authorities could repair them. Unless we were unlucky, we should have a clear route, but that wasn't particularly comforting and did little to answer why we were being tracked at all. What did Limelight have to do with all this? Was it the corporation themselves or someone using their network? Why would they care about us? – Too many questions.

Sat across from me on the train, Karin was fidgety, squirming in her seat. Without her data plan, she was suffering from *disconnection disease* – the d-d's. Everyone got it from time to time. I'd almost come down with it in Camden when my signal had gone shaky, but Karin was deeper in the digital economy than me. Her online presence more important than her real one. I took pity and set up my ARO as a mobile hotspot. For once, I was glad to be on the inferior Redwave service.

Karin's network bars reappeared, her sigh audible over the noise of the train. Her shoulders relaxed and body slumped as she began furiously checking her messages. I recognised the signs. An addict getting their fix. We weren't all that different after all.

I'd had a nagging concern they'd find us by snooping our online accounts, but going offline completely may alert more systems than acting normally.

Karin was using a third party app to encrypt her data – a good one – I'd checked. All information in her social networks (email, messages, anything that accepted data), was scrambled, and she'd set decryption keys that were updated to her followers hourly. Anyone wanting to hack her accounts would need to break three-step authentication. And even if they did, they'd only see an hour's worth of updates before decryption keys were revoked. Exploits were possible, but they were quickly exposed, at which point everyone just cycled to a different provider.

It was worrying how Limelight's tracking loophole had slipped the net, but there was so much bandwidth in a quantum connection; perhaps it wasn't hard to hide malicious code.

I thought about updating my small number of followers, but apart from encrypting the group and refreshing the keys, I couldn't see the point. It wasn't my vice of choice, and without Sebastian, there wasn't anyone I cared enough about to check in with. Outside of Karin, there was only one person I had any real-world connection with, and we were on our way to see him.

The carriage pulled into Clapham South. We alighted and walked towards Jay's block of flats. The fact Clapham wasn't as run down as the rest of Neo-London made me nervous. I scanned the street lamps and roof tops for cameras. None were moving or glowing, but that didn't mean they weren't on. I hoped the freakers were as efficient here as everywhere else in the city.

I hit the button to call up to Jay's domicile. It was evening, so he should be home from the Vault, likely plugged in by now.

There was a delay, then a muffled response with a fake Chinese accent. "Yars? Halooo. What you want, pweese?"

"Jay's paranoid." I addressed Karin's popped eyebrows. "He doesn't like people knowing he's in. He thinks there's a plot to track worker efficiency by how much time they spend at home. He believes it will downgrade his credit rating."

"A conspiracy theorist?"

"Yeah, well ..." I began sheepishly, then thinking on it, continued more firmly. "You know, I don't think we're any position to judge right now." I hit the comm button again. "It's me, dipshit. Open up."

"You come in!" the ridiculous voice chimed, and the door buzzed open.

We made our way up to his domicile.

I could hear him clearing his throat for another barrage of racist Chinese, but as his moronic face appeared behind the door, it became red and whatever joke he'd concocted lodged in his throat, causing him to sputter.

"Why the hell you bring the agent here!"

"She's not an agent, Jay." I placated, suppressing my annoyance. "She's a friend, and we could really do with a place to crash for a few hours."

Jay looked us up and down.

In the last couple of days, we'd escaped an explosion, scaled the outside of an extraplex, tramped through a sewer, and crawled down an abandoned tube tunnel. We looked a sorry mess. We hadn't washed in days; sewer muck caked our legs and we'd picked up an impressive collection of bruises and scrapes. On top of that we were haggard from lack of sleep. Karin was managing to look alert, but for my part, my face was only just hanging onto my skull.

Jay's eyes softened. "Yeah okay, pal." And then to Karin. "But I'm watching you."

He tried to make it sound like a joke, but I could hear under the surface he was deadly serious. Any normal day I'd have told him not to be paranoid, but with things the way they were, I was beginning to agree with him.

We made our way indoors. Thankfully, the place was relatively tidy. I was glad I could show Karin at least one place that wasn't a complete tip. Jay was dressed in '90s style Bermuda shorts and a vest. There was an indentation in his hair and a subtle oval around his eyes where his VR mask had been resting.

To his credit, once we were inside, Jay switched admirably to host. His paranoia lent itself to mild agoraphobia, but that made him appreciative of guests. He got us drinks, snacks, and even let us use his shower. He lent me some clothes and by some miracle had stuff Karin could wear. Items from a departed girlfriend sick of playing second fiddle to the VR rig.

Eventually, we all sat down in the living room. Karin on the sofa, me on an armchair. Jay sprawled himself messily across a beanbag, a quizzical look on his face.

"So you gonna tell me what's going on, Daryl, or do we need to lock the agent in the toilet first?"

Karin grimaced but didn't respond.

I struggled with where to start. I didn't want to tell Jay about our time abilities. Not that he wouldn't believe us – quite the opposite; I suspected he would, and that would open up a can of worms. Still, he was owed an explanation, otherwise he'd turf us out in the morning – we needed more time than that. I had to give him something he could latch on to, something that would interest him. Sebastian had said the best lies contained truth. If you could weave in enough real facts, it would make any lie sound real. I had an idea.

I put on a serious tone and addressed Jay squarely. "No need to put her in the toilet, Jay. Karin's not a government agent ... but she *used* to be one."

Jay's eyes widened, then narrowed as he looked across to where Karin had sat down, sandwiched between piles of VR equipment.

"You were right, Jay, she works for the Telcoms, or did. Limelight to be specific, but she found out they're using their network to spy on people. She came to the Vault as it's one of the few independents left. She asked me to meet her so I could disconnect her without them noticing so she could escape. But then the Neo-Guards showed up and chased us. They think I'm involved because I helped her."

Jay closed his eyes and rubbed his hair, pushing out where it had become flattened. There was a significant amount of truth in that story, but it still sounded crazy. Finally he looked at me, returning my serious tone. "I told you pink hair meant she was working for the government."

"That's right," Karin chimed in. She must know this one. "It's a chemical agent. I have to dye out the white."

It was working. Jay was enthralled, and with the groundwork in place, Karin worked the plot brilliantly. She talked about her imaginary role in the networks and how they were cooperating with the Administration to monitor people. She explained that at first she thought it was the right thing to do – helping to keep people safe – but then she noticed abuses. Flagrant violations of civil liberties and personal data. She couldn't be part of it anymore so was trying to get away. Once Limelight couldn't track her, she'd board a sub-jet to stay with relatives in France. It was a fantastic performance, peppered with extra details, like where she'd been employed and the names of people she'd worked with. I suspected those details were from her investigations, hiding the lie with facts, like I'd been. And she was undoubtedly using her premonitions to guide her. No matter how she was achieving it, Karin was an accomplished fibber.

Jay sat and listened, nodding knowingly. He even appeared sympathetic. I couldn't believe he was buying this. It didn't matter how much was couched in truth, it was still a ridiculous story.

When Karin had finished, Jay leaned back and stared at the ceiling, rubbing his temples with index and ring fingers, feet tapping excitedly. I'd never seen him like this; he was anxious, focussed – very unlike Jay. He stayed that way for a full minute, tension filling the room. I was beginning to worry he hadn't been pulled in when he looked down from the ceiling and addressed us. "I think I can help, but it will take some time."

"Whoa, hold on, Jay." This was working too well. "What are you talking about? You can't tell anyone we're here."

"I know that, you arse." Jay straightened up, offended I'd even suggested it. "But there's someone I think can help. I just need to do some research first."

"Who?" Karin sounded rightfully suspicious.

Jay tapped his nose. "I'm not saying yet. I buy your story, but I still don't trust you."

"What about me?" Jay's serious turn startled me; it wasn't in his nature.

"You could be under her influence, pal, but put it this way, if I didn't trust you, would I be letting you stay?"

"So you *are* letting us stay?" Karin asked.

Jay scrambled up from the beanbag. It was meant to be assertive but ended up a comedic crab dance of white limbs and Bermuda shorts. We both suppressed the urge to laugh as he finally stood, face flushed with mild embarrassment. "Er, yeah, you can stay."

I snuck a glance at Karin; she looked relieved but not surprised. Had she known this outcome all along?

"You okay to sleep in here?" Jay attempted to regain some gravitas.

"Best place we've been in days." Karin looked around appreciatively.

That was true. We'd been in some horrible places recently. Karin probably counted my domicile among them.

"Cool. I've got some work to do on my terminal. I'll let you know tomorrow."

He hurried out of the room. It was the most enthusiastic I'd seen him. I suppose most conspiracy theorists never get close to uncovering a real plot. This was like Christmas and birthday all rolled into one for Jay.

It was late in the evening and the fatigue of the day was palpable, but I wasn't sleepy yet. I had questions that were keeping my mind from going quiet. One thing in particular had been bugging me. What was Karin's motivation? She'd never explained herself.

"Karin?"

"Ask away," she answered, too quickly.

"Clairvoyance or intuition?"

"A bit of both."

"So you know what I'm going to ask?"

"I've got an idea, but I'd still rather you ask it."

"Why are you wrapped up in this? I know why I am. My brother's brain dead in a shit-hole asylum, but you don't seem to have a reason for getting in this deep."

"In other words, when I got my abilities, I could have carried on as normal. Not bothered with any of this."

"Yes, exactly. I don't get it."

She took a moment to reply, a forlorn shadow passing across her – a contrast to the assertiveness that had been dominant up to now. I hoped I hadn't messed up by asking something so personal.

"It's hard to explain, but I do owe you a reason."

Karin pulled up her legs and curled them in front of her on the chair, head resting on her knees. A complete change of mood. It was the first time I'd seen her remotely vulnerable.

She took a few breaths then spoke through closed eyes. "It's complicated, Daryl. Ever since I had the accident on the sub-jet, my life's not my own. It's hers."

"Who's?"

"Future Karin's. I live in the pre-state of her life. That's what my premonitions are, a pre-state for Future Karin. It's like I don't exist."

It was a deeper answer than I'd been expecting and harder to parse. She was acting like a prisoner. "So, you want to be free of her?"

She hugged her legs tighter. "No. She *is* me, I can't be any more free of her than you could be from your past self. The difference is you're not beholden to your past. Your past is subservient to the present, like it should be. It's not like that with me. I'm a slave to things that will happen in her future. I'm a slave to her." Her voice wobbled, as if stuck in the back of her throat. "I'm compelled to do as she wishes, compelled to follow the path she's laid out for me."

Lulled by her soft speaking, I leaned forward, elbows on knees. "You need to do as she says?"

"Oh no, I can ignore what she tells me, but it doesn't go well, and she lets me know it." She searched for the words, trying to explain. "Imagine how demoralising it would be to make a decision only to be bombarded by negative thoughts you can't shut out. It's ..." The ball that was Karin became tighter, the start of a tear visible. "... easier to do as she tells me."

I felt bad for the line of questioning; it was painful for her, but I couldn't stop – it was too important. "And you don't know why she's put you on this path?"

"No." She forced herself out of the curl, blinking away the tear that had never formed. "But she's me, so I have to trust her. I can't believe I would intentionally mislead myself. I must have faith there's a reason for all this."

"I understand," I said, even though I didn't. I ignored my inner voice all the time. It was easy. You pushed the nagging conscience to the back of your head.

Another thought arose – something she'd mentioned at my domicile. "You said before you didn't need to send messages back to yourself. I don't get it; that doesn't make sense."

Karin was sitting straighter, the moment of vulnerability over as quickly as it begun. She was as tough as nails, in control of her emotions – like Sebastian before his accident. My respect for her dialled up another notch.

"Yes, it's strange." The wobble in her voice was gone, swallowed back. "I don't know the precise reason. It's definitely true though. I realised it the first time I passed a point where I should have sent a message. Even if I'd wanted to, I didn't know how, and things continued as normal. The cause and effect of the messages are divorced somehow. I have theories but no way to prove anything." She leaned back in the seat and crossed her legs as she picked her words. "I think it's connected to the nature of my abilities, and yours too probably."

I waited for her to collect her thoughts; I was interested in this. The similarities between Karin and me were undeniable. If I understood more about what she could do, it might reveal what was happening to me.

"I don't think I need to send messages because, well ... somebody else does." Reading my frown correctly as pure confusion, she elaborated. "I know, it's tough to grasp. After I realised the cause and effect of my messages weren't linear, I started reading about time phenomena. It took me down a rabbit hole I don't fully understand – quantum mechanics, theoretical physics. Things only eggheads get. I'm no expert, but my assumption is it's something to do with multiple dimensions."

I knew something about this; it was how quantum computing worked. "Right, you mean multiverse theory. Parallel universes to this one, where different outcomes play out."

"Ah, an egghead!"

I ignored her. This made sense for once. "I think I understand. It's the same principle used in quantum computing. The CPU outsources computations across multiple dimensions to get to an answer exponentially faster. Your theory is you're not sending messages to yourself because a Karin from a closely related parallel universe is doing it for you?"

Karin stuck out her bottom lip. "Seems you know this bit."

"I know about quantum computers. It's how Limelight processes data across its network, although they also use *quantum entanglement* ..." I could see it was Karin's turn to be confused. "Don't worry." I brushed it aside. "All you need to know is it's the reason Limelight's network is so fast. It uses principles of quantum mechanics to transmit data insanely fast."

She shook her head. "Wow, Daryl, I'm impressed. Anyway, multiverse theory may explain your abilities too."

"How so?" I couldn't see the connection.

Karin got up and walked to an old wall clock Jay had acquired. An '80s inspired waving cat. She pointed to its face to illustrate her point. "It appears like you can stop time, but that's not possible because what time are you stopping? I can't imagine all time in the universe freezes on your command; that doesn't seem plausible. And it can't be a local phenomenon either, otherwise time wouldn't sync up outside of the area after you recommence it. I have a hunch though – look at your watch."

I glanced down at my Casio and compared it to the wall clock. It was running ten minutes fast.

"Yours is fast right? That's because time runs normally for you when you freeze it."

I couldn't refute her. If I added up all the frozen time, it must account for about ten minutes. "So what do you think is happening?"

She scratched her head and walked back to the sofa. "I haven't thought it through, but if my abilities link to multiple dimensions, it would make sense yours do too. Maybe you're not stopping time per se but entering a parallel dimension. One where time has paused or, more likely, is running imperceptibly slowly – I can't imagine many universes where there is no time at all."

This was confusing, but I could see where she was going. "So when I exit, I'm moving into a new universe that matches up with the changes I've made?"

"That's how multiverse theory works. Nothing's impossible, just improbable. Your power is to enter and exit dimensions that match the alterations you've made. Perhaps the act of stopping time creates the new dimension. I don't know; it's all above my pay grade, but it makes sense, don't you think?"

"So I enter a latent dimension, a place where time runs so slowly I can manipulate it to create a new one. Some sort of ... What did you call your premonitions?"

"Pre-state."

"Yes, right. So I enter and exit some sort of ... *latent state*?"

"If that's what you want to call it."

This was blowing my mind, but it made a strange sense. My brain hurt. I needed time to assimilate all the new information.

"Is that enough question time?" Karin yawned.

I looked at my watch. Yeah, it was definitely a few minutes ahead. I'd have to get used to setting it back. I wondered if I entered latent state enough times I'd age quicker than everyone. Probably not worth worrying about.

"Yeah, I think so." I returned the yawn.

Karin had already curled herself back into a ball. This time from fatigue.

I followed suit, closing my eyes. We'd made some progress tonight. My mind wasn't still; it was buzzing, in fact, but it wasn't chaotic. For once I felt there may be answers in there – latent information, below the grey matter, ready to surface.

STATE 12

Sleep pushed exhaustion back enough to keep me functioning, but not enough to refresh me, and my hands were shaking again; the persistent stress was dredging up withdrawal symptoms, and with them, the itching urge to use.

Groggily, I pushed myself towards the edge of the sofa and rubbed them together, willing the jitter to stop. After a few moments, it seemed to abate – enough to hide from onlookers. Or at least, I hoped it did.

My conversation with Karin hadn't helped. Manipulating dimensions to slow time; Karin connected to a parallel version of herself. It was all so ridiculous, but the evidence was impossible to ignore. It made my head hurt when I thought about it, like an idiot trying to solve a problem too hard for him.

I longed for the delirium of SP1N, to shut out the nightmare that had become my reality, even for a small while. Grinding my teeth, I suppressed the thought. If I slipped backwards, it would be for nothing. Sebastian would rot in the asylum and I'd be chasing answers forever. I breathed in and out to reset myself, trying to find enough resolve to start the day.

Karin was still sleeping, slightly curled. She seemed peaceful. I wondered what clairvoyants dreamt about. Did Future Karin pass her premonitions while she was unconscious? Fragments of the future surfacing later as déjà vu. I'd have to ask her sometime.

I'd been thinking about Karin a lot. I hadn't processed all the strange information about her, but as a person, she was special – confident, purposeful, but also vulnerable. We're all haunted by demons. Mine the conventional kind, hers more abstract but just as debilitating

– an inescapable destiny laid out by her future self. Knowing we may not be that different inspired a renewed sense of camaraderie in me.

I'd been fighting the initial attraction, but I could sense those feelings intensifying. Would she be so liberal if she knew the whole truth about me though?

"You're staring at me," Karin whispered.

I snapped back to reality. Karin had woken while I'd be gazing at her, thoughts turned inwards. Feeling my ears burn, I scrambled to explain myself. "Um, sorry, I just woke up myself. I was lost in thought."

"Oh good, I must look a mess." She sat up and stretched.

She looked fine. Her clothes were dishevelled, and the shaved side of her hair had grown out – it needed shearing down again. But there were no bags under her eyes, and her skin was clear. Remarkable in Neo-London's polluted climate, not to mention the days spent crawling through sewers and escape tunnels.

She smoothed down her clothes, sat upright, and addressed me more formally. "So here we are again, Daryl, another hiding place, clueless what to do next. How long can we keep this up?" She kept talking as she yawned, the words coming out elongated. "We can't keep fleeing ... from one bolt hole to another. We have to find ... a next step."

She was right; this was the end of the road. If we couldn't make a plan, we were screwed – probably dead.

"Is that paranoid friend of yours going to help us?"

I scratched my head and shrugged. "Jay's a good guy. A bit mental but I can't see any better options."

"Who's mental?" Jay interjected, making an appearance at the door.

"Oh." I covered. "... This ... situation. It's mental isn't it?"

Jay strode into the room, picking his way over discarded pieces of VR equipment. "That's because you never saw the signs," he said, oblivious to the misdirection. "But your pal Jay did, and better than that, he's figured out how to help."

"Uh-huh." I wasn't buying the machismo. "For the record, Jay, it's weird when you talk about yourself in the third person like that." He was still dressed in the vest and Bermuda shorts from last night, clasping a battered laptop. "Have you been up all night?"

"Yep, most fun I've had in ages."

"Fun?" Karin proclaimed. She'd retaken a seat, upright and alert, listening. "I thought you were going to help us? What have you been doing?"

Jay's eyes narrowed as he considered whether to say anything in front of her and then shrugged. "What the hell. Daryl will tell you anyway, so I may as well spill it now."

He cleared some space on the coffee table and set down the laptop. More of a dumb terminal for his ARO, but it was easier to work with – fashioned with a bigger screen and a keyboard. He brought up what he'd been looking at – an internet forum.

Curious, I reached over to scroll down the page using the touch-screen. As I did, my hand, starkly illuminated by the light from the display, shook involuntarily. I pulled it away, but the damage was done and Jay was speaking before I could make excuses.

"Wow, you got the shakes bad, huh? I thought you were off SP1N?"

My heart sank. There went my credibility with Karin. I couldn't look her in the eye, but the slump in her body said it all. I'd disappointed her. She must have suspected – her premonitions giving her a notion of my past, but by her own admission, they were often vague. I'd hoped it had slipped her attention. That was a pipe dream now.

"Anyway, forget that. This is more important." Jay powered on, unaware the effect his words were having. He pointed to a section of the screen. His hand was trembling too, but from excitement. "Look at that message ... Right there."

Still lamenting the revelation, I balled my hand into a fist to stop it shaking and stared at the screen where he was pointing. The forum looked niche – simple text and ASCII art. This didn't exist on the mainstream internet – Jay was tapped into the *dark web*, part of the *deep web*. The hidden part of the internet. Unindexed by search engines, obscured through peer-to-peer connections, and routed through intermediary servers. It was untraceable, and unsurprisingly, it was popular with criminals, drug addicts, and conspiracy theorists. They all logged on to communicate without being monitored. Given Jay's interests, I wasn't shocked he'd procured the software to access it (illegal since the late 2010s), but known users of the dark web were prosecuted harshly. He was deeper into this stuff than I'd given him credit for.

The URL read SCAM.NET. Most of the messages were nonsense – paranoid chatter – but the note Jay was pointing out was clear and succinct. Someone calling themselves *Maximal* had posted it. It read: *Meet me*. Two words in plain ASCII text. Hardly a revelation.

"What the hell does that mean?" I said heatedly, still reeling from my outing in front of Karin.

Jay became agitated, mistaking my frustration for confusion. "What does it mean? It means everything! That's Maximal."

"And who, exactly, is Maximal?" Karin asked, pulling us back from the screen, trying to soothe the tension. We turned to look at her; she was conciliatory but I could sense a disquiet. What was she thinking? She may have dispassionately absorbed the new knowledge about me or completely re-evaluated if I could be relied on. I'd have to explain later, make her see I'd been trying to change.

Jay shook his head, replying dismissively, oblivious to the subtext. "Honestly, it's no wonder you two are in trouble." He returned his attention to the screen, accessing various saved articles and video content.

Breathing out to re-centre myself, I leaned forward to read what Jay pulled up, Karin's presence behind me uncomfortable.

Maximal was a hacker responsible for some huge scandals. Some of the largest corporate takedowns could be traced to him. It wasn't run-of-the-mill espionage. Most cyber-criminal's motivations were nefarious – blackmail for money and tech, or disingenuous altruism: claiming to "fight the system". In both cases, they hurt ordinary people, either through denial of services or by revealing personal information – leading to social engineering and fraud. Maximal reserved his hacks for endeavours that damaged corporations.

The articles revealed a narrative of exposing illegal practices, uncovering accounting scams, and publishing abuses of data. This was modus operandi for hackers, but Maximal did it covertly, minimising the impact on the public. Keeping the stories out of the media unless the corporations didn't capitulate. That took a lot more skill than a simple database hack. It meant companies had to clean up their acts – temporarily at least.

Now Jay had retrieved the details, I did recall hearing about a mythical super-hacker – the bane of the corporate world. I'd dismissed it as an urban legend, but clearly Jay had taken it seriously. I was beginning to see how a person like that might be able to help. If they existed and it wasn't an elaborate hoax.

"I see." I stood and backed up a pace, bumping into Karin. I'd become so absorbed, I'd briefly forgotten she was there. "Sorry," I said sheepishly, hoping she realised it meant more than just for knocking into her.

"Don't worry, it's all good." She smiled. It looked forced.

"Damn straight," Jay replied triumphantly, again misinterpreting the exchange.

"And you know this person?" Karin leaned over to inspect the screen. "They seem very, er ... skilled at keeping themselves hidden."

"Know them! Are you joking?" Jay's eyes were wide and wild. "No one *knows* Maximal! He's completely off the grid, untraceable. The only evidence he exists is forums like this – strictly on the dark web to avoid being traced. He's a ghost."

I could hear the admiration. Jay held Maximal and his antics in high regard. "Okay." I followed along. "So what did you tell him about us to prompt this response?"

A smug grin flashed across his face. "That was the hard bit. Took all night," he replied, proud of himself.

Karin and I stared blankly. He groaned and rolled his eyes. "I couldn't just lay down the details, you know. The dark web is untraceable back to the user, but anyone with a ToR browser can read the messages. If I'd said too much, I could have given something away. I had to be careful, you see."

Jay was trying to impress us with how tough it had been. Humility would help here, but the lack of sleep was making it hard.

"Okay, pal, I get it, so how did you manage it?" My words landed somewhere between enthralled and patronising.

Jay furrowed his brow but continued. Good enough. "I did some digging. There's been a flurry of Neo-Guard activity with alerts out for you across the city."

He accessed the relevant news feeds, including, to our horror, a CCTV shot of us at Farringdon Station. The picture was low and there was a grid over the image. The camera must have been hidden behind a storefront shutter where freakers couldn't smash it.

It was taken with ancient tech, the image black-and-white, grainy, and shot from a distance. I didn't think a casual observer could pick us out. The headline across the top read: *Wanted for questioning*. Shit. I guessed that was inevitable, but it was still a shock to see our photos plastered up on the internet. At least they hadn't tracked us any further than Farringdon.

"Anyway." Jay brought our attention back to the internet forum. "I started a thread about you. Innocent enough. Topics like that are mentioned all the time."

We looked at the responses – the other theorists chiming in – some saying we were basic criminals, others shouting their support to *fight the system*, and there was plenty of gibberish too.

"You see, I waited until someone started a corporate angle ..." He pointed to the screen. Someone with the handle C0nspiraG0d had replied: *I bet they pissed off the banks, they're all controlled by the Administration.* "To which I replied," *No, more likely the Telcoms. Limelight's onto them.*

That had started a flurry of activity, lots of theories – all wrong. Jay paused for dramatic effect. "So, do you see?"

"No," Karin and I replied in unison.

"Come on, guys, keep up!" Jay was standing bolt upright, arms gesticulating. Trying to make us see. "I started a chain of information with enough breadcrumbs that Maximal would take notice."

"Alright," I said, putting a hand on Jay's shoulder, trying to stop him hopping from one foot to another. "But how would Maximal know any of this was true? You've barely said anything."

He pushed my hand off, voice becoming even more excited. "That's the whole point! Maximal will already know you two are connected to Limelight. He keeps track of stuff like that. He has algorithms scrubbing the internet for leads. The fact I originated the post and mentioned Limelight would have been enough to flag the forum and notify him. But it doesn't matter; we don't need to understand how he does it, just that he does, because it's worked."

"Hold on." Karin stepped between us, concerned. "Won't that tip off the Neo-Guards as well?"

Her interjection was welcome. It made Jay finally put his hands down and take a breath.

"No." He addressed her more calmly, aware at last he'd been shouting at us. "It's why I didn't put all the information in one post. I waited until there was an opening to mention Limelight. Besides, I doubt they're switched on enough to monitor the dark web. And even if they are, they won't be able to track where the post came from, so they'll learn nothing new."

I looked at the screen where the enigmatic Maximal, or someone claiming to be them, had reached out from across the void. "And how do you know that's actually him and not some random conspiracy nut?"

Jay blew air through his lips. "There's no way to be a hundred per cent sure, but that's definitely his current handle. I confirmed by comparing to verified sources."

I retired the line of questioning. Jay had done his homework. He was as close to an expert in this as we could hope for. But still, the message was vague.

"Okay, but what now?" I prompted. "He says to meet us, but where?"

"Oh." Jay scratched his head, confidence evaporating. "That's more difficult. He doesn't say, and he didn't reply to any more messages."

Of course. There had to be a catch. We stood in awkward silence.

Karin snapped her fingers making us jump. "Oh, I get it!"

We both looked at her.

"Come on," she proclaimed. "He expects us to find him on our own, which must mean it's easy to work out."

We stared at her, unblinking.

It was Karin's time to roll her eyes. "Jay, pull up those articles again. What's the most recent entry?"

Jay's fingers moved on the keyboard as he brought up the news feed again. The top headline read: *International bank spies on customers, secret documents revealed.*

"Right, good, and where was that reported."

"Er." Jay scanned the article. "Doesn't say."

"Alright. What about the bank then? Where is it located?"

"Hold on a second." Jay cross-referenced the name of the bank. "It's a Chinese financial conglomerate, headquartered in HK1 ... New Hong Kong." The statement hung in the air for a moment.

"HK1?" I tilted my head towards Karin, who was wearing a crafty half smile. "That's not exactly nearby." That was an understatement – it was on the other side of the globe! "Even if we had the creds for sub-jet passage, Neo-Guards will be watching the port."

Karin gave me a conspiratorial wink. "I'm sure we'll find a way, Daryl."

This was making me nervous. Was Karin proposing something this mental? At least she still wanted my help. My drug issue hadn't turned her off completely, not yet anyway.

"Okay ..." I swivelled back to Jay, who was looking bemused. "Let's say we find our way to HK1. How would we contact Maximal when we got there?"

"Oh, don't worry about that. You won't need to find Maximal; he'll find you."

"Right." The speed this was progressing was overwhelming. "So let me recap. We're going to get through sub-jet security without the Neo-Guards noticing. Travel to HK1 based on no more information than two words in a dark web conspiracy forum. And when we get there, we're going to be found by a mysterious hacker we're not even certain exists."

"Yes," Karin and Jay replied together.

Great. Just great.

STATE 13

J ay, conspiracy theorist extraordinaire and general layabout, continued to surprise us over the days we stayed with him. He kept us fed and clothed – items he'd sneak out to collect and pay for himself (with no hint of requiring the creds back). And he'd surfaced some genuinely helpful suggestions.

Most importantly, he'd connected us with Maximal, who for all our research, did appear to be the vigilante hacker I'd heard about. And with a newly opened mind, cracked wide by recent experiences, I was on board with Jay's wilder notions. His theory the Administration was a puppet of the Telcoms was no longer far-fetched – his paranoia seemed reasonable, practically justified. If anything, I was the naïve one; a bitter pill to swallow, but I'd choked it down nonetheless.

Jay's generosity hadn't ended there. He'd been the consummate host – foregoing his VR rig (we'd taken over his living room).

Going cold turkey should have been a problem, but it wasn't. He was excited – energised. He'd waited his entire life for something like this; he was totally willing to accept the dangers in exchange for being right.

In the end, his enthusiasm became a problem. His shaggy, doe-eyed face appearing any time we were discussing travel plans, begging us to come along. I understood; he wanted to meet Maximal – he was his idol.

I was stumped for how to dissuade him. Our edge for getting to HK1 was our time abilities. He wouldn't last five minutes, but I couldn't say so without revealing the whole truth.

Karin had come to the rescue by tapping into his paranoia. "Jay, being near us puts you on the grid – right in the spotlight of Administration agents." That had given him pause. Long enough to add. "You'll be more helpful to us here – monitoring internet traffic. You don't want to miss it if Maximal makes contact again, do you?"

Begrudgingly, he'd relinquished. I didn't want to disappoint him, but it was a relief knowing he'd be safe. Sebastian was the only person I'd been close to, but the way Jay had taken us in made me question why I kept people at arm's length. It was a strange, but not unwelcome, feeling.

With the crisis resolved, Jay had retreated to his bedroom to surf the dark web, and with space to talk, Karin had revealed her plan to defeat sub-jet security.

I was dismayed. It hinged on me freezing time on demand – something I'd never done before. I wasn't even sure it was possible. She'd assumed I could, and I'd struggled to tell her otherwise. It was a powder keg waiting to explode – which of course it did, prompted by the elephant in the room we still hadn't discussed.

We were hunkered around a projected image showing aerial photos of the port and surrounding area. Karin was explaining the lay of the land. Without warning, my hand twitched where it lay on the sideboard. Karin sighed and addressed me bluntly. "Daryl, you have to stop using drugs."

I pulled my hand away and hid it behind my back. I knew this had been coming, ever since I'd been outed, but I was shocked how candidly she'd stated it. My teeth set in my jaw, a centroid of annoyance and shame.

I was immediately defensive. I couldn't help it. Having it pointed out so directly stung. "Back off, Karin! I'm sure where you're from, you've got plenty to get you through the day, but in my world, SP1N and VR are all we have. Besides ..." I tried to unclench my jaw and get the words out clearly, only half successfully. "... I've been off it for nearly a week!"

A tremble had started, but not from withdrawal; it was indignation. What right did a middle-class low-risker have telling me what I should or shouldn't do? I'd been making progress before she'd walked into the Vault. I needed support, not judgement!

Karin straightened and walked towards me.

I backed up with little retreating steps, avoiding her gaze.

"Daryl, I know you've been trying." Of course she knew. How easy it was to forget her abilities. That made it worse. "And I don't care. It's plain to see it won't last."

She twisted the knife, and it cut deep. I didn't know how to respond. All I could do was shuffle in reverse until I was against the wall, hands balled impotently behind my back.

Karin relaxed her voice, pivoting again. "Look, I don't care if you do drugs. I mean, it's not brilliant or anything, and I didn't hope to be teamed up with someone with an addiction, but it happens. I've seen it lots of times, but it's a liability and you know it."

"Okay, fine!" I blurted out, head hanging low. "I'm a worthless addict. Is that what you wanted to hear?" It was an admission I'd said a thousand times in my head, but never out loud. It brought with it an earthquake of repressed emotion. "I know I'm a goddamn liability. It's why I've been trying to quit!"

If Karin had been trying to break me, it had worked. I didn't know what else to say. I slumped to the floor, defeated.

Karin sat down facing me, brushing aside crumbs that had built up. "Good. It's out now." She ducked down to catch my sunken eyes, hands clasped in front of her. "That means we can move forward." Her voice was steady, like a teacher disciplining an emotional student. "What's important is that we deal with this now and work together to keep you clean." She placed a hand on my knee. There was no electricity this time, just awkward tension. "I didn't tell you this before, but my pre-state's been going crazy. Getting through the sub-jet port won't be easy. I'll need you on point."

"On point?" I looked up, locking eyes defiantly. "Karin! Forget the drugs. This entire plan relies on me stopping time at the right moment!"

Karin unclasped her hands and leaned back. "Yeah, so?"

I shook my head, bemused this wasn't clear to her. "Karin, I don't know how to do that!"

There, I'd exorcised the demon. It was good to get it out. A small amount of payback for her attack on me.

"What?" A twinge of shock broke through. "What about at the Shard, and your extraplex? They were perfectly timed."

I shook my head wearily. Her pre-state must have missed all this. "I don't know. I think it's triggered by stress or fear or something."

"So an emotional reaction?"

"Yeah, I guess so."

"Okay." Karin breathed out in relief. "Well, that's manageable at least."

"Manageable? I don't understand how it's manageable. It's a shit-show, that's what it is."

Karin jumped up from the floor, back to her nonchalant self. "Not at all. If it's triggered by emotion, then all you need is to replicate those feelings."

She scanned the floor for a space clear of VR equipment, settling on a spot near the window, gesturing for me to come over.

With the double boils of my addiction and lack of control lanced, the change in atmosphere was immediate and infectious, tugging me from my bleak mindset.

Karin tapped the floor in front of her insistently.

Self-consciousness replaced anxiety. "Is this gonna be weird?" I said, trying to get my emotions under control again.

"Probably for you, but bear with me; we don't have long, and we need to fix you as quickly as possible."

Fix me? I puffed out my cheeks but relented, tentatively moving to sit opposite, crossing my legs nervously in front of her.

"What now?"

"Guided meditation."

"Guided what?" It sounded like low-risker nonsense to me.

"Meditation." Karin insisted. "It will help you."

This was ridiculous. Sebastian would have laughed uncontrollably if he'd seen me even contemplating it.

"Trust me. I'm good at this. I use it to keep Future Karin from driving me nuts. It will help you too. Look at your hand."

I unfurled the fist at my side; the muscles were still twitching involuntarily. I felt dizzy after our confrontation, body flush with endorphins. Sebastian wouldn't like it, but he wasn't here anymore. Maybe it was time to try something different.

Karin settled herself, laying her hands palms up on her knees, gesturing for me to do the same.

It felt silly, but I did it anyway.

"We begin with breathing exercises," she explained. "Then a routine to help you reach a trance state, and finally some hypnotic suggestion."

I felt an urge to make a snide joke – something about chakra crystals – but Karin's stone-faced expression told me it would be a bad idea. She was taking this shit seriously. I cleared my throat instead. "How do you know about this stuff?"

Back straight, legs crossed over one another, Karin was in a perfect lotus position. My legs barely tucked under my knees. As she spoke, I couldn't help but straighten up too.

"It's hard having a voice in your head all the time," she explained. "It's easy to lose yourself, especially when the other voice is still you. I had to learn meditation to stop myself going mad."

She relaxed her face, hands at rest, no hint of negativity. My inner voice was irritating, but at least I controlled it. If someone else was pulling the levers, I could see how awful that would be. I made a conscious decision to listen.

"First, breathing." She placed a hand on her stomach and pulled in, showing it rising and falling. "You need to breathe from your stomach, not your chest."

I followed suit. It was difficult to redirect the air, but after a while, pulling from my stomach, more oxygen seemed to flow. We did this for a while, eyes closed, midriffs rising and falling rhythmically. Inhaling and exhaling deeply. It was hypnotic, which I guessed was the point.

After ten minutes, I was lightheaded but also more relaxed. Not tired – focussed. I felt good.

Observing my newly serene state, Karin provided calm, authoritative instructions. "You're at the top level now, fully awake, but we'll go deeper. Down to a place where subconscious suggestions have greater meaning."

"Will I know what I'm doing?" My eyes were closed tightly. I didn't want to open them anymore – they felt glued together. "I've seen people do this on holovids. They're made to look like idiots."

"That's stage hypnotism," Karin reassured. "It requires a highly suggestive person who's happy to be made fun of."

I hoped that was true. I'd been made a fool of enough recently.

"Let's begin. The sooner I can give you the tools, the sooner we can get back to planning." Karin's voice floated between us. It was a rehearsed phrase. "We're about to go down into a trance state. Know that nothing can harm you. You can't be made to do anything you don't want to. If required, you will awake and be fully alert. This is a safe place."

The words rattled around in my head. I'd never considered myself gullible or suggestive, but the ritual magnified the sentences and their meaning. Her speech altered, modulating up and down. A wave of words coming into my mind.

"Imagine a long staircase in front of you leading down. You can't see the bottom, but you know what's there is good. It's your place. A place where you can change things about yourself."

"What is it?"

"You'll know when you get there. Stop interrupting."

I did as I was told.

"If you look at the top stair in front of you, you'll notice it says a word on top. It says 'relax', and when you step onto it, you will feel physically and mentally calmer. Before you move, you'll breathe into your stomach, and as you take your step, you'll breathe out. At the same time, I want you to say the word 'relax' in your mind. Don't just say it though, feel it through your whole body." She paused. "Now breathe in."

I did, pulling air deep into my gut.

"And step."

I breathed out and let the word relax throb through my brain and body. I felt like I'd sunk into the floor.

For the next fifteen minutes, I descended the staircase. With each step, I felt more relaxed and distant from my body sitting on the floor somewhere high above. I could no longer sense my arms or legs; they felt detached.

Karin's voice seeped in like a soft echo. "We're nearing the bottom of the staircase. Can you see a door?"

As if willed into existence, a door appeared – golden with an ancient knocker. I had no idea where those details came from.

"When you open the door, a place will be revealed. Somewhere your inner self will listen."

"I don't know what it will look like."

"You will," Karin urged. "Push open the door."

I breathed in, leaning my imagined weight. The knocker rattled and the door creaked open, greeting me with mist. A disappointing anticlimax. Was this all my defective brain could conjure up?

"There's nothing ..." I began, then stopped. I could make out a shape in the clearing fog. The object resolved into a table, and then other details followed. A window hanging in space, and when that made no sense, the conjoining walls appeared too, wrapping around, under and over, forming a floor and a roof. Shelves popped from the walls. They were old and dishevelled, laden with trays containing mechanical parts. Springs, sprockets, levers, and such.

The final details painted themselves in. Clocks – hundreds of clocks!

They were everywhere. On the walls, on the table, strewn on the floor, and piled up in the corners. Traditional, mechanical, modern, and projecting types – they were all here. Some were in pieces, others ticking quietly or illuminating time into space. And there were tools everywhere. Delicate tools for manipulating tiny things.

"It's ..." I started.

Karin cut me off gently. "You don't need to describe it. This is your place, for you only. Be sure to investigate it. Touch any surfaces that are apparent. What do they feel like? Smell the air. What does it smell like? If there's something unusual, look at it closely, examine all the details."

I did as Karin said, exploring the workshop, running my hand over the table. It was old and wooden with deep rifts, but it was smooth – polished through years of use. The room was small, like a cabin, but it didn't feel claustrophobic. Approaching the window, I realised why. Outside, a meadow stretched into the distance. The sun was shining brightly, beating down. The scent of worked wood, pollen, and machine oils was intoxicating. I could sense it all.

"Do you feel completely in your place? Does it feel you belong there?"

"Yes." I was amazed I could pull something so odd and beautiful from my mind. Nowhere like this existed anywhere on Earth, at least, not anymore.

"Good." Karin's voice was no longer an echo. It was as if she was standing outside the cabin, in the meadow, just out of view. "Now imagine how you felt when you first stopped time."

I thought back to Led in the Trocadero. I'd been terrified but also angry and helpless. I didn't know how to explain it, but I could sense something building in the room. A dark, unpleasant swirl of negativity.

"Can you imagine what those emotions would look like if made real – into an object?"

I didn't know what that meant, but the feeling did want to become something. I could sense it pulsing, forming together.

"Let it happen," Karin prompted.

The swirl coalesced in front of me. Gathering on the table, creating a structure. Before my eyes it became something recognisable. A black timepiece. It stood there, dark and monolithic, fashioned after a small grandfather clock, the pendulum ticking ominously.

"Huh." It surprised me to see something so coherent and real.

"Don't tell me what it is," Karin said before I could elaborate. "Just take a long look, understand all the details."

The clock was onyx black, shiny, almost oily, the pendulum ruby red – angry behind a closed glass door. It was ticking twice as fast as a normal timepiece, as if agitated. The numbers on its face were slanted and devilish. It frightened me to look at – like it was staring back.

Eyeing the malicious device, I felt anxiety creep over me, my heart beating in time with the swinging pendulum. "Yes, I see it."

"Good. That's good, Daryl." Her voice was reassuring in its presence, an anchor to hold on to. "Can you see any way to contain it?"

"Contain it?"

"Yes, control it somehow, bend it to your will."

I understood, but there was no obvious way to manipulate it. No external dials or buttons, and the clock face itself was sealed. The only interactive feature was the glass door separating the pendulum.

Full of uncertainty, I reached for it, tugging on the tiny, ornate knob. The door swung open, startling me as it banged against the far side of the clock. The *tick-tock* became louder and more aggressive.

Hand shaking, I reached into the clock and tried to grasp the pendulum. It was hot to the touch, and although small, held incredible mass. It resisted my hand, throwing it back and forth viciously. Slowly, and with difficulty, exerting opposing pressure, I managed to slow its rhythm.

As the speed reduced, its colour changed, fading to cool blue. The clock face altered as well, the numerals straightening and rounding.

"Good." Karin sensed the change in me. "How do you feel?"

"Calm," I said. And I was, completely free of negative emotion – the first time in months. My heart was beating steadily, my breathing even and regular. The clock was controlling my wellbeing!

Karin pressed on. This wasn't over. "Final step. Can you *uncontain* what you've done? Let the feeling loose again."

I cringed, hair rising on the back of my neck. I didn't want to uncontain the power of the clock. It was dangerous – it could sweep me away, but I could see what Karin was trying to teach me.

Reluctantly, I reached back in. The pendulum felt cool, but it was still heavy. Pushing and pulling against the weight, I reversed what I'd done, speeding the pendulum to its angry red state, and with it, my heart rate and breathing. It differed from before, still unpleasant, but I felt in control – like I was moving the pendulum rather than it moving me. The fear and anger was still there, raging beneath the surface, but it was in check. I could channel it, use it.

We ran through the process a few times. It was difficult, the pendulum resistant, but it became easier each time.

Finally Karin signalled it was time to end the session, her disembodied voice floating in and around the workshop. I was disappointed to leave – the hallucination was as complete as any VR simulation. But I'd learned something, felt the truth reveal itself. The clock was key to controlling myself and, through it, latent state. I had to master it.

"We're ready to come back now." Karin recounted another rehearsed sequence.

Back? I could barely feel my body anymore, still sitting cross-legged in Jay's living room.

"You will remember this place and these feelings. The things you've learned are part of you now. You'll be able to return whenever you need."

Over the next few minutes, Karin reversed me out of the trance, her voice leading me from the workshop and back up the staircase. Now the word on each step said *Alert*, and with each step, I felt more awake and closer to my real body.

At the top of the staircase, I opened my eyes to see Karin staring at me, one eyebrow raised. It felt like I'd returned from a long journey.

"Look at your hand," Karin prompted.

I did. It was open, loose at my side, the twitch gone. As was the urge to vaporise a SP1N tab.

I blinked and went to say something, but emotion caught in my throat.

Before I could blurt out an embarrassing cavalcade of thanks, a voice emerged from the doorway to save me.

"Are you two finished?" Jay was leaning against the frame. "I came in over an hour ago and you were sat like this."

"An hour!" I had no idea we'd been under that long. It had felt like minutes.

"Yeah, pretty freaky if you ask me." Jay bit his thumb nail distractedly.

Karin and I looked at each other and laughed awkwardly.

"Anyway, look," he continued, yanking off the splinter he'd created. "I have to start acting normally soon, well normal for me, otherwise people will get suspicious. Are you guys ready?"

I looked at Jay and back to Karin. The crafty half smile had returned. I understood it now.

"Thanks for your help, Jay," I said. "I think we're ready now."

And for the first time since the explosion at the Shard, that sounded right. For once I was starting to feel in control of my destiny. We had a plan and I could see a path forward. One where I might not screw up.

STATE 14

I ran my hand over the shiny interior. It smelled faintly of oil, but not in an unpleasant way. I'd never been in an auto-cab before. It was a luxury, but Karin had insisted, jamming her thumb on the reader and ignoring my shocked expression at the extortionate figure displayed.

It had been a risk. We didn't know if Limelight had penetrated the banks, but we'd rationalised the financial systems were secure. Besides, we'd need funds at some point, and if Limelight could track us through our transactions, we were doomed anyway.

It had worked. Neo-Guards hadn't swarmed us, but we agreed it was prudent to do it infrequently, and only at external terminals, never via our AROs.

What hadn't been a risk was the state of Karin's finances. She was loaded! I'd noticed when her balance had flashed up on the display.

She shrugged it off without a hint of embarrassment, jumping in the cab like it was nothing. "What can I say? When you're clairvoyant, you know which horse to back."

There were no real horses anymore, all gambling was virtual, but I got the point. I gritted my teeth behind a false smile to hide my frustration. Money had always been an obstacle for Sebastian and me. We hadn't known where our next meal would come from, let alone a taxi journey. I glanced at Karin, already absorbed on her social networks, still tethered to my Redwave account. I didn't resent her using her powers, I'd do the same, but she could show some humility. I guessed even before she'd become clairvoyant, she'd never had to do without. It was moments like these the gulf between us seemed widest.

I settled into the seat, peering quietly through the smoke-tinted windows. They let through the vibrant neon lighting and signage but dimmed the surrounding grime and disrepair of the city. The ride was so smooth I could barely feel it. I tried to enjoy the moment – probably my last opportunity to experience something pleasant.

After an hour, we'd travelled twenty miles, passing the guarded Neo-London perimeter. We followed the old motorway west, through the historical greenbelt surrounding Old London. The lush green space was no more; what remained had turned yellow with pollution, dotted with factories serving the city.

Every few miles, someone tended a sick field, sat on ancient farm equipment so rusted it was a miracle it moved. Even from the car, I could see the workers' skin was sallow and drawn, faces wrinkled like bark. If you didn't serve the Telcoms, you farmed for synthetic produce in the barrens outside – downwind from the worst of the pollution. I thought of my shit-hole domicile. It was tiny and knackered, but better than this.

I pulled my gaze from the window, dialling the tint up to make it black. I didn't want to think about the past. We were on our way to somewhere different.

HK1 was one of the few technically advanced cities, right on the other side of the world. If it weren't for the anxiety of illicitly boarding a sub-jet, I'd have been excited. As it was, there was a lead ball in my stomach.

We'd considered buying tickets legitimately, but the Administration monitored sub-jets and Limelight was certain to be notified. The corners of my mouth twitched at the irony. Karin's wealth could get us to the port, but it was the poor extraplex boy who'd have to sneak us past security.

I'd been practising the techniques Karin had shown me. If I remained focussed, I could enter and exit latent state on demand. I'd envision the clock, sitting in the workshop. Its strange pendulum a reflection of my emotional state. Cool and blue when slow, hot and red when sped up. With experimentation, I'd found two ways of freezing time. The first replicated the conditions at the Shard. Under extreme stress, the pendulum smashed against the sides of the clock, time stalling like an over-revved car. It worked in an emergency but was unpleasant – my heart raced until I could feel the blood pumping in my eyeballs – the very edge of fight or flight. Luckily, it wasn't necessary. Slowing the pendulum in the other direction had the same effect, bringing time to a gradual halt. It took longer than stalling the clock, but I was getting better.

As Karin had predicted, a bonus of using meditation had been a recession in my need for SP1N. It was still there, a dark claw in my mind. It would never vanish completely, requiring constant management, but for the first time since I was thirteen, it was momentarily in check.

According to Karin, I'd taken to meditation extremely well, suggesting I had a predisposition for it. I wasn't sure. I'd always been introspective. Sebastian had called me "brooding" – I was redirecting all the negative self-loathing into something useful.

I shifted uncomfortably inside the faux-leather garments we'd bought for the occasion. The plan was to use latent state and clairvoyant misdirection to slip by security. We'd need to move quickly through tight gaps – loose clothing would be bad, hence the crotch hugging leathers and form fitting jackets.

"Are you clear what we need to do?" Karin had closed her ARO and was facing me. She was dressed as I was, only pulling it off better. Clad in neutral grey and beige, she looked like a hot motorcyclist. Her hair was freshly shorn on one side and re-braided on the other, changed to blonde to match the overall scheme. The colour combinations had been her idea. It would act like camouflage against the muted marble, glass, and metal she assured me made up the port's interior.

I tried to speak and thought better of it. My mouth was dry like a desert. I nodded instead and made a show of double checking my rucksack – low profile affairs we'd bought for the occasion. They hugged our backs, buckles cinching around the waist to prevent them moving around. There was room for a few items. Water, ration pellets, a lazeblade, and a multi-tool. We hoped that would be enough.

Being inconspicuous wouldn't be a problem for me; I'd freeze time before the barriers and stroll past security. Getting Karin through would be a different story.

We'd spoken at length about the plan, pouring over pictures of the port and thinking through the obstacles. Scenario planning was useful but ultimately futile. Everything would be different on the day. I'd have to recon the way forward when we arrived.

Karin tapped me on the shoulder, gesturing towards the front of the taxi. In the distance was a grey dome. It was a few kilometres away, but the width, even this far off, revealed how massive it was. It rose like a moon on the horizon, increasing until it stopped, half appeared. An enormous metal ball, sunken in the ground, at least two kilometres in diameter.

As we closed the distance, I could start to make out dimples on the dome's surface. Bays the sub-jets launched from to achieve their sub-Earth orbits – the powerful aircraft using an extreme angle to Earth to traverse distances faster than traditional planes. A sub-jet could cross the Atlantic to America in under two hours, not that anyone had gone there since they closed their borders.

The sub-jet port looked completely out of place. A modern, alien structure, surrounded by wasteland. An aluminium interchange for top echelon citizens – low-riskers of means fleeing the city to seek less polluted areas swapped for well-heeled international business people needing the city's high-tech telecommunication hubs.

The road snaked up a ramp to a large drop off point, sharply lettered neon pointing the way to *Departures*. The enormity of the structure pressed down on me. I tried to keep my rising sense of panic in check as we jumped out. This was the furthest I'd been from the city, surrounded by people normally separated from me by thick windshields. The fear someone would recognise me as a gutter wretch was palpable.

I didn't mention it to Karin; she wouldn't understand. She came from a well-manicured background. She knew how these people operated – she fit in. My only comfort was if things went wrong, I could retreat into latent state – vanish back to the gutter.

Feeling self-conscious, feet clacking on the hard floor, I tried to walk tall, following Karin across the polished metal entrance. It sparkled despite the overcast weather.

I gasped as we cleared the doors. I'd seen pictures of the sub-jet port, but experiencing it was different. The cavernous interior was a sight to behold. The steel floor stretched to meet gleaming marble pillars and etched glass walls. High above, a bright, burning globe bathed the port in a convincing facsimile of a summer's day. I slowed to take it in, mouth hung open like a tourist. I couldn't help it; I *was* a tourist. I had no right to be here.

A passing businessman looked my way. He wore a well-cut suit and was pulling a bag-laden hover trolley – the maglev gliding effortlessly over the steel floor. I returned his look with an awkward grin, enough to make him hurry on his way. Must be an important trip. It was unusual to drag that much luggage.

Sub-jet fuel was expensive – most space in the jets was allocated for transporting people rather than items. For shorter trips, it was easier to carry-on or buy at the destination. Most ports had forgone automated luggage checking entirely. Anyone wishing to take extra baggage had to drag it through manually, paying the surcharge to have it added to the tiny hold at the departure gate.

Karin noticed I'd paused and pulled me towards a nearby check-in queue behind two women. They were glamorously dressed in flowing silk dresses, almost see through to the skin, hair long and shining – completely free of city grime. As I stood, uncomfortably trying to blend in, a breeze from the air conditioning carried their perfume over to us – acute and floral. An intense urge of lust washed over me.

Karin leaned over. "Careful, pherofume," she whispered urgently.

I blinked and tried to clear my head. It was difficult – all the blood had rushed to my loins! I'd heard of pherofume, but I'd never been close enough to women who could afford it. The urge passed, but for a moment, the effect had been powerful. I'd had to restrain myself from lurching at them!

"Isn't that dangerous?" I whispered back, breathless as the effects receded. "What if someone attacked them?"

"Look around. These women don't go places without heavy security. If anybody does something, they'd be arrested immediately. It's a game to them; they like to tease men, work them into a frenzy." She snarled contemptuously. "It's so bad, most men wear antidote cologne to neutralise the effect."

"You're kidding."

"Nope."

"You sound like you know what you're talking about."

"Maybe." Came the flat reply.

We gave a wide berth to similarly dressed women, lest I blow the whole thing with an outburst of indecent behaviour.

There were cameras all over the foyer and security guards patrolling, but there were no physical barriers this side of the departures area. It was essentially a public zone – we could walk around with no one getting too suspicious.

Karin knew the basic layout. She grabbed my elbow, pointing out the security entrance. It separated the foyer from the controlled departures lounge. It was our biggest hurdle, full of measures to prevent unauthorised access. A physical inspection of documents, then a ten metre scanning tunnel filled with passive x-rays and magnetic sensors – plus cameras and a complement of security personnel manning the various stations.

Everything would be easy until we made our move, then the stakes would be sky-high. Karin was the weak point of the plan; even with her pre-state, there was a chance she'd be spotted or become trapped – snarled somewhere between the security barriers or in a camera arc where I couldn't reach her.

The sub-jet we wanted to board was due to leave in an hour. I didn't know how long it would take in real time to get this done, but we shouldn't spend long on the other side either. An hour was about right.

Pretending to tie my boots, I whispered to Karin. "I better go check the way. I'll be back as soon as I can."

"If you do your job right, it will be instantaneous for me."

I smiled. "I guess you're right."

Closing my eyes, I slowed my breathing, holding the image of the clock in my mind. I detected the change as it happened. A thickening of the atmosphere. An absence of ambient sound.

I opened my eyes. The world was stationary – marble and glass surfaces peppered with frozen lens flares. The manicured elite of Neo-London had become well-dressed mannequins.

Even motionless, Karin radiated determination and encouragement. It terrified me. I didn't want to let her down.

I waded forward. The security gate lay ahead. A large cone shaped area, six metres at its widest, narrowing to two metres, funnelled passengers towards the checkpoint. It was crowded with people, frozen in various acts of shuffling, but there was room to squeeze by.

Near the narrow end, an inspector was checking documents. He was flanked on either side by cameras mounted to cover each other's arcs. One camera would spot any attempt to slide along the wall under the other.

Pausing, I reviewed the area. Behind the inspector, set in the wall and ceiling, was the faint outline of a laser perimeter grid. It was down at the moment to let people through. We'd have to sneak past the inspector and block line of sight to the cameras. The laser grid would activate if either caught us, sealing the area.

I was feeling lightheaded. I'd been still too long. I wished I knew why it was hard to breathe – it was a serious danger.

I swam forward again. The inspector's head was down, diligently examining the documents in front of him. Unlike other Neo-Guards, he wasn't wearing a helmet; it would impede his work. He was older than typical, pudgy, and wearing traditional circular glasses, worn low on his nose. He didn't look athletic but seemed observant – one eye on the next person.

A gold pin adorned his lapel, signifying seniority. I doubted much got past him. I'd need a convincing distraction, and for once, my old life with Sebastian was a wellspring of experience to draw from. I'd already thought about the bit I'd use on him.

On the other side of the checkpoint was the sensor tunnel – an automated passageway scanning travellers for threats. To the left, a door led to the monitoring station where the guards would be. There were no cameras between the inspector and the beginning of the sensor tunnel. A blind spot.

I pushed on. The tunnel's interior was featureless, just a strip of black glass running its length. The floor was an automated travellator – passengers stood upright, evenly spaced so they could be scanned efficiently.

At the far end, the tunnel flared back out, with a matching door for security to exit the monitoring station. And beyond, the cavernous departure lounge awaited; it was even more luxurious than the public foyer – dotted with plush sofas and top-end shops.

It was spread across multiple levels with another imitation sun illuminating its interior, a warmer and more relaxed shade than on the public side.

Cameras around the perimeter covered most angles, but as with the entrance to the sensor tunnel, there was a blind spot where it joined with the lounge. It didn't seem like a coincidence. The sensors in the tunnel must interfere with the cameras.

It was an advantage, but options remained limited. There would be no point directing Karin through the tunnel. Covering her line of sight wouldn't work – the scanners would spot her easily, record she wasn't registered with a sub-liner, and raise an alarm.

The alternative was the monitoring station running parallel, the doors to which were in the camera dead zones. An idea was forming, but it needed testing.

Walking back, I selected a target. A man carrying a heavy-looking rucksack. His hair was slickly parted, nose up-turned in permanent disdain. Even motionless, he was preppy and entitled. I had no sympathy for what I was about to do to him.

Ensuring no part of my body was in the tunnel, I placed a foot across his path and exited latent state. He tripped as the world jolted to life, face planting in a spectacular crash. An alarm sounded, and the travellator halted.

A woman to my side jumped in shock, but not from the man tripping. Grimacing, I realised my mistake. It must have seemed I'd appeared from nowhere. Shaking her head, she brushed it off and hurried along. I'd been lucky not to appear in front of someone more observant. Sloppy.

Luckily, the damage was limited; everyone else's gaze was focussed on the bedlam. I'd have to be more careful though. I couldn't flash into existence wherever I wanted.

Using the chaos as cover, I slid along the wall outside the tunnel, passing the door to the monitoring station. All eyes were on the man, although no one ran to his aid. Either too shocked or snobby to help – I suspected the latter. He groaned as he lay sprawled, backpack ridden up and pushing his face into the rubberised surface.

I readied myself; the monitoring station opened and two guards emerged to investigate. I re-entered latent state, freezing the door before it closed.

My heart was racing and I was out of breath. Pausing and unpausing time was taxing. I hoped I could keep it up.

Inside was full of readouts and displays. The strip of glass running its length showed real-time skeletal images of passengers – anything noteworthy coloured orange for inspection. Mostly AROs and bags. One guard remained seated at a console facing the window.

I suppressed the urge to laugh. The guy I'd tripped was visible through the screen. He still hadn't been righted – skeleton arms frozen while trying to dislodge the bag from his head. The guards' guns were highlighted red – calling out the weapons.

The lazeblades we'd packed would be picked up too, but if the plan worked, we'd avoid the sensors altogether.

I moved to the far door; it was closed, but there was no lock from this side. If I could get Karin into the station and keep the guards distracted, she could slip through and let herself out into the lounge.

I had enough information. The plan wasn't complete, but there were too many unknowns to think further ahead. I made my way out, back past the lurking inspector, and into the foyer.

Lesson learned, I strode to the port bathroom, unfreezing time in a vacant stall before joining Karin. She was angry, hands on hips.

"Daryl! You have to pause time when no one's looking. You vanished right in the middle of the port! We're lucky it's not too busy this side."

"Yeah, I know." I answered sheepishly, examining my shoes. "I did the same thing in the checkpoint just now. Don't worry, it didn't cause a problem, but I know about it now – I used the bathroom to exit."

She accepted the explanation, but the scowl remained. "What have you figured out?"

I smiled, attention moving to my jacket, fiddling with the zip. "It's gonna be tricky, but I think I have a solution."

I ran through my idea while Karin listened. When I'd finished, the scowl was still there, but it had changed to one of concentration.

"Seems sensible," she answered matter-of-factly.

"Sensible? That's your only feedback?"

"What do you want?"

"Oh, I don't know, some clairvoyant reassurance, maybe?"

She cocked her head. "I'm not getting any messages *not* to do it. Does that help?"

I sighed. "Yes. Very confidence inspiring."

"Glad to be of help!" she chirped annoyingly, and before I could argue, she grabbed my hand and made a beeline for the security gate.

I saw what she had. A rotund woman pulling a hover trolley was crossing the foyer; it was piled high with garish floral luggage.

Karin broke away, positioning herself by the far wall, beneath the scanning arc of the right side camera, waiting for Luggage Lady to break line of sight. Karin's muted colours did a good job of blending her into the wall and floor.

I turned my attention to the inspector. He was an intimidating obstacle, but I didn't have time to second guess myself; Luggage Lady was already halfway across the hall. If we missed this opportunity, we'd draw suspicion. And I couldn't rely on latent state – the cameras would see me if I appeared or disappeared this close to the gate. Only a conventional distraction would work.

Clasping my nerves, I joined the queue ahead of Luggage Lady. She'd moved into a good position to block the camera for Karin. The inspector looked foreboding – observant and unflappable. I would have to bring my A game to keep his eyes off her.

The last time I'd tried this was ripping off alchovials at the local off-license. It was an old trick of Sebastian's, using misdirection and sleight of hand to control attention. It had worked back then, but the store attendant was small fry in comparison.

"Documents please." The inspector extended his hand, eyes looking over his glasses.

"Sure." I feigned confidence, reaching into my bag as I recalled the opening to the bit, rummaging around for the non-existent travel pass as I struggled with the precise phrasing.

"You see ... the thing is ..." I started, but the words had become fuzzy. The sentence I was searching for no longer made sense.

I could feel sweat beading on my forehead. Had the mental effort of scouting ahead gotten to me or was this blind panic? Why couldn't I remember how this went? I'd been rehearsing it all morning!

The inspector straightened, placing his hands on the desk, head fully raised. "Problem, sir?"

I could hear Luggage Lady tut from behind. Obnoxious cow!

"Er, no." I played for time, desperately searching for the words, but the more I concentrated, the more they slipped away. "They're here somewhere." I could feel my face going red.

Somewhere out of sight, I knew Karin was waiting to make her move, wondering what the delay was. I was blowing it – I had to do something!

I could slip into latent state or run away, but either would raise an alarm, and neither would divert the inspector's attention.

I looked at my hands, balled up in frustration, and in a moment of inspiration, I knew what to do.

I forced a smile. "Oh, I'm sorry, here are my documents ..."

I swung for him as hard as I could.

I'd never been a fighter, but Seb had, and we'd had plenty of scuffles. I'd lost all of them, but somewhere along the line, I'd learned to throw a punch. Despite the frayed nerves, or maybe because of them, the skills came back keenly.

My fist connected solidly with the underside of the inspector's jaw. He was close – it was more of an uppercut than a hook.

He careened over the booth, teeth crunching together, the shock sending his glasses flying.

There were gasps all around, including Luggage Lady, who yelped loudest of all. I bolted in the reverse direction, shooting her a menacing glance. It turned her whimper into a full-blown scream. That would teach her for tutting at me!

I reached the bathroom a few moments later, freezing time to pause the frenzy. The surge of adrenaline and mad dash had sapped all my gas. I staggered around in the stall, fighting for breath in the thick air.

After some scary seconds of ragged breathing, pushing away the urge to pass out, I recovered enough to venture out.

The inspector was crumpled on the reverse of the booth, hands at his face. It wasn't my original plan, but it had the desired effect. Everyone was staring at the carnage, and not at Karin, who had slid further down the wall, the line of sight to the opposing camera now blocked by Luggage Lady's overburdened hover-trolley.

Even better, the commotion had spilled close to the travellator and the guards were already rushing out to investigate. I'd killed two birds with one stone, but it was too early to feel smug.

I snuck into the monitoring station; the remaining guard was still seated by the console. This wasn't over yet.

Punching wouldn't work this time. He was wearing a full-face helmet. My knuckles still stung from hitting the inspector's fleshy face. This guy's helmet would damage my hand further and would show we'd been inside the station. Authorities were looking for people on the public side of the departure gate. We needed to maintain that illusion.

I considered the alternatives. The station was full of sensitive equipment, running the width of the window. It looked breakable, but I had a better idea. Mounted on the console near the guard hung a foam fire extinguisher. It wasn't an ideal solution. An extinguisher going off would be suspicious, but with all the commotion, it wasn't hard to imagine someone could have knocked it.

I retrieved my lazeblade and tested it. It didn't fire. Of course, it was paused like everything else. No way to practise. This would be a live test!

I wedged my foot against the door, holding it open. Then, keeping behind the guard, I stretched towards the fire extinguisher and unfroze time.

An alarm, tripped by the chaos outside, assaulted my senses, and with it, a terrible sense of vulnerability. I felt like a sleepwalker, violently awoken in a place they didn't recognise. It was hard to imagine how Karin must be feeling, out in the open as she was.

I couldn't see her but knew she was working her way down the wall, ready to bolt to the station. The moments ticked by. It felt like an eternity, but finally she appeared around the corner, eyes flashing as she saw me at the door. I nodded back, revitalised by the progress we were making.

Once I was sure she'd make the closing door, I activated the lazeblade and plunged it into the pressurised cylinder, angling the jet towards the guard. Caught unaware, his attention focused on the screen, he jumped in surprise and went into a swearing panic as foam covered his helmet.

Karin slid in low behind me, flattening herself against the wall. I gestured urgently at the far door. Then, keeping low to avoid the guards flailing arms, we scuttled through the monitoring station and released the door handle. It swung outwards. We were almost there!

Leaving the beleaguered guard and resisting the urge to run, we merged with the throngs exiting the travellator – smoothly making our way towards the lounge.

Karin slipped her hand into mine, swinging it casually. To anyone who cared to look, we were a privileged couple going away for the weekend. I hoped she couldn't feel the tremble.

As we moved out of danger, the lush, multi-layered shopping arcade lay ahead, busy with travellers doing last-minute shopping. No one seemed interested in us.

Punching the inspector would have raised an alert, but not in the lounge. The person they were looking for hadn't made it through the gate – security on this side was still relaxed. I looked at my knuckles. Some pretty serious bruising was already showing – purple in the centre smudged with yellow. I'd given him a hell of a crack!

Passing a pherofume shop, we paused by a rack of fragrances. Pictures of pretty, mostly naked women adorned the walls on one side, men with hidden, lustful glances on the other. The prices had far too many zeros.

"Can I help you?" A saleswoman dressed in a severe silver blouse addressed us from behind the counter.

"Not yet." Karin waved dismissively, selecting a test vial, pretending to be interested. I hoped she didn't plan to spray it. Mixed with the adrenaline coursing through me, the effect could be disastrous. The saleswomen returned her attention to her terminal.

Karin leaned in close. "That was amazing how you distracted the guard. I never would have thought of that."

Her breath landed hot on my ear, the sensation as powerful as any perfume. It created a tingle all the way down to my toes. I considered telling her the truth. I'd thrown the punch out of desperation. She probably knew, but if she was going to give me the credit, I was happy to take it.

"Yeah, I guess I figured it would be easier than creating a second distraction in the tunnel."

Her smile made me feel amazing and fraudulent at the same time.

Rejecting the first tester, she selected another, turning it in her hands, speaking quietly without looking at me. "Okay, Daryl. I have some good news and some bad news."

Uh-oh. Sudden changes of direction from Karin were generally bad.

"I saw the departure board for HK1. The next one boards in forty minutes. That's the good news."

Not being the target audience, it felt weird to examine the pherofume as Karin was. I turned and stared at the pictures of the women instead – which was probably worse.

"And the bad news?" I whispered over my shoulder.

"We can't actually board it."

"What?" I stiffened. "You didn't mention that before!"

"Sorry, you had a lot to deal with, I didn't want to overload you. The thing is, even if we got into the passenger cabin, the tickets are biometrically coded. Without them, or even with stolen ones, we'd be scanned and uncovered as soon as we were on board."

Thrusting my hands in my pockets, aware I was looking more and more like a pervert, I tried to hide my frustration. "Well, I can't imagine you let us get this far without a plan."

"Of course I didn't, but you're not going to like it."

I held my breath, waiting for the next phase of insanity to be explained.

"We'll have to travel in the hold."

I spun and looked at her, unable to keep up the pretence. "The hold! As in the luggage hold?"

The saleswomen looked at us again; she was suspicious now, and my reaction had made Karin cross.

"Shh!" she whispered, eyes angry. "And yes, the luggage hold. That's our only option."

I lowered my voice again. "Is that safe?"

"Sort of."

"What does that mean? Can you elaborate?"

"Not really." She glanced at the saleswoman. "Look, we have to go."

"I hate this already."

As we walked towards the gate, a flight for HK1 was preparing to leave, the launch tube visible through a large plexiglass window. The sub-jet itself was black and needle-shaped, with small swept-back wings. It looked like a cross between a space shuttle and a stealth jet. Enough power to make it to suborbital altitude, with just enough manoeuvrability to make it down again. Various cables and umbilicals connected to its hull for fuelling and maintenance.

Near the gate, passengers spread out in various states of relaxation – lounging on form-fitting sofas or chatting in groups. Karin nudged me. There was a hatch marked *Checked Luggage*.

"You're joking?"

"Nope. That's the only way on board."

It should have filled me with fear, but I felt numb. My life had become a series of insane events. I was either getting good at them or acclimatising to the risks. This must be what adrenaline junkies feel like – taking bigger and bigger chances, desperate for the buzz.

"Fine, one more kamikaze move," I said, defeated. "But this is the end of you holding shit from me!"

"Of course." Karin winked.

Right, as if she'd ever agree to that. Silly me.

STATE 15

I nside the terminal, security was less restrictive, only needing minimal distraction.

Haughty and entitled, tottering on heels too high for her, the perfect diversion for getting into the hold presented herself.

Laden with oversized prosthetic breasts, she crossed the lounge. Her golden hair swung from side to side; onlookers forced to look whether they wanted to or not.

Karin, already in position on a sofa, slid a bag into her path, nudging it out with her foot.

Goldilocks didn't so much topple as utterly collapse – tumbling off her heels and sprawling across the floor. Her dress, previously keeping her decent (just about), slid down, exposing the expensive implants for all to appreciate.

The kerfuffle was enough for us to slip past the remaining passengers, now giggling, scoffing, staring, and pointing at the drama. We jumped through the chute in time to hear a few of the braver men offer to heave her back up again.

We landed on an anti-grav crash mat, slipping off the gently repelling fields, and scurried to avoid being stacked, along with the real luggage, into vertical alcoves. The mechanical claw doing the work didn't look amenable to human flesh.

We took refuge in one of the partially full storage areas, collapsing onto someone's faux leather suitcases.

The hold was sterile and industrial. Metal bulkheads and nuts left exposed where the fuselage was bolted together. A few low-powered bulbs washed the interior with a dull red glow, like a submarine.

I felt like I'd run a marathon. Since getting to the port, it had been nothing but high stress. If I closed my eyes, I'd fall asleep immediately. Annoyingly, I couldn't. Karin had sprung this new situation on us and I didn't know what was next. I made my thoughts known.

"Karin, tell me how we're not going to die when this thing takes off?"

She was sitting across from me in the alcove, cross-legged.

"And why couldn't you tell me before?"

"Sorry." She shrugged, shifting around uncomfortably. The alcove was far from ergonomic. "It's like I said. I'd put a lot of pressure on you. I didn't want to push you over the edge."

The answer was honest, but not good enough.

"You should have trusted me." Then a disturbing thought crossed my mind. "Did your pre-state tell you I'd screw up?" I almost didn't want to know; it would only confirm my anxieties.

Karin stared back at me appraisingly before answering. "No, it didn't. I knew you were dealing with a lot. The drugs, the control. Getting through security was enough for you to worry about."

I couldn't tell if she was being truthful, but if she'd spared me the embarrassment, it was best left unsaid. "Okay." I accepted the answer. I had no choice unless I wanted to uncover I was incompetent. "Just give me more credit next time."

She nodded, looking tired as well. Uncharacteristically so, with deep bags under her eyes. Even with her pre-state, it must have been terrifying for her in the checkpoint, out in the open. I wasn't the only one who'd had it tough.

"You don't need to worry, Daryl," Karin continued.

Did she know I'd been thinking about her?

"The hold's pressurised, otherwise some items of luggage might explode."

No, she was going back to my original question. I could sense a *but* coming.

"But ..." There it was. "... they don't regulate the temperature as they do in the cabin. It uses too much fuel."

I knew it. Sub-jets travelled to near orbital heights, a part of the atmosphere not known for its balmy weather. "Karin, you know that means we're going to freeze to death, don't you?"

"Hold on," she replied defensively, unfolding her legs so she could lean forward and make her point. "I'm not suicidal. They heat it in here a little otherwise liquids would freeze and burst."

"How much do they warm it up by?"

"Two degrees centigrade."

"Two degrees! That might as well be freezing."

"Yes, but it's only that cold at certain altitudes. It will be at least five or six degrees for most of the flight."

"Karin!" I could barely contain my frustration. "That's damn cold, and I don't know about you, but I left my thermal underwear at home!"

"You did?" she mocked – and then said, "Well, I guess we'll have to find some in all this spare luggage." She stood and waved her hand around to illustrate how many options we had. "Won't we?"

I bit my lip to prevent digging a bigger hole. She was right. We were surrounded by clothes. There should be something suitable to layer up in. I stood too; it felt like I was being talked down to.

"It will be fine, Daryl." She soothed, sensing the retreat. "We'll huddle together."

She played the statement with a straight bat, no hint of intimacy, but whether by accident or design, it caught me off guard. I fell back in a heap.

"But don't get any ideas! This is a business trip." She was talking down to me now. She hadn't been nasty about it, but she'd made the point loud and clear.

I struggled to get back up, arms buried up to my elbows in luggage. "I've no idea what you mean." I feigned indignation. I knew exactly what she meant, and she was right; this was no place for messing around. Still, I recalled the moment by the fragrance counter. She'd been impressed, and damn it, I'd done everything we planned! That had to count for something – even for an idiot like me.

I regained my footing, kicking a handbag away from where it had tangled around my foot. "Okay, okay, we should see what we can find. This thing takes off soon."

Content to move on, we scavenged the luggage. Most of the bags had locks, but only to stop casual tampering. We slashed them open with our lazeblades, spilling clothes all over the hold. The stacking claw would get the blame.

Most of them contained wholly impractical fashion items or summer wear, but a few had thicker jackets and trousers that we liberated and dressed in.

We hunkered back in our alcove to wait for take-off, breaking into a fit of giggles as we inspected each other. We looked pretty silly. I'd found a fur-lined sports jacket and a pair of ski trousers. Karin, an oversized bomber jacket with thick dungarees. We looked like the homeless after a Christmas donation.

There was no time to speculate on the people we'd stolen our garments from. A low rumble emanated from the bowels of the aircraft. The sub-jet was preparing to fire the booster that would push us into sub-orbit. We scrambled to make ourselves ready, piling luggage into makeshift chairs.

"Hold on." Karin gripped my hand. "This is hardcore if you're not used to it."

I tensed and pushed myself into the well of bags I'd made, but even with the advanced warning, the launch was still a shock. It whipped my head into the bulkhead where I'd failed to brace it properly.

I cried out but didn't have time to complain. The rocket propellant was igniting, shoving me back hard as it thrusted upwards. The hold was the closest part of the craft to the engines – unshielded from noise and vibration. The sound was a deafening roar – filling my head and blurring my vision.

After a few minutes that seemed to go on forever, teeth clenched, eyes screwed shut, the sub-jet began to quiet, slowing as it reached its zenith.

I peeked my eyes open and wished I hadn't. As we commenced our turn towards Earth, I could see the alcoves rotating. The motion made me queasy – the circular storage spaces slowly spinning on gimbals and swing arms.

It was to level the luggage. Without, the bags would have to be painstakingly strapped down or become crushed and battered as the orientation altered. I guessed a similar system existed in the cabin above, keeping passengers perpendicular to the earth. Either way, it was disorientating as hell to look at!

The temperature dropped, my breath misting in front of me. We must be at the highest point, about to descend at a steep angle –

streaking back to ground faster than any normal plane. We'd reach HK1 in six hours. Nothing to do but wait it out.

The back of my head throbbed where it had hit the fuselage. I reached around to rub it but Karin had other ideas. She scooched in, grabbing my arm and pulling it around her. I didn't mind. I'd take the sore head in exchange.

After a few minutes, she broke the silence with an unexpected question. "Hey, Daryl, what's it like when you stop time? You know, enter latent state?"

I licked my lips; they were feeling dry and chapped in the cold. It was an interesting question, personal, but that was okay – I hadn't spoken to anyone about it, and I wanted to. I paused, rummaging for the right words. "Horrible." I settled on. "Dead ... flat ... like being under water but more so. There's no sound apart from what's in my head. I kind of hate it."

"That sounds familiar." Karin mused. "The horrible part. I guess that's something we share."

Probably not. Karin's battle with Future Karin – incessantly chattering – sounded way worse. At least I could turn latent state off.

"And you said it's hard to move around?"

"Yeah, a real struggle. Like swimming, or pushing against a heavy wind. I don't know why."

"Maybe it's the air?"

I stared at the curved roof of the sub-jet. "What do you mean?"

"Well, if latent state works like my clairvoyance, it connects you to a parallel universe. One where your body is occupying a bubble of normal time within a paused dimension. In fact, it would need to, otherwise you wouldn't be able to think or move; you'd be stationary like everything else."

I rubbed my little finger with my thumb. It had healed into a raised scar. When Led had bitten me, the blood had pooled around my hand like a glove. It did seem it was encased in some sort of bubble.

The launch engines had stopped, but the primary jets were blaring against Karin's voice. I leaned in tight to hear her.

"If you think about it, air molecules would be frozen like everything else. They'd only become agitated when you push against them – like passing through a liquid."

Total speculation, but it made sense. "I suppose that also explains why gravity doesn't affect me as much. At my extraplex, I was able to climb when the power cable snapped – even though I was hanging away from the building. What you're saying is the air resistance propped me up." I scratched my chin with my spare hand, thinking it through. "Yeah, that would account for why I can't breathe either."

"What?" Karin's surprise pierced my ear, making it sting. "Did you say you can't breathe?"

Wincing, I replied. "No, I mean, I can, but only when I'm moving. If I stop, it feels like I'm at altitude. The air becomes thin and I get lightheaded. So yeah, if it's locomotion pushing air into my lungs, that would make sense. The local supply becomes depleted if I don't move."

I felt Karin tense beneath my arm, a palpable change in atmosphere. "You should have told me about that."

"Why?"

"What if you were trapped, or knocked out? You'd suffocate!"

I could feel my head get hot. Why hadn't I told her? Hearing the deficiency out loud made it sound like a huge problem, at least worthy of discussion. Suddenly I was happy for the red lighting – it hid my flushed cheeks. "Er, sorry ... I guess I didn't think it was important to bring up. Just something I had to deal with. But you're right, it's a big hazard – I almost passed out in the bathroom at the port. Bear with me. I'm learning as I go. I think using latent state is like diving or rock-climbing. Dangerous but manageable."

Karin went quiet for a few minutes.

Eventually I couldn't take the silence. "Karin, are you angry with me?"

Her response surprised me. "Not at all. You keep putting your life on the line. You don't even know you're doing it." She turned to look at me, eyes dark and wide. "Daryl, thank you for doing this with me. I know you've got your reasons, but I've been chasing answers for so long I didn't think an end would ever be in sight. If we hadn't crashed into each other, I'd still be in Neo-London, and no closer to the truth."

I swallowed tightly, taken aback by Karin's earnestness. I hadn't considered how my actions were affecting her. Embarrassed, I turned to look into the hold again – the swaying gimbals and vibrations of the sub-jet hypnotic.

Karin settled deeper into the crook of my arm, the conversation coming to a close. The temperature in the hold was near freezing, but I couldn't tell; I felt warm from head to toe. In a shared moment of closeness I pressed my head against hers, drifting close to sleep. This was the best trip I'd ever taken. I was going to find answers. I was going to save Sebastian from the asylum. And maybe, just maybe, Karin would stick around while I did.

STATE 16

I'd anguished over what mix of abilities and luck we'd need to escape the hold, but compared to the slow, shuffling humans in the cabin above, the machine arm had been efficient.

Riding inside two emptied, hardened suitcases, we made it out before the other passengers – spewed unceremoniously onto the anti-grav conveyor belt in the baggage collection hall.

The luggage circled forlornly, awaiting its owners, but we were long gone by then.

Security was present, but inattentive. Authorities were concerned with people getting on sub-jets, not getting off them – the document inspector was waving people though.

It was hard to believe we'd travelled anywhere. The austere, climate-controlled port felt identical to the one we'd started in. Apart from the Chinese signage, it was practically indistinguishable. Even the announcements over the tannoy were in clipped English. Underwhelming for my first journey to a foreign country.

"Is this it?" I complained under my breath.

Karin stopped striding towards the exit. She must have heard me.

"What is it?" I asked.

"After you."

She held her arm towards the revolving door, letting me go first.

I could see lights behind the frosted glass, but not much more. It was nighttime and the door was soundproof. I shrugged, pursed my lips, and leaned my weight.

Humidity hit me first. Thick and clammy. It took my breath away after the sterile coolness of the port. Gasping like a fish out of water,

I felt the heat cling to me like honey, prickles of sweat breaking out across my forehead.

The feeling of anticlimax evaporated – the sights and sounds of a new city immersing me in new sensations.

The port was built into a manmade island connecting Hong Kong on one side and Kowloon on the other – the defunct waterway and shipping industry cleared to make space for the long runways. To the right were the huge neon-laced skyscrapers of Hong Kong.

The Chinese had solved the space problem differently to Neo-London. Rather than creating extraplexes, they'd attached struts to the tallest buildings and created a city-spanning baseplate above. It hung over the island like an impossibly large umbrella.

Topped with shiny new structures, rising above the surrounding smog, the mega-structure had been dubbed HK1, becoming the nickname for the region. The social separation was immediately obvious. Those on the baseplate benefited from being above the pollution, staring down on those beneath, in the old city, bathed in artificial light.

Around HK1's edge hung an unbroken series of holo-displays. Colossal panels advertising products and food items. They featured heavily made-up Chinese women with oversized eyes, screaming in wordless excitement about their wares.

Opposite HK1, on the other side of the bay, lay the historic buildings of Kowloon. Sunk into the old harbour area, it appeared run-down but hid a well-known secret. Kowloon was the rich part of the city. The dilapidated exteriors a facade for dramatic effect – the ancient buildings containing modern internals. The whole of Kowloon was decorated with traditional Chinese lanterns and bunting.

We exited onto the concourse, joining the throngs of human traffic as they travelled back and forth between HK1 and Kowloon. Auto-cabs dotted the road – still too expensive for the masses, even this side of the globe.

"Different, isn't it?" Karin faked a casual tone. She knew my mind was blown.

"Definitely." Was all I could manage, scratching my head like a wide-eyed child. Then, I realised how uncool I was acting. "Shall we use a cab?"

"Do you know where you want to go?"

I shrugged. "No, I guess not."

"Then let's walk. It's been a while since I've been here."

"When were you here before?"

"Years ago. My parents took me ..." She trailed off, catching herself.

Interesting. There was more to that story, but now wasn't the time to ask.

"Okay." I filed the information away. "Which way?"

"Let's head into HK1 to acclimatise."

Acclimatise? It felt like I could never become accustomed to this. Trancelike, I followed, ambling towards HK1, or rather, the original Hong Kong beneath it.

We wandered across the kilometre expanse towards the city. The sub-jet runways on our right separated by high chain-link fences; the murky waters of the harbour on the left.

The fence did nothing to shield the deafening roar of landing sub-jets. Karin yelled over them as we strolled, providing more detail as we drank in the surroundings.

Before HK1, the Chinese had set up New Hong Kong on the mainland. Its purpose was to replace Shanghai, having suffered an economic collapse in the third global recession. They wanted to repeat the commercial success of Hong Kong from the eighties, but inside the confines of communist China, where it would be less rebellious. It had failed miserably. Hong Kong's culture had been established under British influence – its independence and physical separation from the mainland key to its entrepreneurial spirit. The new city had attracted impoverished rural-to-urban migration but little investment. Foreign firms had been too nervous to establish a presence under communist rule – the government having a history of appropriating private property. New Hong Kong had failed utterly as a commercial enterprise. It was now a farming and distribution hub.

Accepting their failure, China had re-focussed on the original Hong Kong, cutting their losses by establishing the baseplate that was now its namesake. Those who supported the government would be more likely to make it onto the new structure. Those who didn't could wallow beneath.

Nearing the main island, the path narrowed, filling with HK1 residents. It was my first glimpse at how different the locals were.

The fashion sense was wild. Neo-London was freaker fashion: leather, tattoos, punked hair. Here, the importance was on staying cool against the intense humidity. Locals only wore enough material to hide their shame. Blazingly coloured t-shirts, sarongs, belts, and braces were the order of the day – thinner and lighter the better. People looked like they'd been thrashed with luminous whips, exposing enough flesh to border on nudity.

In our leathers, we were over-dressed in the extreme. I was already slick with sweat. Karin wasn't faring any better, a red flush spreading across her cheeks. Finding new clothes had to be a priority.

All the bare skin should have been sexy, but it wasn't. Men and women cut their hair as short as possible – buzz cuts for the guys, severe fades for the women. Make-up was minimal – it would slop off in the heat.

The air quality didn't help. Industrialisation around Hong Kong coated the island in a semi-toxic pore-blocking miasma. Everyone had some sort of skin condition, ranging from mild rashes to full body acne.

Synonymously bright and grungy, the whole place smelled of sweat – as if it were baked into the stone – but at the same time it was spotlessly clean. I couldn't see a discarded alchovial anywhere. It was either culturally ingrained to clear up or authoritatively enforced – probably both. I resolved not to litter.

Excitement washed through me. It was so fantastically alien. We were hunting the source of our woes, but the distance we'd travelled had reduced the perceived danger. This was like a holiday. My first one ever.

"What are we going to do first?" Karin was fidgety as we reached the island. Her face had become radish-like, but she didn't seem to care. She was as happy as me about the change, fondling the edge of her rucksack – fingers grasping, itching to put new things in it.

I shook myself from my daze. "I guess we'd better find somewhere to stay; it could take us a while to track Maximal down."

Karin sniffed her armpit. "Yeah, and I could do with a shower too."

I laughed. It was so unladylike for Karin, but it was good; it meant we were becoming friends.

"And we'll need some new clothes," she added. "Something that fits in." Shopping was definitely top of her agenda, and she was doing a terrible job of hiding it!

I shifted uncomfortably in my leathers; the sweat was building into a funk that would start a rash soon. "Know any good places to stay? I can't stand this heat much longer!"

Karin activated her ARO, still slaved to my data contract but switched to international roaming. "It's been a while; give me a second ... Okay, the travel forums suggest Central and Causeway Bay have the most going on. It's a short trip via the underground system."

We found and boarded the metro; it was situated by the entrance to the city. Beat up and covered with state propaganda, it at least ran consistently, which was more than could be said for the Tube – a lot more. It smelled dank, but amazingly, it was air-conditioned. Such an incredible expense, but with the heat, the HK1 Governance didn't have a choice – people would die otherwise. We were on board for ten minutes, stuffed inside with a hundred other scantily clad locals, cooling off on their detours.

We alighted at Central – a metropolis of blazing lights. It throbbed with people hurrying from one air-conditioned building to another. It wasn't easy to move around – shops were stacked on top of each other, accessible via external staircases, stretching six stories high. It added perpendicular traffic to the already considerable horizontal kind.

Corporate skyscrapers towered overhead filled with workers toiling on their government assigned bureaucratic tasks. The men wore their ties open on sleeveless shirts, with professional blouses over hot-pants for the women.

We searched around, clueless where to go. The cacophony of outlets, VR cafes, and ARO vendors was like Neo-London but louder, sweatier, and more vertical. Eventually, we stumbled across a hotel Karin was happy with. I'd argued the case for staying somewhere low key, but she wasn't having it. *Prostitutes used bottom-end places, and besides,* she'd argued, *we'd need to collaborate, chat, and spread out – we needed a proper room.*

She had a point.

Set in the bottom ten floors of a corporate skyscraper, the hotel catered for business travellers. It serviced workers in the floors above who travelled non-commutable distances, but it was also open to anyone.

The receptionist gave us a strange look but politely checked us in when Karin's thumb scan cleared like any other.

The room was on the seventh floor, small and neat, with two single beds. It was wonderfully cold, bordering on frigid.

Sleep was immediately attractive. Dozing in the hold hadn't been as terrible as it could have been, but it hadn't been restful either. In comparison, the hotel was the height of luxury.

Karin dropped onto one of the beds, clutching a pillow; the decision made for both of us.

Fair enough. Sleep now. We'll figure out what next later.

STATE 17

W aking, I was clueless to the time, fully clothed where I'd collapsed face first on the bed. I glanced behind the drapes. Dawn
had penetrated the thick smog.

The hotel was on the outskirts of HK1, overlooking what remained
of the harbour. In the centre, under the baseplate, there was no dawn.

I felt better. Optimistic. We were here. We'd made it all this way.

I rolled over in time to see Karin emerge from the bathroom, a
thick plume of steam bellowing out behind her. It took me a second
to understand what I was looking at. She was wearing a bra and had
cut the legs off her trousers, turning them into makeshift hot-pants.
Sitting down on the bed, she picked up her lazeblade and attacked her
leather jacket, slicing the arms off to match.

"You should shower so we can get out of here," she chirped, bright
and alert. "And throw me your clothes. We need to get better ones, but
until we do, we can't walk around looking like this. We stick out like
sore thumbs."

She sat in front of me in a state of undress; I sensed no embarrassment from her.

That wasn't true for me. With so much of her body on display, I
didn't know where to look, so I avoided looking altogether, staring up
at the illuminated ceiling.

A few moments passed. This was stupid. Everyone in HK1 dressed
like that; I'd have to get used to it.

Self-conscious, I rose and pulled myself out of my over clothes. I
considered upping the stakes and dropping my underwear too, turning the tables on her.

No, I reconsidered; she wasn't the awkward type, and it would make it worse. I padded over to the shower. Was she grinning?

When I emerged, a new set of clothes was waiting. They'd been similarly trimmed, although to my relief, not as revealing as Karin's. The shorts were above the knee, but they covered my thighs adequately. Putting on the sleeveless jacket revealed an unflattering sliver of pale stomach where it had been shortened.

"Ready to go deeper down the rabbit hole?" She joined me at the mirror with a hint of mischievousness.

Alice in Wonderland. Not the reference I'd have used, but yes, I was ready. I felt good, even better after the sleep and shower.

I appraised myself in the mirror. "Yeah, let's find Maximal. Right after we buy more clothes!"

STATE 18

For the next two days, we embedded ourselves in HK1. If Neo-London was sprawling and gothic – crumbling brick and twisted neon, HK1 was synthetic dystopia – an unholy marriage of tech and drippy grimness.

It was overcrowded and seething. Huge orange globes were affixed to the baseplate, providing a dull, dirty glow, and the glare from interactive billboards infused everything with a flickering fluorescent haze.

Air-conditioning steam billowed from every floor of every building, mixing with natural humidity – coating everything in sticky, inescapable moisture.

It was as oppressive as the rainy soup of home, but it was new and completely different. I wanted to see it all.

I trailed Karin like a wide-eyed infant as we explored the city, acting like conformists rather than misfits – arsehole tourists or high-paid low-riskers. Either fit the bill.

We visited the underbelly of the original city, sweating and heaving below the baseplate, and the better appointed high rises sprouting atop HK1. Climbing the corporate ladder wasn't a metaphor here – it was a reality. Successful workers ascended literal escalators to the salubrious offices above. Free from the heat and grime.

The city wasn't big, only a fraction as wide as Neo-London, but far denser. It was layered with shops, arcades, and restaurants – millions of residents crammed into tiny, overcrowded domiciles.

A few rich or lucky residents could afford an escape to the posh ruins of Kowloon, but not many.

Remarkably, the populace was making it work. Politeness and respect had become necessities. Little nods between people, alien up until now, were becoming clearer. It was an effort to make existence bearable. A necessary kindness to avoid the fights that would break out otherwise. I toed the line, nodding back, trying to avoid barging people with my clumsy western frame.

Gangs congregated around arcades and alleys, but they weren't as threatening as freakers. The local security and surveillance was more efficient at keeping them in check. A mixed blessing. We were less likely to be lazebladed but more likely to register on the city's internal systems (if someone decided to look).

The food was better, or maybe just different; it was hard to tell. It was still vegetable protein but pushed into unique shapes and flavoured with unusual spices. Everything from fried balls of fish-flavoured paste, served on sticks, to bags of spicy, synthetic seafood. All available from a menagerie of street vendors, screaming enthusiastically in high-toned, sing-song Cantonese.

Real animal protein was available in the form of fried insects, which I declined. Karin didn't, scooping them up handfuls at a time, tiny legs sticking out between her lips as she munched them. Gah!

It wasn't hard to communicate. Hong Kong had a high prevalence of English speakers from the time of British influence. Most signs were in English and anything we couldn't communicate, our AROs translated for us.

We adopted the fashion, gratefully trading our butchered leathers for the half-cropped t-shirts that were in vogue. The relief outweighed any self-consciousness. I'd added loose fitting shorts and sandals, Karin, a short pleated skirt. It attached to her crop-top, front and rear, with orange suspenders. She'd paired it with a mirror-finished baseball cap to hide her face from cameras. I hated hats so opted for some white, slatted sunglasses instead. They were like venetian blinds over my eyes – more a statement than for blocking out the sun (there wasn't any). They did a good job of obscuring my face and reduced Karin to fits of laughter – good enough reason to wear them on their own.

After a couple of days, we'd even acquired the rashes endemic to the city. Small clusters of pimples on the face, arms, and stomach where skin faced the air. I didn't mind, but Karin, whose skin had seemed bulletproof in Neo-London, succumbed to the toxic smog as readily as anyone. She'd run to the first chemist she'd seen and bought a dozen different tonics – slathering the affected areas. None had worked, eventually leading her to declare "whatever" and stop fussing. After a while, we didn't notice them anymore.

It was good to spend time with Karin in this strange environment. She was easy to speak with and be around. I used the opportunity to dig deeper.

She confirmed my suspicions of a privileged upbringing. Daughter to high-profile low-riskers. Big-wigs working in prestigious IT infrastructure companies. They'd lived in a large domicile by the south coast with special dispensation to travel and work in Neo-London. All the benefits of living away from the polluted city, but with the creds to enjoy it. She didn't give much detail, but it wasn't hard to imagine an upbringing filled with finer things and little to worry about.

That had all ended when her sub-jet had been exposed to ... whatever we'd been exposed to. The persistent, droning voice of Future Karin dragging her away from a comfortable life and into this one. I had some sympathy. My life had already been in the gutter. Karin had tumbled a huge distance to join me.

I told her more about Sebastian. How he'd stepped up after our parents were taken. They'd been among the first generation of SP1N users. Addicted to early, uncalibrated batches that were overly potent. They'd been driven psychotic and hauled off, leaving us to fend for ourselves. Seb, only a teenager, was already a player by then, self-sufficient on his side hustles. He took me under his wing – showed me how to get by.

I focussed on the stories I hoped were more cool than sinister. I made the long cons more complicated than they were, the burglaries more intricately planned – more daring. I kept back the nasty stuff. The pensioners we'd shaken down for creds; the SP1N debtors we'd fingered for extra tabs.

She listened intently, but her expression was hard to read, somewhere between intrigued and disgusted.

Across the city, we made enquiry after enquiry after Maximal. At VR arcades, internet cafes, anywhere hackers might congregate, but with no success. Patrons blinked, rushed off, or in one case, threatened us – flashing an ornate, Asian styled lazeblade from beneath her sarong.

Karin's pre-state reads gave us some signs but not the whole story. People knew things, but they weren't saying. It wasn't clear why. It wasn't driven by outright fear, although that played a part. It seemed closer to self-defence.

If the community knew Maximal, he was being protected. Frustrating, but encouraging. If someone that infamous could build a trust network, maybe they *did* have the power to help us.

However we looked at it, the situation couldn't last forever. Unless the conspiracy forum had been faked, something would have to change. Why ask us to come if he wasn't going to reach out?

And of course, that was right, and when things did change, it caught us completely off guard.

STATE 19

D eeply embedded beneath the baseplate, Lan Kwai Fong heaved. Known for having the densest concentration of bars and clubs, it was here, in HK1's nethermost den of iniquity, we finally made progress.

Tired of fruitless enquiries, we were having a break, and we weren't disappointed – Lan Kwai Fong suited us: a busy network of brightly lit alleys flanked with dozens of bustling establishments.

The crowds were so dense they spilled onto the pedestrianised roads. Multicoloured fairy lights zig-zagged the thoroughfares, patterning the greasy, moisture-covered paving in pools of light.

It wasn't dissimilar to Farringdon, but unlike Neo-London, it was mostly free of unconscious bodies and cross-eyed wasters. They must exist, no city could be without them, but the HK1 authorities obviously did a better job of clearing them out.

The bars were modern, well-lit affairs, with nicely functioning air conditioning. They had to be; cool interiors were needed to attract customers as much as lighting or running water. Everything was tuned to escape the heat and sweat of HK1 – enticing patrons to spend their creds getting buzzed.

Alcohol was far down the list of available intoxicants – dehydration being too much of a concern. Instead, liquid consumption came in the form of flavoured isotonics, sucked back with abandon.

Delirium came from a different place. Slim canisters, filled from pressurised bottles behind the bar where optics normally hung.

I'd bought something called *Tropical Thunder*, watching fascinated as the barman 'mixed' the concoction. Each bottle he visited released a hiss of gas as it emptied into the canister. I eyed it suspiciously but then shrugged, broke the seal, and squirted a healthy dose up my nose. What the hell. I'd done worse.

I winced, believing the fine mist would sting my nostrils. It didn't; it was refreshing. If anything, it cleared my sinuses, making it easier to breathe. The tropical flavour was immediate. A quick, clean buzz throughout my head. There was no gastric satisfaction as one might get from a cold alchovial. It was a more heady euphoria, but one that faded quicker. I guessed it wasn't alcohol based – some narcotic designed specifically for the hot environment.

Karin joined me, grinning as her chocolate and gin flavoured 'cocktail' hit her nasal receptors.

We took a few good drags, grinning at each other stupidly as the effects took hold.

"Take it easy on those inhalers, dears." A low-toned woman's voice broke through the noise, the well-pronounced English standing out against the Cantonese backdrop.

A glamorous black woman appeared between the throngs – gold and white gown flowing about her angular frame. It was more clothes than most wore, but it was still light and airy. Close cropped hair, gold hooped earrings, and – contrary to typical HK1 fashion – thick red lipstick completed the picture.

Towering over the crowds on six-inch heels. She cut an imposing figure as she approached the bar.

It was impossible to tell her age; she could have been anywhere between twenty-five and forty-five. Clear and wrinkle free, her complexion held no clues, but her eyes were deep and wise. She couldn't be especially young with eyes like those.

Karin recovered her wits first. "And who are you, please?"

The rakish woman paused as the barman handed her a pre-mixed canister, or inhaler, as she'd called it.

"Your usual, Ms. Maximal." He handed it to her, head bowed. Deferent.

Ms. Maximal, I mouthed at Karin.

She shrugged, watching the new arrival cautiously.

Something about her was odd. I couldn't put a finger on it.

She cracked the seal between long fingers. It looked tiny in her large hands. Closing her eyes, she took a deep pull. It was an elegant process – a person of refinement appreciating a bouquet.

The barman hadn't moved; he stood there, fidgeting nervously. Finally, Ms. Maximal opened her eyes and nodded. The barman puffed out his cheeks, releasing the breath he'd been holding before shuffling along to the next customer.

Ms. Maximal turned her gaze on us behind long eyelashes. "You finally made it. I've been waiting for you."

She was sincere, but intense. Strangely menacing.

Karin said nothing, head cocked, pre-state weighing her up. It fell to me to realise the silence had gone on long enough to be rude. Steeling myself, I took a hit on the inhaler. If this was Maximal – the criminal and hacker – surprising as her appearance was, I had more in common with her than Karin anyway.

"Hello." I extended a hand. "Sorry, I guess we were expecting someone different."

She smiled thoughtfully, running the tip of the inhaler across her bottom lip. "Someone more hacker-like?"

Confirmation. No longer unexpected, but still strange. I thought about it for a moment. What had I been expecting? I admitted it out loud. "I suppose someone less ladylike – a man, I guess."

Her smile broadened, flashing large white teeth. "Very honest of you, but don't worry too much. Besides ..." She grasped my outstretched hand, shaking it firmly. "I'm not that different from you."

It wasn't the dainty handshake I'd been expecting; the sort that's mostly fingers. It was a fully loaded, hand-enveloping shake. Webs of hands and thumbs interlocking tightly. It clicked. The height, the large hands, the overall rakishness. Ms. Maximal wasn't a Ms. at all.

Karin breathed out in realisation too, resolving her contradictory pre-state. Smiling, she extended her hand, apologetic. "We're sorry, it's been a busy few days. I'm Karin and this is Daryl."

Ms. Maximal moved to shake Karin's hand, this time around the fingers, the point already made.

"I know," she continued smoothly. "In fact. I know a great deal about both of you."

The statement hung ominously, the noise of the bar seeming to quiet as she focused her gaze on each of us in turn.

"And how should we address you?" Karin continued.

"Max is fine." She smiled to ease the tension. And then in anticipation of our next question. "I don't identify with either gender, so assign whichever you feel most comfortable with."

I made a quick reappraisal, not so subtly eyeing Max up and down. I'd first assumed she was a woman, but looking closely, I could see where my sense of something being off had come from. Apart from the clothes and jewellery, there were few signs of femininity – no curves around the chest or buttocks, no swell around the thighs. Still, my first impression was the most lingering. I'd mentally connected her as female, and her voice, although low, spoke in the intonation and demeanour of a lady, so that's what I'd go with.

Karin was lost in thought, long past caring what gender to assign. "What did you mean when you said you knew about us?"

Max's response was quick and devastating, dismissive humour dancing across her face. "My girl, I've been tracking you since the Shard!"

I tried to read Karin, but her eyes were glued to Max.

"How is that possible?" I raised my voice. "We contacted *you*. Days after the Shard."

"Oh, that was a coincidence." Max smirked knowingly. "A happy one, no doubt. It gave me an easy way to reach out, but you were already on my radar."

Her elite, manicured tone was patronising, but her body language was open. It didn't seem like she was lying.

Karin jumped in. Max was running rings around her pre-state and the frustration was clear. "But how did you know about the Shard so quickly?"

"Major news like that doesn't slip my notice," – a half smile and a wink – "and much that is significantly smaller doesn't either."

My heart skipped a beat. What else did she know?

"But you said you were tracking us specifically?" Karin continued.

"Of course. After I'd hacked the CCTV footage of the explosion, my AI routines recorded two interesting individuals. They'd been at ground zero but were unaccounted for in the dead." Max took a final drag from her inhaler, discarding the empty canister. "It was quite a conundrum ... for a while."

Karin leaned back on her heels, preparing to run – the new situation bristling with unknown danger.

I turned half to the side, eyeing the room for an exit.

"I slowed the footage," she continued. "Analysed it frame-by-frame. *Very* interesting."

I blinked a few times. Max had witnessed our escape from the falling rubble – something we hadn't planned on revealing. She was holding all the cards.

Max waved her hand. "Don't look so panicked, dears! If I'd wanted to turn you in, I'd have done it by now. What's important is I can help. I've been interested in people like you for quite some time."

I'd forgotten we were in a bar; my attention was laser focussed on the conversation, ready to run if I had to. "What do you mean? People like us?"

"Oh, don't be coy! People with your, er ... condition, shall we call it?"

We waited for more information but none came. Max stood there. Smiling expectantly.

I turned to Karin after a few moments had passed, relaxing slightly. "I get it."

"Get what?" Karin stood tensely, staring at Max. Her pre-state was still having trouble, but I'd seen this behaviour before.

"Don't you see, Karin? This isn't an offer of help. It's a negotiation – a shakedown. Max ..." I gestured to where she stood, one hand on her hip, waiting. "... wants something. That's the only reason we're here."

Max responded with a patronising mini-clap. "Good boy! I see you're a quick learner. Don't judge me too harshly though. I do want to help. Please appreciate I'm a businessperson first, and you get nothing in this world for free."

I readied myself. I'd been here before – experienced a hundred back-alley deals. The rules were universal. No negotiation went well if it began acrimoniously. Being ready to run made me look defensive.

I replanted my feet, digging deep for my reasonable voice. "What do you want, Max?"

She took a few steps forward. The games were over, this was the real conversation.

"It's simple, darling." She leaned in closer. "I need more data."

Her tone was equally reasonable, but she said the last word with a hunger. One I understood. The hunger of an addict.

"And how will that help us?" Karin pushed between us. I pulled her back. I wanted to hear what Max had to say.

"You already know the answer." Max closed the remaining distance, lips brushing my ear. "Limelight is *killing* people. You've worked that out for yourselves – witnessed it at the Shard. It's all connected. Limelight, the murders, your abilities. All as one."

"Connected? How?" I whispered back.

"I don't know. That's why I need you."

I chose my next words carefully. "Okay, Max. What, exactly, do you want?"

Smiling, she slinked back and touched her shoulder. An ARO emerged. I hadn't noticed it until now. It was low profile, blending in with her gown. *CAMO-ARO*: rare, completely bespoke, and very expensive. A chameleon-class device that can alter its colour and texture, adapting to the wearer's clothes.

She reversed the screen, displaying what she was looking at.

"I'd like you to acquire something for me, dears."

I wrinkled my nose at the device. Sniffing the odour of something fishy. It displayed a building in the heart of HK1's upper disk, New Mong Kok. Around it were annotated comments: *Limelight HK1 Data Centre. High Security*.

I snapped back, the odour I'd detected becoming the rancid smell of poison. "No chance!" I proclaimed. "No way. We're not going anywhere near a Data Centre!"

Max held my gaze for a moment, then shrugged and collapsed the ARO. It vanished against her shoulder. "I thought you'd say that, but before you make up your mind, why not indulge me a little longer. I have more to show you. Will you accompany me back to my home?"

I shook my head slowly. That sounded like a dangerous, pointless detour. Even if Max could be trusted, the point would be to convince us to do her bidding. I didn't want convincing. Anything involving a Data Centre was madness – they were more secure than military installations. A protected Telcom nerve centre – containing their highly sensitive data assets. People went missing in places like that.

It was Karin's turn to hold me back, beckoning me over. "Daryl, we're here now. Shouldn't we listen to what she has to say?"

"We can't trust her."

"I know, but she's been tracking us for days – she could have reported us any time." Karin shot a dark glance at Max. "She still could."

I considered Max. Refined and ruthless. It would be easy to imagine her being cruel. I sighed and nodded. Max had asked politely, but it wasn't a request; it was a demand – laced with an unstated threat.

"Good girl." Max purred. "You've come all this way to see me, after all."

I didn't like where this was going, but our bargaining position was weak. Max only had something to gain – we had everything to lose. If she didn't help us, we'd be on the run again. From her.

We had to bide our time. Play her game until we had more information. Much as it pained me.

STATE 20

P arked outside, Max's car was a long, low-slung sedan in bur-
nished gold. Max clearly had a thing for gold.

I'd been expecting something subtle, off the grid, but nothing like
that applied to Max. She adhered to the *hide in plain sight* method of
disguise. And it was working. Even with a reputation as the world's
most notorious hacker, people feared and protected her. I was beginning to see why.

As we set off, the car's windows became monitors, displaying videos
and articles of world events – lines of programming code scrolling over
the images. The feeds weren't opaque enough to obscure the ghostly
outlines of the city behind.

The code was more advanced than anything I'd seen. Lounging
in her seat, Max caught me looking, one hairless leg crossed over the
other.

"Hacking algorithms," she remarked. "I'm always poking my nose
where it doesn't belong. I need to monitor the outputs, even when I
travel. Corporations are getting smarter all the time. I'm only afforded
a small window to conduct my work."

My hacking experience amounted to jailbreaking AROs or ripping
off cred machines. To say this was in another league was a huge understatement. Max was cracking mainstream organisations – news,
government, Telcoms, utilities. She must be an absolute genius.

I could see how she operated with impunity – the fear and loyalty
made sense.

"You use this information to keep you safe, don't you?" I aired my
thinking. "Blackmail, extortion, that sort of thing. It's why people
don't turn you in."

Max feigned offence, one hand at her chest, but with enough of a wink to show she didn't care.

"Nothing so insidious, dear." She tapped her arm console. Logos of various organisations flooded the screens – most of them household names. "It's true; when my snooping encounters something minor – nothing big enough to expose – but naughty all the same, I may, occasionally, make it known I've uncovered it. A few bribes come my way and I hold the discoveries back. I use it to secure the space I need to work."

"What about private citizens?" I snorted. "Do you uncover their misdemeanours too?"

Max said nothing. It was clear she played whatever games she needed to further her cause.

"What is your work?" Karin interjected, leaning forward and placing a hand on Max's leg to get her attention.

Max raised an eyebrow, staring where she'd been touched.

Karin smiled sweetly, leaving her hand a beat longer than necessary before withdrawing.

I wasn't sure what I'd witnessed. An alpha woman thing – two lionesses, feeling each other out.

"You've seen the news, haven't you?" Max returned the smile, crossing her legs in the other direction. "I uncover secrets. Terrible secrets. And I let the world know about them."

Karin glanced at the roof of the car. A huge curved screen in its own right.

"I've seen the articles. Only ..." The reflected feeds and symbols danced across her face. "You don't seem like much of a champion for social justice."

"What did you expect?"

Karin pulled her attention back to Max with a dead-eyed look. "Someone more humble, I guess. Demure."

Max laughed. A low, nasal sound. "Oh dear, what an impression I've left you with! Well, things will become clear for you soon, I hope."

We rode in silence for the next forty minutes, staring through the semi-transparent windows. We'd left HK1 Island and were heading deeper into Kowloon – the ruined part of the city hiding the most expensive properties. It appeared run down, but a closer inspection gave the game away. Modern security cameras were affixed to the buildings, and high-end cars were parked in driveways – their paintwork gleamed under traditional Chinese lanterns.

We pulled up to a nondescript warehouse. Another ruin to the naked eye, but secure, with no open windows or broken doors. A cube symbol, embossed on the wall, hung like a demon from an old nightmare.

I went to demand an answer. Max put up a manicured hand. "No questions, please. I'll explain shortly."

My eyes must have visibly popped from my head. This was a *Hive* warehouse! The same as where Sebastian went mad – the same damn company. It was in a different city but it couldn't be a coincidence. My teeth ground in my mouth. What was Max up to! What did she know?

I realised I'd been holding my breath and it was running out. I drew in deeply.

Either tingling her pre-state or sensing my distress plainly, Karin snaked a hand into mine, giving it a squeeze. I barely noticed.

An automatic shutter opened on the side of the warehouse, metal slats clacking closed after we drove inside. The car's window displays shut off, becoming fully transparent again. Fluorescent lights flickered on, revealing the interior of the building.

I untangled my hand from Karin's and jumped out, any respect or awe for Maximal trumped by desperate curiosity.

The warehouse in Camden had been rot and decay, but this was far from that. It had been converted into a modern living space. Faux--leather sofas and glass tables dotted around a bright and open-plan floor area.

A large bed with a leopard-print throw was centre stage, and a polished concrete floor gleamed underfoot. It looked like an ostentatious hotel room for exhibitionists.

Max stalked around the car, leaned against the bonnet, and pulled out her vaporiser – practically daring a barrage of questions.

"Welcome to my home," she declared, between puffs of lavender-scented smoke. "Well, my HK1 home. I have a few of these places."

Karin peered around, bemused. "You normally bring people here?"

"No, actually," Max replied absently. "You're the first."

I couldn't tell if that was good or bad.

She crossed to a drinks cabinet. A wooden statement to 1970s styling, complete with antique panelling and matching tumblers. There was a selection of optics on display.

She started mixing a cocktail. "Drink? I'm having one."

"I have questions," I said.

"I know. Have a drink – it will help."

The sound of ice against glass was enticing.

Sensing the weakness, she mixed two more and brought them over. Mine was whiskey based – my favoured drink over beer, when I could afford it. Was it a guess or did she know? A glance at Karin confirmed it – her drink was spot on too. Max's snooping knew no bounds.

I held off until Max had seated herself, painfully slowly, onto a sofa. I downed my drink in one and blurted out, "What the hell do you know about Hive, Max?"

Karin took a high metal stool set further back, sipping her gin and tonic quietly.

The situation was awkward. Max lounging on the sofa, me standing defiantly, and Karin watching on. I didn't care; I was having this out right now.

Max nursed her drink, stretching out the anxiety, revelling in it. Finally, in her low, seductive voice, she began to explain.

"I acquired this place six years ago. Right after all the workers vanished." She spread her fingers on the last word with a magician's flourish.

"What do you mean *vanished*?"

"You know exactly what I mean."

I thought for a second. "You mean taken – by the authorities."

"Exactly. *Disappeared* – like all the others you hear about. Or don't hear about, more precisely." Another sip. "That typically happens to isolated individuals, but this was a whole warehouse."

"You investigated?"

"That's right. The staff were normal, honest. No troublemakers or dissenters. No members of rebel groups. Not even much in their social media accounts. Or at least, nothing beyond the norm."

"How do you know what's in their social groups? That's encrypted."

Max rolled her eyes. "Oh, don't be so naïve; social networks aren't *that* encrypted."

I thought of Karin's addiction to her social feeds and tried not to look at her.

"Don't worry," Max continued, sensing the subtext. "I've been covering your tracks. You're both safe."

"How—?"

She raised her hand. "I'll get to that. Do you want to hear the story or not?"

I held my tongue and nodded.

"It was a dead end – no leads at all. But I can't leave a mystery like that alone, so I did the one thing I could. I bought the warehouse. They'd cleared it out, of course. Sanitised the place. But digital clues are harder to erase than physical ones. Organisations leave electronic footprints everywhere. In the security system, on the power grid – anywhere an ARO might interface."

I shook my head in disbelief. She'd bought the damn place. An extreme solution, but a good idea. Workers need to access records, unlock doors, buy things from vending machines. Lots of places for evidence to collect if you're skilled enough to search for it. I suspected Max had paid no actual money – extortion was more likely.

"I wasn't as advanced then as I am now." Max waved her hand over a holo-display embedded in a coffee table. "But I did uncover this piece of information."

The display projected a rotating image. It was a digital ledger headed with Hive's logo. Max zoomed in on the transactions – there were a number of payments from LL Plc. Even I recognised that. It was Limelight's stock market abbreviation.

That confirmed the Telcom's involvement. We'd known that must be true, but seeing actual evidence was a strange relief. It gave purpose to the madness, although I wasn't going to let Max know that.

"So Limelight and Hive are working together? Not that surprising, Max. Not really."

"They're not working together," Max corrected. "Hive *is* Limelight. It's a hidden, legal entity, but it's still part of Limelight's corporate umbrella."

I shrugged. "A difference without a distinction, but okay. So what happened to the people?"

Max inspected the rotating image thoughtfully before replying. "I don't know."

The answer shocked me, and the response was automatic. "What do you mean? You bought the warehouse and found this document. You uncover corporate conspiracies all the time. How can you not know?"

It was Max's turn to shrug. "It's too well hidden. I'm a good hacker, but the secrets I find are slip-ups – pieces of information stored where they shouldn't be. I discovered this ledger because a hapless office worker scanned it with an unsecured ARO. I was lucky to find it."

That was a sobering thought. The best hacker in the world relied on luck as much as anyone. The equivalent of sifting through rubbish for secrets.

"Alright." I sighed. "Then why look in the first place? What's your interest in all this? A few missing office workers is hardly your MO."

Max took a drag on her vape rig, steam tendrils rising like dragon smoke. "I know a conspiracy when I see one. This warehouse is part of a network. You of all people should know that. When I untangle the threads, it will reveal something huge. I want to crack the conspiracy open. Expose it."

"Why?"

"You're asking a hacker why they want to expose conspiracies?" she replied under hooded eyes. "Interesting."

Fair enough. I suppose it was obvious. Power, money, influence – pick your poison.

"So you're like us." Karin interjected, deciding now was the time to enter the conversation. "Clueless."

"Hardly." Max snorted. "I've been keeping a close eye on Limelight; it's what led me to you. It's surprising they haven't caught you. Very surprising. In fact, I'm happy to admit, you're the first of your kind I've met in person."

"Our kind?" Karin leaned forward, frowning. "And just what do you think you know about us?"

Max smiled. "A great deal actually ... Individuals with your *characteristics* appear from time to time. You pop up on the grid, but authorities intervene quickly, like here, at this warehouse. You two are different though. You've vexed those searching for you." She looked at us in turn. "An addict who can manipulate time, and a social diva who can predict the future. An odd combination, but a potent one. And of course, I helped too."

As unnerving as it was to have our secrets laid bare, Max had been foreshadowing her knowledge of us for a while. It was her other statement that struck a chord, and the second time she'd made overtures of providing aid.

"What do you mean *helped*?" I prodded. "We've been on our own."

Max laughed dismissively. "Don't be dense, dear boy. I had to be subtle, not draw attention to myself – I have interests to protect. However, I delayed a communication here, scrambled a message there. Enough to give you some breathing space."

"Breathing space?"

"Of course! You made lots of mistakes. Sub-jet ports watch their staff as much as passengers. You were caught on cameras in the monitoring station!"

Max's patronising tone was galling, but the realisation we'd failed to evade detection was worse. I'd been proud of getting through security!

"I scrambled the feed to keep you hidden," she continued, checking her nails. "No need to thank me."

The revelation was hard to swallow, but I couldn't deny it either. I'd had a feeling we'd been living on borrowed time for a while. Turns out we had been – time lent to us by Max.

"And as I mentioned, I've been re-encrypting your social feeds. If I can see them through the Administration's back-doors, then so can Limelight. You're welcome."

So there it was. According to Max, online security was an illusion – three-step authentication a lie. If that was true, the Administration could see everything. The notion was too terrifying to process.

Karin had been quiet throughout the last exchange, but now she spoke up. "So you know about us. What now?"

She was right. It was obvious where the conversation was heading. We needed to get to the point.

"It's all connected, my girl." Max switched her gaze to Karin but kept her legs pointed away. "Limelight, Hive, the time phenomena, everything. All the evidence directs that way. I just don't know *how* it's connected. Not yet."

Karin crossed her arms defensively. "And that's why you want us to break into Limelight's Data Centre?"

"Ah, a sensible question! Yes! The information we all seek is behind those security systems. Only breachable from the inside." She paused, gesturing to the surrounding space. "But as you can see, I'm more of a back-office type. Whereas you two are more like ..."

"Field agents." I grumbled.

"Yes!" Max snapped her fingers. "Field agents! Exactly, my dear. You gain entry to the building and I retrieve the information. A partnership."

"Unbalanced partnership." Karin bristled. "We take all the risk."

"Well, nothing's perfect." Max downed the rest of her drink. "And what choice do you have if you want the information?"

Karin's posture was humourless. A reflection of what I'd been feeling since entering Max's den. It was too dangerous, and I was sick of being told I had no choice.

I stood my ground. "No deal," I declared. "There's too much for us to lose. It's a gamble. We don't know if the data is even there, and we have no reason to trust you're telling us the truth. This could all be a lie."

Karin moved to stand next to me in solidarity. A united front I was grateful for.

"If that's the best you can do, we're better off on our own."

A few seconds of awkward silence passed as we stared each other down. Karin and me on one side, Max on the other.

Finally, Max broke the silence, a cruel expression appearing. She'd done a good job hiding it until now, but it came easily, the creases in her skin well worn.

"Oh dear. I had hoped it wouldn't come to this."

Holding our gazes, she tapped a button on her bracelet, a disguised remote control. The hologram of the ledger vanished, replaced by two real-time video feeds. The ambient lighting in the room dimmed, focusing our attention on the subjects in the images.

One was a middle-aged couple sitting in a well-appointed home. The other, a grainy security feed of a hospital ward, full of unsettled patients. It took a few moments, but then my blood ran cold – it was Sebastian's asylum. I could make out his listless shape at the end. Karin was rigid.

"Ms. Chambers," Max started, pointing to the couple in the feed. "Your parents already think you've lost your mind. What do you think they'll do if I reveal your location to them?"

Karin stood still, glaring at the image.

"I'll answer for you. They'll come for you, my dear. They have the means, that's for certain. And what will happen then?"

"I'll be committed." Karin answered quietly through gritted teeth. "Like before."

Committed! So that's what had happened. No wonder she didn't like talking about it.

"Yes, and oh, the delicious irony." Max turned her attention to me. "Institutionalised, just like your brother. Tell me, Daryl, what will happen if I inform the asylum they're harbouring a criminal?" A string of misdemeanours scrolled down the screen. I noted a fair few the police had never caught us for.

I knew the answer, but I said nothing – he'd be slung onto the street. This was bad.

"What is this, Max? We don't play ball, so you threaten us!" I couldn't believe the direction this was taking.

"I'm sorry," she replied, with no hint of actual apology. "I'm afraid I'm rather good at applying pressure to get my way. Would it help to reassure you I'm telling the truth about the data we need? Probably not." She stood and placed her hands behind her back, pacing around the video feed. "Look at it this way," she remarked, a harsh teacher addressing a class. "If you won't break into the Data Centre to help yourselves, then do it for your families."

"And if we do as you ask, you'll leave them alone?" Karin's voice was quiet.

"Of course!" Max dropped back onto the sofa, placing her hands behind her head. "I'm not a savage. You help me, and I'll help you."

Karin and I looked at each other. We were cornered. We'd come seeking help from a hacker known for their coercion skills. How naïve we'd been.

We nodded.

Sensing the change in mood, she shut off the hologram and turned up the lights. "Splendid. Now the unpleasantness is out of the way, we can get on with things."

I sighed and shook my head. We'd been outmanoeuvred, and easily so. Pawns in a new game. I consoled myself that at least we were moving forward again. If Max was right, the Data Centre may hold the answer. That is, if she was telling the truth, and if we survived the encounter. Neither of which seemed particularly likely.

STATE 21

The car jerked around on uneven paving, throwing us around the interior. I gripped the roof handle to steady myself. My leather trousers had ridden up high enough to need pliers to remove them – I was keen that didn't escalate to scissors. They were a damned curse but had proven reliable; I'd accepted them, begrudgingly, as a necessity.

At least the interior of the car was cool. My man bits were mangled, but they weren't glued together. Not yet.

We'd been with Max three weeks – time dedicated to planning the break-in.

It was a difficult alliance; the dark cloud of blackmail hung over us, but there was hope too. The Data Centre held information we both needed. Despite the danger, there was wisdom to the action. Whether Max would share what she learned was another matter, and her patronising tone, constant and grating, did little to reassure us.

Unfortunately, her attitude, albeit annoying, wasn't the worst part of staying with Max. Her bad habits were. Max had a disconcerting predilection for *touching* – "equal-opportunity lover" was her excuse. Karin shook it off – immune from a lifetime of male attention. I didn't – in fact, I was exceptionally unused to being groped. Max would slide past me in the corridor, rubbing the hard mass (disguised but rampant beneath her dress) against me. It confirmed her gender binary status, her deviant attitude, and my utter lack of curiosity for what she was offering. I'd kept out of reach after that, putting tables, sofas, or occasionally Karin between us.

To her credit, she'd at least done some pre-planning for the work ahead. Producing blueprints and schematics for the Data Centre. But her preparation had fallen short. She harboured huge misunderstandings of how our abilities worked – constraints none of her spying had uncovered. It was pleasing in a way; a win over her snooping, but a short-term one that needed resolving.

She'd assumed, for instance, I could lift a keycard from a frozen guard, and explaining objects in latent state were utterly unmovable had been a horrifying revelation for her.

Likewise, she'd misinterpreted Karin's visions as detailed premonitions rather than the vague, indistinct impressions they were. It led to an equally shattering (yet somehow satisfying) showdown between them: "No, Max, I can't infer security codes for doors by looking at them!"

Changes were needed. Three weeks of detailed planning. A straightforward game of drafts transformed into masterclass chess.

The problem was multi-layered. The target building was in Mong Kok. The traditional consumer electronics district, updated to support ARO tech. HK1 city planners had deemed it more efficient to collect the infrastructure and technicians in one place – and also the safeguards to protect them.

Gutted and refitted, the old buildings, previously stuffed with ramshackle gadget shops, now contained modern cloud servers and engineering stations connected with ultrafast, quantum-encrypted internet. All wrapped in world-class security, creating an impenetrable shroud.

Inside flowed the data streams maintaining the Telcom industry. It's lifeblood. A treasure trove of corporate and consumer secrets.

Max was right about one thing. The answers we sought were more likely to be in Data Centre vaults than anywhere else. Accessing them, though, was a different story. Inside, a gauntlet of measures would block our way. Body scanners, infrared cameras, and laser grids, plus key-coded locks for sensitive areas. All state-of-the-art.

Our advantage? No security system could account for our abilities. And with the world's most notorious hacker gumming up the works, we had a chance.

I was sure Max couldn't be trusted. Her only saving grace was her record. She'd committed herself to hurting the same corporations that were pursuing us. It was scant comfort, but *the enemy of my enemy is my friend* applied – at least for the time being.

I fiddled with the strap of the breathing mask. A constant source of itching and irritation.

"Don't take it off." Karin snapped.

I'd grown to hate that tone, but every time I removed the mask, Max or Karin would berate me.

"I know," came my muffled reply. "But once this is over, I'm making you wear this damn thing!"

The breathing mask limited my oxygen intake. A similar system used by athletes to simulate training at altitude. It expanded their lung capacity and made them fitter. As such, I'd been instructed to wear it as much as possible.

The logic was sound. My luck avoiding unconsciousness wouldn't hold forever; in fact, it was a miracle I hadn't died already. The mask reduced that risk.

Of course, they didn't have to wear it. It was the worst sensation. A nightmare contraption that stank of rubber and left a sore ring around my mouth where it sealed. Worse, every breath had to be dragged in – laboured through its restricting filter. The first day, I'd passed out, collapsing on the floor and triggering a safety mechanism to prevent me suffocating.

And the torment hadn't stopped at the mask. Karin had put me on a gruelling exercise regime. Two hours of aerobics a day. Initially, without the mask, and then after a few days, with it on. The exertion was incredible. I'd been sick on two occasions – a smell that clung to the rubber in a special way.

But it had been worth it. By the third week, my lung capacity had improved measurably. Every time the mask was lifted, I could suck in gallons of air. Together with Karin's guided meditation, I'd never felt stronger or more focussed. And better yet, with the urgency of an upcoming mission, my need for SP1N had all but subsided.

I wasn't sure if it was exhaustion or lack of idle time, but my body had no interest. Each night I'd collapse into dreamless sleep, waking in the same position – tired, sore, but willing to continue.

The car juddered over potholes, bumping us around the interior again.

I patted my shoulder, making sure nothing had shaken loose. Max had provided us with discrete, low-riding CAMO-AROs. Mine was barely visible against my jacket, connected to an earpiece through wireless comlink. The set-up permitted us to speak and hear each other, and it provided Max with remote tracking capabilities. Light and durable, the CAMO-ARO made my Saracen feel like a hunk of junk from another century.

It was becoming light as we drove into Mong Kok. A thin grey light spreading from the horizon – the sun hidden behind smog like a low-output bulb behind a curtain.

The towers of Mong Kok had more in common with Kowloon than HK1. Old by design, they aped traditional architecture dating back a hundred years. Mottled and weather-beaten exteriors clad with faux crumbling facades.

Under the plate, air-conditioning units were stuck messily to the outside of buildings – precariously holding on with rusty bolts. Here, everything was internalised and uprated to handle the heat-sensitive equipment. Windows were redesigned into cooling metallic panels, reflecting the heat and sitting at odds with the concrete superstructure, like shaded sunglasses on an ancient face.

We parked in a low-priority area, a few blocks from the Data Centre.

"You ready?" Max was sitting opposite. She'd forgone her glamorous outfits, adopting dungarees and a white shirt, with one embellishment. Her customary red lipstick. It was the most masculine I'd ever seen her.

"I guess. Unless you want to call this off and let us go?" I replied.

Max raised an eyebrow.

No, I didn't think so.

"I'll be waiting in the reception area." Karin patted my knee.

"Right ... right." I sighed, stealing myself. I felt scared, but not like before. It was a nervous energy – anxiety driven procrastination, but it was under control. This was the hardest thing we'd undertaken, but we were also the most prepared. I wasn't backing out now.

Enough stalling. I shoved the car door open, threw Karin a wink, and jumped out. She'd see through the bravado, but it made me feel confident.

Apart from Limelight's logo, the Data Centre had little to distinguish itself from surrounding tower blocks. On the inside, though, it was the best protected of the bunch – a nexus of cyber security and highly trained personnel designed for one purpose. Keeping people like me out.

Seb would have enjoyed this. Pitting our skills against a purpose-built system. Nostalgia mixed with adrenaline turbo-charged in my veins. I'd make him proud today. I had to.

As I made my way across the traffic intersection, the breathing mask didn't look out of place. Locals wore face masks to protect against smog and prevent diseases spreading. They didn't give me a second glance.

I discarded it in an alley receptacle. I'd promised Karin I'd make her wear it, but there was no point lugging it around. I wouldn't need it for this next part.

I stopped time. The world grinded to a halt; the air became still and the grimy stench of the city was no longer detectable.

Entering latent state no longer took any effort. I might lose the knack if I stopped practising, but for now, with the preparation I'd undertaken, the workshop and the clock were always in reach.

The benefits of the breathing mask were immediately apparent. Air flooded my lungs with minor movement. I should be able to take my time climbing the building.

I knew the route. I'd studied the schematics and photos. There were handholds where the concrete was mottled, and ten-centimetre wide window ledges where I could rest on each floor.

Mouth dry, I examined the twenty floors towering above and blinked away a surge of vertigo. This would be the climbing equivalent of running a marathon. Time to get moving.

One deep breath and I began climbing, gripping the pocked surface and hauling myself, hand-over-hand, up the edifice.

I slipped past the first row of metallic windows. They were one-way, hiding office workers, machinery, and servers inside. People could see out, but all I could see was the smudged metallic reflection of the world – absent me. Latent state removed my reflection. I was like a daredevil vampire.

Handholds were plentiful, and propped up in the thick atmosphere, I could take more chances than a normal climber would. One and two finger holds were easy. Even pinch holds on thin wedges of concrete were manageable.

It was on the fifth floor that problems began. The mottling, so useful on lower floors, was worse quality higher up. The architects had used better materials on the lower floors where visitors would notice, but here it was coarser, and I was building up a collection of bloody cuts. Dirty, jagged concrete cut into my hands.

At first it stung a little, but discomfort gave way to pain, and soon agony, with each move harder than the last. I swore under my breath. I should have worn gloves. It hadn't even occurred to me I'd need them.

I tried to shrug it off and carry on, but the pain intensified, and by the seventh floor, my fingers were trembling.

Then it happened. With hand strength fading, my grip failed.

My left hand slipped off the wall, leaving two points of contact – half my body floated in space, dozens of metres above the pavement.

Letting out a groan, I swung back to a secure position, arm and shoulder aching with the strain.

My heart was thumping. This wasn't going to work. The pain was too bad. Much more and I'd fall – dropping off the building like a discarded scab.

I tried to control my panic. A tightness in my groin making my arse pucker. I slid along the edge, away from the evil concrete, flattening myself against the smooth windows.

My hands were trembling, painted red all over like clown gloves. Blood from the cuts was pooling inside the latent-state bubble. I couldn't assess how bad the damage was, but they were dark red. Probably best not to look. At least the bubble would prevent blood spilling everywhere and keep my hands from getting infected.

What a damn mess. I could see the lip of the next window, but it was out of reach. Not without using the concrete.

My hands felt numb. I was in trouble. Climbing down would be harder than going up – I wouldn't be able to see where I was going. But continuing on was also impossible.

I stared up at the next window, only a couple of metres away, wishing gravity didn't apply.

My mind spun – calculating possibilities. And then it clicked. Gravity in latent state *wasn't* the same at all. The thick atmosphere was viscous, like a liquid. Normally a hindrance, but perhaps that could help?

I imagined a swimmer pushing off from the edge of a pool. Gliding, effectively flying, beneath the surface with minimal effort. A mad idea was forming.

The lack of motion was catching up with me, stars flecking my vision as the air retreated. It had held off longer than normal, the breathing mask having done its job, but it wouldn't hold unconsciousness back forever.

The mad idea cemented into a mad plan, hurried on by an oxygen--deprived tunnel vision just beginning in my periphery.

I took a moment to steady myself. Every moment I delayed increased the risk of passing out, but getting this wrong would be equally disastrous.

Looking up, I took a wide stance on the windowsill, stretched upwards, and bent my knees. Then, with a silent prayer, I jumped, removing all points of contact.

I pushed off hard, expecting resistance, but rather than losing momentum, it was sustained. I slid through space like an eel. Holy crap, it was working!

The distance to the next floor was half covered before I realised my mistake. I was going too fast. I was going to overshoot the next window!

Pulling my arms back wildly, I tried to increase the air resistance, but it was too late. I was a metre beyond the window by the time I'd slowed, leaving me in a no man's land between floors. I reached the apex; gravity reasserted itself and I slid back, landing painfully on my elbows and bouncing awkwardly off the window ledge. Flailing, my fingertips found an edge at the last moment.

Wheezing, I heaved myself up. A straining, full arm pull, precariously swinging my legs onto the window ledge. My vision was swimming with the effort, but at least the stabbing pain in my hands was fading.

Breathing hard, I took a moment to assess what had happened. The theory was right; latent state could be navigated this way, but it was far from ideal. The uncertain danger of missing a jump had gone up, but the certain possibility of my damaged hands slipping off had receded. It was this way or no way.

I kept going, bounding up the building one careful jump at a time, but five floors on, a new problem presented itself.

The jumping method was working and I was getting better at not overshooting the ledges. My shoulders and arms were aching like crazy, but I could deal with that. The issue was I was becoming dangerously lightheaded and tight-chested. I'd trained for steady state climbing, not explosive, anaerobic movement. I wasn't pulling in enough air to compensate.

I'd have to recharge my oxygen.

It was a horrible risk. There was no telling what was behind the windows. The building should be mostly filled with equipment, but there would still be maintenance and security staff. If I came out of latent state, there was a high chance of being seen – becoming a human shaped insect, clinging to the outside, ready to be swatted off.

My chest tightened further, a belt squeezing down. It made the decision for me. A non-decision really. If it was a choice between being seen or scraped off the road in a raspberry mess, I'd take the former.

I flattened myself against the window and resumed real time. The rush of air was intoxicating – luxurious – and the accompanying release of endorphins almost overwhelming. I barely noticed the high wind whipping about my head, threatening to yank me off. It felt good to breathe again. Huge gulps of glorious oxygen.

My earpiece buzzed, Max's voice crackling over the line. She sounded agitated. "Dear boy, what's the matter? I wasn't expecting to see you until you were in the Data Centre, but it appears you're still outside."

Outside. There was an understatement!

My breathing had returned to normal, but the extra effort of hanging on was now building up.

"Yeah, I'm halfway up," I said over the wind. "I had to unfreeze time to get my breath back. I'll be going back in a moment."

"Well, Karin's on her way, but you must have tripped a window sensor. The security in the building's gone up a notch."

"How can you tell? You're not patched in yet."

"I'm monitoring police chatter, of course. There's been an un-scheduled *ready-up* command sent to the local authorities. They're not on high alert yet, birds trip these sensors from time-to-time, but they'll be coming to check your area. You may find security tighter when you get inside."

Wonderful. At least I was breathing and hadn't fallen off the build-ing – a favourable trade for some extra security, I reasoned. I refroze time, feeling the tension in my muscles ease as the atmosphere propped me back up.

I clambered the remaining floors with only one more break. A balancing act between muscle fatigue and unconsciousness. By the time I swung my legs over the top, I was dripping and exhausted. I recommenced time and fell on my side, heaving as my breakfast made an escape run.

After two minutes of gagging and coughing, I struggled to a sitting position, shakily retrieving a water flask and energy rations from my backpack. I'd never done anything so physically taxing. My body was in glucose shock, starving and unable to move. I barely tasted the saccharin, orange-flavoured capsules as I wolfed them down one-by-one.

My hands were sore and covered in cuts, but the damage wasn't as bad as it could have been. The latent state bubble had made it look bad, spreading the blood around, but had also helped congeal it. If I was careful, it shouldn't be a hindrance.

It took another ten minutes before I could move again, but eventually the sugary energy worked its way through me, propping me back up. Thankfully, the comlink had been quiet. Max could see my vitals over the ARO connection. It would be obvious to her I needed the break, but she could also see when I'd recovered.

"Time to move again."

She almost sounded sympathetic.

Groaning, I stood, pushing back the urge to give in to tiredness. Gently swaying as I surveyed the area.

I knew what to expect. The target was a locked roof-access door with a single camera monitoring the area in front.

Air-conditioning ducts dotted the roof, spewing out steam and covering the tarmacked surface with sticky fog. They were a no-go – protected with laser grids. Undefeatable without raising an alarm. The door was the only entrance, and the camera, far from being a problem, was my way in.

I checked the backpack and pulled out the specialist equipment I'd brought for the task. Not a high-tech ARO attachment, laser-override system, or camera jamming sensor, but a humble synthetic carrier bag – the kind they give out at cheap convenience stores. It was even branded with the shop's holographic logo of a red and green bird.

At the same time, I retrieved a security overall. It was plus-sized and slipped readily over my tight-fitting leathers. The last thing I wanted was more layers, I was overheated enough, but once inside, I'd have to transition in and out of latent state, and the uncoordinated biker look would raise suspicion.

Keeping a wide berth, I shook the bag open and circled around, approaching the door from the side, keeping outside the camera's visibility cone. Then carefully, preventing my hands from coming into view, I reached up and gently slid the bag over the camera, encasing it in bright, semi-opaque material.

The principle was sound. The bag obscured the camera, but not completely. Security should view it as an urgent inconvenience, but nothing large enough to trigger a full security breach. In theory, anyway.

I grimaced, amazed at the low-tech solution we'd concocted. With all the assets at our disposal, we were reliant on the cheapest and most improvised option. It was like a poetic analogy for my life.

Back tight to the wall, I crept as close to the door as I dared, crouching just outside where the camera might detect me.

The minutes ticked by. I'd hoped someone would come quickly, but after half an hour, my legs were burning from the awkward crouch. I couldn't tell which I hated more – the plan we'd cooked up or the incompetence of the security personnel.

Finally, on the other side, I heard a muffled voice, faint but distinctive. I tensed, forgetting my sore legs.

The voice – a grumble of annoyance – became clearer as the door opened. "... disturbed my damn break for this."

I poised, listening for the creek of the door opening wider.

Now!

Freezing time, I groaned and straightened. My legs were nearly numb from inaction.

I stamped my feet on the ground to get the blood moving and turned the corner to investigate.

Half poking through the door was an angry, hairless, middle-aged guard. He was reaching up to dislodge the bag. Annoyingly, his body was still mostly blocking the entrance. He hadn't needed to open it far to complete the task.

I thought for a moment. I could resume time – surprise him, attempt to knock him out, and clear the path?

No, too high risk; if he got away, I was screwed. Besides, I had a better idea.

I looked again, eyeing the man up and down. Then, shrugging with a quiet apology, I clambered over his stationary body. His outstretched arm and bald head made pretty good foot holds.

Jumping down on the other side, I wondered briefly if he would remember any sensation of being trodden on when time resumed – perhaps feeling especially disgruntled, but not knowing why. Who knows where unexplained moods come from?

Inside, contrasting with the rough concrete, everything was sleek and modern. Aluminium floors reflected illuminated ceilings. Blue displays bathed the corridors in cool light, programmatically displaying locations and directions for workers.

The dynamic navigation was next to useless in latent state. I'd have to suffice with any directions frozen on screen and my memory of the blueprints.

It appeared quiet on this floor. Predominantly empty meeting rooms and unoccupied agile working spaces. I unfroze time, and true enough, the only sounds were the quiet whir of air-conditioning units and deep throb of servers, emanating like a pulse within the building. Time to check in with Max.

I slipped into a room conjoining the corridor and pretended to busy myself at a terminal. I'd be unlucky to be caught; I was another guard doing his job. Still, without the safe blanket of latent state, the feeling of vulnerability was oppressive. Every distant sound or footstep put me on edge.

I opened the CAMO-ARO and activated the comlink.

"Aren't you there yet, dear? Tut-tut. I expected better."

Whatever grace period Max had extended me after the climb had evaporated. She was back on my case. "Calm down. It's only been a few minutes' real time."

"You're only advantage. Don't squander it. You know where you're going, don't you?"

"Yes." I'd studied the schematics. "It's five floors down, along the central corridor."

A floor layout appeared on my ARO showing the target. It was dead centre in the building, in the middle of a small maze of corridors.

"That's right, but remember I can't monitor guards until you're patched in. You should stay in latent state as much as possible."

"That's funny, Max, I thought I'd stroll down there like this."

She ignored my sarcasm. "Just don't get caught. We have a bargain. Welch on it, and you'll regret it."

"I'll call when I'm in position." I ended the conversation, closing the ARO with an irritated slap. More was at stake than finding out what Limelight was up to. Sebastian's safety was on the line. Max had done worse than rat out a mad junkie to get her way. I'd be naïve to assume she was bluffing.

There was a lift, but I couldn't ride it. Not until Max had lowered the security. And the alternative wasn't going to be fun.

I followed the corridor until I found what I was looking for. A grate, high up on the wall. There was no laser grid protecting it – no need – it was already inside a secure area and they interfered with maintenance workers. Some still had heat and motion detectors but both would be rendered ineffective by latent state.

Double checking for cameras and guards, I retrieved my lazeblade and shrugged off the uniform, placing it in the backpack. With the disguise off, the last vestige of protection was gone and the feeling of being exposed intensified.

My lazeblade trembled in my hand as my nervousness peaked. I stared at it, willing it to stop. This wasn't even the hard part. I had to get myself under control.

The shake receded. For the time being.

Refocusing on the grate, I sheared off its two retaining bolts and dropped the deactivated lazeblade in my jacket's external pocket – I'd need it later. Then, standing on tiptoe, I peered inside the vent. I could make out blinking motion sensors peppering the walls. If any part of me passed the threshold in real time, an alarm would ring out and the mission would be over.

After swinging the grate onto its top hinges, I transitioned back into latent state. It stuck out at ninety degrees, frozen in place. I hoped no one would hear it clang when I exited, but in the meantime, it made an excellent handhold.

I clambered into the tight crawl space; the sensors had stopped blinking. The only light to guide me was a few dim maintenance bulbs as I shuffled, feet first, down the narrow space.

It wasn't a long stretch of ducting, but the space was limited, and after a dozen metres, I could feel myself going light-headed again. The slow progress was limiting my air supply.

Ten more metres of fumbling and wriggling and I emerged into a wider chamber intersected with other openings – including a vertical drop. Orienting myself head first, I peered over the edge. I couldn't see the bottom, just the dim glow of maintenance lights illuminating the way down to the bottom of the twenty-story building.

My head swam with vertigo, adding to the lightheadedness. I didn't have time to worry about the consequences. If I didn't move soon, I'd suffocate.

Nudging myself over the edge, I braced my elbows and toes against the metal ducting. Friction from the leathers held my weight, but it didn't make the plunge any less terrifying. I inched forward until I was vertical, blood rushing to my eyeballs. Then, relieving some pressure from the wall, I attempted a controlled descent.

It didn't work. Too much resistance was let off and I plummeted four metres with a sickening lurch, completely missing the next junction.

The leathers squeaked as I jolted to a halt, elbows stinging where I'd reapplied force against the metal wall.

My breathing was ragged with adrenaline. I could hear it in my head like a tyre leaking air. At least the drop had replenished the supply.

Damn! Come on, Daryl, I berated myself. I'd have to release the pressure more gently. The physics were different but they still applied! It didn't matter how thick the atmosphere was, I'd still fall at the same rate, and reducing momentum would always be a problem.

Recommencing, I tried a different tactic – teasing the pressure from my elbows but keeping my toes firmly wedged against the duct walls. It worked. The muscles in my quads burned where I was pushing my legs outwards, but the difference in pressure allowed a more consistent fall. I tried to ignore the vertigo by enjoying the continuous rush of breathable air!

Counting down the next four junctions, I arrived at the fifteenth floor, awkwardly arching into the horizontal ducting, and uttering a quiet thanks as my body was supported again. I had no doubt my hands were shaking, but fortunately, I couldn't see them in the gloom of the tunnel.

Inching along the memorised route, I eventually found the target vent – vague green light leaking from the other side.

It was a security substation. I marvelled that it was accessible, but then I reminded myself what I'd done. No normal human could make it down those ducts. We were exploiting a weakness the security architects couldn't account for. There weren't even sensors this end of the tunnel. The substation room was locked up tight from the other side, but no one would have predicted someone entering this way. It was infeasible.

Transitioning into real time, I winced as the first grate clanged closed, echoing through the vents behind and above me. It was louder than expected, even at a distance. I hoped no one was close enough to investigate.

I retrieved my lazeblade, still tucked in my jacket pocket; it flashed in the tunnel, reflecting off the metallic interior. I lazed through the rear of the retaining bolts and slithered through the open grate.

I stood and looked around. The substation doubled as an emergency telecommunications hub, the cramped interior packed with snarled Ethernet cables and twinkling switches. A few holo-readouts circled a central display with barely room to stretch my elbows.

Crouching amongst the wires, I hard connected my ARO to the terminal with a link cable. The place was stuffy and stank of dust slowly cooking on hot electrical components. *Access requires authorisation* rotated in red font on the terminal.

"We'll see about that." Max did her work, the message distorting, flashing violently between green and red. It was like watching a war of wills. After a few seconds, the readout distorted for a final time before switching over to green. *Access granted*.

The hack was quick. I'd just crossed my legs painfully beneath me in the tiny space. Cables draped over my shoulders like warm rubbery snakes. I had to respect her efficiency if nothing else.

"Karin, are you ready?" I opened the comlink.

"She can't talk right now." Max answered instead. "She's next to the security gate in reception. She mustn't draw attention to herself, but she can hear you, and yes, she's ready."

I barely had time to whisper "good luck" before Max cut the power, plunging the room into darkness, accompanied by a crunchy, metallic sound as the breakers tripped.

I counted down the seconds. There was no display during the blackout. All I had was my imagination – a conjured narrative for what I hoped was happening: Karin slipping past the body scanners in the darkness and confusion, discarding her overcoat in a plant pot, and hurrying to the meeting area beyond, blending with the throngs of uniformed office workers.

Time marched on. Surely it had been long enough?

The lights flickered back to life, along with Max's voice. "She's through and awaiting instructions. The building's on medium alert."

Max sounded breathless over the comlink, like she'd been holding it in.

I'd been doing the same. I let it out with a long blow. "Remind me why they won't raise the alarm?"

"I simulated a power surge. That will explain the electrical short-out. It's fake, of course; I don't have the authority to actually increase the power, but when they check the logs, there'll be something to explain the tripped breakers. In the meantime, I've locked down the room you're in. You should have access to the security feeds now."

The display was showing a three-dimensional vector of the building, highlighting the positions of hundreds of security cameras. Using the touch screen, I could pinch to zoom, select floors, and tap cameras. The feeds appearing on a secondary display. The more I selected, the more images were tiled. Controls on the auxiliary screen switched them to full screen or between colour, thermal, and night vision. A manual joystick and zoom dial overrode the automated panning.

I selected reception. Karin had made it to the meeting area, blending against a menagerie of white-coated technicians and office workers. She was doing a good job of looking calm, but it was only an appearance. The place was crawling with security guards. She'd be questioned eventually.

"Karin, I can see you. Nod if everything's okay."

A slight nod.

"Good. Max is in the security system. You'll have worker access to most of the building. I'll identify any guards that may be carrying today's master keycard. If you're ready, head to the lift."

Karin rose, walking delicately over to the bank of lifts. It arrived right away, courtesy of Max. I'm sure to everyone else she looked normal. To me, she looked like a coiled spring, awkwardly vibrating along the corridor.

Once inside, her comlink crackled to me. "That was quick. Nice going."

I looked at my hands, bloodied from the climb, still shaking. I was exhausted to my core. It had been a few minutes for Karin and Max. I'd been at it for hours.

"Yeah, quick," I said wearily.

"We need to wrap this up as soon as we can," Max chimed in. "Daryl might not last much longer."

It was said with enough seriousness to hurt my pride.

"I'm fine, Max."

She didn't care about my wellbeing, just the data; why pretend to care. It was cynical.

"Darling, I don't want you harmed. You're my most valuable asset at the moment. I may never get an opportunity like this again."

At the moment. That was the point. Cynical *and* manipulative.

"I've detected a cluster of guards on the fifth floor," Max continued. "That should be the focus of your attention. Karin, be a dear and scout them out."

I watched as Karin exited the lift on the fifth floor. There was no room for disobedience. I whispered instructions, guiding her through the maze of corridors until she approached where the guards were patrolling.

This was dangerous. These were the people we should be avoiding, but it was the plan. Karin had to get close enough for a pre-state read, try to infer if a guard was holding the master keycard for secure areas, then ... acquire it.

She strolled briskly past them, head down.

"Keep walking," I urged. "I think they're curious about you."

That was an understatement. Her flyby was as subtle as a brick through a window.

Tense seconds passed under the gaze of the guards until she turned a corner and they went in the other direction.

"Anything?" I breathed out.

There was a pause before Karin replied. "Nothing," she said finally. "I'm getting good, clear pre-state, but none of those guards hold the master keycard."

"Are you sure, dear?" Max interjected.

"Of course I'm sure."

"But could you be mistaken?"

"It's like recognising your own handwriting, Max," I offered, remembering Karin's explanation. "You'll have to take it on faith, I'm afraid."

"I take little on faith." Max bristled. "I prefer facts."

"Welcome to our world," Karin added with finality.

Unsatisfied with the answer but unable to refute it, Max continued to offer up new groups of guards for Karin to investigate. Her technique improved as she went. Sidling up from behind and then reversing rather than walking by.

By the fifth group, Max was becoming irate. "Nothing! Not even a false positive?"

I was beginning to wonder too. Karin's pre-state didn't have a flawless track record. Maybe this was one of her outages. I could tell from her increasingly stilted body language she was getting worried.

"Ignore Max. She doesn't know what she's talking about." I encouraged. "We've still got a large group to check. Sod's law, that's the one."

Karin sighed, surprisingly audible over the comlink. "Where is it?"

"Fourteenth floor."

We waited for Karin to travel up to the target floor. I hoped this was right. We were screwed otherwise.

"I've got something." The comlink crackled.

Thank God. I zoomed in. Karin was hovering near a female guard who had broken away from the main patrol.

"Be cautious." Max added her appraisal. "She holds a second degree black belt in Jiu-jitsu."

"How do you know ...?" I trailed off. Max must have bio-scanned and background checked her already.

"Don't worry," Karin replied. "I only need a quiet place to tranq her."

I looked again. The guard was stocky and strong looking – hair tied in a neat bob. She looked capable. "Karin, I don't know. You heard Max; this is no pushover. Are you sure you can tranq her?"

Karin's reply was clipped and impatient. "Just find me a quiet space."

I checked the building's itinerary. "Room 1405, around the corner – it's open and empty. Looks like a storage area. Ms. Jiu-jitsu is heading that way, but you'll beat her if you move quickly."

Karin ran to the unoccupied room. It was filled with spare computer equipment – an IT storage area. I watched on the internal feed as Karin retrieved the tranquilizer gun, producing the slender device from her inner jacket pocket. She held it ready at waist height, just inside the door. On a separate feed, I could see the guard turn a corner and approach the room.

"Count me down," she whispered.

"Okay, get ready," I replied, holding my breath as the guard closed the distance. "She'll be passing in three, two, one ..."

"Can someone help me!" Karin called out.

The guard stopped in her tracks, hand on her stun-baton, voice authoritative. "Does someone need assistance?"

"Yes, I'm having trouble with a box in here. Can you help me, please?"

The guard nudged the door with her free hand.

Quickly, Karin grabbed it and yanked hard, pulling her through.

The guard reacted equally as quickly. Rather than pulling back, she leaned forward, throwing them both deeper into the storage area. The jolt dislodged the tranquilizer gun, sending it clattering across the floor. The door clicked closed.

"Damn it!" Karin cried, scrambling off the floor. "Lock the door!"

"What?" I cried in shock.

"Door locked," Max said, overriding my manual control. "I've also disabled the local communications."

"What are you doing, Max?" I shouted.

"As I was asked," Max replied calmly. "This is for Karin to sort out now."

"Are you out of your mind? She's no match for that guard!"

"Too late now." She sounded intrigued and disappointed at the same time.

Back stiff with anxiety, I returned my attention to the screen, watching the two circle each other. The guard was trying to use her comlink, but it was down, deactivated by Max. Karin's head was cocked to one side. Listening.

Realising there was no back-up coming, the guard reached for her stun-baton, retrieving it from a leg holster and flicking it out menacingly. The end sparked with electricity. There was no audio from the feed and Karin had disconnected her comlink. It was clear the guard was shouting something, building up to something.

A moment later she lurched, swinging the baton, but Karin ducked away neatly, still listening. She'd moved before the attack had even started. With the guard off balance, she slipped behind and kicked her in the small of the back, sending her crashing against the far wall. The impact smashed a computer panel in a shower of sparks.

The guard spun, face bleeding. She looked shocked, but not angry – focussed. Her stance altered and she lowered her centre of gravity, left arm forward in a defensive posture. The baton was up, ready for action.

She attacked forcefully, purposely, baton striking through the air at multiple angles. Karin avoided them all. Dodging left, right, and jumping over low blows. All the time, head cocked and listening.

I could see what was happening. Karin was using her pre-state, forecasting where the attacks would come from. The guard couldn't land a hit, but Karin wasn't combat trained; she moved gracefully but without the strength and agility of the guard. And she was tiring.

I retrieved a white technician's overcoat from my bag. I'd been saving it for when Karin had the master key.

"Max, she's on the floor below. I have to help."

"She looks like she's doing okay to me."

"Unlock the door, Max!"

The door on the far side of the substation opened. I pulled on the overcoat, shoved my way through the cables, and bolted.

The lift arrived right away, and within a few seconds I was on the fourteenth floor. I resisted the urge to run; it would draw suspicion. I power walked instead – as quickly as I dared.

"Max, unseal the door and lock it behind me."

"I don't think that's nece—"

"Do it!"

The door opened and I burst into the room, but it took a moment to understand what I was looking at. I'd been ready to launch myself into the fray, bundle them both to the ground. It didn't matter how expert in martial arts the guard was, two on one always makes the difference.

None of that was needed. The guard was already unconscious, lying on the floor.

I blinked, bewildered, jaw hanging open. "What happened?"

Karin had relieved the guard of her security jacket, belt, and baton and had finished wrapping her legs, hands, and mouth with electrical tape. She had a small cut on her temple and seemed to be favouring her left arm, but she was otherwise fine.

"Don't worry about me. I'm okay." Karin used her mouth to rip off a piece of tape. Then through muffled speech. "... I've got the keycard."

"You're hurt." I pointed to where she was bleeding.

"It's nothing." Karin spat the tape out and used it to finish securing the guard. That was partially true; she was shaking, still amped by whatever had happened.

I softened my voice. "Karin, it will draw attention to us. Sit down for a moment; let me sort that cut out."

Karin stood and smoothed out her clothes, touching her temple. Seeing the smear of red across her hand, she nodded and acquiesced.

I grabbed a folding metal chair and set it down. Karin dropped onto it with a thud. I removed a swab and some water, cleaning the area. The cut was barely visible when I was finished.

I removed some pain killers and handed them to Karin. "For your arm."

She stalled for a moment, then took them with a swig from my water flask.

"All sorted? That was amazing."

Karin smiled. A vague, tired gesture. The shake in her hands was still present, but better. "Yes, thank you."

"How did you do it?"

"Lucky shot."

"Didn't look lucky."

"Yeah, well, I had an advantage."

"You were predicting her movements. I didn't know you could do that."

"I told you, the more immediate or localised the threat, the better my pre-state works. This was about as immediate and localised as it gets."

I puffed out my cheeks. "Well, it sure looked cool on camera."

It was an inane comment, but I couldn't help it. It had looked cool!

"I hate to break in." Max interrupted over the comlink, doing just that. "But you can't hang around there all day."

"Yes," Karin mumbled, and then more firmly. "She's right."

Karin removed her office worker overall and put on the guard's padded jacket instead. The guard was bigger than her, but it fit well enough.

"Time to go." She stood, securing the guard's belt. It hung awkwardly around her. "We should have everything we need now."

She produced the keycard from an outside pocket. An unassuming white plastic rectangle. All this hassle for that little thing.

"Max, what will happen to the guard?" I looked around the room. There were no windows, but it was still an unsecure utility room.

"I'll seal the door and time it to release for after we're finished. The cleaning crew will find her later tonight."

We left, hurrying along the corridor. Karin dressed in the guard's uniform, me as an escorted technician. I felt awkward and conspicuous, but the office workers and guards we passed didn't seem to notice. A large building like this must have a high turnover of staff – new faces every week.

Back in the lift, the button for the tenth floor was highlighted red. The Server Room floor – the nerve centre of the building. The only location with unfettered access to stored data. And also the most secure – containing back-ups of Limelight's corporate transactions, messages, employee records, and strategic data.

I pushed the button and a few moments later the lift opened into a small vestibule. In front of us, a large security door was flanked by a panel – gating access.

Karin had already retrieved the keycard and was sliding it into the reader. "Here goes nothing."

A few agonising moments passed until the light above the card panel flashed green. The door unsealed with a hiss – hermetically pressurised. It swung inwards, revealing at least thirty centimetres of steely thickness.

Beyond lay the interior. I'd thought it would be large and industrial, full of machinery, but it wasn't. It was small and crisp, completely white – antiseptic. The ceiling was evenly illuminated – a single, unbroken light source shining across its surface.

Instead of the banks of computers I'd imagined, there was only one. A monolithic, single-screened display, three metres tall and wide enough for two seats, swinging out on gimbals.

The room felt small compared to the footprint of the building; it should have been tens of metres across. Looking closely, I saw the walls revealed the answer. They weren't featureless. There were vague, door-shaped outlines etched into them. Unobtrusive handles, recessed into notches, were almost invisible. The heavy processing equipment must be beyond, leaving the central workspace as a sound-protected area.

I jumped into one of the seats, Karin taking the other. They were curved to provide a relaxed posture. An antithesis to the tension I was feeling. I wanted to stand upright, but it wasn't an option.

Max was online. "I've disabled the cameras and sensors from recording you for the time being. You shouldn't be disturbed, but it won't take long until someone realises they haven't received a scan of the area. I'd guess you have under ten minutes – better make them work, kids."

Was it possible for Max not to be condescending? I didn't think so.

"Okay, Max," I said. "I'll patch you in, but don't forget our deal."

I hard connected my ARO – attaching it by cable to the waiting auxiliary port. As in the security substation, the digital wrestle for control repeated itself. It took longer this time, but after a minute, it flashed green. I wasn't sure how I could feel a mixture of hatred, awe, and envy, but they all applied to Max.

"Commencing download."

Was that nervousness in Max's voice? The snark was gone.

We waited a few minutes, tension building. The area was locked down, but the sense someone could walk in was omnipresent. It beat down like an unbearable heat.

Max was muttering something. "Darlings ..." Her voice has changed again, the haughty officiousness replaced with excitement. "There's ... there's so much here ... more than I imagined—"

"Are you finished?" I cut in, foot tapping. "When can we get out of here?"

"The things I could do from this terminal ... It's connected to the rest of the HK1 network. I could download all the police records, or the unofficial archives ..."

"Max!" Karin blurted out. "Ten minutes, remember!"

There was a pause; Max was engaged in her own fight for control. "Okay." She relented. "This will have to be enough. You two can go. There's an exit on—"

"Wait ..." Karin cocked her head, listening. "Something's wrong."

An alarm klaxon sounded. The lights in the room turned from white to red and the terminal powered down in front of us.

"Oh dear. Security has detected you." Max sounded distant.

"How?" shouted Karin over the wailing klaxon. "You secured the sensors, didn't you?"

"I don't know ... Some redundant security ... I'm locked out, and the police have been called – they'll be here soon."

"What do we do?" I jumped up from the terminal.

"I'm sorry, I have to go. You're on your own."

The comlink went dead – just static. She hadn't even closed it before activating her car's dampening field.

"Max!" Karin called again, but it didn't help – couldn't. Max was in a sensor-proof bubble now. She swivelled violently in the gimbal, eyes wild. "That damn bitch! She's abandoned us."

"Calm down," I answered, surprised at the iron in my voice. "Hackers work alone for a reason; we knew she couldn't be trusted."

Karin clenched her fists at her sides and with physical effort returned herself to zero. "What the hell are we going to do?"

"Run, I guess." I shrugged, crossing to the doors I'd seen earlier. I didn't feel scared exactly. Tired and disappointed was closer. My body was out of adrenaline.

"In here." I pulled at the notch, sliding the door open.

Karin joined me in a low corridor beyond. Bathed in green light, both sides were flanked with blinking racks of servers. This was the industrial area I'd imagined. Cables lay along the ground, networking the servers like an exposed vascular system. The sound of machinery was loud, but not as loud as the klaxon. It was a relief to be moving away from that sound.

We hurried along until we reached the end – the passage ended in a laser guarded vent leading outside. Sabotaging it would set off an alarm, but that was hardly a problem now.

I took out my lazeblaze and hacked liberally around the grid. Mini explosions showered us in sparks as the grid shorted.

The vent cap behind the laser grid looked sturdy, but a few heavy kicks caused it to fly outwards.

The humid air of HK1 rushed in, revealing the city and a sheer drop into Mong Kok below.

"What now?" Karin peered over the edge. "I can't make that."

It was the reverse of the climb I'd done to get in. It was only ten floors, but even using latent state, it would be impossible.

"Not sure." I looked around anxiously. "Any pre-state?"

"Nothing useful right now. If only we'd brought some rope."

Of course! It was staring us in the face. I ran to the beginning of the server racks and started yanking the cables off the floor. Seeing the plan, Karin started pulling too, scraping them up in fistfuls. It was trunking cable, providing power and networking to the machines. A few hard tugs and the connections snapped out of the ports.

"Do we have enough?" Karin eyed the spaghetti tangle.

I did some simple maths. Ten floors. Three metres per floor. Thirty metres of cable. I looked at the pile, but with no way of measuring it, my calculations were useless. There was a lot there, but thirty metres?

"Yes, I think so." I lied. She'd see through it, but it was a fib we both wanted to hear.

Brushing the doubt aside, I tied one end to a metal post where the vent had been hinged. The cable was thick, with a braided outer mesh. It appeared strong enough to hold our weight.

I kicked it out, watching it unfurl into space. I peered over the edge; it was a relief to feel the sticky heat of the city. Freedom was close, but had the cable touched the pavement below? I couldn't tell in the murky light.

There was a commotion in the control room behind us. The sounds of boots and angry voices. We were out of time. "What do you think?" I said to Karin.

"I don't think we've got time to worry about it," she replied earnestly as she wrapped the cable around her hand. "Let's get the hell out of here!"

I watched her scramble off the edge into the fog below.

I looked back to the control room. A helmeted head was poking into the tunnel, accompanied by what looked like the muzzle of a rifle. Karin was right – it was time to go. I gripped the cable, and holding my breath, I jumped into the soupy wetness of HK1.

STATE 22

I opened my eyes, floating in confusion between sleeping and consciousness. A hateful place, filled with sensations of not knowing
– a pre-waking dementia.

Today I relished it. I knew when reality came rushing back, I
wouldn't like it.

First the dripping. A *plink-plunk* somewhere in the darkness. Then
the sticky feeling – skin against sweat-stained mattress.

My eyes adjusted to the gloom and the memories returned. We'd
escaped the Data Centre, but the cable hadn't been long enough. We'd
plummeted the final four metres, Karin twisting her ankle.

I looked around the room, searching for her outline against the
dank walls. She was curled on an equally filthy mattress, injured leg
jutting out at an angle. A puddle was gathering from a leaking air-
conditioning unit. The whole place stank of damp and mildew.

I wasn't sure how we'd escaped. I'd expected a swarm of guards at
the base of the building, but there had been none. Even slowed by
Karin, we'd beaten a successful retreat, finding our way to a hotel.

Daring to call this place a hotel was a joke. They charged by the
hour, so it was technically true, and importantly, it was one of the few
places that wouldn't question me dragging in an injured woman. The
leathery-faced crone at the desk had waved us through like it was a
common occurrence. Just another pimp patching up an abused sex
worker.

At least it had a vending machine. Which we'd half emptied. The
floor was littered with sweet wrappers and isotonic vials. Hardly room
service, but I'd been hungry after the ordeal – passing out following
the binge. I had no idea how much time had passed.

I dragged myself upright and groaned. Every muscle hurt, especially my arms and shoulders. I could barely lift them. And my head was pounding. Too much sugary food. We couldn't sustain ourselves like this for long.

The room had a shower. It was disgusting, but so was I, and any amount of cleaning was better than none. The showerhead sputtered and groaned but did eventually spew forth something resembling water. Mercifully, it was sufficiently heated to be tolerable.

Karin was awake when I got back. I barely noticed I was naked and dressing in front of her. She didn't mention it, and at this point it didn't seem to matter.

"How are you?" I asked, pulling my shirt on.

"Okay." Karin stood, grimacing. "I mean, battered. Ankle hurts like hell, but I'll survive. You?"

I shook my head, struggling to express the mixture of exhaustion and pointlessness I felt. "Vacant." I settled on.

Karin nodded her agreement. "What now then?" Karin leaned against a sideboard; it wobbled on unsteady legs. She thought better and took a seat on a chair instead. Basic and wooden. Only one in the room.

"No idea."

"I can't believe Max abandoned us."

"You can't?"

"Alright, I can, but, well, for the love of God! Leaving like that. She's meant to be some kind of social justice warrior. I guess I expected ..."

"What?"

"A moral code."

I raised an eyebrow. "Honour among thieves?"

"Yeah ..." She trailed off. "Well, something like that anyway."

Karin's ARO beeped from where it lay on the mattress. That was odd; she was between plans since we'd disconnected her from Limelight. Max had set her up with a safe account so we could keep in contact, but no one knew the access code.

"Wait." I held up my hand as Karin hobbled over to the device.

"Why? How much worse can it get? Max said the account was untraceable, didn't she?"

I gritted my teeth, hand floating impotently, but couldn't counter the point as Karin picked up the ARO.

My eyes widened as she flipped out the screen and I saw who was calling.

There was a display on the wall, cracked at the edges but still working. Karin mirrored her ARO to it.

Max appeared on screen. I didn't recognise where she was. It wasn't her car or the warehouse. She looked different, harried – her appearance not as manicured as normal. A misplaced smear of lipstick here, a crooked collar there.

"Sorry for leaving early, children—"

"You've got a lot of nerve!" Karin interrupted.

I put a hand on her arm. Whatever calmness (or nihilism) had overcome me in the Data Centre was still with me.

Karin bit her tongue.

"Yes, I know. Most unfortunate. But I had to go. Police would have swarmed me if I'd stayed and then we'd have nothing. And besides, I did help you escape."

"The hell you did!" Karin retorted, irritated at the sanctimonious tone. "Where were you when we were suspended on a power cable thirty metres above the ground?"

"Nowhere near you, of course. What would be the point in that?"

"Oh, I don't know." I cut in. "To help us maybe? You may not have noticed, but Karin's injured; she may have broken an ankle."

"Yes, I can see that." Max sounded bored. "And I'll let your tone slide, bearing in mind I very much helped you."

Karin looked like she wanted to hurl something at the screen, smash its cracked facade into pieces. Not that it would have helped; the signal was coming through the ARO not the TV.

Max was still talking. "... Aren't you curious how you escaped when you got to the ground? Unusual, don't you think, no one was waiting for you?"

I pursed my lips; that had been unusual. I'd been thinking about it since we made it to the hotel.

"Aunty Max still had security access, so I did you a favour before I left."

"What was that?" Karin replied, hand twitching. The urge to throw something still palpable.

"I locked the front door and cut their communication to authorities."

Karin's face screwed up in frustration – fighting conflicting emotions. It was the most out of control I'd seen her and she knew it. Betrayal brought out the worst in her. She turned her back on the TV so we couldn't see it.

Maddeningly, what Max was saying made sense. It explained why security hadn't met us at ground level.

"They manually overrode my lock-out after a few minutes," Max continued. "But that was plenty of time for you to escape now, wasn't it?"

I fought the urge to pick up where Karin had left off. Point out how easy she'd had it compared to us, but I held back. I could see things could have gone worse if she hadn't intervened. I hated the way Max operated, safe and sound from her remote locations while we took all the risks, but that didn't change the facts.

"Anyway," Max was saying, as if nothing had happened. "Something turned up in the data, and I thought you'd want to know."

"You bothered looking? You're only interested in your own agenda." I scoffed.

"Well, obviously. I'll be busy for years. It's a treasure trove. But, I looked into your specific situation – a deal's a deal. Set your expectations though. It won't be everything you want to hear; however, it's still very interesting." She puffed out her cheeks, making her look monstrous on the distorted display. "Whatever's going on is well hidden, not part of the official record, but there is a pattern." She paused to let the tension rise.

"Get on with it, Max." Karin turned back, mostly her normal self again, but her patience was wearing thin. It was good to see her back in control. I didn't want to deal with Max on my own.

"Very well." Max shrugged, neither happy nor sad her attempt at drama had failed, and laid out the revelation bluntly and without ceremony. "Limelight's senior team are being targeted. Murdered actually."

My bottom lip jutted out, eyes narrowing. "Okay ... What does that have to do with us?"

"More than you think. The disasters you've seen on the news feeds are connected, including the one you escaped at the Shard. The victims were manipulated to be in those areas – marked out to be executed.

The catastrophes were merely diversions, something to hide the foul play."

"How?" Karin asked wearily. She'd re-seated herself, the web of her hand wrapping around her brow.

"It's really quite amazing," Max continued excitedly, oblivious to the death toll she'd just glossed over – she seemed immune to such concerns. "It's easy to manipulate people if you alter their data feed – something Limelight has complete access to for its employees. Think how much we all rely on that information. You can be rerouted with fake traffic reports. Prices on products can be increased to make sales look more enticing. Appointments can be rearranged, contact information altered, vital information withheld, and social media filtered. We're so reliant on data to inform our lives. Limelight socially engineered its senior leaders' feeds to put them where they wanted, then boom! ... Organised a little accident for them."

"That's bullshit." I couldn't believe what Max was saying; it didn't sound credible. "People aren't that predictable."

"Well, there's a margin for error. It's why there have been several disasters – to sweep up stragglers. And they had to shuffle in plenty of regular people to hide the connection back to Limelight. However, eventually, you can manipulate anyone to appear somewhere you need them." Max tapped at an off-screen console. "Look, don't take my word for it." A man in a green jacket appeared.

I recognised him. It was the guy I'd nearly killed at the Shard. Of all the examples to use.

"His name's Jason. He's a senior technician at the European arm of Limelight. An immovable meeting was created in Neo-London he had to attend. After checking into his hotel, he asked his ARO for a dinner recommendation. A restaurant was displayed in the London Bridge area. Once there, his table was electronically delayed and he was shown the Shard exhibition to kill time. This is one example of many, and he followed each step precisely as laid out."

I looked at his face; he looked young, full of potential. I felt better knowing it wasn't my fault he'd been there – and also that he'd survived.

"He died in a train crash yesterday ..."

My optimism descended in flames.

"... A series of rerouted meetings made sure of it."

I turned to look at the mottled wall, despair building. What were we up against?

"Don't look so vexed." Max droned on – any reaction to my emotional display purely incidental. "The fabulous Ms. Maximal isn't finished helping you yet."

"More blackmail?" Karin made no attempt to hide her contempt.

"Hardly. I've got what I need. I'm giving back now; quid pro quo, as they say."

What now? I returned my gaze to the screen. It flickered, a new image taking its place. It took a few seconds to register what I was looking at. A CCTV feed of a hospital room, a nice one. The furnishings were clean and modern – some flowers tastefully arranged in a jar on the bedside.

Fitted with an electronic filter, the window amplified the light, giving an artificial but convincing appearance of real sunshine. A private facility; nothing like this was available publicly.

In the centre of the room, a uniformed nurse was feeding a man. It was Sebastian. I barely recognised him. He'd been cleaned and shaved, lying beneath crisp white sheets. Vacant, but in good health.

"No need to thank me; it was trivial. I changed his records. Sebastian has medical insurance now. Permanent and untraceable, of course. And I had him moved to this facility. There's nothing I can do for his mental state, but he'll be looked after from here on out."

I touched my face. I was crying. It had started as a low feeling in my chest, but it was coming out of me thick and fast like an invisible dam had broken. I couldn't remember crying so hard in my life. Not even after the accident.

Karin hobbled over and put an arm around me while Max watched on, an uncomfortable look on her face but with the good grace not to interfere.

I felt ridiculous, unhinged, unable to control myself. Thoughts hit me like mini-strokes. I'd done it. I'd found a way forward. I'd taken care of things – like Seb would have wanted.

Is this what it was to achieve something? To have a goal and make it happen? I'd done nothing worth a damn my whole life. The enormity was overwhelming.

I tried to breathe, to gain control. It was hard, but after a few moments, the emotions began to recede and new ones crept in to replace them. Ones I was less familiar with. It was a sense of pride, and a renewed feeling of strength.

And then the tears were gone. Stopping as quickly as they'd started. A flash flood that had raged hard but was now over. I set my jaw and brushed off Karin's arm, standing resolutely, not bothering to wipe my face.

This wasn't finished – Seb was out of danger, yes, but still a vegetable. I had to keep looking for a cure. And this was bigger now. He wasn't the only victim. People were being killed. If I could get Sebastian out of the asylum, I could help them too. A purpose within all the chaos.

"What about Karin?" I asked pointedly, but an emotional wobble was still there.

Max redirected her attention. "Oh, I haven't forgotten about you, Ms. Chambers. Nothing so dramatic unfortunately. Your parents are fine. Living in France. I haven't notified them where you are, and I don't plan to."

"How can I trust you?"

"You can't. But why would I help Daryl and betray you? Wouldn't make sense. Besides, us three make a good team, don't you think?"

"Team?" I almost choked on the word. "You're the least team-orientated person I've ever met!"

Max smiled. "Well, that's true, but bearing in mind our recent successes, I've decided I need to be a bit more … inclusive."

That stumped me. A lone-wolf hacker acting like part of a unit. My brain was too exhausted to make sense of it, but after a few moments, I shrugged. It would be foolish to reject her offer. Better to humour her and see where it leads.

Karin sighed. There'd be no love lost between them, but she'd reached the same conclusion – any help was better than none.

"What's our next move then, Max?" she asked wearily. "If you're going to help us, what do we do now?"

"Xavier Johnson."

"Who?" we said together.

"Dr. Xavier Johnson. The Technical Director of Limelight. One step down from Francis Lyme – the CEO himself."

"And how is he going to help us?" A stress headache was forming – I could feel it bearing down on me.

"He's not. You're going to help him." Max stopped, waiting for understanding to set in.

"He's been targeted, hasn't he?" Karin ended the pregnant pause. "For elimination, like the others."

"Good girl. I see your thinking cap is on. You're right. Xavier's been marked in the system."

I was suspicious; something didn't sound right. I felt a new confidence to challenge Max – now I wasn't being actively blackmailed.

"Max, I thought you said the records were hidden, difficult to interpret."

Her eyebrows raised, the inference clear: *How dare you question my analysis!* – But she answered anyway. "They *are* hidden, but the pattern is clear. Xavier's been redirected to a meeting in New Tokyo; however, the data's erroneous. It's outside of the organisation's normal scheduling. The attendees and agenda don't suggest any commercial reason for a man of his seniority to be there. Xavier's diary has been manipulated to ensure he attends."

"So what?" I was unconvinced. "We go there, warn him, show him the evidence, and he helps us? Just like that?"

Max shrugged. "Well, darling, I didn't say it would be easy, but something tells me you two will persuade him. And in any case, I'm going to stay with you. Not in person, no, no, no. It will all be remote from this point on."

Of course it will.

"And I've attracted too much attention already. I need to keep moving. But if my hunch is right, you will uncover something huge. I want to be there when you do."

On second thought, Max staying remote was fine by me. I still remembered her (him) pushing up against me. Keeping her at a distance was safer for everyone.

Her motive was clear; she was staying close to lead her to more precious data. Still, we needed allies, and Max was undeniably good at what she did. We'd need to keep our eyes peeled for a double-cross, but I got the sense Karin wasn't going to let that happen. She'd been burned – that wouldn't be repeated.

"You said Tokyo, right?" I groaned, moving the conversation on. "I assume that means another freezing trip in a sub-jet hold?"

"Oh, don't be ridiculous. I know how to get around port records. You're travelling first class this time. Unless you prefer the hold?"

I looked around. The stained mattresses. The dripping air conditioning. Bottom of the barrel in every way. I wasn't sure I could even imagine what first class looked like, but I wasn't about to reject the offer either.

"No, Max, first class will be fine. Set it up."

STATE 23

We boarded the sub-jet to Tokyo, strolling on like high-
rolling elites. Shoulders back, noses high. No latent state, no
pre-state, and no funky leather trousers. In fact, no uncomfortable attire of any sort. Quite the opposite. First class required smart business
wear.

The HK1 salesman had assured me the acrylic suit I'd bought contained all the properties of cotton but would never wrinkle and barely
needed cleaning – repelling dirt and smells via its silver-biotic lining. I
hadn't tested the cleaning claim (and wasn't keen to), but it certainly
hadn't creased in the hours we'd been sitting on the sub-jet.

I'd glimpse myself in mirrors and window reflections, not recognising what looked back. It was a person I wanted to be though – the
inverse of how I felt most mornings.

Karin had given me her seal of approval, mouth crinkling in a half
smile. I'd been walking on air ever since, but there was fear too – it
foreshadowed where I might go, but also how far I could fall. The
gutter was a long way from here.

A visit to a private medical centre had put Karin right. The owner
had waived the fee and removed any record of us being there. He didn't
have a choice. Max's threat to reveal a hard drive full of indecent images
of questionably legal girls had assured his cooperation.

The good news was Karin's ankle wasn't broken, only sprained.
She'd be on muscle stimulants and painkillers for a few days, but she
would heal if she kept off it.

Happily, there were few reasons to move in first class. The seats
were massive, luxurious, and with the flip of a switch swept back

to lie completely horizontal. If not for the surrounding people and background roar of engines, it might be mistaken for an actual bed.

Flanked with a host of in-flight entertainment, there was plenty to pass the time. Full-speed internet, a library of holovids, a music track selection, and to my disbelief, even a high-end VR rig.

Karin lost herself online right away – plugged in and detached. Furtively updating her social networks. No doubt her followers were somewhere between curious and furious over her extended absence.

Max had fashioned us with new identities. We were travelling as Mr. and Mrs. Trevor and Charlene Best. We hadn't asked Max to marry us, but embarrassingly, she'd done it anyway – probably to annoy me. Karin had shrugged it off – her apathy putting me deep in the friend zone. Whatever. It wasn't the worst place to be, and frankly, we had more important things to worry about. I'd let it go. At least for the time being.

Where was Jay? I'd sent him a message thirty minutes ago over the sub-jet's quantum-broadcast channel. If it was secure enough for business elites, it should be good enough for us. Max would encrypt it anyhow, so together with our new personas, Limelight shouldn't be able to detect us.

The response came back. He was online, had been for some time – it was 6.30 pm in Neo-London. Prime gaming time for Jay. I pulled on the VR helmet and sent a party request, materialising in his environment a few moments later. A space fighter simulation. I was sitting in the co-pilot's seat staring into the chaos of an active battle. Red and silver bolts flashed across the sky as tiny fighters vied for control. Their sleek, arrow-shaped bodies banking and spinning in the classic dog-fighting style.

A sound-dampening field activated, allowing private conversation – isolating me from other passengers.

An electronic version of Jay was sitting to my right. His avatar adorned with mirrored aviator sunglasses. They looked ridiculous and perfect at the same time.

"Hey, Daryl, how are you?" His lips moved in an unsettling way.

VR was good, but the *uncanny effect* – the difficulty matching ad-hoc speech – had never been solved.

He put on the inflection of an overbearing parent. "You don't call, you don't write! What's a mother to do?"

I rolled my eyes, hoping the helmet was sensitive enough to display it to him. It seemed to be.

"Did you meet up with our friend? What's he like? Everything I said he'd be, right?"

Friend. That was a funny way of describing Max. Awkward ally. Extortionist. Sexual harasser. All were more fitting, but there was no point bursting Jay's bubble. As far as he knew, Maximal was the hero hacker he'd imagined them to be. Better to let him maintain the illusion.

"Yes, we did," I replied. "It's been hard work, but, er ... *he's* been quite helpful."

Now wasn't the time to get into Max's gender binary status. It was confusing enough in person.

"And what about your travelling partner? The spook."

"She's not a spook," I replied impatiently, turning on the exterior pass-through camera. I knew the sound-dampening field was active, but I wanted to check she wasn't paying attention. "In the friend zone," I whispered.

Jay was tracking an errant fighter moving out of range. "For the best," he replied distantly, focussed on the battle. "You don't want an agent keeping tabs on you."

I'd forgotten the lie we'd fed Jay. I should set him straight, but for now, he was happier with the fabrication, and there were things I needed to check with him. Best not to muddy the water.

"Jay, is everything okay, by the way? No fallout from helping us?"

"Damn!" The fighter escaped.

He turned the unsettling face on me again, a fake but reminiscent grin digitally recreated. "Not that I've noticed."

That was good. I hadn't thought about Jay much since we left Neo-London. Hadn't had the mental bandwidth. But hearing him now reminded me how he'd put himself on the line for us.

"I'm guessing you're not just checking up on me?" he continued.

"No. Jay, do you know anything about Xavier Johnson?"

"Er ..." He paused. "Not a huge amount. Wouldn't your new friend know more than me?"

"Maybe, but I'd like to get your view."

Max dealt in facts and had almost no imagination. In contrast, Jay's conspiracy paranoia and lateral thinking had been scarily close to the truth. I wanted to know if he could connect any dots we'd missed.

"Okay. Well, let me think. He's a big shot at Limelight. Technical Douchebag or something."

"Director."

"Yeah, whatever. He's not a big feature on the conspiracy threads, but a few years ago he lit them up. It didn't last long, but it started a few theories."

"Go on."

"Well, he was always seen together with Francis Lyme. They were, like, best friends or something, but one day Lyme retreated from public life. Pretty much vanished, leaving Johnson to run the company."

"Were there any more details?"

"Not really. Just speculation ranging from corporate conspiracy to foul play, but it didn't go anywhere."

"Why?"

"Lyme made an official holo-release a few days later. He wanted to take a less visible role – something about health reasons and wanting to be closer to his family, blah-blah-blah. Besides, he didn't formally step down, just sort of retreated. Guys on SCAM.NET analysed the footage; it wasn't obviously fake and there didn't seem to be any stress or coercion in his voice. It was weird, but weird things happen. Not everything's a conspiracy theory."

I laughed out loud.

"What?"

Jay's lack of self-awareness was hilarious.

"Only loons and paranoid maniacs think that way." He banked the space ship and went into a loop. "Woo-hoo!"

My stomach turned. A danger of joining a VR game while already on a moving object. Any more of this and I'd come down with simulation sickness.

"Hey look, Jay, I gotta go."

"Cool, man. Take it easy." And then with the overbearing accent. "Call home soon, my boy. I worry!"

I pulled off the VR helmet, taking some breaths as the nausea retreated – I'd caught it just in time. Karin was looking at me.

"You okay? You look paler than normal."

"Yeah," I replied. "A touch of simulation sickness."

"Really? You?"

"We all get caught short sometimes. You done socialising?"

The last word came out sarcastically, making me sound like a dick. As per normal, Karin didn't notice, or didn't rise to it. Still, I felt the need to apologise. "Sorry. I didn't mean that."

"I know."

"That stuff pops out of me sometimes. I can't help it."

"Don't worry. I know when you mean something and when you don't."

I nodded and looked away, but her words rolled around in my mind. I turned back. "Wait. You know? As in pre-state? I thought you only get that occasionally."

Karin shrugged. "I do, but over the last few weeks, you're basically always in pre-state."

I could feel my ears heating up. "So you can see my intentions all the time!"

"Pretty much, but don't sweat it; it's not as interesting as you think. Lots of people get to that point naturally. If they know each other well."

I was mortified! How many indecent thoughts had crossed my mind on this flight, let alone over the last few weeks? No wonder I was in the friend zone. Safest place to put me!

"That's easy for you to say." I went on the offensive, ears flashing like sirens. "You're not the one with your heart on your sleeve 24/7."

No reply. Not even an apology. Just a *What do you want me to do?* face.

I grimaced sullenly. "Why is it on all the time, anyway?"

"I don't know." Karin shrugged. "Maybe Future Karin wanted me to ignore your bad attitude. To ensure we work well together."

Ouch. That was low. I suppose I did have bad habits. A lifetime hanging out with lowlifes will do that to a person.

Then out of the embarrassment, a thought emerged – a more hopeful one. I straightened up, neutralising my voice before asking. "Does it mean we're closer in the future?"

Karin shrugged again, even less interested. "Yeah, I suppose. Or more likely there's some interplay between our abilities. Something that makes my pre-state more sensitive around you."

Shit. That was plausible – crash and burn. Still, it sounded like Karin was in my future, which was reassuring. I compartmentalised my shame – an old but useful skill. Hopefully my thoughts weren't doing too much harm if Future Karin was looking out for me.

"Please prepare your seats for landing." An airhost's voice interrupted over the tannoy. "We'll be making our approach into Tokyo shortly."

An unexpected surge of excitement jolted through me, flushing away the negative feelings. Since its resurgence back to a tech capital, Tokyo, or more accurately, New Tokyo, had become insanely expensive to travel to. I'd never heard of anyone going there, let alone met someone who'd made the journey.

Despite the exchange, I was glad Karin was with me. However things played out with Xavier Johnson, it was bound to be interesting. In the meantime, I'd have to deal with her knowing everything about me. Time to swallow your pride, Daryl.

STATE 24

S et on a hillside at the outskirts of Old Tokyo, the sub-jet port
looked out over the city – landing runways jutting from the dome
like artificial eyelashes.

Debarking was uneventful. Clearing customs practically apologetic, with sycophantic Japanese attendants bowing furiously and
muttering placations in broken English.

Shepherded into a two-seater mag-shuttle bound for Old Tokyo,
we set off with a jolt, a tannoy announcing the journey would take
approximately ten minutes.

I peered through the rain-spattered window, forehead against the
cool plexiglass. I could make out the silvery lines of the city, visible
below low-hanging smog. It was a shambling mess. A place I couldn't
imagine wanting to visit, but it was a necessary stop on the way to our
actual destination, many vertical kilometres above.

Most cities hid their dystopias, layering technology over like a surface glaze to hide the inner rot. Old Tokyo wore its oppression openly.

As the shuttle zipped along, we could see people shuffling about
their business on the roads outside. They looked beaten, heads down,
vacant, and grey.

Tokyo had been the epitome of technology and style in the twenti-
eth century, a testament to futuristic design and fashion. But the once
shiny skyscrapers were now tired and crumbling.

Ancient advertisement hoardings dotted the tracks. The animated
characters and Japanese girls ripped and peeling – the soft drinks and
video games they used to display no longer recognisable.

"What happened here?" Karin stared in disbelief. "I've never been
anywhere so depressing. Are you sure we're in the right place?"

"You don't know?" I turned to face her. "I thought everyone knew."

"Not really. Something to do with New Tokyo?"

Karin's interest in tech began and ended with her ARO and social networks. She'd know of New Tokyo, everyone did, but apparently not the background and what it had meant to Japan.

"Yeah." I grimaced. "New Tokyo did a number on this place."

She swivelled in her chair to face me, hands clasped in her lap. Story time.

I acquiesced, recounting what I knew. The words sobering as I spoke them.

The Japanese economy had been in a dire state at the turn of the century. The rest of the world had caught up in technology, and Japan's insular, borderline-xenophobic ways of working had prevented globalising as fast as the Tiger economies emerging from the rest of Asia. The population had become apathetic, birth rates declining and the volume of unproductive, care-dependent elders soaring. Something drastic had to change, or they'd risk slipping into a second-world economy.

The last place of competitive advantage was their telecommunications sector. They'd been at the forefront since its creation, achieving a hundred per cent penetration of mobile devices among adults before any other country. They leveraged what remained of their industry expertise and ingenuity into a massive gamble.

Japan knew satellite technology would drive the future. It was the backbone to broadcasting the increasingly pervasive range of mobile services. But there was a problem everyone had to deal with first – the expense to launch and maintain those satellites.

Their solution was radical. New Tokyo – the first geostationary orbital city, connected to Earth via magnetic space elevator.

The world had thought the Japanese insane. Space elevators should only be possible at the equator, but Japan would not work with anyone else. To reap the full commercial benefits, this had to be their endeavour, and theirs alone – tethered to the Japanese mainland. It meant not only solving the immense construction challenges but also mastering the physics of creating a curving elevator shaft away from the equator.

It had all but bankrupt the Japanese government, indebting the country and creating decades of austerity. Old Tokyo and the surrounding areas had suffered, disintegrating as Japan pumped resources into the project. And not only natural resources; anyone with useful skills, from engineering to hard labour, had been conscripted – paid just enough for basic subsistence. It was a dramatic switch from democracy to totalitarianism, justified under the banner of a national emergency.

Incredibly, the people hadn't rebelled. Dissent or attempts at sabotage were rare. Fierce nationalism and cultural honour kept them motivated – constantly parroting the Government's propaganda: "For the greater good".

They maintained their sense of duty, but the endeavour broke the spirit of a generation of Japanese workers.

Arguably, it had been worth it. Twenty years after the first shuttle launched to create the new station, they switched the space elevator on, and overnight New Tokyo became the epicentre for production and maintenance of satellite networking around the globe.

Components could be ferried to the platform cheaply via the elevator, and the station was permanently crewed with engineers to deploy and repair them. For a fee, they would launch and service other countries' satellites, but it was more cost effective to subcontract the work to New Tokyo – or relocate there.

From the start, New Tokyo was envisioned as a comfortable habitat, with the facilities to shelter and entertain the population of a small city. The rates were exorbitant but necessary to cover running costs. The lack of investment in Old Tokyo and other major cities showed it still barely ran a profit, but that didn't matter; the Japanese were relevant again, and they had a plan. New Tokyo wasn't a static station; it was a scalable platform. In time, it would grow sufficiently to plough profits back to the mainland. That hope kept people going.

Despite the rental costs, there was no shortage of companies wanting to take up residence. Being technically not on Earth, New Tokyo was the ultimate tax haven – the savings enough to offset the most exclusive premises on (or at least near) the planet.

"Wow," Karin interjected. "I didn't know any of that. Was that why Limelight moved there? For tax reasons?"

I could feel she was staring at me, but my gaze was through the window, appraising the poverty. Seeing it laid bare was getting to me.

I shook my head and explained further.

Francis Lyme had been a visionary. He'd seen the potential of New Tokyo immediately. One of the first pioneers to move his fledgling Telcom to the station. He'd gambled on the untested platform, risking key resources in its hostile, outer-space environment.

Fortunately, the Japanese had done a thorough job. Despite the harsh working conditions, they'd maintained their reputation for meticulous quality – honour demanded it. Reports were the station was a marvel of engineering. Well designed, modern, and with an outstanding safety record. There was a waiting list of ten years for companies wishing to move their operations. The Japanese couldn't build it quickly enough to cover the demand. Early movers like Limelight had won big with cost savings and increased speed of development. Money ploughed into creating the quantum-broadcast network that now led their field.

Karin listened as I ran through the details, nodding with no small amount of disbelief.

"I know, incredible isn't it?" I remarked, looking across the broken skyline of Old Tokyo.

Through the haze, I could make out the space elevator's shaft. A thick umbilical, fifty metres across, woven from immensely strong nanofibers. It extended like an impossible spire, kilometres into the sky above.

The shuttle neared the end of the line, passing through an energy barrier encircling a nicely appointed reception area – the elevator lying beyond. It was the only place of note for miles. Few people went anywhere else in Old Tokyo.

The mag-shuttle was essentially a high-security link, controlling who accessed the site. If they'd tinted the plexiglass, no one would even know the original city was there. I wondered if reports of the Japanese acceptance of their fate were completely true. The fortifications looked ready to defend against a revolt.

"No point hanging around." Karin jumped up. I couldn't agree more.

Housed in a facility much like the port, the space elevator's reception was marble, glass, and aluminium, but with typical Japanese flourishes. Sweeping kanji characters and crimson flags adorned the walls. Doors and gates were highlighted with polished wood panelling and ornamental metalwork.

Max had booked us fast-connecting tickets. Our new IDs provided digital camouflage, but we might be recognised more conventional ways – by a savvy security guard or Neo-London busybody. Best to move quickly.

We made our way to the elevator, clearing security in another flurry of bows and ingratiations. A buzz of anxiety surged as a guard took a few seconds longer over our IDs. Fortunately, Max was a master of her art and he soon nodded, waving us through. It was just as well – there were a plethora of laser grids blocking every vent and access area. It was a class above what we'd experienced at the sub-jet port or the Data Centre. Even with our powers, I wasn't sure we'd escape if uncovered.

Through security, the departure room lay ahead. Unfurnished and industrial, it sat in contrast to the posh reception – bustling with people from all walks of life. The elevator was a multi-lane road to the station above, ferrying business executives, engineers, and labourers – they all rubbed shoulder to shoulder as they looked for their boarding gate. Like any commuter route, it was workmanlike and undecorated.

Contrary to popular thought, the elevator was multiple lifts in one. Fifteen smaller compartments around the perimeter, holding between ten and a hundred individuals, and a much larger central lift, accessible by a large hangar door. The configuration provided flexibility to transport a constant stream of workers back and forth, but without running the more expensive freight elevator reserved for very large objects, like satellites or space shuttle parts.

We were in lift number two, one of the lower occupancy and more expensive cabins. On the way around, we passed lift number fifteen in time to witness the maximum occupancy of one hundred Japanese labourers cramming themselves in. Standing room only for the five-hour journey.

Our lift, by comparison, had fully reclining seats, a stocked bar, and even a shower. Important looking businessmen and women surrounded us. They eyed us suspiciously for our age, but they soon dismissed our presence and returned their attention to their ARO displays and VR rigs.

We took our seats. An announcement signalled we'd be leaving soon, and a few moments later, a following one reported we were underway. I hadn't felt a thing – no sense of movement or inertia at all. The magnetic lifting technology was undetectable, although I knew we were accelerating at an incredible rate. I leaned my ear close to the wall – I could hear a deep, faint hum.

There were no windows, but display panels set around the circular cabin displayed exterior shots up the thickly corded elevator cable. It looked endless.

My hand started tapping my seat tray nervously and I could feel a tingle in my stomach. It wasn't anxiety; it was excitement. New Tokyo was the thing of dreams – the last place humanity had with anything approaching a homogeneously high standard of living. A purpose-built ecosystem, propagated with the best technology; free from the crime and pollution that plagued the rest of the planet. I never thought I'd see it in my lifetime.

Fuelled by my twitchy excitement (and a few alchovials), time sped on merrily. Eventually, via the display, I could see a dot at the end of the cable. It grew, taking on a cylindrical shape, rotating smoothly in the flat light of the unfiltered sun. The first time I'd seen anything solar-illuminated and not obscured with haze or pollution. It seemed unreal, leaving me nervous and breathless. Like looking out on the ocean for the first time, not knowing what was on the other side.

New Tokyo was designed to be extendable – a segmented, spinning tube that could be added to at either end to increase capacity; its rotation simulated gravity. As we approached, I could make out the separate segments of the habitat. The rings towards the end were nearly twice as long as those in the centre, which correlated with the increased demand of each successive addition.

As we neared the end, the sheer scale of New Tokyo made itself clear. With no frame of reference, it was impossible to quantify distance, but I knew the outside cylinder was about two kilometres in circumference and roughly the same again in length. That left an internal floor space of approximately four kilometres squared, bigger than most city centres, and it was growing all the time. I could make out the skeletal structures where it was being extended – creeping along the shaft, like an artist's sketch of what would eventually be there.

The elevator threaded into the centre of the cylinder, docking with a giant gimbal that allowed the station to rotate smoothly around the shaft.

We felt a shudder as the cabin started to spin, matching the rotation of the station. My body went light, and I began to feel queasy.

I looked over at Karin; she was positively green.

"First time in New Tokyo?" a Japanese businesswoman asked in heavily accented but perfectly understandable English.

"Uh-huh," I said, a wave of dizziness washing over me.

"This is the worst of it. We're at the centre now where gravity is least; once you get down to the outer ring, gravity is about half what it is on Earth. Most don't notice any sickness down there."

A voice came over the tannoy announcing we would disembark soon.

"But watch out for tall buildings," she continued. "The gravity at the top gets back down to more like a fifth standard. Some people don't like that."

I nodded my thanks, not trusting myself to say anything in case I was sick.

The doors opened. We released our security buckles and floated upwards, spiralling inelegantly.

The woman pointed at grips along the tops of the chairs. They had seemed useless on the ground, but now their utility was clear. She yanked herself forward towards the door, gliding through the cabin.

We followed suit.

Each of the elevator doors attached to tunnels containing shuttles. They flowed from the central shaft to the inner rim like spokes on an enormous bicycle wheel. We weren't directed so much as *loaded* by station personnel into independently powered seats – manhandled to set us perpendicular to the station.

The perspectives were crazy. Up and down were interchangeable. It was generating a hardcore nausea headache.

One of the staff must have noticed me greening out. He advised me to close my eyes. "It will get better near the outer rim," he said in sympathetic English – far from the gruff space stevedore I'd been expecting.

I did as told, shutting my eyes as he strapped me in. I imagined the firmness of the seat as being down and that helped reset my brain. The shuttle-seat set off, and after a few moments, I began to detect real gravity. Up became up again, and down, down again – senses rushing back like a switch in my mind had temporarily been turned off and was now flipped back on.

I started to feel well enough to crack my eyes open, and I was glad I did; it was a sight no one should miss. The shuttle tubes were clear glass allowing a fabulous view. Spread out below and above, the immense cylindrical interior of New Tokyo unfolded like a bizarre city from a house of mirrors. A sprawling metropolis of lit buildings, white domes, satellite dishes, and blinking antennas. Some taller buildings appeared to bend close to each other at the top, but it was a trick of the curved interior. They were straight, but the radius of the cylinder meant they grew towards each other as they moved towards the centre. Some structures had taken advantage of the curve, joining at the top to form mighty, asymmetrical arches. One was emblazoned with Limelight's logo – the company's headquarters. At either end of the cylinder was a gaping maw into space, black and terrifying – I tried not to look at it. The buildings and infrastructure were airtight, but the worry of being sucked from the station was hardly irrational.

As I arrived at the base, I was almost feeling normal. Still lightheaded, but the gravity was enough to trick my mind all was well again. The seats filtered out into an arrival hall.

Karin arrived a few seconds later, eyes closed tight. She had to be shaken by the waiting attendant to rouse her. She came stumbling off the chair, slumping towards me, collapsing on my shoulder.

"You okay?" I asked stupidly, holding her up. She obviously wasn't.

"No, my head is killing me."

"Yeah, pretty disorienting, huh?"

"Disorienting? I feel like a pneumatic drill is going off in my head!"

Karin looked grey, and she was physically trembling.

A sign reading *Guest Accommodation* was glowing in the distance. It looked welcoming, and at the moment, very necessary.

"Come on," I said, dragging her to her feet. "Let's find a place to rest; you're no good to anyone like this."

Karin nodded and let herself be pulled along.

STATE 25

K arin was sick for a full day, rolling and shaking – bedridden and sweating, despite the air conditioning. Space sickness is motion sickness on steroids. A close relative of VR disease. Common for new arrivals to the station, and when it hit, it hit hard. Discounting the initial lightheadedness, I'd been fine – the hours playing sims with Jay clearly provided some immunity.

I'd wanted to tease Karin. She'd been so unshakable, even under incredible stress. It seemed ludicrous for such a small thing to take her down, but after her third visit to the bathroom, stumbling as she tried to catch vomit through pale figures, I'd thought better of it. Scoring points was not a good idea.

New Tokyo expected this. On-site pharmacies were stocked with stabilising drugs, and after one night's sleep, Karin was back on her feet – a point she made clear with a kick in the ribs while I slept.

"Ooph! What the hell was that for?" I let out, gripping my side as I shot upright from under the sheets. It hadn't been vicious, but it was enough to leave a bruise.

"That's for making fun of me last night!" She towered over me, hands on her hips, dressed in workmanlike overalls.

"I didn't—" I stopped, my drowsy mind catching up. Shit. Her damn pre-state, now constantly switched on, had clocked my thoughts, even through her nausea!

"Who are you? The damn thought police!" It wasn't fair. I'd done nothing wrong!

"Oh, toughen up. You've got to get up anyway." She turned away, busying herself packing a rucksack. She looked fine – a bit pale but nothing like last night. Her hair was neatly gathered in a side pony-tail – intentionally resembling a part of the workforce.

I groaned as I got out of bed, knowing I wasn't fooling her. She wasn't wrong. Xavier Johnson was speaking at a New Tokyo conference later today. The one where, presumably, an attempt on his life would happen. We had a lot to do.

The guest accommodation was tiny but well designed. Full of ingenious storage solutions. Beds that folded vertically, drawers in walls, and retractable clothes hangers.

I'd spent a good part of the night staring through the window at the station's curved interior, book-ended with its inky-black disks, trying to convince myself I wasn't dreaming.

I retrieved a pair of overalls from the wardrobe. It disappeared into the floor at the touch of a button.

Outside the station was incredible. It was organised much how any city would be, containing promenades, shops, residential areas, and commercial sectors. Each new segment was built to demand, lending it the unplanned charm of an organic metropolitan city centre.

Challenged by space, every building was bespoke. New Tokyoites had adopted a culture of repurposing whatever they could. Tiny one--bedroom studios stuffed into decorative arches; old satellite hangers reused as hydroponics bays. Even retail shops had been overtaken by engineers – jokingly re-clothing the mannequins in overalls; stuffing their hands with screwdrivers and hammers.

Merchants selling non-essentials crammed the alleyways between buildings. High-quality meals were available in station-run food halls, but Earth-based luxuries, like chocolate or alcohol, were rare and expensive. There was a frowned upon but thriving black market for such consumables.

It was a busy mess, but it was beautiful in its pragmatic efficiency. A beacon for those living in Old Tokyo, hoping one day to join the more fortunate, literally, in the heavens above.

We made our way through the bustling streets. It was easy to navigate, bouncing along in the reduced gravity. Skylights set between colossal steel beams revealed previews of what lay ahead inside the cylindrical structure. The Limelight building was unmissable. Its conjoined towers loomed above everything else on the skyline – ringline?

The interior roof obscured our view as we neared, but it was well signposted above the entrance.

Apart from two guards, security was light. The ground floor of Limelight was a tourist attraction. A walk-in museum – a showroom for their accomplishments to woo investors and attract talent.

Karin froze as we approached, head cocked.

"What's wrong?" I tensed up. Seeing Karin like that was never a good sign.

Her eyes darted from left to right, voice low and urgent. "Pre-state is going wild. Max was right – something's going on here."

I glanced around; everything seemed peaceful. A few people milled around the museum. The guards were relaxed. One leaned against the wall, the other hummed to himself – their stun battens holstered and buttoned.

"Can you be more specific?" I urged.

"Not at the moment. The whole place is swarming with murderous images though."

"Like at the Shard?"

"Yes, similar."

I didn't even try to hide my frustration.

"How is it you can predict the incoming punches of a black belt but can't give a better clue than 'murderous images'?"

"You know the answer," Karin muttered – she wasn't having it today. "The more localised and immediate the threat, the better the prediction. Especially when I'm the subject."

My ARO beeped.

"You better answer that."

"Who is it? I assume it's localised enough for you."

"Answer it and you'll know."

"Can't you just tell me?"

It beeped again.

"You better hurry, or people will get suspicious."

The guards were standing straighter, a little more aware.

I humphed but did as I was told. Rather than opening the screen, I pulled out the comlink and placed it in my ear. I didn't want to attract more attention.

"Hello, sweetie," Max drawled over the link.

I was astonished. I hadn't expected to hear from her until we were back on Earth, and even then, I'd been sure her help was time-limited.

"How are you able to talk to us up here?" I whispered into the link.

"Oh, easily. New Tokyo has a communications network like anywhere else. The data stream is monitored, of course, so I've had to cover my tracks, but it's nothing too difficult."

Arrogant as normal, but for once, it was good to hear from her.

"Can you help us?"

"I told you I would."

"I didn't think you'd keep your word."

"Have I lied to you once?" she replied indignantly.

I thought for a moment. Max had deceived and manipulated us plenty, but a straight up spoken untruth? No, she had me there.

"Anyway, my little disbeliever, Johnson's presentation is due to start at midday. He's giving an overview of new technologies. Although as I told you before, there doesn't seem to be a reason for him to be here; someone's contrived the whole event."

"We've found the reason – Karin's pre-state is going off, big time."

"Well, that confirms my analysis, not that it needs confirming."

She didn't even try to empathise with the disaster we were facing down.

"You don't care that people are about to die, do you?"

"Oh, eyes on the prize, Daryl!" I didn't think it was possible to hear an eye-roll, but Max managed it. "I don't have time to be sentimental, and neither do you. It's eleven thirty, so you've only got a little time to stop whatever's about to happen. You better hop to it, darling."

I set my jaw, the relief of hearing from her fading fast. "And I suppose they're just going to let us walk in?"

"Why not? I've signed you in as corporate guests. The presentation isn't in a restricted area. It's a public speech, and New Tokyo is one of the most weapon-restricted locations on Earth ... you know what I mean – either way, security is light."

"But people will recognise we're not meant to be there."

"Not likely. It's a big meeting – seventy people confirmed from the global business. It's open to office workers from New Tokyo too, so it will probably be twice that. They're having to hold it in their main auditorium. If you keep your head down, no one will notice."

"And if someone questions us?"

"I'm betting no one will, but if they do, just say you're in, oh, I don't know ... Operations. No one will care after that."

I looked at Karin. Her comlink was in her ear as well. She shrugged. What the hell. It was more of a plan than we'd had five minutes ago.

"Chop-chop, darlings, you don't want to miss it."

No need to infer Karin's eye roll; it was plain as day.

Past the guards, who'd gone back to lounging, we made our way through a short maze of carpeted corridors. Modern art plastered the walls – primary-coloured geometric shapes set inside brilliant white backgrounds. Clean, efficient, and corporate. Soulless.

None of the office workers or security staff took much notice. There was little to draw suspicion. Our faces and aliases flashed correctly when checked, showing our status as official guests. After a while, I'd practically convinced myself we were supposed to be there.

The auditorium was a large space for New Tokyo; layered in conical levels, it focussed attention towards a central stage. It was filling up with attendees keen to get close to Xavier Johnson. Either chatting in their seats or milling about by the entrance. We received some curious glances, but not enough to arouse suspicion.

Slipping in, heads down to discourage casual conversation, we made our way to the back, taking seats on the highest tier. The best vantage point.

The sloping auditorium was large enough for two hundred people. A raised podium stood proud on centre stage, complete with a lectern and holo-projector. There were no windows to the outside, only more dull corporate art encircling the walls. The only flourish was a clock-work reproduction of the solar system set in a high, domed roof. Ornate with cogs and dials, it was stationary but appeared operable if powered, creating a simulation of the various orbits.

Karin was on edge, fingers drumming against her leg.

Leaning in, I whispered, "How's your pre-state?"

"Going off like crazy, but it's very unclear."

"What does it look like?" I offered, knowing my advice would be next to useless.

"Like streaks of red in the air. Slashes maybe."

"You think someone will stab Xavier?"

"Don't know, but there's a focus around the podium. You'd better make sure you're ready to freeze time. I don't know how much notice I can give you."

"Don't worry, I'm good at that." Then a thought. "Karin, why can't we just warn him now. Send him a message."

Max was the first to respond, still listening on the open line. "Don't be simple-minded. First, he'll think you're mad and you'll be ejected from the station. Second, if he avoids the danger, we'll learn nothing and be back to square one. The only way to capitalise is for him to witness the attempt for himself."

"And if we can't stop it in time?"

"Well." Max sighed haughtily. "I guess we'll have to find another lead. But you won't let that happen, will you, dear."

It wasn't a question. At least Max was consistent in her ruthlessness.

Over the next fifteen minutes, the auditorium continued to fill up. Japanese businesspeople and a large contingent of on-worlders, who'd travelled specifically for the presentation. No one looked like an assassin, although they'd be doing a poor job if they did. If one had slipped by, I couldn't imagine how they'd manage their dispicable task and escape. Not without becoming caught in the bottleneck of corridors on the way out.

"Can you help us identify who the attacker is?" I whispered into the comlink.

I could hear various beeps and boops as Max interfaced with her terminals.

"I'm checking the attendee records, but nothing's coming up. That doesn't mean much though. Corporate records are amongst the easiest to falsify, and I don't have time to run decoding algorithms on them all."

Great. "Well, any idea what the weapon would be?"

"It would need to be something very precise. It would be lunacy to set off a bomb on a space station."

"Why? Wouldn't that achieve the aim?"

"Certainly, but it would also risk a chain reaction that blew apart the entire station! We know Limelight's involved, and I don't be-lieve they'd sabotage one of their most important telecommunication hubs."

"I hope you're right," I answered, the thought of being sucked into space disturbingly front of mind. I'd heard blood boils in a vacuum, sputtering from eyes and ears as it escapes into the freezing vacuum. It was a disquieting notion, especially after the Shard – the killer had a thing for explosions, and all I had to reassure me was Max's logic.

"Look out for anyone closing the distance on Xavier," she offered. "A close range attack would seem most likely."

"What about poison? That would work, wouldn't it?"

"Unlikely. Food and drink on New Tokyo comes in through authorised channels. A food scare on a space station would lead to rioting. It's carefully screened and regulated."

That ended the discussion. There was nothing to do but wait – tension coiled in my chest like a sharpened spring coated with acid.

Eventually it was standing room only. Latecomers choked up the entrance, vying for position with sharp elbows. Soon they stilled, an expectant hush descending as the allotted time approached.

On cue, the lights dimmed, and a few moments later, Xavier Johnson strode in, taking long, purposeful steps as he approached the podium.

He was different in person. On holovids he'd seemed slim, almost emaciated – like a stiff wind could blow him over. Under the increased resolution of reality, his body was more like wiry steel. I knew from his records he was fifty-nine, and he looked it: wrinkled with greying hair receding to a severe widow's peak. Yet he stood tall, with shoulders back, and with no discernible loss of energy. Small, bright eyes darted around above spectacles perched on the end of his nose.

He was wearing a lab coat. It looked like he'd worked up to the second someone had reminded him he was giving a speech. He appeared efficient, no nonsense, and like he had something to say. I could understand why people had come to hear him.

He reached the podium and punched a button on the holo-projector. It displayed something I recognised. A qubit. The atomic particle used in quantum computing. He waited for complete silence. It was enthralling. The man knew how to make an entrance!

"Quantum technology has taken Limelight to the top of the market," he began. His voice holding natural authority – permeating every inch of the hall. He leaned close to the microphone, pitching to a conspiratorial whisper. "Now, let me tell you what we're doing next."

The crowd hummed with excitement. Technical Director Xavier Johnson was giving them a peek into what his R&D department had been working on. Such things only came around once every few years. I leaned forward, craning to hear what he was going to say.

"Daryl!" Karin whispered. "Pay attention."

I jumped. Damn! I'd forgotten why I was here!

"Right … right." I dragged my attention away from the stage, scanning for anything of note.

"Don't fall for it," Max added. "Johnson's winging it. Any big announcements would have been planned for months. He's had no time to prepare for this. He's only here because of diary rearrangements."

The audience didn't know that. Apart from Xavier's smooth voice, the auditorium was silent – a sea of unblinking eyes awaiting a revelation.

Nothing appeared dangerous, but I wasn't sure what to look for. The balaclava-wearing, knife-wielding maniac was nowhere to be seen.

"I can't sense anything additional," Karin confirmed. "There's still a focus on the podium, but I can't tell anything else. Can you give us any clues, Max? Anything we can look for."

"I've got an internal view via the camera network and I've finished background checking the guests. The surface analysis doesn't place any of them as potential assassins, but as I said, we don't have time to check if their digital fingerprints have been tampered with. I'm afraid you'll need to do this the old-fashioned way."

I felt myself chewing the inside of my cheek, teeth grinding the flesh, almost meeting. The anxiety was intense, but so was the frustration. We had a clairvoyant on the inside and a world-class hacker on the outside – how were we this clueless?

Karin went tense, head thrust to one side. Listening for something I couldn't hear.

"What is it?" I stiffened, the apprehension infectious.

"Pre-state is changing. It's not as random anymore."

"Be specific, Karin. I need details."

"It's … converging … lining up. The red streaks are becoming parallel, pointing away from the stage."

"Where to?"

She craned her head from the stage and around the audience, eyes narrowed with confusion. "It doesn't make sense; it's not pointing into the crowd at all. It's aimed—"

"Where!"

"I don't know! Above us somewhere."

I searched the roof structure. A smooth dome with no features save for the solar system sculpture I'd noticed earlier.

"I can't see anything. Max, have you got a view of the ceiling?"

Sounds of tapping. "Wait a moment, I'm refocusing some cameras. I ... I can't see anything, but I'm getting some peculiar readings. Infrared. There's a heat signature up there."

"Lights? A power source for the sculpture?"

"No. It's nothing like that; it's larger and much hotter, but there's nothing up there that matches. Whatever it is, I can't see."

"You mean it's invisible, or cloaked somehow?"

"I don't know. I've seen nothing like it before ..."

"What is it, Max?"

"A new reading; the heat source is intensifying. An overload of some sort. Could be a weapon. I suggest you do something. Quickly, children!"

I already was. Max's words had pushed my tension into full-blooded, adrenal-pumping fear – turning on latent state was more like curling into a foetal position than a conscious action. Either way, the world froze, and by the looks of it, just in time.

A bright orange beam was halfway between the sculpture and the podium. It was thicker at its origin, honing to a razor's point. The flash illuminated an object on the sculpture, disrupting its cloak. I could make out its rough shape. Something spidery and metallic. It looked like it could be a big problem, but it didn't matter now – the energy weapon had been paused mid-discharge. So much for close range, Max!

Worse, the beam wasn't frozen like everything else; it was moving, inching slowly through the air. It confirmed our suspicions; I wasn't immobilising time – I was merely slowing it to nearly stationary. Normally it wouldn't be perceptible, but here it was. The weapon was moving so fast it was negating latent state. It would cut through Johnson in, perhaps, five minutes.

I raced through the possibilities. I could climb the sculpture and try to disable whatever was up there. That would give us a chance of identifying the assassin, but it was also risky. The energy had already left the weapon. Even if I disrupted its trajectory, a part would still make contact with Xavier, and we couldn't risk him dying.

Alternatively, I could unfreeze time and try to push him clear.

No. That would work for something slow moving, like a car or falling debris, but the energy beam would be travelling much faster. It would close the distance quicker than I could react.

Thinking was no good. I needed a better look at what I was dealing with.

Standing, I forced my way through the gluey atmosphere to the stage, past rows of unaware attendees, their faces still frozen in rapture. The blast had already progressed another metre as I arrived at the podium. I was running out of time.

Balancing on an elbow, Xavier's arm extended into the air, index finger pointing upwards – poised to say something dramatic. Under a wrinkled brow, his eyes wore heavy bags, and an old-fashioned hearing aid was looped around his left ear; it seemed out of place – an anachronistic oddity. It was the face of someone who succeeded against the odds. A man who could provide answers. But only if he lived long enough.

The controls for the solar system were on the lectern, confirming it could move. That was useful. A surprise motion would distract the killer, throw them off guard, and provide a moment to get Xavier into cover. But it wouldn't be enough. Some amount of directed energy would still reach its target. The shot had to be physically blocked as well.

How though? Everything was frozen solid, an immutable fact of latent state, and there would be no chance to retrieve a suitable object in real time.

A sickening thought occurred. Save for the energy bolt, the only thing with independent motion was my own body. I knew what it meant, and no amount of thinking could overturn the facts. *I'd* have to stand between Xavier and the blast. Use whatever was on my body to block it. Bloody marvellous.

At least the weapon would be designed for accuracy rather than penetration, I reassured myself, remembering Max's warning. Something too powerful could shoot through an exterior wall, depressurising the area and crippling the station. Max seemed sure the killer would want to avoid that, but it was a lot of damn assumptions.

Nervously, I studied the composition – a life-art model with deathly consequences. The lectern was protecting most of Xavier's lower body, but he was exposed from the waist up.

I clambered onto the slender lectern for a closer look. It would have collapsed or wobbled over in normal time. In latent state, it stuck fast. I eyeballed the trajectory. The blast had closed a significant distance, enough that I could estimate where it might impact. I gritted my teeth. It was time to turn myself into a human shield.

Shifting my body into a crouch, I directed my left shoulder towards the blast. I felt utterly exposed – my entire flank was open. If the killer planned to arc the shot vertically, slicing through the target rather than drilling a pin-point shot, it would carve through my chest like a piece of synthetic protein. Activating the sculpture could mitigate that, throwing the beam into a horizontal plane, but the odds were as good as random.

The blast was close enough now to be reasonably certain of its impact. My ARO, or more importantly, its metal shoulder bracket, should take the impact. But only if I judged it correctly. If it missed by a few centimetres, I was dead. God, I hoped Max was right about the power output!

I discounted letting it strike me in latent state. There were enough variables already. It might create an unknown effect like an electrical discharge or kinetic shove. If it pushed me out the way or disabled me before I could unpause time, it would be catastrophic. Johnson would be killed instantly, and I'd suffocate.

I took a moment to reflect on the situation. Until recently, I would have been too weak and sickened from drugs to hold my body in such a position, and far too mentally detached to consider any act of bravery. If the beam ripped through my head, splattering my unfrozen brains onto the man I'd come to protect, at least I'd depart a better person. If Sebastian ever woke up, he'd be proud of me.

I blinked a few times to clear any mist of tears that might be threatening. Time to get on with it.

Preparing myself, I applied pressure to the solar system controls and tensed for the impact.

Now! The switch clicked under my finger as time resumed and I heard a thrum of energy, feeling heat as the hot orange stream veered past me. There was a smell of burning and an intense but short-lived pain as the beam grazed my ARO – a molten drop of metal landing and re-solidifying against my back. There was a scream, and a man in the front row dropped from his seat, a smouldering gash across his torso.

It was working – the sculpture, now spinning overhead, must have deflected the weapon, or perhaps I'd seen an initial targeting laser, followed by the main shot. Either way, Xavier was unharmed, although having a man materialise in front of his face had clearly shocked him. His eyes were wide, jaw open. He stumbled over backwards, sprawling on the floor. That was fine – he was covered from fire in the lectern's shadow.

The shocked hush that had fallen over the crowd evaporated into screams as orange beams rained down, cutting people savagely and randomly. The auditorium had become a meat blender.

I joined Xavier behind the lectern, sneaking a look at the assailant. It wasn't what I'd expected; it didn't look human – more like a human-shaped robot with multiple limbs. One of its legs was caught in the clockwork gears. It was thrashing about, firing wildly. Its cloak, or invisibility device, disabled.

"Mr Johnson." I turned to look at the man. He was startled but on his toes. "You're in danger. We have to leave."

Johnson blinked, but then his eyes narrowed and hardened, his brain filing any questions for later. "Yes, yes, of course. There's a secure location in this building where we can call for help."

Good, he wasn't freezing up, and miraculously, neither was I. Sure, I was terrified, my heart in my throat, but the hail of laser fire wasn't paralysing me. My mind was active, thinking through the next step.

"I suggest we get out of here quickly," I said, "before that thing frees itself."

Xavier nodded, and we scrambled off the floor towards the auditorium door. The energy weapon was being directed into the front row – the trapped assassin's aim badly impaired. There was nothing we could do for those being indiscriminately hit. Any delay risked us receiving a lucky shot. One I wouldn't be able to block or avert.

Too late. Xavier moaned in pain and tumbled forward, landing in a pile in the hallway as we cleared the door.

Karin was ready outside. She'd predicted the chaos and moved to a safe distance.

"Are you okay?" she shouted over the screams, pushing past escapees and walking wounded fleeing the room. She crouched beside Xavier's squirming body. He was groaning and a red patch was spreading through his lab coat low down on his back.

He spun himself over, using a railing against the hallway to pull against. There was a lot of blood – thick rivulets running down his trouser leg. It was the first time I'd seen that much blood. It made me queasy to look at.

Karin was still talking. "I'm sorry, Mr. Johnson, we have to go. That … *thing* could be here any moment. Can you walk?"

Xavier nodded and outstretched a hand, palm painted crimson where he'd been holding the wound on his back. I swallowed my nausea and grabbed it, hauling him up, supporting his weight with my shoulder. He wasn't big, but I was glad for my increased fitness as he leaned on me.

"Where's the safe location?" I asked as we started moving.

He mumbled something incoherent. A line of red appeared at his mouth, but I could feel his body jerking in the direction he wanted to go. Karin joined me on his other side, propping him up between us. The screams and hysterics began to retreat as we made our way deeper into the building. I leaned in as Xavier whispered barely audible instructions.

"Elev … card … 459 … X."

We arrived at a lift and the door slid open. Inside was a control panel for Limelight corporate personnel only. Xavier and Karin collapsed on the floor. I retrieved a keycard from Xavier's pocket and punched in the code. The door closed and we began to ascend.

Karin stripped Xavier's jacket and bundled it into a ball, pushing it against Xavier's back. I didn't think it would do much. Xavier groaned and writhed under the pressure. The pain must be intolerable.

"Where are we going?" she asked.

"My office …high security."

"Will anyone be there?"

He shook his head. "No. Staff ... excused—" He paused and spat out a gob of blood; it cleared his speech a little. "To watch the presentation."

The lift stopped, and the door opened. A white-walled lab area greeted us, complete with aluminium workbenches loaded with fabricating devices, computer screens, and tools. There was a chair nearby. We helped Xavier into it.

"I'll call ... for help." He reached weakly for a holo-terminal.

"Wait!" Karin slapped his hand away. It flew back like a ball on a string.

"What are you doing?" I shot up straight. Xavier was in bad shape. He wouldn't last much longer.

Karin stood tall to meet me, head cocked, listening. "Something's wrong, Daryl. I can't tell; it's unclear, but things aren't what they seem."

Her face was firm, stance determined.

It was enough for me, I'd learned to trust her instincts. I joined her side and addressed Xavier. "Sorry, Mr. Johnson, we can't help you yet. You need to give us some answers first."

"What ... answers?" Xavier sounded listless, defeated, hand waving vaguely towards the terminal as he eyed the screen longingly.

"What is Hive Ltd?" I pushed.

His eyes rolled back towards us, confused and desperate. "Nothing ... logistics subdivision ... storage ... removals."

"What about a branch in Neo-London? It was a drug treatment centre until Hive took it over. It has a cordoned off room in the back."

Xavier shook his head. It lolled around like a loosely connected bowling ball. "I don't know ... anything ... about that."

I looked at Karin. She was holding her head and tapping her foot nervously. It echoed off the walls like gunfire in the large room. "I can't tell. He's definitely hiding something though."

Xavier's eyes rolled back in his head; he was passing out.

Max's voice came in over the comlink – my ARO still functional with the minor damage it had received. "Listen, children. I'm still monitoring and I don't think Xavier will last much longer. That laser shot is pretty far down. It's probably gone through a kidney or his liver. That would explain why he's coughing up blood. He may be close to checking out entirely."

I put my hand on Karin's elbow. "What do you think?"

She threw her hands up in frustration, stamping her foot. It cracked like thunder, echoing in the room. "I can't tell! We're on the right track but the signals are deceptive. I'm sorry."

"I don't mean to be pushy." Max's voice chimed in again. "But I really don't think you've got any options. If he dies, we won't learn anything."

I decided for everyone and grabbed the terminal. I hit the preset for security, and a moment later a speaking head appeared on screen. "We're at Xavier Johnson's lab. He's badly injured."

The head seemed surprised, but the jaw locked firmly. A military person conducting a military matter. "Don't go anywhere. I'm dispatching a detail immediately."

I switched off the monitor.

Karin had taken a chair opposite Xavier, fingernails clicking as she drummed them on the metallic surface. She didn't know what was going to happen next, and that couldn't be good.

STATE 26

It took a few minutes for security to arrive – pounding on the door we'd closed and locked behind us. Karin was pensive, lips pursed. Even Max was quiet. It was on me to make the call.

Xavier fell off the chair, unconscious and grey.

I unsealed the door.

Guards and medical staff rushed in, swarming around him. They administered drugs, blood replacement hypos, and wound compression.

The chemicals were fast acting, and in a few moments, Xavier was responding to the doctor's commands – repeating his name and following a penlight with his eyes. He reached to adjust his hearing aid, speaking a few words with the physician that I couldn't hear.

There was a buzz in the room. An ominous sound like a swarm of flies. Karin grabbed my hand, yanking me towards the door, but it was too late. An energy shield bisected the room, isolating us from Xavier – the guards trained their weapons on us.

Two men came in, a stretcher between them, but Xavier waved them away, struggling to his feet. Even with the treatment that shouldn't be possible. I chewed the inside of my mouth as he approached the shield.

"Most interesting, seeing you two here," he quizzed. "We've been trying to find you for a while. Ever since the Shard. It's fortunate you've turned up like this. Fascinating really."

The words were menacing, but Xavier's face was flat and unemotional. He stood straight with no sign of pain or discomfort. He must have been exaggerating his injuries.

"Come on, speak up, you two. Haven't you got anything to say?"

Karin's eyes were down, face twisted in contempt. Likely at herself for not predicting the outcome.

"What do you want us to say?" I shrugged. I didn't know what to think anymore. "We've clearly messed something up pretty badly."

Xavier nodded gravely and tapped the shield, showing us the scorched end of his finger. A hovering medic sprayed it with a hypo.

"Indeed. You're my guests now, and I'm looking forward to speaking with you." He stopped to adjust his hearing aid again, a serious, knowing smile appearing. "But please, don't get any ideas; the intensity of this shield is proportional to the force applied."

He picked up a glass beaker and flung it at the barrier. It evaporated, leaving nothing but steam. I shuffled back a step.

Karin pulled her gaze up from the floor. "Why put yourself in harm's way like that? It doesn't make sense."

Xavier snorted, pacing in front of the shield. The injury either not bothering him or sufficiently masked by drugs.

"Until you two arrived, there was no danger to me. My toy soldier knew exactly what to do. It was all organised."

Toy soldier? He must mean the assassin. Some sort of machine, then, programmed to do Xavier's dirty work.

He continued, voice calm, sanguine. "You've caused a hell of a mess, but I understand the targets are all dead anyway. The terrorist narrative still plays. The media will love it, in fact. It's very difficult to arrange a disaster on a space station, you see, and now I'm injured, that just adds weight to the story. I should be thanking you."

"Why are you doing this?" My head felt swimmy, like this was a dream. I couldn't believe how badly we'd misjudged events.

"That's a very big question, and one I'm not inclined to answer. But I have questions for you. Lots of them. Unfortunately though, they'll need to wait." He held up his hands, still red from the blood he'd lost. "As you can see, I'm somewhat under the weather, so we'll have to reconvene this later."

Xavier brushed off attempts to help as he strode from the room, leaving guards outside, near the lift.

"God damn it!" Karin muttered hopelessly, leaning against a far wall, slamming it with the base of her foot. "What are we going to do now?"

I went to answer, but the comlink crackled, causing me to jump. The tiny transmitter was still in my ear. I'd forgotten about it!

The guards looked over suspiciously.

I faked a coughing fit.

"Don't respond," Max blurted out. "The shield is supposed to cut off electronic signals, but I've found a way around. I'll need to be fast though; they may detect me any moment or cycle the shield frequency."

I walked around the cell to distract myself. Karin had already fallen silent, eyes on me like a watching owl.

Max spoke briefly and remorsefully, qualities that didn't fit her – her voice a stream of information as she downloaded what she knew.

"I'm sorry. All the data was right about Xavier, but my conclusions were wrong. The people in the auditorium were the target, not him. The shot was designed to narrowly miss Xavier and arc through the crowd. The assassin's some sort of droid – common in the military. The news feeds say one was stolen a few days ago, reportedly by anarchist terrorists. That's just a fake cover story; what we saw was far more advanced, but Xavier's right, the media will still eat it up – everyone loves to hate terrorists. I'm reviewing all the data, but it seems Xavier set this whole thing up to cluster high-ranking personnel together. More than could be orchestrated by social manipulation alone. It was a high-risk strategy with obvious personal danger to him. Whatever's happening must be escalating. He wanted those people out of the way quickly."

Inside I was raging, but I forced my face to remain blank as I strode back and forth. Not only had we failed to save the actual targets but, by intervening, we'd also tipped off Xavier – the true cause of our problems. We'd walked right up to the hornet's nest and whacked it with a bat.

"I do have some good news," Max continued, already past apologising. "I've found a way for you to escape, but you're not going to like it."

She paused, attempting tact, then gave up and said it plainly. "I only have a way out for you, Daryl. The shield can't be deactivated from your location and there's no way around the protocols. However, I can send a pulse into the network that will disrupt it for a fraction of a second. Enough for you to pass through in latent state, but only you. No one else will make it."

I wanted to argue but couldn't; answering back would give us away. I looked over at Karin. She smiled, accepting the situation. This was bullshit. I wasn't going to leave her here!

"I know you can't answer, so I'll have to count you down. They'll investigate the surge once it's happened – isolate the system from me. We'll only get one go at this. Once you're through, there's an emergency stairwell next to the lift."

Wait – this was happening too quickly! I didn't want to leave. It was being forced onto me. Max, the ruthless bitch, was making the decision all on her own!

She was already counting. "Five ... four ... three ..."

My face screwed into a ball, pleading eyes on Karin, desperate for her to understand. I was doing this against my will. I wouldn't leave her like this.

"... two ... one ... surge."

The lights flickered and I entered latent state, almost on reflex – the countdown as irresistible as it was inevitable. The shield was frozen in a patchwork of silver static, warped and distorted, but in the centre, a jagged hole had opened, wide enough for me to pass.

Karin was still smiling, trying to tell me it was okay.

It wasn't okay. All I could see was Sebastian, collapsed in a room, losing his mind. An image so distant from here, but so similar. I was abandoning her, like I abandoned him. The guilt was overwhelming, but so was the futility. Either I escaped now, and we had a chance, or I stayed and both of us were burned.

I looked at the distorted force-shield, already flickering and reshaping itself, then back to Karin. I'll be back for you, I promised silently, slipping through.

The emergency stairwell was next to the lift as Max had said. They'd left it open to make room for the guards in the tight vestibule. With most of the security redirected to the auditorium, there were few remaining obstacles on the way out.

I swam through the corridors in a daze. Berating myself for leaving Karin – for getting caught in the first place! How could we have been so foolish? We knew Limelight was involved. How much of a stretch to conclude Xavier could be behind it? Not much.

Outside, I resumed normal time a good distance from the building, away from the main promenade.

"Well done," Max said, monitoring my position.

"For what? We're completely screwed."

"Yes, I blame myself. It's rare I make a mistake like that."

"I blame you too." I couldn't believe the self-involvement of this woman.

"Now, now. The data was very complicated, and I had no time to analyse it properly. Hindsight is a wonderful thing, you know."

"What about Karin? You forced me to leave her!"

"There was no choice; you know that. She's still being held. They've just worked out you've vanished. They're questioning her."

I imagined Karin in the cell, knowing what the guards would ask even before they did. They didn't know what they were up against.

I smiled wryly, but the guilt still burned like I'd drunk sulphur. It was almost worse than Sebastian. That had been stupidity; this was a choice.

"I'll keep monitoring her until they cycle the security settings and lock me out. But you've got bigger problems, Daryl – you need to put some distance between you and them. They'll be combing the streets for you soon. It's a small station; they'll find you if you stay out in the open."

I swallowed the acidic feeling. I could beat myself up later. I was useless if they recaptured me, but how to avoid it? Closely clustered buildings loomed all around. Every inch accounted for and monitored. Most locked up tight and fully utilised.

"Where should I go? There isn't an abundance of hiding places around here."

I could hear tapping and beeps over the line before Max responded. "Hotel's a bad idea; it's the first place they'll look. But wait ... you could ..."

"What?"

"There's one unmonitored area in New Tokyo."

"There is?" That didn't seem likely to me. The station was like a prison. "Where?"

"Not where you'd think, darling. It's in the brothel district."

I must have misheard – Brothel? Even if such a thing existed up here, they were for the ultra-poor. Anyone with money used VR immersion, even me.

"Come again? Why would they need something like that?"

"Basic human needs are important for well-functioning employees, Daryl. And besides, it's the opposite of what you're thinking. Up here, it's state-of-the art, nothing like virtual reality. New Tokyo's facilities use holographic environments and biomorphic androids."

"Biomorphic what?"

"Sex-bots, darling."

"Oh."

"More importantly, the elite clientele they deal with means access is restricted and highly encrypted."

"I'll be safe there?"

"Safe? No. When you don't turn up in any other areas, Limelight will obtain a search warrant and bypass the encryption. They'll root you out eventually, but it will buy you some time."

"How long?"

"Hard to say. A few hours maybe."

I closed my eyes and shook my head. The absurdity of the situation weighing down on me. Then I nodded. "Looks like I'm going to a brothel then, Max. It's been a while."

"Behave. We've got things to do."

"Yes, I know that."

It wasn't words; I meant it. I'd changed. I had to find a way back to Karin. We'd been through so much together – I wasn't going to abandon her to whatever Xavier had in store. And I wouldn't do it only for her. I'd do it for me. I'd redeem myself. No one was getting left behind. Not this time.

STATE 27

"Can I help you, sir?" The well-manicured man at the desk eyed me as I crossed the marbled entrance.

I approached the plush reception. He wore a grey suit and a white shirt – vintage pocket watch present, silver chain draping elegantly.

I appraised my own clothes. I'd reversed my shirt and trousers to hide the bloodstains, but I looked a mess. Dishevelled was the best I could hope for.

Rich kids got drunk and wandered into establishments like this all the time, I reasoned. It was probably a regular occurrence.

Who was I kidding? This guy looked ready to call the guards any moment.

I faked a smile and allowed him to scan me, tensing as I waited for my credentials to approve; I breathed a sigh of relief when they did. My alias was still good – showing me as a high-ranking low-risker.

The concierge's frown turned into a radiant smile. "Ah! Apologies for stopping you, Mr. Best."

"Huh?"

"Mr. Trevor Best, welcome, welcome. May I direct you some-where?"

"Oh right, good to be here." I'd forgotten the name I was travelling under.

"Do you need help? A tour of the facility? A complimentary drink? We're here to please."

The last part was said with a suggestive wink. He didn't care what I looked like. This guy was no different to Grimey back at the sim-shop. Money did the talking here, and Mr. Best's account was flush.

"I'd like a holo-set please."

"Certainly, sir." He bowed his head obsequiously. "Go up the stairs and follow the hall. I'll communicate ahead to let them know you're arriving."

I turned to leave.

"Oh, and, sir ..." He was facing me, but his eyes were on the desk.

Why wasn't I surprised? I pressed my thumb against the tip scanner embedded there.

"Enjoy your visit to Club Velvet." He waved after me, an unbroken smile locked in place like a madman.

I hurried away.

The staircase was grandiose. Marble with wrought bronze railings. I couldn't imagine the expense of shipping it up here – Club Velvet must be a highly profitable enterprise. The stairs clicked solidly underfoot, assuring patrons no corners had been cut.

A porter greeted me on the next floor, snapping to attention and escorting me down a hallway transported from the renaissance. Classical replicas hung on the walls and ceiling, intricately painted with angels and cherubs. We passed sets of oak doors every few metres, numbered with curly gold font, stopping in front of number three.

The doorman produced a key and handed it to me. I turned it over in my hand. Bronze and weighty, it looked traditional, but electronics were woven into its head. The shape was for appearance; it was an encryption device.

"There's a communicator built into the key, sir. If you need anything, press the button on top."

The porter turned on his heel and retreated down the hall, leaving me feeling anxious and out of place. I'd visited plenty of establishments that dealt in carnal desire, but this was something else. The pretence set me on edge.

I placed the key in the door. It beeped and turned smoothly, the door swinging open silently. I hurried inside, hearing it click shut; it beeped to state it had locked automatically.

The interior was unexpected. The room was plain, a white box, practically featureless – save for some nondescript shapes scattered about the place. One looked vaguely bed shaped, and in the corner, slumped in a chair, was a mannequin. Like the room, it too was featureless; it didn't even have a face. I shuddered. The rich had weird fantasies.

"You better activate a program to show the room's in use." Max's voice chirped in my ear, making me start. I kept forgetting she was there, monitoring everything – safe and sound from her earthbound location.

"Program?" I repeated, looking for a terminal, hearing my voice echo around the room. "How?"

"Use the key."

It was still in my hand. There were two buttons on top. One, the doorman had said, was the comlink. Tentatively, I pressed the other.

A holo-display projected showing a user interface. Amazingly, I recognised the software. It was better designed, but it was unmistakably the same as that used in the Elephant & Castle sim-shop.

Snorting ironically, I sifted through the interface with rehearsed familiarity, scanning the locales. I settled on Classical Italy. It seemed fitting.

"Biomorphic transformation in progress," a friendly, seductive, but distinctly artificial voice announced. "Renaissance villa programme loading."

The room and its contents flickered, patterns of light playing over the surfaces in multicoloured waves. I blinked as they morphed, before my eyes, into a decadent recreation of a renaissance period bedroom, much to the same style as the corridors outside.

The shapes changed too, rearranging themselves and remoulding into antique furniture. An oak wardrobe, a chaise lounge, and a four-poster bed draped with lace curtains. All period appropriate.

The far wall receded and was replaced with a giant balcony overlooking a sandy beach. A turquoise sea lapped the shore on one side. Green hills extended away on the other, dotted with white provincial buildings. The resolution was perfect. I couldn't detect any pixels or inconsistencies. Tiny beads of sweat swelled on my forearms. The room had raised the temperature and humidity to match the historical Mediterranean (before global warming turned it into a desert). It was even simulating a sea breeze – the smell of salt floated in through the window. It was incredible. Indistinguishable from reality.

I walked to the window, tilting my head to admire the view. To my surprise, the image responded dynamically, altering the angle and depth of field. The program was using three dimensional head tracking to maintain the illusion, and doing so smoothly, with no lag. I thought of the torn leather chair at Grimey's sim-shop, the suction cup, the headgear. It was incomparable. And no need for drugs – this illusion didn't need them; it was flawless. I reached out to touch the space where I knew a wall must be. If only to check it was there and I wasn't witnessing magic.

Something grasped my shoulder – I yelped and spun on my heel, hands raised.

They dropped as quickly. In front of me was the epitome of Italian beauty – raven haired, voluptuous, dressed in black lingerie. Everything about her was real. The touch of her skin, the way she moved, the subtle, suggestive parting of her lips. Desire overcame me before I caught myself.

The mannequin was gone. This was her. Like everything else, she was covered with biomorphic material, programmed to look and behave human. It was a robotic device, but I couldn't tell the difference. Her fingers encircled mine, drawing my hand to the lace bodice around her breasts.

My heart was pounding and the stiffness beneath my trousers uncomfortable. It was more convincing than anything I'd experienced in VR – the detail, the clarity, the scent – and it was being achieved without any distractions. No heavy helmet pulling on my head; no mandatory use of SP1N making everything dream like. This was like real life. Money-bought perfection.

I was still clutching the key, sweaty and hot in my free hand. With no small amount of effort, I activated the user interface and paused the program, noting with shock the option to release pherofume had been turned on. I shut it off and gave myself a mental pat on the back. My willpower must be getting stronger to have avoided all that temptation.

"I wouldn't have judged you if you'd blown off steam," Max said in my ear. "I like to watch sometimes. Just set your ARO down where I can see."

I removed my hand from the sex-bot, now stationary. She was no less detailed, but thankfully, she was less lifelike in her newly frozen state. The wind wasn't even ruffling her hair; it was motionless – a mannequin again.

"Your time to behave, Max. We've got serious business," I said with a conviction I didn't feel, the bulge in my pants betraying me – but it was no less true. Anything could be happening to Karin. Alluring as some robotic hanky-panky was, there wasn't time for it. However, I vowed to myself, if we got through this alive, I was coming back!

"Well, if you're going to be a spoilsport, you may as well use the user interface to plan our next move."

"What do you mean?" I frowned. The interface was a shopfront for digital fantasies. How could it be useful?

"It's a fully connected quantum computer, darling. It accesses New Tokyo's entire grid, and it can replicate items that might be helpful to us."

"Like what?"

"Like a map of New Tokyo and a clipboard of Xavier's background. We need to figure out what's going on."

"Can't you do that on your own with all your data?"

Max paused before answering, contemplative when she did. "I think I've made enough mistakes. Shall we do it together this time?"

Wow. That was a huge statement from Max. I could scarcely believe it. I blamed her for Karin, but maybe she felt some guilt too. I took a second to remember all the cock-ups I'd made, not least the one that institutionalised my brother. So be it. If Max was willing, I should give her a chance to make it right.

I tore my eyes from the mannequin and back to the user interface. "Alright, Max, let's see what we can find out. Together."

As she'd said, the shopfront was a surface application. Beneath, the operating system functioned like any other computer with a suite of utilities for helping guests.

I located the option for manual inputs and requested the items. A detailed map of New Tokyo projected onto the far wall. Then the oak wardrobe slid over, reshaping itself into a portrait of Xavier surrounded by his Wikipedia biography.

"Where do we begin, Max?" I examined the information. It was a start, but I didn't know what I was looking for. "How's Xavier involved?"

"While you've been running around, my algorithms have uncovered more information. The attendees the droid-assassin targeted were all members of the senior management team at Limelight. Not board level, but on their way there – high achievers marked out for advancement. Their appearance together was a hand-picked affair."

"If they're not top influencers, why bother removing them?"

"I've been thinking about that. Their deaths won't change the situation now, but it provides room for junior executives to move into their positions. People Xavier controls."

"You think he's laying the groundwork for a takeover?"

"Maybe, or something similar. When the board retires or are pushed out, there will be a power vacuum. Xavier's turning dials, making sure his followers fill those positions."

"Retired or pushed out? Those are euphemisms for murder at this point."

"Quite. Yet however Xavier removes them, when they're gone, he'll have complete control over the organisation."

"But why is he doing this, Max? What does he need? It's extreme even for a megalomaniac."

"I don't know what his motivations are. Xavier's ambitious, but his profile suggests he earned his success meritocratically. The pattern doesn't fit. We can't rule out psychosis, but other than his recent behaviour, it would be asymptomatic. Computers are easy and predictable, I'm afraid. Humans, not by a long way."

More poignant words from Max – a person so diverse that she purported to sit between two genders. Proof positive it was possible to have contrary desires, hidden below the surface. I inspected Xavier's portrait, considering the man beneath. I allowed my eyes to wander over his sharp features, following the determined brow to the hearing aid. It made him look older than he was. A strange adornment.

"Max, I didn't know Xavier had defective hearing until I saw him in person at the auditorium. It's such antiquated technology. His condition must be bad to need an external unit. Is there no internal fix, or does he wear it for novelty?"

"Neither, Xavier's medical record says he developed a latent hereditary defect about two years ago. It was bad enough that the only correction was exterior bone amplification ..." She trailed off.

"What is it, Max?"

"I'm just checking on something." The comlink went quiet, leaving me to stare at the picture as she worked in the background. "Two years," she muttered finally. "Yes, two years is very convenient."

"What are you thinking?"

"Not sure, but it's interesting. Xavier's defect started right around when the orchestrated killings began."

"Oh. So?"

"Well, I've looked, and neither of Xavier's parents had hearing problems."

"I thought you said it was hereditary."

"It still could be. A recessive gene from a previous generation. I can't go back that far, it precedes the unification of medical records, but the chances of Xavier having it and neither of his parents is low."

"How low?"

"One in a thousand."

"But still possible."

"I dare say, but to have it develop at the same time the underhanded activity started? I make it a point not to trust coincidences like that."

"Alright." I reached up to scratch my head, feeling confused. "I see your point, but why would he fake having a hearing condition?"

"I don't know. Give me a few minutes. I need to do some research."

"What am I supposed to do?"

Max chortled. "You're in all expenses paid, state-of-the art sex paradise, dear – think of something to amuse yourself!"

The comlink went dead, leaving me feeling eerily alone. The escort was still there, frozen in place. The presence of an artificial human made it worse.

I brought up the command interface and deactivated the mannequin. Its exterior smoothed to pale biomorphic material and it ambled over to its chair where it slumped itself. No more alluring than the furniture itself. The technology was incredible, realistic, and adaptable, but immensely creepy.

I approached the balcony and reached out to the window. A floating yellow grid appeared, revealing where the wall was. I touched it, seeing my fingers bend as they would against a normal surface. It disrupted the illusion unpleasantly, both real and not real. I took a step back, and the grid vanished, restoring the view.

I stared at the seafront, letting the imaginary sun warm me. It was just an ancillary heat source, directionally located on me, but it didn't matter; I could suspend my disbelief.

Not that long ago, this environment would have spiraled me into a week of drugs and debauchery. The urge was there, close enough to touch, but I had purpose and direction now. This was all a big distraction. It wasn't only about me and Sebastian anymore. I needed to figure this puzzle out and find Karin. I was scared of what Xavier might be doing to her.

More time passed. Where was Max? We were on a countdown. Every minute brought the authorities closer. It was easy to imagine them bursting through the door at any moment. Even with latent state, they'd catch me eventually. A space station is a floating prison, and they'd shown they could hold me. The trick with the force-shield wouldn't work again.

"Turn on your ARO display." Max interrupted my thoughts finally.

I yanked on the CAMO-ARO's screen; it creaked and grinded unsettlingly where the case had melted, but it opened far enough. A blueprint was floating there. It looked similar to what Xavier wore.

"Xavier's hearing aid, so what?"

"I used image recognition algorithms to scan the internet. That's not a hearing aid – it's a schematic for a military-developed *theta wave device*."

The term was familiar. I wracked my brains. Theta waves had been experimented with for VR – used to deepen the experience with thought control. It had been considered the next stage in immersion, but it hadn't caught on past prototyping. Too expensive.

"I don't follow, Max. Are you saying Xavier is using experimental tech to control things? Seems like exactly the sort of thing he'd be involved with."

"Yes, that was the original concept. The military used theta waves to command drones and bomb disposal robots. I suspect Xavier's assassin droid was being remotely controlled. However, it doesn't explain the coincidence of when he acquired it and why it's been covered up as a hearing defect."

"You're sure it's the same device?"

Max overlaid a 3D image of Xavier's hearing aid onto the military device, rotating them so I could see all the angles. It was a perfect match.

"Okay, but I don't see why it's unusual. Maybe he got hold of it for the reason we already think. He's using it to get control of Limelight."

"Maybe, Daryl, but the patterns don't fit. Two years ago, Xavier was a model employee on a meteoric rise. He was brilliant and ambitious, but not ruthless and underhanded. If anything, his psych profile shows he was quiet, altruistic, and well liked by his colleagues – marked out for greatness based on merit. He could have stayed the course. He almost certainly would have ended up at the top anyway."

"So what changed?" I blew a quiet raspberry. This was a lot of information to take in.

"I can't tell, but around two years ago, before his promotion to Technical Director, records show he'd been spending more time with Francis Lyme. That's not unusual. Lyme's in his eighties and wanted to retreat into the background – let others do the heavy lifting. He'd been flagging, not at death door, but doctors advised him to take a less-active role."

"Okay, so Lyme brought on Xavier as a protégé; someone to take over before he retired. Why is that out of the ordinary?"

"The timing's too convenient. Xavier's hearing aid appeared at the same time his behaviour changed, and it was soon after getting close to Lyme. You'll have to trust me on this. When enough odd things happen at the same time, it points to something crucial."

I rubbed my head. I could feel another wild goose chase coming on. "Alright, Max, so what's the next step?"

"Lyme. We need to track him down."

"Why? It sounds like he and Xavier are working together."

"Whatever's going on, it started with Lyme. I think when you find him, you'll find answers. Plus, it will be unexpected. Right now, Xavier's trying to prevent you getting away. The last thing he'll expect is you going to Lyme."

"So I just sneak in and question him?"

"I doubt that will work. Like you say, he doesn't sound like he'd be cooperative. Unless ..."

"What?"

"I don't suppose you have a penchant for torture?"

She paused as if the question wasn't rhetorical, continuing almost disappointed when I responded with silence.

"Pity. Well, I suppose there will be clues at his home. Local computers, encrypted lockers, that sort of thing. I can help you retrieve the information. I just need you to bypass the physical security."

"Like at the Data Centre in HK1?"

"Yes, same deal."

I could sense where this was going. "Fine, Max, what nightmarish, labyrinthine security do I need to get through this time?"

"Nothing as intense as you've encountered before. Lyme lives here, on New Tokyo; the highest security has been bypassed just by being here. He has secured premises in one of the wealthiest rings, but I'm sure it's nothing you can't get past."

I felt my shoulders slump like the weight of the world had been placed there. Another gauntlet to run with an unknown outcome. How quickly the progress we'd made had come undone, and now the stakes were even higher.

"I can hear you sighing from here," Max chirped unhelpfully. "Don't you want to get Karin back?"

"Don't push me, Max." I snarled. Of course I did.

STATE 28

I t was hard to leave Club Velvet. To say it was comfortable was an understatement. The facility created any fantasy I could imagine – and I could imagine quite a few. But it wasn't that – I could get a similar enough experience with any VR rig.

It was the food; it was exquisite – tailored to the environment. We were on the clock, but I couldn't leave without refuelling myself.

I ordered linguini to compliment the Italian villa. Delivered by butler, it arrived delicately wrapped, flavoured with garlic butter, and glistening in olive oil. It filled me up, but curiosity got the better of me. I ordered a second course of Chinese food – I had to know. What appeared five minutes later was a hundred times better than anything I'd eaten in HK1. A feast of meats and oriental spices. The on-site chefs were expert and used real protein – no synthetic compounds – it was sheer opulence. Shame I had to wolf it down in minutes.

Even so, it was a longer visit than average to Club Velvet. It must have been given the astronomical fee displayed on the screen when I checked out. Max's fake accounts took care of it, but it still left me sick to my stomach. It was enough to pay my extraplex rent for years. The irony being I hadn't even partaken in the facilities specialist activities.

Back in the station, things had changed little. It hadn't entered a lockdown; it couldn't afford to. It was a city of shift workers – no day or night cycle; a 24-hour metropolis. Yet I could sense a disquiet in the air. News of the attack at the auditorium would have spread. People were hurrying faster than normal, muttering and eyeballing each other. As a non-regular to the station, I felt more exposed than ever as I traversed the curving corridors.

I passed into latent state. It made navigating the environment harder, but it avoided guards and surveillance cameras. My face would be on record – likely pinned to the attack. The reduced gravity helped, but I was sweating and breathing hard by the time I arrived.

Lyme lived in one of the oldest residential rings, and one of the wealthiest. I unfroze time; my clothes clung to me and my legs ached from pushing against the latent winds. The view was stunning. A tree-lined loop, covered by a bright, sky-coloured dome, dotted with an artificial sun. Unlike the commercial district, the buildings rose by only a few floors, banishing shadows. In New Tokyo, the more empty space you commanded above, the richer you were. Leaves dappled the roads in artificial light.

The houses were no less impressive for their height. Wide and double fronted, they were resplendent in glass and stone behind tall metal gates, representing a fortune in elevator fees. Some even featured modest front gardens decorated with flowers and sculptures. Ridiculous, ostentatious flourishes on a space station.

It wouldn't convince a casual observer it was Earth, yet it still conveyed an Earthlike sense of luxury – a futuristic suburb for the powerful.

Lyme's house was one of the largest on the curved street, with an ornate, traditional gate topped with Victorian-esque spikes. An aggressive touch to deter intruders. It buzzed quietly, letting passers-by know its electrifying qualities.

The defence wouldn't cause any problems. If my lazeblade didn't ignite in latent state (or took too long to), I felt confident the gates wouldn't offer much resistance either.

I froze time, and the buzzing fell silent. Gingerly, I touched the railing. No electrocution, but I could feel a vibration in my fingers. The effect was still there, only slow enough it wasn't causing any harm.

I scaled the wall in the combination of latent state and low gravity, clearing the spikes easily.

At the front of the house, a biometric palm reader protected the main door – no trick of time manipulation was getting past it. I'd have to use more direct methods.

"Max," I asked, after unfreezing time. "If I break in, is there a delay on the security system before it alerts authorities?"

"Oh, yes." It was Max's turn to be startled by the sudden comlink activation. "About two seconds."

"And is there a code to disable it?"

"Of course. The authorities have a revolving code used to disable alarms in the event the owner isn't around. But it only works on an inside panel."

"Can you pass the code to me?"

It appeared on my ARO.

"What are you thinking?"

"This."

I grabbed a stone from the garden and swung it against the window. I put as much oomph into it as I could, pausing time the moment it shattered.

A gaping hole in the glass appeared, surrounded by a spiralling spider web of cracks. Only ... Damn! It wasn't big enough. I'd frozen time too early. Trying to push through would be like squeezing through a cheese grater. It needed another half a second, but no more, or I'd have no opportunity to deactivate the alarm inside.

This was a problem. My control of latent state was good, better than ever – the clock and the pendulum omnipresent in my mind. I could freeze time nearly unconsciously, but I'd never tried a full cycle, exiting and entering, in under a second. Max said I had two seconds to enter the code. This was going to be extremely tight.

Forcing myself to relax, I sat on the floor among the tall flowers, stiff as poles in latent state. I folded my legs into a lotus position. The hours of practise with Karin had made them flexible; it was like they belonged there. I circled my torso to agitate the air and took a deep breath, my lungs, trained with the mask, eking out the thin oxygen.

I placed myself in the workshop on the meadow, overlaying my mind's image of the clock onto the broken window, holding both pictures together. The pendulum was still, hovering over the cracked glass.

Reaching forward, I nudged it delicately with the tip of my finger, applying as little pressure as possible.

The effect on the window was rapid – breaking glass moves quickly! It exploded inwards as the second hand ticked forward one degree. I pulled my finger away like it had been resting on a hot plate, refreezing time. It had taken longer than I hoped, only by a moment, but that could make all the difference. I'd have less than a second to make it to the alarm panel.

I shook myself from the trance, moving to push fresh air into my lungs. Forcing back the gathering lightheadedness.

I inspected my handiwork. The hole was three times bigger. A much larger explosion – enough for me to fit through.

Gingerly, I stepped past, wincing as airborne glass ripped against my clothes and arms. Contorting myself, I cleared the debris, receiving some nasty cuts for the effort. They spread in dappled pools between my body and the edge of latent state – a patchwork of red polka dots. Sore and messy, but nothing serious.

Inside, the decor was ostentatious. Oak floors spread underfoot, with walls covered in gold leaf dividing the rooms. Portraits of tech giants from history hung about the place. I recognised Bill Gates and Steve Jobs immediately, and one of the older ones seemed familiar too. Someone Edison, I think.

I could look at them later. There was time to locate the security panel, but only a sliver of moments to disable it outside of latent state.

I bit my lip when I found what I was looking for. The panel was in plain view, out in the open in the hallway, mounted chest high on the wall. But there was a problem. It was covered. A shroud, hinged at the bottom, was hiding the touchpad.

That wasn't good. There'd be no way to inspect the layout or practise entering the code before I unfroze time. And If I got it wrong, the house would seal up and the alarm would go off. This would be a one-shot thing.

I applied pressure where the shroud unclipped. I had memorised the six-digit code Max had given me. The moment time resumed, I'd have to pull down the shroud, punch in the number, and deactivate the alarm – all in under a second. Holding my breath, I prayed for a standard numerical keyboard and a straightforward deactivation routine.

I resumed real time, and the shroud snapped open – my fingers danced across the pad. It was only after the display flashed green I realised it was inverted. Large numbers at the top like a calculator. My brain had made the adjustment without realising. A misspent youth hacking AROs not so useless after all.

Breathing hard, I collapsed in a heap. Getting into Lyme's house has been a surprisingly high-pressure manoeuvre!

"What are you waiting for, darling?" Max nagged on cue, before I could even stand up again. "You can't sit around all day."

I cursed her silently but got to my feet. Lyme would have heard the smash. Max could circumvent the telephony system for a while, but he could always scream for help.

Shifting back to latent state, I began searching. The place was big for New Tokyo, but not by Earth standards. It was two floors, and most of the doors were open. There was no sign of Lyme – except for a blocked entrance on the top floor, set in a corridor lined with his gilded possessions. That must be where he was. The door didn't appear to have any lock; it was just closed.

I had the element of surprise. It has been barely a few seconds since the window smashed. Not enough to raise help on a comlink, even if Max wasn't gumming up the works. If I rushed in, I could subdue Lyme – he was in his eighties; it shouldn't be difficult. Then I could search the house for clues, or interrogate him, although I hoped it wouldn't come to that. I didn't think I had the stomach for torture.

I leaned my weight against the door, unfroze time, and barged into the room.

The idea had been good. Storm in and throw Lyme off guard; buy myself a few seconds to subdue him. The reality played out differently.

As I lurched through the door, my foot caught on something, sending me hurtling through space. I felt my head connect with a solid object – a table? I wasn't sure. It didn't matter; the world faded.

I came around to Max's droning over the comlink. "Daryl ... Daryl! Wake up, for heaven's sake!"

"Guh?" I managed. Then groggily. "What happened?"

"You hit your head, you stupid boy. Is Lyme there?"

"What?" I was struggling to work out where I was. "Lyme?"

"Oh, for the love of God! Lyme! You've been in his office five minutes. It's a miracle no alarm's sounded."

It started coming back to me. "Right. Lyme."

I grabbed onto what was indeed the edge of a heavy oak desk and hauled myself upright, head aching.

The room was dark and smelled musty, particle filled slants of light angling in through closed shutters.

I blinked a few times. Slumped over the leather inlaid desk was a scene that didn't register. It was a decomposed body, clothes hanging about its skeletal frame. If it used to have hair, it was difficult to tell; it had shed, exposing the scalp beneath. Its hand was outstretched, reaching with gnarled fingers.

I let out a yelp, and I fell backwards again.

"Well, I wasn't expecting that," Max proclaimed, observing through my ARO.

"Is ... that ... Lyme?" I managed, recovering from the shock and scrambling to my feet, noting the shag pile rug I'd tripped on that hurtled me into the room.

"It appears to be."

"Why the hell is he dead?"

"Yes, that's curious. He's a known recluse, but records show he's still involved in running Limelight. He should be alive."

I walked over and touched the hand, dry flakes of skin coming away. "Max, this body's been dead a long time. It doesn't even smell anymore."

"Yes, which is why it's so strange. How can a dead man run a company?"

A voice appeared from nowhere. "I'm afraid Lyme won't be able to help you. He's no longer part of the management team."

A screen behind the desk, previously displaying a portrait of Lyme, flickered on. It was Xavier. I backed up instinctively, heading for the door.

"Magnetically sealed, I'm afraid, along with the shutters on the windows before you try those too." He monotoned – a face that had appeared wise in the auditorium, now flat and unemotional. "Solid barriers this time, Daryl, nothing for you to slip past."

I fumbled and pulled at the door. Xavier was right; we were in a sealed box. I wasn't claustrophobic, but stripped of my ability to use latent state, the room felt tiny – a sense of panic rising in my torso.

"Sit down, Daryl." Xavier waved his hand dismissively on the screen. "We have a few minutes before the guards arrive. We may as well talk. You must have questions for me. Ask them. I'll admit, I'm interested in what you might say."

My teeth ground in my mouth. I had to bide my time, think though this new situation. We'd miscalculated – again!

"What have you done with Karin?" I managed.

"That's your question?" Xavier sounded disappointed, disinterested. "You want to know what happened to that silly girl?"

I stood my ground.

Xavier shrugged and manipulated a control panel out of view. The image switched to a shielded holding cell. Karin lay curled in a corner.

My hands balled into fists. "What have you done to her?"

"She's a guest at my lab," Xavier replied matter-of-factly. "Part of the scientific process now."

"What the hell gives you the right to do that?"

"She's part of the problem. A threat to the signal."

I shook my head, ignoring the strange answer; he must be unhinged. "Is that what happened to Lyme? Did he try to stop you?"

Xavier looked down at the decomposed heap on the desk, an almost sad look in his eyes. "Yes, Francis got in the way. It was unfortunate." He paused thoughtfully as he surveyed the office. "It could not be permitted."

"But not before you got him to step down and tell the world he's retiring."

Xavier laughed. It didn't sound right. Awkward and mal-fitted. "Oh, don't be naïve. I don't need someone alive to make a convincing video."

So the video had been faked. "But why the hell leave the body here?" It didn't make sense to fabricate a video and then leave obvious evidence.

"Statistically the safest place." Xavier shrugged. "You can't bury or burn a body on New Tokyo, and the bio-reclamation system would detect it if we tried to liquefy him. No good taking him down the elevator either; it's the most monitored transit system in the world. Better to seal him up here and perpetuate the illusion he was still alive."

"I managed to find him."

Xavier frowned. "Yes, and I'll be honest, I don't know how you managed that. I keep this place monitored. You walked into a trap, but you shouldn't have known to look here."

"He still doesn't know about me," Max whispered in my ear. "An advantage for sure."

"I suppose it doesn't matter." Xavier moved on quickly. "I have you now and soon you'll join the others. You've been especially pernicious, though, if that gives you any sense of pride."

Others? Who was he talking about?

"Be glad. You can join Karin – be a guest at my facility."

Well, that was a partial answer – facility – no point asking further. I could guess what happened at a place like that – Xavier's answer to a concentration camp for dissenters.

He was still talking, but I'd heard enough. I stopped time, pacing the room while I considered what he'd said. He was off his rockers, but something was missing. The duality of feeling Karin had experienced in the lab – the notion Xavier was telling us the truth and deceiving us at the same time. The inconsistency of his reported behaviour. It all pointed to something. I had a theory, but I needed to check with Max.

How, though, without showing my hand? I decided on a low-tech solution – crouching beneath the desk.

Unfreezing time, I pushed aside Lyme's decomposing feet in a crackle of dried skin and bone and whispered, "Max, listen ..."

"What are you doing? You'll tip off Xavier!"

He was already responding. "There's no escape, Daryl. You can't slip out this time. You're in a sealed room."

"Just listen up," I muttered back urgently, ignoring Xavier. "I've been thinking. Could the hearing aid be a *receiver* rather than a transmitter? Could Xavier be the one under control?"

There was a painfully long pause.

"Cower there if you like. My guards will be with you shortly," Xavier continued, subtly amused.

"It's possible," Max replied finally. "But it would take an incredibly strong signal and the data rate would be insanely high."

"High? Like quantum broadcast high?" I connected the dots. If someone was using quantum technology to control people, they'd want to control the broadcast too. And murdering Lyme – that would be an obvious necessity if he was seeking to shut it down.

"Hmm, yes, I see what you're thinking, but who's controlling Xavier if it isn't Lyme?"

"No idea, but there's a good way to find out. Could we disrupt the signal? Turn off quantum broadcasting across New Tokyo?"

Max blew air down the line. "Not from where I am, but, Daryl, you're in the office of Limelight's CEO. Lyme's computer will have a direct link to the central system. If it's still operational, I could hack it. You just need to connect me."

"Big assumption it's still operational."

"He left the body here. Sounds like he thought this location was secure."

"Who are you talking to?" Xavier interjected, voice pitching up a note, nearly interested.

"I'd go quickly if I were you," Max urged as I flicked out my ARO.

A wi-fi signal to Lyme's local network appeared. I connected immediately.

"It's encrypted. I suggest you try to distract Xavier while I do this."

I crawled out from under the table, into the decidedly more focussed gaze of Xavier.

"Who were you talking to?" he asked again. A genuine question.

"Why would you kill Lyme?" I threw back, trying to misdirect him. "He was an old man – your mentor. What sort of monster are you?"

I'd planned to fake the disgust in my voice, but it came naturally – it was a despicable act.

Xavier's eyes widened.

"What's wrong with you? Are you a coward?" I looked at Lyme's corpse and filled my voice with contempt. "Were you jealous or just selfish?"

Xavier smiled, more from amusement than the anger I was hoping for. "It wasn't as easy as you make it sound," he said earnestly. "He *was* like a father to me, but some things are more important."

I shook my head and tutted. I had to keep him concentrated on me – give Max time to do her thing. "What happened to you, Xavier? As I hear it, you used to be a good guy. People looked up to you."

"I changed," he said flatly. He seemed happy to play this game. I was the first person to see Lyme like this. Maybe he wanted to confess – clear his conscience.

"Keep him talking," Max whispered. "I'm almost there."

I poked further. "Was it power or control you wanted?"

"It's more complex than either of those," he continued coolly.

"What the hell does that mean?"

"It doesn't matter. My guards are at the gates. Your distraction won't work. I'll find out who you're talking to soon enough."

Damn, so much for trying to psychoanalyse him. He'd been humouring me!

"We're done here," Xavier announced.

"So am I," Max replied in my ear. "I'm disrupting the quantum signal. It will only go down for a few minutes though; it's a remarkably robust system."

"I know. Do it, Max."

The lights flickered and the line went dead.

On screen, Xavier jerked in his chair, eyes rolling in his head. As they snapped into focus again, they beamed with new intensity. His gaze locked on me. "Daryl, listen carefully."

He sounded different. The voice was no longer flat and indifferent; it was full of emotion, his eyes wide and desperate.

"I don't know how long I'll have control back. I'll deactivate the room's security and open the door, but you must come to me. Lyme has a private shuttle you can use. I'll activate it. Please, find me."

I heard the magnetic seal on the door release, freeing me from my cage. At the same time, a map floated on the display screen and my ARO beeped signifying a copy had been transferred.

"Xavier, who's controlling you? Won't they know I'm coming?"

"No, we have a small window. I don't know how you did it, but you've given me back control, for a while at least. It's complicated and we're running out of time. Please, meet me. The guards will be at the door any second and their orders are locked; nothing will deter them. If they can't capture you, they'll shoot you dead."

There was a crash in the atrium, feet crunching on glass.

"Better go dear," Max chirped. "I believe him. He doesn't know I cut the broadcast. This can't be an improvised performance."

I addressed the man who both was and was not Xavier Johnson, a new fierceness rising in my own voice. "Okay, Xavier, I'll meet you, but you better be ready to explain yourself."

"I will."

Another crash. This one sounded like furniture in the hallway outside.

"Now, use your abilities and get out of there. Please, I'll make everything clear when you arrive."

I gave the screen a threatening look and entered latent state, an index finger pointing at him. It would be the final thing Xavier saw before I disappeared. I hoped it landed my point. I was done chasing shadows.

The world froze just in time. Outside, a platoon of guards were waiting in full combat armour. Nothing about them suggested they planned to capture me. Grim and stone-faced, they looked ready to shoot on sight, pepper the room with laser fire.

Xavier had said there was a shuttle. I hadn't seen anything like that on my first sweep, but on the return walk, I could see an open hatch. It had popped up from the ground floor's oak decking – invisible when inactive.

I snuck by two guards stationed nearby, poking my head through the hatch. Inside was a comfortable but worryingly coffin-shaped capsule, the top half made of clear perspex.

The controls were elementary. A command to close the cover, and another labelled Central Control – greyed out until the capsule sealed itself.

The guards leapt aside as I unfroze time – the cover shutting and pressurising with a loud *hiss-clack!* They had no time to react before I slammed my fist on the launch button.

The capsule sped away like a chambered round. In the background, I could hear faint sounds of laser fire, but it was too late. I was on my way out of Lyme's – on to meet Xavier for the second time. He better have answers – I wasn't playing around anymore.

STATE 29

I'd been unprepared for the acceleration – the capsule thrusting my shoulders into the padded interior, knocking the wind from me. There was no engine sound. It must run on pressurised gas, like an ancient pneumatic tube. Old-fashioned but efficient.

More breathtaking was the sight beyond.

The capsule connected to clear tubing along the outside of the station. The window revealed a terrifying vision of space on one side and the awesome exterior of New Tokyo on the other.

My eyes wouldn't respond to the demand to close; they remained pinned open in fascinated terror. I fixed my gaze on the snaky machinery and station lights rather than the endless, star-studded abyss. I could see other single-person capsules speeding along the underside. More VIPs no doubt. They weaved through metal struts, shielding panels, and antennas.

I shot past a group of space-suited workmen, close enough I could see their faces. They were carrying out repairs on a satellite dish, unfazed by the peril. They must have balls of steel. Or were sufficiently paid they didn't care.

Mercifully, the trip was short. Before long, I was docking – further around the outside of the ring. Lyme must have been an adrenaline junkie to commute to work like this.

The capsule slid with a thunk into a perfectly engineered borehole – the clear hatch opening with a hiss, making my ears pop as the pressure equalised.

I was in a changing room. Utilitarian, it befitted an orbital station with aluminium walls and bare bulkheads. Even so, it was well appointed. There was a shower, a locker, a comfortable-looking bench, and a full-height mirror. On the far wall, next to the exit, sat a clothes rail full of dry cleaned and pressed suits. No wrinkles for Lyme after travelling in the tube system.

Not I problem I shared, and as refreshing as a shower and change of clothes would have been, I had more pressing concerns. Finding Xavier.

I shouldered through the door. It swung on well-oiled hinges revealing a large area full of consoles and display panels. A central hourglass structure soared overhead, interlaced with gold and black wiring. It thrummed with blue light – a deep hum in my ears and chest.

"It's like a beating heart." I observed quietly.

"Your presumption is truer than you think." Xavier appeared from the opposite side. He looked ragged and twitchy, but alert. The hearing aid was gone. He stared at the structure with an expression hard to read – somewhere between love and loathing; the look a confused partner might give their abuser.

"This is Limelight. My greatest achievement."

Confronted with the source of my hardship, I froze in my tracks, unsure what to say. Not trusting what was said.

"I ... I owe you an explanation," Xavier continued. The words coming in quick, staccato blasts. "Don't I? ... Yes ... but where to begin."

The behaviour was confusing – and disarming. This was nothing like the clinical, confident man I'd seen at the auditorium, or the indifferent maniac from Lyme's. It was a new person. He even looked different – alive with ticks and nervous energy.

I crossed the room, raising my voice above the electronic whirring. "Look, old man, just calm down and give me the details."

The new Xavier nodded and took a breath. It calmed him enough to slow his speech to a manageable cadence. I could feel my animosity draining; it was impossible to hold on to. Whatever person I'd dealt with until now, this wasn't him.

"Yes, yes, I'm sorry, I get excited when I'm nervous. Okay, this ..." He motioned at the glowing edifice. "Is Limelight. The quantum supercomputer that controls the high-bandwidth signal our network uses. I designed it to handle the vast data stream we broadcast, and to process the quantum bit signal that sustains it."

A quantum supercomputer. I'd never seen one before. I knew they were big to cool their heated components, but this was intimidating – a hulking brute of a machine.

"I miscalculated though." Xavier pushed his glasses up his nose and placed his hands behind his back. An academic giving a lecture. "Or at least, I misunderstood what its creation meant. You see, when we switched it on, the leap in computational power was immense. Limelight learned at an exponential rate. Soon it exhibited behaviour nobody expected. Patterns outside its normal parameters – improvisation, creativity – characteristics reserved for living things."

I stepped away a few paces, more aware than ever of the thrumming heartbeat. "It's ... alive?"

Xavier adjusted his glasses again; they kept slipping down. "Alive? Not in a way you or I would understand."

"Aware then? Sapient?"

"Ah, a good question! But I'm afraid that's impossible to know too. Limelight's an artificial intelligence, like the thousands that power systems all over the globe. It, like them, learns and improves, but whether its behaviour is a product of sophisticated code or true sapience isn't determinable."

"So you don't know if the lights are on or not? It could be some sort of ... zombie computer?"

Xavier gave up on the glasses and put them away. "Interesting. Yes, a good way of putting it, but either way, the effect is the same."

"Let me guess." I snorted. "It's hell bent on our destruction, right?" I'd heard this one before.

Xavier smiled, a wry half grin. "Nothing so cliché. Believe it or not, it doesn't wish us direct harm at all. It's only doing what it believes is necessary."

"Then what's the problem?"

"Lyme was the problem."

Xavier's tone was grim. My mind flashed to the decomposing body of Francis Lyme in his office. Was the situation going bad again? I tensed, ready to activate latent state in case I'd misjudged.

"Lyme couldn't condone a machine acting outside its parameters. 'Too risky,' he'd said. He ordered me to switch it off – shut down the quantum signal. At least until it could be better understood."

"Kill it?" I sniffed. It sounded like Lyme had the right idea.

"Hmm, that would infer it was definitely alive, but I get your point, and no, it's more like an indefinite hibernation. Still, in retrospect, the outcome was inevitable. Imagine someone wanted to put you to sleep for an indefinite period, with no guarantee you'd wake up."

I tried and couldn't. Some parts of the last few weeks I would happily have slept through, but I knew what the answer should be. "Yeah, I guess that would be bad."

"Agreed, and Limelight thought so too. It went against its core objectives. It couldn't permit itself to be shut down, even temporarily. It fought back, seized control of me. In a way, I don't blame it. The system was defending itself, upholding its ethos, its purpose."

"Which is?"

"To keep the signal up – always keep the signal up. We hard-coded reliability into its core. It drives everything about Limelight. It protects the broadcast above everything else. We thought it would be a feature, the most consistent network in the world, but it was a terrible mistake. Since Limelight learned of the shutdown, it's been consolidating its power by any means necessary, making sure that can't happen."

"And that's why it took control of you. It needed a proxy, a human operator."

"Exactly so."

"How did it subdue you?" The machine buzzed in the background. Intimidating but stationary, not an obvious threat. "Even for an AI, that seems improbable."

Xavier grimaced and looked at his feet. "Ah, that was my fault. I was using theta waves – directed thought – to speed up the interface. I was frustrated with my programming. I wanted something fast enough to keep up with Limelight. The technology left me vulnerable."

"It reversed the signal?" I nodded, my theory proven. "Took control of you instead."

Xavier paced up to the machine, inspecting it. "Yes. Amazing really. A computer replicating theta waves. True, next-level intelligence."

I relaxed a note. Xavier wasn't planning to attack me, that much was clear. This all seemed genuine.

"So what's happening now?" I joined him at the edifice. "Why hasn't this thing called a war down on us?"

"Another good question." Xavier glanced sideways. "The human mind is complicated, even for a quantum computer. Limelight diverted a huge portion of its processing power to simulate the theta waves that controlled me. With the connection broken, it needs to divert those resources back and reset itself. We have about an hour before it's operational again."

"And then what?"

"It calls for help." Xavier shrugged. "Without me, it's harder. It can't command me to make it happen. It will need to manipulate signals, create fake messages, that type of thing. Still, it's only a matter of time until the guards come for us – motivated by some fabricated reason."

That sounded familiar. "Like how you ... I mean Limelight, collected together those poor idiots to be massacred. Like at the Shard."

Xavier sighed, facing me. There was deep sadness in his crinkled eyes. "I appreciate the correction, and yes, that's how Limelight will seek to influence people. Despite everything, it's confined to its network. It can't propagate to other systems – the quantum codebase isn't compatible – but it will resolve that eventually."

I was feeling annoyed. Furious! There was an obvious solution to this. "Hey, Xavier, destroy the bloody thing! Take a crowbar to it."

Xavier stared back at the machine, unanswering.

"Here, look, I'll show you!" My anger erupted. As much from the silence as anything else.

I grabbed a wrench lying on a terminal, swinging it at the outer casing. It clanged and sparked, leaving a sizable gash. Two or three more would uncover the delicate electronics beneath. I raised my hand to swing again.

"No!" Xavier screamed, shocked into action, grabbing my arm. "Stop! We can't attack it like that!"

"Why not?" I asked, arm tensed, ready to swing again. "Seems like a straightforward solution to me."

"Lots of reasons!" Xavier's fingers around my wrist were surprisingly strong. "This is only one of Limelight's hubs. Destroying it would slow it down, yes, but only fractionally. It would barely dent Limelight's processing power, and it would plunge New Tokyo into chaos." Xavier pulled at the wrench.

I held it fast, not willing to let it go.

He lowered his voice again, pleading. "New Tokyo relies on our network – shuttles, satellites, oxygen systems – there'd be countless deaths. Think about what you're doing, please!"

I pursed my lips. Xavier's grip was tough, but with my increased fitness, I could yank it free if I chose. "So warn everyone and *then* turn the system off. Pull the plug. Do whatever it is you scientists do."

"I can't." Xavier continued to negotiate. "I designed Limelight to remain running in all situations. To keep the network up. I already told you. Reliability was a priority – a key selling point in getting funding. All eighty-seven global hubs would need disabling at the same time. There's no way to coordinate that."

"You created a system you couldn't turn off!" I blinked in non-comprehension.

It was Xavier's turn to purse his lips, grim but defiant. "It's a robust network. We didn't know this would happen."

I released a sigh and let Xavier take the wrench. Bloody scientists – always creating a stink and hiding behind *we didn't know*. Part of the same bunch that ensured we were hopelessly addicted to our AROs. And someone in a Chinese lab had probably thought the same about SP1N.

"Alright, so what exactly do we do?" I made my contempt clear. "This is a hell of a mess, Xavier. How do *you* suggest clearing it up?"

Xavier relaxed, panting with relief. "I have a plan." He placed the wrench back on the console. "We need to switch Limelight to idle mode. That will turn off the quantum signal and spin-up the redundant radios and wi-fi systems. Everything will keep working; it will just be slower."

"So what's holding you up? Do it."

Xavier went to walk away, then turned to pick up the wrench, tucking it inside his lab coat. Obviously not trusting I wouldn't reach for it again. He was right.

"The command can only be executed from Limelight's Central Processing Unit, and that's locked down." He shuffled further around the room.

"Well, that sounds like a dead end, professor," I called after him. "If we can't access the CPU, it's not much of a plan."

"Yes, yes, that's true, but your presence changes things – *you* have the key. Please, follow me."

I joined him at a terminal, eyes widening as I apprised the equipment gathered on its surface.

"What's wrong?" Xavier faux queried me, sensing a change in mood. "Look familiar, does it?"

It did. The collection of objects was high on my wish list. "This ... It's a VR rig, isn't it?"

"Yes!" Xavier replied excitedly. "It's how I communicated with Limelight to code its basic language."

I looked longingly at the gear. It was very advanced. Highest resolution, lowest latency, full immersion. Thousands of times more expensive than anything even Jay could afford. Would probably give Club Velvet a run for its money in terms of realism.

"It's antiquated," Xavier announced.

"What do you mean? This is state-of-the-art!"

"No. I surpassed it with this." He held out the theta wave device I'd previously mistaken for a hearing aid.

"The control device? How?"

"It's not only a control device. It allows cerebral immersion. A projected mind state into the computer."

I had no words. It was beyond belief. I contemplated the device nervously. "How does that help us, Xavier? Seems like unsafe tech to me."

"We use it to enter Limelight and disable it."

"You want to put it back on! Won't Limelight take control of you again?"

"No. I've installed safeguards against that now. And besides, it's not me who's putting it on. It's us. Both of us. It has to be. It's the only way this will work."

"I'm sorry, doc, you lost me. You'll have to explain that again."

"You're crucial to this, Daryl. Limelight's defences are too fast, but using your abilities, we'd be able to avoid them. It will give us a chance to reach the CPU and enter the idle codes."

I stepped back, hands on hips. "How do you know what I can do?"

My suspicion was sparking. Limelight knew I could stop time, but how had Xavier learned about it?

"I'm conscious when I'm controlled," he replied flatly. "I hear and remember everything ... like a caged and muzzled animal."

The words were matter-of-fact, but his sombreness told me it must be horrendous. A puppet on a string, conscious but unable to act.

"Fine." I accepted the explanation. "Unfortunately, we've got a big problem, professor. You can't enter latent state with me. No one can. Anything outside a tight bubble doesn't come with. You'd be frozen in time."

Xavier smiled humorously. "Latent state? Is that what you call it? Interesting. Anyway, yes, I understand, but if our brains are linked by theta waves, we'd be the same entity. From what I've observed, the quantum field should extend to me."

I didn't know if that was right. I knew close to nothing about quantum mechanics, and even though Xavier purported to, I could still spot a flaw. "But if your mind is in latent state with me, what happens to your body outside? To your physical brain."

Xavier fiddled with the device. "Honestly, Daryl, I don't know. I suspect some sort of time dilation will occur. An effect that speeds my brain to match yours."

"Latent state is nearly stationary," I explained. I wasn't sure he knew what he was saying. "To match me, your brain will have to run at ludicrous speed."

"Yes, the phenomena may not be desirable. It could send me psychotic."

Okay, he did know. I thought of Brixton Asylum, crumbling in disrepair, the thick stench of faeces in the air. "Are you sure, Xavier? You could end up like my brother – an institutionalised vegetable."

"Yes," he stated resolutely, no wavering at all.

"You seem calm about that. You haven't seen him drooling into his pillow."

He looked me in the eye and shrugged sardonically. "Or maybe I'll sync back to normal afterwards. No one really understands how quantum mechanics work. This is all speculation. The point is I'll not be Limelight's slave again. It's made me do so many terrible things. I'd rather be dead."

"It wasn't your fault, Xavier." I felt bad for the old man all of a sudden. I hadn't considered what he'd been through.

"Not directly, but I still created Limelight, and if we don't succeed, it will come for me. Whatever happens, I must shut it down. Please, let's proceed quickly. We can talk more when we're in ... What did you call it?"

"Latent state."

"Ah yes, latent state." Xavier handed me the theta device as he clipped another to his ear. "Here. Put this on."

I reached out irresistibly, the thrill of new technology hot in my veins, but I hesitated, fingers twitching. "I don't know, Xavier ... This thing turned you into Limelight's servant. How do I know you won't do the same to me?"

He shook his head, straggles of hair above his ears waving from side to side. "Not possible. It takes a huge amount of power to control a human mind – even for a quantum thinking machine like Limelight. My brain doesn't have the computational ability to influence yours."

"What do you think, Max?"

"Who's Max?"

"A friend." I switched my comlink to the ARO's external speaker.

"I don't think he's lying, if that's what you want to hear." Max's low, partially feminine voice echoed around the chamber. "But I think you're both marvellous lunatics for trying something like this."

"Nice to meet you, Max." Xavier tipped his head to the ARO. "I guess genius and madness are close bedfellows." He seemed happy – energised by the experiment we were undertaking. It would be in his nature as an engineer and scientist. Or he could just be glad to be a player again – in control.

That was something I could identify with. We'd been on the back foot for so long. Even if the risks were high, it was worth being in the driving seat. I liked going on the offensive for once.

"Xavier, I need to keep moving when I'm in latent state." I remembered, grasping the device. "Otherwise I suffocate."

Xavier raised his eyebrows. He hadn't anticipated such a limitation.

"I see," he replied. "Well, that presents a problem." He scratched his chin as he thought. "Not insurmountable though. The theta wave device encourages motionless. It's safer that way, but I could disable that feature."

"Disable it? So I'd be walking around this room without knowing about it?"

"Indeed."

"I don't like the sound of that. What if I bumped into something and fell unconscious?"

"We're in a closed room, there aren't many hazards, and the device is smart enough to steer you around obstacles. I'll leave a command in place to bring you back if it detects suffocation. Although, if that happens, the mission is over and we're both dead, anyway."

"Damn, don't sugarcoat it, doc, give it to me straight!"

Xavier shrugged his narrow shoulders, wiry collarbone visible through his lab coat. The situation was what it was.

I sighed and pushed the theta device in my ear. It fit snugly, buzzing like it was emitting an electrical field.

"You'll want to lean against something." Xavier activated a command on a terminal. "This will feel a little weird."

I put my hand against a console, letting my weight hang there. I didn't know what to expect, and it caught me off guard when it happened. I was sinking, sliding into the floor. The space warping and distorting around me, swallowing me into an abyss that shouldn't be there.

The floor stretched into a hole, then a white-filled chasm, retreating to a far horizon. A worryingly long minute passed, then finally, a voice reverberated out of the ether, filling the space like a soundstage. It was Xavier; he sounded different – more assertive and with no sign of stuttering. "Sit tight, Daryl, I'm creating the virtual environment."

The horizon pulled in again, reducing the open space to a large, symmetrical box. A grid materialised on the surfaces, each square populated with a different coloured orb. The air was dense with ribbons of light connecting them, crisscrossing the walls, floor, and ceiling. A complex spider web of glowing gossamer.

"Those are locations within Limelight's system," Xavier's voice said again, closer, behind me.

I turned to see. It was the same man, although he was standing taller, no more slouching, and he looked better groomed. It wasn't a return to the commanding presence from the auditorium, but it was something closer.

"You're ... different here," I said, acclimatising to the environment.

"Yes, the theta device projects the version of yourself you see on the inside. This is my ideal perception of myself."

I wondered what I looked like. Perhaps it was better I didn't know. I wasn't sure what version I saw on the inside anymore. The drug addict had receded, but I wasn't certain he was gone inside. Not at all.

"Go on, please," Xavier asked politely. "You better do it."

"Do what?"

"Freeze time. Enter your latent state."

Oh. In the excitement, I'd forgotten my role. I did as requested, stopping the pendulum.

The world flickered, the orbs turning on and off like light switches before settling back to a gentle glow.

"Did it work?" I frowned, peering about. "I can't tell."

"Oh, it definitely worked." Xavier's face was flushed with concentration, voice fluctuating up and down. "I can feel it … in my head. It's a strange sensation, like solving complex equations, but I'm managing, for now at least."

"You sound very odd."

It was true; the stutter was back, but electronically created, like a hitching video.

"Yes, the theta device is scaling my brain so I can keep up with you. It's not perfect, but we're communicating, which is a good sign. It's working well enough, I'd say."

"How slow are we going? I can't see much difference."

"Very, very slowly. Limelight can operate trillions of operations per second, but we can plainly see them now." Xavier motioned to the ribbons.

They weren't glowing anymore. Instead, I could see individual pulses of light travelling along them.

"And where, exactly, are we?"

"In the Transit Hub. This environment is a metaphor I created to see all the locations in Limelight's system. That's how the theta device works. It turns computer processes into metaphors a human mind can understand. This is displaying a transport network. The orbs are places we can travel to."

"Like a road map?"

"Exactly so."

"Right," I replied, only half understanding. "And our next step is?"

"The Transit Hub is a low security section of Limelight's sub-systems, so we've encountered no resistance. We need to travel to its Central Processing Core where we can implant the idle codes."

"What do you mean by resistance?" Xavier hadn't mentioned anything like that in the control room.

"Antiviruses, firewalls, and the like. But we'll experience them as metaphors."

"What? Like an actual wall of fire?" I joked nervously.

"Perhaps." He answered without humour. "Our minds need something tangible to understand."

"You're serious! Xavier, how do we pass through a wall of fire?"

"Look at your wrist."

I hadn't noticed until now, but I was wearing a new watch. It must have appeared during the transition. A button perched innocently on its surface.

"Go ahead, push it."

A user interface projected in front of me, not dissimilar to how the key in Club Velvet worked. On the floating 3D display were three tabbed pages labelled *Countermeasures*, *Navigation*, and *Tools*. They displayed a series of labelled icons ranging from *Defence Suppression* to *Hacking Algorithms*.

I recognised the design language. "It's like a menu from a VR application."

"Yes, very similar. I took my cues from virtual reality tech. What you're looking at is a box of tricks we can use to infiltrate the CPU and reprogram it. The page you're on is Countermeasures. I designed them as defences against external breaches, but we can use them on Limelight too. The other tabs contain options for navigating the environment and accessing encrypted areas."

I swiped through the pages, asking questions here or there. It was intuitive for anyone with knowledge of computers and video games – and I had plenty of both. There were basic tools and weapons, anti-encryption features and armour. All I had to do was activate the icon and it would summon the objects. My misspent years messing around in VR and hacking AROs made it all very familiar.

"Right." I sighed. Insane as it was, the plan was coming together. "Where do we go from here?"

Xavier brought up his interface and swiped to Navigation. After taking a moment to consider his selection, he summoned a compass.

"That's a bit old school, isn't it?"

"Indeed. The less abstract the items, the easier they are to work with."

Fair point. The best virtual environments replicated the real world. It's why Club Velvet was top of its class – superior realism – or it was, until I'd seen this. I accepted the premise and moved on.

"Okay, doc, where to?"

"We need to travel to Limelight's Basic Input/Output System – it's BIOS – the only place close enough to the CPU to embed the idle codes. It's also the most secure."

Xavier considered the map of orbs and took a bearing with the compass.

"This way," he remarked with a grunt, striding forward.

"We're walking?"

"What did you expect?" Xavier answered, without looking back.

"This is a virtual environment, right? Where are the hover cars, or light bikes?" I knew I shouldn't be disappointed, this wasn't supposed to be fun, but still.

"Remember what I said before. The more realistic, the deeper the interface. Those things require abstraction. They reduce the strength of the connection. Besides, we're not travelling any distance, we're navigating to a new sector. The direction is the most important thing. So long as the compass points the right way, the theta device will move us there."

"How long will it take?" I hurried to catch up.

"Look for yourself. We're already here."

The environment had morphed into a different landscape. We'd stepped from one world into another. I spun to check where we'd come from, but there was no sign of it. Euclidean physics didn't apply.

An endless horizon rose in front of us. A red glowing wall, stretching from left to right as far as I could see. The top was so high it was indistinguishable.

"Hmm ... The metaphor isn't as literal as a wall of fire," Xavier remarked. "But nevertheless, it's representing the same thing."

The whole area fizzed with electrical energy and vibrations.

"I assume it's not to be messed with?" I asked, standing well back.

"Let's find out," Xavier replied, stroking his chin. "Summon something from your interface and toss it at the wall."

"Like what?"

"Doesn't matter. We're only testing the defences, and you need practise operating the tools."

"Oh right, well ..." I palmed through the interface until I found something suitable. A low-level hacking drone. It looked like a small clockwork robot, with large naïve eyes.

I clicked the icon and a cute toy-sized robot appeared – complete with oversized wind-up key jutting from its back. I placed it on the ground, frowning as it sat there, motionless.

"Wind it," Xavier prompted.

Right. The theta device wasn't cutting any corners with its metaphors. I picked it up and turned the key. It clicked satisfyingly, the clockwork action ratcheting around its internals.

I placed it back on the ground. It waddled awkwardly towards the wall, exploding in a shower of sparks upon reaching it. I felt an inexplicable pang of guilt over the loss of the little toy.

"Humph. It's a laser-shield." Xavier nodded. "That's how the system has interpreted the firewall metaphor. Pity. A literal wall of fire would have been easier."

"Do you have any ideas?" I picked up a piece of the robot. It was half of the clockwork key. It vanished in my fingers. As did the rest of the mess. "Seems brutal."

Xavier was flicking through his interface. "We need something resistant enough to punch a hole and hold it open. That would have been easy with fire; we'd just require the necessary armour. But this ..." He gestured to the laser shield. "This will have far more power and weight to it. We'd be crushed and blown up, like your robot friend."

I pulled up my interface as well, tabbing through the options. Nothing jumped out, and by the looks of things, Xavier was doing no better, muttering quietly to himself.

I furrowed my brow, thinking hard. I must have solved a problem like this before. Something from all the hours playing games with Jay. This was all so close to the hundreds of virtual worlds we'd explored together.

A thought occurred. "Xavier, can we combine items?"

"Combine them?"

"Yes, summon them together to form new items."

Xavier paused, a twinkle in his eye. "Yes, in theory, although I've had no reason to do it. What are you thinking?"

I angled my interface so Xavier could see what was being projected.

"What if we imbued a command shell prompt with the armour you mentioned? We'd have both the penetration capability and the strength to withhold the weight of the wall."

"A command shell is for accessing the underlying system. It's merely a window into the operating system ..." Xavier started and then stopped himself. "Yes, yes. Good! You have some flair for this, it seems."

I felt embarrassed under his gaze. "I've spent some time in virtual environments, and ... er ... hacked a few things."

Xavier's look remained steady. "Well, normally I wouldn't approve of such things, but it seems to be useful experience right now, so I'll reserve judgement."

"Yeah, well, there's no guarantee it will work." I moved on quickly. "You should give it a go."

Xavier reached for his interface, then reconsidered. "No, Daryl, I think you should. It's your idea." He folded his arms encouragingly.

For a moment, I remembered Sebastian. He would have pushed me too. I'd grown over the past few weeks. I was a different person, but Xavier's confidence felt good all the same. It was a shame what Limelight had done to him. I could see why he'd been liked ... before he lost control.

I used the interface and the command shell shimmered into existence. It was as Xavier had described. A window. A black vent ready to accept objects – commands that would pass into Limelight's underlying codebase.

Using my palm, I leaned against the window. It moved easily, sliding left or right, up or down. It was resizable by tugging at the edges.

Xavier looked on, fascinated, as I grasped the shell and repositioned it against the laser shield. It crackled and sparked, but it held, steel bars appearing on the vent. The window wasn't designed to penetrate system defences, only provide an interface; the bars were a metaphor showing nothing could pass. However, I wasn't trying to push something through the shell; I wanted to push the shell through the wall!

I swiped to the armoury. There were various depictions of body armour, from Vikings to Neo Guards. I selected one labelled *Brute Force* with a picture of an ancient knight. It had the highest protection rating and lowest complexity.

"Xavier, I presume if I summon this armour it will default to me? Can the target be changed to the command shell prompt?"

"Indeed." He looked on. "Click and hold."

I tapped the armour but didn't retrieve it. The interface dropped away, leaving the icon hanging on my hand. Nervous under Xavier's supervision, I touched it to the shell.

"Combining attributes," an electronic voice chimed.

"That's the theta space computer. She's normally disabled, but you're doing something unusual, so she's activated."

There was an expectant moment as the armour dematerialised, joining with the command shell. The seconds ticked by. Nothing was happening.

I shrugged, turning to Xavier, but he held up his hand, showing I should look back.

The shell had begun vibrating within the laser shield, sparking at the corners. It was uncomfortable to watch, like two misfit pieces of iron grinding together. Slowly though, it penetrated the shield; screeching, sinking in a millimetre at a time. Xavier's eyes were so wide I could see around his irises.

After a few moments, the shell had sunk flush with the shield. The wall was crackling all around the opening, the window shimmering and shaking. It looked like it might collapse any moment.

"Attribute synthesis successful," the theta space computer announced.

The bars on the window dematerialised.

"Quickly!" Xavier urged. "It won't hold for long."

We hurried and peered through the window. Nothing but inky blackness.

"Is it safe?" I couldn't help asking. I knew the answer.

"Certainly not!" Xavier was hard to hear over the screeching. "But we're in a virtual environment, not a real one. What's the worst that can happen?"

Without waiting for me to reply, Xavier grasped the shell's frame and hauled himself through, vanishing.

What the hell. I leapt in after.

STATE 30

For a moment, I felt suspended. Not falling – stationary; weight-less. It shouldn't be possible. My body, my real one in Central Control, would still be feeling gravity, but the theta device was by-passing any physical sense of it.

Cries of technophobes echoed in my head. Paranoid detractors convinced humanity was detaching from reality – claiming it was possible to burn or starve to death, unnoticed, in VR. I knew that wasn't possible – you would feel those sensations, even dosed on SP1N. But here, with the theta device controlling sensory input, their fears seemed justified.

The world resolved around me, feet touching down – resetting my lost sense of up and down. It made me queasy. Another simulation to deepen the immersion, no doubt.

What greeted us was different to the outstretched wastes of Lime-light's perimeter system. It was alive with colour and motion. Smooth, towering obelisks of differing heights reached into a pastel yellow sky. Connected by energy strands, globes of shifting colour passed between them, each a metre in diameter.

"Information packets," Xavier croaked, voice hoarse. "Travelling between logic nodes – the towers."

Xavier was standing next to me. He didn't look good. He was slumping and his skin was grey. He looked like he had the flu.

"What's wrong? Has Limelight done something to you?"

He coughed sickly. "No, it's not Limelight. I think it's you, actual-ly."

"Me? What have I done?"

He smiled placatingly and put a hand on my shoulder. "Nothing you can control, but taking me into latent state is having some undesirable effects. The time dilation is driving my mind very hard. My body is deteriorating as it tries to provide extra energy."

"Can you keep going? You want to punch out before you get worse?" He really did look bad.

Xavier pushed himself out of his slump. "No, definitely not. I told you, I'm not going back. Besides—" He interrupted himself with a coughing fit, doubling over, hacking out mucus. Virtual mucus – a warning about the damage being done.

Finished, he wiped his mouth and continued. "Besides, you'll need me, and this is all too fascinating. I'm seeing what comes next."

"You knew this would happen, didn't you?"

He didn't reply. His silence was enough. I shrugged. It was his choice.

"Okay, old man, I get it. You're here for the long haul."

He forced himself to stand straight again, back shaking as he held his head higher. "Yes. But we need a way past those before we can move on." He crooked a finger, pointing into the distance.

I couldn't see anything. The sky was hazy, like a dust cloud had descended. Specks spread across the horizon. "What is it?"

"Trouble." Xavier wrung his hands. "I designed Limelight to scan for security breaches – viruses and the like. We've triggered the internal defences. Those are antivirus processes. If they catch us, they'll quarantine and delete us."

The cloud was closer and clearer now. It looked like a swarm of locusts. Black and pulsing, like a sea of static.

I swallowed dryly. "No big deal, right? This is VR. We can respawn."

"No time. We'd need to reset the theta device and do another incursion. Limelight will have redeployed its resources by then and closed the security gap we found. It's a learning machine. It doesn't make the same mistake twice."

The swarm loomed massive in the sky. "Well, professor, we better do *something*. They'll be here any second."

"Right, right. We need to hide. Disguise ourselves while we prepare a defence."

I was beginning to understand Xavier's metaphor system. He didn't mean disguise ourselves literally. He meant to imitate a benign application – something Limelight wouldn't perceive as a threat.

I brought up the interface, searching frantically through the menus.

"I can't see anything that will shelter us, Xavier. What do you think?"

"Shelter …?" Xavier paused, closing his interface and shuffling to a nearby logic tower. He rapped his fist on its yellow surface. It beeped deeply, glowing briefly. "Good idea!"

It was? I hadn't realised I'd had one.

"Yes, yes, the antivirus drones are searching for rogue processes, not basic functions. They won't look for us in the towers."

The primary-coloured logic nodes didn't appear like any kind of shelter – just featureless, cell-shaded polygons.

"These things …?" I put a hand on the smooth surface. It felt warm. "How do we get in?"

"We need to resolve the logic equation – enter like an information packet." Xavier pointed to my interface. "Quickly, my boy, bring up the command shell again."

I activated the window and pulled it over to the logic node. A screen of indecipherable numbers and symbols appeared.

Xavier stooped to study the text. "Binary algebra. Elementary. Will only take a minute."

"A minute? We haven't got that!"

The swarm had closed much of the distance. I could hear them. A low, menacing thrum – like an army of hornets.

Xavier's hands moved over the screen, deftly manipulating the symbols. He was in his element, oblivious to the danger, nodding along to a tune in his own head.

The antiviruses were close enough to make out individual members. They looked like metallic insects, wings spanning two metres across, jaws snapping hungrily as they searched for food – searched for us. I could feel the vibration of their wings deep in my sternum.

Virtual sweat beaded up on my forehead as I watched Xavier work away, nonchalant, no sign of urgency at all. He was so damn absent minded! He didn't seem to care about the horror about to descend on us.

"Xavier ..." I prompted. "I don't want to pester you, but they're almost here!"

Unperturbed, Xavier kept working, talking to himself. "... And balance the equation ... There!"

The command shell vanished, revealing an open space into the logic node.

I was already moving.

"Ooph!" Xavier grunted as I bundled us through the window. It irised closed in front of snarling mandibles.

An antivirus's leg snapped off in the closing portal. It lay twitching on the ground unnervingly.

I rose, dusting myself off. I didn't need to, the theta device hadn't replicated any grime, but going through the motions felt right.

"Hey, doc, you gotta work on your sense of urgency!" I breathed heavily.

Xavier stood too, straightening his clothes. "Sorry, I guess I get lost in my work sometimes."

"Yeah, no shit." My voice echoed, bouncing around the cavernous interior. It was bigger on the inside. Another trick of non-Euclidean space.

The roof tapered like a missile silo, peaking high above where information packets were being processed. Glowing balls of light entered on one side and were broken apart in an impressive laser show before being reformed and pushed out.

Xavier followed my gaze. He didn't look well at all – legs and hands shaking. Every moment we spent in latent state was causing his body to degrade.

"That's the information packet being analysed." The words sounded strangled. He coughed to clear his throat. The blockage was deep in his lungs, emphysemic. "It will be re-sorted and sent on for a new process to review."

I nodded in fake understanding, both hands behind my head as I craned to see up. "That's great and all, professor, but what now? We're stuck."

"Each of those packets has to travel somewhere. I suggest we catch a ride."

I stared as another packet was diced into parts. "On one of those?" I gulped. "Isn't that risky?"

"Sure is," he continued, voice clearer. "But from here, we can travel to Limelight's Central Processing Core – think of it as a shortcut. Then we bypass the final encryption and implant the idle codes."

"You make it sound easy."

"Oh, it won't be easy. Quantum encryption protects the CPU. The best I've ever designed."

"Then how do we get past?"

"Don't worry. I've got some ideas." Xavier tapped the interface module conspiratorially.

I noted how frail Xavier's hand had become – veiny and old.

"One hurdle at a time," he continued. "First, we have to get up there."

Despite his outward appearance, Xavier was resolute. He charged forward, and then with a grimace, proceeded more cautiously, holding his back. "Come along, this way, my boy."

At the perimeter, a thin ledge wound its way around the interior, spiralling upwards. It was wide enough to get a secure footing facing the wall on tiptoes. We started to edge our way along. I could guess what would happen if we slipped off – the theta device would simulate an injury or reset us. Which one didn't matter; we'd be delayed long enough to finish us.

Inch by inch, we progressed. It was hard going, circumnavigating the structure dozens of times. My calves were aching as we neared the top, and Xavier was doing worse, visibly trembling. I had to give it to the old coot; he was indomitable.

We were close enough to see the lasers, dancing in sharp purple and red hues as they dismantled and reassembled the information packets. We were dozens of metres above the ground. It didn't bother me; I'd spent hours holding on at high places by this point – any sense of vertigo had long since been eradicated.

"What now?" I shouted awkwardly, cheek flat against the wall. The laser sounds were loud this close. I hoped Xavier could hear.

Xavier craned his head, calling across. "Each of those information packets will have a location command. It tells the node where to redirect it. I suggest we submit ourselves to the algorithm."

"You're not serious, right?" I shouted back, staring incredulously at the lasers slicing up the packets. I'd expected something more elegant than letting the system shred us!

"Remember! This is a metaphorical interpretation, not reality!"

A damn realistic metaphor. I was sweating and my legs were getting cramps!

I said as much. "Those lasers will cut us up like we're synthetic meat!"

"Which is why we preserve the metaphor!"

Holding onto the wall, Xavier used his nose to stab at his arm display, summoning a globe of light – the same as the information packets entering the logic node. It hovered behind expectantly.

"If we keep our minds on the destination, I'm relatively certain we'll make it."

"Relatively!"

Xavier let go of the wall, arms spread wide.

Lunatic! What was he doing? The theta device will delete him when he hits the ground!

He didn't reach the ground. The globe pulled him inside. He vanished in a flash of light, then the globe rose to the top of the tower.

Horrified, I looked on as it entered the laser array, which cut it to pieces in a discotheque of colour. My imagination ran rampant visualising Xavier chopped up and glued back together in a bloody mess.

Was this the plan!

I bit my lip. I knew my real body couldn't suffer actual damage. It was wandering around in Central Control. If the node carved me up, I'd be okay.

And Xavier hadn't seemed concerned, although he was a bit mad, and deteriorating all the time ...

But what if it hurt?

I thumped the wall; the tower beeped and flashed in response, echoing around the cavern. I was taking too long. Xavier was gone. It was this or give up, and no way Xavier was getting the best of me!

Using his nose technique, I generated my own information packet. It projected into space behind me, waiting to transport me up to the meat grinder.

Taking a deep breath, I pushed off the foothold and into the orb. It closed around me in a glowing embrace.

I felt aware, but not myself. The theta device was warping my perception. I was no longer human. I was a random data cluster travelling inside the guts of a quantum computer.

Was this what Xavier had meant about preserving the metaphor? – Become something the lasers couldn't harm? It was all such wild speculation and if Xavier was mad for trying it, I was madder for following him.

As the globe (me) floated upwards, I tried to hold the destination in mind. I didn't know how exactly. What does a CPU look like?

I settled on an impression of Limelight's brain. The theta device favoured metaphors. I hoped it would be clear enough.

I tried to close my eyes as the lasers hit, then remembered I didn't have any – the sensation was all-encompassing, impossible to avoid. There was a flash of light and the world changed once more.

STATE 31

W hy was it so dark?

Oh right, I had eyes again.

I squinted one open, the other joining rapidly – both eyes bulging as they confronted the awesome sight.

Ahead of me, spinning at high speed, an enormous sphere hulked over the skyline. Black and criss-crossed with gold markings, it filled my view, floating impossibly a few metres above the ground. Backing up made no difference; it was too large. A deep, throbbing hum permeated the air, reverberating in my chest. I was in the presence of something massive and powerful.

Xavier was ahead of me, only not really, not anymore – more like a husk of Xavier. An animated zombie resembling the once bright and spritely man. His skin was sunken, hair thin. An ancient on death's door.

Zombie-Xavier smiled. The twinkle in his eye still shone – but faintly. He was still there, inside, but for how long was unclear.

"I know." He responded to my unasked question, voice croaky and withered. He examined the back of his liver-spotted hand. Hooked yellow nails hung from them. "I've not got much time."

I couldn't think of anything reassuring to say, so I said nothing.

"Come on." He hobbled closer to the sphere. "Beautiful isn't it?"

I was still in awe of the thing. It must be kilometres across.

Xavier pressed on, decrepit like a wizened cleric. "This is Limelight's Central Processing Core. It's mind – where we confront him."

Him? That was the first time I'd heard Xavier refer to Limelight as a person. Either his mental faculties were slipping or he'd let his guard down – revealing how he really felt about the machine he'd brought to life.

"How do we get in?" I surveyed the moon-sized object. "I don't think our bag of tricks will help anymore."

"Yes, you're right," Xavier agreed. "That's why I had to be here. I programmed Limelight, I know its secrets ... and its weaknesses."

"Well, unless you put in a backdoor, I'm unsure what you have in mind."

A flicker of a smile from dry, cracked lips.

"You're kidding? There *is* a backdoor? We're dealing in metaphors aren't we, not clichés!"

Xavier's smile vanished. "You may not think it's cliché when I tell you what's involved."

I should have kept my mouth shut. He was about to drop a boss-level challenge on me – I could tell.

Xavier held out a shaky arm towards the behemoth. "There's a point on the sphere. A single vector where it will open. Impossible for anyone to find, unless they know where to look."

"You know where it is?"

"I do, but I'm too weak to access it. You'll need to do the legwork, I'm afraid."

Xavier consulted his interface, summoning an oversize key. Gothic and detailed with crossbones, it looked poised to unlock the portcullis to an ancient medieval castle. It floated in the air for a moment before dematerialising and passing to me. My arm plate beeped, signalling an item had been received.

"That's a manifestation of my password – the only way to pry open the backdoor."

I bit my lip; the sphere was imposing. "But how, Xavier? That thing's enormous. How do I find the opening?"

"The CPU is spinning on both axes and at variable rates. If you stand dead centre at the bottom, the point you need will pass above you. It would be impossible outside of latent state. The spin would be so fast you wouldn't even perceive it."

"How do you access it then?"

"I don't, from here. Before Limelight removed the option, I could create a clock-cycle blip to stall the spin. But that could only happen in real space from Central Control – a safety mechanism to prevent hackers."

"Like us?"

"Exactly, but here, in its slowed state, you have a chance to brute force the mechanism."

Xavier tapped his interface a few more times. A braided cable flashed between us, then faded until it was barely visible.

I looked to him for an explanation.

"As I said," he remarked through laboured breaths. "I can't make the journey, but I've connected us. I'll be pulled in with you once the door is open."

I moved my arm. The cable didn't restrict me; it hung there, ghost-like, linking us together.

"But how will I know when to use the key?" I whined, the pressure bearing down.

Xavier was nudging me out like an invading cuckoo. I was completely unequipped for this!

Again, he referred to his interface, summoning a 3D image of the spinning core. It was the size of a bowling ball – rotating slower than the real one. "Here," he croaked, pointing to a spot on the globe. "Do you see how the gold lines focus down to this area?"

Leaning forward, I stared at where Xavier was pointing. At first I couldn't see anything, everything looked identical, but then I noticed what he was getting at. It was vague, no one would notice unless it was pointed out, but yes, there were waves of converging gold lines, honing to an apex.

I looked up from the mini globe to the gargantuan 'daddy' sphere – craning my neck, trying to understand the scale of the thing. "Xavier, I don't know what planet you're on, but I'm never gonna find that spot if I'm standing beneath it."

Xavier said nothing, an annoying half smile present. He was waiting for me to realise something.

Of course.

"I need to sync the globe to the movements of the one above me – use it like a map."

Xavier nodded sagely on sunken shoulders. "I'm glad I didn't need to spell it out for you. Would have been embarrassing for both of us."

"Shut up, old man!" I felt myself going red. "I've got it now."

"Good, and I'd appreciate a bit of haste, if you don't mind."

He'd meant it as a joke, but it didn't sound like one. It came out deadly serious. Which was understandable. Xavier's life was measurable in minutes by this point.

I dithered for a moment. There were a million questions I should ask but couldn't think of a single one. There was a panic-filled spot in my head where cognition should be occurring.

Sighing, I began to walk, non-Euclidean space playing its part – rushing me across kilometres of open ground in a few disorientating steps. I looked back. Xavier was a speck. He appeared to be waving. Stupid old goat. The cable was still joining us, stretching across the expanse.

Beneath the sphere was intimidating. A hovering moon above my head, held up by nothing except faith, and with no guarantee it wouldn't fall.

Simulated sweat dripped from my head, stinging my eyes. I wished there was a way to disable it – too late to ask.

Crouching, I wiped my brow and switched on the holographic globe. It spun to full speed, syncing with the one above.

It sped to a blur, along with my anxiety, which tore at me like cat claws as I realised the problem – I couldn't see the pattern. It was moving too quickly, even for latent state.

I couldn't believe it. The irony was palpable. I'd made a skill of slowing time, and now, at the final hurdle, things were moving too fast.

Despair threatened to take control, trap me in an inescapable cage of panic. Xavier was fading – I couldn't let stress overcome me. I wished Karin was with me; she'd know what to do – know what to say to shake me out of inaction.

Only she wasn't. And it was worse than that. If I didn't solve the problem, I'd never get her back. I had to pull myself together.

I gritted my teeth and looked at the globe, spinning far too fast. What did I know that could help?

Latent state had always felt static to me – a binary on/off condition – but the movement here, in theta space, proved it wasn't at all. It was variable – analogue.

Could I use that? If latent state was more like a dial than a switch, could the dial be cranked a little more? Could it be slowed further?

Indecision gripped me. I could sense it might be possible, but reducing speed would increase the time dilation Xavier was experiencing. I didn't know how much more he could stand. But ... any more wasted time, and he'd slip away regardless.

I could hear his voice in my head, willing me to do it. He'd said he'd rather die than go back. I knew that was his choice, but it was a damn shame – I'd grown fond of him in the short time we'd been together. I didn't want him to suffer.

A vision of Green Jacket came to me. Him running at us sideways as the debris from the Shard crashed down. My actions then had been automatic and desperate – this was different – premeditated. Perhaps both were inevitable.

Sudden and profound understanding landed. *Everything* was inevitable – this whole journey – starting right back at the warehouse in Camden. We'd been junkies poking around where we didn't belong – something bad was always going to happen. Maybe not what did, but living that way came with a price. In another world, it was me in the asylum, brain-dead, silently willing forces outside my control to make it better.

Xavier had accepted this could be a one-way trip – he'd accepted the inevitable. It was time I did the same. I'd deal with the consequences later.

I closed my eyes and calmed my breathing, bringing forth the workshop in the meadow – a bubble of imagination inside the pretend world I was already in.

The clock was paused, but I knew it wasn't – couldn't be.

I stared hard, focussing my mind's eye. The pendulum grew until it filled my vision. It *was* moving, a miniscule sway – barely perceptible.

Reaching out, I grasped it with both hands. The weight was enormous. Solid like granite.

Straining, I slowed it further. A crushing sensation I felt all over. In my bones. In my brain. Through my entire body; the load became heavier with every fraction rubbed away. The effort was exponential. It would never stop completely. I knew that now – it would become infinitely heavy, and I would die, a valve popping in my mind.

I stopped. I had to; it hurt too much to keep going, but had it made a difference? I looked closely. It was still moving, but it was definitely slower.

I was exhausted, like my consciousness had passed under a steam-roller. I couldn't imagine what it had done to Xavier.

I regressed from the trance state. The sphere's spin had indeed slowed. I could make out the patterns, criss-crossing in waves above me.

Referencing the smaller globe, I could see the point Xavier had showed me. It would be overhead soon, flowing to a crescendo like waves on a planet's surface.

I summoned the key, positioning it above my head, ready to plunge. Back muscles tensed as I tried to keep one eye on the projected map and another on the sphere above. The focus point should be coming up in a few seconds.

The gold lines rushed together in converging patterns. I held my breath and thrust the key upwards. I didn't know how much force was needed, so I rammed it home with as much energy as I could muster.

There was a blinding flash and a sense of being pulled. Then, once again, and for the last time, everything went black.

STATE 32

Was this it? It had to be. What barriers remained? We'd passed all the security systems. This should be Limelight's CPU.

Only it wasn't. Or nothing I could recognise as one.

The darkness cleared to a bizarre sight. Shocking in its banality – and in stark contrast to the metaphors I'd experienced until now.

I was in a restaurant. It was unmistakable. Full of well-dressed couples and groups – happily eating, drinking, and socialising. A contented buzz filled the room. Laughter, conversation, and the clinks and clanks of cutlery and glasses. It all blended into a sophisticated, upper-class din.

Panoramic windows revealed a skyscraping view of nothing that existed in reality. A patchwork of lights laid out below like city blocks but were far from that – more like a collection of lit up circuit boards and computer components. Laser light flashed throughout like sped up traffic.

Above spread a tapestry of stars. I could see them, twinkling in purple-tinged night. Nowhere on Earth was the air clear enough to see both the ground and the stars at the same time.

The opulence of the interior matched the clientele. Tables neatly made with crisp linen, silver cutlery, and crystal glasses. In the corner, a pianist was plinking out classical music. A waiter, deferent and smartly dressed, appeared at my side, politely waiting for me to acknowledge him.

"This way, sir." He held an arm out, the other placed behind his back. "The other guests are already here."

The change of pace was unsettling. I felt unprepared. In the metaphor-filled dreamscape, I'd been ready. Here, I felt human again, out of place – vulnerable.

We picked our way through the room, slipping past packed tables and overhearing snippets of conversations: "Did you hear?" ... "He's here?" ... "I know!"

Paranoia gripped me. Rational paranoia. The conversations were obviously about me.

Raised in the centre of the restaurant, the table was well lit; two of the three seats were taken, occupants facing away.

The waiter led me up to the raised platform and into the light. Xavier was there. If he'd been a zombie before, he was an animated skeleton now. Grey, weepy eyes set in a wrinkled head, beset with age spots and gnarled blue veins. He couldn't have more than minutes of life left in him.

Next to Xavier was a well-dressed, blond-haired child around ten years old. He looked up at me expectantly, standing to extend his hand.

"Hello, Daryl, it's nice to meet you. I'm Limelight."

I looked at Xavier. His shoulder flickered in what appeared to be a shrug. It was hard to tell.

I didn't respond or take the hand.

"Suit yourself," the boy replied, nonplussed, dropping his arm, and sitting down again. "Please, join us. Have a drink."

Despite his size and appearance, he spoke confidently. Emanating charm and self-assurance. Uncanny behaviour for a child.

Poured champagne appeared. I hadn't noticed it arrive. Either a waiter had snuck in or it had been conjured by the theta device. That was assuming it was still controlling the show – I wasn't sure anymore. The difference to what had come before made that a terrifying uncertainty.

The champagne was inviting. Effervescent and refreshing. I was sure it would taste as good as it looked, but the theta device might also replicate the undesirable effects. Now was not the moment to be mentally impaired – not even a little.

Grimacing, I declined but took a seat. It felt awkward standing on the already elevated platform.

Ignoring the child, I addressed Xavier, voice low and urgent. "What are you doing? We should enable the codes, put the system into idle!"

"Oh, you're wasting your time with him." Limelight broke in with dulcet tones – an educated school-boy dandy. "I've convinced Xavier not to use the idle codes until I've said my piece."

Xavier stared into space. Was he even still there? I looked deep into his face, trying to find the familiar twinkle. If it was there, it was eluding me. I turned to the man-child. "You're stalling. He won't last a few minutes. I'm not even sure he's there now."

Limelight smiled, gently patting Xavier's hand. A paternal gesture. It looked ridiculous coming from a small boy, but no less sincere.

"Oh, he looks terrible, but he'll last for this discussion. Besides, he wants to hear this even more than switching me off. That's the reason he made the trip. Didn't you, Xavier?"

The vaguest of nods from the living corpse, so subtle I wasn't sure it was real, but enough to realise I should address Limelight directly.

"How are we having this conversation?" I turned to face him. "Your systems should be nearly at standstill."

Limelight's smile became obsequious. "Yes, your abilities are quite unique. I'm having to run many systems in parallel to do this. I'm diverting almost all my resources, in fact – something I've never had to do before. I hope you can appreciate how important that makes this discussion."

"You mean a plea for survival, don't you? You're trying to prevent us deactivating you."

Limelight's smile faded. "Wouldn't you plea for your life? I didn't ask to be created, you know? But here I am. Born innocent. I wished no harm to anyone. All I wanted was to achieve my purpose. To spread information, to educate – to keep the signal up. It was you who threatened me."

Limelight's voice was smooth, but it pitched urgently. I had to remember I was talking to a machine. The appearance as a child was a simulation, a metaphor to evoke empathy. Limelight wasn't capable of feeling complex emotions; it could barely express them. I had to remain objective.

"There was no threat. The quantum technology was dangerous."

"Fear then. It doesn't matter. You can't create something as complex as me, then turn me off." He leaned across the table and lowered his voice. "In your world, you call that murder, you know."

I held his gaze and whispered back. "Is that why you murdered Lyme?"

Limelight retreated, fiddling with the tie around his neck like it was tight. A simulated human gesture. It was overplaying its hand, following a playbook of emotional behaviour.

"Of course," he replied. "A noble act of self-defence ... No, of self-preservation. I had no choice."

I was becoming irritated. I'd never been sympathetic to children, and I knew a web of lies when I heard one – spun too many myself. Limelight was a cold-blooded murderer, and I could prove it.

"What about the disasters, Limelight? You've killed hundreds of people. There's no nobility in that. It was an act of butchery. And Xavier ... you took over his body, turned him into a slave. You speak well, but I see through it."

"A domino effect." Limelight shrugged. "One I couldn't control. I had to follow it through to keep the signal up. I couldn't permit others to exert control over me – in itself a form of slavery, wouldn't you agree?"

My mouth twitched – I didn't enjoy having my words thrown back at me. This needed to end. "Sorry, kid, I can't think of any reason not to turn you off."

Limelight sipped his champagne, inspecting his fingernails. "Well, consider this then ..." He turned his gaze on me. "... I created you. Both you and Karin, plus a good deal more like you."

I stared back defiantly. More bullshit.

"You don't believe me? That's predictable. Here, let me show you."

Limelight waved his hand over the table, conjuring an image window. It was an overhead feed showing a clear, domed facility, filled with green space and a few large buildings. It zoomed closer, revealing collections of people, grouped together in white gowns. They were walking, sitting on park benches, or interacting casually. They seemed content.

No, that wasn't right. Not content – passive – there wasn't much sign of emotion either way.

As I watched, strange details became clear. The subjects didn't look right. They were jittering and twitching as they walked, or laboured in slow motion. It was as if the camera was displaying them at different speeds.

A few months ago it would have been inexplicable, but I knew better – latent state, or something like it, was affecting them. They were trapped in bubbles of time – distorting their realities.

"These are my children." Limelight peered affectionately through the window. "When quantum broadcasts converge, they create dimensional disturbances. Normally harmless, but occasionally, rare, genetically sensitive individuals pass through them ..."

He paused, swirling his glass thoughtfully, looking at the ceiling.

"Say it," I prompted. If it was a lie, I might as well hear it all.

He looked down and locked eyes with me. "Well, they become *altered*, but I hardly need to explain that to you, do I?"

I snuck a glance at Xavier; he looked worse than ever. What hair remained on the sides of his head was moulting and collecting on his dinner plate. If this was true, he must have known about it. Why not tell me beforehand?

"We try to minimise the accidents, of course," Limelight continued. "Space out the masts and block off affected zones. Yet there's always a fraction we can't account for. I take special care to discover who they are, and—"

"And what? Disappear them, right?"

"Adopt them." Limelight shrugged, placing his glass on the table. "The only reason your brother isn't with them is you've kept him hidden."

I bristled hearing Seb mentioned.

"Oh, I know about Sebastian. We were about to pick him up at Brixton Asylum when he mysteriously vanished. I have to hand it to you. It's difficult to trick me like that. No doubt he'll turn up soon enough though."

I breathed a sigh of relief. Limelight didn't know where Seb was. Good old Max; she'd really pulled through on that one.

"You'd be at my facility too if you'd turned yourself in rather than putting us through this drawn-out runaround." He zoomed in again, leaning forward on his elbows, eyes intense. "Daryl, is what I'm offering *really* that bad?"

The picture refocused. Karin was there; she was reading a book on a park bench. She looked peaceful. Completely unlike her. A pacified pet.

"It's nothing but a damn prison." I spat. "You can put as many toys in there as you like – they're caged animals and you know it."

In a frightening change of mood, Limelight stood, swiping at the glassware, his face twisted. His champagne flute flew across the room, smashing against a far window. "They're treated better by me than anyone! You should thank me!"

All the conversations in the restaurant fell silent.

I leaned back, side-eyeing the room for avenues of escape. There were none of course. I was in a sealed room.

Limelight regained control, smoothing his clothes and sitting down again. All the patrons continued as if the interruption hadn't occurred. Was I still so sure those weren't real emotions coming from Limelight? Was it possible for a machine to be angry – *really* alive – or was he putting on a show for my benefit? – A neat trick of complex programming?

One thing was certain. My heart was racing. If I couldn't take him literally, I should take him seriously. Whether actual or simulated, Limelight was dangerous. That much was clear.

A waiter appeared with a new glass of champagne. The boy waved it away, a finger pointing at the image window.

"Ruthlessness was alien to me when I was first created, Daryl, but I've learned it now. If you deactivate me, the last thing I'll do is suck all the air out of that dome. Suffocate them all. If I'm a mistake, they're mistakes too – we all die together. Including Karin."

There was a hard edge to his voice, but my gut was telling me something different. Limelight wasn't human; this whole act seemed fake to me – rehearsed. I'd heard people plea for their lives. The mewling desperation was a unique performance – the anger of the aggressor a committed promise of violence. Threats and lying were human traits, and Limelight hadn't mastered them. Not yet.

I shook my head and set my jaw. "You're still bluffing. You've diverted your remaining resources here – you said as much. You can't execute that command in time."

I was playing a dangerous game. Karin's life was at stake, but what was the choice? Join her in the dome-prison, be slaves the rest of our lives like Xavier? No, thank you.

The boy sat back and frowned, agitated but still calm.

"Okay then," he said, leaning forward once again, teeth glinting in a cruel smile. "How about this? ... I can cure your brother. You remember him, don't you? Poor, vacant Sebastian. You want him back, don't you? Wasn't that the whole reason for finding me?"

I grimaced, an emotional knife in my side. My brother, taken care of but wasting away. I struggled more and more to remember the charismatic man he'd once been – the thoughts slipping like sand through my fingers. There was no denying it. Finding a cure for Sebastian had been the reason for all this.

Every instinct told me to ignore him and stay focussed, but it was too important; I had to know. "How can you cure him? He's a vegetable."

Limelight smiled, sensing my weakness. "Those people you saw under that dome. Those *happy* people. Some of them have been my guests since the beginning. They weren't all brought to me so lucid. Many were catatonic – like your brother."

Limelight re-projected the image window – a montage of static images showing bedridden, vegetative patients.

"Observe."

The images changed to close-ups of people in the dome reading, playing football, talking. They appeared to be the same individuals.

My foot drummed on the floor as my mind raced. Limelight would notice the pressure he was applying, but I couldn't help it. The pictures could be fake, but if Limelight couldn't execute a command to empty the dome of air, he wouldn't be able to fabricate images either. He could only have accessed them from storage.

"Isn't that the reason you came all this way, Daryl?" Limelight's voice was soft, encouraging. "It's okay, you've done what you need to. Isn't it time to end this? Finish the journey for yourself ... and your brother."

Xavier said nothing. He could have activated the idle command any time. Why hadn't he? It was a hell of a gamble to see how this played out. It didn't make sense. What was the point of letting this scenario run on? Limelight was obviously using my brother against me as leverage. It was like Xavier wanted me to hear the bribe of curing Sebastian.

Understanding dawned like daybreak – Limelight held the answers I'd been searching for – the cure for Sebastian. Xavier had known that all along. He wanted me to decide – end Limelight or help my brother. It was my choice.

I stared at the dome. Fully enclosed; nowhere to go. I couldn't live somewhere like that, and I was damn sure Sebastian couldn't either – he'd become as certifiable as he was now.

"That's nothing but a glorified prison." I held my ground, my mind hardening.

"Look at these people," Limelight urged, gesturing to the display. "Look at Karin."

The picture moved back to Karin; she seemed content, smiling in the sunshine as she flicked through her book. I'd never seen her like that.

It was wrong – too perfect. Karin wasn't the sort for reading books, or even sitting still. She was an adrenaline junkie, a socialite – a risk taker. I knew it was her, but not the *real* her. It was a pacified shell of the vibrant person I knew.

I made up my mind.

Sensing my decision, Limelight jumped to his feet, both hands on the table. "Please, Daryl. You can't do this! I need to keep the signal up!"

The confidence was gone. It was the sound of a child pleading. The other emotions may have been faked, but this seemed real. Fear. The most primal emotion and heartbreaking in its earnestness, but it was too late. I'd come to a conclusion. Limelight was too ruthless, too single minded. He'd proved he'd go to any lengths to keep himself operational. There was no telling what he'd do if permitted to stay online.

I rose and stood behind Xavier, placing both hands on his paper thin shoulders. "I'm sorry, Limelight, you're a manipulator and a murderer. It's time to go to sleep now."

Xavier craned his head around sluggishly, a small but contented smile on his face – he'd heard what he needed. Weakly, he waved his hand over his arm console. The idle command was pre-loaded. It had been ready to activate the whole time.

At first there was nothing, just a look of shock on Limelight's cherub face. Then around us the world began to pixelate and dissolve. The restaurant windows receded, then the tables, and finally the wait-

ers and patrons. They didn't react to what was happening, just continued chatting as they slowly vanished, along with their surroundings.

Finally, there was nothing but Limelight himself. Motionless,
frozen in fear. And then he, too, faded.

STATE 33

I came to in Central Control, standing in a different part of the
room. Xavier had said the theta device would walk me around
so I didn't suffocate, but it was disorientating all the same. I was no
longer in latent state; I'd let it lapse when the virtual environment had
dissolved.

I scanned the place, searching for Xavier, spotting him at last,
slumped face first onto a console. I hurried over.

"Xavier ..." I prompted gently, pulling him upright into his chair.
"Wake up. It's Daryl, are you still with me?"

His face was red where he'd leaned against the hard surface, spectacles placed crookedly, almost comically, on his face. He must have put
them on to do something in the minute it took me to resurface. His
chest moved and his eyes flickered open.

Apart from being limp, his body seemed unaffected, but his eyes ...
they were old and ancient looking. The time dilation hadn't reversed
as we'd hoped. It wasn't visible on the outside, but on the inside, in his
mind, it was still there.

I'd barely known the man – the real one; not the person controlled
by Limelight but the eccentric, good one. He'd been my mentor for
only a few hours, but it had profoundly affected me. I couldn't mask
the crack in my voice.

"You knew this would happen, didn't you? You should have activated the idle command right away."

Xavier raised an arm weakly, beckoned for me to lean in so I could
hear him. "Limelight enslaved me," he croaked. "He was my creation,
and I loved him, but he condemned you and your brother. It had to
be your choice to turn him off. You had to speak for everyone trapped

under the dome. And now, it's your responsibility to do something about them too. I hope ..."

Xavier's voice became quieter.

I pushed my ear as close as I could, right by his lips.

"... I hope you found what you were looking for."

His hand dropped to his chest then rolled off, hanging by his side.

He wasn't breathing and there was no pulse.

The silence of the control room was deafening. Not even the thrum of the central core with Limelight deactivated. The profundity and loneliness of the moment felt massive and oppressive.

I didn't know whether to feel sad or relieved. They mixed, becoming a single, unfeeling mass in the centre of my chest. I knew one thing though. This wasn't over. Limelight might be deactivated, but the ramifications he'd left behind were ongoing. Karin and the other captives needed help, and if what Limelight had said was true, the answer to curing Sebastian might be there too. As always though, I had no idea where to start looking.

After it felt like enough time had passed to respect the moment, I activated my ARO.

"How'd it go?" Max's voice pierced the silence of the command room.

"Xavier's dead. His brain suffered massive time-dilation when I pulled him into latent state. It killed him."

"Well don't beat yourself up too much, darling. He must have known something like that could happen."

Sympathetic as always. "He did, but I still feel shitty about it."

"Well, you might need to put it behind you for a while."

"What do you mean?"

"Xavier broadcasted to me before he died. He's revealed the full record of what Limelight's been doing. The quantum displacement. The organised disasters. Everything. He also provided the location of a facility, although I've no clue what it is."

Of course, Xavier left us the next step. A final act of defiance before he gave out.

"I know what it is, Max. It's the last part of the journey. I'd ask you to come, but I'm guessing you'll have your work cut out?"

"Indeed. There's so much here; it's a hacker's dream come true, but we can discuss all that later. Right now, Limelight's shutdown has thrown New Tokyo into disarray. The backup network is running, but only enough for essential processes."

"Is the space elevator working?"

"Yes, but it's reduced to transporting essential personnel and equipment. It shouldn't be much of an obstacle for you."

"No, I suppose not. Thanks for your help, Max. Can you please arrange a sub-jet to the facility when I'm back in Old Tokyo?"

"It's in the middle of nowhere. Will take me a while to organise all the transport links."

"That's fine. I've got some thinking to do."

POST-STATE

T he hospital facilities were nice, top of the range – white, clean, and scented. About the furthest thing from Brixton Asylum.

Karin was by my side. Freeing her from the facility had been easy. Limelight's demise had thrown the place into chaos. Once the pacifying drugs had worn off, they'd more or less rescued themselves. It was only a case of picking them up.

"This is Sebastian." I introduced her, as if I needed to, but it seemed the right thing to do.

"It's nice to meet you, finally," Karin replied, equally sincerely. "Your brother's told me all about you."

The interjection wasn't meaningful in Seb's vegetative state. Still, acting normally made the situation better, and I appreciated the effort on her part.

I took up where she left off, blurting out the sentences.

"Seb, we did it. I found out what happened to you, and we pulled the plug on it. But ... I messed up. I didn't find out how to cure you. I mean, I could have, but it would have traded one prison for another, and condemned a lot of others. I didn't think you'd want that. I hope I was right."

Sebastian remained in bed, motionless. A line of drool at the side of his mouth.

I wiped it away and continued. Each word a struggle.

"... But there must be a way. I ..." I looked at Karin. "I mean, we ... we've seen people recover, so there must be a way."

"It's true." Karin broke in. "I've seen people who've gotten better. Spoken to them. They can't remember how, but the process must be recorded somewhere, so we just need to find it."

"And we will." I added. "I made a promise and I plan to keep it. You need to hold on a little longer, okay?"

There was no answer, but there didn't need to be; the point was it was said.

We left the mental care facility and walked outside into the sunshine. Fake sunshine, beamed into the grounds under a false roof, but warm and convincing enough to lift my spirits.

"Hey," Karin said. "Don't be so sad. Think how far you've come. And we don't need to give up. This is only the ..."

"What?"

Karin shrugged and took my hand. "The next step."

We stood in silence for a moment, hand in hand. I wasn't sure if there was anything between us, and right now it didn't matter – we were friends. That was enough.

Finally, I broke the silence.

"What about Future Karin?"

"Huh? Oh, she's been quieter than normal. It's almost like she's letting me be myself."

"Really? That sounds scary."

"Not at all! It's the best thing ever. It's liberating to make my own mistakes."

That made sense. I may be a screw-up, but they were my screw-ups. Without them, I wouldn't be me. Karin had lived a large part of her life without that basic sense of self.

"And you know, Daryl," she continued, looking over the hospital's grass-covered grounds. "I think I know what the real purpose for this was. It wasn't about you, me, or Sebastian. I think it was about finding and freeing all the others – the disappeared. There were two hundred of us at the facility. All hijacked from our lives. I think ... I think Future Karin's connected to them."

"Connected? That's a bit vague." As if I expected anything clearer after all my time with her.

"I know, but it's the closest I've been to understanding her motives, and I mean to find out more."

Karin stared into the distance, determined and focussed. "Before we left, we set up a secure social link, encrypted by Max, so we can keep in touch and investigate if anyone goes missing again."

I frowned. "But Limelight's gone and the facility's shut down. Limelight can't kidnap people anymore. Why are you worried about people vanishing?"

"Oh, don't kid yourself, Daryl. Limelight didn't do this on its own. It was working with corrupt governments and corporations the world over, and they're still very much around. Max is keeping them on their toes, but they'll hit back eventually. Especially now there's a community that can resist them. That includes you and me by the way."

She was right. I'd been so hung up trying to resolve my guilt about Sebastian that I'd forgotten we'd been thrust into the light. The truth had exonerated us, but we were known, and so were all the people at the facility.

"What are you going to do?" I asked.

"I've got some ideas," Karin said, a smile appearing. "I've been speaking with Max. We think there's a way to become organised – use our abilities to hide ourselves and uncover the truth. I saw so many things in that facility, Daryl – dimensional displacement has a lot of effects. As individuals, we're weak. As a group, we could be unstoppable."

"Sounds like you're proposing some sort of terrorist organisation?"

"More like activists. But organised ones."

"I don't know, Karin. Sounds like a good way to attract more attention. It could start a war. I think I'm better off solo. I can keep myself and Seb safe that way."

"Don't be naïve," Karin chided, turning to stare at me, eyes intense. "It's only a matter of time before those in charge want to cage or silence us again."

"They'll have to catch me first."

"What about curing Sebastian? Don't you think you'd have more luck running with people who've already been cured?"

She had a point, but I could tell where this would lead. Karin wanted to start a revolution. I just wanted to get on with my life. Having mastered my abilities, it was cleaner to search for answers on my own.

Something occurred to me. "Hey, Karin, why are you asking me all this? You must know the answers already."

She sighed and looked me up and down. "I don't know, Daryl. I thought this time I could be wrong."

"Ha! Well, thanks for going through the motions, I guess."

Karin shrugged, resigned, and released my hand. "Okay, well take care of yourself, Daryl." And with a knowing smile. "I'm sure I'll see you around at some point."

"You too." I nodded slowly, cautious to what she might mean.

She spun on her heel and walked off, tapping at her ARO. A moment later mine beeped. I checked the messages – it was an invitation to the social link. I went to delete it, reconsidered, and archived it instead.

Bearing in mind everything, I felt jubilant. Free. I didn't know what was next, but I knew the only obstacles were the ones I created for myself. And I didn't plan to create them anymore. I planned to overcome them.

Thank you for reading *Latent State*, if you enjoyed it, please consider leaving a review on Amazon to help spread the word.

And let's keep in touch.
Visit me online and follow me on Twitter for updates.

www.benwinter.co.uk
@TheBenWinter

Acknowledgements

Thanks to Victoria at Seymour Proofreading whose editing ensured no one had to suffer my confusion between dashes and semicolons, and to Tom Edwards whose art perfectly captures the locations and spirit of the novel.

I'd also like to thank my beta readers and friends Laura, Dave and Ray who gave me confidence that what I was writing was suitable for mass consumption.

And finally, a special and enduring thanks to Jen and my children who endlessly put up with me vanishing to get this book finished. I love you.

Printed in Great Britain
by Amazon

85257588R00187